Marketing Management

A European Perspective

Marketing Management

A European Perspective

Susan Norgan

 Addison-Wesley Publishing Company

Wokingham, England • Reading, Massachusetts • Menlo Park, California • New York
Don Mills, Ontario • Amsterdam • Bonn • Sydney • Singapore
Tokyo • Madrid • San Juan • Milan • Paris • Mexico City • Seoul • Taipei

Many of the designations used by manufacturers and sellers to distinguish their
products are claimed as trademarks. Addison-Wesley has made every attempt to
supply trademark information about manufacturers and their products mentioned
in this book.

Cover designed by Viva Design Ltd, Henley-on-Thames.
and printed by The Riverside Printing Co. (Reading) Ltd.
Typeset by Meridian Phototypesetting Ltd, Pangbourne.
Printed in Great Britain at the University Press, Cambridge.

First printed 1994.

ISBN 0–201–54447–4

British Library Cataloguing in Publication Data
A catalogue record for this book is available from the British Library.

Library of Congress Cataloging in Publication Data
Norgan, Susan.
    Marketing management : a European perspective / Susan Norgan.
        p.   cm.
    Includes bibliographical references and index.
    ISBN–0–201–54447–4
        1. Marketing – Management.   2. Marketing – Europe – Management.
    I. Title.
    HF5415. 13. N67   1994   93-50928
    658.8'0094 – dc20   CIP

Preface

This textbook has been written with three objectives:

(1)　To familiarize students with core theory of marketing management.
(2)　To identify ways in which contemporary business practice influences how this theory can be put into operation.
(3)　To track key moves towards a Single European Market which have a significant impact on marketing practice.

How does the structure of the book support these objectives?

Firstly – the 17 chapters are organized into three parts to reflect the coherent development of marketing theory and practice. The sequence of chapters mirrors the logical progression of concepts, analysis and disciplines necessary to deliver a product to its customer.

In many respects, core ideas are introduced in the order in which a trainee product manager's experience of the market evolves. The one exception to this is the early focus on strategic management issues. The European management model tends to exclude junior managers from this level of strategic involvement.

Part 1　Corporate and marketing strategy and management issues; identifying the customer through needs and behaviour; defining and measuring target markets; market research.
Part 2　The marketing mix; product, price, place (defined here as the logistics of provision), and promotion. Significant attention is paid to elements of the promotion mix.
Part 3　The complete marketing plan and portfolio analysis; looking to the future with new product development and the impact of information technology on traditional marketing methods.

Secondly – The accepted theory is interwoven with examples from the contemporary business world and includes application of key concepts to the not-for-profit sector. Recent research in specific areas is highlighted and supported by a comprehensive reference listing to each chapter.

Thirdly – Combining the moves towards the Single European Market with marketing theory and research has presented a dilemma: whether to incorporate these into the body of each chapter, or to deal with these issues separately. The chosen route is a 'European perspective' to each chapter. In these sections, the specific EC issues relevant to the core material of the chapter are identified.

As a result of the Maastricht Treaty, there is a move towards the use of the term European Union (EU) instead of European Community (EC). Use is made of the latter (EC) throughout this text for consistency with references cited.

Subject to entry negotiations during 1994, the European Community will expand to 16 Member States from January 1995, with the inclusion of Norway, Sweden, Finland and Austria.

It is recognized that the 1990s represent a period of rapid change with respect to European market integration. However, the focus on areas of strategic importance, and identification of key EC Directives and case law, provide a valid framework of marketing analysis. It is inevitable that new law and EC decisions will affect operational details.

Table 1 Interaction between marketing theory and practice and other disciplines.

	Human resource management	Quantitative methods	Financial management	Psychology and social sciences	Logistics and operations
Part 1 Strategic Marketing Management and Customer Needs					
Ch. 2 Contemporary Marketing Management	X				
Ch. 3 Strategic Marketing Decisions	X				
Ch. 4 Buyer Behaviour				X	
Ch. 5 Segmentation		X			
Ch. 6 Market Research		X		X	
Part 2 The Marketing Mix					
Ch. 7 Product Positioning	X				X
Ch. 8 Pricing		X	X		
Ch. 9 Distribution Channels and Logistics					X
Ch. 10 Advertising		X		X	
Ch. 11 Sales Promotion		X			X
Ch. 12 Direct Marketing		X	X		
Ch. 13 Selling and Sales Management	X			X	X
Part 3 Marketing Planning and Responding to Change					
Ch. 14 Complete Marketing Plan and Budget	X	X	X		X
Ch. 15 Portfolio Analysis			X		
Ch. 16 New Product Development	X				X
Ch. 17 Impact of Technology on Marketing Methods			X		X

Overlap between marketing and other business disciplines

At its broadest level, marketing is an integral part of the management of resources to achieve organizational objectives. This means that marketing management is not an isolated activity, but must overlap and integrate with other functional management areas such as financial management or logistics and operations. In parallel with this, some marketing theory finds its basis in, or makes use of, the tools of other disciplines. Significant among these are psychology and social sciences, quantitative methods and human resource management.

The objectives of individual chapters will determine how far these areas of overlap are examined in the text. So that students can identify these in advance of detailed study, Table 1 provides a simple reference grid on a chapter-by-chapter basis.

Acknowledgements

Special thanks are due to the following for help and support while writing this book.

Firstly, the reviewers, whose comments and suggestions were built into revisions to the final text. Special acknowledgement is due to Tim Nightingale for his help in compiling the chapter objectives and problems and assignments as well as undertaking to proofread the book.

Secondly, thanks are due to colleagues at Greenwich University Business School for helpful comments on sections of the text. The support of the Business School Libraries at the University of Greenwich and the University of Westminster in tracing references is also gratefully acknowledged.

The permission granted by authors, institutions, companies and others for reproduction of text, figures, tables or interviews is acknowledged with thanks. Every effort has been made to trace owners of copyright to gain permission for material reproduced.

Finally, I would like to thank my parents for unfailing support. This book is dedicated to them.

Susan Norgan
London, April 1994

Contents

6   Marketing research   162

13 Selling and sales management 421

PART 1

Strategic marketing management and customer needs

1 Setting the scene: marketing management and a unified Europe

Chapter objectives:

- to define marketing management
- to establish the link between marketing and added value
- to outline the planned characteristics of the Single Market
- to identify the marketing benefits of a unified Europe and its strategic influences

Definition of 'marketing management'

Contemporary marketing management involves a wide spectrum of responsibilities – from proposing brand strategy to approving the media plan; from briefing the salesforce to agreeing the 12-month sales and profit budget. The degree to which a marketing manager has control over key resources (money and people) will depend on a range of factors, of which the most important are:

- corporate culture
- the target market (consumer or industrial; mass or niche)
- the nature of the product (complexity, value)
- relationships with external providers
- changes in the external environment (affecting market, or employment patterns)

Many of the factors influential in creating a management environment for marketing professionals are explored in Chapter 2. Possibly the most significant of these is the prevailing culture of the organization. How does the Chief Executive view the marketing management function? What has the traditional area of marketing responsibility been? Is the organization finance-led? Some of these questions can be addressed by investigating the organization's definition of marketing. The reader is offered a choice of three, which will define the role that the marketing concept plays in the short- and long-term success of an organization.

(1) Marketing can be defined as the satisfaction of customer needs through the deployment of organizational resources (money and people) so that organizational objectives are met in the longer term. These organizational objectives may be defined in terms of profit, sales, or return on capital for a profit-seeking company, or expressed in the form of market penetration, leadership or positioning. For the not-for-profit sector, quantification of objectives may take the form of specified quality or amount of service provision against a pre-defined budget. Such performance targets have become common in the public service domain.

(2) The marketing concept may also be viewed as the creation of added value to a product or service to differentiate it from the competition. This added value can be created through superior benefits, features, service elements or the nature of the advertising message. It is through this process that brands are created. Brands are perceived by their purchasers as meeting needs in a more precise way than would an unbranded or 'generic' product.

The use of the term **'added value'** in a marketing context is explored later in this section of the chapter.

(3) The creation and development of a customer base is an alternative, but narrower, definition of marketing.

It is this third aspect of marketing that is most evident through advertising on television, in the press and in the various incentives which arrive through the letterbox or are prominent on products or retail displays. For companies marketing to other businesses, there is heavy reliance on the salesforce to maintain profitable relationships with existing customers and to cultivate new customers.

The visible signs of marketing in this third definition are just the tip of the iceberg of the marketing management process. Considerable management time is spent in evaluating past performance, identifying potential market opportunities, analysing market research data and screening proposals for innovation or change. These activities are necessary before products are developed, advertised and made accessible to the potential customers.

The first of the three definitions of marketing is the broadest in scope, and suggests that marketing – far from being simply one of the functional areas of management such as production or finance – is at the core of an organization's philosophy and operations. For many consumer-goods companies this has been the reality for several decades. The marketing activities of multinationals such as Unilever and Procter & Gamble (and of IBM in the industrial sector) became icons of best practice because these organizations were driven by the optimal use of resources to meet customer needs. However, even 'market-driven' organizations can lose a sense of direction when dogma displaces customer awareness.

Contrasted with the market-led organization is one that focuses on the product. This is a frequent phenomenon where there is a high level of technological input. Alternatively, the lead culture may be dictated by financial management in day-to-day control. This is a feature of holding companies which see operating subsidiaries in terms of financial assets rather than market players.

The prevailing culture of an organization may be so deep-rooted that a catalyst is required for the adoption of a market-led approach in which the customer's needs are viewed as paramount. The catalyst for change may take the form of a new Chief Executive, new competition or a sudden market decline. The organization's transformation may not be rapid, but will involve the infiltration of new ideas and working practices at every level.

Marketing and added value

The increasing importance attached to the marketing concept in the public sector found its origin in the need for accountability in terms of achieving value for the customer against a specific cost of provision. Progress towards these aims has been supported by quality management and quality audits as specific processes.

At the broader level, a customer is seeking 'value for money' for a product purchased. Similarly, a consumer identifies with specific values in a brand, when these match needs.

All of these management and customer expectations can be identified within the concept of marketing as value-added.

The term 'value-added' is invariably associated with taxation in Western European countries, and the tax is levied at each stage of the supply chain. A company will be charged the going rate of tax on the sales value of the goods, having achieved that value through production, processing or provision of a product or service. In the case of a service, the value to the customer may be created through the provision of expert advice (as in consultancy or securities broking), or it may simply be the transportation of a product from point A to point B. If the product becomes more accessible to the customer at point B, then value is added. This is where the term takes on a distinct meaning within a marketing framework, although the definitions below are drawn from the world of accounting.

> 'Added value is the increase in market value resulting from an alteration in the form, location or availability of a product or service, excluding the cost of bought out materials or services'
> (ICMA, 1974).

The customer is prepared to pay the price for a product at a specific point in the supply chain because of the values built into it through the preceding stages. An intermediary such as a wholesaler or retailer is prepared to offer services associated with distribution, merchandizing, advertising and selling because the value added will support a price to the customer which will cover the intermediary's costs and provide a profit. This means that the added value also takes on a meaning associated with the profit motive, as the following definition highlights:

> Added value is 'the wealth the reporting entity has been able to create by its own and its employees' efforts'
> (The Accounting Standards Committee, 1975).

There would be an intuitive expectation that all expenditure for goods and services at a level that reflects the values placed on them by customers would equal the income obtained by the value-creating organizations. This expectation is formalized in the way in which a country's economic performance is measured. Thus there are three levels at which added value can be identified and measured:

(1) the customer
(2) the firm
(3) the national economy

The areas in which added value takes on significance at each level are illustrated in Figure 1.1, and important issues are now explored under each of the three headings.

Added value for the customer through benefits

Some early proprietary remedies and patent cough medicines developed a loyal group of customers because the products did what they promised (helped alleviate symptoms) and made the patient 'feel better'. Some of the customer benefit came from the security of a remedy that was trusted because of the familiar name and pack. The initial advertising on posters and in newspapers reinforced this feeling. So the added value for the customer was through measurable medical benefits and the perceived benefit of reassurance.

In identifying how to provide this extra reassurance, the marketing company needs to understand the underlying customer motivation better than the customer himself. How this is translated into advertising values is the responsibility of the creative team. The product strategy is the straitjacket of objectivity provided by marketing management. The advertising agency's responsibility is to superimpose a personality on the brand, which can be profiled in terms of attributes.

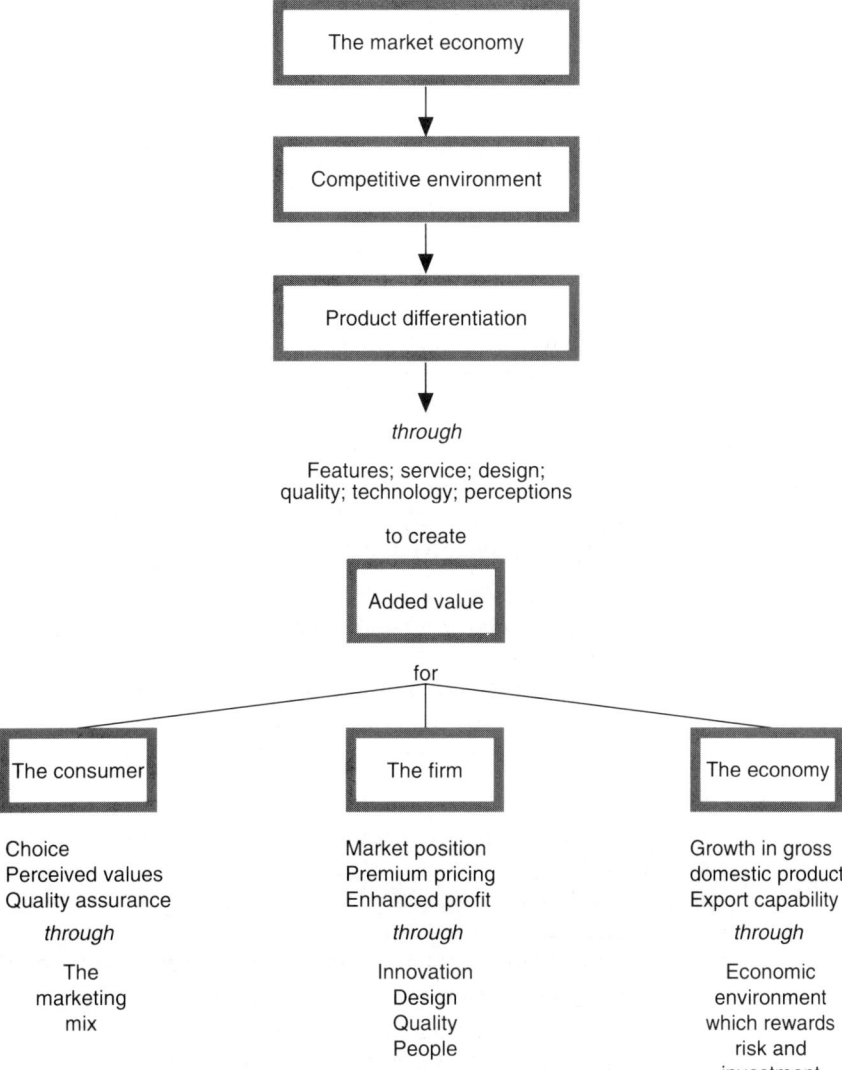

Figure 1.1 The creation of added value.

Because the benefits to the customer are built into the brand through the marketing process, the price/value relationship is different from that for an unbranded, generic product such as aspirin BP. The customer is prepared to pay a higher price for the branded product, but there are costs associated with providing the brand's superior benefits.

Added value and the firm

The UK official Census of Production has used the concept of **net output** as a measure of individual company performance to incorporate into an aggregate measure of the **gross domestic product** for the economy. Since 1973, gross output has been derived by adding together:

- sales of goods produced
- receipts for work done and services rendered
- value of capital goods produced for own use

Firm inputs are then subtracted from this figure to give a value for net output. The firm inputs are:

- raw materials and components
- goods for merchanting or factoring
- payment for individual services and work given
- duties payable
- increase in value of stock

Accession to the EC has meant that the UK has adopted a common definition for value added as applied to the firm, and which is more narrowly focused than the earlier definition of net output. This is because further firm inputs have to be subtracted, which are:

- payment for rent of buildings; hire of plant
- commercial insurance premiums
- bank charges
- cost of professional services, post, transport and royalties
- cost of licensing motor vehicles
- rates (excluding water rates)
- depreciation

Advertising would be an input cost to be subtracted under this narrower definition.

When these additional inputs are subtraced from net output a figure for **net value added** is derived. Apart from the necessity of filing these returns for government statistics, a firm may make use of its value added for internal or external purposes. For example, it can be used internally for comparing performance with previous years. It could be used for informing employees about performance and for involving them in seeking to improve this through incentives related to value-added targets.

This links added value to productivity, which most companies strive to improve in one of two ways: either by achieving more out of existing resources – materials, labour and plant – or achieving the same performance with fewer resources.

The added value of a firm might be used externally to impress shareholders (particularly large institutional investors), but this would set a difficult precedent if, in subsequent years, the performance did not compare favourably with the past or with other companies in the same industry.

However, traditional measures of productivity do not include the value that the customer places on a brand. A good example is the Goodyear tyre which has been advertised on the basis of 'a reputable product, of known value and superior quality' since the 1920s. The Goodyear attitude to advertising is that it is the tip of the iceberg, and would be less productive if it were not supported by strong distribution, a quality product and an effective salesforce (Martin, 1989).

Each of these inputs cost money, but can be justified if the price supported by the added value creates a profit performance that is better than the industry average.

There is a temptation to reduce advertising spend when there are pressures to reduce costs – such as in a recession. However, such action can mark the beginning of a downward spiral of perceived value, price and profit.

Added value and the national economy

A direct measure of added value for industry sectors within each national economy would provide an ideal comparison of the true marketing performance of sectors across EC Member States. The facility for measurement is available through the value-added tax collecting authority in each country.

Added value can be viewed as a measure of wealth creation at the level of the national economy. Taking the aggregate across all firms, the excess of sales value achieved over costs is the 'national profit' which accrues to different interests within the economy and this can be 'spent' in different ways:

- The shareholder has an increased dividend which can be spent on consumer products or reinvested in more shares of the same company, or in totally different shares.
- The small business owner sees improved profits which can be spent on consumer products, ploughed back into the business or invested in alternative ways.
- The employee may receive a bonus, commission or profit-sharing. Alternatively, the firm is in a position to pay higher wages across the workforce because of improved productivity. However, this increase in wages would also be considered an input to be subtracted before reaching a figure for added value for the firm.
- The government imposes taxes on enhanced company profits, individual earnings or consumer spending. This increases the national budget available for such areas as health, education and social support.

The balance of trade between national imports and national exports is influenced by the level of added value in the two components. If a nation exports low added-value products, which could include raw materials with minimal processing, and imports products with high added value (such as high-technology consumer products or engineering equipment), then there is the danger of a balance-of-trade deficit. This is because the nation exporting the high technology can charge a premium price for the value added before export.

The importing nation is dependent on high volumes of raw material exports of its own to compensate. Alternatively, a nation might increase exports of services to counteract increasing imports of manufactured goods. However, the nature of the 'product offering' of a service will determine how much of the value added is exportable, and how much is part of the service delivery in another country.

Added value and the nature of competition

Competitive strength at the firm and national industry level is dependent on the development of expertise and productive capacity which give rise to products and services with a relatively high added value. This requires investment in people by way of education and training, and in research and development to create new technology. Countries with cultures that favour such costly inputs invariably succeed in the longer term through the competitive edge of products favoured by the customer. This increases market share and provides profits that may be invested in the development of future products.

If an organization is to focus on added value as a route to success in the international marketplace, then it must view marketing as a coherent, strategic planning process which is followed by detailed implementation of plans and constant monitoring of performance. If this approach is not adopted, then market opportunities will not be correctly identified nor successfully exploited. Essential to this is a culture which encourages long-term commitment to innovation, with the facility for attention to detail at every level of operation to control quality and costs.

The objective of creating the highest possible added value in a product consistent with customer needs and organizational resources is the underlying philosophy to the chapters in this textbook. Complementary to this is the creation of an open Europe, which will increase market opportunities through a reduction in operational barriers. The larger market will provide European firms with the incentive to compete with the other global players – USA and Japan.

Planned characteristics of the Single Market

The long-term aims of the European Community (EC) were embodied in the original Treaty of Rome and further clarified in the Single European Act of 1986 and, more recently, in the Maastricht Treaty. These agreements provide the legal framework within which the European Community moves towards one integrated market comprising 12 Member States (*status quo* in 1993). It is possible that, by the year 2000, there could be 16 or 17 Member States.

This far-reaching legislation set out plans for a single market with the following characteristics:

- free movement of goods, services, capital and people;
- a common external tariff for goods entering it;
- harmonized taxes;
- coordinated foreign policy;
- a common economic policy with movement towards a single currency;
- promotion of common conditions of employment, welfare and human rights;
- furtherance of free competition between companies from all Member States under conditions of a 'level playing field', to encourage economies of scale in serving a larger market.

Responsibility for the gradual process of harmonization rests largely on four EC institutions:

(1) *The Council of Ministers*   This is drawn from the governing party in each Member State. The Council of Ministers meets periodically to agree policy on specific areas such as employment, immigration, the environment, social welfare or economic policy. The responsible minister in each Member State attends council meetings on relevant issues: for example, the Minister for Employment will represent the Member State at council meetings on the Social Charter, and the Minister for Home Affairs will attend meetings relating to immigration.

(2) *The European Commission*   This is made up of 17 Commissioners drawn from the 12 Member States. The Commission takes on the role of the civil service for the Community, but can also initiate legislation. Each Commissioner is allocated to one of the 13 policy areas. There are approximately 10,000 support staff, excluding scientific research officers.

(3) *The European Parliament*   This is made up of 518 democratically elected members with the number of representatives from each Member State dependent on its population. The Parliament does not pass laws, but discusses proposals and makes amendments to proposals and draft EC law, which are then submitted to the Commission to be enacted as directives.

(4) *The European Court of Justice*   This is situated in Luxembourg and comprises 13 judges with six Advocates-General to assist them. The Court has wide jurisdiction in relation to non-compliance with Community legislation. The decisions of the European Court take precedence over national laws of Member States, and there is no appeal against its rulings. There have been significant decisions where an individual or organization has taken a case to the European Court and won judgement against official actions of a Member State, thereby bringing about a change in the national law or its interpretation.

Problems in moving towards a single European market

The aims as outlined reflect the *status quo* of a **Common Market** moving towards an **economic union** by the end of the 1990s. However, there are three factors which must be recognized in any assessment of the speed with which total market integration can be achieved. Firstly, there are differences in perceptions of the nature and purpose of the Single Market on the part of individual Member States. Secondly, much of the planning and groundwork towards a unified market took place in an extended phase of economic growth in Europe. Implementation under conditions of recession or low growth may prove more problematic. Thirdly, the world political order underwent a major change with the downfall of the Communist regime in the USSR and East European bloc. Reunification of East with West Germany is the most significant outcome, but there are various political and economic implications for a Single European Market which, until then, had been viewed as predominantly 'Western European'. Ten key issues have been identified as inhibiting the smooth transition to a single market.

(1)   The President of the European Commission, Jacques Delors, has a personal vision of the EC as a political as well as economic union. Individual Member States do not necessarily share this vision, as this replaces national sovereignty with executive powers accorded to the Commission, which is not a democratically elected body.

(2)   The policy continues of using a large part of the EC budget for subsidizing a level of food production in the Community which is not matched by demand. This maintains prices at an artificially high level, with the accumulation of unsold food in store. There is a strong political lobby from certain Member States to maintain this *status quo*.

(3)   There is financial pressure on richer Member States to fund those less economically developed. West Germany, France and the UK have been net contributors to the EC support fund, while Spain, Portugal and Greece have been beneficiaries.

(4)   The break-up of the Communist bloc in Eastern Europe and its conversion to independent market economies has led to competition for investment resources between East and West Europe.

(5)   Resistance by the UK to moves towards a single currency has led to an 'opting out' clause in the Maastricht Treaty. The major concern is the loss of sovereignty over economic policy and, particularly, taxation.

(6)   Resistance by the UK to implementation of the EC Social Chapter and enforcement of a minimum wage could lead to a distortion of the 'level playing field'. The UK's concern is the inability of companies to compete with non-European labour costs if there are prescribed employee benefits. (On an index basis for 1991, hourly compensation costs for manufacturing workers were – Germany 123, Netherlands 107, Italy 92, France 89, UK 73 and Spain (1988) 64.)

(7)   Resistance by Member States to harmonization of consumption taxes may distort the pricing mechanism and artificially maintain borders. However, there has been reasonable convergence in standard rates of value-added tax.

(8)   Variation in levels of corporation tax applied in different Member States will influence companies to locate for tax advantage rather than to exploit market opportunities. Corporation tax does not currently feature in the agenda for harmonization.

(9)   Wide variations in financial reporting requirements for companies across Member States, and differing local rules relating to acquisitions by companies from other Member States, provide further distortions to the 'level playing field'.

(10) The impact of German reunification on economic and monetary convergence has cast considerable doubt as to whether a single currency is a realistic expectation for the EC by the year 2000. As this is an important adjunct to the creation of a single market, this issue is explored here in greater depth.

The benefits of economic and monetary union

The Maastricht Treaty is the most recent manifestation of EC intentions to create a single European currency by the year 2000. There are several stages necessary within economic monetary union (EMU) to create the conditions that will make this single currency possible. Membership of the exchange rate mechanism (ERM) was one way of ensuring that the economies of Member States began to meet the convergence criteria through fixed bands for currency fluctuations. However, events in the currency exchange markets in 1992 and 1993 severely disrupted the ERM, and plans for a single currency across all Member States appeared unrealistic.

What would be the benefits of a single currency as part of a move towards a single market?

(1)   This would eliminate the financial risk associated with currency exchange rate fluctuations for a company involved in cross-border trade.

(2)   There would be a reduction in transaction costs of cross-border buying and selling, through elimination of bank commission on conversions from one currency to another in the course of trade.

(3)   Operation of a trans-European financial market would be faster, simpler and cheaper, and this would provide positive support to other forms of trade between Member States.

The opportunity to exploit these benefits now appears remote since the UK left the ERM in September 1992 and the further crisis affecting other major European currencies in August 1993. This disruption in the ERM reflected strains on Member States attempting to achieve

Table 1.1 Strategic influences featured in the pan-European perspective for each chapter.

Chapter	Social	Financial	Influences Legal	Technical	Environmental
(2) Contemporary Marketing Management	National cultures and their impact on organizational culture Building the European team Business ethics	EC Member State support for small and medium-sized enterprises	Effects of Member State laws on marketing practitioners		
(3) Strategic Marketing Decisions	Impact of national culture on mergers and acquisitions		Nature of the contract between principal and distributor Local laws for establishing subsidiary or brands office EC competition law and conditions for referral of merger or acquisition EC law on state subsidies	European environmental policy: – Air pollution – Energy efficiencies – Environmental labelling – Packaging – Water quality	
(4) Buyer Behaviour	Language and cultural barriers to cross-border selling	Cross-border payment	EC judgements on agency and distributor agreements EC Directives on procurement for high value contracts EC law on selling direct to the the consumer		
(5) Segmentation	EC demographic influences Effects of national culture on attitudes	Consumer buying power across EC Member States			
(6) Market Research	Language and comprehension issues in research		Confidentiality and data protection law across Member States		
(7) Product Positioning and Creation of Added Value		Pan-European financial services	Acceptance of professional qualifications across Member States EC protection of trademarks EC ruling on information sharing EC Directive on product liability	EC rulings on technical specifications Food labelling	Differing attitude towards environmental issues across states 'Green' labelling
(8) Pricing		Currency: – Fluctuations – Differing rates of value-added tax across Member States	EC competition law regarding dominant market position and price fixing		Transport costs and border issues

Table 1.1 (continued)

Chapter	Social	Financial	Influences Legal	Technical	Environmental
(9) Distribution Channels and Logistics	Retailing patterns The Social Chapter	Cost of different transport modes Price fixing in road haulage	Deregulation of EC road haulage Types of physical distribution agreements		Impact of the Channel Tunnel
(10) Advertising	Culture effects in pan-European campaigns Availability of media as a result of differing cultures	Differing media costs across Member States	EC Directive on misleading advertising EC Directive on cross-border broadcasting	Specific product issues: – Tobacco products – Pharmaceuticals – Financial services Satellite broadcasting	
(11) Sales Promotion	Attitudes towards consumer incentives		Member State restrictions on sales promotion techniques Cross-border promotions		
(12) Direct Marketing	Different geo-demographic classifications		Data protection law	Availability of databases	Increasing volumes of non-targeted mail
(13) Selling and Sales Management	Language and culture issues in recruitment and training	Salesforce remuneration	Member State legal requirements for recruitment		
(14) Complete Marketing Plan and Budget		Problem with the European Monetary System (EMS)	EC Directives relating to common accounting standards	Impact of information technology	
(15) Portfolio Planning	Social payments by companies	Importance of consumption taxes and corporation tax levels in determining location Decisions on where to invest	EC Directives relating to company law		
(16) New Product Development	Culture and innovation	EC-funded research	EC judgements on technological agreements European patent Copyright		
(17) Impact of Developments in Technology on Marketing Methods		Electronic financial transactions	EC Directive on cross-border banking	Corporate information systems Cable TV Value-added data networks	

convergence of their economies through stable exchange rates. The conditions for monetary union included the need for convergence on four economic measures: interest rates, inflation rates, national deficit and gross debt stock.

The feasibility of achieving convergence was also severely strained by the unification of West and East Germany, with a one-to-one conversion of the two currencies not mirrored by equivalence in productivity across the two regions. As a result, Germany became a net absorber of capital and raised its interest rates in order to secure this inflow. This put upward pressure on the Deutschmark, but, in the absence of revaluation of the German currency, financial market pressure resulted in a fall in the values of other major European currencies relative to the Deutschmark. This meant that exchange rate fluctuation was greater than that allowed by the constraints of the ERM. The power of the international money markets was ultimately greater than the political will of Member States, and greater than the financial reserves available to them to support their currencies.

Marketing benefits of a unified Europe

The broad objectives of the Single Market are not limited to the achievement of economies of scale in order to compete with Japanese and US companies. The elimination of barriers to trade would also create the conditions for improving corporate cash flow and margins. However, this would be achieved through a longer-term commitment to serving the world's most demanding customers, providing quality products and service responsiveness by way of enhanced organizational capability.

The Cecchini Report (1988), published by the European Community, predicts that the elimination of non-tariff barriers will provide the conditions for an overall fall in prices as a result of increased competition, which will stimulate demand. This should lead to an increase in production volumes for the most competitive and successful organizations, whose costs decrease. This provides the opportunity for improved margins.

This scenario involves the restructuring of industry as not every corporation can gain market share. European Community law, as currently enacted, strikes at the heart of protectionist measures taken by individual Member States. The Community is ostensibly neutral towards the issue of public versus private ownership, but the creation of an open and equitable market is supported by European competition law and the Commission's hard line on state subsidies to individual organizations.

It is these issues that feature in each chapter's European perspective section, which focuses on strategy and the market environment. To identify where key European influences are located within these sections, Table 1.1 provides a chapter-by-chapter guide, classified by strategic influence.

Significant impact on marketing strategy will arise through developments as a result of the Social Chapter, as these affect employment costs and location decisions. Similarly, environmental law must be considered in development, production and delivery of a product.

At the operational level of marketing management, specific areas of Community policy and law must be addressed at the planning stage, whether this involves details of implementation on pricing, distribution and advertising, or selling across more than one Member State.

Organizations that invest money and management time in planning on a pan-European basis are more likely to reap the opportunities and rewards available through the creation of an open European market.

Problems and assignments

(1) Using the narrow definition of **marketing management** (the creation and development of a customer base), describe the process involved for one of the following:

(a) a multinational company marketing a pet food brand;
(b) a medium-sized cleaning contractor for offices and factories;
(c) a charity collecting for famine relief.

(2) How may 'value-added' be defined at the aggregate national level?

(3) A company invests resources in creating value for the customer in a product or service. How is the company rewarded, and how can this reward be used?

(4) In what ways are financial resources used to produce customer values in:

(a) an electronic component?
(b) an advertising campaign involving television and press?

(5) Identify the tangible and intangible values to the customer in the following:

(a) a proprietary, branded medicine sold over the counter;
(b) a mobile telephone;
(c) a rail transport network.

(6) What are the major benefits to organizations established and trading in the Single European Market?

(7) Discuss the key problem areas associated with the Single Market.

(8) How will the existence of the Single European Market enable European companies to compete more effectively with major corporations established in Japan and the USA?

(9)   How important a part do differences in language and culture play in the development of a pan-European business?

(10)   Identify and discuss the impact of major EC legal moves towards harmonization on key business decisions in product positioning and pricing.

(11)   How far has EC harmonization been achieved in areas affecting promotion mix divisions?

(12)   How important is monetary union with the establishment of a single European currency to the ideal of a truly single market?

References

Cecchini Report (1988). *The European Challenge 1992: The Benefits of a Single Market.* Wildwood House

Institute of Cost and Management Accountants (ICMA) (1974). *Value Added, an Appreciation for the Accountant concerned with Industry.* London: Heinemann

Martin D.N. (1989). *Romancing the Bland: the Power of Advertising and How to Use it.* AMACOM (Division of the American Management Association)

2 Contemporary marketing management

Chapter objectives:

- to identify the role of marketing management in organizations
- to describe the functions and responsibilities of the marketing manager
- to compare management style in the traditional organization with that of the 'customer-led' organization
- to identify the key issues in developing a pan-European marketing management structure

Company history, culture and management style will dictate how far and how fast the 'marketing concept' is adopted by any organization. Students with knowledge of and experience in an organization will recognize attitudes, behaviour and market performance reflecting a position along a continuum. For some industrial companies, 'marketing' is but a service to other functional areas, and there is no control over resources or expenditure. Undergraduate students will benefit from an understanding of how contemporary marketing management has evolved from the limited and traditional concept of marketing (definition 3 in Chapter 1). Many of the roles and activities have *not* been abandoned, but incorporated into new organizational structures and methods of achieving objectives. In the customer-led organization, marketing management acts as a pivot to integrate the activities of other departments.

This chapter is divided into three sections to explore this evolution:

(1) The role of marketing management in traditional organizations.
(2) The 'market-led' or 'customer-led' organization and the management of change.

(3) Marketing management of the 1990s and beyond (including marketing ethics).

The role of marketing management in traditional organizations

A simple model of the three levels of marketing involvement in corporate decision-making and activities is shown in Figure 2.1.

Corporate strategy is frequently written in terms of 'where do we want to get to?' Targets defined in terms of market share, new product acceptance or customer satisfaction levels will indicate adoption of marketing principles at the highest level. Alternatively, corporate objectives are primarily financial and these are translated into **marketing strategy** and objectives by marketing management. Strategic tools and practices are explored in Chapter 3, and ways of **segmenting** markets and deciding on target groups are the subject of Chapter 5. Decisions in these two areas are often feasible only with the aid of information from **market research** (Chapter 6).

The **implementation** stage or 'How do we get there?' will include marketing activity as one of many functional areas: finance and accounting, production, human resource management (also called 'personnel management'), research and development, logistics and distribution. Departmental titles will vary with the nature of the product and company culture.

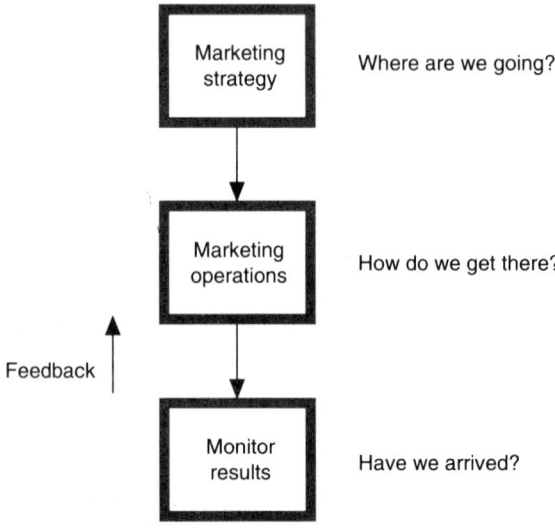

Figure 2.1 Three levels of marketing involvement in corporate decision-making and activities.

Where strategic decisions have been taken about the **marketing mix** for a given product or service, implementation of marketing plans involves day-to-day management of each of the elements of this mix:

- **Product** benefits and features (Chapter 7)
- Setting the **price** (Chapter 8)
- **Distribution channels** and intermediaries (Chapter 9)
- **Promoting** the product (Chapters 10 to 13)

Success in implementation will often reflect the time and attention devoted to setting **marketing plans** (Chapter 14).

Monitoring of performance is critical to establishing whether the targets (often short-term) are being met, and whether activity needs to be adjusted in order to respond to market conditions. Measurement of performance will frequently take the form of sales and financial indicators, and these will be compared with the annual budgets set in relation to deployment of resources.

Feedback from the market will also indicate where major resource decisions are needed with changes in strategy. This may involve reassessment of the range of business activity of the organization through **portfolio analysis** (Chapter 15). Decisions made as a result of this may lead to **new product development** (Chapter 16).

Non-market factors in corporate decision-making

How much authority over resources is vested in marketing personnel will depend on the lead culture of the organization. The importance of adjusting resource allocation against market and customer needs is frequently recognized through management response to periodic market research or audit data. The absence of syndicated or proprietary data for many industrial markets means that resource decisions are frequently made on non-market judgements. There are other factors which cause managing boards to give less weight to the needs of the marketplace:

- *Short-term financial considerations*   Earnings per share, share price, possibility of an unwelcome takeover bid, entering the Unlisted Securities Market (USM).
- *Shortage of investment capital*   Needed for high-tech research and development or marketing support for a new product. Where this is taken from profits, it reduces profit available for distribution to shareholders which means the share may be marked down by financial institutions.
- *Industrial relations*   Production of competitive products may mean flexible working practices which the workforce will resist.
- *Changes in the external environment*   A credit squeeze on consumers (through high interest rates), new laws.

- *Internal politics*   Survival at the personal level for a manager may mean avoiding the high risk or high expenditure route; possible dominance of a financial or engineering culture.

Authority versus responsibility for the marketing manager

Responsibility for achieving sales against a plan may be vested in the **marketing director** (where there is heavy commitment to advertising for a consumer product) or the **sales director** (if the main source of business momentum is through personal selling). In some organizations, this may well be the same person with a composite title. (See Chapter 13 for exploration of these issues.)

In each case, there is an assumption that effective deployment of resources in the context of a competitive market environment will achieve the desired results.

Authority of a manager may be defined through **span of control** over other personnel: a marketing director may be responsible for personnel controlling four areas of functional activity: the product group managers, market research manager, advertising manager and the promotions and incentives manager. Each of these managers will have a department over which they, in turn, have a span of control. The degree of control over aspects of employment not directly related to day-to-day marketing duties will depend on the level of support from central management departments.

Authority may also be defined in terms of **financial control over a budget**. The manager is responsible for allocating a particular sum of money in a 12-month period across activities which will achieve targets. The amount of money will determine the level of authority. A marketing director in a large UK consumer goods company will have control over tens of millions of pounds primarily for television and press advertising. A marketing manager in an industrial company may have control over a budget of only £100,000, for example, to produce technical sales literature and organize regional seminars.

Responsibility of a manager is defined in terms of the results expected as a result of the endeavours of the personnel under their control, and as a result of wise allocation of funds against specific activities. Under the traditional model of the firm with a hierarchical structure, how far managers are **answerable** for results varies with the culture of the organization. Under the US and British models, the very high levels of pay of senior managers and board directors relative to the rest of the workforce would suggest that answerability rests at a senior level. This reflects the more global authority vested at this level to influence the way in which the business is managed.

There are three factors which make definition of responsibility a complex issue:

- Business performance is recognized to be a measure of cooperation and collaboration across functional departments. It is not always possible to break down 'performance' into constituent parts and allocate these against departments or individuals. Where there are performance expectations of a discrete team, then the team will get the credit. This issue is explored later in the chapter in the discussion of organizational structure based around project teams.

- Should the performance expectations be long-term or short-term in nature? A new marketing director may be employed to inject strategic marketing skills into an organization whose market position needs to be re-established through product innovation and professional selling. At the same time, current sales levels must be maintained to protect cash flow to finance research and development.

   There is a danger that the drive for profitability in the short term may damage prospects for the long term. Many brands suffered market share losses of two or three percentage points in the period 1979 to 1981 because of management's drive for year-on-year profit growth in a recession. The subsequent expenditure on advertising to restore brands to their original positions far exceeded the original profit gains.

- Where these two factors are recognized, there is a variety of measures which can be used to measure performance:
   - gross sales
   - market share
   - return on capital
   - net sales
   - brand penetration
   - stock turn
   - gross margin
   - brand awareness
   - direct product profitability
   - net margin
   - customer service

Relationship between title, pay and responsibility

Where responsibility for performance is passed down a traditional **hierarchical structure**, then there is the assumption that the relevant authority over resources passes down at the same time. So, for example, a **product group manager** in a frozen foods company will be answerable for sales of the consumer products within the group, where advertising and sales promotion are the major allocated expenditures. Alternatively, an **area marketing manager** for a range of microcomputers would be responsible for the region's sales performance, where new customer recruitment

Internal relations	External relations
Senior management	Advertising agency
Research and development	Promotions supplier
Engineering pilot plant	Advertising media
Finance and accounting	Design agency
Production and quality control	Market research company
Production planning and forecasting	Printers
Purchasing	Other suppliers
Legal	Technical standards
Logistics and transport	Trade associations
Sales (if not incorporated)	Customers:
Customer service	End-user
Public relations	Intermediaries

Figure 2.2 Key internal and external relations of a product manager.

occurs through sales seminars and technical follow-up. In this case, the costs can be charged directly to the region.

Where responsibility for performance is not matched by delegated authority or control of resources (money or people), then a **stress** situation is created for the manager. A **job description** should identify the areas of responsibility *and* the span of control, defined in terms of budget or personnel, or both.

It is human nature to maintain control, but to delegate answerability. Corporations resolve this dilemma in one of two ways:

(1) *High pay – high responsibility*   This is the route adopted in many US companies where **product managers** are effectively 'general managers' for single product businesses. Because costs can be allocated accurately against individual products, such managers are responsible for profitability as well as sales performance. Individuals taking on these responsibilities will typically be educated to Masters level, and have significant business experience. There will not be direct line authority over other functional departments, but the skills and expertise of the product manager will be recognized through cooperation from other departments for mutual success. The key internal and external relations of a product manager are illustrated in Figure 2.2.

(2) *Low pay – low responsibility*   This has been the marketing management route traditionally adopted in British industrial companies. Where the marketing function has been accepted as playing a valid part in achieving corporate results, this is frequently viewed in terms of 'support' activities. The title and remuneration will reflect this role. Some of the titles used and functions associated with them are described in Table 2.1.

Table 2.1 Alternative titles and responsibilities of marketing personnel.

Brand manager/ product manager	'Champion' of the product inside and outside the organization. Responsible for sales performance against a marketing plan with expenditure allocated against advertising, sales promotion, selling and public relations. Responsible for briefing on product improvements, market research and relaunch advertising strategy.
Marketing manager	Responsible for allocation of marketing expenditure over several products, with line authority over product managers. May also have responsibility for all or part of the salesforce activity.
Market development manager	Responsible for building a customer base in a particular business sector or geographical region. This may involve use of an existing product form and advertising strategy, or development of new ones to meet market needs.
Marketing services manager	Provides a support service to managers responsible for meeting sales objectives. Services would include: market research, sales literature, promotion materials, audio-visual presentations, advertising liaison.
Marketing operations manager	Ensures that marketing plans are implemented effectively through planning and coordination of internal resources; interfaces between marketing and salesforce; promotion planning of materials and stocks; activates response to feedback from customers and salesforce.

Internal relations of marketing management

The large number of internal contacts of the product manager illustrated in Figure 2.2 reflects the breadth of marketing influence in an organization. The absence of line responsibility over departments whose cooperation and commitment are needed means that interpersonal skills feature high on the list of prerequisites for marketing managers.

Contact with other departments can range from the simple 'housekeeping' areas of expense control and forecasting demand on established products, to more demanding team leadership involved in developing new products from idea creation through to market launch.

National culture plays a part in determining the degree of cooperation across functional roles and departments. For example, Japanese culture promotes the interest of the group before that of the individual. This gives rise to the search for consensus on a particular course of action before it is implemented. The decision-making process may take longer, but once complete, the whole team shows commitment to the chosen route. This culture facilitated the introduction of **quality circles** in the late 1950s. Quality circles were the brainchild of Professor Kaori Ishikawa, who wished to bring craftsmanship back to groups without losing the efficiency of American flowline production methods. A small group of workers was trained to identify, analyse and solve work-related problems, and present their solutions to management. Quality circles were first tested in Japan in 1962 at the Nippon Telegraph and Cable Company, and the successful concept swept through Japan.

Table 2.2 Potential areas of conflict between marketing and other functional departments.

Department	Department needs	Marketing needs
Production	Mass production Long runs Long lead time	Customized products Many variants Short lead time
Engineering and R & D	Exact specification Long development period Highest quality product	Flexible specification Rapid development Highest quality for specified cost
Purchasing	Economies of scale Minimal inventory	Variants to suit needs Inventory cover
Finance	Detailed fixed budget Minimum marketing expenditure Smooth cash flow Tight credit control	Flexible budget Maximum marketing expenditure Phased marketing expenditure to capture seasonal sales Flexible payment terms
Sales	Limited number of fast-moving, competitively priced lines Frequent promotions High discount levels freely available	Mix of lines with good profit, including slow sellers Few promotions with specific objectives Strict policy on discounts to protect gross margin

By contrast, many developed Western countries encourage individualism, which is seen as a source of creativity and leadership potential. However, this makes the achievement of consensus more difficult, particularly among the highly intelligent creating a negative team dynamic classified as the 'Apollo Syndrome' (Belbin, 1981).

A further cultural problem in the UK is that an **adversarial process** is dominant in politics, the law and industrial relations. This encourages a process of challenge and counter-argument between groups with different vested interests. This culture intensifies conflict where the potential for this exists between different functional departments in a company. Marketing is the natural focus of innovation within the organization, and where change is resisted, the opportunities for conflict will increase. Examples of these are given in Table 2.2, where the goals of finance, production, research and development and purchasing, conflicting with those of marketing, can lead to disarray and poor corporate performance. Skills in negotiation to achieve compromise on individual issues will mark out the successful marketing manager.

External relations of marketing management

Most of the external contacts of marketing management are suppliers – whether of creative ideas (advertising agencies), promotion materials (promotion agencies or printers), or information (research or audit companies). Some contact may occur with suppliers of primary elements of the product in order to establish quality criteria and detailed specifications. The degree of contact with customers (end-users or intermediaries) will depend on the nature of the product and the existence of a sales team acting as the prime interface here.

For new product development, suppliers are the external members of the team appointed to get the product to market. Where they are supplying intangible services the communication skills of marketing management are critical to success. The liaison role will involve frequent briefings on needs, and interpretation and feedback on proposals and submissions. There will also be negotiation of costs.

External relations of marketing management will include informal **networking**, where the individual brings to the position a capacity for developing relationships with no immediate benefit to the organization. However, over time, benefits accrue through exploitation of knowledge, resources, opportunities and referrals (Sonnenberg, 1990).

Expertise and skills for contemporary marketing management

The wide-ranging role of marketing management in the context of these internal and external contacts means that market knowledge and creativity alone are not sufficient for resolving complex marketing problems. The demands of short-term budgetary control and long-term business development mean that a broader range of aptitudes, skills and experience is needed by contemporary marketing management. These are classified under three headings in Table 2.3:

- analytical
- interpersonal
- creative

Table 2.3 Expertise and skills required for contemporary marketing management.

Analytical	Interpersonal	Creative
Budgeting	Appraising	Brainstorming
Forecasting	Briefing	Briefing
Planning	Delegating	Evaluating
Reporting	Liaising	Innovating
Researching	Motivating	Interpreting
	Negotiating	
	Organizing	
	Recruiting	
	Representing	
	Team-building	

The sophisticated management information available through developments in technology and reduction in computing costs puts added pressure on marketing management to comprehend, interpret and respond. This requires a level of training in other disciplines that permits communication with other functional managers, which inspires credibility and cooperation. Quantitative skills are paramount here, to provide good rapport with finance managers, production planning and logistics.

Organizational structure and effective marketing management

Where **marketing management** is perceived and used as one of the functional elements necessary to achieve operational objectives, then its effectiveness will be assisted or constrained by **organizational structure**. Using the broadest definition of 'marketing' – meeting customer needs and organizational objectives – the choice of organizational structure will frequently reflect the relative importance attached to the needs of the customer and the needs of the organization.

In this marketing context, three types of organizational structure are explored:

- hierarchical
- matrix
- project team

Hierarchical organizational structure

The hierarchy of this, the most traditional form of organization, is represented by the pyramid with top management at the pinnacle and the lowest rank of worker at the base. The number of management layers between the two determines how high or flat the structure becomes, and this is critical to communication and motivation.

Under this model, top management has ultimate control over decisions. The enterprise is structured along functional lines to make the most effective use of specialist knowledge, skills and experience. For the one-product enterprise this structure is effective. However, as the enterprise diversifies, the amount of information that top management has to absorb expands beyond human capacity to analyse. Under the pressures of operational decisions, strategic planning is sacrificed.

One solution to this problem is the multi-division organization, where the functional structure is replicated for each product or product group. This reduces the information to be processed for effective decision-making at the divisional level. However, top management in some organizations has been shown to be unwilling to decentralize decision-making and to fail to implement the necessary control systems to support such decentralization (Hill and Pickering, 1986).

Divisionalization assumes delegated responsibility for pricing, pay and incentives, cash flow and strategic planning, if the division is to be a true **profit centre**. In marketing terms, responsibility would be defined in terms of product positioning to meet customer needs so long as financial objectives were also met. If there is cross-trading between divisions, then transfer pricing should reflect external market conditions.

In reality, divisions in many organizations have the status of **cost centre**s, where specific operations are to be conducted within budgets allocated by central management. Cross-subsidies can occur from one division to another where transfer pricing *does not* reflect external market conditions.

Research into the UK insurance industry indicates that, on average, 50–60% of divisionalized companies operate as profit centres (Ingham, 1991). Some twenty per cent go a stage further in delegated authority by operating as **investment centres** although there is generally consultation with central management on investment decisions.

The hierarchical structure is best suited to the 'housekeeping' mode of marketing management, where there is little outside or inside stimulus for change, where corporate emphasis is on minimizing operating costs and communication is primarily vertical and 'top-down'.

Matrix organizational structure

Business is characterized by two main types of activity:

(1) Specific, non-recurring objectives involving particular tasks. From a marketing perspective, such activities would include a new product launch, a cost-reduction exercise on an existing product, or training of a new group of intermediaries on the technicalities of a product. At the more general level, there may be a financial or production focus to the activity.

(2) Regular, repeated activity which requires functional specialisms organized to achieve economies of scale. For marketing specialists this would include briefing a market research company, evaluating a media plan or monitoring retail audit data for sales performance.

The challenge of business organization is to accommodate both forms of activity. The **matrix organization** is one way in which the dual design can operate effectively.

In the formal matrix structure there are **dual reporting and control mechanisms**. This permits the functional control and expert input necessary to maintain the company's position. At the same time there is the flexibility for the specialist to be a member of a task-directed team under the influence of a different management structure. The matrix structure is illustrated in Figure 2.3, where functional management represents one side of the grid and project management forms the other side.

The balance of authority between the two reporting structures can lay along a spectrum, and Galbraith has identified three points along this spectrum which he labels 'coordination', 'overlay' and 'secondment' (Bresnen, 1990).

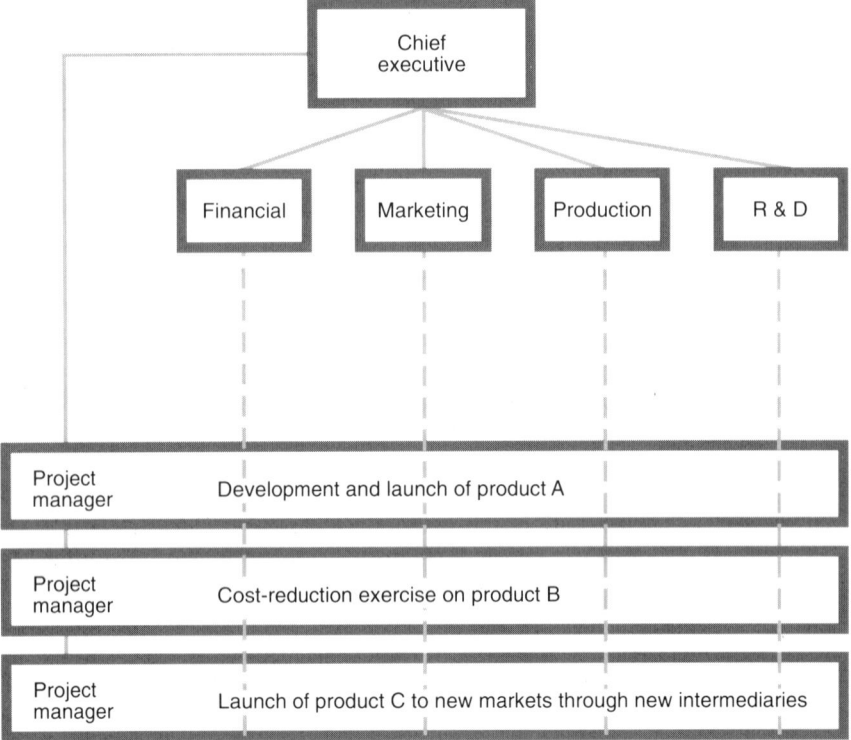

Figure 2.3 Example of matrix organization structure.

With rapid advances in technology a major task or project may be initiated without a clear view of the end result. This leads to **task uncertainty**, which is added to the **task complexity** associated with many major projects. Dual management control provides organizational benefits in this demanding environment. However, there are also disadvantages to the matrix structure:

- conflict of reporting goals leading to stress for the individual;
- vague delineation of responsibilities in one or both areas;
- increased responsibility for a member of a team, without comparable authority.

Many organizations operate a matrix structure which is not formalized, but accepted as an effective way of achieving business objectives *and* providing managers and specialists with development opportunities outside their narrow functional role.

Organizational structure based around project teams

In contrast with the 'housekeeping' or product maintenance approach to marketing management, the development of new products and successful market launch requires the synthesis and application of diverse skills and knowledge. These are frequently drawn from managers with specific functional responsibilities who also contribute to a special project on a part-time basis. The functional skills that they bring to the project can range from scientific and technical to financial and commercial, from creative and design to statistical and analytical.

The type of knowledge, skills and experience necessary for an individual to make a significant contribution to a new product development team will depend on the nature of the product to be brought to market. There are key differences in the features of consumer and industrial products which require contrasting expertise, as illustrated in Table 2.4.

There is a further dilemma in project management: how are such knowledge and skills to be harnessed for the success of the project? What is the management process and is an autocratic or democratic route preferable for a timely outcome?

Table 2.4 Different expertise required for project teams in consumer and industrial marketing management.

Consumer	Industrial
(1) Customers number hundreds of thousands, which leads to *mathematical norms* to buying patterns. Quantitative skills are needed to identify these through research, modelling and forecasting. Standard skills can be applied to a wide range of markets.	Customers are fewer (tens or hundreds), so *mathematical norms* may not exist or may be difficult to identify. Extrapolation skills and thorough understanding of the product and market are needed.
(2) Because of the importance of *branding*, creative skills are needed for design and innovation to meet emerging, identified consumer needs.	Because of the importance of *technical superiority*, there is a high premium on scientific knowledge and electronic engineering capability.
(3) *Communication* of the product benefits is based on *advertising*, which requires understanding of consumers' cognitive response.	*Communication* of the product is based on technical knowledge and support through intermediaries or salesforce.
(4) *Pricing* is linked to product positioning and advertising expenditure. Skills needed to control expenditure to optimize sales performance.	*Pricing* depends on product costs. Skills needed to control development and manufacturing costs.
(5) *Pricing* per unit generally low and non-negotiable. Therefore low authority vested in sales personnel.	*Pricing* per unit generally high and negotiable. Therefore authority vested in sales personnel, who also need negotiating skills.
(6) *Interpersonal* skills needed for management of complex *internal relationships* to bring products to market.	High level of *interpersonal* skills needed for liaison with customers, to identify and fulfil their organizational needs.

A **project management** culture thrives on – and responds to – change. The organization of skilled resource is arranged around one-off tasks rather than sequential and repeated activity. The importance to marketing management is that such an approach can focus on (changing) customer needs and how to meet them. The coexistence of project management teams alongside traditional line management means that checks and controls are still in place but that communication can also flow horizontally.

The success of this approach for marketing activity lies in the definition of project management:

> 'Project organizations are characterized by matrix structures and groups, and individual specialists who are encouraged to show initiative and make contributions at all levels. They emphasize added value rather than cost control. Because people can manage and work on assignments at different levels, status come not from who they are but from what they do'
> (Firth, 1990).

A management team is composed of individuals bringing to the group not only specialist knowledge, skills and experience, but also personality differences and behavioural tendencies. Top managers of an organization may take the intuitive decision that a team of highly intelligent managers will produce the best results for a specific project. Alternatively, there is a tendency for organizations with an identifiable culture to recruit and put into management teams individuals with similar personalities and behaviour patterns.

Either of these scenarios is likely to lead to poor performance, according to research on team-building carried out by Belbin (1981). Analysis of success of teams with differing compositions showed that the best results were evident where individuals brought to the group a range of different qualities and behaviour patterns.

The 'market-led' or 'customer-led' organization

In the traditional organization, response to market changes takes place within a structure that defines relationships between managers and the formalities of information flow. In contrast, the organization that sees itself as focusing on the needs of the market and customer develops informal structures which are most appropriate at the time to meet these needs.

The project team approach is significant here as it lends itself to the major features that differentiate a 'customer-led' organization from the traditional corporation:

- It must be flexible and relatively 'flat' in structure, with few layers of management.

- It must be close to the customer, through constant personal contact, research and formalized feedback mechanisms.
- Information must flow vertically and horizontally.
- There must be response to the information, whether operational or strategic.
- Informed leadership is necessary to maintain cohesion and a sense of direction when management teams are created or disbanded in response to changing market needs.

Response to the market is arguably swifter where decision-making on use of resources is as close as possible to the point of contact with the customer. This means budgets being held at the point of delivery within smaller, autonomous business units, rather than back along the chain of hierarchy within a larger, more amorphous structure. It has been the drive towards better use of resources for providing health services that meet the changing needs of the British population which has led the UK National Health Service to change to this type of organization.

Example: The National Health Service – Organizational change focusing on customer needs

In 1989, the British government issued a White Paper, 'National Health Service – Working for Patients'. This marked the beginning of a revolution in the way in which the largest employer in Europe was to be organized to use a very large part of government spending in order to maintain and improve the health of the nation.

Historically, funds were held by area health authorities which budgeted for the activities of general practice and hospitals in each area. Budgets were set on the basis of past experience and population, with poor information on the actual needs of the catchment area or the quality of health provision by individual institutions. The prevailing management culture was therefore **supply-led**, with no real accountability by medical professionals for provision of service against resources used.

The White Paper proposed radical change through the adoption of an **internal market** in health service provision. Instead of budgets being allocated to units of provision (general practice surgeries or hospitals), they would be attached to units of demand (general practice patient list). Simultaneously, hospitals would have the option to become self-governing trusts outside the control of an area health authority. Such hospitals would be responsible for setting their own targets on provision against a business plan.

The theory was that the internal market would operate through GPs 'buying' hospital services for their patients out of an allocated budget, which would also cover prescribed medicines. Hospitals could set a price against specific operations or treatments, and they would compete with other providers.

The key features of this transition to an internal market are outlined in Table 2.5. It represents the largest exercise in the management of change for any organization in the UK, and there are important organizational behaviour aspects:

Table 2.5 Impact of the Government White Paper on National Health Service reforms.

Status quo before reforms	White Paper recommends	*Status quo* after reforms
No competition between institutions	Internal market	Institutions compete on price and quality
Supplier-led	Choice	Customer-led
Non-profit service	Self-governing institutions	For-profit service
Professionals-led	Stronger management	Management-led
Non-accountability (clinical freedom)	Medical and Financial audit	Accountability of professionals

- inertia to change;
- power of the medical profession;
- transitional arrangements while piloting the new system;
- lack of experience of existing staff in managing budgets;
- ethical considerations in determining medical priorities using financial criteria.

These management issues highlight the need for very different expertise under the new market system. Some of this can be acquired through **training**, but this presupposes a disposition on the part of the individual to make the culture change necessary to adopt new working practices. This culture change is associated with an assumption for the past 40 years that all health needs of the population will be met free at the point of use, and will be publicly funded. The political initiative behind the White Paper is viewed by some as a mechanism for ceasing to commit to this universal provision, with the objective of **privatizing** the National Health Service. The concepts of markets, price and customers are particularly alien to many involved in health provision.

Organizing for success in the small business

In contrast to the largest employer in Europe, an entrepreneur has to be aware of customer needs for small business survival and growth. However, the criteria for success are not necessarily financial, as research among 61 electrical engineering businesses in Yorkshire has illustrated (Foley and Green, 1991). In this study, only 8% of entrepreneurs put financial ambition as the motivating factor for running a small business. Success was more frequently defined in terms of making a product, developing new products or (for cooperatives and community businesses) achievement of alternative goals through different organizational structures.

The type of organization adopted to meet goals becomes relevant as the size of the workforce increases. Only 12% of respondents wanted their companies to expand to more than 200 employees (the upper threshold of a small business). A workforce of 27 employees was seen as the optimum beyond which the owner/manager would have to delegate managerial responsibility for major operational areas.

In contrast with the more analytical approach of business managers in large organizations, entrepreneurs were less concerned with risk, and attributed success to a loyal workforce, hard work and luck. It can be argued that effective use of business planning and marketing enables the entrepreneur to take advantage of market opportunities as they arise. This represents the analytical evaluation of performance although the entrepreneur may use more emotive words.

Leadership for change

The turbulence created by organizational change makes heavy demands on management and leadership skills. This is because there is inevitable resistance to change on the part of some or all of the workforce, depending on the degree of threat to the *status quo* and the position of individuals before and after change.

One of the most significant examples from the 1990s is the renunciation of communism by the USSR and the adoption of free-market principles. The move from a command economy to a buy/sell situation based on an agreed price was a quantum leap that could not be accommodated without new infrastructure. However, this transition was blocked by the lack of cooperation of previous party members who controlled the food supply chains under the old order. As a result, the supply chains collapsed and there were food shortages, which created political instability. This was a very severe test of leadership, when the population had to be convinced that the hardships were necessary for the country to make progress and gain the confidence of the Western world.

At the corporate level, the impact of change on the individual is equally serious where livelihood is at stake, but more commonly it means changing working practices and relationships. The individual has to be convinced that the changes are for the good. Good leadership will invoke a sense that change is managed rather than imposed and will be aware of, and respond to, individual needs. The situation creates individual stress which has to be minimized and managed, and there is a rational response that accepts the necessity for change but an emotional response that rejects it. Effective leadership in such situations will adopt a management style that incorporates the following attributes (Darcy and Kleiner, 1991):

- pragmatism
- active involvement

- flexibility
- sensitivity
- integrity

As the rate of change becomes exponential rather than linear through technological advances, particularly in the field of telecommunications and computing, then this style of management will need to be the norm rather than the exception.

Marketing management of the 1990s and beyond

It is unlikely that traditional organizational structures will be adequate for the task of enabling marketing management to use resources in a way that optimizes market opportunities in the 1990s. The overriding objective for many major companies in the past two decades has been the quest for economies of scale to maximize return on capital. Organization structure supported this goal in an environment in which market growth provided external momentum.

Saturation of many consumer markets means that profit and added value must derive from fulfilling needs through **mass customization** (discussed further in Chapter 5). The emphasis will move from manufacturing to information processing and marketing. There will be a need for highly specialist skills which are more cost-effectively 'bought in' rather than directly employed.

This will lead to a trend away from the vertically integrated organization (manufacturing–commercial centre–distribution), towards a nucleus or core which is primarily information-driven, with a network of suppliers. One form of this is the **marketing exchange company**, where the strategic core can be viewed as the worldwide network of marketing offices and information centres connected by satellite and a computerized information system (Achrol, 1991).

As the amount of specialist information to be processed increases there will be reliance on outside professionals, thus reducing the need for large organizations. Instead, there will be less rigidly defined groups managing projects, where the skill emphasis will be interpersonal as well as intellectual. In such a scenario, the generalist rather than the specialist may be better equipped to survive constant turbulence. Human capital will come to be regarded as an internal and external resource as relationships with suppliers become more like alliances than simple contractual arrangements. Networking at the individual and organizational level will be essential for the marketing manager. This will provide the mechanism for accessing influence, knowledge, leads and resources which may be the key to competitive edge (Sonnenberg, 1990).

Table 2.6   Features of 'visionary' management and organizations.

Influence	Reaction
(1) Removal of barriers (physical, legal, financial).	Formation of new alliances and different commercial relationships.
(2) Speed of communication.	Ability of managers to absorb information and respond.
(3) Business activities will be simultaneous and not sequential.	More complex working environment makes multi-skill demands on managers.
(4) Better educated workforce.	Greater demands on management and leadership for motivation.
(5) More rapidly changing market environment.	Flexible team-type organization perpetually in a state of flux.
(6) Increasing tension between traditional business objectives and concern for the individual and the environment.	Leadership that can exploit this tension to create a business structure conducive to innovation and successful marketing.

These considerations bring into question what exactly is meant by a **firm** or **business enterprise**. At one end of the spectrum, the corporate entity is a facilitator for a series of contracts. At the other end of the spectrum, the strategic core of the firm can be considered to comprise visible assets, such as technology, finance and people, as well as the invisible assets of interpersonal skills, culture and ideas which set the organization apart from its competition (Aoki *et al.*, 1990). In this sense, the value of the individual contracts between the firm and internal and external associates is more difficult to quantify than suggested by the legal definition.

Whatever the definition, the need for **vision** on the part of managers will be intensified by the impact of the technological and economic environment on the nature of competition. Some of the features of this new vision are outlined in Table 2.6. Organizations that recoil at the need for different types of leadership and more flexible structures will find the most able and valuable employees fleeing to pastures new.

European perspective

The pan-European business has the potential for being more complex than some global corporations. This is because certain global businesses have developed through identifying territories where market needs, culture and language are broadly similar. Some multinationals have expanded through links with the old British Empire (Beecham before the merger with Smith, Kline French, and Anglo-Dutch conglomerate Unilever spring to mind), but penetration of European markets was later and slower. Similarly, in some UK industry sectors, there is a stronger relationship with the USA than with Europe; there are historical reasons for companies that supply defence equipment taking this approach, but the retailing sector is motivated more by the expected return on capital.

Diverse cultures and languages across the 12 Member States will remain a barrier to cross-border business. The commercial benefits of pan-European marketing accrue from identifying similar needs – and in serving them, accommodating minor differences at the same time. The moves towards harmonization in commercial, legal, social and economic fields for the 12 Member States will, in time, cultivate convergence of consumer and industrial needs as well as reduce operational impediments to trade.

The role of corporate management in this process is to promote the same ethos and goals in other Member States as have been the key to success in the home market. This filters down to marketing management through the strategy for each product or service. This will translate into product benefits and design (with quality paramount), creating access to this product for the target market through a specific distribution network, and communicating the product message through appropriate media.

European product management

The first choice of any European marketing manager should be to adopt in other Member States as much of the successful 'product formula' from the home market as is indicated through market research and testing, and is practicable. This route focuses on a pan-European image for the product as well as achieving economies of scale. Marketing managers in subsidiaries invariably try to stamp an individual identity on products destined for their markets. Carefully directed strategy, strong communication links between head office and subsidiaries and interchange of marketing personnel are measures designed to reduce this tendency.

Where customer needs in Germany may be similar to those in the UK, there will be differences in laws, technical standards, industry codes of practice and commercial culture. These differences will affect the way in which a marketing manager implements a marketing plan from one Member State to the next, however similar the underlying product strategy. The following six examples illustrate the wide-ranging influence on marketing operations:

- The nature of a contract between a software design house in the UK and a French distributor giving rise to a different balance of rights than a similar contract in the UK.

- Legal restrictions in Belgium to giving high levels of discount on the price of an industrial tool that is going out of production; however, this approach would be permissible in other Member States.
- Higher road haulage charges in Germany than in the UK and Italy, increasing the cost of product access; UK hauliers would not be allowed total freedom to operate for internal German deliveries.
- Differences in requirements for efficacy evidence from clinical trials for drugs across Member States. There is also the issue of different rules as to how trials on human volunteers may be conducted.
- Considerably less television airtime available in Germany for advertising a new shampoo than is available in the UK or Italy. The quality of airtime (and audience measurement) may also be lower in some Member States.
- More stringent requirements as to space, layout and exits for a branch office in some Member States as a result of safety regulations. Higher social charges on employers would also increase costs.

Taking the broad areas of responsibility of the European marketing manager, each is affected by differences in laws and practices, making the pan-European task significantly more complex. Some of the key issues are summarized in Table 2.7. The move towards harmonization in each area will reinforce the marketing manager's ability to think and act 'European'.

The European Commission's attempts to gain consensus and convergence have had a chequered history. In some areas – notably competition law in relation to exclusive distribution agreements – there have been significant judgements and precedents. In others, such as pricing, there have been fewer cases that provide companies with guidance on what is acceptable under Commission rules. In highly specialist areas such as television advertising or sales promotions, providing short-term incentives, the principle of subsidiarity has been reinforced, leaving a very confused scenario in each sector of marketing practice. The power of industry groups in lobbying the Commission cannot be underestimated in attempting to predict the course of future EC directives.

Developing an export market is costly, with pay-back often taking longer than the same launch in the home market. This is one reason why British companies have preferred to extend the product range at home rather than entering other territories. A second reason is the lower gross margin achievable. (**Gross margin** is the amount left from the selling price after product costs and marketing costs have been deducted: the remainder covers overheads and profit.) With the harmonization process far from complete, costs in other markets will inevitably be higher and EC rules on pricing may prevent recovery of the optimal margin through charging what the market will bear.

Table 2.7 Areas of responsibility of a marketing manager affected by diverse laws and practices across Member States.

Marketing responsibility	Areas of diverse laws and practices across Member States
Product design	(1) Technical standards (2) Safety laws (3) Consumer protection
Research and development	(1) Product testing; requirements and limitations (2) Patent law
Market research	(1) Laws on confidentiality and privacy (2) Data protection law (3) Acceptability of sampling methods and questions (4) Stage of industry development
Advertising	(1) Restrictions on air-time (2) Laws on product claims and comparative advertising (3) Acceptability of message type (cultural and religious) (4) Trade-mark law (5) Stage of industry development
Sales promotion	(1) Legality of specific incentives (2) Value perception in relation to cost (3) Stage of industry development
Direct marketing	(1) Data protection law (2) Cultural view of personal intrusion (3) Quality and reliability of the postal service
Personal selling	(1) Law in relation to contract between principal and agent (2) Restrictions to selling in the home (3) Licences required for specific products (such as financial services)
Distribution	(1) Laws against anti-competitive practices (e.g. vertical integration, exclusive distribution agreements) (2) Traditional intermediary power (wholesalers, brokers) (3) Licensed hauliers, cabotage
Pricing	(1) Inclusive elements: service, training, parts (2) Legality of discounting (3) Tendering formalities (4) Currency of quotation (5) Additional product costs due to excise duties on raw materials and statutory employee social provision

Skills and knowledge of the European marketing manager

Within the ideal portfolio of skills of the marketing manager shown in Table 2.3, there will be particularly heavy demands on the interpersonal skills of the European marketing manager. In order to attain development and acceptance of a pan-European strategy and forward plan, the ability to motivate a multi-cultural team and gain consensus on major issues as well as day-to-day operations will be paramount. Understanding and acceptance of differing cultures on the part of the manager will provide a role model for subordinates. Foreign language capability will be a significant tool in increasing mutual cooperation of managers across borders.

There are three routes to effective European management:

- higher education
- experience
- training

Many younger managers adopt a positive European route to their careers through studying for an international qualification in business at undergraduate or master's level. This is reinforced by experience of working in European subsidiaries. Large companies build a valuable resource through the creation of an informal network of managers who have moved across borders.

The management seminar can be used for international training purposes in two modes:

(1) *Context-driven*   The topic chosen for exploration and group work is not specific to the company but enables managers to acquire new ideas and attitudes which can be applied later. Examples would be: new ways of looking at employee relations, EC pricing judgements, cultural influences on distribution.

(2) *Task-driven*   In this type of seminar a specific corporate opportunity or development acts as the focus for brainstorming and group activity. The terms of reference would be linked to Europe with delegates from several European markets. This exercise could be used as the seed-corn for a marketing development project, and at the same time encourage new attitudes and modes of behaviour.

Managers who take a pan-European view of markets at an early stage in their careers are more likely to contribute towards a company culture moving in that direction away from a home market focus. The intransigent attitudes of more mature managers trained along traditional functional and national lines could prove the greatest impediment to change.

A company with ambitions to become European in philosophy and business mix must have a strategy for informing managers of changes taking place in the EC, including the successes (or difficulties) in the process of harmonization. Some organizations, such as ICL, have appreciated the importance of this education process, appointing a senior manager with responsibility for it. This constant updating process can take the form of seminars, in-house literature or a networked database.

An early induction into the process of European integration can give managers an insight into how rapidly changes will occur in their own area of responsibility. At the corporate level, the likely impact on the business can be assessed and strategy evolved to take advantage of the opportunities arising from the enlarged market and reduce threats from potential competition in other Member States. Competition will also come from US companies which view the European harmonization process as one of several global changes to monitor. Their management-updating methods will ensure that every directive is scrutinized for the way in which products and operating methods are affected (Miller, 1990).

Adopting a pan-European marketing strategy

The first stage in the process of pan-European marketing is acceptance that this is desirable at the **strategic management** level. For most companies, the focus will be on products already established in one or more EC Member States. The experience gained from past success will provide a basis for a more consolidated approach to operations, and a possible blueprint for penetrating new markets. The initial assessment process will require three questions to be asked for each product.

(1)   What are the common features across countries?
(2)   What are the differences where convergence is possible? These differences will be identified through examination of **laws, technical standards, commercial practice** and **customer needs**.
(3)   What are the differences that have to remain?

Each organization will adopt a list of pan-European brands according to the balance between the convergent elements, (1) plus (2), and the divergent elements, (3).

The costs associated with convergence will mean that changes will be phased according to economic choices – new packaging materials when stock of the old material has been used, new electronic components as the original become obsolete, compatible software designed during the normal upgrading cycle. Good timing can reduce costs of convergence, but not eliminate them entirely. There are also risks attached to change, and researching consumer acceptance is vital for major brands. The local agent or salesforce can be used for smoothing relations with business customers in the process of changing technical product specifications.

The short-term costs of convergence will be weighed against the longer-term opportunities for market penetration with economies of scale. This is part of the strategic planning process at the European level, which is explored in the European perspectives of three chapters of the book:

Chapter 3:   Strategic Marketing Decisions
Chapter 15:   Portfolio Analysis
Chapter 16:   New Product Development

Pan-European marketing implementation

The second stage of the European marketing management process is **implementation**. Every aspect of product presentation, performance, delivery and communication has to be scrutinized for compliance with laws and commercial practices of individual Member States where the product is to be marketed. Marketing managers must also judge the direction that the European Commission will take in harmonizing controls in such areas as advertising, consumer incentives, product liability and high-pressure selling. The detailed implications of issues outlined in Table 2.7 are explored in the European perspectives of the relevant chapters.

Since this text is not product-specific, students and practitioners have the opportunity to apply some of the facts, trends and conceptual structures to markets in which they have some experience. Alternatively, they can identify industries where harmonization will mean radical rationalization in the medium to longer term, provided that national governments no longer subsidize industries of national importance, under the threat of EC punitive judgements.

As an example, the corporate banking industry attracts complications over and above those outlined in Table 2.7 when operating across European borders. This is because every transaction takes on some of the features normally associated with business management at the aggregate level (Stevenson, 1989):

- currency risks
- tax implications
- trans-border data flow
- time-zone differences
- different banking procedures
- different regulatory conditions

Implications for, and the role of, financial services industries in EC harmonization feature in three further chapters:

Chapter 14: the way in which banks can support corporate moves to budget and conduct financial reporting on a pan-European basis; the consideration of doing business in ECUs.
Chapter 15: the likelihood of achieving economies of scale through pan-European operations in banking.

Chapter 17: the role of electronic trading between banks in supporting faster and better logistics between supplier and customer.

In many respects, attitudes and adoption of new working practices supported by information technology within the banking infrastructure will determine the pace of cross-border business alignment in many other industries. This is because the flow of financial information will be the bedrock of **performance evaluation**, which is the third key area of activity for a market-driven organization.

At the macro-level, debate over the Maastricht Treaty focused on concern that national governments would lose sovereignty over key policy areas. The possibility of a single currency and a non-partisan European bank featured heavily in this debate. However, even before the UK entered the European Monetary System (whereby the pound sterling was linked to other European currencies), some major companies believed that the biggest stumbling blocks in creating an open European market were fiscal and monetary policy rather than managerial issues. Allied-Lyons, Lucas Industries and the retail combine Storehouse demonstrate this attitude (Ferguson, 1988).

As these issues are explored in other chapters, the focus of this section will be on the *cultural aspects of managing organizations*. It is assumed that every market-driven organization strives to achieve a balance between meeting corporate objectives and serving the needs of individuals – whether customers, employees or members of the local or international community. The issues are explored under four headings:

(1)   Importance of national culture in managing the organization.
(2)   Building the European marketing team.
(3)   European policy and the small business.
(4)   Ethics in business – the marketing dimension.

Importance of national culture in managing the organization

Alternative models of managing the organization have already been identified (hierarchical, matrix and project teams), and these approaches are identified with Western management theory and practice. However, diverse cultures within Europe will affect the way in which the application of these models is perceived. For example, how far is authority attached to an individual through his or her qualifications and track record, or is managerial authority bound up with the formal functional role, regardless of individual competence? Will a matrix reporting structure be alien to certain national cultures?

Table 2.8   Different perceptions of organizations as a result of national culture.

Organizations as political systems	French and Italian managers perceived a greater political role for managers inside and outside the organization than Danish, British, Dutch or German managers.
Organizations as authority systems	French, Italian and Belgian managers reported a more personal and social concept of authority. Managers from the USA, Switzerland and Germany reported a more rational view of authority that regulates interaction between tasks and functions.
Organizations as hierarchical relationship systems	There was a greater likelihood of a matrix structure being accepted in the USA, the Netherlands and Sweden. A matrix structure would not be as readily accepted by French and Italian managers.

Source: Laurent (1983).

Laurent (1983) made a significant contribution to understanding the diverse national concepts of management. He used a 56-item questionnaire on 817 respondents from nine European countries and the United States. The respondents came from groups of upper- to middle-level managers attending various INSEAD development programmes in the late 1970s. Correlation analysis was conducted along country not individual lines, to reveal significant country differences along three main parameters (see Table 2.8). The national differences in the way in which organizational structure and managerial roles are perceived (as identified by Laurent) will affect the success of changing organizational structure to meet European market needs.

Multinational organizations cultivate corporate cultures which are viewed as critical to success at the international level as well as in the home market. There is a presumption that this corporate culture (often finding its roots in the philosophy of the founder) overrides the influence of national culture. This has been shown *not* to be the case (Laurent, 1986), as deep-seated managerial assumptions are strongly shaped by national cultures, and these appear not to be deflected by corporate culture.

Laurent summarizes findings across groups of managers working in affiliated companies of a large US multinational firm:

> '*German* managers believe that creativity is essential for career success. In their mind, the successful manager is the one who has the right individual characteristics. Their outlook is rational: they view the organization as a coordinated network of individuals who make appropriate decisions based on their professional competence and knowledge.
>
> '*British* managers hold a more interpersonal and subjective view of the organizational world....They view the organization

primarily as a network of relationships between individuals who get things done by influencing each other through communicating and negotiating.

'*French* managers look at the organization as an authority network where the power to organize and control the actors stems from their positioning in the hierarchy.... They perceive the ability to manage power relationships effectively and to 'work the system' as particularly critical to their success.'

Such differences are deep-rooted, and even in the enlightened era of the 1990s it is unlikely that a definitive corporate programme of training, management seminars and cross-border transfers can do more than enhance mutual understanding and cooperation.

Such understanding of cultural differences is also critical to determine what is acceptable behaviour at the interpersonal level in dealing with foreign nationals from other organizations. Cultural formalities, particularly at the introduction stage of a protracted negotiation or partnership, can shape perceptions of the individual and the organization that outlive an initial commercial agreement (Hawkins, 1983).

Building the European marketing team

Many of the facets of global team-building can be employed at the European level; an initial disadvantage for many organizations is that the closeness of European markets has meant that they have been viewed as an adjunct to the home market, administered through an export department, with little strategic analysis of market needs. The formation of a European team involves a change in attitudes and working practices, with senior management commitment vital at every stage. Success in the process depends on five factors identified as **experiential guidelines**:

- strategic assessment of European marketing management needs;
- formal agenda of meetings and seminars;
- development of an informal network;
- shared experiences at the operational level;
- integrated projects – where feasible and cost-effective.

The pan-European mailing is an example of how this process can be used to integrate promotion across several Member States. There is then a logistical choice as to whether customer access to the product or service is also coordinated from a centre, or whether local provision is preferable for cost and quality reasons.

The harmonization of postal rates across Europe has eliminated cost barriers to integrated direct marketing campaigns. However, there is also a need for:

- database compatibility (the same information on prospects held in a similar format across countries);
- knowledge of legality of copy used and incentives;
- competence in creating foreign language versions of the communication;
- understanding of how the response will be handled for each market from the perspectives of customer requirements and logistical constraints.

The net result should be enhancement of the process through message, presentation and administration, and cost benefits from shared creative and economies of scale in print and mailing.

From this example, the process of European marketing appears relatively straightforward. The difficulties emerge in applying the process where product specifications and marketing practices differ across markets for legal reasons. Two markets are highlighted as suffering particularly from this scenario, the pharmaceutical industry and the car market.

Example 1

The European car has become a reality for some major producers – but there are still barriers to reaping all the economies of scale which could accrue from pan-European production. Differing technological and ecological standards between countries lead to flexible production technology that is at odds with large-scale output.

For example, in October 1992 the Dutch government ordered that all car wrecks, used tyres, batteries and waste would have to be recycled from 1994. The legislation to enforce this became necessary because of a shortage of space to bury rubbish.

Manufacturers targeting Europe with new models must decide whether to adopt the necessary specifications for all cars produced (estimated to cost 250 guilders per car), or whether to have a specific production run for the Netherlands.

Example 2

Sterling Drug used management development to build a world-class global team for its International Division, which has a $1.1 billion turnover. The plan was developed opportunistically, but there was a formal **people task-force** in the same way as task-forces were instituted for other critical areas (Fulmer and Goodwin, 1991). Two core management development programmes were created – one for senior managers which focused on global strategic thinking, and one for key managers who reported to them. This programme included a computer simulation of the decision-making process.

Team development in the International Division was such a success that the process was extended to the corporate level. The decision was made to integrate international and domestic activities by 1991, as a commitment to becoming a global force in pharmaceuticals.

The decision to change the organizational structure to accommodate strategic business development for a broader spread of geographical markets is often implemented through gradual evolution of a traditional hierarchy to new communication and reporting networks. The matrix structure can take into account both **product** and **regional** demands, but this can prove inflexible and complex. Some nationalities also have greater difficulty in fitting into this structure.

There are three coordination concepts that help to integrate country-based criteria within a central administrative process (Meffert and Bloch, 1991):

- The lead country concept for a product or product group (this need not be the home market).
- Regular communication circles: to coordinate decentralized international activity, especially where there are significant country needs.
- Global coordination groups: this provides a forum for representatives of the host country enterprises to present and discuss market needs, and to develop standard development routes. This has particular application for Europe.

Team consensus on the way forward is likely to be a better route to success than imposition of a uniform approach by the head office. Shared information (particularly from syndicated or customized market research) is one route to mutual understanding of differing market needs, and can set the agenda for coordinated projects. There will always be the need for local expertise, however sophisticated the European database becomes as a reservoir of knowledge for an integrated marketing approach.

European policy and the small business

In 1986, there were approximately 13.5 million enterprises in the European Community. More than 91% of these were micro enterprises (less than 10 employees), half of which are self-employed without employees. Small and medium-sized enterprises (SMEs), with more than 10 and less than 500 employees, represent 8.5% of the enterprises, but account for 45% of employment.

It is because of their significance for national employment as well as their potential for growth that SMEs attract the attention, endeavours and budgets of individual EC Member States. The focus of support and protection from burdensome administration differs across Member States according to underlying policy and the government department responsible for SMEs.

Most European policy affecting SMEs is initiated by other directorates, and a focal point for the small business lobby is therefore critical to fair representation. However, there are indications that, as so often happens at the national level, a merger of DG23 into DG3 (Internal Market and Industrial Affairs) is under consideration (Small Business Perspective, 1992). The increasing importance of small businesses to economic growth in Member States will mean that their governments will have to listen to this lobby group; should representation at EC level disappear, then the opportunity to coordinate policy will have been sacrificed to political expediency.

Ethics in business

Most of the accredited literature on business ethics originates from the United States, where this subject is now an integral component of MBA programmes and similar higher degrees. It is explored in the context of European marketing and business development for two key reasons:

- A **market-driven** organization is, by definition, meeting the needs of a defined public: these needs include a perception of the organization as dealing honestly and fairly. There is also acceptance that there is corporate responsibility towards a wider community – at the local, national or international level. This could involve a balance between serving market needs and preserving natural resources or controlling harmful atmospheric emissions.

- **National cultures** impose different standards of behaviour on individuals and organizations. These can operate through accepted commercial practices, formalized codes of practice or legislation. Each market sector within each country is characterized by a mixture of these three. Developing a pan-European business philosophy and set of ground-rules becomes a complex task for organizations in markets where there are diverse practices.

At the macro-level, can commercial and industrial practices be judged against common standards? Would these apply to both a **free-market** system and a **centrally planned** economy as existed in the USSR and Eastern Europe before the collapse of communism? It is simpler to address ethics issues at the level of the corporation and the individual. Here, the dilemma is *'What balance should be struck between the profit interests of the corporation and the interests of society at large?'*

The traditional professions have a reputation for honesty and fair dealings which is protected through stringently applied codes of conduct administered by professional bodies. Lawyers or accountants who fall foul of the rules face serious sanctions. A person who operates within the business sphere with different knowledge, skills and experience suffers from a lack of clear perception on the part of the community as to the **moral ground rules** that dictate behaviour.

This individual has the additional dilemma of reconciling personal business ethics with those of the employer. Where there is reasonable convergence between the two in relation to dealings with suppliers, customers and the public at large, then the individual will not suffer moral discomfort. However, if there are sufficient individuals whose ethical standards differ from those of the employing organization, then there emerges an **ethics gap**. This is the difference between individual ground-rules and those of the organization (Carmichael and Drummond, 1989).

Where there is a wide ethics gap, the individual may find alternative employment as the only solution to excessive distress caused by conflict between personal moral standards and the activities to which they are a party. Where serious malpractice is identified, then the individual may need to follow conscience in reporting this to the relevant authorities. This can have serious consequences where, for example in Switzerland, such 'whistle-blowing' can contravene laws relating to confidentiality of commercial secrets, and result in criminal charges for the individual.

Ethics and the marketing dimension

The marketing manager has a responsibility to the organization for providing a product or service to the customer and meeting sales and profit targets. In this process, there is a variety of relationships in which the marketing manager is revealing standards of moral behaviour endorsed by the company. Each marketing relationship falls into one of two categories: firstly, that of the business arena, or secondly, the public arena, as illustrated in Figure 2.4. Where the customer relationship is with an individual consumer, then this falls into the public arena, and will be scrutinized by bodies protecting consumer interests or by specific lobby groups.

Some pressure groups recognize the marketing process as one of manipulation, hyperbole and 'puffery' without viewing communications in the context of contemporary attitudes held by a significant part of society. On the other hand, some companies take the view that any commercial act is acceptable if it remains on the right side of the law: this means taking no moral standpoint of their own in business dealings. These are extreme cases, and most organizations identify and work to a set of ground rules that reflects generally accepted standards of behaviour.

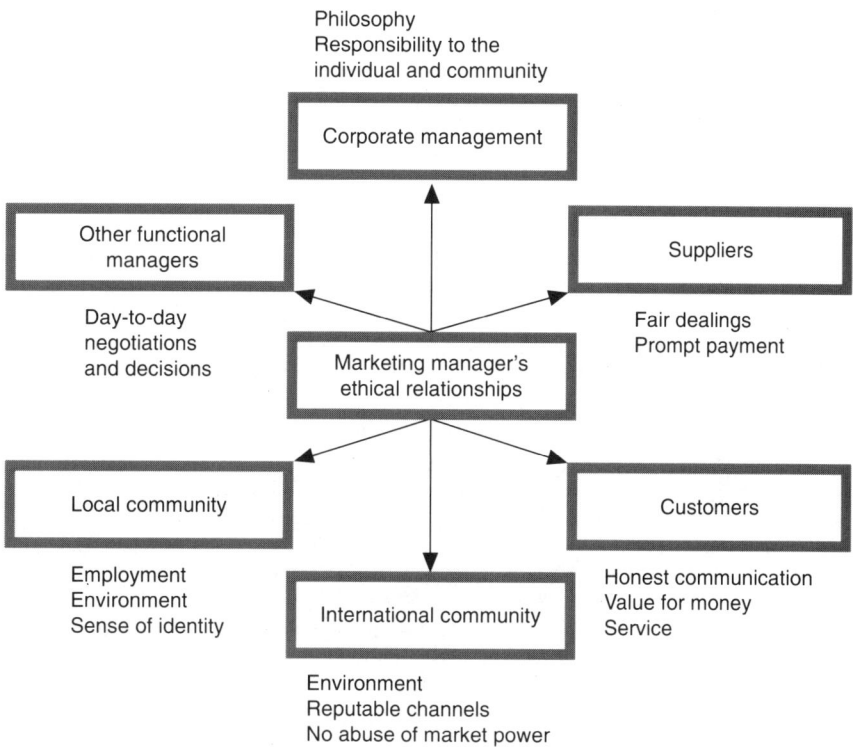

Figure 2.4   The ethical relationships of a marketing manager.

This does not mean that the marketing manager does not have to face ethical dilemmas in the course of fulfilling the role. Some of the situations that could give rise to moral conflict within the organization or between the company and its set of public forces are highlighted in Table 2.9. The examples chosen illustrate issues that fall within the marketing domain. The student might identify in which situations convergence between individual ground-rules and corporate ground-rules are essential to resolve the problem.

A reference framework for ethical behaviour to which individuals and the employing organization would be committed would generally provide straightforward solutions to these problems. As well as encompassing relationships with customers, suppliers and the community at large, it would also lay down ethical principles by which conditions of employment and the process of managerial accountability are judged.

This would require the commitment of company directors to ensure that there was reasonable consensus on the style and content of such a code of practice. It should then be communicated throughout the organization on a regular basis. This would comply with Donaldson (1989) in

Table 2.9 Examples of ethical dilemmas facing marketing management.

(1) Finance department invoices customers at list price in a period when the salesforce has sold against volume discounts. Only 20% of customers notice the error.

(2) In order to maintain gross margin on a concentrated fruit drink, the juice level is reduced without altering the product description on the packaging. Some customers use the drink as their primary source of Vitamin C.

(3) Selling a financial investment package that is inappropriate to the needs of the customer, but provides the best profit margin to the company and the most attractive commission to the seller.

(4) Promoting a nutrition product that has been successful in developed economies to less-developed markets where poor literacy could lead to misuse.

(5) Use of the 'development risks' defence for marketing a drug available only on doctor's prescription, but which is later shown to have serious side-effects. Initial clinical trials had indicated this risk was present, but was not significant.

(6) Use of 'scare' tactics in literature for accident insurance addressed to individual households.

(7) A senior sales representative is made aware of a significant sales support budget, when negotiating provision of army supplies to a country where bribery is an accepted part of doing business.

(8) All suppliers are paid by a company at 60 days from receipt of invoice, regardless of the terms of business indicated on the invoice and undertaken when the contract was made. A small advertising agency used by the marketing department has indicated that they will be in serious financial trouble if their invoice is not paid within the specified 30 days.

(9) The export department of a reputable fitness equipment manufacturer consistently refuses to meet an agent from another European country who wishes to import the equipment. The manufacturer supplies small quantities to select outlets in this export market at a high transfer price.

taking the position that 'the systematic handling of values in business and industry is no more impossible in principle than is the systematic treatment of problems of motivation, order and control in the empirical management literature'.

The driving force for a company to do this is not simply esoteric: there are increasing pressures from the customers on whom it depends. Concern for the environment is no longer the prerogative of fringe groups: such attitudes are now mainstream. The morality of a product or service is now judged by such ventures as **ethical portfolios** whereby investors can choose to exclude certain types of products (such as tobacco) from their financial planning. These pressures will force companies to seek greater cohesion between their public face and their private business dealings.

Problems and assignments

(1) Discuss the relationships between a marketing manager and other functional departments in a 'for profit' organization. Indicate where conflict may arise and how this may be resolved.

(2) How may the performance of a marketing manager be measured? Could such measures be used validly in performance-related remuneration?

(3) What are the key external relations of a marketing manager? What is the relative importance of these in (a) a business to business context and (b) consumer products?

(4) What are the relative advantages and disadvantages for marketing success of a matrix management structure compared with the traditional functional line management structure?

(5) In which areas of marketing activity would a project team approach be the preferred management route to success? Give your reasons.

(6) What are the major impediments to successful brand management on a pan-European basis for:

    (a)   a product where the strategy is dictated from Head Office?
    (b)   a product where local management has discretion on positioning and advertising?

(7) Apply an analytical technique for evaluating whether to manage the following products on a pan-European or single country basis:

    (a)   an electronic switching component for factory process control;
    (b)   designer spectacles;
    (c)   private health insurance.

(8) Discuss the cultural factors which are critical in implementing a matrix management structure across several EC Member States.

(9) A French car manufacturer and a British Jeep manufacturer have set up a joint venture for the development and pan-European launch of a new fun 'roadster' vehicle. What organizational structure would you recommend for the joint venture? Suggest formal communication and training activities for its inception.

(10) Why are ethical issues of product management made more complex when operating across European borders? Make reference to the different ethical relationships of a marketing manager.

References

Achrol R.S. (1991). Evolution of the marketing organisation: new forms for turbulent environments. *J. of Marketing*, **55**(Oct.), 77–93

Aoki M., Gustafsson B. and Williamson O.E. (1990). *The Firm as a Nexus of Treaties*. London: Sage

Belbin R.M. (1981). *Management Teams: Why They Succeed or Fail.* London: Butterworth-Heinemann

Bresnen M. (1990). *Organising Construction, Project Organisation and Matrix Management.* London: Routledge

Darcy T. and Kleiner B.H. (1991). Leadership for change in a turbulent environment. *Leadership Organization Development J.,* **12**(5), 12–16

Firth G. (1990). Introducing a project management culture. *European Management J.,* **9**(4), 437–443

Foley P. and Green H. (1991). *Small Business Success.* Paul Chapman Publishing

Hill C.W.L. and Pickering J.F. (1986). Divisionalisation, decentralisation and performance of large UK companies. *J. of Management Studies,* **23**

Ingham H. (1991). Organizational structure and internal control in the UK insurance industry. *The Services Industries J.,* **11**(4), 425–438

Sonnenberg F.K. (1990). How to reap the benefits of networking. *J. of Business Strategy,* **11**(1), 59–62

European perspective

Carmichael S. and Drummond J. (1989). *Good Business – A Guide to Corporate Responsibility and Business Ethics.* London: Business Books Ltd, pp. 91–93

Donaldson J. (1989). *Key Issues in Business Ethics.* London: Academic Press, p.166

Ferguson A. (1988). Take Europe by example. *Management Today,* Nov, 111–115

Fulmer R.H. and Goodwin J. (1991). Building a global team at Sterling Drug. *Executive Development,* **4**(3), 12–13

Hawkins S. (1983). How to understand your partner's cultural baggage. *International Management,* Sept, 48–51

de Koning A. and Snijders J. (1992). Policy on small- and medium-sized enterprises in countries of the European Community. *International Small Business J.,* **10**(3), 25–39

Laurent A. (1983). The cultural diversity of Western conceptions of management. *International Studies of Man and Organization,* **13**(1/2), 75–96

Laurent A. (1986). The cross-cultural puzzle of international human resource management. *Human Resource Management,* **25**(1), 91–102

Meffert H. and Bloch B. (1991). Globalisation strategies: their implementation. *Industrial Management and Data Systems,* **91**(5 November), 3–9

Miller L. (1990). Managers up to date. *Training and Development J.,* **44**(9), 35–37

Hands off DG23! (1992). *Small Business Perspective,* no. 4, July–August

Stevenson B.D. (1989). Product management in corporate banking. *International J. of Bank Marketing,* **7**(1), 17–21

3 Strategic marketing decisions

Chapter objectives:

- to describe the use of analytical tools for determining corporate and marketing strategy
- to identify the key stages in the strategic planning process
- to explore strategic options for entry to markets in other EC Member States
- to outline the impact of European environmental policy on corporate and marketing strategy

Introduction

Major multinational companies based in the USA or Japan have had the advantage of building marketing and technological strengths by serving the needs of large home populations. This, combined with opportunistic expansion abroad, sowed the seeds for the global businesses with which European-based companies are striving to compete. The elimination of barriers to the movement of goods, money and people within an open European market of 330 million people will provide companies based in Member States with the same home market advantages as these US and Japanese multinationals. However, results will depend on the speed of enactment of the various Directives, and on agreement by the Council of Ministers in the sensitive areas of social and fiscal harmonization.

Although a completely level playing field may not exist in Europe until the end of the 1990s, the changes that have already taken place add to the complexity of the environment in which companies must devise strategies for survival and growth. This process will not be without pain, as the moves to promote competition and reduce tendencies to protect national suppliers mean that there will be casualties in the search for economies of scale. There is likely to be a shock-wave of closures and rationalizations as the full impact of open competition in traditionally protected markets is felt. Where over-capacity has been disguised through state subsidies and artificially high prices charged by monopolies, the enforcement of EC competition law will encourage companies to face up to inefficiencies.

Simultaneously, at the operational level, managers will need to be conversant with the effects of Directives already in force on their areas of influence. The fact that there is little synchronization in the implementation of Directives makes this a complex task. For example, the Seventh Directive relating to harmonization of financial reporting has been implemented by most Member States, yet the final position as to the legal controls on broadcasting and sales promotion are far from clear. The principle of subsidiarity means that the laws of Member States take precedence where there is no strict EC interpretation, leading to confusion and the possibility of restrictive practices.

Although EC coherence will be elusive at the operational level until well into the 1990s, clarity of purpose will be vital at the strategic level if an organization is to prepare itself for the full impact of inevitable market changes. Traditional **strategic planning tools** will be necessary to deal with the more complex environment. Each organization must consider a far wider range of options for the way forward due to the multiplicative effect of the variables introduced by EC harmonization. These can be viewed in the context of the analysis of the **external environment** which is an essential precursor to defining **corporate strategy**. This discipline will apply whether the organization's goal is to include only one Member State or all 12 in the strategic plan, or whether Europe is but one region to be considered in a global blueprint for profitable growth.

The balance between investment for the longer term and profitability in the short term will be dictated by the prevailing culture of the organization and the external pressure from shareholders. Where the latter is dominant, as with large institutional investors looking for continued profits growth, a strategy for expansion into other Member States may be inconsistent with such pressure if margins achieved in the home market cannot be replicated. This scenario is illustrated by the fact that French, German and Benelux supermarket groups have made considerable progress in entering the markets of other Member States, whereas UK groups have not (Thompson, 1992). The average net margin of the major UK grocery retailing groups is 5–7%, whereas in France, Netherlands, Belgium and Germany, the average net margin is 0.5 to 1.5%. Even allowing for greater buying power, logistical efficiencies and advanced use of information technology on the part of the UK companies, the probability of matching UK margins abroad is low. So how will these retailing groups achieve growth in the future?

This dilemma illustrates the role of strategic analysis in determining the **company mission**, which is a short statement of corporate intent, including a definition of the market in which it sees itself, the company approach within it, and the nature of the relationship with customers and employees. The move to a European territorial definition of **the market** marks out those organizations which have embraced a pan-European strategy.

Following analysis of the external environment, strategic options are further reduced by **industry profiling** for each area of business activity, and by an evaluation of the company's ability to harness inner resources to meet the challenges of these key industry sectors. This evaluation takes the traditional form of a **SWOT analysis**, looking at company strengths, weaknesses, opportunities and threats.

When the longer-term strategy is defined (longer-term for retailing could be three years, whereas for a pharmaceutical company this would be ten years), **resource allocation** against the different business activities will require the application of portfolio analysis techniques as described in Chapter 15.

An understanding of the resource–reward equation for each business area will enable the company to formulate a distinct **marketing strategy** for each product group. Moving to this step without a detailed understanding of financial resources and constraints, and of the historic performance pattern against use of these resources, will increase the risk of failure to meet marketing and financial objectives.

An evaluation process is also necessary at the product group level in order to reduce marketing options based on **competitive analysis**. Use can be made of the concept of the **product life cycle** to help in determining the timing of investment to achieve growth, and when to expect pay-back. There is a range of **market entry options** for a new product, and a choice will be made based on the nature of **product differentiation** and the strength of existing and likely future competition. Finally, the marketing strategy is implemented through the marketing mix – **product** positioning and features, **price**, **distribution** and **logistics** (incorporating the **place** of product access) and the **promotion mix**. A sound marketing strategy can be undermined by poor implementation, and the theory and contemporary application of these areas of the marketing mix form the substance of Chapters 7 to 13.

An overview of the components of the strategic decision chain explored in this chapter is shown in Figure 3.1. Strategic routes for entering new territories, whether EC Member States or markets in other continents, are summarized in Table 3.1.

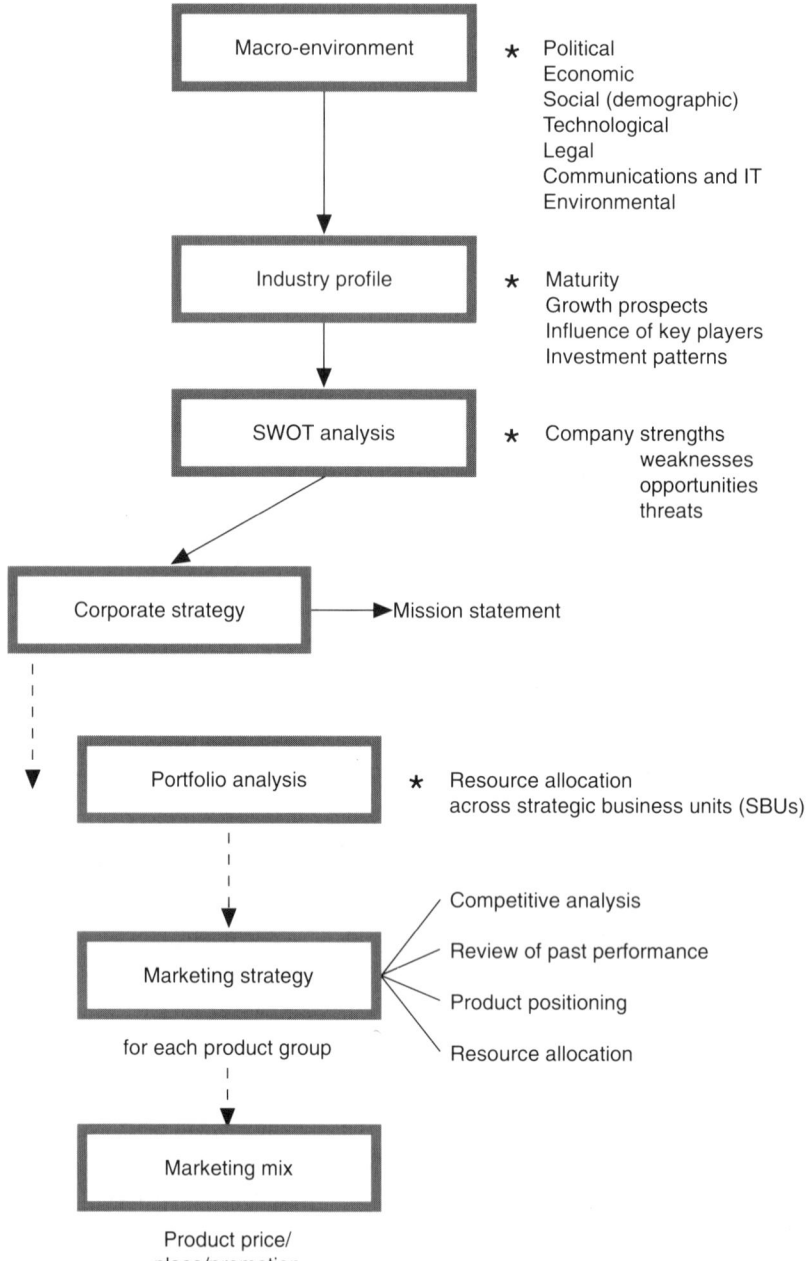

Figure 3.1 The strategic planning process.

Defining corporate strategy

Evaluating the macro-environment

For a company that is market-led, changes in the **political, economic and social environment** will be significant at two levels: firstly, these influences have a direct bearing on strategic decisions such as investment and employment policy. Secondly, they affect the markets in which the company operates through consumer confidence and changes in spending power. Over a longer time-scale, these influences work their way up the supply chain so that all intermediaries are ultimately affected. Tightening of government spending affects the military, education and health institutions as buyers of goods and services, and the severity of such changes will determine whether structural changes occur in specific industries. Contracting out of refuse collection, hospital cleaning services, homes for the elderly and the management of prisons are examples of the implementation of political ideology with far-reaching effects within existing financing and employment structures.

Contemporary issues and influences within each of the key macro-environmental areas are summarized in Table 3.1. Politically motivated changes in taxation or loosening of restrictions on the operation of financial markets can lead to rapid expansion of consumer spending and availability of capital and financial services. This was the UK scenario in 1987/1988. The subsequent recession as interest rates were raised to curb inflationary growth in money supply was longer than expected due to the restrictions on monetary policy once the UK had entered the ERM. (See the European Perspectives section of Chapter 14 for a fuller explanation.)

Demographic changes can be considered as part of the broader social trends, but shifts in attitude towards the role of women and towards the relationship between work and leisure have also led to new markets emerging. Differences in attitudes between generations are created through the higher incidence of working mothers, the higher divorce rate leading to second and third families, and greater ethnic mixing. This means that the family must be redefined and that economic aspirations change as education becomes critical to advancement (Waldrop, 1991).

In spite of the trend towards global provision where needs are homogenous on an international basis, minorities now have the courage and legal rights to maintain lifestyles redolent of traditional cultures. These groupings are of sufficient economic importance for companies to identify and serve specific needs. The emergence of cultural nationalism manifests itself through language, religion and custom, and the most significant trend in the 1980s was the Islamic revolution which took Western cultures by surprise (Naisbitt and Aburdene, 1990).

Table 3.1 Evaluation of the macro-environment.

Political	Move towards socialism and state intervention, or towards a free market with privatization and laissez faire; changes in taxation: general or product-specific; effect of government borrowing on interest rates.
Economic	Stages in the economic cycle: (1) high growth rate for GDP with industrial investment, increased spending power of individuals leading to new market opportunities (2) Slower growth with more stable markets, period of consolidation for industry (3) Recession: restructuring of industries suffering from over-capacity
Social	(1) Demographic trends (2) Longer life expectancy (3) Changing role of women (4) Increased leisure with job sharing (5) More educated population (6) Decreasing role of the nuclear family (7) More cosmopolitan society with greater cultural mix
Technological	(1) Automation (robotics) increasing productivity but reducing need for semi-skilled and unskilled labour (2) Increase in product obsolescence (shorter product life cycles) (3) Cost of research for new products becomes barrier to entry and threat to company survival (4) Importance of biotechnology
Legal	Move towards tighter controls or greater leniency in laws relating to acquisitions and mergers, monopoly power, government subsidies, sharing of information, employee conditions of service, financial reporting.
Communications and information technology	Diversification of broadcasting with specialist channels; interactive facilities for home shopping (consumer) and electronic data interchange (business-to-business). Trend towards moving information to workers rather than moving workers to the information. Companies with state-of-the-art IT gain competitive edge.
Environmental	Pollution controls on factory effluent; recycling of materials; replacement of ingredients harmful to the environment or the imposition of tax penalties to encourage product switching. Reduction in carbon dioxide emission levels in energy production and for vehicles.

The speed of the implementation of EC directives by Member States, and the gap between existing national provisions and the *status quo* after harmonization, will determine the turbulence of the **legal environment**. The EC has shown itself to be particularly effective in curbing anti-competitive activities of companies identified as occupying dominant positions in specific markets. However, the EC task appears more daunting where government monopolies are concerned, as in the case of French subsidies to the publicly owned telecommunications company.

Strategic decisions are influenced by the company's capacity to disseminate information throughout the organization, and by management capability to analyse and react. The status of **information technology** and the timing and level of investment in it will be a key determinant of competitive edge. Its interrelationship with, and effects on, traditional marketing methods are examined in Chapter 17.

At the consumer level, the **broadcasting** revolution with satellite and cable television posing a threat to established national channels is providing the mechanism for creating international aspirations and lifestyles. However, it is early days for consistent attitudes to be evident across borders. For example, company response to **environmental issues** will be in tune with consumer attitudes in specific markets, where these have been researched adequately. Government action in the form of laws relating to factory effluent, recyclability of materials and product ingredients harmful to the environment will be increasingly expensive for companies to implement. Those organizations (such as Procter & Gamble) which include within their marketing strategy an identification of consumer trade-off between product efficacy and concern for the environment will retain market share in the longer term.

Industry profile

The second stage of information analysis takes a narrower focus on industry performance and future prospects. Senior management is charged with monitoring and reacting to significant industry changes in the short term, but the discipline of a regular, formal review of structure and trends over the longer term provides a sound foundation for strategic decisions on investment for future success.

The data gathered for this stage is critical to detailed portfolio analysis: percentage growth rates of markets and degree of maturity; level of concentration and market shares; degree of influence of key players and investment patterns. Internal company performance data in the area of sales, profitability and return on investment is combined with this industry profile to provide a comprehensive database for the analysis stage.

The amount of management or specialist time devoted to strategic analysis will depend on the nature of the business portfolio, current needs for re-evaluation of strategy, and corporate culture. For a company that is essentially a holding company for a range of unrelated businesses such as Hanson plc, portfolio analysis will be part of the day-to-day work of the financial management team. The **strategic planning** tools chosen will depend on:

- the performance criteria chosen to evaluate strategic business units (SBUs);
- historic practice;
- data availability;
- financial or market orientation of top management;
- the ability to build monitoring and control mechanisms around the performance criteria.

At least 30 different strategic planning tools and techniques can be identified (Webster *et al.*, 1989). Some of these are described here or in Chapter 15. There is wide variation in the amount of data required and the level of sophistication of quantitative analysis across these management tools. They traverse the spectrum from a marketing focus at one end to strictly financial analysis at the other. Some are essentially tools of market research within the company or industry (the Delphi method and focus groups). Others, such as the McKinsey 7-S Framework, devote more attention to organizational structure and culture through seven key issues: strategy, structure, systems, style, shared values, staff and skills (Peters and Waterman, 1982).

SWOT analysis

Analysis of strengths, weaknesses, opportunities and threats can be applied to the organization as a whole or applied to key areas of activity. Brainstorming sessions involving multidisciplinary teams without hierarchical constraints on thinking are valuable at this stage. Unprompted suggestions will flow from managers with a detailed understanding of the organization and its performance. However, specialist bias of the team might lead to inadequate coverage of all relevant activities and outside perceptions of the organization. A prompt list is useful in this situation (Table 3.2).

Where a significant list of factors might feature under each of the headings in the SWOT grid, that is strengths, weaknesses, opportunities and threats, there will be consensus on the most important factors. Decisions can be made on the key **strengths** on which to build for the future, and which **weaknesses** will be most damaging to the business if not remedied. A quantitative analysis can be designed for assessing the seriousness of **threats** to the business (such as restrictive laws or innovation from a competitor) and the probability of occurrence. Measures for attractiveness of **opportunities** and the probability of success reflect the kind of analytical tools used in portfolio analysis and planning.

Table 3.2 Checklist for SWOT analysis.

Marketing	Logo, image, media, budget, salesforce coverage, market feedback, customer satisfaction, market share, distribution channel, intermediaries used
Financial	Sales growth, gross profit, net profit, stock turn, liquidity, return on capital, earnings per share, share price, ability to raise capital
Organizational	Management structure, expertise, leadership, motivation, communications, teamwork, training, recruitment, systems, support
Product	Benefits, features, differentiation from competition, costs, technological edge, research and development, process, investment, success in innovation
External relations	With the City, with shareholders, with the general public, with the local community, with customers, with the media

Action plans will reflect the outcome of this type of analysis plus the resources available to implement them.

While this analytical review of a business is commonplace in the for-profit sector, it requires the injection of different attitudes and expertise into the not-for-profit sector for such methods to be adopted.

Marketing strategy

When corporate strategy and resources allocated against business units or divisions have been agreed by top management, divisional managers have responsibility for formulating a marketing strategy for each product group within their scope of authority. The way in which resources are allocated will influence the outcome. In a traditional **top-down** organization, competitive bidding for resources may occur at the product level, but no higher.

An alternative approach is illustrated by the Japanese company Matsushita where each division gives 60% of pre-tax profits to headquarters, and keeps 40% to update facilities or for expansion or new technology. Managers have resources for future marketing plans depending on past success and are therefore, to some degree, masters of their own destiny (Pascale and Athos, 1986). This contravenes the traditional portfolio management approach to business strategy and operations. The real market test of management is extended in Matsushita through each division's freedom to source externally, while at the same time there is the possibility of internal purchasing through a transfer pricing arrangement.

Where authority for decisions on market entry and support is devolved to the divisional level, then the **competitive analysis** for each product category will also occur at this level. This will involve in-depth analysis of the information covered in the SWOT checklist under the marketing and product headings.

Continuous market feedback is essential for an accurate picture of how the products and services provided meet customer needs. In industrial markets and the business-to-business sector this means staying close to the customer with formal communication routes at senior level, and informal feedback sessions such as seminars. For repeat purchase consumer goods, the market research programme will include periodic surveys among users and non-users of the brand to identify usage patterns and attitudes. Japanese car companies commission regular audits of their customers to identify any vulnerability to competition.

However, new concepts reach the drawing board before there is definitive proof of changing needs: the car manufacturer must anticipate and, in some respects, dictate customer needs if the company is to retain and improve market position. This involves risk, and detailed analysis of marketing and financial performance of previous and existing car models will provide ammunition for supporting such decisions.

The product life cycle

Traditional marketing theory embraces the concept that a product has a limited life expectancy due to the changing pattern of demand, competitive forces, and obsolescence resulting from advances in science and technology. When sales are plotted against time for most products there is a recognizable pattern to the curve as illustrated in Figure 3.2.

The product life cycle is an analytical tool which attempts to identify distinct stages in sales history. There are patterns to investment and profitability associated with this sales curve, which can be used to plan the use of resources in implementing marketing strategy. The product life cycle assumes that product sales pass through four distinct phases: introduction, growth, maturity and decline, and that different strategies and use of resources are needed to ensure success at each stage.

This is a relatively blunt management instrument for supporting marketing decisions through provision of information on:

- the phases of product performance;
- how long these phases are likely to last;
- relative cash flow at each stage.

Companies with a track-record in a specific market will have the advantage of drawing on data and life cycles of similar products for predictive purposes. However, even in this situation, there are limitations to the use of this analytical tool, as it does not provide information on:

- changing usage patterns in the total market;
- what the competition is doing;
- major technological breakthrough;
- when innovation is needed to protect market position.

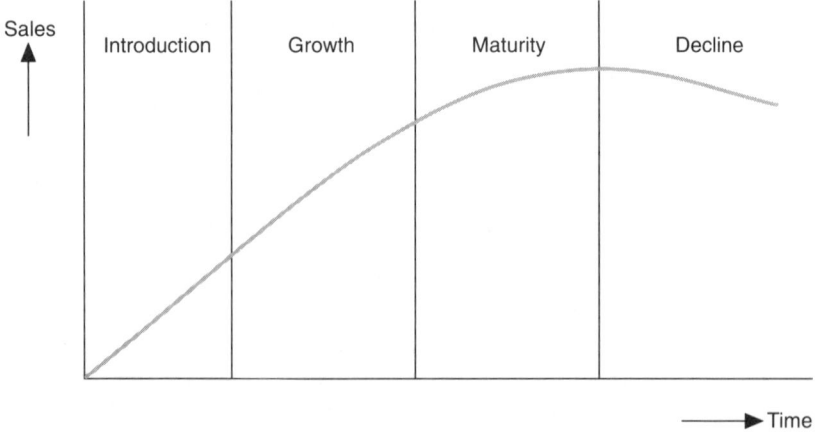

Figure 3.2   The product life cycle.

In spite of these limitations, the phases of the product life cycle can provide management with a strategic planning framework based on the following features of the curve.

Introduction

When a product is launched there is commitment to investment in research, design, production, advertising and distribution. For repeat purchase consumer products, the major part of investment will be in heavy media campaigns to achieve awareness and trial. For other consumer products, such as high-definition television, and for industrial products with a high technological component, the investment will be heavily focused in research and development. This results in a cash drain on the company, justified by a strategy of technological superiority to attract innovators among the target market. The first entrant with a new product has a greater chance of achieving a higher price, higher market share and higher profit margin.

To reach the innovators, the company might choose to use selective distribution in the introduction phase, and promotion will be pioneering and informative. The investment in this education process and the quality of the message will determine the level of demand. The speed of adoption and initial sales curve cannot be predicted with any accuracy in those industries where sophisticated test marketing is not a viable option.

Growth

The rapidly rising sales curve in this phase indicates the position where cash begins to flow into the business to finance the sales infrastructure supporting the new product. With the growing number of customers, there is also likely to be increased competition as established companies defend their industry positions through matching the product, or increasing distribution pressure on existing brands. There is a danger of withdrawing advertising support too soon in this phase as establishment of a significant market share can lead to market dominance for the future, but this requires management nerve and cash resources.

Maturity

The rate of increase in sales slows in this phase. The plateau of the sales curve indicates that it is becoming more difficult to attract new users to the product category, or that those that still exist are adopting competitive products. This arises through the diverse range of products now available at lower prices. This puts pressure on the company to reduce prices and accept lower margins, or to implement a cost-cutting policy, with possible negative effects on quality and service levels.

An alternative route to profit maximization in the mature phase is to maintain perceptions of product superiority through advertising support, maintaining a price differential. This has been successful in product areas as diverse as detergents, pre-prepared meals and household textiles. In industrial markets, the security of a supplier with expertise and service provision will often mean more to a customer than a slightly lower price. However, aggressive sales promotion may be necessary to encourage brand switching in a saturated market, and specific campaigns would involve discounting or extra value at no additional cost to the customer.

Decline

Where sales decline as the product is superseded, expenditure to support the brand is reduced to the minimum level consistent with maintaining a core of loyal customers and maximizing profits. Distribution policy is reassessed as heavy discounting may deter traditional stockists, with the danger of over-stocking outlets positioned on price alone. The product range is evaluated to delist slow sellers and rationalize inventory. Management will assess the option and possible timing of product withdrawal.

The scallop-shaped curve

There is evidence that products do not necessarily reach the decline stage as preventive marketing action can maintain brand position over decades. This requires constant attention to customer needs and regular product improvements to maintain competitive edge. Packaging and brand presentation through advertising are updated such that the changes are virtually imperceptible to brand users.

There may be a major shift in product positioning where scientific advances permit new performance claims. An example is the move from advertising platforms of cleaning power and oral freshness for toothpastes to anti-caries claims with the inclusion of fluorides as active ingredients. Where the sales curve showed a decline, the relaunch of a brand with new performance claims and significant investment in advertising can lead to an upswing in sales and market share. Where this occurs periodically, the life cycle curve takes on a scallop shape as shown in Figure 3.3.

The life cycle for **fashion products** can take place over months rather than years, as is the case for a spring or autumn season's range of designer clothes for women. There is high risk associated with this sales curve, so it is not surprising that a policy of minimal investment is followed by UK fashion houses. German and American fashion houses offset the risks associated with the high-fashion end of the product range through investment in conservative, quality coordinates which are not necessarily associated with a particular fashion season, and which have export appeal.

Figure 3.3   The scallop-shaped curve.

Market entry options

Broader strategic options facing a company with a wide portfolio of products are explored in the context of the Ansoff Matrix in Chapter 15. At the single product level (or narrowly defined range involving small variations in product features) there are two alternative strategies based on product positioning and price – these are **market skimming** or **market penetration**.

Market skimming involves charging a high price for a product or service that is entirely new to the market, providing exclusive benefits for which the narrowly defined customer base is prepared to pay a premium. The speed with which market entry takes place depends on the quality and quantity of promotional support targeted at a narrow audience. Financial success for the product may be best served by maintaining an exclusive image and usership in the longer term; alternatively, the development of a broader franchise would be the correct strategy if competitor entry was anticipated. It would not make sense to finance product education through advertising, only for the competition to reap the sales benefits.

A strategy of market skimming is associated with higher profit margins gained on a smaller sales volume.

Market penetration involves market entry at a price that will be attractive to a wider target audience, although there will still be initial dependence on the innovators to lead the way in usership and product acceptability. The market penetration required to provide an adequate return at this entry price will only be achieved by significant advertising support. This scenario requires a detailed sensitivity analysis at the planning stage, to identify the optimal combination of variables – price, advertising support and level of distribution. Profitability will not be achieved immediately, and cash resources may be needed for up to three years to finance market share growth until a dominant position has been achieved.

An alternative way of viewing market entry is in relation to the competition:

- As **market leader** through distinctive product positioning and significant promotional support (IBM, Mars, Coca-Cola, Adidas, Kodak films).
- As **follower** through less distinctive differentiation of product benefits and features, but focus on value for money through competitive pricing. Absence of major advertising campaigns is often compensated by clever publicity (Amstrad, Virgin Airlines).
- As **market nicher** through serving the specialist needs of a narrow user segment, thus avoiding direct conflict with those companies with greater resources competing in the volume market (Bang and Olufsen, Club Méditerranée).

The strategic decision to serve a market niche might be the only option for survival as an independent company. Avon Tyres, based in Wiltshire, is a prosperous company dwarfed by multinationals such as Goodyear, Pirelli, Michelin and Continental. Avon survived the period of over-capacity in the tyre industry and changes in product specification by contracting operations and concentrating on two niche markets – high-performance motor cycle tyres and high-performance car tyres (Crainer, 1990).

Financial risk of market entry is particularly acute where new technology is involved. Research among 14 companies marketing high-technology products and based in the UK showed favoured risk-reducing strategies to be as follows (Beard and Easingwood, 1989):

(1) Share the technology (19%).
(2) Position the product through concentration on early adopters (45%).
(3) Win market support through establishing a leading reputation, or by focusing on opinion leaders (28%).
(4) Reduce the risk of adoption through encouraging trial by leasing, or other forms of absorbing customer risk (9%).

However, the fourth option increases the financial commitment of the marketing company where it has already undertaken heavy investment in technology.

Porter's analysis of strategic options

According to Porter (1980), the competitive situation can be described by five forces: supplier power, buyer power, degree of existing competition, threat of entry and threat of product substitution. Porter identifies three strategies that may be successful within this scenario:

(1)   Cost leadership
(2)   Product differentiation
(3)   Market focus

The market for financial services in the UK underwent considerable change in 1988 when building societies were accorded many of the freedoms traditionally associated with the clearing banks. This led to intense competition in areas such as savings accounts, mortgages and insurance. The strategic option available to new entrants to the market reflected Porter's scenario (Speed, 1990).

The larger building societies had the financial resources to invest in computer support for new services, and showed a distinct cost advantage over the clearing banks. This advantage became apparent through the ratio of operating costs to average assets. Smaller building societies needed to focus on serving local needs. Television advertising for the Liquid Gold Account at the Leeds Permanent Building Society highlighted one route to a product differentiation strategy.

Information technology as a competitive strategy

The market for financial services is just one area where the information technology (IT) capabilities of the provider will determine whether an organization will succeed in the longer term. The cost disadvantage of poor administrative support where this is lacking or outdated could be such as to threaten the survival of an organization. (This is illustrated by the hostile bid by Lloyds Bank for Midland Bank in May 1992. Lloyd's strategy was to reduce operating costs through enlarging the customer base of a merged bank – requiring the loss of some 1000 retail outlets and 20,000 jobs. The bid was withdrawn as it had attracted scrutiny by the Monopolies and Mergers Commission, whereas the opposing bid from Hong Kong and Shanghai Bank had not.)

In such situations, information technology provides the support to reduce operating costs and enhance the management decision process. However, IT can also be used as a strategic weapon, as illustrated in the following three examples:

(1)   Incorporation of microcomputers into domestic appliances to monitor and control energy use.
(2)   The use of electronic data interchange (EDI) for provision of a delivery service from one regional despatch point, where the order was received in another region (e.g. Interflora).
(3)   The adoption by a publishing group of a new business strategy to market systems that incorporate electronic media for information retrieval.

These examples illustrate the way in which IT has the potential for changing strategic direction through:

- creation of totally new products;
- enhanced service provision;
- reduced cost-base allowing entry to new markets.

New strategic routes available through propitious use of IT are in addition to the tactical cost and decision-support advantages (Diebold, 1986).

European perspective

The uncertainty attached to key areas of EC harmonization means that companies must make strategic decisions without knowing the full impact of changes five or ten years hence. However, they can plan in the knowledge that there will be continued momentum towards the creation of a level playing field with implications for increased opportunities within the enlarged market; but there will also be cost penalties where market-wide standards imposed are higher than those of the individual Member State, as for social benefits or controls to protect the environment.

Companies that do not research European needs for their products or take the initiative in establishing a presence in one or more Member States will be at a strategic disadvantage during the 1990s. Competitors will reap the benefits of operating in the enlarged market with economies of scale feeding through to lower prices and the capability to invest in product innovation.

Strategic routes for corporate entry to other Member State markets

The options open to a company for expansion into other Member States will depend on:

(1) The stage of development of the business in the home market; resources might already be stretched through rapid expansion there.
(2) Access to capital in order to fund penetration of new markets.
(3) The capabilities of management in overseeing the building of a new offshoot, including language ability and an understanding of the local culture.
(4) The nature of the business: for example, collaboration with foreign partnerships to provide Europe-wide services would be advisable in

the professions, where success depends on detailed knowledge of local laws and business practice. Where new technology is not revealed through patents but maintained as proprietary and secret processes, then a company would have no option but to locate plant strategically through a wholly-owned subsidiary within an enlarged Europe.

The six strategic options available to an organization are summarized in Table 3.2.

Table 3.2 Strategic options facing a company in entering another Member State market.

Option	Considerations	Next stage
Export from sales office in home base	Strength of home base Ratio of export to home sales Infrastructure for administration Time-scale for growth Effect on margins	Locate sales office abroad or appoint agent
Use of agent or distributor	Degree of delegation for developing new market Track-record of appointee Financial resources of appointee Nature and terms of agreement Termination conditions	Open branch office or subsidiary

Start subsidiary	Need for:
	  Local expertise, lawyer
	  Existing contacts
	  Manager commitment – locally recruited or seconded from headquarters
	  Good communications with headquarters (language?)
	  Property purchase or lease
	  Compliance with local laws
	  View on corporation tax
		Business development:
		  Allow local practices or impose corporate style
		  Assess need for local production

Joint venture	Equity split and control Terms of reference (which markets, technology sharing) Leading culture and management Mechanism for resolving conflict Possible contravention of EC law	Sustain or change legal status with majority shareholding
Merger	Complementary market and technological strengths Efficiencies to be gained Combined market share Possible referral to EC Mergers Commission	Decide which company sets the lead in culture and language

Acquisition	Same considerations as for merger with additions:
	  Availability of cash or access to capital
	  Local laws preventing hostile bid or foreign predator; possible limit to stake-holding
		Policy choice: acquired unit accountable for results or absorbed into prevailing culture

Exporting from a home base

This is the 'first step' towards establishing sales in a new territory. Of the options for entry, it carries the least financial risk. A company generally embarks on developing exports when the home business base is secure and large enough to provide the cash flow for financing the export activity. This is necessary as an export customer base will take time to develop and payment arrangements will be more complex.

The disadvantages to this approach for developing exports are:

- Insufficient market attention from export sales managers responsible for specific territories but based at head office.
- Administrative support has to be provided by the head office sales services, with possible conflict of duties.
- Lower margins generally associated with export sales because of higher costs of transport and procedures. These margins are frequently compared directly with those for sales in the home market.

There is the option of using an **export house/agent** to administer shipments and deliveries of goods, associated paperwork and financial transactions. This takes the place of administrative support from within the company, but the cost of using an export house/agent would reduce the margin on sales. Such expertise and structure may provide more consistent customer service.

For the small business it is particularly difficult to isolate market facts and identify opportunities with this approach. However, there may be no option if a major customer starts to operate in another European country. Information will be needed on local technical requirements and procedures if the business is not to be lost. In the longer term, there will be high demands on management time and working capital, but the small company cannot afford to ignore Europe even if implementation of the substance of EC Directives appears daunting. Businesses as diverse as property development, landscape gardening and manufacture of leisure craft are forging a path there (Batchelor, 1989).

Appointment of an agent or distributor

A company taking this route to develop export sales relinquishes some measure of control over how market opportunities are exploited. A **sales agent** will take responsibility for creating awareness of the product range and winning orders, but will not take legal possession of the goods. Financial risk is reduced on the part of the exporter by eliminating the need to create a sales infrastructure in the new territory. However, an agent may not want to devote exclusive attention to one customer, but will sell complementary ranges to the same customer base.

Compliance with local laws on the form and level of payment to agents is necessary. For example, sales staff in France have significant rights on commission payments and to the business attached to their territory under the *Voyageur Representant Placier* (VPR) Statute. Under EC law an agent will have an automatic right to compensation on termination of their appointment.

A **distributor** will buy the product and sell on to the customer in the export territory. The financial profile required for this level of involvement means that there is generally tighter vetting of potential distributors. If they are given **exclusive distribution rights** for a Member State or region within it, it is critical that their track-record indicates that they have the resources and expertise to develop sales to an agreed target.

The nature of the contract will determine the scope of responsibilities and form of payment. The use of a local lawyer by the exporter is advisable for negotiation of the terms and conditions.

Where a distributor has exclusive rights over a specific territory, the exporter must ensure that the terms of the agreement do not contravene EC competition rules. For example, the rules would be breached if rights to one market are conditional on the distributor refraining from making passive sales across a national border to another market, where the price is higher and could be undercut by parallel imports. Permitting such conditions would be contrary to the concept of a single market. Dunlop was fined by the European Commission in April 1992, for maintaining artificially high prices for Slazenger sports equipment through restrictive distribution agreements.

Establishing a company office

This strategy involves greater risk in that there are higher costs associated with leasing or owning an office building and with employing personnel. Significant management time will be needed to identify the resources needed, and to acquire office premises and recruit staff. However, presence in the market indicates commitment to its development, with the facility to get closer to customers which is necessary where long-term relationships need to be developed.

Traditionally, there have been three stages to this strategy, as indicated below. As more and more companies look for a strategic location to serve the wider European market, this historic pattern is breaking down and centralized production, marketing and sales administration replaces the country-by-country approach.

(1) Set up a branch office to develop and administer sales, with product delivered from a factory in the home market. Local management is responsible for meeting sales targets and managing local employees.

(2) Open a subsidiary company registered in the new territory. A managing director and board is appointed to take commercial and legal responsibility for operations. The directors are judged by head office on financial performance and business development.

(3) Set up production facilities in the new territory. This requires a significantly greater level of investment, and will follow an analysis of how best to serve the needs of the enlarged market through strategically placed product sourcing.

Whichever of these three options is chosen, local contacts and knowledge and the commitment of managers from head office are prerequisites for success. There will be exposure to local employment legislation and, depending on the legal status of the corporate presence, to local taxation and reporting requirements.

The search for the right location for corporate expansion into the single European market has become something of a science for US and Japanese companies in particular. Intel of California, looking for the right site for computer production, took only three months to choose the Republic of Ireland. The task force charged with recommending a location used as their criteria labour relations, demographics, skills, site availability, incentives and costs (Duffy, 1991). In contrast, Japanese companies take longer to make a decision and require more detailed information (such as Toyota in looking for its first European assembly site).

Skilled labour availability scores high on the list of criteria for location for high-tech manufacture and research and development, and can outweigh high labour or property costs or the incentive of development grants offered by alternative regions. Local advice on property is essential as the terms for commercial leases vary across Member States. Where the normal lease in the UK will be for 25 years, those in other countries are shorter: Belgium nine years, France three, six or nine years, Germany five or ten years, Italy six years and six years' option, Spain three, five or ten years.

Joint venture

The risk of entering a new market can be reduced by forming a joint venture with a company that is established in the new territory. The criteria of assessment for potential partners will be very similar to those used for merger studies, as there is a need for complementary expertise, market coverage or technology. However, the degree of commitment to the partnership is dictated by the nature of the legal agreement, and alternative forms are given below.

- Formation of a jointly owned subsidiary to exploit new technology or market opportunity. The equity split between the partners can be equal or unequal. Care needs to be taken with the competition rule.
- Agreement to pursue joint research and/or development in a specific area where resources needed would preclude each partner from taking action independently. The agreement would specify how the results of the research should be used to the commercial advantage of each party. Agreements which involve sharing of information could be subject to scrutiny by the European Commission for any contravention of competition rules. (See Chapter 16 for examples of EC judgements on technological agreements.)
- One party to the agreement supplies technical know-how and product specifications for local production, and the other party contributes purchasing and marketing skills and a distribution network.

There are two potential areas of conflict in agreements of this type. Firstly, there will need to be a 'lead culture' for the joint venture to be managed on a day-to-day basis, and secondly, as the venture becomes successful, the parties to the agreement may take differing views as to the best strategy for the future and the level of financial involvement appropriate for each.

Example

Iveco Ford Truck was formed as a joint venture between Iveco UK (part of Fiat) and Ford Heavy Truck Division. Each partner had 48% shareholding, with the balance held by Credit Suisse. Iveco was a leading European manufacturer of trucks and Ford wished to disengage from unprofitable activity in this sector of the market (IPM, 1988). The lead culture was provided by Iveco, which insisted on performance-related pay and gave a higher status to production and engineering than would have been the case under Ford management. The culture change was facilitated by commitment at top management level, a period of time for the process changes to filter through (with training programmes built in), and regular departmental interchanges between the UK and Italy.

One of the main catalysts for international joint ventures is political instability of the market in which the partner looking for growth wishes to invest. By taking on a partner with national status, the risk of losing investment capital is reduced through more favourable treatment by the local government. Alternatively, national law might limit any foreign investor to a maximum of 50% equity stake in a local company.

The loss of total control over finance, operations and marketing inherent in a joint venture, or loss of confidentiality on technical know-how, would be so unacceptable to companies with a very distinctive management culture that this is not considered a strategic option.

Acquisition

This strategic route provides an established company infrastructure as a vehicle for market penetration. Time can be saved in the competitive race for market share but there are risks to this approach. The cost of the purchase must be justified in terms of longer-term profit potential, and accurate predictions of future performance are difficult in a rapidly changing European legal environment.

- Does the acquired company's product range fit into the existing business portfolio from the perspectives of expertise, market coverage and technological strategy?
- Will financial and management resources of the acquiring company be stretched by the acquisition?
- How different is the organizational culture in the acquired company from that of the parent, and will key personnel leave before the businesses are fully integrated?

There are three types of acquisition:

(1) *Horizontal*   Where the two companies have similar product portfolios and the acquiring company establishes a higher market share but with reduced operating costs (example: acquisition of Bournville by Nestlé).

(2) *Vertical*   Where a supplier is acquired to gain control of raw material or component sourcing, with downward pressure on product costs. Alternatively, a distributor might be acquired to ensure effective penetration of the market and limit the amount of competition using the same channel (such as brewers acquiring hotel chains; the divestment of public houses by the major UK brewing groups as a result of a Monopolies and Mergers investigation indicates pressure in the reverse direction to restore competition to the market).

(2) *Lateral*   This involves the purchase of a company with products unrelated to those of the acquiring company, and indicates a strategy of diversification (the Hanson Trust is an example of a successful 'holding company' which looks at new acquisitions from the point of view of current under-performance and asset value).

The advantage of gaining local managers with market knowledge and experience can be exploited through sensitive handling of integration at every level. The injection of new national cultures and languages into the existing organization can be used as a catalyst for creating a pan-European outlook.

Where an acquisition within the enlarged European market would create a company passing a threshold level of turnover, it will be scrutinized by the European Commission (DG4) for possible contravention of competition rules. This process is explained in detail later in the chapter.

Merger

Where a company is looking to expand its operational base but is unlikely to do this through organic growth, and where the financial resources are not available for acquisition, merger with another company is possible. There should be a fit between the two organizations in the areas of:

- product range (complementary products would provide the opportunity for more productive use of sales and distribution resources);
- complementary geographic coverage;
- technology (there should be complementary research and development strengths, or alternatively one partner has a high research profile but lacks the expertise and infrastructure to exploit market opportunities);
- customer base (the integration of different sector specializations creates a formidable market force).

Rationalization of the combined operations would be necessary for achieving cost economies, and would be likely in the following areas:

(1) Production and distribution
(2) Marketing and sales
(3) Computing and management information
(4) Research and development
(5) Product design and customer research

Consideration of strategic plans and financial evaluation would precede decisions on closing plant and reducing staffing levels. Once decisions are made, swift enactment reduces the negative impact on morale of speculation and uncertainty among employees.

In a market with derived demand such as the packaging industry, strategy must be customer-led, and this was the philosophy of the group formed through the merger of UK's Metal Box and Carnaud of France. Metal Box had a worldwide reputation for research and development whereas Carnaud was the smaller company without the same resource base but with a culture that responded to market needs with creative packaging solutions. The problem of merging the two management structures and cultures was solved through the adoption of a triangular framework for each of the four key markets, with the customer at the top of the triangle (Clutterbuck and Scholes, 1990). This pattern was replicated at divisional and product level.

Mergers are also subject to scrutiny by the European Commission if the size and market influence of the combined organization meets certain conditions. Examples of EC judgements are given later in this chapter.

Effects of a barrier-free Europe on industry concentration

The overriding objective of the European Union is to create an enlarged market free of trading barriers and protectionist measures characteristic of the Member States before their involvement with the Community. This provides the conditions for companies to achieve economies of scale in production, physical distribution, advertising and administration. The Cecchini Report concludes that, in the longer term, the macro-economic consequence of EC market integration will be an average 4.5% increase in gross domestic product and an average reduction of 6.1% in consumer prices.

The mechanisms through which these gains will be made at the corporate level are:

- Removal of government protection in procurement in the public sector (worth up to 15% of EC gross domestic product).
- Greater competition in consumer markets as companies take advantage of the removal of trade barriers.
- European Commission action against unlawful discriminatory pricing.
- Production located to meet the needs of an enlarged market, with savings on tooling, labour and overheads.
- Convergence of technical standards so that one product specification meets the needs of several individual markets.
- Efficiency gains feeding into higher profit margins, with increased corporate investment in research and development.

This process will be accompanied by industry restructuring, as over-capacity in key national industries is eliminated through competitive pressures. Industry rationalization will be painful for large and small businesses alike, and survival will depend on inherent market strength in the longer term, and cash reserves to finance the business through market turbulence in the shorter term.

The period of rationalization will differ between industries, depending on the degree of protectionism to be dismantled. However, four distinct stages have been identified in corporate response to what is the biggest environmental event in contemporary business history (Gogel and Larréché, 1989). These are:

(1) *Mobilization*   A period of corporate awareness and research, with identification of opportunities and threats.
(2) *Strategic turbulence*   Strategic moves by forward-thinking companies give rise to competitive edge but with some risk as the regulatory environment is still in flux.
(3) *Competitive struggle*   Exploitation of the new legal environment by companies striving to maintain and develop market position.
(4) *Competitive equilibrium*   Whatever industry rationalization is necessary has occurred by this stage and the new market dynamics become apparent.

Corporations with the financial resources will use acquisitions as the fastest route to strengthening market position. This will have the effect of increasing the pan-European market share of the few major companies who already dominate a particular industry. This consolidation process will go beyond the level of **industry concentration** necessary for companies to reach scale economies approaching those of American and Japanese companies.

The mechanisms for harmonization outlined above will have a particular impact on the level of concentration in industries where there has been either excess capacity or government protection or both. These include banking, telecommunications, transportation, food and beverages, publishing and business services such as consulting, accounting and advertising (Buzzell and Quelch, 1989).

The more liberal takeover environment in the UK and the economies of scale achieved through serving a vast and essentially homogenous American market mean that companies from the UK and USA are already in strong positions in Europe. For example, a study of the product/geographic strength of 39 major companies in the European food market included 12 UK companies (representing 49 products) and 11 US companies (representing 42 products). The remaining 16 companies came from five countries – Italy, Germany, France, Netherlands and Switzerland (Gogel and Larréché, 1989).

It could be argued that companies from Continental Europe had fundamentally different strategies from their British counterparts in that they did not aspire to high market share in several territories in key product areas. However, the size of companies such as BSN of France, Nestlé of Switzerland and Unilever (Anglo-Dutch) and the importance of their respective food brands suggests that where the strategy was possible through resources and legal environment, it was enacted. This leads to the question of why markets are more concentrated in the UK than in other European Member States.

Reasons for high levels of concentration in UK industries

Two relationships are well established for consumer goods markets:

(1)   positive correlation between awareness and market share;
(2)   positive correlation between market share and return on capital.

To exploit these relationships, companies have developed strategies of increased market power such that key industry sectors (petrol, brewing, confectionery, processed food, detergents and cars) are dominated by a few companies with significant market shares. Other industries with a history of public sector ownership but transferred to the private sector by flotation are characterized by virtual monopoly (telecommunications, electricity, gas and water industries).

Where market power has been achieved over time, seven contributory factors have been identified from the external environment and operating conditions prevalent in the UK. These are shown in Table 3.3. The enigma faced by companies that have achieved market power in the UK is that the regulatory framework evolving in the European Community will create obstacles to market penetration through these routes. This means that in some cases, alternative strategies for growth in a barrier-free Europe will be needed.

One argument put forward for the greater market power of consumer goods companies in the UK is that the homogenous attitudes and subsequent purchasing behaviour of consumers in the UK provide companies with economies of scale in meeting mass needs. Such attitudes and behaviour are not replicated in other large European Member States, where regional cultures and economies and impact of the weather and neighbouring states can produce diverse consumption patterns. The island geography of the UK plays a part in this phenomenon, but some explanation can be provided in the importance of television as both a leisure pursuit and advertising medium in fashioning attitudes. Two features serve to dilute regional differences; firstly, the majority of programming is networked rather than locally produced and secondly, pre-produced material from the USA can dominate peak viewing times. The common language has facilitated this trend. The popularity of American programming would be expected to be less in other Member States where English would be the second or third language.

Table 3.3 Forces in an open European market curtailing traditional methods of achieving market penetration.

Traditional route to UK market power	Restrictive force in an open European market
(1) Heavy commitment to networked television advertising to create *awareness*.	Fragmented pattern of television airtime availability across 12 Member States.
(2) Sophisticated sales promotion techniques to achieve *product trial*.	Stricter controls on sales promotion in some Member States, with EC policy unclear.
(3) *Premium pricing* supported by brand differentiation leading to high *gross margin*.	EC competition policy makes discriminatory pricing illegal.
(4) Control of the *distribution* chain through vertical integration (petrol, brewing).	EC scrutiny of restrictive clauses in distribution agreements.
(5) Dominance of major *retailers* with replication of high street pattern throughout the country.	Increased importance of small, specialist retailer in Continental Europe.
(6) Continuous reassessment of costs, with downward pressure on labour costs and overheads.	EC Social Charter specifies minimum wage, social benefits. Legal limit to working week.
(7) The hostile takeover bid encourages short-termism and creates market power. Referral terms for scrutiny by the UK Monopolies and Mergers Commission are discretionary.	EC Mergers Commission exerts control on takeover activity with strict terms for referral; the principle is avoidance of potential abuse of market power.

Rather than homogenous behaviour patterns being indigenous, the higher level of expenditure on networked advertising could be argued to be a cause rather than a result of this phenomenon. The advertising industry is also self-regulating, with greater freedom as regards products that can be shown on television and executional style. Supporting the creation of mass awareness is a highly sophisticated **sales promotion** industry, where the use of sampling, free gifts, competitions and money-off incentives takes place in one of the most liberal legal environments in Europe.

A highly concentrated **retail structure** gives added momentum to manufacturers' drive for high market share. Replication of the same pattern of grocery and clothing outlets in every high street limits consumer choice; and the merchandise mix will reflect retailer focus on fast-moving lines and those which give the best margins through sizeable discounts for bulk purchase.

The imagery created through advertising supports a price premium for many leading brands and, in the case of new concepts or technology, may be priced at what the market will bear. Under this pricing strategy, the markets of different Member States may be at different stages of development, thus leading to discriminatory pricing. This phenomenon will become less common as needs and purchasing patterns become more homogenous; but until then, the European Commission will react to complaints over discriminatory pricing using the judgement in the 1978 United Brands case as the lead policy (see Chapter 8).

Even in the recessionary conditions of 1991–92, many consumer companies were able to report increased profits achieved not through business growth but by **cost reduction**. Moves towards harmonization of employment and social security legislation will mean that costs in these areas will increase rather than decrease for UK companies. Some Member States have legally imposed conditions that go beyond the minimum EC standards, so that any company setting up operations there will not take with them the UK cost advantages.

Arguably the greatest obstacle to replication of high market shares in other Member States is EC **competition policy** in relation to **mergers and acquisitions**. The terms of reference of the UK Monopolies and Mergers Commission in overseeing horizontal acquisitions are less stringent than those of the EC Competition Directorate. Specifically in cases of vertical integration where a manufacturer has control of the distribution chain, the Monopolies Commission reports lack the force of law in ensuring that competition is restored to the marketplace. The enforced divestment by breweries of public houses was one of the few examples where the UK authorities imposed sanctions. In other markets such as those for petrol and cars, recommendations made in preliminary reports from the Monopolies Commission have been diluted for the final report following lobbying by major players in the market.

EC mergers policy

As of 21 September 1990, the conditions for referral of a merger to the EC Mergers Commission came into force. The existence of different merger controls for individual countries meant an uneven playing field and possible conflict of interest between the European and national dimension. The conditions for a potential merger to fall within the remit of Brussels are:

(1)   The worldwide turnover of the combined companies must be more than 5000 million ECUs.
(2)   Turnover in the EC is to be more than 250 million ECUs.
(3)   Not more than 66% of the turnover of either partner is to be in any Member State.

These conditions ensure that the Community competition dimension is significant enough for the Commission to become involved. If a potential merger does not meet these conditions, then it may be referred to the national merger authority. The European Commission has one month to adjudicate as to whether the merger falls within its terms of reference. When it first took on these powers, it was estimated that 50 to 100 such decisions would be needed each year.

Although judgement is announced by the Competition Commissioner, the team of specialists within the Commission, including economists, statisticians, lawyers and accountants, addresses three questions in relation to the potential merger:

(1)   Does the merger constitute a concentration?
(2)   Is there a Community dimension?
(3)   Will the merger have a negative influence on competition?

Some mergers fall outside these conditions through the nature of the deal or the structure of the business after the merger. For example, Hoylake's takeover bid for BAT Industries involved junk bonds and was not necessarily a competition issue. The Commission also takes a view on the consequences for the consumer and employees where corporate decisions will be made regarding plant closures.

In contrast, the takeover bid by Tate & Lyle for the British Sugar Corporation would have created an entity with nearly 95% control of the processed sugar market in the UK, which accounts for 20% of the EC market. Since Tate & Lyle have a policy of importing cane sugar whereas BSC sourced within the UK, there were powerful lobbies at work when this bid was referred to the UK Monopolies and Mergers Commission.

The purchase of the British Rover Group by British Aerospace was subject to scrutiny by the European Commission and conditions were negotiated before it could go ahead. The main issues were plant closures and rationalizations, which were viewed as reducing the danger of over-capacity in the EC motor industry, and state aid, which can distort competition (Competition Law, 1989).

The issue of state subsidies

The protection of national economic interests has been the overriding concern where the governments of Member States have provided financial support to state-owned companies. Such subsidies are now investigated by the European Commission for distortion of competition within the open market. The differing political climates of individual Member States has given rise to differing levels of publicly owned enterprises as a percentage of the total economy. The UK Conservative government's privatization programme meant that, by 1986, public enterprises accounted for only 7% of the UK economy, whereas in France it was 12%, and in Italy, 15%. Greece and Portugal also have higher levels than France, where the EC has taken a particular interest in state subsidies.

There is nothing in the Treaty of Rome which forbids government industrial ownership, and the general principle by which a state subsidy is judged is that it is acceptable so long as private shareholders would have made the same financial decision.

The attention paid by the European Commission to French takeover activity is understandable when the presence of state-owned companies in key industries is taken into account (see Table 3.4). As cross-ownership between public sector companies increases, there is the possibility of the government transferring responsibility for subsidies away from its own depleted coffers to successful public ventures. For example, two state-owned banks took equity stakes in two public sector industrial companies in 1991. Crédit Lyonnais took a FF2.5 billion stake in Usinor–Sacilor, and Banque Nationale de Paris took a FF1 billion stake in Air France (Duffy, 1991).

In the context of state aid to industries, the Commission has to tackle state energy monopolies, steel cartels and French proposals for govern-ment aid to the computer and electronics industries. Monopoly in nuclear power, for example, can lead to high electricity prices. Alternatively, the state can subsidize the primary industry to create artificially low prices for electricity, preventing competition from a non-national supplier. In both scenarios, the principle of the open market determining price is violated, and the Commission has to choose the legal route to redress. The ultimate beneficiary will be the European consumer, but the battle against national interest will take some years to win.

Table 3.4 Incidence of public ownership in French industry.

Sector	Public sector company
Banking	Crédit Lyonnais Banque Nationale de Paris
Insurance	Union des Assurances de Paris
Computers	Groupe Bull
Airlines	Air France (took over UTA and Air Inter, the internal airlines)
Steel	Usinor–Sacilor
Oil	Elf Aquitaine
Electronics	Thomson CSF
Cars	Renault
Water	Water assets publicly owned: private companies bid for contracts to manage assets and water supply at the local level

The **strategic options** open to competitors in the European computer industry appear limited if they wish to compete with the likes of IBM and DEC. The French and Italian traditions for state subsidies (Groupe Bull in France and Olivetti in Italy) are no longer legal recipes for survival, where the British and German competition is forced to survive under strict market conditions. The creation of a major European force through merger appears a likely outcome, but this could fall foul of the Commission if the combined market share is unacceptable.

European environmental policy and corporate strategy

The original aims of the Community were economic but the legislative framework allowed for the enactment of policies in other areas. Formal recognition of EC **environment policy** came with the Single European Act of 1987 (Articles 130r–t). The first two provisions of Article 130r lay down the objectives and governing principles:

(1)   'The objectives of EC policy are to preserve, protect and improve the environment; to contribute towards protecting human health; and to ensure a prudent and rational utilization of natural resources'.
(2)   'The principles governing EC action are that preventive action should be taken, that damage should as priority be rectified at source and that the polluter should pay'.

The principle of subsidiarity exists for environmental law as in other areas. A Member State is free to take more stringent action than the Community, although the Commission needs to be informed under the 'environment information agreement'. The Commission is then in a position to amend EC law if appropriate.

As European environmental law takes effect, companies based in Member States whose prior laws were less rigorous will find themselves at a strategic disadvantage. In areas such as gas emission, industrial process effluent, non-biodegradable packaging and energy consumption, companies will need to examine the costs and time-scale of compliance. In some industries the costs of necessary equipment will result in business closure or merger. Those businesses that had anticipated events would have allowed for necessary investment and forecast effects on prices.

The seven key areas in which the European Commission can impose standards are shown in Table 3.5. A balance has to be found between altruistic concern for conservation of resources with a reduction in waste harmful to the environment, and the increased costs to industry and the

Table 3.5   Effect of European environmental policy on corporate strategy.

Environmental policy	Strategic impact
(1) Controls on harmful gas emissions, to reduce long-term damage to the atmosphere and improve air quality.	Increased costs of power generation, trend away from coal-sourced power. Cost impact on heavy chemical industries and road transport.
(2) Promotion of energy efficiencies in the home.	Improved specifications for house design and construction materials. Improved design for appliances – possible eco-labelling.
(3) Incentives for improved energy performance of cars.	Technological routes: Improved aerodynamics 16-valve engine (as against 6 or 8) Improved tyre design.
(4) Controls on raw materials used in consumer products and industrial processes, to reduce harmful effluents. Eco-labelling is an early, voluntary measure.	Will affect: Product and process costs Investment in e.g. filtration equipment Product efficacy Development of concentrated products; 'less does more'.
(5) Controls on raw materials used in packaging and disposable products, to reduce toxic waste and encourage recycling.	Will affect: Product and process costs Product protection and aesthetic appeal Handling procedures.
(6) Controls on import of key ecological resources (such as rainforest timber).	Change in product specifications. Search for ecologically sound alternatives.
(7) Quality controls for water supply: framework set by Directive 80/778 for drinking water, and Directive 76/160 for bathing water.	Will affect: Investment costs for water companies Perceptions of quality and demand.

consumer. This balance is further complicated by the necessity for European companies to compete in the global market with their Japanese and US counterparts. Where there are significant costs attached to compliance with EC environment law, companies will be at a disadvantage compared with competition from the Americas or the Pacific region if environmental standards there are less demanding.

Of world carbon dioxide emissions, Western Europe accounts for 15%, Eastern Europe 25%, North America 27%, and Japan and the Pacific 7%. Regions heavily involved in supply (and export) of energy products carry a disproportionate responsibility for pollution. However, a simple per capita comparison gives an indication of differences in perceptions of harm done to the environment and laws in existence to limit this damage. For example, the US State of Massachusetts has an Energy Conservation Law, whereas the UK has no legal standards for appliance efficiency and the Energy Efficiency Office is charged with informing the public and encouraging voluntary compliance from industry.

Two **market mechanisms** are available to encourage industry compliance with environmental standards:

(1) Eco-labelling as planned by the Community. This will create consumer demand for products designed with the environment in mind, which in turn will put pressure on companies to respond to protect market share.

(2) Pollution taxes: lower excise duty is evident for lead-free petrol. However, 15% of total UK carbon dioxide emission is caused by car exhaust fumes, and research by the Oxford Policy Unit suggests that such a tax would need to be in the region of two to three pounds sterling per gallon to have a significant impact on this source of pollution.

The seven areas of EC environmental influence are examined in the context of legal and market mechanisms for compliance.

(1) Air pollution

The EC is concerned with four types of controls:

- limits for particular gases or substances such as lead, asbestos, nitrogen oxides, CFCs and smoke;
- standards laid down for products causing substantial pollution, including petrol and gas oil;
- limits on pollution from particular industries such as power stations and municipal incineration plants;
- international action to protect the ozone layer through control of emission of greenhouse gases.

Firm EC action is evident in the area of limits to car exhaust gases for cars with differing engine sizes; these came into force for new models and new vehicles on 31 December 1992. This involves the compulsory fitting of a three-way catalytic converter (Directive 89/458 (OJ L226 of 3 August 1989)).

(2) Energy efficiencies in the home

This is an area in which the voluntary initiatives of the EC are overtaken by the more positive action of individual Member States. Culture plays a part in the adoption of energy-saving practices and appliances in the home, as well as the capacity for the average standard of living to absorb the costs and limits to consumption inherent in such moves. Scandinavian countries have traditionally taken the lead in this area.

(3) Improved energy performance of cars

EC Directives are not yet apparent in this area, as the initial focus of action has been to reduce harmful pollution. Universal sanctions would be difficult to impose where there are different rates of technological advance between manufacturers. An alternative approach would be consumption tax incentives for car models which meet higher specifications on performance/petrol consumption. Alternatively, a reduced rate of corporation tax could be used to stimulate research and development.

(4) Environmental labelling of products

Proposals for EC eco-labelling were adopted by the EC Council of Ministers in 1992. Some national schemes have been in existence for some time, such as the 'Blue Angel' eco-label in Germany. This is concerned with the constituents of the core product rather than with packaging or ancillary elements. For example, paint products qualify if they contain less than 10% of environmentally harmful solvents, where the level in normal products is 40–60%. German consumers have grown to accept reduction in performance as the price to pay for environmental advantage.

Table 3.6   Environmental policy and detergents.

Phosphates	Active ingredients in detergents which pollute water and increase the incidence of green algae. Five European countries have banned or restricted the use of phosphates.
Consumer labelling	Detergent packs may carry the descriptions 'environment friendly', 'environmentally friendlier', 'green product', "ecological formula'. So far, there have been no objective criteria in the UK or for the EC by which the consumer can judge these descriptions.
EC eco-labelling	The product must meet objective criteria applied to the four stages of its life cycle to qualify.
Ecover	This product has one per cent of the detergent market in the UK. Phosphates have been replaced by zeolite. This active ingredient is less polluting, and is acknowledged to be a less effective cleaning agent.
Albright and Wilson	Manufacturers of phosphates, whose research shows that use of Ecover leaves a zeolite deposit on textile fibre after washing.
Procter & Gamble	Invested in research to develop detergent products that minimize harmful effects on the environment and yet optimize product performance. Moving towards more concentrated products.
The marketing dilemma	How much loss in product performance are consumers prepared to tolerate to protect the environment? What price premium are they prepared to pay for ecologically sound products?

The European eco-label will be more comprehensive and is designed to replace national schemes in the longer term. To merit the award of this label a product will need to comply with objective standards set by an expert panel through four stages of the product life cycle:

- raw materials used
- industrial processes involved
- packaging
- final disposal

Initially, the scheme will invite voluntary compliance, and food, drink and tobacco products are excluded.

Detergent products have attracted considerable interest as the size of the consumer markets means that manufacturers are exposed to public relations threats from lobby groups which, over time, become a significant commercial threat from hardening consumer attitudes. Some key issues for this industry are highlighted in Table 3.6.

(5) Packaging materials and toxic waste

An EC proposal in preparation in 1992 embodied two principles:

- enforcement of a reduction in the amount of packaging waste gener-ated in each Member State;
- border-free movement of packaged products within the EC; this means that Member State laws in relation to environmental packag-ing cannot be used to discriminate against entry of products from another Member State.

The ultimate EC objective is that only packaging which can be reused or 'recovered' is put on the market, and each item would be labelled to show the category that it falls under.

With respect to packaging, Directive 85/339 (OJ L176 of 6 July 1985) requires Member States to establish four-yearly waste reduction pro-grammes for approval by the Commission – and this applies to most kinds of sealed drinks containers. The policies adopted should include con-sumer information, promotion of **recycling** and collection initiatives and efforts to increase the proportion of **returnable containers**.

Although this 1985 directive gave each Member State considerable freedom in the methods of achieving the objectives, the differing pace of compliance between countries has created the reality of divergence, whereby Brussels has to focus on convergence seemingly 'after the event'. In the interests of free trade, the European Commission attempted to stop Denmark from insisting that beer and soft drinks be sold only in refillable containers. The European Court of Justice overruled this verdict and proclaimed that environmental considerations should take precedence over free trade.

Germany has traditionally had the strongest environmental lobby of all Member States and, in response to this, Germany's packaging ordinance was passed in April 1991. This obliges retailers to take back packaging from consumers, manufacturers to retrieve it from retailers and packaging companies to reclaim it from manufacturers (Cairncross, 1992). The effects of this are far-reaching: companies within specific industries cooperate to put the ruling into practice; new service and processing industries emerge to act as facilitators; over 70% of bottle fillings are now multi-trip.

If these standards become the norm for Europe, there will be a major impact on **new product development** and revolutionary **distribution** strategies will be needed to ensure compliance.

In 1992 the Commission was preparing a proposal designed to minimize emissions resulting from the incineration of hazardous wastes, through the promotion of 'best available technology'. This would cover air emissions and those likely to pollute water or soil. Existing incineration plant is likely to have a three-year reprieve to reach acceptable standards, with operating licences possibly reviewed every five years.

As well as increasing disposal costs for particular industries, there will be cost penalties for the provision of municipal services, as toxic constituents remain in the consumer packaging and disposable product chain. There will be indirect pressure on Member States to reduce these elements (certain plastics, for example) in order to contain waste management costs at the local level. The alternative mechanisms for payment for the specialist waste management necessary to meet targets will be:

- local taxation of the individual;
- local business rates;
- direct charging of the industry responsible for the toxic waste through a levy;
- a special sales tax on products which give rise to toxic waste, so that market forces will operate in favour of environment-friendly alternatives.

(6)   EC control of imports

International agreements on the conservation of rare or ecologically important resources (such as rainforests) will result in EC import bans. Controversy surrounding the 'North/South divide' at the Rio Environmental Summit in June 1992 focused on the need for less developed nations to harvest and market rare resources in order to guarantee economic growth in the face of opposition from the developed world. However, some developed nations, notably the USA, were also adamant that national economic interest should take precedence over global environmental considerations.

(7) Water quality

EC Directives on water quality focus on levels of 129 toxic substances in what is known as the 'black list' (List 1). There is also a 'grey list' (List 2) of less toxic chemicals.

Individual Member States have fallen foul of the EC objective standards for drinking water. In particular, unacceptably high levels of nitrates have been found in drinking water in agricultural areas of the UK (Draft Directive on Water Pollution caused by Nitrates, COM(88)708 OJC 54 of 3 March 1989). This poses investment problems in relation to special filtration and monitoring equipment for the local water supply company. The regional water authorities have been privatized and are therefore under pressure to produce high profit growth for the shareholders. This leads to a potential conflict of interest on safety limits for such chemicals as nitrates. Higher contamination levels may be found to be acceptable as a trade-off against less financial commitment to up-to-date filtration plant or reservoir management. Alternatively, the price of water must increase to cover investment.

Environmental overview

Although EC Directives and proposals on environmental issues are creating a strong legal framework for harmonizing actions, if not attitudes, this has to be seen in the global context. Where a 'European border' can be enacted for goods, capital and people, this is not a reality for atmospheric emissions, pollution of the seas and consumption of world resources.

Damage to the environment can be measured on a global scale, and global solutions are needed in key areas (such as compliance with the target of 25% reduction in carbon dioxide emission set at the 1988 Toronto Conference). Only this will ensure that competition between suppliers from different continents is consistent with common standards for protecting world resources and ecology. This means international agreement on the economic sacrifices that have to be made in the interests of the quality of life of future generations.

Corporate strategic response to an open Europe

The impact of European harmonization at the industry level and examination of EC judgements under competition law provide an appropriate backdrop to exploration of corporate attitudes and actions in relation to Europe.

UK companies

In 1989, the British Post Office interviewed 500 managing directors of a representative sample of UK companies. At a time when moves towards harmonization were gathering momentum, relatively complacent attitudes were apparent: 65% had no specific strategy for meeting competition in the single market, and 78% had no plans for additional representation in Continental Europe by the end of 1992 (Berry, 1990). The same questions asked of European top managers revealed a slightly greater readiness for the challenge of Europe, but the level of inaction was broadly comparable.

The competitive threats facing UK companies are understandable in view of this lack of strategic planning. In contrast, large multinationals with a base in the UK see the approach to Europe as just one aspect of a strategy to meet the needs of a **global market**. Numbered among this group are Monsanto, Rank Xerox and Ford.

Companies with a strategy for Europe have adapted their human resource policies to provide an international management team, and three other issues are identified as laying the strategic foundations for success (Coulson-Thomas, 1990):

- Definition of objectives in terms of customer requirements (or outputs) rather than resource inputs.
- Operational focus on building networks rather than bureaucracy and implementing processes rather than procedures.
- Defining the 'home market' as Europe rather than the UK.

US companies

The potential threat of 'fortress Europe' was not viewed seriously by two-thirds of US companies who had no formal strategic plans for Europe, according to a survey by Booz, Allen & Hamilton (Berry, 1990). One argument put forward for this lack of planning during the pre-1992 period was the difficulty of predicting the outcome of the 279 EC Directives due to be approved by the end of 1992. Those companies awaiting the definitive out-come of this phase of regulatory harmonization will be out-manoeuvred by competitors who have already made strategic moves to protect and streng-then market position in the inevitable industrial restructuring process.

Such moves involve risk, but this is reduced through use of the most advanced forecasting services used in combination with a comprehensive analysis of a company's European business portfolio. The prospect of a pan-European market can act as a catalyst to rationalization or investment in Europe which US management might otherwise have neglected.

For some companies, the legal concept of a combined market of European states does not alter strategy determined some three decades ago. In the computer market, IBM's share of European information tech-nology revenues in 1989 was just over 20%. Other American companies with smaller market shares have shown the same commitment to viewing Europe as one market – including DEC, Unisys and NCR. Four aspects to strategy are identified as contributing to the establishment of a firm footing in Europe (Miles, 1990):

(1)   Attitude towards Europe as a single market.
(2)   Recruitment of local managers for European subsidiaries.
(3)   Positive nurturing of corporate culture in subsidiaries outside the USA.
(4)   Promotion of a consistent range of products or services that are tailored to meet local needs.

The higher visibility of major US corporations in penetrating European markets disguises the role played by smaller businesses. Those with fewer than 500 employees account for more than 12% of the value of US goods exported directly by manufacturers or through their sales offices. An additional 9% of the value of US exports were handled indi-rectly through wholesalers and brokers. Many US export analysts believe that although the major corporations will continue to be the dominant players in their respective markets, real growth will also be generated by small to medium-sized businesses (Kaikati, 1990). This will be achieved through small companies exporting for the first time, and medium-sized companies increasing the frequency of export shipments. As the business builds, such companies can then explore the strategic options for growth in Europe outlined earlier in this chapter.

The enactment of a single European external tariff for individual product categories entering from such markets as the USA will render redundant Article 115 of the European Community. This allowed Member State governments to prohibit indirect import of non-EC goods through another member country, and resulted in different prices for the same product across Europe. When internal frontiers are dismantled, some Member States are concerned that this will benefit US and Japanese imports more than European goods if the external tariff is set too low.

Canadian companies

The common language and Commonwealth link provide the historical framework for success of Canadian companies in the UK. The recession of 1990–93 did not dampen optimism regarding future prospects given the opportunities provided by the Single European Market.

Nearly 150 Canadian companies based in the UK were polled at the end of 1990, and the results showed that business activity would increase, according to these key findings (Armstrong, 1991):

- 68% thought that the UK was the easiest European market to penetrate;
- 65% viewed the moves to harmonization as enhancing their European market share prospects;
- 52% expected to expand UK operations.

The UK is therefore at a strategic advantage from the point of view of inward investment from Canada for exploiting pan-European markets.

Global opportunities for European companies

Three hundred of the largest multinationals account for 20% of world trade. The success of international strategies for companies to be numbered among this group depends on:

(1) Accessibility of markets in territories other than the home market (through lack of legal and financial barriers).
(2) A threshold size of market in these territories with sustained levels of growth.
(3) Economies of scale within the organization allowing the penetration of markets from a lower cost position for equal or higher value/quality than offered by the local competition.

One of the benefits of an open Europe is to create the opportunities for companies to develop market positions that allow them to compete on equal terms with US or Japanese multinationals. In theory, this is possible. However, the timing of legal and fiscal moves for harmonization coincides with external events which could work against this initiative. These include:

(1) Increased concern for the environment, and a percentage of gross domestic product of Member States which will be allocated to this, whether through the cost element of corporate compliance, taxation or the market mechanism (consumers choosing to spend more on products designed and distributed with due regard for the environment).

(2) Lower economic growth rates for developed nations, as the high penetration levels for traditional consumer products mean that there is saturation in some markets.

(3) The possibility of protectionist measures on the part of other nations in response to what are perceived as unjust external European tariffs (as made evident by the USA in increased tariffs for imports from the EC).

The achievement of economies of scale will depend on identification of pan-European target groups, and the use of new technology to capture the market and gain cost efficiencies. Companies aspiring to this will need to recruit the brightest and the best managers, and make a commitment to investment for long-term success.

The emergence of new global European companies is a possibility in high-growth markets such as biotechnology and telecommunications.

The full impact of the 'peace dividend' will take time to flow through into demand: in the old Eastern bloc countries, national resources once commandeered through central planning to service the military will be available for meeting the needs of the new consumer. However, this consumer needs a wage, and the process of reconstruction will provide the demand and supply sides of the equation in the emerging market economies.

The 'peace dividend' could be viewed as a mixed blessing for the economies of the USA and some European countries, most notably the UK and France. This is due to the historically high levels of government financing for research and development to support military projects with national defence and export potential (see Table 7.4 for an international comparison of government funding of research and development). There were inevitable civil sector spin-offs to technological advances for defence, and the reduction in research funding could jeopardize technological edge in related industries such as telecommunications, satellite technology, use of lasers and robotics. However, reduced business opportunities for supplying national defence procurement agencies will stimulate the search for alternative use of corporate financial resources to provide an acceptable return on capital.

The EC initiatives on research and development under ESPRIT (European Strategic Programme for Research and Development in Information Technology) is an example of commitment to specific fields of research which will provide technological edge for European companies on a broad front. Other examples are the RACE, BRITE and EURAM programmes (see Dudley (1990) for an explanation of these research activities).

The flexibility of operations needed to comply with EC Directives as they are implemented can be reduced where industries have applied concerted pressure on the Commission to take into consideration market needs and logistical constraints. The lobbying process in Brussels is complex and a sophisticated army of lawyers and public relations consultants represents the diverse interests of those most affected by legislation (Plachta, 1990). The size of the Brussels bureaucracy (approximately 10,000) means that it is unable to access all information on market background or commercial impact of a new Directive. It is therefore open to pressure groups to provide response to proposals so that the best way forward is identified for submission to the Commission.

Problems and assignments

(1) Apply a macro-environmental analysis to a profit organization of your choice. Indicate where corporate strategy will need to change in response to one or more key influences.

(2) Compare and contrast the strengths, weaknesses, opportunities and threats (SWOT analysis) for two retailers competing in the same merchandise sector.

(3) How useful is the concept of the product life cycle in assisting a company's strategic market planning? What are the limitations of the PLC as an analytical tool?

(4) Discuss the strategic market entry options for launching the following products in the home market:
   (a) compact video camera,
   (b) motor insurance.

(5) What are the relative advantages and disadvantages of launching products in other EC Member States through:
   (a) exporting from a home base using a sales office,
   (b) using an agent in the host market?

(6) Discuss the alternative models available for establishing a corporate presence in another EC Member State. What are the implications for launching a service through each of these models?

(7) Discuss EC mechanisms for ensuring that the principles of free competition are applied across the 12 Member States.

(8) How will the EC mergers policy influence corporate decisions on growth strategy in Europe?

(9) With reference to the seven EC environmental issues explored in the chapter, discuss the statement:

   'Pressure on companies to adopt strategies which protect the environment will be exerted by the consumer rather than the force of law.'

(10) Does a unified European market represent a threat or opportunity to major corporations based in the USA and Japan?

References

Crainer S. (1990). A niche for high performance. *Marketing Business,* October, 14–15

Diebold J. (1986). Information technology as a competitive weapon. *International J. of Technology Management,* **1**(1/2), 85–99

Easingwood C. and Beard C. (1989). High technology launch strategies in the UK. *Industrial Marketing Management,* **18**, 125–138

Naisbitt J. and Aburdene P. (1990). *Megatrends 2000: Ten New Directions for the 1990s.* New York: William Morrow & Co

Pascale R.T. and Athos A.G. (1986). *The Art of Japanese Management.* London: Pengiun

Peters T.J. and Waterman Jr. R.H. (1982). *In Search of Excellence.* New York: Harper and Row

Porter M.E. (1980). *Competitive Strategy: Techniques for Analysing Industries and Competitors.* New York: Free Press

Speed R. (1990). Building societies: new strategies for a competitive era. *The Service Industries J.,* **10**(1), 110–123

Thompson K.E. (1992). Food for thought on the competitiveness of British industry in post-1992 Europe. Paper presented at the *'Studies in the New Europe' Conference,* Nottingham University, April

Waldrop J. (1991). You'll know it's the 21st century when.... *Public Management* (USA), **73**(1), Jan, 2–6

Webster J.L., Reif W.E. and Bracker J.S. (1989). The manager's guide to strategic planning tools and techniques. *Planning Review* (USA), **17**(6), 4–13

European perspective

Armstrong I. (1991). Firms confident for 1992. *Canada Today,* no. 29, June, 4–5

Batchelor C. (1989). The European Single Market: beware an ostrich mentality. *Financial Times,* 14 March

Berry J. (1990). Way back in the year 1992. *J. of Management Consulting* (Neth), **6**(2), 29–33

Cairncross F. (1992). How Europe's companies reposition to recycle. *Harvard Business Review,* March/April

Clutterbuck D. and Scholes E. (1990). Packaging Europe and the globe. *Marketing Business,* June, 8–10

Dominant position (telecommunications): Mercury case. *Competition Law in the EC,* **12**(9), Sept 1984, 251

State aids (motor vehicles): the Rover case. *Competition Law in the European Community*, **12**(5), May 1989, 119–120

Monopolies (telecommunications): Commission Directive. *Competition Law in the EC*, **14**(5), May 1991, 103–104

Cookson C. (1991). Is it the end of the Golden age? *Financial Times*, 15 January

Coulson-Thomas C. (1990). Yes, we have no blueprint. *Director* (UK), **43**(7), Feb, 73–74

Dudley J.W. (1990). *1992: Strategies for the Single Market*. London: Kogan Page

Duffy H. (1991). Sophistication enters for search for ideal locations. *Financial Times*, 4 January

Economist (1989) Water industry: storming the barricade. *The Economist*, 14 October

Gogel R. and Larréché J.C. (1989). The battlefield for 1992: product strength and geographical coverage. *European Management J.*, **7**(2)

Greener A. (1989). Rewards and risks for the drinks industry in the new Europe. *Admap*, June, 13–17

Griffiths J. (1991). More mergers in prospect for car industry. *Financial Times*, 12 April

IDS and IPM (1988). *1992 – Personnel Management and the Single European Market*. Incomes Data Services and the Institute of Personnel Management

Kaikati J.G. (1990). Opportunities for smaller US industrial firms in Europe. *Industrial Marketing Management*, **19**, 339–348

Miles R. (1990). Breaking down boundaries. *Computing* (UK), 4 October, 22–23

Plachta J. (1990). High pressure. *Marketing*, 26 April

Quelch J.A. and Buzzell R.D. (1989). Marketing moves through EC cross-roads. *Sloan Management Review*, **31**(1)

Roney A. (1990). *The European Community Fact Book*. London Chamber of Commerce and Industry (Kogan Page), pp. 9–11

Tate S.J. (1990). The European property market: setting up a European office. *J. Tate Pennigtous Law*, Winter 1990–91, 5–7

Thornhill J. (1991). Tissue-makers look to clean up in Europe. *Financial Times*, 18 March

The Times (1991). Freeing the phones, and other articles. *Times*, 6 March

4 Buyer behaviour

Chapter objectives:

- to understand how the concept of buyer behaviour is important for both consumer markets and industrial or organizational buying situations
- to relate buyer behaviour at the macro level to different means of customer segmentation
- to understand each of the buying influences' needs in tandem with the organization's culture in the industrial sale
- to run through a brief history of the most salient models of consumer buyer behaviour
- to apply the principles of buyer behaviour to a wider European context

Introduction

Traditional marketing theory requires the practitioner to have some knowledge of how the prospect or potential customer is likely to behave in response to communication about the product. Where significant advertising budgets support repeat-purchase branded consumer products, practitioners are armed with this knowledge, gained in a systematic and, increasingly, computer-driven process. Sadly, the track record for the industrial and business-to-business sector in understanding complex behavioural issues is less complete.

Market research identifies a target market at the individual consumer level and the process of segmentation attempts to group individuals into **subsets**. Members of any subset will respond to a similar message on account of similar needs.

It is frequently through broadly similar behavioural patterns across a sufficiently large number of individuals that these subsets emerge. The behaviour may relate to purchase or use situations for an existing product

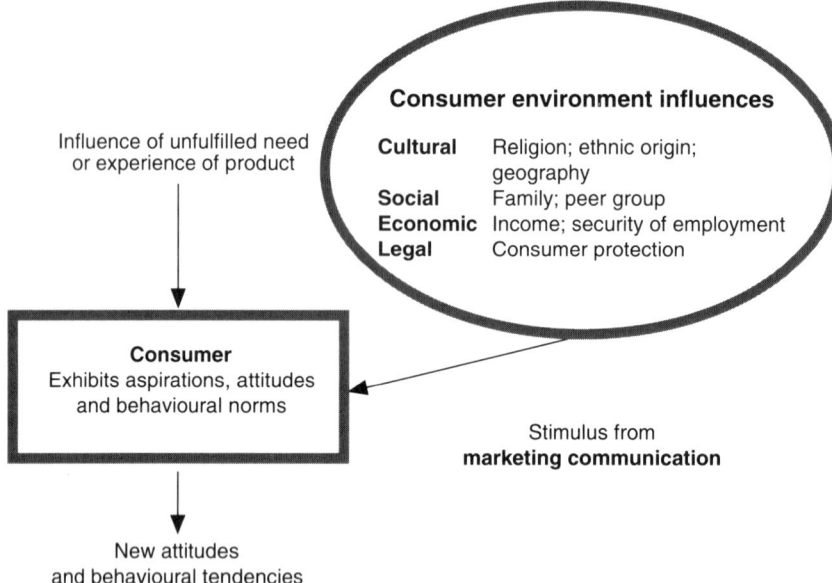

Figure 4.1 Influences on consumer attitudes and behaviour.

group. For a totally new concept, product form or mode of delivery, recourse has to be made to areas considered influential in the purchase decision.

In this situation, predictions are made of future behavioural response based on knowledge of determinants of behaviour. These may be social status, lifestyle, economic or family circumstances, or any of the influences illustrated in Figure 4.1. Overlaid on the net behavioural tendencies will be marketing activity, the objective of which is to influence the outcome.

The links between influences and behaviour are tenuous and complex. This is why new product launches are viewed as high-risk activities. The traditional approach of consumer goods companies and their advertising agencies is to conduct research among the perceived target group, form a hypothesis regarding the most likely stimulus to a positive behavioural response, and design the product message accordingly.

It is the underlying theory to this approach which is explored in the first section of this chapter. This extends into evaluation of the key aspects of behaviour at the macro-level – where consumers are grouped into tens or hundreds of thousands. At this aggregate level, statistical norms in behaviour can be identified, and rules emerge.

The second section of the chapter deals with **organizational buying**. This is inherently complex due to the conflicting needs of different individuals within the organization who have a stake in the purchase decision. These individual needs then overlap to a greater or lesser degree with the more objective needs of the organization.

Where the individual has an attitude, an organization has a culture. Both must be addressed to match product to needs in the selling situation. This section concludes with a guide to **negotiation** – now an integral part of marketing where major contracts and sales of high-value products are at stake. Successful negotiation is the ultimate stage of understanding buyer motivation and behaviour at the organizational level.

Consumer behaviour: some alternative models

'Advertising would be a simple proposition if the advertising man had the ability to read the individual human mind' (Woolley, 1914).

A vast array of academic research and proprietary market research has blossomed since the 1960s, built on the hypothesis that the consumer psyche can be probed to discover the antecedents of choice. Knowledge of these influencing factors can then be used to direct marketing activity in order to achieve the desired behavioural outcome.

Much of this work finds its foundation in cognitive psychology, which uses highly structured research methods to measure such activities of the human mind as:

- perceptions
- imagery
- retention
- recall
- intention to purchase
- awareness
- attitudes

Cognitive information processing

Research into the type of psychological parameters listed above is conducted within the framework of a model of consumer decision-making which assumes that the consumer knows that information has been received and that behaviour is modified as a result. In other words, there is cognition on the part of the consumer. This process of cognitive information processing is described in some detail by Foxall (1983), whose schematic representation of the process is illustrated in Figure 4.2.

This model of consumer information processing simplifies the complex array of factors that act to influence the final outcome – purchase or non-purchase. The individual filter of information received will be fashioned by current needs and interests. The link between short-term and

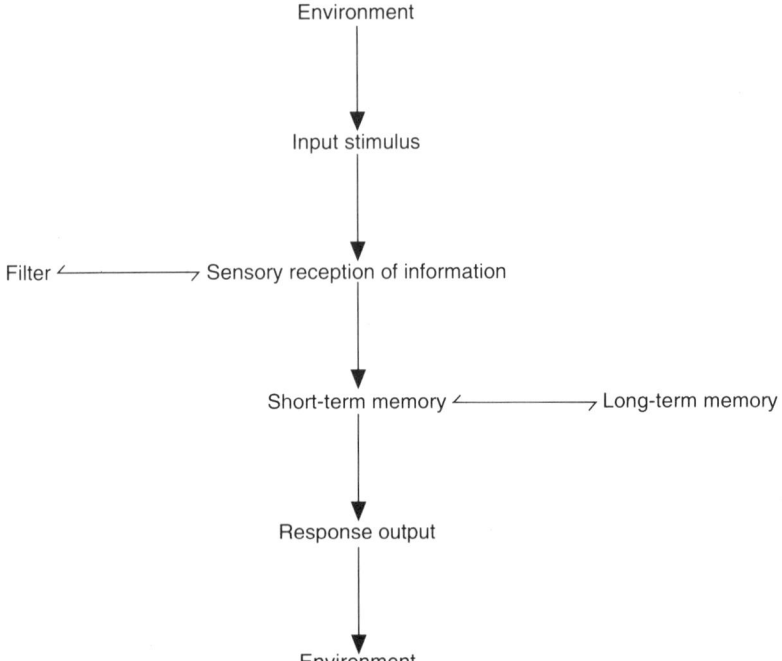

Figure 4.2   Cognitive information processing in the individual (Foxall model).
Source: Foxall G.R. (1983). *Consumer Choice.* Basingstoke: Macmillan Press Ltd

long-term memory is one of the more complex areas of psychology in which empirical evidence to date has only scratched the surface of human comprehension of the underlying process.

Howard–Sheth model of the purchase decision process

Howard and Sheth (1969) focused on the stimulus–response sequence with their model of consumer choice, shown in Figure 4.3. This clearly identifies the role of attitude formation as a key step in the purchase decision process.

The assumed relationship between attitude and purchase lies at the heart of much of the market research into attitudes. Advertising is created in the belief that it induces a selected attitudinal change which is necessary before a behavioural change.

Definition

An **attitude** is a mode of thinking towards an object or idea, which has come about through cognitive evaluation of information, through emotional response and through past experience. An attitude can be positive or negative, transient or long-term and lead to active or passive response.

Three main components of attitudes have been identified:

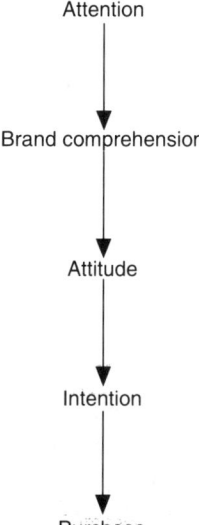

Figure 4.3 Howard–Sheth model of the purchase decision process.
Source: Howard J. and Sheth J.N. (1969). *The Theory of Buyer Behaviour.* New York: John Wiley & Sons, Inc.

(1) *Cognitive* The thinking component of awareness, knowledge and comprehension. This could be considered as 'self-persuasion' (Perloff and Brock, 1980).

(2) *Affective* The evaluation, liking and disliking that form the feeling component of an attitude, whereby advertising can appeal to emotions.

(3) *Conative* The action tendencies that result from the attitude or belief. These may be translated into a measure for 'intention to purchase'.

An advertiser is interested in attitudes only if they are predictive of purchasing behaviour. Research has shown only tenuous relationships between the two. However, attitudes may be indicative of behaviour whereas research is highly specific in terms of individual needs, context and time-scale.

Maslow's hierarchy of needs

Given the complexity of attitude formation, it is not surprising that there is no single theory that explains human motivation and behaviour. However the **hierarchy of needs** proposed by Abraham Maslow as far back as 1943 was influential in the development of advertising theory and practice. Maslow proposed that each individual has a set of needs which is organized in a predefined hierarchy, and this determines the order in which the individual will seek to satisfy the various needs.

Under this theory, physiological needs such as hunger and thirst are satisfied before the needs for security and protection (manifest through the quest for housing). Higher up the hierarchy come social and emotional needs, which are satisfied before the need for self-esteem and status. Maslow places the needs for self-development and self-realization at the top of the hierarchy (Maslow, 1970).

There are two qualifying features:

- more than one category of need may be satisfied simultaneously;
- not all individuals follow this precise pattern.

This model was a useful reference point during the decades when the Western world was experiencing a rapid rise in living standards, and advertising was a significant influence in channelling expenditure into specific types of consumption. However, its relevance at the turn of the twenty-first century must be seen in the context of attitudes moving away from 'conspicuous consumption' and towards preservation of natural resources and the environment. With increasing levels of education and the speed of technological development, individual perception of needs will become highly specific and their satisfaction will require a more complex array of offerings.

The theory of reasoned action

The model proposed by Fishbein and Ajzen (1975) is based on the premise that human behaviour is directed by reason and is under conscious control. Behavioural intention is then stated in terms of two components:

(1) Attitudes towards performing the act in a specific set of circumstances;
(2) The subject's normative belief about how the act will satisfy social pressures or influences.

The model can be stated simply as follows:

$$B \times BI = Aact + SN$$

where:

B $\quad$ = overt behaviour;
BI $\quad$ = behavioural intention;
Aact = attitude towards performing the act;
SN $\quad$ = subjective norm (compliance with what others think should be the act).

To illustrate the use of this theory, the subject of an undergraduate student contemplating the purchase of a personal computer to produce word-processed assignments is explored in Table 4.1.

Table 4.1 Fishbein Theory of Reasoned Action: application to purchase a personal computer by an undergraduate.

Salient choice outcomes	Column 1 Importance evaluation	Column 2 Option A	Column 3 Option B
(1) High quality presentation of assignments	+5	0	+4
(2) Ability to work at own convenience	+3	+2	+2
(3) Learning tool	+2	+3	+1
(4) Affordable	+3	+4	+1
The sum of Col. 1 × Col. 2		24	
The sum of Col. 1 × Col. 3			31

Referrants	Column 4 Motivation to comply	Column 5 Option A	Column 6 Option B
(1) Tutors	+4	+2	+4
(2) Fellow students	+2	+3	+3
(3) Parents	+3	+4	+1
The sum of Col. 4 × Col. 5		26	
The sum of Col. 4 × Col. 6			25

There are two purchase options:

(1) *Option A* Low cost, range of software included in price, poor quality printer.
(2) *Option B* Higher cost, only word processing software included, higher quality printer.

The student will evaluate each of these options against outcome criteria which are given importance scores. This process is illustrated in the first part of the table.

In the second section, motivation to comply with the perceived preference of a 'referral group' is scored, as is the student's normative belief of what the preference would be for each group.

The results of the scoring process indicate that option B is preferred by the student on the basis of outcome, whereas option A is the marginal winner based on perceived views of the referral groups.

It is the translation of theory into brand attributes which gives the advertiser the opportunity to identify which end-results are important to the buyer and to match the advertising message to this outcome. For example, a toothpaste brand may prevent gum disease and ensure fresh breath. The researcher must identify the relative importance of these two attributes to the buyer, and must have the brand scored on these attributes (along with other brands in a structured test).

For an established product, the theory provides the advertiser with the opportunity to change a belief about brand performance on a particular attribute. However, the product performance in use must match the advertising claims. If it does not, then there is a gap between expectation and performance. This is known as **cognitive dissonance**. It is a serious inhibitor to repeat purchase.

Social, cultural or economic influences can change the relative importance of brand attributes. In some instances, public opinion can swing rapidly on a particular issue (such as biodegradability or the potential for recycling). In such situations, the advertiser may be forced to strengthen brand positioning on a specific attribute. This is an expensive defensive tactic, and may be avoided by monitoring changing attitudes on a regular basis. Environmental aspects to product performance and packaging illustrate the potentially complex application of the theory of reasoned action. The individual must assess the environmental impact of the product, and will have perceptions of peer group pressure to comply with 'environmentally acceptable' purchasing patterns.

The elaboration likelihood model of persuasion

Petty and Cacioppo (1981) identify two distinct routes to attitude change which are emphasized in the literature relating to social and consumer psychology. The first is the **central route** by which attitude change results from a person's comprehension and learning of information relevant to the issue or product. One hypothesis of this model is that attitude changes via this central route are relatively enduring.

The second route to attitude change is called the **peripheral route**. The hypothesis here is that the change occurs not because an individual has consciously considered the merits of the issue or product, but because of the cues in the message associated with it. Typical cues might be the endorsement of the product by a celebrity or an expert, or in-use situations with cues relating to social status. The model proposes that the attitude change via this route is only temporary.

The authors of the model reported empirical evidence that when the subject had a high involvement with the product, attitudes changed through the central route. Where there was low involvement then attitudes were affected by the peripheral route. The research construct involved four different advertisements for a fictitious brand of disposable razor (Petty and Cacioppo, 1983). The messages were varied in terms of message arguments (strong or weak) and type of endorsement (celebrity or average citizen). The subjects were motivated through reward to have a high or low involvement with the product.

The results of the research generally fitted the hypothesis of the Elaboration Likelihood Model. High involvement subjects had a higher positive reaction to the product when exposed to the cogent product arguments than when the arguments were specious. The nature of the product endorser had a significant impact on product attitudes only under low involvement.

A further result of the research was that the correlation between attitude and purchase intention for high-involvement subjects was higher than the same correlation for low-involvement subjects. The researchers claim that this result suggests that attitudes formed through the central (cognitive) route will be more predictive of behaviour than attitudes formed via the peripheral route.

Consumer behaviour at the aggregate level

The models already explored give indicators to the process of persuasion, but there is still the implicit assumption that the attitude change measured by **intention to purchase** bears a linear relationship to actual purchase. The advertiser is, after all, interested in the sales response to a campaign. An alternative way of looking at buyer behaviour is at the **aggregate level** – in which individuals are grouped in a target audience, and their response to a particular marketing stimulus is measured across the group. This approach forms the basis of test marketing, as the results are more reliably predictive of a larger group comprising the same type of individuals.

Companies and advertising agencies that place greater reliance on direct marketing to stimulate sales are frequently unconcerned about the process of persuasion at the individual level. The focus of these organizations is on evaluation of historical response data at the aggregate level. General rules about response rates and spending levels are deduced and then used as a forecasting base for future marketing activity. There is a general equation which acts as a foundation to this aggregate approach for a single repeat purchase consumer product.

$$\text{Volume sales}_t = \text{Number of customers}_t \times \text{Average frequency of purchase}_t$$

where t represents a specific period of time (month, quarter or year).

For the direct marketing approach to evaluation of campaign performance, a more elaborate version of this fundamental equation can be used to understand the components of sales response. This is explored in Chapter 13. This equation also underpins extensive empirical research which formed the basis of repeat-buying theory.

Repeat-buying theory

When Ehrenberg and Godhardt's 'repeat-buying theory' (Ehrenberg, 1972; 1988) was first published, it led to a considerable amount of rethinking about the purchase patterns for consumer brands. From empirical research among consumer panellists, Ehrenberg was able to deduce simple mathematical rules which provided predictive tools. Before presenting these, some contextual background is necessary.

The consumer makes three major decisions relating to purchase which are of interest for predictive modelling:

(1) Whether to buy the given product class at all
(2) If yes – when?
(3) If yes – which brand?

Ehrenberg's study of a wide array of consumer panel data shows that most people tend to develop habits of buying one or a small number of brands, each fairly regularly. This would be expected intuitively from the desire to 'habitualize' low-risk purchases, once satisfactory outcomes have been experienced through product trial.

It would be expected that the incidence of repeat-buying for a brand will depend on a number of factors. These could include:

- the nature of the product
- usage habits
- level of advertising
- consumer promotions
- attitudes towards the brand
- purchasing patterns for competitive brands

However, Ehrenberg's empirical research shows that regular patterns of purchasing behaviour exist for a brand, and that the variations in values associated with this behaviour can be explained by one single measure. This measure is the average rate of buying per buyer in the specified time-frame.

This finding applies particularly to stationary markets where there is not rapid growth or a number of recent market entries. This **market equilibrium** would apply to such markets as toothpaste, toilet soap, margarine, soap flakes and coffee.

In the general equation for volume sales given above, the number of customers can be interpreted as the level of penetration for the brand. This is generally expressed as the percentage of the population buying in the time-frame, and can be compared with the penetration levels of other brands and of the product sector.

Ehrenberg's empirical data showed that it is the penetration levels of brands that will show significant differences, rather than the average rate of buying per buyer, which will tend to be more or less the same across brands within the product sector.

What does this mean for the advertiser trying to increase market share? For an established brand, advertising means keeping the product message in the forefront of the consumer's mind through planned repetitions of the message at appropriate intervals, and by reinforcing **salience**. There is correlation between brand share, brand penetration, salience and preference (McDonald, 1988). For the established brand, a decline in the importance attached to advertising may mean the danger of longer-term decline in brand share, if other brands maintain their advertising spend (sometimes known as **share of voice**).

For the new product, a significant launch advertising campaign will create awareness and, if the message arguments are convincing, purchase will follow. Where the product sector is relatively undeveloped (such as private health insurance in the UK), then the communication plays an educative and informative role for the total sector as well as for the individual brand. Timing of a campaign can be as important to success as the quality of the message, as economic and social factors will play a part in determining the relevance of the message to the target audience.

Multi-brand buying

Ehrenberg extended investigation of empirical evidence to the situation in which more than one brand is purchased. It was found that the proportion of a population buying any two brands, X and Y, in a period can be predicted from the penetration levels of X and Y. This has implications for sales promotion activity. In the situation where a brand is in a 'steady state' with a fairly constant level of penetration, then sales promotion activity can be expected to increase sales in the short term through bringing more buyers into the net, and increasing the penetration level. This will be at the

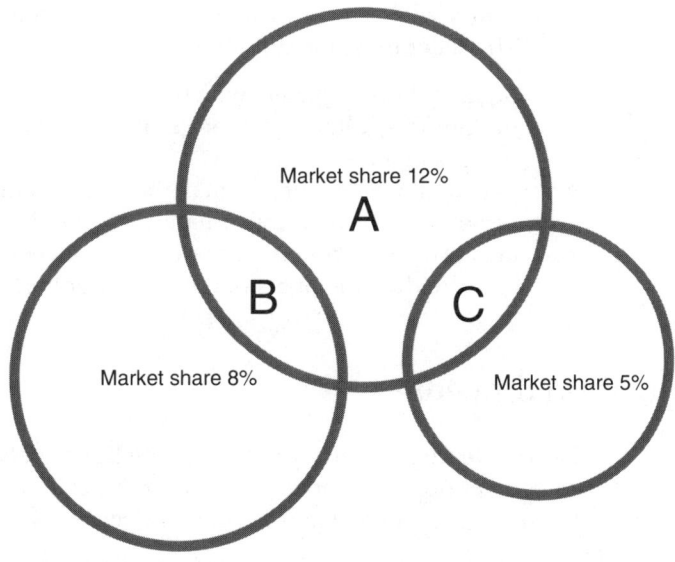

Brand switching between
A and B > A and C

Figure 4.4   Ehrenberg's theory of brand switching.

expense of other brands for that purchase occasion, and hence the objective of brand switching is fulfilled.

According to Ehrenberg's theory, the level of switching from individual competing brands will be in proportion to the penetration of each brand. This is illustrated by sales promotion for Brand A encouraging switching from Brands B and C, as shown in Figure 4.4.

As a general rule, for an established brand, sale promotion cannot:

(1) Significantly increase the average buying rate per buyer (although purchases may be brought forward); or
(2) Bias the brand-switching process from other brands out of proportion to their relative penetration levels.

However, a brand relaunch may use the opportunity to encourage different uses or different usage quantities, in which case the broad rules above would not necessarily apply.

Organizational buyer behaviour

Buying decisions for organizations invariably involve a network of individuals, each of whom has a greater or lesser degree of influence on the outcome. This makes the buying process more complex than for the individual consumer, and also takes place over a longer time-scale, particularly where considerable financial commitment is involved.

The seller must identify three components of the buying process:

- organizational needs, which tend to be objective, rational and measurable, although there may also exist political and cultural dimensions;
- personal needs, which may be socio-political, linked to career progression or financial situation, or based on ego fulfilment;
- area of overlap between organizational needs and the personal needs of individual members of the buyer network.

Organizational needs

Before identifying key members of the buyer network, it is necessary to categorize organizational markets. Organizational needs will be affected by the market context and business objectives within each category.

(1) *Producer markets* Buyers of raw materials, components and labour to create added value through the production of an end-product or service. These organizations may be driven by directly serving the needs of consumers, in which case influences on consumer buying

behaviour will have a direct effect on the organizational buying behaviour. This means that purchasing requirements are derived from the primary consumer market.

An example of this scenario is the demand for Lycra materials by companies manufacturing ladies' casual clothes. The higher spending on leisure and the drive towards a healthier lifestyle has increased the incidence of sporting pursuits in which Lycra garments are viewed as both comfortable and fashionable.

An alternative scenario is the company purchasing aluminium foil and board for production of food packaging. The need to sell to the food processer creates an additional layer of derived demand.

(2) *Reseller markets* Intermediaries such as wholesalers and retailers, creating added value by making the product accessible. Buying policies will be influenced by the need to make a margin on the buy/sell process.

(3) *Institutional markets* Traditionally covering the government sector and other non-profit organizations such as charities and trade associations. Buying behaviour will reflect moral and humane con-siderations, as well as a political framework for operations in the case of national government agencies.

Government buying in the UK can be split conveniently into the national government sector and the local authority sector. Both sectors have been subject to the move towards privatization during the 1980s, which has had a significant impact on buying policies and procedures.

The national government sector

In the national government sector, defence procurement remains strictly in the public sector, and national security needs influence the choice of supplier. In contrast, the energy and water industries fall within the private sector, and the profit interests of shareholders of gas, electricity and water companies determine buying policies. In the situation whereby national monopolies become private monopolies, then buying behaviour may become tougher through greater accountability to the shareholder compared with the less stringent demands of the amorphous body of taxpayers. Sector-specific conditions apply to the buying process in education, transport and health.

In education, the possibility for schools to 'opt-out' of local education authority control means that a budget calculated on a pupil *per capita* basis is managed directly by the school head. This has the impact of reducing the buying power of the local education authority, and imposes buying activity without the advantage of economies of scale on a head teacher with little formal training or experience in the buying process.

In transport, deregulation of buses has led to greater diversity of provision, with competition on some routes and the scaling down of vehicles used according to route needs. The privatization of rail transport remains controversial, with some commentators unable to envisage the nature of competition on a single track, for example between London and Gatwick or Birmingham and Coventry. The level of investment in engines and rolling stock would be determined by commercial rather than public-sector spending criteria.

Moves in the National Health Service towards self-governing hospital trusts and fund-holding general practitioners have reduced the buying power of local health authorities. This has had the effect of creating an internal market within the health service, whereby the funds follow the patient from general practitioner to hospital for specialist consultations, operations and treatment. Hospitals as providers can compete on speed, quality and cost of treatment. The management will therefore learn to identify and respond to a new type of buyer behaviour, whereby optimal use must be made of restricted budgets to serve the greatest possible number of patients.

The local government sector

Buying at the local government (or local authority) level is invariably structured in a set of policies and procedures which have two broad objectives:

- to ensure that the best value for money is achieved for the catchment population who are funding services through a local tax;
- to maintain scrupulous dealings with suppliers with respect to the way in which contracts are allocated.

These requirements result in invitations to short-listed suppliers to **tender** for a project or contract – in other words, the submission of a price quotation along with a specification of what will be provided for the price. Such tenders may be **open** (available for all to see) or **closed** (submitted to the prospective buyer in confidence).

Historically, local authorities have employed their own in-house departments for provision of such services as street cleaning, school meals and parks and recreation management. During the late 1980s and early 1990s, national government policy encouraged local authorities to invite tenders from outside agencies to fulfil specific services. The momentum was created by the view that companies operating in the private sector could offer a more focused service at a more competitive price.

Internal departments were encouraged to tender for services along with commercial companies in a process called **market testing**. Quality issues were considered important, in response to a political environment in which agencies were encouraged to put the customer first. This customer was empowered to demand a minimum standard of performance, details of which were specified in a **customer charter**.

Industrial buyer network

Members of an organization who influence a purchasing decision do so through authority vested in them by the nature of their managerial capacity or specialist function. General types of roles in the process have been identified which are equally applicable to industrial buying and the public service sector.

The **gatekeeper** controls the way in which contact is made with decision-makers, and may also act as a filter on information reaching them. The receptionist or personal assistant can resist attempts by sales-persons to make appointments for personal visits. However, tactfully handled, such situations can be turned to advantage through the seller obtaining information on key personnel and their working methods.

One member of the buying organization may have identified a need, and is set the task of reviewing alternative products and suppliers. This **suggester** may be a specialist such as an engineer, research scientist, or software systems manager, or a non-specialist intent on improving per-formance within their own department or sphere of influence. It is critical that the needs of this member of the buyer network are satisfied, since he or she represents a potential advocate for the supplier within the network.

When there are major capital spending plans within an organization, specialists will be called upon to provide management with advice, infor-mation and product trial results, as appropriate. These **influencers** may represent the most demanding link in the buyer network. For example, companies like AWD Bedford, Volvo and Leyland-Daf would be invited to tender for the supply of the British Army four-by-four truck or 'tactical load carrier'. Each potential supplier would have to commit to significant investment in the development of a prototype which would then undergo rigorous testing by the buyer. Under the terms of a fixed price per vehicle contract, each supplier would strive to achieve measurable superiority for their vehicle on key endurance and ease of use criteria.

The ultimate **decider** in the buyer network may not be readily iden-tifiable by the prospective supplier. This is the member of the organization with the authority to sign a contract. This authority may arise through management seniority or expertise as a specialist. Other members of the buyer network could disguise the level at which buying authority is held in order to maintain control of communication with suppliers. Alternatively, this approach would form part of the official delegation process, so that the decision-maker relies on the research and advice of subordinates and specialists.

Some organizations have a designated **buyer** role, whereby a whole department will have responsibility for communications with suppliers. This official buyer may have authority to sign some or all purchase requi-sitions or contracts. Alternatively, the role of the buyer may be to make sure that purchasing procedures are followed, and to monitor supplier practices and the price and quality of their products.

The buying team at companies with the resources for sophisticated management services supported by information technology will use forecasting models to predict changes in costs of raw materials and components. The buyer will then be in a position to negotiate with existing suppliers regarding price increases.

A more formal acknowledgement of individual roles within a buying team is the committee approach to purchasing. At committee meetings, the detailed activities of members of the team will be specified, reviewed and acted upon. Where a high degree of consensus of the team is required for buying decisions, then there is less scope for supplier influence at the individual level. The focus of selling will be on organizational rather than personal needs.

A structured approach to choosing a supplier

As organizational needs are more objective and quantifiable, what tools are available to help in supplier choice?

Historically, competitive bidding was the predominant method for choosing suppliers, where price was the key, and often only, determinant. However, the importance of **quality** in every aspect of production or service provision has led to a broader range of choice criteria for many organizations in vetting suppliers.

A structured approach to assessment of supplier capability through a performance ratings system can provide a framework for monitoring input aspects of an organization's own quality improvement process. This approach, adopted at Kodak (Aleo, 1992), can involve measures of acceptance rates of incoming goods and of supplier delivery performance against agreed timings.

Even more complex approaches to the procurement process involving a wide array of assessment criteria may not necessarily lead to better decisions. Case studies reveal the use of up to 14 criteria for supplier evaluation, whereby each member of a committee gives a weighting to each criteria, and then rates each supplier's system against these criteria (Mattar *et al.*, 1992). Calculation of the total weighted factor score for each system permits ranking of the offerings against needs. The researchers propose a method of exclusion of suppliers who cannot meet minimum standards of performance on specific product criteria, linked with pairwise comparison, as a more robust approach.

Personal needs of the buyer

In most business relationships the personal needs of the buyer representative will not be discussed. However, some account must be taken of these needs in selling and negotiating. The buyer will reflect attitudes through behaviour and what can be termed personal style. Signals can be read by the other party to adapt his or her own personal style and presentation to best suit the needs of the buyer.

Wilson Learning Corporation of the USA has developed a reference framework of social styles which is used by sales trainers and consultants on both sides of the Atlantic. This concept makes use of two dimensions in Jung's theory of behaviour. Firstly, the **assertiveness** scale allows for the assessment of behaviour on the degree to which a person 'tells' or 'asks' in the communication process. Secondly, the **responsiveness** scale indicates the personal level of emotional response to an idea or situation.

Some people are more fact-oriented, others prefer to respond on the more subjective, emotional level. When these two scales are combined, a grid of four typical styles emerges which illustrates four different 'comfort zones'. Individuals prefer to operate within their own comfort zones, and therefore respond more positively to those who exhibit the behaviour traits of the same social style. Figure 4.5 illustrates these behavioural styles and characteristic behaviour for each of them; the guidelines in Table 4.2 will help the seller to identify the personal style of the buyer and to adapt the presentation accordingly.

For each of the four areas of social style there is a primary response to stress, called **back-up** behaviour. The driver becomes authoritarian, the expressive will show an emotional outburst, the amiable will acquiesce and the analytical will attempt to avoid a situation of stress or conflict.

The perceptive seller will read the behaviour signs of a buyer, interpret these in terms of social style and then adapt the approach, presentation and closing techniques to that personal style. This flexibility will provide a greater degree of assurance that the personal needs of the buyer are met in the sales process.

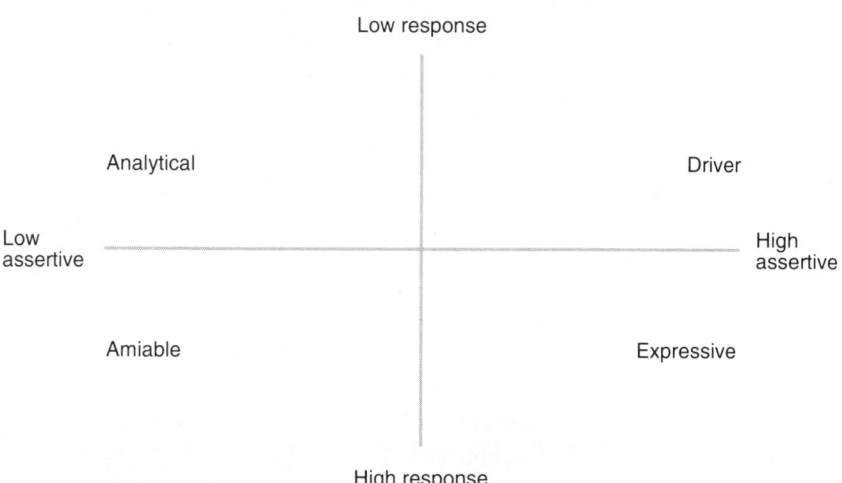

Figure 4.5 Wilson Learning social style recognition.

Table 4.2   Characteristic behaviour for social style recognition (Wilson Learning model).

	Driver	Expressive	Amiable	Analytical
Behaviour	Results-orientated Wants to know the bottom line Interested in the broad picture Demanding of others Takes short, summarizing notes	Appears to be easygoing and low key Relates on a personal level Extrovert, trusting Dislikes paperwork and detailed facts	Appears to be easygoing and low key Works at friendship, loyal Company worker, cooperative Pays attention to detail	Pays great deal of attention to facts Needs full information Low key, listens carefully Takes detailed notes
Decision-making	Easy, based on facts and personal knowledge	Easy, based on instincts and relationships	Difficult, needs reassurance from others	Difficult, needs to assess all the facts
How to sell to	Keep presentation short Talk bottom-line results Close quickly	Keep presentation dynamic Use third-party stories rather than facts Build rapport at emotional level Close quickly	Needs lengthy presentation Low key, friendly approach Build rapport at personal level Avoid pushing for a close	Needs lengthy presentation Cover facts and figures in detail Keep presentation low key Close after all questions answered

Negotiation

The process of negotiation involves two parties moving from different starting positions in relation to needs, and reaching a mutually acceptable outcome. It can take place between individuals or teams, and may involve only one meeting or take place over an extended period. For commercial transactions, the negotiation process occurs towards the completion of a sale where the buyer wishes to strike the best possible deal in granting a major contract.

Price is frequently the subject of negotiation, and the buyer has greater negotiating power during periods of recession. For the seller of a complex product or service, reducing the price to that which the buyer would ideally wish to pay could mean a low or non-existent margin on the deal. For the buyer, the initial price quoted by the seller may be higher than the budget available. Both parties need to move from their ideal positions, by making concessions, to reach a mutually acceptable price. Each party adjusts position within an area known as the **negotiating zone**, which is illustrated in Figure 4.6.

Skilled negotiators take into account both the personal roles and needs of the other party, as well as the needs of the organization which

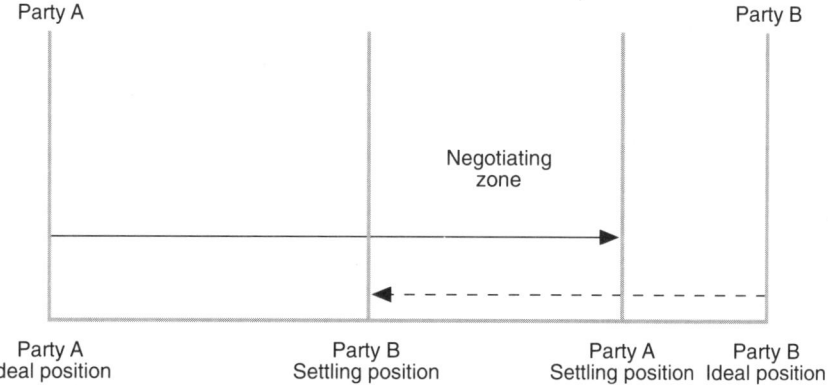

Figure 4.6 The relative position of two parties in negotiation.

they represent. The process therefore makes use of the theory already explored in this chapter. There are five key stages which can be identified in the negotiation process:

(1) Preparation
(2) Exploration
(3) Proposal stage
(4) Bargaining stage
(5) Closing stage

Preparation

Each party should identify the ideal position and settling position. For the buyer, this settling position may be a ceiling price. Concessions that can be made will be identified and given some order of importance, and consultation with other members of the organization may be necessary here.

The information needed from the other party should be identified, together with the strategy for obtaining it. This information is needed to determine the strengths and weaknesses of the other party in bargaining on key issues. Tactics for revealing information on one's own position should be planned, as should the roles to be played by individual team members.

Exploration

In the early discussion stage, each party is exploring the other party's position, probing for information and testing assumptions. It is important to pick up signals to confirm assumptions, including body language.

Proposal stage

When it is clear that no more progress can be made without one party making a conciliatory move, then a proposal or concession should be tabled. The seller may table a proposal to include extra service elements if the buyer agrees to the price already proposed. The buyer's response will determine whether further specific concessions are needed.

Bargaining stage

When there is positive response to the buyer's concession, then an equal concession should be requested in return, for example: 'If we reduce the price specified by 5%, could we expect you to pay on delivery rather than the normal terms of 30 days from invoice?' The nature of the concession demanded from the buyer will depend on the degree of competition for the seller and the importance of the contract in meeting sales targets.

Closing stage

When no further concessions are forthcoming, each party must decide whether conditions are right for concluding negotiations. One party – frequently the seller – will ask the other party to confirm that agreement has been reached, and the key areas should be summarized. The terms of agreement should be confirmed in writing after the meeting, so that both parties are clear on the outcome.

If the seller pressurizes the buyer into an agreement, there may be buyer dissatisfaction with the terms, which may lead to problems in the relationship. A successful outcome to negotiation is that in which both parties believe they have struck a good bargain.

Cultural influences on the nature of the relationship between buyer and seller

The role that negotiation plays in the purchasing process will depend on national and corporate culture. Historically, it has played a greater role in Europe than America, as the nature of the relationship is perceived differently. In the 1980s, the American approach was dominated by 'the market' and therefore bid prices were the dominant influence on supplier choice. The relationship that followed was conducted very much at arm's length, and fear of competitor substitution was the dominant influence in contract compliance by suppliers.

In contrast, the European buyer will be more prepared to consider long-term relationships with fewer suppliers. The choice of supplier will be made on social as well as technical qualities, which will be assessed in the process of short-listing for negotiations (Cova and Salle, 1991).

However, it is the competitive nature of the global market which is making major organizations with an Anglo-Saxon tradition review relationships with suppliers. There are two contemporary features of buying which are forces for change: the pace of improved technology and the move towards **just-in-time** procurement.

In order to guarantee technological superiority of their own product, buyers need to identify the lead technology among suppliers. This requires greater collaboration and sharing of information which takes a relationship into the realm of an alliance, as distinct from the traditional adversarial position. It also requires commitment over the longer term, if each party is to benefit from the arrangement.

Similarly, the impact of just-in-time procurement on the distribution chain has been predominantly one of cooperation such that boundaries between supplier and customer become blurred. This is particulary evident where major capital investment is necessary for suppliers to 'lock in' to the logistical processes of dominant customers. (These issues are covered in more detail in Chapter 7.)

Where markets are showing lower growth records or even saturation, then price competition is paramount. American companies are therefore also under pressure to reduce costs, and dealing with a large number of suppliers on a short-term basis can increase the transaction cost element of the final product. This, as well as undue dependence on particular suppliers, is driving many American companies to seek closer ties or alliances with their vendor base (Sriram *et al.*, 1992).

European perspective

The complexity of the relationship between buyer and seller depends on the nature of the product or service, the organizational cultures of the parties to the agreement, and the personal styles and needs of the individuals involved in the transaction. These issues are also influenced by industry structure and legislation at the national level.

When considering the selling process across borders in the enlarged Europe, the picture is further complicated by problems of language and culture. There are also moves towards EC harmonization in such areas as procurement of products and services where the contracts are of a high value, and agency agreements. Recent EC Commission judgements on exclusive sales agreements or restrictive clauses in distribution contracts also provide clear indicators of where historic practice would be considered as restricting free competition in a borderless Europe.

These issues are considered in the context of how companies selling across borders will have to make adjustments in attitudes and working methods if they are to take advantage of new opportunities. There is specific focus on pan-European selling for the industrial and business-to-business sectors, although direct selling to the consumer is included.

Selling in a new market

Issues of language, culture and national business practices can create barriers to trade when a company is at an early stage in establishing sales in a new market. Under these conditions there are four ways in which the company may proceed:

(1) Sell direct from the UK office
(2) Use an **import house** from the new market
(3) Use an **agent** in the new market
(4) Use a **distributor** or **wholesaler**

When a company's products become established within the new territory, other options become available: the setting up of a branch office or a fully owned subsidiary, arranging a **licensing agreement** with a company with an established sales and distribution network in the market, or setting up a **joint venture**. A decision to develop through one of these routes would be considered part of corporate strategy, and they are therefore explored in the pan-European context in Chapter 3.

Selling direct from the UK office

This is essential where the product involves specialist expertise as well as hardware, so that senior executives can define the customer problem and propose the appropriate solution. Products that fall into this category are mid- to large-frame computers, distribution or handling systems, and highly specialist plant and machinery that requires detailed follow-through during installation and start-up.

Other areas of selling involving high-value capital goods will also require experienced negotiators, so that elements of the contract relating to price, inclusive service provision and any penalty clauses are agreed to the satisfaction of both parties. The increasing importance of the **information society** means that consultancy and project management will also be sources of cross-border revenue. This means that executives and professionals must make a greater commitment to visiting the new market, understanding local needs and communicating with local advisers or members of project teams.

Use of intermediaries

The choice of intermediary will depend on degree of product expertise required, market coverage offered and level of financial involvement. The criteria to be applied are the same as those explored in Chapter 7, with the added dimensions of language capability and understanding of national laws.

Where a high degree of technical expertise is required and relationships with customers take time to evolve, the appointment of a **distributor** will be the preferred option. The distributor agreement will set out the terms of business in relation to delivery of product, terms of payment, customer service levels required, responsibility for promotion and development of a sales territory. The conventions of doing business in the new market may well differ from those of the home market, and a degree of compromise may be necessary in finalizing agreements. Nuance of language could lead to misunderstandings, so the advice of a local lawyer would be essential to protect the interests of the principal.

Where products are less complex and the company wishes to maintain control of physical distribution, then the use of **sales agents** is an option. The agent's prime role is as an 'order getter', through an established network of customers (possibly retail outlets), or by creating new business through representing the principal at trade shows, or by advertising or cold-calling. National laws relating to agency agreements must be observed, including the way in which commission on sales is paid (including payment on residual sales when the agency agreement is terminated). An agreement would normally also cover the period of the contract, territory involved and responsibility for promotion. The principal should identify other product ranges that the agent carries, to be sure that these are complementary rather than competitive, and to establish that sufficient resources will be available to develop the principal's interests.

Some initial research on the new market is essential before making major contractual commitments, and to identify industry features that affect the sales operation. For example, where an agent in the UK might take on responsibility for one of eight easily defined geographical territories, the market in Germany might focus around three major cities, Hamburg, Stuttgart and Munich, and three agencies would be sensible. Similarly, the larger geographical areas of France and Spain would merit industry analysis to identify the most effective form of agency coverage.

Trade shows and exhibitions

Exhibiting in an international trade show is one way of identifying and recruiting potential sales agents for individual Member States. A short-list can be drawn up and strong candidates invited to the UK site for interviews and familiarization with the company and its products.

Where the company does not have the resources for a national field salesforce, the **trade exhibition** may be the only available route to awareness of the product name and features, and the development of a tailor-made prospect list for mailings and sales appointments. Availability of specialist advertising media may encourage spending in these to the detriment of trade shows. This may be one explanation for differences in attitudes towards exhibiting at trade shows between UK companies and those in Continental Europe.

Some observers see the international trade shows held in the UK as the poor relation of those held in France and Germany, where exhibition space can be twice the size of the UK's largest venue, the National Exhibition Centre. The 'international' nature of a show can be gauged by the number of European and other overseas exhibitors, and by the mixed European profile of the visitors. Most British trade shows cater for a predominantly home market.

However, there are signs that British attitudes towards the importance of trade shows are changing, with companies spending up to 40% more on this type of promotion; yet these still get low priority within the marketing budget. According to the Incorporated Society of British Advertising (ISBA), UK companies spent about £700 million on show participation in 1988, which represents nearly 10% of advertising budgets. In contrast, German companies spend nearly 20% of advertising budgets on trade exhibitions (Cobb, 1990). If UK companies are to penetrate other Member States with their products and services, then representation at key trade shows is essential. This will require commitment in terms of planning horizons, management time and budgets, and the use of professional services to design and construct displays which measure up to the standards set by competitors from Europe.

Legal effects of EC harmonization on pan-European selling

These fall into two broad categories: firstly, individual distributor or agency contracts and the EC interpretation of the terms of each contract under Article 85(1) of the Treaty of Rome, to determine whether the contract upholds the spirit of free trade. Secondly, EC Directives on procurement of goods and services where the contract exceeds a specified value have significant implications for companies in the way that they advertise for tender, evaluate offers and come to a buying decision. The principles of extending sales opportunities across traditional borders are also extended to the public sector, where national interests have historically biased procurement towards local suppliers.

EC judgements on agency and distributor agreements

Where distributor agreements provide for exclusive distribution rights within or across EC Member States, then there is a likelihood that such terms would infringe Article 85(1) of the Treaty of Rome. Depending on the nature of the market, the influence of the parties to the agreement on the market and the specific terms of the agreement, there may be conditions for exemption under Article 85(3). However, Commercial Agency Agreements are treated more favourably and do not, as a rule, fall within the scope of Article 85(1) if they involve true agents who do not carry out any other business on their own account.

Three decisions of the European Commission illustrate the way in which free-trade policy is applied to distributor agreements.

Example 1

In the case of Bayer Dental, the EC was concerned by the condition of sale under which packages carrying a registered trade-mark may be supplied to third parties only in unopened form, distribution being limited to a single Member State on the grounds that resale in other Member States may give rise to a breach of intellectual property rights (*Competition Law in the EC*, 1991). The Commission took the view that the restrictive clause was an integral part of the contract and it ran counter to the principles of free competition within Europe, even if parallel imports were unlikely.

Example 2

The Eighteenth Report of the EC on Competition Policy provides a second case which throws light on their view of restrictive clauses. It involved contracts between the Nutrasweet Company for the supply of sweetener Aspartame to the Coca-Cola Company and to Pepsico Inc. Clauses in the contracts related to agreement by the two purchasers that they would purchase all their Aspartame requirements in the Community *exclusively* from Nutrasweet until 1990. Since the three companies had major shares of their respective markets, the EC required that these exclusive supply clauses were removed from the contracts, to enable other suppliers of the sweetener to enter the market.

Example 3

A third case involved agreements and concerted practices between Tipp-Ex and its exclusive distributors of correction products for the typing market in France, Beiersdorf and Diffusion Marketing International. These distributors agreed not to sell to customers who sell the products covered by distribution contracts in other Member States. This arrangement was judged to infringe Article 85(1) of the Treaty of Rome (Commission Decision 87/406/EEC). On appeal, the Commission verified the judgement, indicating that the creation of absolute territorial protection designed to hinder parallel imports was contrary to the Treaty, and that ignorance of the infringement was not a defence, as the purpose of the conduct was to restrict free competition (*Competition Law in the EC*, 1990).

EC legislation relating to procurement

In 1986 total purchasing controlled by the EC public sector was worth ECU 530 billion, which amounts to 15% of the Community's gross domestic product. Even allowing for goods and services which are inherently non-competitive, it is estimated that contracts worth between seven and ten per cent of GDP could be open to competitive tender across the EC (Cecchini Report, 1988). In fact, the value of contracts awarded to non-national companies by the public sector is minute. Transport costs and the ability to provide after-sales service are considerations that prompt local purchasing, but there are deeper-seated cultural and protectionist reasons for working with national suppliers.

In early moves towards an open market, the EC Directives on public works (1971) and public supply contracts (1977) did not make an impact on these protectionist policies, as it is difficult to enforce rules where purchasing is decentralized. However, the EC persevered with legislation some ten years later. This promotes competition with the twin objectives of creating downward pressure on prices and creating robust European industries better able to compete with Japan and the USA.

New public works and supplies Directives came into force in 1990, and Directives on sectors that were hitherto excluded (telecommunications, energy, water and transport) took effect by the beginning of 1993. The EC has taken the precaution of defining mechanisms for legal enforcement.

The EC allows three possible approaches to awarding a contract:

- open
- restricted
- negotiated

This is provided that, in most cases, there has been a prior call for competition. The policy of the Commission is that the buyer can 'choose the cheapest' or the 'most economically attractive' option – but the criteria on which this decision is to be made have to be made clear to all tendering parties in advance.

Professional purchasers take the view that the EC is imposing administrative procedures on buyers which will not enhance cross-border trade above the level that organizations would encourage or seek out anyway to fulfil their own needs. It is claimed that the procedures fail to recognize the input of professionals into the buying process – through influencing, advising, investigating technical specifications, and negotiating (Harvey, 1989). These procedures also assume that the tender process is always the best form of procurement on the part of public authorities, who have shown recent trends towards more commercial approaches, more typical of the private sector.

The new rules apply to all public buyers such as local authorities and hospitals; the majority of large and medium-sized European companies in nearly all sectors will be affected as potential bidders. The contracts covered must be over ECU 5 billion for works contracts, and ECU 200,000 for most supplies except for water, transport and energy, where the threshold is ECU 400,000, and telecommunications, where it is ECU 600,000 (Kellaway, 1990).

The buyer must advertise the contract in the *Official Journal*, and this must be at least 52 days ahead of the deadline for receipt of bids in the case of an open tender. If the tender is to be restricted, the buyer must indicate the objective criteria to be used for selection of the bidders.

A major obstacle to complete freedom in supply is differing technical standards in individual Member States. The EC has attempted to overcome this potential excuse for not considering non-national suppliers by working towards convergence on several thousand standards across a wide range of industries (Haigh, 1988). There is some way to go towards achieving this. Meanwhile, according to an amending Directive of 22 March 1988 (EC Directive 77/62) buyers must define technical specifications relating to each applicable contract 'by reference to national standards implementing European Standards, or by reference to common technical specifications'.

What does this mean for the seller?

The enforced advertising of requirements by the buyer means that more information is available about buyer needs, but this excludes sensitive commercial information (such as price of the accepted bid, which is submitted to the Commission in confidence).

Companies can develop a more accurate picture of their own competitive position within the wider European market through the following steps:

(1) Monitor information on new contracts in their specialist fields, advertised in the *EC Official Journal*.

(2)   Identify whether their product or service meets the outline specifications.
(3)   Identify the additional cost elements of delivering to the other Member State and of providing after-sales service. How will these elements affect price competitiveness?
(4)   Monitor the outcome of the bid procedure for individual contracts; who was awarded the contract and why?
(5)   How does the successful company compare in terms of resources, and how do their products compare on technical specification and quality? (Attendance at an international trade exhibition may be the best source of information.)
(6)   Identify features and benefits of own products which provide competitive edge, and highlight these in advertising material available in key European languages.

Language and cultural barriers to cross-border selling

The ability to communicate in the language of the buyer provides the seller with advantages that go beyond the simple discovery of needs and transmission of information about the way in which these needs can be fulfilled. Selling in the language of the buyer indicates a willingness to move towards their position in personal and organizational terms, and shows that some cultural understanding exists through the process of learning the language.

The historic nature of international travel and trade for each Member State has influenced the fluency of its population in foreign languages. Education systems have also played their part in maintaining compulsory foreign language teaching. The outcome is a wide variation in fluency across Member States. Two thirds of the Dutch speak English, and two thirds also speak German. Over 40% of Germans speak English, but only 18% speak French. The Danes also show a good proportion of the population able to speak English and German. Other countries show a less impressive profile, with the French and Italian records at much of a par. The British performance is the poorest on foreign languages (apart from the Irish), with only 15% speaking French, and 6% German (Danton de Rouffignac, 1990).

Political and business focus on Europe has created the demand for UK employees able to speak at least one foreign language. This has influenced foreign language provision in higher education, where courses are offered as part of the pathway towards a degree in another specialty. Where resources and student time permit, the method of learning a foreign language can have a significant bearing on the individual's capacity to appreciate the values and culture of the foreign national, particularly when negotiating. One proposed approach focuses on two ideas (Beneke, 1983):

(1) A **contrastive** approach in which study of the points of difference between two languages brings about a greater understanding of the nature of communication, and the need for empathy.
(2) An investigation of the **concept**s being described by language: a **cognitive** approach as opposed to mechanistic.

However, in a personal selling or negotiating situation there are other important aspects of the encounter which can influence the success of proceedings. These are related to body language and other nuances of culture, some of which are highlighted in Table 4.3.

There are two overriding features of doing business with those from another culture and in another language. Firstly, it is necessary to identify how important personal trust and empathy are to the buyer. Signals about success in this area will tend to come from body language and the way in which negotiations develop. Secondly, good communication takes place in the context of a set of common assumptions. This is more difficult to achieve across different cultures, and a negotiating team might request a preliminary meeting in which influencing issues are discussed to identify common ground from the outset.

Table 4.3   Some cultural aspects of selling and negotiating across borders.

Body language	(1)	How much personal space is considered polite?
	(2)	Is too much eye-contact considered threatening, or too little as a sign of lack of commitment to a position?
	(3)	What seating arrangement matches the formality of the situation?
Social convention	(1)	The duration of preliminary 'niceties' as a prelude to the main discussion.
	(2)	Speed of moving through an agenda. The distinction between work and leisure may not be as marked in southern European countries as in northern cultures.
	(3)	The degree of involvement of each member of the negotiating team: observance of seniority.
Nuances associated with language	(1)	Degree of assertion: Germans expect knowledge and facts to be stated; British understatement needs to be decoded to identify true position.
	(2)	Value placed on individual views as against the team or corporate position.

Cross-border payment

As cross-border trade increases, so there will be increasing complexity of financial transactions. Where many companies quote prices in ECUs, the status of transmission of funds in Europe is a long way from the utopia of dealing in a single currency across 12 Member States. The current complexities add to administrative costs and payment delays when selling across borders. An added dilemma in searching for new customers is their willingness to pay on time. Companies in Denmark and Germany have a good record on payment, whereas those in UK, France and Italy are slow payers, in comparison.

According to Intrum Justicia – which claims to be Europe's largest debt collection agency – British business is the worst for settling bills, paying in an average of 78 days, a month later than the normal time in Germany and Scandinavia (Kay, 1992). The problem had become so severe for small businesses that the UK Conservative government has imposed an obligation for companies to disclose their policy and record on payment of bills in the annual report (Budget Statement, March 1992).

Lobbying of the EC is in train to encourage harmonization of interest rates on outstanding debts, to give companies the right to be represented in court without a lawyer and to legislate that the cost of debt collection should be met by the slow payer. These principles are already applied in Germany, Netherlands and Scandinavia, and France has similar legislation in the pipeline. Were this to be law in the UK, small companies would be reluctant to apply these rights in the case of large, influential clients for fear of jeopardizing a large percentage of their overall turnover.

Selling direct to the consumer

It is recognized by the European Commission that contracts undertaken in the privacy of the home or in other non-business settings could be signed under conditions that would not prevail in the normal business setting. Therefore, such selling situations are covered by a Directive 'to protect the consumer in respect of contracts negotiated away from the business premises' (Directive 85/577/EEC).

The Directive specifically excludes:

- sales initiated by the consumer,
- those affecting immovable property,
- contracts for less than ECU 100,
- foodstuffs and drinks (such as bread and milk) delivered by regular roundsmen,

- contracts for the supply of goods and services,
- insurance contracts,
- contracts for securities.

Individual Member States have codes of conduct for direct selling, and certain product areas such as financial services are covered by specific legislation. The publications of the British Direct Selling Association set out a code of business conduct in relation to employees and agents, other companies operating in direct selling and in relation to retail customers (DSA, November 1990 and March 1991).

Problems and assignments

(1) What are the implications of the Ehrenberg research into buyer behaviour for the sales promotion industry?

(2) Give examples in an organizational buying situation of the three components of the buying process – organizational needs, personal needs and the overlap between the two.

(3) In which market areas would you expect trade shows and exhibitions to be accorded greater importance than media advertising? Why?

(4) Under EC Directives, public contracts over and above a specified size must be put out to open tender across the Single Market. Discuss the reasons in the short/medium term why local suppliers are still being preferred.

(5) In transposing the organizational buying/selling situation from a domestic to a European context, what additional factors would need to be taken into account?

(6) Where would you go in order to find the information required to answer question (5)?

(7) As a sales manager for a company selling specialist printing presses, how would you go about deriving your marketing strategy for a move into Europe?

(8) A small to medium sized enterprise (SME) has been selling its special breakfast cereal formula in the UK for many years. What steps would you advise the MD to take prior to trying to break into Europe?

References

Aleo Jr J. P. (1992). Redefining the manufacturer–supplier relationship. *Journal of Business Strategy*, **13**(5), September/October, 10

Cova B. and Salle R. (1991). Buying behaviour in European and American industry: contrasts. *European Management J.*, **9**(4), December

Ehrenberg A. C. S. (1988). *Repeat Buying*, 2nd edn (1st edn 1972). London: Charles Griffin/New York: Oxford University Press

Fishbein and Ajzen (1975). *Belief, Attitude, Intention and Behaviour: An Introduction to Theory and Research*. Reading MA: Addison-Wesley

Foxall G. R. (1983). *Consumer Choice*. Basingstoke: Macmillan Press

Howard J. and Sheth J. N. (1969). *The Theory of Buyer Behaviour*. New York: Wiley

Maslow A. H. (1970). *Motivation and Personality*, 2nd edn. New York: Harper and Row

Mattar S. G., Macdonald R. J. and Choo E. U. (1992). Procurement process: decision by exclusion and painwise comparisons. *OMEGA, Int. J. of Management Science*, **20**(5/6), 705–712

McDonald C. (1988). Repeat-buying refreshed. *Admap*, September

Petty R. E. and Cacioppo J. T. (1981). *Attitudes and Persuasion: Class and Contemporary Approaches*. Dubuque, Iowa: William C. Brown

Petty R. E., Cacioppo J. T. and Schumann D. (1983). Central and peripheral routes to advertising effectiveness: the moderating role of involvement. *J. of Consumer Research*, **10**, September

Puloff R. M. and Brock T. C. And thinking makes it so: cognitive responses to persuasion. M.E.

Ridoff and Miller G. R. (eds) (1980). *Persuasion: New Directions in Theory and Research*. Beverley Hills: Sage Publications, pp. 67–9

Sriram V., Knapfel R. and Spekman R. (1992). Antecedents to buyer–seller collaboration: an analysis from the buyer's perspective. *J. of Business Research*, **25**, 303–320

European perspective

Beneke J. (1983). The values of cultural studies in the training of cross-cultural negotiators. *European J. of Education*, **18**(2)

Cecchini Report (1988). *1992: The Benefits of a Single Market*. Hounslow: Wildwood House, pp. 16–17

Cobb R. (1990). Shows of force. *Marketing*, 26 April

de Rouffignac D. (1990). *How to Sell Europe*. London: Pitman, pp. 34–35

Direct Selling Association (1990). *A Consumer's Guide to Shopping at Home*

Direct Selling Association (1991a). *Code of Business Conduct: A Member's Relationship with other Members and their Salespeople*

Direct Selling Association (1991b). *Code of Practice. A Member's Responsibilities to their Retail Customer*

DTI. *Export Europe: Overseas Trade Services. Notification of Requirements in Federal Republic of Germany for Itinerant Selling*

Exclusive distribution (correction products): The Tipp-Ex case. *Competition Law in the EC*, **3**(6), June 1990

Export restrictions (dental products): The Bayer dental case. *Competition Law in the EC*, **14**(2), February 1991

Haigh L. (1988). EEC proposals alarm public sector buyers. *Professional Engineering*, November, pp. 19–20

Harvey F. (1984). The purchasing prospective. *Purchasing and Supply Management*, May, 34–38

Kay W. (1992). Getting the bills paid on time. *Business Life*, Meadway Publications, February, 30–34

Kellaway L. (1990). Procurement in the EC: market beginning to open up on bigger contracts. *Financial Times*, 4 April, p. 14

Woolley E. M. (1914). Finding the point of contact. *Advertising*, Vol. VI of the Library of Business Practice, New York: A. W. Shaw, pp. 25–26

5 Segmentation

Chapter objectives:

- to identify discrete groups of customers within a wider universe, who share relatively similar needs or characteristics as determined by a range of factors
- to apply the principles of market segmentation within the wider context of a marketing strategy
- to consider the implications of segmenting markets across the Single Market

Introduction

The use of the word 'universe' in statistical sampling for market research is apt when one considers the nature of a target market. In the era of global marketing, a multinational might well consider the world population as its natural market. At the other extreme, a direct marketing company with a sophisticated data management system might regard its target market as the individual with highly specific needs which can be met with custom-designed products communicated through highly personalized messages.

In practice, most companies operate on the basis of a target market positioned on the wide scale between these two extremes. The process of market research will determine the needs, behaviour and attitudes of actual or potential customers and a selection of a grouping within the total 'universe' for the product type will be chosen as the target market.

Use of information gleaned through market research to define these groupings is the process of **segmentation**.

Market segmentation

Market segmentation is the process of dividing the total perceived market into subsets, in each of which the potential customers have characteristics in common leading to similar needs from a product or service.

Identification of segments will require judgement based on the analysis of data. This data might be expensively obtained and highly detailed – as, for example, in the cluster analysis of demographic, income and attitudinal data of buyers of high-performance cars. On the other hand, business-to-business marketing often requires decisions based on research among a representative sample of customers in key industries – as, for example, in the supply of printing inks.

The purpose of market segmentation is to identify the segment with the *best potential on a range of criteria*, and to target a product or service at users or potential users in that segment. The product benefits, features and advertising message will be positioned against the needs of this target group.

Example

In 1987, Barclays Bank launched its Connect card. This card would allow personal banking customers to debit their bank accounts when shopping in retail outlets that accepted the card. The card also has the functions of a cash dispenser card and cheque guarantee card. The bank would make profit by charging the retail accounts a discount on the ticket value.

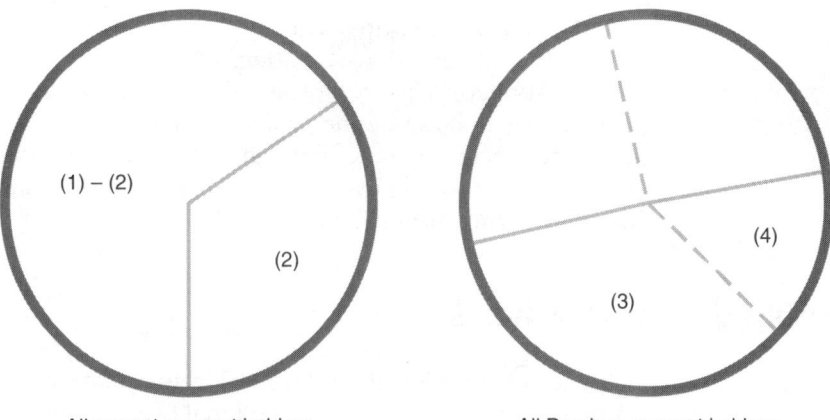

All current account holders   All Barclays account holders

    (1)   All holders of a current bank account
    (2)   All holders of a current Barclays bank account
    (3)   Barclays current account customers who debit the account
          at least six times a month for other than cash withdrawal
    (4)   Barclays customers who do not go into overdraft

Figure 5.1   Possible segmentation for Barclays Connect card.

In launching the card, the issue for Barclays was to identify one or more segments within their existing customer base (or even outside it) at which to target the new facility. The choice could be made from the following selection of sub-groups, which are also illustrated in Figure 5.1.

These sub-groups illustrate ways that Barclays might segment their market for the new Connect card depending on their revenue and profit objectives.

If the maximum number of accounts is the target, then the first two sub-groups would appear attractive. However, it would be very expensive to reach the first of these groups through advertising, and information on banking and spending habits would not be as readily available as for other, narrower groups.

If conversion of unprofitable personal accounts into profitable accounts was the objective, then Barclays might wish to focus on the third and fourth sub-groups listed.

Classification of market segments

Market segmentation is based upon the identification of certain **characteristics** common to a sub-group. These characteristics may belong to the product, the buyer (or prospective buyer) or the purchase occasion. There must be a clear and recognizable method of scaling the characteristic to facilitate division of the total user group into sub-groups.

For example, buyer age is easily classified by groups such as 18–25, 26–40, 41–50 and so on. Income levels are similarly easy to classify, but attitudes and lifestyles do not always lend themselves to such clear demarcations. In such situations, a battery of questions might be used; cluster analysis applied to the response will identify sub-groups which can be given names to describe the general bias of the group. For example, the title of 'boy racer' identifies the segment of male car buyers who are looking for the thrills and power of a racing car but who have modest means and some family responsibilities.

Product characteristics

One way of dividing the total market is by key product attributes or features. These may be of the functional type such as efficiency, speed of operation, simplicity or economy. Alternatively, aesthetic considerations could be important.

For industrial markets where the buying decision process will be complex, involving different functional managers with different needs, a series of objective criteria is likely to apply to comparison of products. Some of the likely criteria on which a manufacturer might choose to segment the market are listed in Table 5.1.

Table 5.1 Product characteristics for segmenting industrial markets.

Direct benefits	Indirect benefits
Simplicity of operation	Reduced stockholding
Less labour required	Fewer customer complaints
Higher operating speed	Increased sales
Lower energy requirement	Lower insurance premiums
Less machine down-time	Lower capital requirement
Less environmental pollution	Improved quality perception
Less space required	Competitive edge
Safer operating conditions	Improved profitability
Access to technical advice	

Cain (1969) defines appearance as 'the outward expression of the quality of the product and is the first point of contact with the user'. As companies find it increasingly difficult and expensive to achieve product differentiation through function then attention will be turned to aesthetic aspects of design. The more sophisticated and educated customer will also demand that the visual and tactile senses are pleased at the same time as the core need is satisfied. This applies particularly to consumer markets where increased standards of living have meant that penetration levels for everyday products have reached a plateau and sales must be achieved through product replacement with a more sophisticated model.

User characteristics

Characteristics of the user are the most commonly used classifications for segmentation because these are the easiest to identify and subsequently measure through market research, particularly in consumer markets. Some of the more common user characteristics are shown in Table 5.2.

Geographic classification is important in two significant areas of market research. Firstly, where regional boundaries for consumers more or less approximate to television reception areas, correlations can be established between product message and attitudinal and behavioural response. Secondly, decisions on the location of new retail outlets will rest on detailed examination of catchment areas and how populations in different towns are likely to respond.

At the broader level, needs will vary by region if there are distinct differences in income levels and discretionary spending (when essentials like housing, utilities and food have been paid for) by region. Tastes and social attitudes will also vary.

Analysis of a customer list by the address postcode has provided the most detailed segmentation now available, and relies on the advances of information technology specifically in database management and

Table 5.2 User characteristics that feature in market segmentation for consumer products.

Characteristic	Typical classification
Geographic	North, south County or canton Urban, suburban or rural Urban by size of population: – cities greater than 0.5 million – cities 0.1–0.5 million – towns 50,000 to 100,000 – towns less than 50,000 Postcode of individual household
Demographic	Age: 0–15,16–25, 26–35, 36–45, 46–55, 56+ Sex: male, female Family size: 1 adult, 2 adults, 2 adults + 1 child, 2 adults + 2 children, etc. Education Income level Socio-economic based on occupation of head of household:[†] A Higher managerial, administrative or professional B Intermediate managerial, administrative or professional C1 Supervisory or clerical, and junior clerical C2 Skilled manual workers D Semi- and unskilled manual workers E State pensioners or widows, casual or lowest grade workers Family life cycle: single; young married, no children; married with young children; married with older children; older married no children at home; older, living alone
Psychographic	Lifestyle Personality: introvert, extrovert, high ego-drive, low ego-drive, independent, group worker
Usership	Non-user, current user, past user, potential user Heavy user, medium user, light user Regular, special occasion
Attitudes	Towards product area Towards brand Towards usership and use situations
Benefit sought	Utility, convenience, luxury, economy, etc.

[†] Socio-economic grades used by The National Readership Survey (NRS), which has been administered since 1968 by The Joint Industry Committee for National Readership Surveys (JICNARS).

manipulation. Methods of segmentation which rely on these facilities are discussed in detail later in this chapter.

Demographic classification is the most apparent in the literature and market research up to the early 1980s, because of the ease and convenience of describing users by characteristics defined by their relationships with other persons or organizations. For example, age is an absolute measure only in the sense of the chronology of the body. In terms of demographic classification, it permits the individual to be compared with others in the same or other age groupings with the assumption that needs could be different as a result of the age difference.

Similarly, income level defines a relationship with a peer group on the financial dimension. Socio-economic groupings define relationships with others in terms of the occupation and the prestige attached to it. Given that perception of position in society begins to draw on individual attitudes which are more difficult to categorize, then intuitively one would expect this demographic classification to be less satisfactory for many segmentation exercises. This is borne out by the considerable debate and rethinking which has accompanied the use of this classification in market research circles.

This dissatisfaction with traditional demographic breakdowns, and the greater facility for data analysis which computers have provided, has led to an increased focus on the **individual** as the generator of segmentation parameters. These can be identified and explored with disregard for the traditional classifications, leading to segmentation through user characteristics that relate to physical and psychological needs.

Market research companies with a tradition of rigorous sampling techniques and sophisticated analyses are now able to provide more user-specific data on purchasing habits, attitudes and lifestyles so that their clients can make more informed decisions on product and media targeting. Examples of these are examined later in this chapter.

Use or purchase situation

Some markets lend themselves to analysis and segmentation through the use or purchase situation. For example, whether a person is eating out at a restaurant for convenience, business or indulgence and pleasure will provide a simple structure within which to segment the market according to the provision of the divergent needs of these three groups.

This type of analysis is appropriate for many emerging service industries in which location and timing of service provision are crucial to optimize sales and minimize costs.

Conditions for successful segmentation

Identification of broad segments within a market is initially an intuitive activity, particularly where data is sparse and many assumptions have to be made. However, when market research is commissioned or syndicated data is purchased then more intellectual rigour should be applied to the segmentation process. This is not just as an academic exercise, but provides a valid framework within which to make decisions regarding the use of resources in supporting products in the marketplace.

Five key questions need to be asked about any market segment that is proposed as a marketing opportunity:

(1)   Is the segment measurable?
(2)   Is the segment accessible?
(3)   Is the segment substantial?
(4)   Is the segment sustainable?
(5)   Is the segment actionable?

The criteria on which answers to these questions will be judged will vary across companies. Influences on their decision-making will include whether the organization is involved in manufacturing as well as marketing, the level of investment required for the product category in terms of both time and money, and the return on investment seen as reasonable for the sector.

With these factors in mind each of the questions will be explored.

Is the segment measurable?

Marketing management is charged with producing quantified targets so that sales and financial objectives can be met. Progress at various stages of marketing activity will need to be measured to assess performance to date. The common performance parameters used will relate to the 'market' which generally means one or more segments. So percentage market share and penetration targets have as their prerequisites reliable measurement of the segment.

For an established product with a significant market presence and a sizeable advertising budget, changes in usage patterns and underlying attitudes need to be monitored on a regular basis. Such detailed measurement has to be a practical possibility. Consumption patterns of repeat purchase products with 'lifestyle' connotations can change rapidly as fashions change and the late adopters take over from the experimenters as the target market. Will the standard measurement process take account of this?

With new product development where considerable expenditure is necessary – for example, on new software development, engineering plant, or clinical trials for a new drug – then the potential market size and share must be measured as accurately as market research tools permit to allow for assessment of financial risk and return.

Is the segment accessible?

A viable market segment is one in which the individual buyer can be reached by the advertising message *and* delivery of the product.

This is particularly pertinent for business-to-business marketing where a specialist service is destined for businesses that are heterogeneous in the sense that there is no common way to communicate with them (through a specific medium) or to deliver to them through a common distribution network or agency.

A wholesaler of fashion garments would find it easy to advertise to the niche market segment of expensive boutiques through fashion shows, exhibitions and trade magazines. Personal selling through regional agents would support this activity. National carriers would provide a garment delivery service where the wholesaler was not of a size to support its own delivery service.

In contrast, access to the Japanese market for personal computers has been frustrated by system compatibility problems. NEC is a dominant player in the Japanese market, with around two million PCs installed and with 52% of all sales in the year to 31 March 1989. A group of computer makers formulated the AX or Architecture Extended Standard which would operate as both an English-language AT compatible and a Japanese-language MS-DOS machine, to compete with NEC.

Unfortunately, initial AX machines were often partially incompatible with each other in Japanese mode, while the versions of the English-language MS-DOS operating systems chosen by each company were not fully compatible; so product design problems compounded those of access to this NEC-dominated segment (Financial Times, 1989).

Is the segment substantial?

The definition of substantial in this context will depend on the economies of scale for production and marketing. The segment must be large enough to provide a viable level of business for the organization with a pre-determined set of costs so that profit is available, whether in the short or long term.

Clive Sinclair's C5 electric car was targeted at the enthusiast who already had the standard saloon for essential travel. Unfortunately, there did not appear to be enough people in this segment to warrant commercial production runs of the invention.

The Body Shop started as a retail outlet in Brighton selling naturally based products in simple containers. The demand in that catchment area indicated that these products were serving a substantial and hitherto untapped segment of the market. On a national basis, this segment proved capable of supporting a retail chain which developed on a franchise basis throughout the 1980s.

Is the segment sustainable?

The essential question here is about **how long** the market segment will exist and the relationship between this time-scale and the period necessary for an adequate return on investment.

In the electronics field, companies producing state-of-the-art equipment cannot afford to use obsolete components and saturation of an innovative component is achieved over a short time-scale. This puts pressure on the component supplier to have a rolling programme of product improvement and innovation in order to maintain dominance of a segment or to offset the risks of it disappearing altogether through changes in the end-user market.

Fashion or 'lifestyle' market segments are particularly vulnerable to an early demise. In the stationery market the segment serving the young, ambitious executive was taken by storm by the **Filofax** personal organizer. The proliferation of cheap imitations meant that all potential buyers of the product type came into the market within a few years. By 1990, the corporate profits of the originator of the product idea were looking very sick indeed.

Is the segment actionable?

Management time and research expenditure will be set against identification and measurement of market segments. Although intellectual rigour is an important feature of such activity, it should not camouflage the need for identifying early on whether progressing down a particular segmentation route will produce a **viable action plan**.

When a segment has been identified as providing a business opportunity which meets all the criteria under the first four questions, then the resources and reputation of the organization must be scrutinized to put together the marketing plan. This will show how the target market is to be reached with a clear message about the product suitably positioned against the needs, habits and aspirations of the segment.

If sizeable impediments still exist in putting together this plan then the viability of the market segment must be questioned. Similarly, if the right media to reach the target audience do not exist (including a suitable mailing list), and the cost of a salesforce or use of agents to spread the message and obtain orders is prohibitive, then there are significant risks attached to targeting against this segment.

Use of linear averaging for segmentation decisions

Linear averaging is a method of ascribing numerical values to alternative decision routes facing management. It is a general aid to decision-making which can be used in several areas of marketing, namely portfolio planning, segmentation and the choice of distribution channel. It is also called the **weighted factor score method**.

Linear averaging requires management to list the major factors that the company should consider in choosing a market segment. A **weight** (W) should be assigned to each factor such that the sum of these weights is 1.0. Taking an individual segment, each factor should be given a **rating score** (R).

The rating score is multiplied by the weighting for each factor and then the resultant figures added to give an overall **global utility index**:

$$\text{Global utility index} = \sum_{\text{factors}} W \times R$$

Comparison of the global utility index across the various segment possibilities provides a quantitative basis for decision-making.

In the example of the segmentation possibilities facing Barclays Bank in the launch of their Connect card given earlier in the chapter, each of the four segment options listed may be subjected to this linear averaging process to help identify the best segment for targeting this card. This process is illustrated in Table 5.3.

Table 5.3 Use of linear averaging for segmentation decisions. Example: segment options for Barclays Connect card.

	Weighting (W)	Rating score (R)	W × R
Segment 1			
All holders of a current bank account:			
Size	0.2	5	1.0
Accessibility	0.3	2	0.6
Long-term prospect	0.2	2	0.4
Profitability	0.3	2	0.6
Global Utility Index			2.6
Segment 2			
All holders of a current Barclays bank account:			
Size	0.2	4	0.8
Accessibility	0.3	3	0.9
Long-term prospect	0.2	3	0.6
Profitability	0.3	2	0.6
Global Utility Index			2.9
Segment 3			
Barclays current account customers who debit their account at least six times a month for other than cash withdrawal:			
Size	0.2	3	0.6
Accessibility	0.3	4	1.2
Long-term prospect	0.2	4	0.8
Profitability	0.3	4	1.2
Global Utility Index			3.8
Segment 4			
Barclays customers who maintain their accounts in credit:			
Size	0.2	3	0.6
Accessibility	0.3	3	0.9
Long-term prospect	0.2	3	0.6
Profitability	0.3	4	1.2
Global Utility Index			3.3

Explanation of the values in Table 5.3

Three of the factors that have been chosen for assessing the four segments for Barclays Connect card are directly linked with criteria for successful segmentation – namely, size (substantial), accessibility and long-term prospect (sustainable). The fourth, profitability, is an important measure of whether **action** should be taken in respect of that segment of the market.

Segment 1

This is by far the largest segment as it includes *all* holders of a current bank account, regardless of clearing bank. However, reaching this target group could be difficult as Barclays would only hold their own customers' names and addresses in a data bank, and mailing to such a wide audience would be very expensive.

The conversion rate of mailings to customers would be expected to be low and there would be a wide spectrum of usage rates for the card. These factors would affect profitability and long-term prospects.

Segment 2

This is the second largest segment, and is easily accessible to Barclays, but the cost of reaching all current account holders with the promotion material would be high. The loyalty factor would be expected to influence long-term prospects compared with segment 1, but the wide targeting would lead to a modest take-up rate for the card and the average frequency of use would be less than for segment 3, thus reducing profit expectations.

Segment 3

Potential card carriers in this segment share the characteristic of frequent use of the bank account for retail purchases. As Barclays do not charge the customer for debiting the current account, in this way profitability would be significantly improved if Barclays received a discount on these transactions through use of the Connect card. The segment is smaller than the first two, but is easily and cost-effectively reached.

Segment 4

This is also a smaller segment than for the first two and would be more difficult to access unless the computer alert system for registering an overdraft also maintained this as a 'flagged' event for later recall on the selection of a mailing list. As customers who maintain their accounts in credit would not pay bank charges, then profitability could be increased through their use of the Connect card.

Since there is no evidence of frequent retail purchase and the lack of an overdraft suggests spending with restraint, then the long-term prospect is less rosy than for segment 3.

Different approaches to segmentation analysis

Linear subdivision of a market

The simplest method of segmentation relies on a linear process of sub-division of successive strata within a predefined market. This approach is commonly associated with definition of the market segments by product characteristics. Using the example of medicines for cold relief, Figure 5.2 illustrates this approach.

This approach is valid for market segmentation if research indicates that sufficient customers classify their needs along this product form parameter. In practice, relief for specific symptoms of the cold might be a stronger determinant of product choice; segmentation on this parameter would then prove more useful for product positioning.

Classification by product type remains a strong feature of market research data in the ethical pharmaceutical field, that is, in an industrial market where the product and promotion are aimed at the general medical practitioner. Many pharmaceutical companies use the chemical property of the drug as the segmentation variable and then find difficulty in targeting to a medical audience that is motivated by patient need.

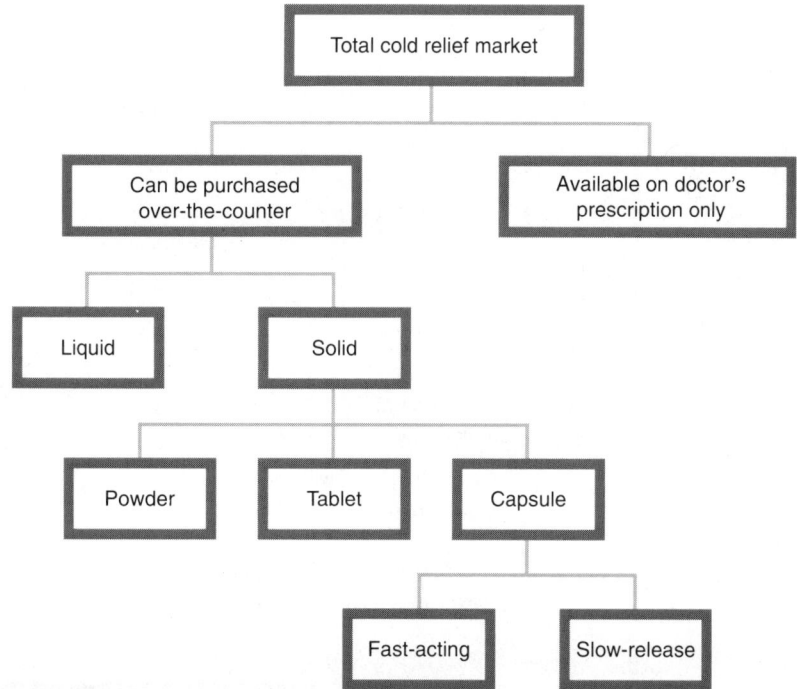

Figure 5.2   Segmentation of the market for cold relief by product characteristic.

Lidstone (1989) proposes a linear approach to segmentation (which he calls the 'cascade') built around the needs of the patient. He illustrates this with the starting point of his cascade as 'relief of pain and inflammation' rather than the traditional 'anti-inflammatory drugs'. Through the choice of the 'pain' branch of the tree, the segments of soft tissue pain, joint pain, muscle pain, bone pain, etc. emerge for assessment of size and trends. Further segmentation is possible by demographics to provide the facility for comparison with the demographic profile of a regional health authority's catchment area.

Cross-tabulation by characteristic

The most useful cross-tabulation exercises involve the selection of any *two* from user characteristic, product characteristic and use/purchase situation characteristic, and the identification of discrete market segments defined by these two parameters. A grid is produced by scaling along each parameter, and the boxes of the grid represent potential market segments. Not all of these boxes will merit the acknowledgement of a discrete segment, as illustrated in the grid for textured wall-coverings shown in Figure 5.3.

		Product characteristic			
		Visual and textural appeal	Safety, fire retardant	Acoustic properties	Hard-wearing
User characteristic	Industrial		Laboratories Hospitals		
	Commercial	Luxury offices Hotels Galleries		Sound studios Hotels	Restaurants
	Domestic	Luxury homes			Standard household

Figure 5.3 Segmentation of the market for textured wall-coverings.

In the cross-analysis of Figure 5.3, there are 12 possible segments of which six are recognized as providing potential marketing opportunities. These six would then be examined for viability from the point of view of size, accessibility and profit potential.

It could be argued that the classification used for the **user characteristics** is somewhat arbitrary; use should be made of official classifications wherever possible so that there is a valid basis of comparison for data from different sources when investigating segment size and trends.

Cross-analysis of data on dimensions of **user characteristics** and **use or purchase situation characteristic** provide possibly the most actionable segmentation data, as specific user groups can be linked directly with a measure of volume sales. This permits targeting of advertising to those people who represent important consumers of the product group.

The link between behaviour and attitudes

So far, this chapter has explored characteristics of users, products and use or purchase situations which are tangible or visible and which are measured in ways that are practicable and straightforward.

The most accurate measure of consumer behaviour for a marketing company is sales performance. However, this aggregate figure does not give any clues to the pattern of purchase and motivation at the individual level. The vast array of data generated by market research companies on behaviour relies predominantly on the **reported behaviour of a statistical sample**. There are intrinsic errors in data of this type, but superior data would be difficult and costly to obtain.

Even this type of data has limited use for the advertiser as it explains *what* is happening, but not *why* it is happening. In other words, the motivation of the individual for behaving in a particular way cannot be deduced. This problem has not changed over the decades and was succinctly stated in 1914:

> 'Advertising would be a simple proposition if the advertising man had ability to read the individual human mind'
> (Woolley, 1914).

This perennial problem has led to the emergence of a vast array of market research techniques and academic papers, particularly since the 1960s. These are built on the hypothesis that through market research techniques the consumer psyche can be probed to discover the antecedents of choice. Knowledge of these can then be harnessed to exert marketing influence on the individual to behave in a particular way. More particularly, individuals can be assigned to groups with similar predispositions to facilitate targeting. This is the process of **segmentation by attitudes**.

An attitude is a mode of thinking towards an object or idea which has come about through cognitive evaluation of information, emotional response and past experience. It can be positive or negative, transient or long-term and lead to active or passive response. The more important theories relating to consumer attitudes and how these relate to behaviour are explored in Chapter 4.

Segmentation based on attitude measurement

The single attitude statement throws some light on a consumer's predisposition to purchase, but is not conclusive evidence of it. For example, when researching into preferences for unusual action holidays against the standard package tour, the simple question below might be used:

	Agree completely				Disagree completely
	(1)	(2)	(3)	(4)	(5)
I like to spend my holiday sunbathing by the sea					

When cross-analysed by demographics, response to this statement would assist the targeting of standard Mediterranean package holidays, but would not identify the potential market for unusual action holidays.

However, if a battery of questions was asked relating to desire for new challenges, attitude towards personal fitness, need to be in a group situation and so on, the combination of answers to these questions should pinpoint an appropriate target group.

The Target Group Index (1969–1989) includes a 'lifestyle' section in which respondents are asked 186 questions relating to habits and preferences. These are organized randomly on the questionnaire but fall into 12 broad groups such as finance, shopping and diet/health.

Cluster analysis

Where measurements from a population sample have been taken on a range of dimensions, the analytical technique for identifying sub-groups where the members of the sub-group resemble each other on certain, preselected dimensions is known as **cluster analysis**.

This technique is particularly useful for analysis of response to attitudinal questions, and does not presuppose any fixed groupings. The number of groupings is determined by the cluster pattern which can be seen through two-dimensional representation, or numerically through computer print-out.

Psychographics

This is the name that is given to the evaluation of the clusters or segments that are found through cluster analysis of response on a range of attitudinal questions. People within the same age band or income band could show very different psychographic profiles.

Where identifying the clusters has involved statistical rigour, **naming** the clusters involves creativity and an understanding of the process of inference in communication. Leading advertising agencies appear to have spent as much energy in creating names for their psychographic or lifestyle segments as in generating them in the first place.

According to their Cross Culture Consumer Characterization, Young and Rubicam describe the trend-setting and trendy as 'reformers' while McCann Erickson calls them 'avant-gardian'. Greenpeace and companies selling lead-free petrol would target towards this group.

'Mainstreamers' according to Young and Rubicam are 'belongers' according to Taylor Nelson; advertising for Abbey National, the *Telegraph* and Pedigree Chum would appeal to this group. Those who are badly off and becoming desperate are not excluded from this type of lifestyle analysis; Young and Rubicam see this group as the 'struggling poor' (Clayton, 1989).

The Target Group Index classifies women into clusters according to their attitudes towards their appearance. The names for these groups range from 'self-aware' and 'green goddess' to 'unconcerned' and 'dowdies'. One danger of this approach is that a particular group can take on a higher profile than is justified by the size of the segment. A second danger is that the name can live on when the segment has all but disappeared.

In spite of these dangers, psychographic segmentation is useful in providing a tool of cross-analysis with usership data.

Segmentation in industrial markets

The link between behaviour and attitudes and the resultant segmentation on psychographic dimensions are very much a feature of market research and analysis for consumer goods. The accessibility of members of the general public for market research and the homogeneity of individuals making the buying decision means that this type of data has a sound statistical foundation for marketing decision-making.

Where the potential customer is also involved in the supply of an added-value product or service, then the total market takes on a more heterogeneous character and information about that market is not so easily obtained. This makes the segmentation process more heavily reliant on judgement linked to limited information. Also, progression from

Table 5.4 Classification for segmenting industrial markets.

Geographical	Level of intensity or dispersal of customers
Number	Of customers
Size	Of customers; by turnover or number of employees or level of demand for product
Level of technology	Of customer; whether machinery is state of the art, superseded or obsolete
Buying processes	Through agents; through open tender, sealed bid, through centralized buying department
Buying criteria	Price, quality, delivery, service support, etc.
Buying quantities	Size of order, frequency of order
Prevailing attitudes	Open to new suppliers, value existing relationships
Competition	Monopoly, oligopoly, many competitors
Customer's competitive position	Market leadership, one of many, minor player

segmentation on behaviour towards segmentation based on attitudes is further complicated by organizational buying, where several individuals will be seeking to satisfy their own, as well as the corporate, needs.

Starting from first principles, there are certain key classifications that can be used in the initial stage of a segmentation analysis for an industrial market as illustrated in Table 5.4.

Assessment of market segments based on some of these criteria will require previous experience of related markets or a sizeable market research exercise to possess sufficient hard data to make the segmentation actionable.

Where information to facilitate segmentation on these parameters is difficult to obtain then reliance will be placed on the more familiar **needs/benefit analysis**. This can be carried out with more general information about the products, performance and policies of potential customers.

Needs/benefits segmentation

Rothwell (1983) highlighted the importance of identifying customer needs through feedback during industrial product innovation. His study showed that of 33 innovations in the field of medical equipment, 25 were initiated by the user. In industrial design, this continuous assessment of customer needs and the process of developing matching benefits are crucial to gaining a competitive edge.

Taking the example of electronic control panels for factory machinery, a needs/benefits analysis can be approached by taking a range of advantages as listed down the left-hand column of Figure 5.4. A

	Need intensity	**Need stability**	**Need diffusion**
Reliability	High	High	High
Quality	Medium	Medium	Low
Acceptance by workforce	Very high	Low	Medium
Logistical improvements	Low	Medium	Medium

Figure 5.4 Needs/benefits analysis for industrial markets (example: electronic control panels for factory machinery; market segment: bottling plants).

particular market segment can then be classified according to the **need intensity, need stability** and **need diffusion** of each of the listed benefits. The production and service capabilities of the supplier company would then be matched against this grid for each segment to identify the best target market.

Need stability and need diffusion both relate to the sustainability of the market segment, once a company has decided to target against it. Will the rapid pace of change in the customer's market make them reluctant to invest in the new machine? If there are innovators among customers willing to take on board new technology, how fast will this adoption process trickle down to others in the same market segment?

Where new technology is involved in positioning against a particular market segment, it is important to gain an understanding of the attitudes of the customers within it so that a forecast can be attempted at the likely adoption time-scale. For example, if electronic control panels were to be sold on the benefit of reliability, it is likely that bottling factories would want to adopt this new technology within a short time-scale to gain cost advantages through constant speed of operation and less down-time through electronic failure.

This market segment's diffusion process could be represented by Figure 5.5, where 42 potential customers are broken down into three groups to represent their attitude towards process innovation (gleaned by market research) and therefore likely take-up time for the control panel.

From the perspective of business potential, it is important to know not just how many companies are in each of the diffusion groups, but how much business each represents. Very often, the market leaders will have

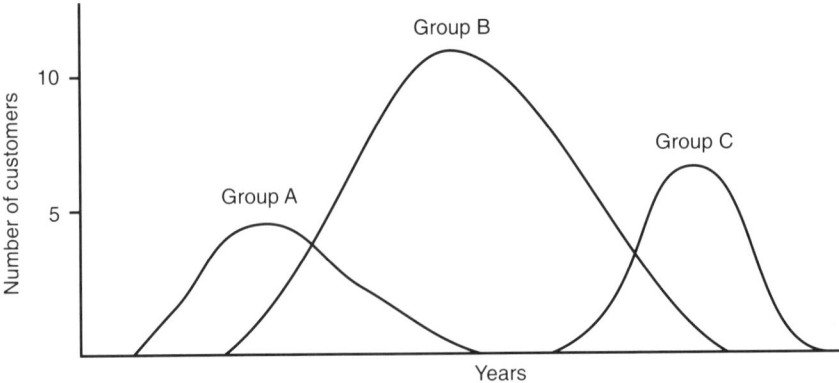

Figure 5.5 Diffusion process for new electronic control panels for bottling plants.

the resources and desire for efficiency leading to early adoption of new technology. Where they account for a significant amount of the buying power in an industrial market, then the laggards may not constitute sufficient business to rely on this product alone, and other innovations should be in the pipeline.

Advances in segmentation methods for direct marketing

Computer software packages now available provide companies marketing in the industrial or consumer sector with sophisticated tools to reach specific segments in a highly targeted fashion. Companies relying on traditional direct marketing methods for reaching their audience are in a position to design and use their computer database in a way which suits their operating procedures and gives them a competitive edge in satisfying customer needs. Companies may also purchase computerized lists of private households which are segmented by postcode and by housing classification (such as ACORN data by CACI) and which give indications of socio-economic status.

However, the reality is far from the ideal for most operating companies. Computer hardware may not be compatible with the preferred software, or the custom-built information system may no longer be state-of-the-art, unable to provide the preferred mailing list selections or sales analyses.

Given the constraints of the database and the computer system, there are certain key steps required in the use of information technology for effective segmentation.

Defining and reaching a market segment using a computer database

(1) Define the parameters to be used to identify:
  (a) The customers (or potential customers); for example, the size of business; end-use; household size.
  (b) The purchasing pattern; for example, frequency of purchase; value of order; products purchased.
(2) Use these parameters for data input against each customer or potential customer who is identified by a unique customer number. Each piece of information is set against a classification code, and this system of coding information against the individual customer number is called **flagging**.
(3) Special analyses of historical sales can be specified by using selected codes for customer characteristics or purchase characteristics. By cross-analysing data across two characteristics at a time, key segments can be identified.
(4) A mailing list which coincides with a key segment can be selected by using the codes relating to the desired characteristics.

It is important to consider all possible information-flagging requirements at the stage of setting up the database, as the information cannot be coded at a later date once it is on computer file without the additional work of repunching the hard data. On the other hand, there has to be a realistic assessment of future analysis and selection needs against the additional cost of the more detailed data input.

The ultimate market segment – the individual customer

At the beginning of this chapter the mass market was discussed in terms of heterogeneous individuals whose needs are assumed to coincide in order to suit the shotgun marketing approach of a company that does not choose to segment its market.

Following the intricate journey through a wide array of segmentation techniques we have reached the final thesis – *the proposition of the individual as the ultimate market segment*. This ideal is reached when a custom-designed and delivered product or service is communicated through a personalized message to each person or household. This communication could take place by mail, telephone or, ultimately, by interactive computer link. The latter development could take some years to materialize for the majority of the population.

Davis (1989) identified the individual as the ultimate segment when he coined the phrase **'mass customizing'** to describe the way in which individual needs could be met – not just at the luxury end of the market, but for everyone.

The key to this approach is computer-aided design (CAD) and computer-aided manufacture (CAM). From fashion shirts to household paint, from interior design to family cars ... the effects of sophisticated design information transmission and robotics are beginning to make themselves felt in the marketplace.

The power of the database and the direct relationship with the customer can already be felt in the approach of the large financial institutions, who advertise custom-designed financial packages for the individual through personalized messages which arrive on the doormat periodically. Intangible services are easier to manipulate to satisfy each individual's need.

The question still remains: how long will it be before 'The computerized assembly line can bring customized products within the reach of the average person' (Davis, 1989)?

European perspective

The Single European Act of 1986 committed the Member States of the European Community to completing the internal market by 1992. This means that there will be convergence towards common laws and practices for the supply of goods and services. However, this Act cannot legislate for **uniformity of demand** across Member States.

Where companies are marketing consumer products to more than one Member State, they will be structuring the product message and the vehicle of product delivery in the context of potentially different consumer response patterns. These patterns of behaviour will be influenced by population structure, relative economic status, social networks and the resultant group aspirations, culture and a complex array of attitudes created by the interaction of these forces.

Changes in attitude are invariably precursors to changes in behaviour – and the former take time to evolve in the absence of high-intensity, mass-media campaigns. Familiarity with the lifestyle of a neighbouring nation is enhanced by cross-border travel. Increasing affluence and the reduction of physical barriers (of which the Channel Tunnel and high-speed trains are examples), will mean that 'early adopters' of a hitherto foreign product will command even greater commercial significance.

The challenge for a company marketing on a pan-European basis is to identify common strands of attitudes and behaviour. These can then be mobilized within communication and distribution strategies for a target group which transcends national boundaries. Within this context, then, the traditional concepts of segmentation theory apply.

The exploration of the key determinants of pan-European segmentation requires the identification of major differences between Member States on demographics, social groupings, buying power, and expectations. Examination of culture is beyond the scope of this chapter, although examples of different behaviour within specific product or service categories will illustrate its importance.

Demographic influences

In 1989, the total population of the EC was 325 million, this figure for the 12 Member States having grown by only 3.2% since 1979. In October 1990, the 18 million people of Eastern Germany combined with the West to form a unified Germany with a total population of 79 million, the highest of the current Member States. This gave rise to a new EC population total of 343 million.

Germany, France, Italy, Spain and UK account for 84% of the EC population. Each of the other seven nations contributes less than 5% each, and their total contribution of 16% of the population has to be served by a potential 'Euromarketer' on the basis of seven languages and theoretically as many different cultures. The market opportunities in the smaller Member States will therefore need to be weighed against the additional logistical and language input necessary to exploit such opportunities.

The existence of the Benelux agreements facilitates a more homogeneous approach to 25 million people. However, there are obvious attractions for a marketing company to focus on the needs of the major countries, assuming sufficient purchasing power at the national level.

From an analysis of the data in Table 5.5, it is evident that companies positioned in the child and youth markets have stronger opportunities in Spain and France than in Germany, judged purely from the perspective of demographics. The positioning of health and leisure services for the 60+ age group has particular attractions in Germany and UK.

Economic influences

Although economic indicators at the national aggregate level camouflage differing levels of affluence of groups within a country, they do provide an indication of relative spending power. Statistics from 'Eurostat – National Accounts' for net national disposable income across the 12 countries have been compared with population figures to provide an index on a *per capita* basis, and these are shown in Table 5.6.

Belgium, Italy and Netherlands have similar spending power *per capita*. France and UK appear well matched on this dimension, and the

Table 5.5   Population structure in the five largest countries of the EC.

Age group	France (%)	W Germany[†] (%)	Italy (%)	Spain (%)	UK (%)
0–4	6.7	4.9	5.0	6.2	6.4
5–9	6.9	4.8	5.6	7.2	6.2
10–14	6.9	5.0	7.1	8.4	6.3
15–19	7.7	7.4	8.0	8.4	7.8
20–24	7.7	8.8	8.5	8.5	8.4
25–29	7.5	8.1	7.6	7.8	7.6
30–39	15.4	13.9	13.7	13.1	13.8
40–49	11.5	14.1	12.9	11.2	12.1
50–59	10.9	12.3	12.2	11.4	10.7
60+	18.8	20.7	19.4	17.8	20.7
Total	100.0	100.0	100.0	100.0	100.0
Total population in millions	55.75	61.14	57.40	38.91	56.85

[†] before unification.
Source: Percentages based on data from Eurostat (1990).

figure for Germany exceeds all others (prior to unification). The index figures for Spain and Greece fall well below those for other nations.

However, the way in which this spending power is distributed across the population is of more importance to companies focusing on narrow target groups as against the mass marketer. Precise data here is less readily available, and recourse is made to occupational classification. This is far from ideal where the two-income family is commonplace and where the earnings of some groups of manual workers could exceed earnings of some white-collar workers. However, the data in Table 5.7 is indicative of key similarities and differences across the biggest five Member States.

Table 5.6   Net national disposable income *per capita* at current prices and current exchange rates (1989), on an index basis (value for all 12 EC countries = 100).

Country	Index value
Belgium	102
Denmark	105
West Germany	112
Greece	58
Spain	78
France	108
Italy	102
Netherlands	103
UK	107

Source: Calculated from Eurostat, National Accounts ESA (aggregates) 2(c).

Table 5.7 Occupation for the population aged 18 and over within the five major EC Member States (%).

	France	W. Germany	Italy	Spain	UK	All EC
All white collar	43	50	29	18	47	39
Management	19	22	6	4	15	14
Other white collar	23	28	23	14	32	25
All blue collar	19	30	45	38	46	36
Skilled	9	16	15	17	20	16
Other blue collar	10	14	30	21	26	20
Never worked	39	19	26	44	7	25

Source: Reader's Digest (1990).

The very low relative figure for 'never worked' in UK reflects the higher percentage of young people finishing full-time education by 16 years of age (69%) compared with 48% for the EC as a whole. In contrast, the figure for West Germany is 15%, with a high percentage of young people following a craft training to age 18 or above.

Aspirations

The aspirations of a nation's people are heavily influenced by past experience, linked with political propaganda. Given the past affluence of West Germans, it is not surprising that the penalties of unification in terms of personal economic sacrifices are revealed in consumer surveys of the time. The lower percentage of West Germans who believe that they are 'living comfortably' compared with respondents from other EC nations is a measure of the perceived drop in economic expectations (see Table 5.8).

Table 5.8 Economic expectations across the five major EC Member States.

	France	W. Germany	Italy	Spain	UK	All EC
Percentage believing that they are:						
Living comfortably	25	11	32	21	29	25
Coping	50	62	41	53	46	49
Finding it difficult	20	18	21	17	16	18
Finding it very difficult	4	6	6	7	8	6

Source: Reader's Digest (1990).

Perceptions of economic well-being – as against real levels of spending power – are invariably more important to consumer confidence and the resultant expenditure on non-essentials.

Perceptions of functionality

Marketing companies cannot change diverse product usage patterns across EC countries in the short term, as these have evolved through differing cultures and the harnessing of culture and prevailing attitudes within effective advertising campaigns.

Breakfast cereals feature in 90% of British homes, but only 39% of French, 25% of Spanish and 17% of Italian households. Conversely, 'real' coffee can be found in 93% of Italian and West German homes, 87% of French homes but only 40% of British homes (Reader's Digest, 1990).

Attitudes towards, and purchasing patterns of, such mundane household items as disinfectant and floor polish are skewed across the Member Nations reflecting both needs and advertising message. Some of the most striking differences are to be found in national preferences for home-made meals using fresh ingredients in French, Spanish and Italian households, as against the popularity of convenience and frozen foods in the UK. Such patterns will mean that pan-European opportunities for the major British-based food conglomerates will need to be clearly identified through market research. Success in the USA and the UK will not be automatic pointers to significant market share in the enlarged Europe.

Easier access to markets through reduced paperwork, tariffs and improved physical distribution across national frontiers will not induce Europe-wide acceptance of a product just by virtue of its accessibility at a reasonable price.

The market for over-the-counter (OTC) medicines provides further evidence of 'usage barriers'. The French prefer suppositories, the Germans may prefer a brand in powdered form, the British take tablets and the Dutch and Belgians are used to sprays. This generalization appears oversimplified, but serves to illustrate the problem facing a pharmaceutical company wishing to market a uniform product delivery system across Europe.

The company Boots plc is in the enviable position of developing, producing and marketing to the consumer its own-label OTC medicines. However, this UK market strength was of no avail in the launch of Nurofen (a branded tablet competing with generic aspirin products) in Italy, Spain and Holland. Consumers in these countries were not prepared to change from established analgesic habits, in spite of significant advertising support (Gourlay, 1991).

This illustrates the difficulty in creating a 'Eurobrand' where the key benefit must be relevant across national boundaries and must be capable of communication through mass media. True economies of scale will be derived where uniformity of name, packaging, product form and benefit can be achieved for a brand. For the pharmaceutical industry, this difficult task is further complicated by national regulations relating to product testing, registration and permitted distribution. Harmonization in these complex areas is some way off, and companies must look to the optimal trade-offs in sales revenue versus marketing costs and patent life expectancy following product acceptance by national regulating authorities.

Differing national needs are similarly evident in the holiday market. Where the 'package holiday' is a common feature in Germany, Britain and Denmark, there is a greater propensity for a do-it-yourself approach to accommodation and travel among the French, Italians and Spanish. The influence of good weather and proximity of attractive coastline is acknowledged. This means that greater attention will need to be paid to novelty, cost-effectiveness and convenience if such habits are to be changed with targeted package holidays.

As well as addressing different needs, the multiple sector of the British travel market (Thomas Cook, Lunn Poly, Going Places) will need to assess the importance of catering for the individual, and whether this approach is compatible with the economies of scale and subsequent low margins of traditional package holiday provision. There is evidence to suggest that the British are also now tempted towards higher value-added holidays, and are deserting companies offering only mass shipment to sunnier climes.

The fact that this trend coincides with the loss of duty-free business through tariff harmonization may tempt companies to raise prices. However, the opening of the Channel Tunnel will be an incentive for travellers in both directions to put together personal itineraries. New technology will provide the opportunity to book direct through computer link with hotels, airlines and car hire; this provides the customer with the facility to bypass the travel agent (Boyd-Adams, 1988).

It remains to be seen whether harmonization of data-links will occur on a Europe-wide scale, and whether German or British tour operators will be the first to invest in order to reap the prize of market leader.

Attitudes and lifestyle

'Lifestyle' segmentation has become an accepted ingredient of the market research portfolio of consumer goods companies at national level. Research companies and advertising agencies are now looking at ways of classifying groups based on social values and subsequent behaviour patterns across national boundaries.

There are three key problems with this type of analysis:

(1) Defining values that are important across nations (often dependent on judgement derived from market experience);
(2) Producing a research tool that is valid and actionable in each nation (for example, the vocabulary and style of question within a questionnaire would need to be tested in different countries for comprehension and willingness to respond);
(3) Assessing how the pace of change (fast in Spain, slow in Britain) will influence how 'attitude groups' emerge across national boundaries.

Two organizations have pioneered work in this area: the International Research Institute on Social Change (RISC) and the more commercially focused AGB Research. The latter carried out a two-stage study over 15 countries using the same questionnaire, and looked at quality of life, shopping habits, market trends and key values affecting behaviour. Sixteen 'consumer types' were identified throughout Europe, and subscribers have access to information on how these groups behave and how to communicate with them successfully (Miles, 1990).

Difficulties inherent in segmenting on a pan-European basis

When the characteristics of a market are explored in the context of segmentation analysis, comparing profiles across national boundaries adds a further series of obstacles which are highlighted in Figure 5.6. One central theme is dominant: how easy is it to obtain the relevant information for each market, and is it valid to compare the data when obtained from different sources?

The degree of risk associated with strategic marketing decisions based on a segmentation approach is illustrated by the banking sector. This risk can be reduced by stringent comparison of corporate strengths versus competition in each segment. For example, in retail banking the criteria below would provide the framework for this type of analysis:

(1) *Size* Coverage, capital for investment, awareness of name, economies of scale.
(2) *Degree of specialization* Current accounts, savings accounts, consumer loans, credit cards, insurance.

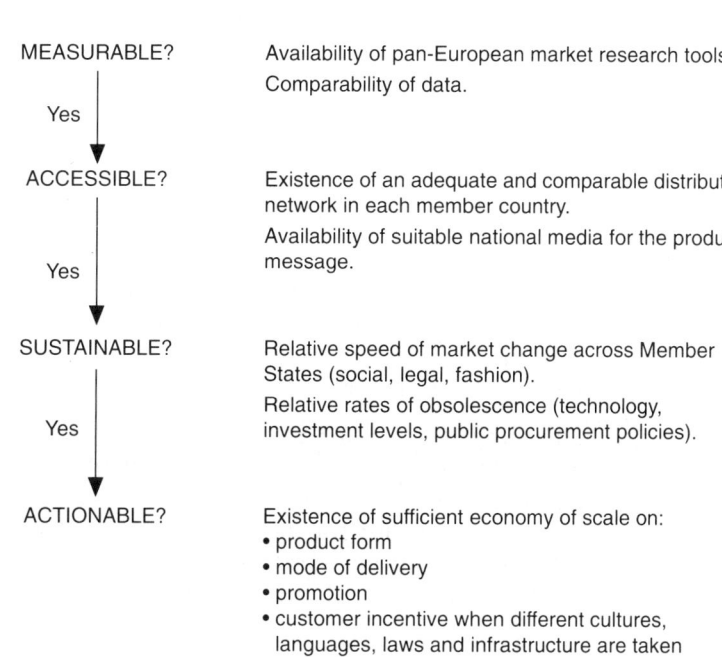

Figure 5.6 tree content:

Across EC Member States, is the segment

MEASURABLE?   Availability of pan-European market research tools.
                     Comparability of data.
Yes

ACCESSIBLE?   Existence of an adequate and comparable distribution
                     network in each member country.
                     Availability of suitable national media for the product
Yes   message.

SUSTAINABLE?   Relative speed of market change across Member
                     States (social, legal, fashion).
                     Relative rates of obsolescence (technology,
Yes   investment levels, public procurement policies).

ACTIONABLE?   Existence of sufficient economy of scale on:
                     • product form
                     • mode of delivery
                     • promotion
                     • customer incentive when different cultures,
                       languages, laws and infrastructure are taken
                       into account.

Figure 5.6   Validity of segmentation on a pan-European basis.

(3) *Current level of penetration of services which constitute product strength*
     Example: possession of cash dispenser card:

West Germany	38 %
Italy	16 %
Great Britain	60 %
France	53 %
Spain	30 %

     (*Source:* Reader's Digest Eurodata)

(4) *Status of implementation of advanced technology*   Influences ability to
     deliver cost-effective service in transactions.

(5) *Capability of product differentiation*   Added-value of services or
     competitive rates of interest.

When these complex issues are taken into account, only the major players will attempt a true pan-European strategy. One suggestion is that in the medium-term banks operating at a transnational level are likely to fall into one of four categories: the true 'pan-European', the 'super-regional', the 'regional' and the 'niche' (Andrews, 1989).

Problems and assignments

(1) Outline the segmentation options for two of the following consumer markets. Make reference to user characteristics, product characteristics and purchase-use situations:

    (a) books
    (b) music cassettes
    (c) dog food
    (d) children's clothes
    (e) personal computers
    (f) wallpaper

(2) For each of the two markets chosen in question 1, show in grid form one approach to segmentation. Use Figure 5.3 as your model for creating the grid. Indicate your estimation of the relative size of each segment by the size of a circle drawn in the relevant square of the grid.

(3) Propose a possible segmentation approach to identify target markets for the launch of a new investment plan to customers of a clearing bank.
As a group exercise, use the linear averaging technique to choose the most appropriate target market for the investment plan based on the criteria of size, accessibility, level of competition and long-term potential.

(4) How would you apply the Howard and Sheth model of the purchase decision process to a significant purchase that you have made in the past year? (Refer to Chapter 4 as well as this chapter.)

(5) Discuss the advantages and potential shortcomings of the cluster analysis approach to identifying target groups from 'lifestyle' statements in market research. Illustrate your answer by reference to the women's fashion market and the car market.

(6) Construct a needs/benefit analysis for an industrial market of your choice. Use Figure 5.4 as your model.

(7) Discuss the potential inadequacies of the following when used in segmentation:

    (a) Linear subdivision of a market (as in Figure 5.2);
    (b) Classification of users by socio-economic groupings;
    (c) Use of the 'total number of users of a product field' as a target market for a specific brand within the product field.

(8) As a coursework project, choose a consumer market and research whether it is possible to segment by the same product features and user characteristics across three European Member States. On the basis of your findings, recommend whether the same target market could be proposed for a new product to be launched in all three Member States.

(9) What is the relative importance of (a) cultural and (b) economic factors in determining whether a single target group can be used for a consumer financial product, across several Member States?

References

British Market Research Bureau. *Target Group Index.* Volumes available from 1969 to 1989

CACI Ltd. *A Classification of Residential Neighbourhoods.* London: CACI

Cain W.D. (1969). *Engineering Product Design.* London: Business Books Ltd

Clayton S. (1989). Divide and rule. *Campaign,* 24 March, 51–53

Davis S.M. (1989). Future perfect: mass customizing. *Planning Review,* 17(2)

Financial Times (1989). Personal Computers. 27 September

Lidstone J. (1989). Market segmentation for pharmaceuticals. *Long Range Planning,* **22**(2)

Lynn S.A. (1986). Segmenting a business market for professional services. *Industrial Marketing Management,* **15**(1)

Rothwell R., Schott L. and Gardiner P. (1983). *Design and Economy.* London: The Design Council

Woolley E.M. (1914). Finding the point of contact. *Advertising,* Vol. VI of the Library of Business Practice. New York: A.W. Shaw, pp. 25–26

European perspective

Andrews S. (1989). Banks's winning gambits for 1992. *Institutional Investor,* June

Boyd-Adams E. (1988). The retail leisure travel industry: pressures for change. *Transport Marketing* UK, **1**(2)

Eurostat: (3) Series C, *Population and Social Conditions,* 1990.

Gourlay C. (1991). Over the counter and across the sea. *Marketing,* 28 March

Miles L. (1990). Gateway to Europe. *Fortune Tellers,* April 26

Reader's Digest (1990). *Eurodata – A Consumer Survey of 17 European Countries.* Sponsored by the Reader's Digest Association Inc.

6 Marketing research

Chapter objectives:

- to understand the role and function of marketing research in marketing management
- to examine the various facets of market research – qualitative and quantitative – as well as when to use which
- to examine the six key stages in any market research process
- to understand the role of market research agencies for different research tasks
- to see how market research should complement a company's wider management information system

Introduction

In an increasingly complex business environment, information is a powerful tool of competitive edge. The degree to which a company will seek and use accurate and problem-specific information depends very often on corporate culture rather than need. The management cultures of multinational companies such as 3M, GEC, Nestlé and Procter & Gamble inculcate a dependence on reliable and expensive information, both internally and externally generated, for marketing decisions. In smaller, entrepreneurial companies, an 'instinct' for the market, which can often be justified on the basis of years of experience, replaces information and market research to suit egos and bank balances alike – but very often this has only short-term success.

Chapter 7 describes the importance of product positioning and defining key benefits which will mark a product or service out from the competition, appealing to, and satisfying the needs of, a specific target market. A company that takes these decisions without the right information is taking considerable **risk** in terms of investment in production capacity, inventory, advertising expenditure and salesforce time.

Every company operating in a market has access to published statistics and data. However, this type of information, which is one component of **desk research**, only tells half the story. The missing part is the specific information relating to where the company intuitively believes that there is market demand which it has the expertise and resources to meet. The insights, observations and statistical data resulting from a programme of primary **market research** and the decisions made on the basis of these results will be significant determinants of success.

Market research can be defined as the collection and analysis of data relating to a specific marketing problem, and which has been conducted against clearly defined objectives, such that conclusions can be drawn from the results that aid in the decision-making process.

An example of the importance of market research is in the mass market for cars, where features that were optional extras in the early 1980s became standards for the bottom of the range by the end of the decade. It was important for European car manufacturers to identify the changing expectations of their customer base in the face of competition from Japanese imports. **Tracking studies** would be carried out at suitable intervals which would monitor attitudes of a sample of customers and non-customers defined as the target group for a particular model range. From analysis of the data it would be possible to identify which features were essential to retain and possibly increase market share, and those features that could be considered as optional against a specific add-on price.

Balancing market research cost against risk

Highly sophisticated market research studies such as that described for the car market are very expensive (measured in tens and sometimes hundreds of thousands of pounds); but the risk incurred if this information is *not* available could be measured in millions of pounds of lost sales, longer-term loss of market share and under-utilized production lines.

Each organization must weigh the cost of a specific programme of market research against the financial risk of taking marketing decisions *without* the information that this market research would yield. Companies marketing a wide range of branded repeat-purchase consumer goods with the backing of tens of millions of pounds of television advertising are committed to annual market research budgets which themselves can reach a million pounds or more. This would include the purchase of bi-monthly **retail audits** from market research providers such as A. C. Nielsen, and **household purchasing audits** from such organizations as Audits of Great Britain (AGB).

However, an industrial company selling specialty cleaning chemicals on a regional basis with more modest sales targets would take a different perspective on the market research budget. The stage of development of the business would determine how much information was needed on the customer base, and there would be few (if any) standard market research products which could be purchased 'off-the-shelf'. This means that a market research company would need to be briefed on a specific problem to be solved on a once-only basis at an agreed cost. Very often, this level of cost must be weighed against sales potential rather than against risk to existing business.

The market research process

There are several important stages in the market research process where specific marketing information is needed with a finite time horizon linked to specific decisions. A structured approach is needed for the process, as errors or omissions due to taking short-cuts cannot generally be remedied at a later stage.

Problems that might arise are the choice of a population sample which is too small to give statistically significant results at the 95% confidence level (the norm for market research projects, and discussed later in the chapter); or the use of incorrect quotas for age groups and income levels to reflect the population of the target market; or the use of questioning techniques that make coding and analysis of the results complex and expensive.

The six key stages of the market research process are highlighted in Table 6.1 (where the relative time-scale for each stage of the process is illustrated for an industrial marketing problem).

(1) *Problem definition* Is there an aspect of product performance that needs to be tested? Do minimum levels of customer service need to be improved to match prevailing market conditions? Are changing social attitudes creating new target markets for existing products, and how should the benefits be presented to the new audience?

Very often, the problem is identified through management or specialists keeping up-to-date with literature on the market or through observation and feedback from the salesforce or distributors. Problem recognition and desk research tend to proceed in parallel until the next stage becomes apparent, when a **market research brief** is prepared by marketing management for an in-house market research department or an external agency.

(2) *Market research design* This will often take the form of a proposal on the best way to achieve the required information with the appropriate degree of statistical validity. Discussion at this stage will

Table 6.1 The market research process for an industrial marketing problem.

Stage	Activity	Duration
Problem definition	To establish the level of awareness and penetration of the products of a major European specialty chemicals company in the UK. The products are sold through an exclusive agent with its own salesforce. The market research is being carried out independently of the agent, but with their knowledge. Parent company produces **research brief**.	1 week
Market research design	Market research company produces a **research proposal** in response to the research brief, recommending methodology, sample size and structure plus cost estimate. When this is agreed, **questionnaire design** and **field force recruitment** can take place.	3 weeks
Data collection	Field force (e.g. 6 interviewers) interview 150 company buyers selected on a quota basis (company size and geography). Structured questionnaire administered to identify frequency of category purchase, products purchased, awareness of client's products, visits made by agent, influences on purchase decision. Some open-ended questions.	4 weeks
Data analysis	Completed questionnaires checked for completeness and errors. Computer input and analysis of results; manual analysis of response to open-ended questions.	1 week
Presentation of results	Summary of key findings at a meeting (top-line results). Full report submitted to client.	1 week 2 weeks
Conclusions	Client reviews results and makes decision on future sales strategy, including relationship with current sales agent.	1–4 weeks

revolve around the number of stages that are necessary, the methods to be used (for example, whether qualitative or quantitative methods are more suitable) and the estimated cost. Management will have a budget limit against which the research design will be trimmed if the original proposal involves unacceptably high costs. The integrity of an external market research agency is paramount when the budget set is too low to achieve a valid result. A solution which might be suggested is the use of an **omnibus survey** which provides quantitative research at lower cost but which is generally a compromise on the ideal (discussed later in this chapter).

(3) *Data collection*   Within this stage is included the structuring of the population sample, briefing of interviewers who will carry out the fieldwork, followed by interviewing or observations. Follow-up is required to fulfil quotas or check whether the research has, in fact, been carried out according to instructions.

(4) *Data analysis*   This traditionally time-consuming aspect of the process has been revolutionized by sophisticated computer programs. The degree to which coding of response can take place through the use of structured, closed-ended questions makes a significant difference to processing time and costs. Sometimes the cross-analyses of response will be specified in the brief, where the

questions asked are straightforward and where there is an intuitive understanding of the direction which the results will take.

However, where there are more complex batteries of questions asked, particularly in relation to attitudes and lifestyle, the correlation between these parameters and purchasing behaviour may only be determined through more complex factor analyis, involving an iterative process in which the most significant relationships are identified through trial and error.

(5) *Presentation of results* The skill with which data is presented in tabular form or by highlighting key findings can influence perceptions of what is important and 'actionable'. There is a convention in many larger companies that a presentation of the 'top-line' results is made before the full market research report with detailed findings is available.

Researchers should present findings in the context of what is a statistically significant result and what could be considered purely a function of the sample used (this is explored later in the chapter in the section on 'sampling').

(6) *Conclusions and recommendations* The level of involvement of market researchers in making recommendations on strategy will depend on their relationship with the decision-makers. For example, a researcher working within the marketing company is likely to be familiar with the dilemmas facing the organization and can interpret the results in this context. However, there is the concomitant danger of corporate politics influencing the way in which results are presented. Where results and decisions are likely to have a ripple effect through the organization, the outside research contractor can present results with a dispassionate view.

Who should carry out market research?

The simple and immediate answer to this question is those who are professionally qualified and experienced to advise on, structure and implement a market research programme against a specific brief. In the UK, membership of the **Market Research Society** indicates a level of competence and professionalism which any major corporation would find acceptable to guarantee confidentiality, proficiency and ethical conduct of a party to whom they have awarded a market research contract.

For the larger companies, this question takes on a broader meaning, in that they have the resources and the kind of market research budgets which justify the employment of in-house specialists. However, such organizations are also aware of the need for flexibility in the way in which this market research budget should be spent to address the information problems associated with changing and emerging markets. In practice, a large proportion of the budget for a company involved in repeat-purchase consumer products will be spent on regular retail or household audit data, with the balance available for specific tracking studies, *ad hoc* market research (including that for new product development) and market research personnel.

Escalating salaries for market research personnel during the 1980s has meant that companies with large budgets have adopted a lean approach to the specialist department, where market researchers act as the filter for briefs from marketing management to specialist research agencies. At the same time as they are embellishing or restricting briefs, they are acting as a quality control mechanism on the output of companies carrying out major research projects. There is also a negotiation function involved in the purchase of audit data, where representation in several key markets can bring significant cost benefits.

Smaller companies, whose market research needs would not justify them employing their own specialists, have to buy the services of the most appropriate market research company for a specific project. Very often, the choice is narrowed swiftly by an appreciation of the market research technique best suited to the brief, and those companies which specialize in such techniques (such as focus groups, hall tests, concept and advertising testing, in-home placement tests, usage and attitude surveys and other methods which will be explored in the course of this chapter). In some cases, the advertising agency with whom a major account resides will also act as a filter on market research briefs related to the product being advertised, and can act as the bridge between the client and the market research company. A standard 17.5% commission may be charged as a handling fee on the value of the market research contract, or a 'one-off' management charge can be agreed with the advertising agency.

Desk research

This is commonly undertaken at an early stage of a market evaluation, product marketing review or market research problem definition, in order to identify the information that is available (sometimes at the cost of a subscription or one-off payment for a research report). This is also known as **secondary research**. Marketing management is then in a position to identify the gaps in information that have to be filled through the commissioning of **primary research**, which means the customized field-work undertaken to a specific market research brief.

Secondary sources that are frequently used in the definition and assessment of markets are summarised in Table 6.2.

Also included within the definition of **desk research** is the collection and analysis of internal company information which is part of the **management information system**. This is generally split into:

(1) *Financial performance data* For example, profit as a percentage of sales, return on capital, net current assets as a percentage of sales, gearing. These measures can be compared with competitors in the same market, or with companies active in markets in which the organization is considering entering, to identify whether the same ratios are achievable.

(2) *Sales data* The kinds of analyses that are useful are:
   (a) Absolute volume sales by product and product group on a monthly basis over several years.
   (b) Moving annual total of volume sales on a monthly basis over several years (this shows the trend without the seasonality factor).
   (c) Sales by customer group or large individual customers.
   (d) Sales by type of intermediary or form of distribution.
   (e) Frequency of order split by customer type and size.
   (f) Average size of order split by customer type and size.

For some projects, particularly of an exploratory nature, activity does not progress beyond the **secondary research** stage as there is sufficient information available to ratify a 'stop' decision for the project. This will invariably mean that market growth prospects and competitive activity are not compatible with the achieving of corporate targets with predefined resources. These types of decisions are explored in more depth in Chapter 16.

Table 6.2 Information sources for UK market desk research.

Consumer markets	Industrial markets
DTI statistical returns from industry and commerce available as the 'Business Monitor' series	DTI statistical returns from industry available as the 'Business Monitor' series

Office of Population, Census and Surveys (OPCS) publications:
  Population Trends (Q)
  OPCS Monitors (Census information 1981, 1991)
  Family Expenditure Survey (A)
  General Household Survey (A)
	Commercial directories:
	  Dun and Bradstreet
	  Kelly's Directory
	  Kompass
	  Key British Enterprises

Periodicals:
  Campaign
  Economist
  Financial Times (Special Surveys)
  Grocer
  Marketing Week
  Mintel
  Retail Business
	Specialist trade magazines
	Economist

Company annual reports and sales literature Store visits Electoral register	Company annual reports and sales literature Trade exhibitions Trade associations

Syndicated research

There are several large, international market research companies that have developed expertise and techniques in specialist areas or markets, and they offer data collected on a universal basis to several clients at a cost far lower than would be the case if a client had conducted the research on an individual basis.

For industrial markets, companies such as Arthur D. Little and the Stanford Research Institute (SRI), both with headquarters in the USA, provide major market reports in such areas as electronics, fibre optics or pharmaceuticals. These organizations guarantee confidentiality of data collected from individual companies, and make available to the subscribing clients information at the aggregate level. In view of the high levels of investment and working capital needed in such markets, there are often fewer than 20 prospective clients for any one commission. This illustrates the need for the market research organization themselves to 'research' the market, and to develop the capability to work at an international level.

For consumer goods markets there are two forms of **audit research** which are available on a multi-client basis and which make extensive use of the theory and constraints of **quantitative research**. The first of these is **retail audit** data of which the most widely used is the bi-monthly data collected, analysed and reported by A. C. Nielsen. A wide range of consumer goods is covered by the **Nielsen Index**; companies operating in the field of repeat-purchase items are at a severe disadvantage without this data, which shows bi-monthly movements in retail sales volume and value, market share, retail penetration and stock levels (and particularly, the **out-of-stock** position). The data is presented aggregated for total GB, and also presented for individual television areas. It is also presented in different reports for type of retail outlet.

The Nielsen audit takes a representative sample of retailers, including multiples, independents and cooperatives across grocers and chemists as well as confectioners, tobacconists and newsagents (abbreviated to CTNs).

Retail audits are based on the following equation for assessing sales in a specific time-frame:

Opening stock for period (checked last audit)		Net deliveries since last audit		Stock held at present audit		Sales to consumers during period
	+		−		=	

A different type of audit is carried out by AGB, who arrange for a household panel to report retail purchases. The data obtained is grossed up to produce a bi-monthly report on volume and value sales of specific repeat-purchase consumer product groups and for individual brands. This data permits tracking of brand shares at the consumer-use level.

A third major syndicated source of consumer usage data on a wide range of consumer products is the **Target Group Index** produced by the **British Market Research Bureau**. These research volumes are based on comprehensive interviews of a nationally representative sample of 25,000 people over two weeks each year. The classification of respondents by heavy, medium and light usership of the product group and individual brands, together with an analysis of readership habits, provide useful information for advertising targeting.

The large sample used for the Target Group Index means that the data produced is reliable for quite detailed analyses at the brand level. However, its publication only once a year means that it provides only a 'snapshot' of the market at one point in time, and the leading consumer goods companies and advertising agencies need to subscribe to this in combination with other audit data to be sure of having the most recent and comprehensive market data at their fingertips.

Different market research methods

There are a large number of different techniques that can be used to collect purchase and usage data, measurements of attitudes, evaluation of concepts, products and advertising executions and statistics on television viewing and press and magazine readership. At the broader level, these different methods fall into one of two categories: **qualitative research** or **quantitative research**. Specific methodologies will be explored under these two headings, together with suggestions as to the kind of marketing problems that each methodology is capable of solving. Some of these research methods stand alone in providing discrete answers to specific marketing problems. The value of other techniques is in their complementary use alongside or in sequence with other market research methods.

Qualitative research

In this broad category of research, the sample used for interviewing or observation is *not* chosen for statistical validity in respect of the population under study, but is used to provide an insight into prevailing motivations, attitudes, habits and changing needs.

The line of questioning used is highly exploratory and sufficient flexibility can be built into the interview or discussion framework to follow up relevant leads as they emerge. To exploit these opportunities for new information and ideas, highly qualified psychologists are generally employed to structure and conduct this type of research. This is even more critical when the line of questioning may lead the respondent into areas of discomfort where deeper feelings and motivations are not easily revealed.

In-depth interviews

In this type of qualitative research, individuals are selected from the key customer groups or potential target groups, and are interviewed in a formalized and structured way. The scope for open-ended questions and answers will depend on the nature of the product and the psychological depth of information required on the motivation underpinning product purchase and use.

This type of research technique is very popular in industrial markets where customers are frequently clustered on a geographic, industry or need basis, and the alternative of a large-scale quantitative survey would not yield significantly better information when judged against the relative costs. In-depth interviewing of major customers and those at the leading edge of technology in their fields can be highly instructive as to future product and service requirements.

For consumer products, this technique can prove useful as a prelude to a broader study of habits, attitudes and needs, particularly in relation to durables, which involve a high purchase price and more complex attitudes towards brand choice and the in-use situation. Given the highly competitive markets for cellular telephones, this would be an ideal method for identifying purchase criteria which can then be employed in a quantitative study.

Focus group

This qualitative research technique is also known as a **group discussion**. It involves ten or twelve individuals from the target market together in a room where the discussion is led by a moderator (generally a qualified psychologist). The discussion starts with a broad topic acting as an umbrella for the specific areas that will be explored later in the session. It is important that individuals begin to talk openly and eliminate the normal inhibitions of speaking in front of a group of strangers. The members are chosen as far as possible to create homogeneity within the group, so that 'factions' do not emerge, and one or two individuals do not take on the mantle of spokesperson for the whole group. This is where the moderator's influence and ability to direct the discussion are crucial.

For the **exploratory research** stage of a major market research programme to determine the marketing mix for a new product or for the relaunch of an existing product, as many as eight or ten focus groups will be run, so that different age groups and socio-economic groups as well as users and non-users can be involved. There will also be an appropriate geographic spread of research groups.

For consumer products, the omission of this stage even when quantitative research is carried out can be dangerous. This is because a significant change in product perceptions, attitudes and usage habits might only be revealed under such exploratory and 'open-ended' conditions. The most sophisticated and rigorous questionnaire applied to a large sample of the target group could exclude the most important parameter of product choice if this has not been identified beforehand.

The focus group is generally associated with consumer research because of its value in identifying underlying feelings and motivations. In recent years, a modified version has emerged called **technical focus research**, which has proved useful in revealing the attitudes of business people towards companies that they do business with, and the reasons for not choosing to do business with others. It helps to identify what customers view as important in a product, and what trade-offs they are prepared to make. It can also be of great value in segmentation and has led to new product niches which would otherwise have remained undiscovered (Rostky, 1986).

Projective techniques

These research methods move out of the realm of direct questioning of respondents about their conscious acts and thoughts into the territory of the subconscious. This requires the skills of a psychologist to provide stimuli which elicit a reaction that can be interpreted in terms of underlying beliefs and motivations.

One such method is **word association**, where words are presented one at a time and the respondent mentions the first word that comes to mind. An extension to this approach is **sentence completion** where a whole sentence is presented to the respondent who finishes it. This is a sophisticated form of open-ended question and requires detailed analysis to deduce actionable results. Moving further along this spectrum, there are the techniques of story completion and picture completion. The 'ink blot test' is the most extreme example of the use of psychological testing in market research, where respondents are asked to identify the shapes formed by ink blots.

In times of budget constraints, management will be under pressure to have clearly defined objectives for all market research undertaken, and in this climate some of the more extreme projective techniques might be difficult to justify in terms of less actionable results that are likely to emerge from them.

Quantitative methods

Quantitative market research involves the observation or questioning of a **representative sample** of the chosen population, such that the research results can be interpreted as applicable to the whole population. This means that the sample size and structure are chosen so that the measures and statistical outcome are real and not spuriously achieved through sampling error.

So, for example, a company might wish to identify whether the benefits sought from a breakfast cereal differ between the users and non-users of their brand. If the pattern of results shown in Table 6.3 emerged from research among a sample of 500 respondents, there would need to be an indication of whether the difference in the percentage figures were real **(statistically significant)** or a function of the sampling error.

Table 6.3 Percentage considering certain attributes to be very important in a breakfast cereal.

Attributes	Users of the brand	Non-users of the brand
Nutritious	72	77
Good-tasting	81	74
High in fibre	45	53
Low in calories	38	47

There are simple statistical tests which would reveal whether these differences were significant, and this is explored further in the later section on sampling.

Where large samples are to be structured with **quotas** from different categories of a population (the common ones are sex, age, socio-economic group, geographic area and current or potential product group usership), then sufficient time has to be built into the research framework to allow for **recruitment** according to the quotas. For example, simple random sampling in a high street of shoppers would be simpler and quicker than making sure that each of six different categories of shopper is filled to the correct quota in four different parts of the country. This latter route also adds to the cost.

There is a socio-economic classification commonly used in consumer surveys. This is the one devised by the Joint Industry Committee for the National Readership Survey (JICNARS). (See Table 5.2). This organization has been disbanded and the social grading system has been taken over by National Readership Surveys Ltd. It uses the convention of identifying the occupation of the head of household according to the following classification:

A   Higher managerial, administrative or professional.
B   Intermediate managerial, administrative or professional.
C1   Supervisory, clerical, junior administrative or professional.
C2   Skilled manual workers.
D   Semi-skilled and unskilled manual workers.
E   State pensioners, widows, casual and lowest-grade earners.

The interviewer collects the occupational information and makes a classification of the respondent. This is then checked by skilled analysis at the research agency.

A significant service industry is now growing around the identification of target groups by household composition and lifestyle, which in turn, can be linked to housing type. One company providing a comprehensive service based on the **Census of Population** is CACI, whose **ACORN** classification of housing type linked with postcode provides a sophisticated method of segmenting and targeting for individual consumer products and services.

The success of quantitative market research rests on two key areas:

(1)   Data collection
(2)   Sampling

In the market research process, the sampling frame would be determined before the data collection stage. However, it is sensible to explore methods of data collection first, since the choice or limitations here will have an influence on the sampling procedure.

Data collection

There are two broad categories of data collection: **questioning,** which involves verbal or written response from the sample of interviewees; and **observation,** where individuals in a sample or on a panel are knowingly or unknowingly observed in their behaviour relating to a particular product or service. The different techniques in each category are listed below and explored one by one:

(1)   Questioning techniques
    (a)   Personal interview
    (b)   By telephone
    (c)   Postal survey
    (d)   Computer response
(2)   Observation techniques
    (a)   Personal
    (b)   Diary
    (c)   Instrument

Questioning techniques

Personal interview

The use of a structured questionnaire by a trained interviewer provides the opportunity for gathering highly detailed information with a greater likelihood that it is accurate than for other methods. This is because the interviewer is in a position to make an instantaneous judgement on classification of the respondent or to probe response if doubt arises as to accuracy or validity. There is the inherent danger of bias through inappropriate prompting, but training should highlight avoidance techniques for this. The way in which the **questionnaire** is structured and coded will also be a determining factor in the degree to which the interviewing protocol is adhered to by the interviewer.

Although this is the preferred data collection method for a variety of quantitative research studies, there is still the inherent inaccuracy introduced through respondent **recall** of past behaviour, where this is being investigated. The traditional questions relating to purchase behaviour – 'bought within the past week', 'bought within the past month' or 'bought within the past six months' – suffer from an approximation process within the mind of the respondent which increases with the time elapsed since the activity in question.

Because this type of quantitative research is very labour-intensive, it leads to significantly higher costs than for other methods of data collection.

Telephone interview

This type of research is becoming increasingly popular for reasons of speed and lower cost compared with the face-to-face interview. Using a 'scripted' questionnaire approach, a typical interview may take only one or two minutes, and use can be made of off-peak telephone rates to minimize costs. Computerized dialling of numbers listed on computer file can also reduce the amount of interviewer time spent reaching members of the sample who are repeatedly unavailable. There is also the advantage of speed of implementation of research by this method. A company may brief on their needs and the specification drawn up, with interviewing complete within a week. This would be valuable where there has been a significant downturn in a service area (such as air travel during the Gulf War) and management needs to minimize staffing costs where these can be controlled to match changing demand.

The major disadvantage of this method is the interviewee attitude to invasion of privacy, if the researcher is telephoning private households. For research into business activities and attitudes, the respondent might not be willing to spend time answering questions where there is no perceived benefit to the business or the individual. For these reasons, the success rate in achieving valid interviews is lower than for personal interviewing, and a larger sample base needs to be drawn to guarantee the desired number of interviews.

Postal survey

This is an inexpensive method of research using a structured questionnaire which requires self-completion by the respondent. It suffers from the disadvantage of low response rates, which can fall to 5% in some instances, where there is no incentive for the individual to respond and where there is low interest in the area of research. However, there are research situations where the response rate can reach 30 or 40%, where the sample chosen is highly selective and the respondents identify that they, or their organization, will benefit from cooperating.

There is an opportunity cost of responding on the part of the individual in the sample and this is balanced against any reward which might be offered for completing and returning the questionnaire. This might be prepaid (imparting a sense of obligation to complete), or a promise of subsequent reward (with the attendant risk of non-receipt of what was promised). Three different monetary **incentives** were used in research to explore their effects on mail survey **response rates** (Lorenzi *et al.*, 1988).

Computer response

There is a higher level of investment involved in this method of data collection, through the installation of computer hardware in respondents' homes and training the panel in the use of appropriate programmed response. This approach is therefore more commonly associated with longer-term studies or the collection of repeat data. There is the advantage of instantaneous feedback to stimuli such as television advertising, and the facility for **electronic data transmission** means that there is no need for costly and time-consuming coding of information as the analyses and aggregate results will be provided automatically through centralized computer instructions.

Observation techniques

Personal observation

Where the monitoring of behaviour of one person by another is the chosen form of data collection, then it should be unobtrusive, as 'obtrusive' observation is likely to influence the behaviour under observation and therefore affect aggregate results.

An area where this technique has been applied successfully is in the observation of pre-purchase behaviour, where reliance was previously placed on shoppers' recall. Seventy groups of shoppers were observed in the Park Shopping Centre, Belfast to provide an insight into the nature of shopping behaviour (Brown S., 1988).

In this research, 60% of shopping expeditions were found to be multi-purpose, and all but 18% of the observed groups entered one of the 'magnet' stores, of which there were three. Observation was restricted to retail outlets entered by the groups, and no attempt was made to monitor in-store behaviour for fear of attracting attention. This highlights the limitation of the technique.

Another accepted form of observation is the monitoring of 'shopping behaviour' under laboratory conditions, where a panel is free to spend money on a range of products including the test brand after being exposed to advertising developed for a new or relaunched product, along with the advertising for unrelated product categories. In such **test laboratories**, the fact that behaviour is observed is just one of the distorting features compared with the 'real life' buying situation.

Diary observation

There are three approaches to the collection of data on the purchasing behaviour of individuals on a research panel:

(1) A regular (often monthly) visit by a research auditor to the home, where the packaging of specified product categories is located in a special receptacle, so that the brands, sizes and variants can be checked and reported.

(2) The individual panellist keeps a diary record of the purchases made, and this information is sent to the auditing company at agreed intervals. This second approach is less costly, but relies on the diligence of the panellist for accuracy and completeness of the diary record.

(3) Product bar coding allows for electronic scanning by the members of the household, and electronic data transfer reduces time and costs associated with traditional auditing methods.

The diary method is also used as a recognized method for supplementing 'metered' measurement of household television viewing. The advantage of the diary technique is that it records *who* is doing the watching, whereas the meter can only measure when the television set is switched on, regardless of the members of the household who are (or are not) watching at the time. However, this diary information is subject to errors of **recall** and incomplete knowledge of activities of household members, particularly the young.

The diary method is also appropriate for recording intimate details of day-to-day life where these are required, for example, in research into medical conditions and the alleviation of symptoms which trial drugs are intended to deliver.

Observation through instruments

The television meter is an example of this approach; another is the use of **physiological testing devices** which give automatic readings on emotional response to advertising. These include the **psychogalvanometer**, which measures the electrical resistance caused by increased activity of the sweat glands in the palms of the hands and fingers with emotional arousal.

Another of these instrument techniques is the **pupillometric test** which is used to measure pupil dilation as the panellist views television commercials or focuses on printed advertisements. Positive reaction is indicated by greater relative pupil dilation. **Voice pitch analysis**, where variance in voice pitch during verbal feedback is compared with a baseline level, is linked with the amount of emotional involvement in advertising viewed by the panellist.

Sampling

Most market research exercises involve sampling in some form, where a limited number of members of the total population to be surveyed are selected to represent the population: but this is not always the case. The **census of population** for a country is an example where every member of the population being researched has details about their whereabouts and attributes recorded on a specific day.

This is a rare form of research as it is expensive. For example, the UK Census carried out in April 1991 involved 117,000 researchers or 'enumerators' visiting 200 households each and collecting a completed form about the residents of each household. The government of the day can justify this type of research for the value of information it provides on the age profile of the population, ethnic breakdown of the country, the state of the housing stock, the employment status of each adult, their state of health and the transport they use to get to work. This then facilitates more effective planning of housing needs, health care, infrastructure and employment support. The very high cost of this type of census means that it can only be carried out once every ten years. However, the results obtained, when stripped of personal details, also act as a reservoir of very accurate market research data for those organizations able to afford it.

In the more frequent situations where a sample must be taken to represent the total population or 'universe', the researcher must ensure that this sample will be as representative of the population as possible, so that the results obtained for the sample can be taken as applicable to the total population. There will always be a statistical error associated with the sampling procedure, but this can be minimized where the rules of market research procedure are observed. So, for example, samples of 2000 or fewer are commonly taken to represent the 45 million adults in Great Britain.

Where the target population has been defined, the sampling unit must be identified and a sampling frame chosen which will ensure the right balance is achieved between different constituent parts of a population, if these exist. There are two broad approaches to sampling catering for different market scenarios and research needs: probability sampling and non-probability sampling. These are now explored in more depth.

Probability sampling

The theory of sampling rests on the probability that a number of members of the group are representative of the group. There are three different approaches.

(1) **Simple random sampling**, where every member of the population has a known and equal chance of selection.

(2) **Stratified random sampling**, where the population is divided into mutually exclusive groups (such as sex, age and socio-economic groupings) and random samples are drawn from each group. When equal proportions are sampled from each group then a **uniform sampling fraction** occurs, and often reflects incomplete knowledge about the population. The existence of each population grouping is understood, but the relative importance of each group is not known.

(3) **Cluster sampling**, where the population is divided into mutually exclusive groups and one or more groups are chosen for interview. This might be the approach of an industrial company researching customer needs across a wide range of industries and geographical areas. The company might choose to research all companies from industry A in area 1, and all companies from industry B in area 2 and so on. However, care would be needed to ensure that there was a sufficient degree of homogeneity across areas in terms of each industry's characteristics.

Confidence limits

Values obtained from research among a sample are approximations for the values for the population as a whole: there will be some degree of sampling error. The way in which the numerical data tends to fall around an average value is known as the variation. A measure of the variation of any distribution of values is known as the **standard deviation**.

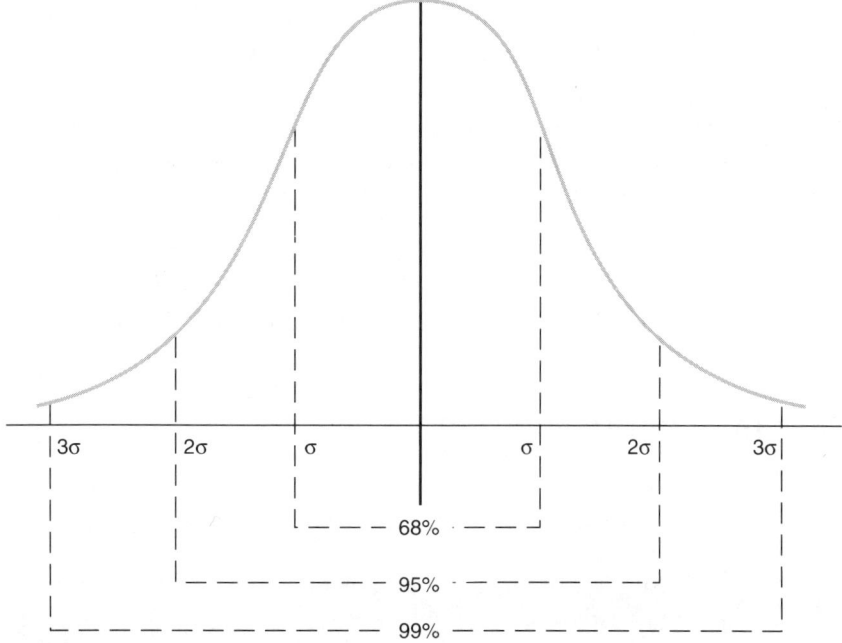

Figure 6.1 Normal distribution curve showing the importance of the standard deviation.

The standard deviation of the sampling distribution is known as the **standard error of the mean**. As the size of the sample is increased the standard error becomes smaller.

The standard deviation is defined by:

$$\sigma = \sum \frac{1}{n}\,(x - \bar{x})^2$$

where:

n = the number of items in the sample;
x = the individual reading;
$\bar{x}$ = the mean.

Figure 6.1 shows the **normal distribution curve** and illustrates the way in which the measure for part of the population deviates from the mean across the total population. Researchers can choose the level of confidence at which they wish to work in terms of the variation in a measure for the sample which is due to sampling error alone.

Given that variability in a population is measured by the standard deviation, a researcher can work at the following confidence levels:

- **68% confidence level**, where there is a one in three risk of the sample mean being outside the range covered by ± one standard deviation from the mean.
- **95% confidence level**, where there is a one in twenty risk that the sample means is outside ± two standard deviations from the mean.
- **99% confidence level**, where there is a one in a hundred risk that the sample mean is outside ± three standard deviations from the mean.

It is common practice in market research to work at the 95% confidence level. Very often, the increase in sample size and therefore cost is not justified by the marginal increase in statistical significance achieved by working at the 99% confidence level.

For a detailed analysis of the impact of sampling error on quantitative market research results and how this is influenced by research design, the student is referred to Chapter 4 of Crimp (1990), which also has a comprehensive section of statistical tests (compiled by E.J. Davis).

Non-probability sampling

There is the alternative option of choosing a sample without the random element: there is a deliberate **weighting** introduced to reflect certain characteristics of the population. This is introduced to make the sample similar in structure and composition to the population that is being investigated.

One form of this is **judgement sampling**, where the sample is chosen for the significance of the individual members within the total population.

This would be particularly valid for some types of industrial research where 80% of the potential demand for a product or service might be generated by 20% of prospective customers (an example of the 80/20 rule). In this situation, the sample chosen would include much greater representation from this 20% of prospects than their absolute number would justify.

Alternatively, groups within a population are identified and a sampling frame is designed which specifies a quota against each group. This is a form of **quota sampling** which is very common in consumer research, as the population on which an organization requires information on buying, usage pattens or attitudes is unlikely to be exactly like the total population in make-up. So, for example, a sampling frame for research into the types of films to show at a local independent cinema would include a heavier quota of 18–25 year olds than would be representative of the local population, as younger people visit the cinema more frequently than the population taken as a whole.

Non-probability sampling illustrates the balance that has to be struck between statistical rigour and common sense applied to the specific marketing problem facing management. The way that information obtained from quantitative research is used will be influenced by the sampling frame, and competent market researchers will draw the user's attention to the limitation of the data reported.

Questionnaire design

The degree to which a market research exercise is implemented through a formally structured questionnaire will depend on the nature of the information to the gathered and the research method that has been chosen for the task. The moderator of a focus group session would use a framework of leading questions and ideas to prompt the specially selected group into responding in an open and informal way. However, this would differ markedly from the highly structured format of questions applied to a sample of several hundred respondents in a quantitative survey. An in-depth interview with an industrial buyer to determine reasons for particular purchasing decisions would be structured to the extent of not omitting any key areas, but would be sufficiently flexible to allow aspects of corporate needs, culture and operating methods to feed into the response.

Questionnaire design will take place during the third stage of the market research process (market research design), although it will follow the definition of information required and a decision on research methodology. The questionnaire may be used to gather information on past behaviour, attitudes to situations, perceptions of products or services and behavioural intentions. The value of results obtained will depend on the way in which each question is phrased and the sequence in which questions are placed, as both of these factors can lead to response **bias** which may invalidate findings. Where this is possible, for example in providing a range of prices for the respondent to choose the price at which he/she would be likely to purchase, then bias in the response towards the prices higher in the list can be eliminated by reversing the order for half of the sample.

Where more than one interviewer is involved in administering the questionnaire, there can be no room for ambiguity in the questions as interpretation and prompting will differ between interviewers, which means that the results have not been obtained in a consistent way.

Questions should be reasonable in terms of the degree to which a person will be prepared to give an answer (for example, relating to personal habits or earnings), or in terms of their ability to remember events from the past (purchases made in the past week, month or year).

There are three influencing factors which need to be taken into account in devising the questionnaire: **comprehension**, **costs** and **coding** (the three Cs).

(1) *Comprehension* Each question must be clearly understood by the respondent so that it can be answered in the format specified. This requires the use of vocabulary and sentence structure that avoid ambiguity and reflect terminology in common use among the sample interviewed. Balanced against the need for clarity is the avoidance of 'leading' questions which have a tendency to provoke one form of reply more than another, thus creating **bias**.

Comprehension of questions will also be influenced by the order in which they are asked, as this provides a logical framework of reference for the respondent. However, this framework can also pose a danger in leading a respondent from a generic area of research (such as attitudes to a healthy lifestyle) to a more specific line of questioning (such as purchasing patterns of butter versus poly-unsaturated fats). The respondent will be aware of why the second line of questioning is taking place, and might adapt responses to give the impression of a healthy diet. In such a situation, the order of questions might be reversed to obtain an accurate measure of behaviour, with well-constructed attitudinal questions to follow, possibly using a **Likert Scale** (see Table 6.4).

Where a questionnaire is self-administered, such as in a postal survey or panel diary, comprehension and ease of response become even more critical to the success of the research, as there is no interviewer present to explain or clarify.

(2) *Costs* The longer and more complex the questionnaire, the longer it will take to be administered by a trained interviewer, which will increase costs. This is directly measurable in omnibus surveys, where the client may be charged per question added to the survey across a predefined sample. Where there is a budget constraint, a balance must be struck between sample size and questionnaire length.

Table 6.4 Types of closed-ended questions used in market research.

Type	Example
Dichotomous (choice of two answers)	Yes/No Of interest/Not of interest
Multiple choice (from 3 or more answers)	Buy every week/Once a month/Once a year
Rating scale (gives a measure of assessment of a product or service attribute)	Respondent chooses from: Poor/Fair/Good/Very good/Excellent For example, to describe the service in a restaurant. This response can then be compared with that for other restaurants.
Likert Scale (technique for measurement of attitude)	Respondent is asked whether they: Strongly agree, Agree, Neither agree nor disagree, Disagree, or Strongly disagree with a number of statements such as: 'Supermarket products should be packaged in material which can be recycled'. The response is coded 1 to 5.
Semantic differential	Scale between two words with opposite meanings and the respondent chooses the appropriate point on the scale. Example for coffee evaluation: Mellow tasting 1 2 3 4 5 Bitter tasting

Importance scale	The respondent indicates how important the attribute is to them on the 5-point scale:
	    Extremely important
	    Very important
	    Quite important
	    Not very important
	    Not at all important
	So, for coffee, one respondent might rate price as 'very important' and taste 'quite important'. The aggregate result will indicate which performance parameters are key to success.

Another constraint on the length and complexity of the questionnaire is the ability to hold the interest of the respondent without losing goodwill through excessive demands on the respondent's time. The first stage of the market research process – problem definition – will indicate the information which is essential to obtain, and that which is of marginal importance. The second type should be included only where it does not make the questionnaire unwieldy or too costly.

(3) *Coding* Advances in computer software for analysing response to market surveys have provided the opportunity for obtaining fast and accurate results. But this has imposed even more stringent conditions of encoding each type of response to every question asked, so that the data from a completed questionnaire will be entered on computer as a series of unique numeric or alphanumeric codes. This facilitates direct collation of results across a large

number of questionnaires, and the possibility of cross-analysis, for example, between a specific respondent attribute (such as age or socio-economic grouping) and a particular type of behaviour (such as frequency of purchase).

However, the desirability of coding for computer analysis imposes the need for **closed-ended questions**, where the respondent is *not* free to answer in his own way, but must choose one of the alternative answers provided. Very often, the main choice of response will be supported by the option of replying 'don't know', 'none of these' or 'other'. These answers can be coded, but are less useful in revealing the attributes, habits or attitudes of the respondents giving them, unless accompanied by an **open-ended question** such as 'if other, what are these?' This response will be more difficult to code, and may involve manual collation of results.

Definitions and examples for different types of closed-ended questions are provided in Table 6.4.

A further issue which arises in terms of the order of questions in a questionnaire is the screening of respondents to identify attributes, which might be age group, occupation, earnings (and of course, sex). This process is important where sample quotes are to be filled. These questions which act as the **classification** for the respondent should come at the end of the interview, although the data entry could come at the beginning of the questionnaire.

Piloting the questionnaire

As there is no magic formula for creating a questionnaire that is ideal for a particular research problem, testing or 'piloting' the questionnaire on a percentage of the sample will reveal problems of structure (for example, where a question is used to filter respondents in or out of a sub-sample), problems in comprehension and vocabulary, and potential problems with coding of response. Depending on the size of the sample in quantitative research, piloting between five and ten per cent should allow for the necessary fine-tuning of the questionnaire.

In qualitative research, a less structured interview format for in-depth interviews can be amended after initial interviews take place, so long as the amended structure does not 'bias' the approach towards a preferred outcome.

Measuring consumer perceptions in services marketing

Some of the more complex questionnaires used in market research explore attitudes, and the theories and techniques of experimental psychology have played a part in the development of the more sophisticated approaches. Attribute scales provide actionable results where advertising strategy can be revised to improve the target group's perceptions of product benefits or features.

As product differentiation on tangible dimensions becomes increasingly difficult, market researchers are asked by clients to construct survey techniques which identify more abstract qualities associated with different consumer brands. This is also becoming a feature of research in services and retailing, where **perceived quality** is viewed as critical in assessing overall competitive positioning, and particularly, price positioning. Quality can be viewed as a global value judgement or overall evaluation very similar to an attitude, and can be assessed by dimensions such as reliability, responsiveness, access and competence.

Ten such dimensions were used in the construction of a market research instrument for measuring consumer perception of service quality, called SERVQUAL (Parasuraman *et al.*, 1988). Ninety-seven items were generated to represent the ten dimensions, and each item was cast into two statements, one to measure expectations about firms in general in the service category being investigated, and one to measure perceptions about the particular firm whose service quality was being assessed. Half the statement pairs were worded positively, and half worded negatively, and a seven-point scale ranging from 'strongly agree' to 'strongly disagree' was used with these statements.

The 97-item instrument was refined through use on a quota sample of 200 adults recruited in a shopping mall. The respondents were spread across five different service categories – appliance repair and maintenance, retail banking, long-distance telephone, securities brokerage and credit cards. Analysis of the pooled data resulted in reduction of the 97 items to a 34-item scale, with seven distinct dimensions describing the service quality perception.

A second stage of data collection relating to one firm in each of four of the industries listed and the separate analysis of the four sets of data resulted in the reduction of the 34-item scale to 22 items spread across five dimensions which were given the following labels: tangibles, reliability, responsiveness, assurance and empathy. The authors of this research provide support for the validity of the SERVQUAL scale and suggest a wide range of uses in defining and maintaining service quality.

The role of market research in the brand development process

New product development for consumer markets involves considerable financial risk, particularly where multimillion pound advertising budgets are necessary to achieve viable market shares. The use of carefully chosen

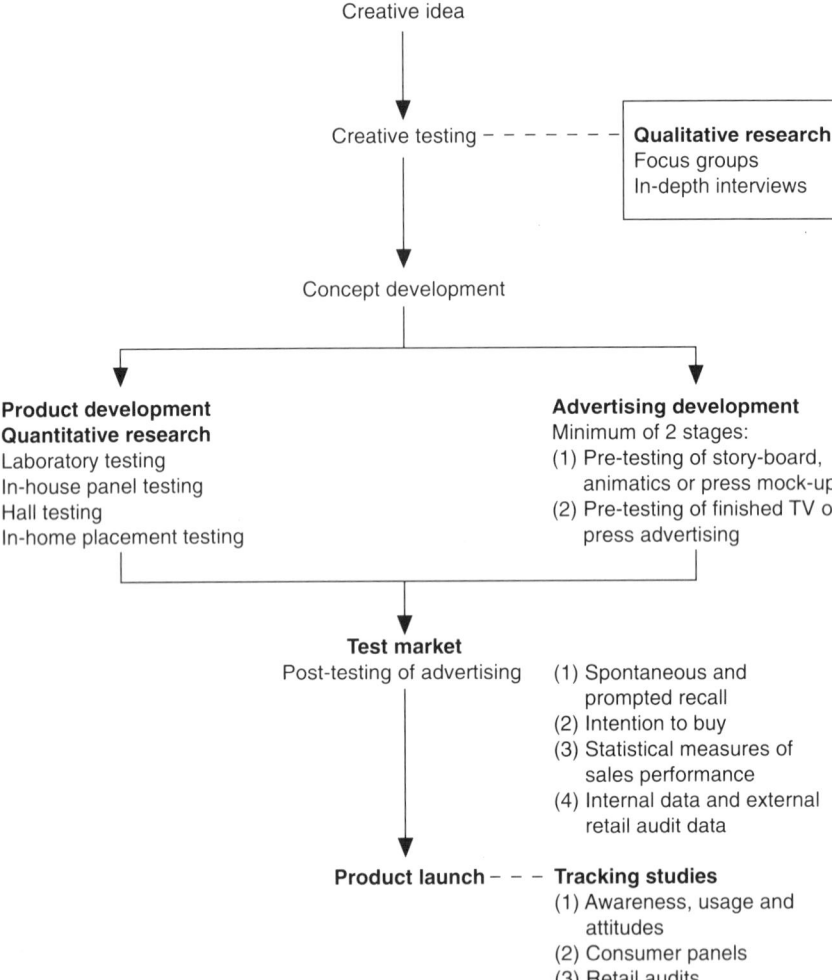

Figure 6.2 The role of market research in the brand development process.

market research techniques at critical stages in the process will serve to reduce risk by providing reliable information on the end-users, their attitudes, habits and perceptions of the product offering.

Whether market research is managed by the innovator's own personnel or by outside market research consultancies (and many specialize in new product development), the wide range of techniques used in the process serves to illustrate their relative capabilities. The brand development process and some of the more important market research stages involved are illustrated in Figure 6.2. From the early stage of testing whether a new product concept is viable (and it may be one of several to be screened), to tracking the performance of the brand once launched, market research plays a critical role in the go/no go decision and in the positioning of the brand in terms of tangible and intangible attributes.

In the early stages, **concept testing** makes use of some of the techniques of qualitative research already explored, namely **focus groups** and **in-depth interviews**. Where a viable new product route has been demonstrated, then the company sets in train the process of developing the concept through **product development** and **advertising development**. The chronological order of events will be determined by the complexity of the product. Product development frequently precedes advertising development, which can be conducted in a matter of weeks after the months or years needed to develop a viable product. However, shorter product life cycles and the fear of premature obsolescence will pressurize management into using market research methods which give the swiftest results consistent with validity.

Typically, product development will start with a **new product proposal** to the research and development laboratory. When the product has reached a stage at which properties and performance need to be tested to assess if the work has been on the right track, then consumer panels recruited from within the organization will be used. Sampling structure and questionnaires tend to be simple at this stage to obtain directional results and to keep the administrative load to a minimum.

When internal panel results indicate that the brief has been met, then this needs to be validated through larger-scale quantitative research.

Quantitative methods for product testing

There are two methods commonly used for testing the performance of a new consumer product, **hall tests** and **in-home product placement tests**. Hall tests are so named because, in the case of consumables, individuals from quota samples are drawn from a public thoroughfare and requested to spend a few minutes evaluating the test product in a hall hired for the purpose. There are several scenarios:

(1) A single test product is evaluated on a range of attributes through scoring, and the degree to which these attribute scores are enhanced through revelation of a brand name, packaging and advertising can be measured as a second stage of the same interview.

(2) Two or more test products can be evaluated against each other through attribute scoring. This would take place in an unbranded format, or so-called **blind testing** conditions.

(3) A test product is evaluated 'blind' against one or two major competitors whose identities are not revealed. Attribute scoring in this situation gives a measure of the test product's performance on key tangible parameters.

(4)   A test product is evaluated in the context of its prospective branding and advertising against a major competitor whose identity is revealed. This could be considered the most realistic of all four scenarios in terms of test conditions, as it emulates the situation in which an individual would be assessing the product after first purchase, including the **halo effects** of brand name and advertising.

The choice of scenarios above will depend on the objectives of the research, but statistically significant results will only be achieved where the sample is sufficiently large and quotas are well structured on a geographical and demographic basis with regard to the target group.

Hall tests can be used as a preliminary stage before **in-home placement tests**. These involve the recruitment of a structured sample of households (or one member of the household) to try one or more products in the home environment for a specific period, and to complete a questionnaire to reveal their assessment of the product(s). For certain categories of personal care products and home equipment, this is the only way to achieve a result that provides sufficient confidence in product performance to permit a launch decision.

Some of the alternative scenarios outlined for hall tests also apply to in-home placement testing. The research format can be 'blind' or 'branded', and it can be a **monadic test** – in which only one product is tested in each household or it can involve a **paired comparison test**, in which each household tests two products. Where there are three alternative versions of a new product to be tested, or two test versions are to be measured against a competitor, then a **round-robin** research design will be needed to ensure comparability of conditions for all three, and the statistical validity of the results achieved.

Some major consumer goods companies exclude the 'blind testing' stage from external research, as it is argued that this is an unrealistic scenario. These companies prefer to move directly to branded in-home testing.

Advertising development

Advertising development involves the testing of alternative executions of the same **creative strategy** (this will specify target group, key benefit(s), supporting evidence and 'atmosphere' or style). For cost reasons, the samples used for this type of **pre-testing** are small and therefore this research falls into the category of qualitative research. It is usually sufficient to provide the directional leads necessary for the advertising agency to proceed along one route. Creative material developed to the next stage can be exposed to further testing, in the form of a story-board, animatics or press advertisement mock-up.

The measures used in this type of research are discussed in Chapter 8, in the section on 'assessing advertising effectiveness'. The validity of much advertising research hinges on the assumed link between measures of advertising recall and product purchase. However, the quality of the message recalled has a bearing on propensity to buy a new product, and it is difficult to establish a reliable benchmark for this before launch, particularly where the product is creating a new category. Experience of systematically pre-testing commercials and subsequently tracking them for several years has indicated that pre-testing does not necessarily provide a yardstick of campaign performance (Brown G., 1988).

The test market

This is an option open to consumer goods companies because there are mechanisms available for measuring sales response in a defined geographical area (through retail audits), and for restricting advertising exposure through a regional television station or controlled distribution of a split-run magazine. This facility is expensive and pre-announces the launch package to the competition, but the multinational companies that practise the science gain advanced knowledge of sales response before committing to an expensive national launch.

The role of the test market in new product development is explored in Chapter 16.

Tracking studies

A variety of tools exist that enable a company marketing fast-moving consumer goods to **track** or evaluate the performance of various elements of the marketing mix. Two forms of tracking studies are retail audits and consumer panels, both of which have already been explored under 'Syndicated research'. A common form of monitoring brand performance is the **usage and attitude survey**. This takes the form of a periodic quantitative survey into spontaneous and prompted **awareness**, brand purchase and attitude measures that monitor perceptions of the brand along relevant parameters. Conducting this type of research at six-monthly intervals (commonly referred to as **'dipstick'** testing) provides an historic perspective on brand performance against advertising weight. However, where a brand is well established, small fluctuations in these readings do not provide actionable results, and some companies have sacrificed this type of brand tracking for more problem-specific research.

An alternative to carrying out customized research is the use of an **omnibus survey**. This is a regular (perhaps weekly) questioning of 2000–3000 people either face-to-face or by telephone, and is a service offered by several major market research companies. A client may 'purchase' a number of questions for a modest fee in order to track more obvious performance measures. This is a blunt but cost-effective instrument for keeping abreast of how the brand is selling in the mass market. Because the sample will be broadly based, this type of research does not meet the needs of companies wishing to have detailed knowledge of the buying habits of a smaller target group (Bond, 1989).

Research aids to media planning

Conveying a brand message to the target audience requires use of the right media at the right time. Where the creative element is the 'quality' of the message, media planning will provide the right 'quantity' of the same message for a specified media budget. In order to select the timing of television commercials and insertion of press advertising in the appropriate magazines and newspapers, up-to-date information must be accessible on **television viewing** figures and **readership** of magazines and newspapers.

Measuring television audiences

In the UK, measurement of television audiences is controlled by the Broadcaster's Audience Research Board (BARB). This organization is jointly owned by the Independent Television Association and the BBC. The contract for the measurement of audience size is held by AGB, and the assessment of audience reaction is provided by the BBC's Broadcasting Research Department, acting on behalf of BARB. This assessment takes place through a self-completed questionnaire by an audience panel.

Competition for available air-time during the mid to late 1980s led to escalating costs in spite of the addition of Channel Four and Breakfast TV. However, at the turn of the decade, recessionary influences took their toll on advertising budgets, which meant that advertisers and their agencies now scrutinize media plans for cost-effectiveness in reaching the target audience.

Subscribers to BARB Audience Measurement receive fortnightly reports or have access to on-line data. Data from the viewing household is collected through electronic data transfer to the AGB computer. Recording of viewing takes place for each set in the household, and the metered information is fed to a central meter with the on-line connection. The information is presented in a way that allows for direct measurement of viewers of a particular spot or programme, assessment of the percentage of the target audience reached and of the cost-effectiveness of a campaign compared with competitive advertising scheduling.

The high incidence of video recording equipment and the growth of subscriptions to satellite and cable TV mean that viewing is more fragmented and this has the effect of introducing a greater degree of error into measurement. With the increasing saturation of key markets, advertisers are looking to reach smaller target groups with tailor-made products, and mass media appear less attractive on the basis of the threshold cost needed for national TV advertising and cost per thousand reached. The limitations to accuracy of audience research due to sample size and instructions to viewers will bear more heavily on smaller and more specialist audiences. Some of the errors introduced through sample turnover and the definition of 'watching' were the focus of attention when Nielsen and AGB began **people-meter** services in 1987 (Twyman, 1988).

Readership research

Measurement of readership in the UK is vested in the Joint Industry Committee for the National Readership Survey (JICNARS). In 1984, the number of titles monitored increased from 120 to 200, and the face-to-face interviewing technique is applied to a sample of 28,500, involving just under 2500 interviewer calls per month. National Readership Survey data is published twice-yearly.

The questionnaire used asks about 'readership in the last year' and the number of issues read. 'Readership' is inevitably higher than the circulation figure for a publication, but the definition of readership is vague (it would include in-depth reading of every page as well as 'skimming' for items of interest). There is availability of readership data classified by occupational status and ownership of household durables. This, together with the narrowly based circulation of certain magazines, allows for more focused targeting.

The weaknesses of readership research are reflected in corporate assessment of the cost-effectiveness of press versus television advertising. In a J. Walter Thompson study, magazines were considered to be 70% as cost-effective as TV, national newspapers 66% and local newspapers 41% as cost-effective (Gullen, 1988).

Limitations of market research

The error introduced by researching among a sample rather than the total population is generally quantifiable and acknowledged by both researcher and user. Similarly, *ad hoc* research is recognized as providing a snapshot of habits and attitudes at a point in time and even information from tracking studies suffers from obsolescence in markets subject to rapid change. However, these limitations can be accommodated when the research is used to address specific problems.

Companies are becoming less tolerant of the fragmented nature of knowledge about the market in which they have to operate when major decisions have to be made in rapidly changing environments. Developments in information technology have led to greater reliance on databases to provide indicators on purchasing patterns and customer profiles. This assumes that the company has the capability to build a database through direct marketing activity or control over retail points with EPOS.

However, such databases rarely provide the necessary insights into prevailing attitudes and emerging needs for identification of new segments, products and services. There is increasing evidence that many companies find a pragmatic route to information needs through a combination of database and market surveys.

For example, a retailer's chargecard database identifies which cross-purchases are made across different departments, but does not know which purchases are pre-planned and which are link or impulse purchases. A survey among a sample of the chargecard customers will reveal the important patterns here (Hochhauser, 1986). The same research discusses the problem of a mail order catalogue company which was successful in generating new customers, but database analysis indicated that these were less profitable than existing customers. A well-constructed market survey among a sample of the new customers and a sample of the existing customers will identify differences in habits and attitudes in an attempt to explain the lower profitability of the former group.

The fact that much advertising research is qualitative rather than quantitative is a tacit admission of the directional nature of findings where the stimulus–response mechanism is not fully understood. Many of the research methods (which employ such measures as day-after recall, product attribute scoring and intention to purchase) were developed in the 1960s and 1970s as indicators of what was happening as a result of an advertising campaign. Sophisticated computer-aided tracking studies and market modelling have usurped this role, and agencies are turning to advertising research predominantly to explain underlying attitudes and motivation. This calls into question the role of the **account planner** who has traditionally been the consumer champion within the agency brand team, and whose main ammunition was the longer-term advertising research data (Grundy, 1987).

Social commentators have indicated that the 1990s will be characterized by a trend toward the search for 'quality of life' rather than 'quantity of life' in developed markets where environmental issues are influencing purchasing patterns. This poses a challenge to research consultancies in providing an early-warning system of changing attitudes, so that marketing companies can respond without compromising their traditional dependency on 'hard' data.

European perspective

The major issues and operational problems of market research are magnified when an organization wishes to conduct research across European borders. The obvious differences in language create a major impediment, but social and cultural factors must also be taken into account. A perfectly acceptable question in one country may be considered intrusive in another.

A major requirement of research data collected across borders is that there should be **comparability**. Measures of awareness and usage of a brand should mean exactly the same, whether the data has been collected from France, Denmark or the UK. This has implications for question design and questionnaire structure if either is to be administered in more than one country.

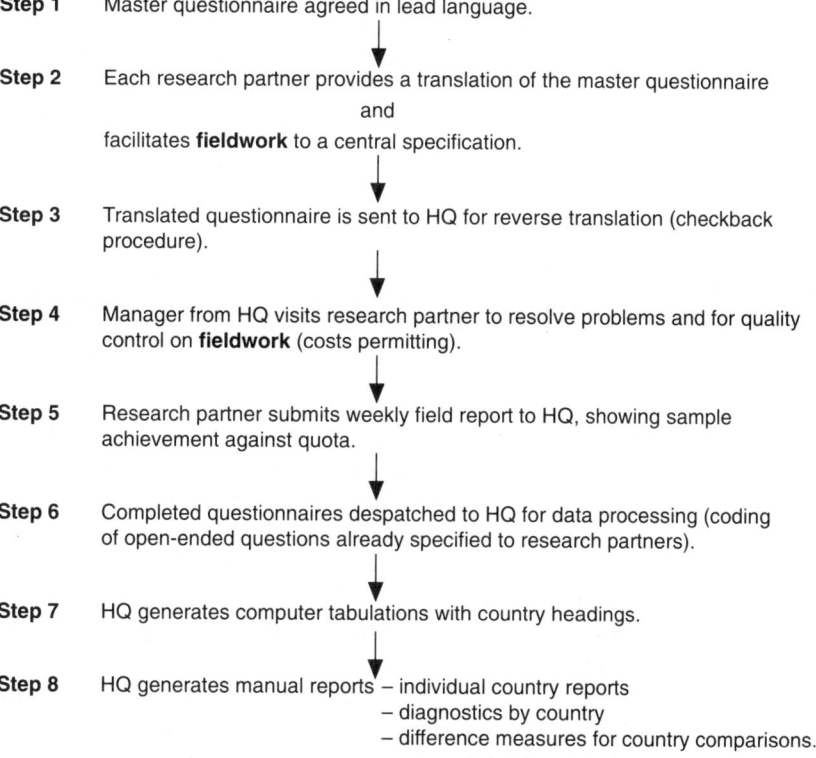

Step 1   Master questionnaire agreed in lead language.

Step 2   Each research partner provides a translation of the master questionnaire
and
facilitates **fieldwork** to a central specification.

Step 3   Translated questionnaire is sent to HQ for reverse translation (checkback procedure).

Step 4   Manager from HQ visits research partner to resolve problems and for quality control on **fieldwork** (costs permitting).

Step 5   Research partner submits weekly field report to HQ, showing sample achievement against quota.

Step 6   Completed questionnaires despatched to HQ for data processing (coding of open-ended questions already specified to research partners).

Step 7   HQ generates computer tabulations with country headings.

Step 8   HQ generates manual reports – individual country reports
– diagnostics by country
– difference measures for country comparisons.

Figure 6.3   Process for managing cross-border market research.
Acknowledgement: This figure was compiled with the assistance of V.A. Research Ltd, London.

The ideal data structure for drawing transborder comparisons is 'single source', where the same sample is used, for example, for deriving purchase, attitude and lifestyle information. This is costly in practice as drawing the right sample (invariably based on socio-economic quotas) may require persistence and, therefore, increased expense.

Some areas of compromise are inevitable where a client requires a particular outcome, but within a budget. The specialist researcher must advise on the sources of error or uncertainty, but must also have confidence in the specialists and field workers in the European countries where research is to take place. The European network built by a consultancy specializing in international research is an integral part of the service offered. The quality of work will depend on constant vigilance in screening European partners and checking sampling procedures and research data.

Because of the complexity and cost of cross-border research, some multinational organizations take a conscious decision to classify brands as 'multinational' or 'single country'. This will depend on the numbers of brand features common across several countries and the importance of these features to the competitive positioning of the product.

The role of the market research agency, consultant or in-house specialist is to optimize accuracy and consistency of research across borders through the kind of stepwise procedure outlined in Figure 6.3.

Financial implications of pan-European research

At the level of the national economy, market research managed across borders is an element of foreign trade. The commissioned agency exports expertise and 'buys' fieldwork from the research partner in another Member State.

This type of transaction has currency exchange risk implications for all parties – client, lead MR agency and research partners. For example, a Japanese car manufacturer might commission a British-based agency to conduct pan-European attitude research. The client would wish to have a price quoted in yen and the research partners would quote for fieldwork in their home currencies. The lead agency would need to hedge against currency movements to ensure an adequate profit.

This adds a further dimension to the work of the lead agency – that of currency speculation. In this respect, it bears the risks of a traditional exporter.

The importance of the right research partner

The quality and validity of research results will depend on uniform attention to detail across countries as specified in the initial proposal from the lead agency. The choice of a research partner in a European country will therefore be made through a screening process, based on:

(1) A reputation and track record;
(2) Entry in national, Market Research Society or ESOMAR handbooks;
(3) Assessment of expertise through conferences and networking.

Problems and assignments

(1) Your advertising agency has suggested it is time for a new campaign for your fmcg product. They have responded to the brief and their creative execution should now be put to the test. Outline a programme of research to test the new campaign.

(2) Your sales director has told you that his sales team is finding it difficult to get appointments in selling your high value precision tooling equipment. He does not know why this is. What response would you recommend in identifying the causes?

(3) Your market research consultants have proposed running a qualitative study with a large sample to be able to understand better consumers' perceptions of your product – sunglasses. Why might you feel uneasy and what could you do to reassure yourself that the investment will be worthwhile?

(4) As a market research expert, your client is a national sports club with 15,000 members. The club's management wants to ask members for their perceptions of the club and the services it offers, but has only limited funds available. Each member receives the club magazine bi-monthly. How would you advise them to proceed?

(5) Market research revealed a gap in the market for a new biscuit brand, targeted at children and teenagers. Your company has developed the brand to meet the need. Put forward an outline research proposal in order to reassure management that your research findings will be representative of the marketplace.

(6) Your company serves a number of European markets. In carrying out market research in all of them, would you recommend using one agency with a network of offices, different research agents in each market, or some other arrangement? Why?

(7) Results from a limited programme of hall tests of a new product are encouraging. Why might you urge your client to err on the side of caution before proceeding?

(8)   A client thinks it is time his company started to sell 'in Europe'. He has approached you for 'market research in Europe'. What recommendations would you make in the first instance?

References

Bond C. (1989). Catching the bus. *Marketing*, 23 February

Brown G. (1988). Facts from tracking studies – and old advertising chestnuts. *Admap*, June

Brown S. (1988). Information seeking, external search and 'shopping' behaviour: Preliminary evidence from a planned shopping centre. *J. of Marketing Management*, **4**(1), 33–49

Crimp M. (1990). *The Marketing Research Process*, 3rd edn. London: Prentice-Hall

Grundy J. (1987). Advertising research – Is it time for a rethink? *European Research*, November

Gullen P. (1988). Is press research merely a currency? *Admap*, May

Hochhauser R. (1986). Market survey, database or a combination of both? *Direct Marketing*, October

Lorenzi R., Friedman R. and Paolilli J.G.P. (1988). Consumer mail survey responses: more (unbiased) bang for the buck. *J. of Consumer Marketing*

Marketing News (1984). New technology 'TRACES' reaction to TV ads. *Marketing News*, 25 May, p. 3

Parasuraman A., Berry L. and Zeithaml V.A. (1988). SERVQUAL: a multiple-item scale for measuring common perceptions of service quality. *J. of Retailing*, **64**(1), Spring

Rostky G. (1986). Unveiling market segments with technical focus research. *Business Marketing*, October

Twyman T. (1988). Which peoplemeter? (which meter, but also which people?). *Admap*, January

---

European perspective

Sources of European marketing information:

Croner. *Croner's Europe*

Department of Trade and Industry (1990). *Marketing Consumer Goods in Western Europe*

Euromonitor (1992). *European Compendium of Marketing Information*

Euromonitor (1992). *European Marketing Data and Statistics*, 27th edn

International Committee of the Market Research Society (1992). *Country Notes – Regional Volume: Eastern Europe*

International Committee of the Market Research Society (1992). *Country Notes – Regional Volume: Western Europe*

London Business School Information Service (1991). *Guide to European Market Information: EC Countries*

Mort D. (1992). *European Marketing Handbook*. London: Pitman

Newman O. and Foster A. (compilers) (1993). *European Market Share Reporter: a Wide-Ranging Compilation of Statistics from Journals and Limited-Circulation Publications*. Gale Research International

NTC Publications (1992). *European Marketing Pocket Book*

Office for Official Publications of the European Community (1993). *Panorama of EC industry*

Other useful information sources:

Economist Intelligence Unit. *Marketing in Europe*. London: Economist Intelligence Unit

Euromonitor. *Market Research Europe*

Euromonitor (1991). *The European Directory of Marketing Information Sources*, 2nd edn

Mintel. *Market Intelligence Europe*

PART 2

The marketing mix

7 Product positioning and competitive edge

Chapter objectives:

- to understand product positioning in the context of the market economy
- to understand the role of the price/quality relationship in product positioning
- to explore the concept of product differentiation in terms of 'value added' – e.g. delivery of product and commensurate service rather than tangible product benefits
- to examine what is a brand and how it is differentiated from its competitors
- to consider the topical subject of brand valuation

Introduction

The term **'product positioning'** is commonplace in traditional marketing theory and practice because these have evolved from the developed free markets of the United States and Western Europe. It took on a significant meaning in what was East Germany only in 1989, when the people there were able to travel to the West and exert choice in how they spent their money on a particular category of goods. In contrast, state-run economies which provide for a staple form of a product to fulfil specific needs (from soap to socks) do not encourage the provision of alternatives as this activity is not rewarded through profit.

Consideration of the most important of the four Ps – the product itself – cannot therefore take place outside the context of the **market economy**. This assumes that individuals pursue their own self-interest in buying the best merchandise at the lowest price while producers seek to sell at the best price in order to maximize the gap between that price and their costs (their profit). The customer's best interests are served by

competition, the most perfect existing when there are no barriers to market entry (such as technological or capital requirements), and no organization exerts more influence in the market than others. In practice, these conditions are rarely fulfilled, and pure market forces are tempered by political, cultural or historical factors. **Oligopoly**, where two or three organizations control supply, and therefore pricing, in a market is common (for example, national distribution of petrol).

The more extreme situation of **monopoly**, where one organization controls the source of supply, and therefore the price, is evident, for example, in the world diamond market where De Beers controls over 90% of supply. The existence of state monopolies is not the preserve of socialist states. Developed economies which have a tradition of democracy have frequently been characterized by state control of utilities (power and water). The state agency responsible for distribution is charged with meeting financial targets for investment as well as covering running costs, and the pricing policy will reflect this. Where the public monopoly becomes a private monopoly, there is a danger that the profit motive can obscure the need to provide a good product at a reasonable price.

This **price/quality** relationship is the pivot around which product positioning revolves in the contemporary competitive climate. As real disposable income increases and all essentials are available to the majority of a population, then the discretionary spending element provides the opportunity to base buying decisions on non-price factors. This is equally true of industrial buying, where reliability and ease of communication with a supplier could be more important than the simple price comparison.

The role of price in contemporary marketing management is explored in Chapter 8. Therefore, the focus here is to identify the phenomenon of **product differentiation** and what it means for the consumer, the firm and the national economy. It is explored in the context of **'value added'**. For the 1990s and beyond, product differentiation will be increasingly difficult to achieve through the traditional route of tangible benefits. There will be increasing focus on *how* the product will be delivered with the emphasis on customer service. A corollary of this is the increasing role that **service industries** play in the national economy. Apart from the lack of a marketing tradition in these business areas, there is a core problem of fashioning products to make them sufficiently different from the competition, and being able to communicate these differences in a coherent way. Two examples are used here to illustrate some of the issues: the financial services sector and the 'health' industry.

The second part of the chapter examines those aspects of business activity which contribute to the 'value added' of a product. These are innovation, design, quality, people and culture.

Finally, the discussion moves from the qualitative to the quantitative, where methods of measurement of attributes which make a **brand** different from its competition are examined. The chapter concludes with examination of the controversy surrounding **brand valuation**, where the intangible asset of goodwill surrounding the brand has traditionally had a value put on it only on acquisition. Why do companies wish to change this accounting convention? In answering this question, an attempt is made to identify the interaction between financial and marketing objec-tives, and to illustrate how the prevailing economic climate can induce 'short-termism' to the detriment of longer-term organic growth of compa-nies through investment in the technology for product development and in the advertising necessary for brand building.

Product differentiation

In primitive societies, tribes would obtain the full range of food and mate-rials that they needed by bartering those that they could produce or har-vest for those that they could not. Even in this situation, there is the element of choice in selecting the highest quality or best 'value' that they could achieve for a given quantity of goods exchanged. As societies evolved, the role of money was to fix a value of 'exchange', and floating exchange rates for different currencies indicate the 'market' that has been created for money itself.

Differences between product offerings were initially 'tangible' – in the taste, size, appearance and texture of food, or the speed, precision and space required for an industrial machine. As companies became more adept at communicating with their customers, so they were able to trans-late evolving customer needs into 'intangible' benefits that were illus-trated and reinforced through advertising. Such benefits as 'reliability', 'modern', 'exotic' or 'healthy' could be imparted without drawing on factual evidence, although some companies would make a point of using this technique to support the brand positioning (Procter & Gamble with Crest toothpaste and Vortex household cleanser).

The power of television advertising in particular could be harnessed to convey imagery through the affective (or 'feeling') communication process as well as the cognitive (or 'thinking') channel, to produce action tendencies based on a total perception of a brand.

What is a brand?

A brand is the representation of all the properties, features and attributes of a product which provide **value** to the potential customer, and this value is greater than the simple sum of the constituent tangible properties. The embodiment of brand value takes the form of visible and easily identifiable signs, designs and words, whose meanings in the minds of the consumer have been established through consistent portrayal of the benefits associated with use or consumption of products available under the name or sign, over time. For some brands, like detergents or confectionery lines, the values associated with them have been built over several decades. However, the single-mindedness of the product strategy does not eliminate the need for change in order to maintain the contemporary appeal of a product, and the small changes that occur, for example, in packaging, invariably pass unnoticed by the majority of brand users, but would be noticed if they did *not* occur.

The increasing availability of mass media has meant that product life cycles (where it is accepted that these are inevitable) are getting shorter. Where 'fashion' plays a dominant role in product perception, then a brand may be in a position to establish notoriety in a matter of months rather than years, as in the case of the Swatch watch. However, companies operating in these markets must protect themselves from the very changes in fashion that have provided success, through constant innovation of products designed for different market segments.

One way of doing this is to extend the 'cachet' of the brand name over several product areas. The name 'Giorgio Armani' conjures up visions of exclusive one-off fashion creations that are rarely seen off the Milan catwalk. The reality of how the name is used to cater for different markets is rather different. The exclusive designs are seen as advertising tools rather than profit earners. Armani has one set of 'diffusion' designs produced in small numbers for smaller, exclusive retail outlets, and another range produced by larger manufacturers for a wider target group. Each range is differentiated from another by price concept and content. This marketing machine also extends to accessories such as perfume and sunglasses. Very few British designers have been able to emulate this marketing approach, as the mass of British consumers has been conditioned by the large retailing groups into using the five per cent of consumer spending that is allocated to clothes on many cheaper items rather than a few well-designed clothes.

Another fashion company which tried to extend the brand franchise is Levi Strauss. In the early 1980s the company extended the Levi's name from jeans to other clothes and shoes. Jean sales suffered, and were only rescued when Levi's returned to the core business and engineered the highly successful 501 relaunch. This indicated that the brand name could not be extended beyond the original product, and other ways would have to be found to develop new business, as the successful introduction of Chinos trousers testified.

Using the 'umbrella' of a strong, established brand name for new product launches is a temptation that is not restricted to the fashion industry. As early as the 1920s, the Wall's meat pie and sausage company looked for ways of augmenting sales in the flat summer season, and decided on ice-cream. Both product areas now sit comfortably within the Unilever portfolio under the Wall's name, but operated by different divisions. In contrast to this entrepreneurial gesture, the risk of launching another product under the Mars name would have been thoroughly researched before the company did, in fact, launch the Mars ice-cream in 1989.

Extension in the use of an established brand name runs the risk of diluting consumer perceptions of what the brand name stands for and, in the more serious cases, of actually damaging the brand name through the wrong associations. This has been the case with some French designer labels where quality control of the merchandise licensed to carry the name has been overlooked.

Corporate image and branding

Many of the large multinational consumer goods companies choose to maintain separate identities for each of their major brands, and to keep a low profile for the company name and associated image. The rationale here is that the vast advertising budget allocated to each major brand is supporting a specific mix of benefits communicated to an identified target group. Adding the company name complicates the message without adding strong 'halo effects' to the brand.

However, the company name would need to be presented in a favourable light to the City institutions, and more targeted public relations exercises would be of most use here, to focus attention on the performance of the organization in managing its portfolio of brands.

Other conglomerates take a different view, and the Lyons Tetley name frequently appears in the final frame of television advertising for new and existing brands. Some advertising to the consumer is more of a public relations exercise than an outright attempt to increase sales. The major petrol companies, BP and Shell, use attractive visuals and a reassuring tone of voice to emphasise damage limitation to the environment. This suggests that the traditional position of market share being determined by distribution strength rather than by product differentiation is under challenge, as perceptions of effects on the environment are increasingly expected to change buying behaviour among a large percentage of consumers.

Corporate identity can replace the brand where the individual product might not be significant enough in its own right, may be too complex to communicate in traditional advertising or where a product may be customized for each customer. A successful case history is the relaunch of the Prudential name and identity (through contemporary design of the virtue 'Prudence' in the form of a woman's head) to take it away from the 'Man from the Pru' traditional insurance origins and to create an image consistent with a major European financial institution (Olins, 1989).

This area is expected to grow in importance where issues of social conscience are likely to interact with aspects of corporate activity. The combined social conscience of several hundred thousand customers will influence boardroom decisions in the 1990s in a way that would not have been possible 20 years ago. This phenomenon is fuelling activity such as Abbey National, the major British building society (and now bank), pledging to plant acres of trees to replace those lost in the production of 450 tonnes of prospectuses issued during its public flotation. It is spawning new businesses, such as the creation of unit trusts with 'conscience' portfolios, which exclude environmentally hazardous products and those by which personal health can be damaged.

The market opportunity created by the new public attitude towards caring for the environment has encouraged companies like Loblaw, a Canadian food distributor, to launch its own-label green brand in 1989. The company chose a range of around 100 products as being environmentally sound (Economist, 1989). Major manufacturers of products traditionally associated with pollution have had to conduct detailed research to identify what quality sacrifices their customers are prepared to make in order to reduce environmental damage. In practice, companies able to make substantiated environmental claims without the product quality suffering will win in the long run, but this will be expensive in terms of research, process and raw materials.

Brand advertising and added value

The creative hook around which an advertising message is built must draw on contemporary lifestyle and culture, while accommodating the key benefits of the strategy statement. Achievement of this balance to the satisfaction of demanding clients marks out advertising that is successful in terms of product sales and market share from advertising that merely wins creative awards.

However, the barriers to achieving this type of success for new consumer products are formidable. As well as needing a significant budget to achieve reasonable awareness and penetration levels, the manufacturer has become a hostage to the buying powers of the large retailing groups, which impose stringent conditions tantamount to the 'purchasing' of shelf-space through discounts. Where the manufacturer can know product performance at store level within weeks, the retailer will know it within hours and can react. The emergence of **generic products** (see Table 7.1) and **own-label products** (see Table 7.2) are case histories of the failure and success, respectively, of the retailers to capitalize on distribution strength to develop added value for their own products.

Manufacturers under pressure to discount rather than spend funds on supporting brand benefits have developed sophisticated techniques for assessing, on the basis of historic performance, whether to spend each extra pound or dollar available for marketing support on retailer discount or brand advertising. Perhaps the most valuable asset in difficult market conditions is a strong negotiating team within national account management.

Table 7.1 The emergence and decline of generic products.

Definition	Commodity food and household lines which were sold pre-weighed in basic packaging, without the additional benefits traditionally associated with branded lines. These **generics** were sold by the major food retailers under their own name.
History	1976: Carrefour launched a line of 50 'produits libres' in France. 1977: International launched a generic range in UK, followed by Fine Fare (1980), Allied Suppliers and Tesco (1981). No generics remained by 1987.
Pricing	Generally 40% lower than branded goods; 20% lower than own-label.
Prognosis	Generics perceived by consumers to be similar to own-label, and this had a damaging effect on the image of these lines. Generics also took up shelf space otherwise occupied by higher-margin lines, and retailer margins suffered (de Chernatony, 1988).

Table 7.2 The success of retailers' own-labels.

Definition	'Own-label products are consumer products produced by, or on behalf of, distributors and sold under the distributor's own name or trademark through the distributor's own outlet' (Morris, 1979).
History	Originated in the 1970s as a cost-cutting exercise during a period of high inflation; retailers encouraged manufacturers to provide grocery lines in the retailers' own packaging at lower prices than manufacturers' branded lines. This protected retailer margins and the retailer market share through lower consumer prices.
Pricing	Originally 10–20% lower than branded alternatives. Some own-labels now perceived as of equal or higher quality (such as Marks and Spencer's St Michael label), with pricing to match.
Trends	Own-labels accounted for £21 billion UK sales in 1986; forecast is £27 billion in 1990, with 27% share of retail sales.

	Own-label as % all sales	
	1982	1991
Safeway	15	40
Asda	8	40
Gateway	6	38
Marks and Spencer	100	100
Sainsbury	53	53
Tesco	33	53

Source: Marketpower.

Prognosis	Examination of consumer perceptions in six product categories (bleach, toilet paper, washing-up liquid, aluminium foil, kitchen towels and disinfectant) indicates that branded products are seen as distinct from own-label, and that this will continue while manufacturers support brands with advertising (de Chernatony, 1989).

Marketing of services

A **service** is the provision of an intangible benefit to a producer, intermediary or consumer in return for payment. This benefit may take the form of improved access to goods, such as through wholesalers and retailers, transportation, telecommunications, repair and servicing of hardware, provision of human resources (employment agencies) and financial resources (banking), training, education and healthcare. The wide range of technical and professional expertise provided in the form of architectural and engineering practices, management consultancy and scientific research contracts to universities contrasts with the mechanistic approach to service evident with the fast-food chains.

There are two stages of evolution of service industries within an economy:

(1) The industrial base has not kept pace with other countries for lack of investment and expertise, and a large part of the workforce must seek employment in providing a service to others, often at low wages or on a self-employed basis. Countries with a warm climate and a tradition for personalized tourist hospitality are typical here. It may also be true of a specific geographical region of an otherwise developed economy.

(2) Following an industrialized phase of economic growth, the climate is created for more service provision for the following reasons:
    (a) increased spending power of the population (a reflection of increased GDP *per capita*);
    (b) technological developments in manufacturing enabling the reduction of labour requirement;
    (c) growth in leisure time;
    (d) demographic trends: an aging population requires more service provision, particularly in health care;
    (e) management skill in exploiting opportunities: there is greater corporate presence in services, having developed sophisticated business concepts through marketing.

Moves towards a freer market through internal legislation and the the external forces of European harmonization have had a strong impact on professional services, where the traditional 'gentlemen's agreement' between client and advisor has been replaced by a more commercial contractual arrangement through the forces of competition. In accountancy, the mergers of leading names to create 'mega-partnerships' has created the opportunity for economy of scale and the marketing of a range of consultancy services as 'add-ons' to the core activity of auditing.

In the legal profession, the increasing incidence of mergers and adoption of the marketing concept occurred a few years after the accountants. The Law Society published *Best Practice – Marketing* in 1989, and the Institute of Chartered Accountants admitted in early 1991 that it was examining the potential conflict of interest where an accountancy firm provides both auditing services and management consultancy to the same client. This followed a series of company receiverships caused through the inability to finance heavy levels of debt incurred for expansion in the mid to late 1980s.

There are two important trends in relation to the area of service provision. Firstly, there is increasing dependence on expertise in a particular functional or resource area. Secondly, where there is the option that a service can be provided in the public sector (government financed and managed) or the private sector, through the mechanism of the free market, then there has been a trend towards the latter.

Example

A major example of the latter trend is the reorganization of the British National Health Service with the introduction of the concept of self-managing hospitals as trusts from April 1991. A major objective of the new approach was that health services should be planned and run with a sensitivity to the needs of the 'customer'. An assumption was made that the best way of imposing the necessary checks and controls to meet this objective was through the providers of the service managing budgets, rather than the traditional method of health authorities allocating funds against estimated need.

The facts outlined in Table 7.3 illustrate the size of the task faced by health service managers in changing culture in order to improve efficiency so that each unit of resource bought more by way of patient care. The pivotal force for success in this change is identified as providing consumer choice (which may be translated into the choice made by a 'budget carrying' general practitioner on behalf of the patient). This, in turn, leads to the need for hospitals to price specific operations and services and for general practitioners to seek the best value, which includes speed and quality of health provision.

Table 7.3 The National Health Service and accountability.

Annual budget	32 billion pounds sterling
Employees	1 million
Hospital beds	285,000
Cases per bed	23 per year
In-patients	6.6 million
Day cases	1 million
Out-patients	36.5 million
Emergency cases	14 million
Theatre operations	3.5 million

April 1991 reorganization To provide better health care and improved services to patients and to give people working in the NHS better job satisfaction.

Underlying principle remains the same National Health Service will be available to everyone, will be paid for mainly out of taxation and will be mostly free at the point of use.

Performance control criteria policy, planning and budgeting, quality, economy, equity, accountability. Ratios appropriate to (1) Hospital Management and (2) General Practice need to be identified and monitored.

The auditing process[†] will identify:

economy	low cost
efficiency	optimizing output from resources
effectiveness	results.

[†]Price Waterhouse, 1990.

The investment made in computer information systems to facilitate these changes was generally focused on cost per unit of patient care (such as specific operations performed, out-patient visits for a given ailment or drugs dispensed). However, as the new form of budget management becomes widespread, there is the parallel pressure to evaluate customer satisfaction. An early example of this was the research carried out by the Community Health Services Department of Riverside Health Authority into customer perception of how well women's health care needs were catered for by the existing Family Planning Clinic (Chambers, 1987). The results indicated that a broader range of services was required by women than simple contraception, and the name of the unit was changed along with the way in which a range of services was available, but with no additional recurring costs.

Theory of service marketing and the needs of the 1990s

Traditional theory expounds four features of a service which distinguish it from other products:

(1)   The main benefit of performance is intangible (it cannot be touched, seen or tasted, although proof of the service having been performed may be, such as the arrival of food in a restaurant).

(2)   Production and consumption are inseparable: this is usually a function of personnel available to provide the service where and when it is needed.

(3)   The service is perishable: some costs are incurred whether or not there are customers at a particular time and place.

(4)   The service is heterogeneous: there is a variation in the provision which is primarily a function of the individuals providing it.

By the nature of the definition of a service, the first point is immutable, but the other three are open to challenge as service providers evolve creative and complex ways of meeting customer needs. This is happening because of three influences: intense competition as some service markets reach saturation (as with financial services), a more educated and informed customer base, and technological developments providing alternative means of delivery.

The concept of inseparability breaks down when considering the provision of information services, where on-line access means that the customer can obtain the service on a 24-hour basis but the 'production' of the latest information takes place at a particular time each day. This is also true for some banking services. In general, service industries have exhibited a higher percentage of total investment intensity going to information technology than other industries. So, for example in 1984, the wholesale sector spent 17.7% of investment on IT, and the retail and repair sector 16.3%, whereas the food sector spent 5.4%, and the drink and tobacco sector 8.3% (Teare, 1990).

The concept of perishability becomes a liability where demand cannot be estimated with any degree of accuracy. To reduce commercial risk, companies are adopting sophisticated ways of estimating and also manipulating demand and are using resources (particularly people) more flexibly to reduce the 'loss' through service supply outstripping demand. In many ways the lessons learnt from the adoption of **just-in-time** production are being applied to the service sector. An outstanding example of this is the daily delivery of goods to supermarkets to match demand.

Wherever people are the main instrument of service provision, then there will be an associated heterogeneity of performance, but competitive forces and the search for excellence mean that recruitment and training programmes within organizations are geared to achieving a high degree of uniformity. Forward-thinking companies in the service sector, from hoteliers to construction engineers, have applied for and obtained British Standard BS 5750. This was originally written in 1979 as a management standard for organizations' quality control. Companies now use it as an assurance of consistent and high quality of performance. Since it requires a manual detailing of every procedure, there is a marked impact on the working culture in an organization.

The traditional concept of the service offering being split into three distinct levels – core service, tangible element and augmented element – is helpful to companies in deciding how to differentiate their product from the competition. For example, all estate agents provide the core service of a link between property buyer and seller with the efficient transfer of information between the two. The tangible element is the office environment which very often forms the first point of contact. The augmented element is the provision of a wide range of back-up services which would include advice on mortgages and insurance.

However, in a very competitive market, the fundamentals of the service should be re-examined in order to provide a solution to customer problems which fit in with their needs and lifestyle. Sellers will be looking for evidence of advertising to prospective purchasers who in turn will be looking for market coverage by the agent. Sellers will be looking for negotiating skill, speed of transaction and convenience. In meeting these needs some agents see accompanied visits of prospective buyers to properties as part of their core service, rather than an occasional inconvenience to be tolerated when the vendor is not at home.

The competitive market for mobile telephone services provides a contrasting situation, where additional 'bolt-on' services are available at a price. Cellnet makes available to its subscribers a link with British Telecom's centralized answering service 'Voicebank' and a radiopager, so that when the subscriber is not available to take a call, a message can be relayed and a return call made. This augmented service turns the potential for one call into three calls, with 10–12% increase in revenue per subscriber.

UK marketing of financial services

The Building Societies Act of 1986 extended the range of services that traditional British building societies could offer the general public, and enabled them to compete with the high street clearing banks in such areas as current accounts with cheque facilities as well as standard saving accounts. The Abbey National Building Society took the further step of becoming a public limited company. In 1988, the Financial Services Act introduced a raft of provisions for the protection of investors, including the polarization of those advising on, or selling, financial products into organizations selling only their own products on the one hand, and those offering independent advice on the other.

These changes, plus the fact that the clearing banks were already offering mortgages, the traditional domain of building societies, meant that marketing of financial services became very competitive. With the credit boom of 1980s, growth in demand meant that the major players were well content with performance. However, high interest rates at the end of the decade and a downturn in the housing market (with which so many financial service contracts are linked) meant a reappraisal of marketing strategies and operational efficiencies.

Major clearing banks needed to assess strategy on several fronts:

- Geographical coverage – high streets were becoming 'over-banked'. Which branches were cost-effective?
- Core services to provide a competitive edge, such as efficient current account management.
- Development of information technology capabilities in line with more defined targeting of products through direct marketing.
- Streamlining of operations, such as centralized cheque processing and regional centres for small business advice, to reduce the cost-to-sales ratio (which was as high as 75% in some banks compared with less than 50% for some building societies).

The level of commitment to the marketing concept within each organization determined how far each was successful in addressing these issues. For example, Midland Bank broke new ground with its distinctive advertising for the First Direct telephone banking service.

Although by the late 1980s all the major banks had accepted marketing as an important functional area, research indicated that just over half of financial service companies interviewed believed themselves to be market-driven as opposed to finance or operations-driven (Hooley and Mann, 1988). The career background of the chief executive officer was primarily in finance or operations, and the status of the chief marketing executive tended to be lower than or equal to counterparts in finance and operations. Of particular concern was the high proportion (two in five) of chief marketing executives without marketing experience before taking on the role. Most of the organizations sampled reported the existence of a specialist marketing department, but its responsibilities were frequently limited to research and promotional work.

Banks, building societies and unit trusts are all becoming aware of the power of the corporate database as a marketing tool. However, effective use of this requires access by those skilled in the segmentation and promotional techniques of direct marketing. Where control of resources remains in the hands of financial or operational managers, there is the danger that competitive advantage will be lost. For example, some clearing banks were in the position of assessing and merging customer data banks as late as 1990. In contrast, some building societies had achieved the more advanced stage of having custom-built software for information access and analysis. Included within this format would be detailed calculations of levels of response to particular mailings, cost per conversion of a prospect to a customer, and profitability per customer. The ability to segment a database by response history and purchasing patterns will be a minimum requirement for the 1990s.

The components of added value

Contemporary marketing theory has been developed in conditions of economic growth fuelled in the past three decades by the increasing affluence and expenditure of individuals in the developed nations. As all tangible needs are satisfied in these markets, corporations must look to less developed markets for growth through sale of their existing products, or must provide demonstrably superior products to satisfy increasing expectations of the home market. To do this, there has to be a commitment to **innovation** with the vision, investment and risk that this entails.

Innovation can take the form of a totally new idea, such as slow-release drug implants, or the value-added element takes the form of a **design** improvement measured in ergonomic or aesthetic terms. The additional benefit has to be sufficient to induce the target market to replace an existing (and possibly, obsolete) product and to pay an enhanced price. Where the in-use experience of a number of customers, for example in electrical appliances, leads to a reputation for **quality** and reliability, then this factor can provide the basis of a price premium. In service industries, consistent quality will be linked with the **people** delivering this service and the **culture** within which they operate. These components of value added are explored in the following four sections.

Innovation as a value-added component

A technological breakthrough will only lead to commercial success where the management skills of the organization are harnessed to exploit the development. In particular, marketing skills are needed to match benefits to needs and to communicate and deliver, while financial skills are needed to ensure an adequate supply of investment capital for the development and launch stages, and to identify the profit rewards following launch.

An inflationary environment has a negative effect on investment plans as companies look to short-term survival, adjusting prices to meet escalating costs and reducing stock levels as recession hits demand. This squeeze on investment reduces the level of innovation, as distinct from invention.

Invention is an idea, outline or model for a new product or process. **Innovation** 'in the economic sense is accomplished only with the first *commercial* transaction involving the new product, process, system or device, although the word is also used to describe the whole process' (Freeman, 1982). Innovation, as perceived as a process, is examined in the context of new product development in Chapter 16.

It was only in the 1960s that many economists began to take seriously the role of innovation in the form of investment in **research and development**. By this time, major companies had formalized the activity through the creation of cost centres and management hierarchies. Past successes fuelled the search for new sources of profit. Companies committed a percentage of research funding to speculative areas where research scientists worked within very wide terms of reference to follow hunches and rely on the forces of serendipity.

The *modus operandi* within those research laboratories that continued to exist into the 1990s reflects a much tighter control on the way researchers use their time, and the reporting systems ensure that commercial objectives remain the driving force.

Government spending on research and development (R & D) reflects different socio-economic objectives in different countries, and is a major influence on national wealth creation. The heavy emphaisis of some nations on defence R & D spending has been justified on the basis of the 'spin-off' effects of the innovations in other fields. From Table 7.4 it is evident that the USA, UK and France placed great emphasis on military R & D funding in the 1970s and 1980s whereas Japan and Germany showed a greater commitment to funding for energy and infrastructure, and agriculture and industry. These comparative statistics have to be viewed in the historical context of the period, but go some way to explaining differential rates of economic growth during the 1980s, both Japan and Germany having successfully invested in innovation which would ultimately translate into export capability at the industrial and consumer level.

One strategy available to the marketing company is that of market leadership. It is an attractive one because the PIMS study (see Chapter 15) indicates that return on investment increases with market share. There is significant evidence to indicate that being first in the market with a new design or technological advantage creates the opportunity to become market or niche leader. This is illustrated by Vauxhall's (General Motors)

Table 7.4 International comparison of government funding for research and development by socio-economic category.

| | Percentage of government funding in 1980 | | | | |
	USA	Japan[+]	Germany	UK	France
Defence	47.0	3.6	14.2	59.4	40.9
Space	14.4	9.3	6.0	2.3	5.0
Civil aeronautics	1.6	–	2.3	3.4	2.4
Health and welfare	15.2	8.3	13.9	3.9	7.6
Energy and infrastructure	15.3	23.8	29.1	10.1	16.5
Agriculture and industry	2.6	32.3	14.3	7.9	11.9

[+]Figures are for 1979.
Source: OECD, 1981. Figures for key spending categories have been aggregated from a more detailed analysis.

introduction of the Cavalier in 1982. This had an impact on the Ford Cortina market share, which dominated the fleet market. Ford responded with the Sierra in 1983, but only regained market leadership in 1986. Ford's profitability in those four years was heavily dented by the share loss and the advertising expenditure necessary to restore it to the level before 1982 (Little, 1991).

The launch of a new car takes years of planning and design but the engineering advances may only be incremental with each new model. A company involved in process equipment will build in technological improvements as they are discovered by the development engineers, in order to stay ahead of the competition. This illustrates the fluid nature of innovation. A company which stands still and withdraws investment from the products of the future will ultimately sacrifice added value, premium pricing and profit margin.

To keep up with shorter product life cycles, an innovative approach to project management is also necessary. The sequential approach (design to engineering to production to marketing) has been displaced by multidisciplinary teams working together at each stage to hasten the product to market.

The major step from invention to innovation frequently needs an enlightened intermediary that acts as a broker of ideas. National culture dictates whether this falls within the remit of a government agency (the Ministry of International Trade and Industry, or MITI, has influence in Japan), or whether market forces alone should dictate outcome. British Technology Group (BTG), the world's largest and most successful technology transfer company, was privatized in 1991. Its traditional success had come from the trust that inventors and potential licensees placed in the group to be impartial in the exploitation of ideas. Ownership of BTG by an industrial company could jeopardize perceptions of this integrity.

Patent protection

So that organizations can protect new inventions while they are under-going testing and commercialization, each novel feature of a machine, component, process or formula may be the subject of a **patent**. By filing a patent application with the relevant authority in each country where commercial exploitation of the invention is both possible and desirable, the novel aspect is protected for sole use of the applicant for a specified period.

Because development periods for products such as ethical pharma-ceuticals can take up a sizeable proportion of the patent life (with extensive clinical and safety trials), there is pressure on the company to maximize price and profits in the early part of the commercial life of the product before so-called 'generics' make their way onto the market. The same pressure encourages the parallel commercialization in several major markets, which requires considerable reserves for marketing and distribution. This has led to mergers within the industry so that individual players have immediate access to key markets.

Design as a value-added component

A company that is technology-led rather than market-led will focus on engineering design as the core product advantage, which can be defined as 'the use of scientific principles, technical information and imagination in the definition of a mechanical structure, machine or system to perform pre-specified functions with the maximum economy and efficiency'. (*Engineering and Industrial Design,* a report of the Committee of the Council for Scientific and Industrial Research).

Even in the early 1970s it was appreciated that industrial design could not be considered in isolation from the user:

> 'Industrial design is tightly interwoven with and dependent on the **socio-economic context** in which it is exercised. It is concerned with the improvement of usability of industrial products which form part of the overall **quality** of a product'.
> (*Development Through Design,* Bonsiepe, UNIDO, Austria, 1973).

Industrial design is primarily concerned with formal properties which can be measured in objective ways:

- speed of operation for a machine
- energy consumption for a given unit of output
- rejects per thousand units produced (quality control)
- machine downtime in transferring from one product to another
- number of operators required (level of automation)
- flexibility: potential use for several products or processes

An increasing awareness of working conditions as part of the 'socio-economic' context has focused on the relationship between people and machines. This evaluation of the **ergonomics** of a new machine or process will include mental fatigue due to repetition, as well as the physical burdens and environment imposed by it. Laws governing health and safety at work will be regarded by some organizations as the standards to which they are operating. Others will see these as the bare minimum, and will strive to achieve a working environment which reflects the same quality standards as the product they are marketing. From small family businesses to major conglomerates, the culture of the organization will be revealed in the level of harmony between man and machine, which sees its reward in a satisfied customer.

The market-led company will identify customer needs now and in the future before setting in train the complex and invariably expensive **design process**. This begins with the **specification** which incorporates features and performance criteria that may include ease of use and maintenance, costs, working life, reliability and appearance. The design team produces ideas that are screened against technical and financial feasibility criteria. The selected idea passes on to the **development** stage with the production of one or more prototypes.

For products where the capital outlay is high, customer feedback at this stage is invaluable, but requires strict control to protect confidentiality. The lengthiest part of the total process can be initial tooling for production, in which quality and performance standards are rigorously applied to make sure that production models meet initial specifications.

Given the incremental nature of much design performance, there is the opportunity for a company that has lost competitive edge on the technological front to catch up with a strong design team and commitment of the necessary resources. A classic example is the development of British Leyland's 1100/1300 series which was based on radical design changes. In contrast, the Ford Cortina was launched with four basic models offering a variety of small changes to different customers (Rothwell *et al.*, 1983, for The Design Council). The customer choice was far wider than provided by BL in the period 1962–67, and while the 1300cc engine was under development, the 1100cc model could compete only at the bottom end of the Ford range and hence BL lost share to Ford. This case illustrates that innovation on its own is not enough for commercial success. There must also be an awareness of how such developments will satisfy the emerging needs of different sectors of the market.

The commitment of different countries to design as an essential partner to technical innovation is reflected in the pattern of trade between nations. Where design makes a product visually appealing as well as technically and ergonomically superior, then the consumer will respond where there are no barriers to imports. Some countries have developed special industry strengths based on traditional culture or government-sponsored effort in particular areas of innovation.

Quality as a value-added component

The intangible aspects of measures of quality for many organizations, particularly those in the service sectors, highlight the contribution of management and worker attitudes, culture and commitment to the provision of a 'quality' product. Although managerial and process controls are necessary to implement a programme of quality improvement, these mechanistic devices are unlikely to deliver in a cultural vacuum.

The famous **quality circles** of Japan were successful because of the long-term commitment of managers and workers at all levels to achieving common goals. If necessary, these goals would be explored and agreed over an extended period in order to assure the commitment of everyone involved in the process.

In Britain, too much emphasis on functional quality control and computer-aided manufacture can obscure the need to see beyond the short-term demands of financial managers and city institutions. A commitment to quality can mean additional costs in both managerial time and enhanced machinery and materials. This has been the traditional defence for acceptance of existing standards of performance. However, Dr W. Edwards Deming put forward the alternative hypothesis that improving quality ultimately brings down costs, develops the market and secures a better return on investment. This view provided the impetus for Japan's post-war industrial reconstruction during the 1950s.

BS 5750 as the international standard for quality systems

British Standard BS 5750 was originally written in 1979 as a management standard for an organization's quality control. However, its current role is more far-reaching. It sets out how an organization can develop, document and maintain an effective quality system appropriate to its own needs. It does not attempt to define the quality standards for a product or service but sets out the principles by which these can be identified and achieved so that a particular industry or set of customers is confident of the quality outcome of a supplier's product.

Small and medium-sized companies have been known to commit considerable resources to achieving BS 5750 because they are aware of the need to reassure customers of consistent quality for survival in lean times as well as growth when the market is buoyant. The step-by-step procedure requires commitment to management control and line procedures which can revolutionize the way in which an organization plans, develops, produces and inspects a product; trained and qualified staff are essential to this process (Collard, 1989).

Quality of relationship between the organization, its suppliers and customers

Information technology is playing an increasing role in service enhancement. This can be achieved through better information on the product, delivered more swiftly and in a form convenient to the customer. This facilitates the purchase decision and can provide an interactive medium for acting upon it.

However, for some products and services, this reliance on computers is supportive to the main provision which is still people-led and involves customer contact. This interface will be a critical element of quality perception.

The traditional view has been that quality perceptions of the organization by suppliers are not important as the relationship is essentially an adversarial one. However, certain US companies motivated by the desire to reduce costs and upgrade quality have moved towards a relationship with suppliers based on cooperation and coordination.

Rockwell's survey among its vendors in USA and selected foreign countries measured perceptions of the organization along ten dimensions including quality, ethics, policies and procedures and organization effectiveness. The same dimensions were tested simultaneously among customers and employees (Goldstein and Howe, 1988).

Based on the results of this research, Rockwell identified an action plan to make the company more customer-centred, obtaining a commitment to quality at all organization levels.

Where an organization wishes to do this, the absence of any clear definition of 'quality' can make the task difficult in the early stages. One approach for services is to close the *gap* between the consumers' expectation of service quality and their perception of that actually delivered (Lewis, 1989). This does not differ significantly from the concept of cognitive dissonance, in which a product does not live up to the expectations built through advertising. However, according to Lewis, there are four ways in which the situation has arisen for a service:

(1) Management's perceptions of customer desires are different from the real desires.
(2) Service quality specifications are different from customer expectations. This could be due to lack of resources or straightforward ineptitude.
(3) The service that is delivered is different from management specifications for service quality.
(4) The way in which the service is described in advertising is different from the reality of service delivery. (This leads to **cognitive dissonance**.)

People as a value-added component

Where delivery of a service is concerned, the commitment and training of the employees who are providing it will be a critical element in the value created for the customer. Organizations in which the culture is geared towards quality at every level will institute mechanisms for feedback from the customer to ensure that standards laid down are being met. Where a retailer such as Marks and Spencer is exacting very high standards from its suppliers, personnel within these companies must also adopt a quality mantle, and be prepared for spot checks without prior notification.

Where a company is taking the financial risk of design, development and marketing of a radically new product, then the quality of and relationships between the functional specialists take on an added dimension. In-house specialists can form a coherent team with knowledge of, and commitment to the organizational culture. An alternative approach is to use a respected and creative design consultant to act as a catalyst for new ideas which are then interpreted by the in-house team of production engineers. The designer Kenneth Grange acted in the capacity of 'consultant design director' for both Wilkinson Sword and part of the Thorn–EMI group. The latter relationship gave rise to his successful design for the Kenwood Chef food mixer, which is just one example of many of his designs which leave their mark on everyday life (Lorenz, 1990). Kenneth Grange was committed to the combination of form and function and believed that products should be attractive to see as well as pleasurable to use. This commitment manifested itself in an ability to work well with clients' engineers through a respect for their technical capabilities.

This type of respect is the cultural norm in manufacturing companies in Germany, who see their position in the market as relying on the quality of the product and their effectiveness at making it.

Brand building and quantitative techniques

The different values that contribute to the branded product have been explored, and the essence of the brand is that the whole is greater than the sum of the constituent parts. This is achieved through communication of key benefits which establish an image of superiority in the minds of the target audience.

Where large sums are invested in advertising, the company must reassure itself that the brand will achieve a viable positioning against competition, both at launch and later in the brand's history as consumer needs evolve.

Measuring brand attributes

The most common form of quantitative assessment of brand performance is by measuring consumer response to **attribute** measures. There will be a battery of properties or characteristics which will be associated with a particular product category. For example, the following attributes might be considered important when assessing the perceived performance of a food mixer: efficiency, flexibility (or suitability for a range of tasks), ease of use, convenient size, visual design, ease of cleaning.

The traditional approach is to take a representative sample from the universe of category users, which can mean a sample of between 300 and 600 respondents. The questioning technique that has yielded actionable results for a large number of consumer products is the bi-polar Likert Scale, and a scale of from (1) to (7) is popular. For in-home appliances there is the added complication that recent experience of more than one model is unlikely, and valid results can only be achieved through the more artificial scenario of in-home placement of the test model among users of either the model to be superseded, or the competitive product.

An illustration of a brand attribute analysis which might result from research into two models of food mixer is shown in Figure 7.1. By aggregating the responses over the total sample, the diagrammatic approach of the analysis provides immediate clues as to the relative strengths and weaknesses of the test model. Action can be taken in the form of product improvement or a changed advertising message or, more frequently, a combination of these two. Before this stage, it is also necessary to have a clear indication as to the relative importance of the different attributes to the consumer.

Moving away from consumer durables to repeat-purchase products, innovation from a competitor or changing consumer needs can create a perceived weakness in a brand in a matter of months rather than years.

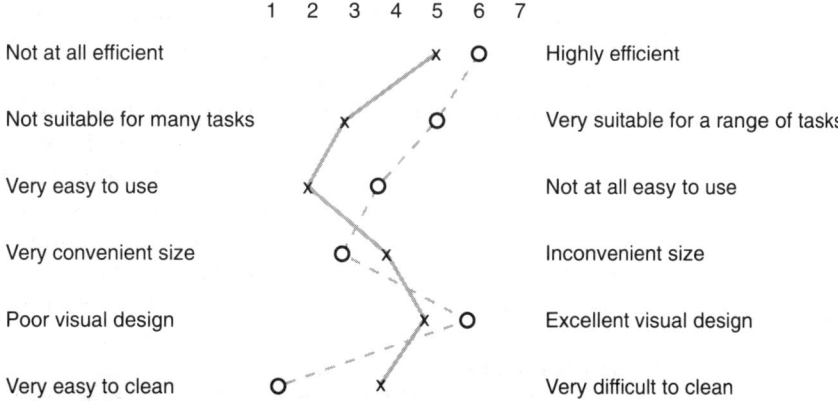

Figure 7.1 Illustration of a brand attribute analysis for competitive models of food mixer.

Changing dietary habits through the quest for good health created the need for decaffeinated coffee and low-calorie soft drinks. Nestlé, with the Nescafé brand, and Cadbury Schweppes were always appraised of changing needs and perceptions through regular market research, and took care to introduce their own 'healthier' products under the umbrella brand name, to pre-empt others gaining share at their expense.

A simpler way of looking at the performance of a number of brands on just two key attributes is the **brand mapping** exercise, in which the scores for each brand on a vertical and horizontal axis are plotted to give a visual position on a two-dimensional grid. This can reveal bunching of brands, market gaps and the reassurance of a unique selling proposition borne out by consumer perceptions.

For major brands like Coca-Cola, maintaining brand leadership means constant attention to brand image, and the collection of image data is a critical activity. Research was conducted in Europe to evaluate the relative merits of two types of scale. The first was the traditional bi-polar scale ranging from (1) to (6) on a range of characteristics applicable to soft drinks. The second was a 'Yes/No' check-off classification against a number of soft drink brands to a selection of criteria such as 'modern'. The parallel sets of **usage and attitude** surveys conducted indicated that as sample sizes get larger, the 'Yes/No' approach is preferred for actionable results, and multi-point scales are more efficient where sample sizes are smaller (Carroll Mohn, 1989).

Contrasted with such well-established brands, the financial services sector is in its infancy in terms of full appreciation of product differentiation and the market research techniques available to achieve it. However, the large sums now spent by British banks and building societies on television advertising means that the younger age groups are deriving a perception of these institutions which does not necessarily derive from past use or current need.

Some qualitative insights into the constructs underlying perceptions of banks and building societies were obtained using Kelly's Repertory Grid technique along with in-depth interviews on a small sample split into three age groups, 16–25, 26–45 and over 45 (Smith and Harbisher, 1989). Building societies were perceived to be relatively distinct from banks but individuals found it difficult to make distinctions between different building societies. The younger age group used constructs with more negative connotations when describing building societies. Banks were perceived by the over-45s to provide efficient service but not to be particularly friendly or caring. Visual identity, promotion (including direct mail) and staff behaviour at branch level are factors which can help to differentiate one building society from another. Each of these factors is distinct from the offering of loan or savings account, where interest rate is the key influence.

The risks involved in launching brand extensions lead manufacturers to conduct considerable 'insurance' research, to protect the umbrella brand from the negative or inappropriate perceptions of the extensions. Research conducted into perceptions of 20 hypothetical product class extensions to six existing brands (ranging from Heineken beer to Vidal Sassoon shampoo) was motivated by the broader objective of gaining an insight into how consumers form attitudes towards brand extensions (Aaker and Keller, 1990). An important finding of the research was that a relationship of a positive *quality* image for the existing brand with the evaluation of a brand extension was strong only when there was a basis of fit between the two product classes. This basis of fit has to be identified through such dimensions as substitutability and manufacturing credibility.

Brand valuation

Brands are the intangible assets of a corporation. This means that they are not valued in the balance sheet in the same way as such tangible assets as stocks, plant and machinery. The current British accounting convention is that the value of brands is classified under the heading of **goodwill**, which is defined as 'the difference between the value of a business as a whole and the aggregate of the fair value of its separable net assets' (Accounting Standards Committee, 1989).

This goodwill is classified into 'purchased' – through acquisition – and 'non-purchased', that is, generated internally or organically by the business. When there is an acquisition the valuation of goodwill is quite straightforward, but this is difficult to measure in other circumstances. After an acquisition, goodwill is perceived to be the balancing figure between the purchase price of a company and the value of the net separable assets, and is written off in current accounting convention.

Brand valuation became an issue in the UK when, in August 1988, Grand Metropolitan announced that it would take the value of recently acquired brands into its balance sheet for £500 million. This was followed by Rank Hovis McDougall boosting its balance sheet by £678 million by placing a value on such brands as Hovis, Bisto and Mr Kipling.

A series of such valuations in the late 1980s was motivated by a wide gap emerging between the book worth of a company and the market capitalization. Stock Exchange rules require companies to seek shareholders' approval for acquisitions worth more than 25% of the company's net worth. Putting a value on brands in the balance sheet meant that this approval was not necessary.

One proposal for accounting for brand values in the balance sheet is through **amortization**, in which brands are seen as assets with an assumption of systematic depreciation over time, say 20 or 40 years. The difficulty here is in knowing the 'useful economic life' of a brand. Another complication is that there will already be a charge to the profit and loss account for the advertising and sales promotion necessary to maintain the brand's position in the market.

One way of assessing the market value of a brand is to take the price premium that it enjoys over lesser-known alternatives and to multiply this by the number of items sold. From this, the present value of the future cash flows attributable to the brand can be calculated. Two more formal ways have been enunciated:

(1) In the UK, with the help of a specialist consultancy, Interbrand, Rank Hovis McDougall developed a method which involved taking the average earnings from a brand over the past three years and multiplying it by a factor reflecting eight criteria which described the product's position in the market and the amount of advertising support (Euromonitor, 1990).

(2) In the USA, a common concept of brand valuation is 'relief from royalty'. The question is asked 'How much would a third party have to pay to obtain the right to use the brand name?'; so, for example, a three per cent royalty rate could be assumed on forecast sales for 15 years, and a suitable discount rate applied (King and Cook, 1990).

Although there has been considerable discussion on brand valuation among the British accounting profession, the general conclusion appears to be that brand values should not be capitalized. The convention appears to be as recommended by the authoritative report 'Accounting for Brands' (Likerman *et al.*, 1989) and that companies may show brand values in the unaudited section of company reports.

European perspective

Potential for emergence of world-class products from Europe

The application of EC anti-competition rules in such areas as takeovers and mergers, exclusive distribution networks and licence agreements is justified by the EC Commission on the grounds of protecting the consumer and promoting competition between companies within the Single Market. However, it could be argued that the body of legislation that is now growing, works against the possibility of 'world-class' products from Europe. This is because the conditions for the necessary economies of scale to compete on price worldwide would have less chance of being fulfilled compared with products generated by Japanese or American companies, which are serving home markets that are larger than individual EC member states.

In spite of this, companies in the USA are justifiably concerned at the need to identify the needs of the European customer in terms of quality, price, location and timing, as they see 'Euro-producers' emerging with a product focus rather than a diversified portfolio.

Some of the features of 'world-class' producers are identified within the context of manufacturing, distribution and systems (Seal, 1990):

- firm management direction
- quality
- cost control – particularly in non value-added areas
- flexibility
- good customer relations

Most of these features are predictable, but the significant area of difference between the 1980s and 1990s is that the traditional areas of trade-off will not be as readily available. For example, consumers will be looking for high-quality performance and competitive pricing. Industrial customers will require flexible supply terms without a cost penalty.

The need to work to high standards in all of these areas requires commitment to team working across the traditional functional boundaries. There is increasing emphasis placed on monitoring levels of customer satisfaction. Feedback through marketing management to product engineers, manufacturing and distribution management facilitates modifications in product design and working practices which ensure competitive edge. Neglect of the customers' perception of added value in favour of short-term profits will increase the risk of customer franchise moving to the competitor who is ready to respond to a faster-changing environment.

In the first chapter, the concept of added value as a measure of wealth creation was introduced. Such data as provided in Table 7.5 shows the trends from 1970 to 1986 in the pattern of meeting customer needs through added value by sector for Europe, Japan and the USA.

Table 7.5 Comparison of added value in the major world markets analysed by sector (percentage basis).

	Japan		USA		Europe	
	1970	1986	1970	1986	1970	1986
Agriculture	6	3	3	3	4	4
Industry	41	43	35	33	42	38
Market services	42	44	47	52	39	43
Non-market	11	10	14	11	15	15
	100	100	99[†]	99[†]	100	100

[†]less than 100 due to rounding.
Source: Eurostat. *Some Statistics on Services,* 7(c), 1990.

The percentage of Japan's total added value contributed by agriculture halved from 1970 to 1986, reaching the same percentage figure as the USA, and just below that of Europe. The most significant difference between the three regions is shown by the percentage contribution to added value from industry. In 1986, this was 43% for Japan but had declined to 33% for the USA and 38% for Europe. This reflects the strength of Japanese consumer goods on the home and export markets, while an increasing percentage of added value in Europe and the USA came from market services.

The fact that this sector contributed 52% of US added value by 1986 reflects an economy vulnerable to recession. Professional services related to economic growth and consumer spending on discretionary services showed a significant downturn in 1990/91. Although the comparable figure for Europe is 43% for 1986, a structural difference in the total market economy is seen from the higher percentage contribution to added value from non-market services, compared with Japan and the USA.

Pan-European marketing of services

Two examples are chosen to illustrate both the effects of, and difficulties in, exploiting the opportunities from a harmonized market for services from 1992.

The financial services sector has two distinct arms in, firstly, the retail banking and insurance market, and secondly, the 'institutional' or corporate sector. The first area has been characterized by a high ratio of labour costs to turnover, and access to broader markets will mean staffed outlets. However, there is a move towards electronic communication, and the bank that is further advanced in information technology and that has the capital available to create retail presence may take up opportunities that others cannot.

However, the greater competition of the open market will exert downward pressure on pricing (Cecchini, 1988). Where the cost of consumer credit is higher in the UK, for example, banks from other Member States might be prepared to offer more attractive personal credit terms, and British banks might be reluctant to accept the lower profit margins on a pan-European basis which such competition would impose.

Article 7 of the EC Second Banking Directive relates to third-party reciprocity. It states that banks from outside the Community (such as from the USA and Japan) which intend to operate in Europe will have their application endorsed only if reciprocal banking access is provided to European banks (Howcroft and Whitehead, 1990). This provision may stimulate merger and acquisition activity on the part of non-European banks rather than an inflow of investment into Europe for organic growth.

The institutional market for financial services is reliant on the expertise of small teams with investment in the latest computer technology making location less and less significant. The traditional strength of London institutions in the fields of insurance and corporate finance could be threatened by government obduracy in the move towards a single European currency. There are signs that Frankfurt is taking increasing prominence as a financial centre, as the German mark becomes pre-eminent in the European exchange rate mechanism (ERM).

A second area of service marketing that falls under the spirit of the Single European Act is the range of professional services that includes the legal, accountancy and architectural professions. The ultimate objective of harmonization in this area is that a professional qualified in one Member State should be free to practise in any other Member State. The reality of the situation even after 1992 will be rather different in that reciprocity is difficult to enact, where definitions of, and training for, professions vary widely across European countries.

Since 1979, a Directive adopted in 1977 allows European lawyers to plead cases jointly with a lawyer from a host country, and to provide other legal services such as consultations. However, diplomas are not recognized, which means that restrictions on the right to set up business in a country without a diploma from that country remain in force (European File, 1989a).

Rather than encouraging mutual acceptance of training and qualifications, the overall Directive relating to professions has in some instances produced the opposite effect. For example, laws were drafted in France and Luxembourg which gave a monopoly of legal advice to locally qualified professionals (Gabb, 1989).

The differences in functions and responsibilities of accountants across Europe are heavily dictated by the differing auditing requirements of individual countries. Where UK law requires that all companies are obliged to have a statutory audit each year (the major reason for the profession numbering some 80,000), German law requires this of a much smaller number of companies, and Spanish, Italian and Greek auditing requirements are sparse by comparison with UK.

According to an EC Directive, all companies of a certain size will need to undergo an audit. However, harmonization of accounting principles will make it much easier for accountants to practise across national borders, as well as giving momentum to the move towards an integrated market. One of the strengths of the US market is the US Generally Accepted Accounting Principles (GAAP), which provides for a common treatment of corporate transactions across the country. This includes treatment of goodwill in mergers and acquisitions, calculation of equity and treatment of reserves (Ugeux, 1989).

Technical harmonization

A major objective of the Single European Act is to reduce barriers to market entry based on different technical standards for products. Hitherto, highly specific product specifications (without reasonable justification on scientific efficacy or safety grounds) could be used to protect home industries from imports from other EC Member States.

The Commission is now vigilant in order to identify where technical specifications for product import authorization are unreasonable. The mechanism by which there is movement towards harmonization of technical standards is through EC Directives for specific product areas or industries. The general principles to which these Directives conform relate to health and safety requirements, freedom of movement within the EC and technical specifications to be drawn up by bodies other than the Commission (for example, the European Standards Body).

For example, the Construction Products Directive of December 1988 applies to all products intended for permanent incorporation into building and engineering works (but not scaffolding and temporary framework). Transitional arrangements exist so that, for example, a manufacturer who produces to a current British Standard and markets only within the UK can continue to do so until a European Standard replaces the British Standard (Boodle Hatfield, 1989).

Another area that is important for multinationals whose food brands traverse national boundaries in the EC is that of food labelling. The Council Directive of September 1990 states that 'foodstuffs bearing nutrition labelling should conform to the rules laid down by the Directive... whereas all other forms of nutrition labelling should be prohibited but foodstuffs bearing no nutrition labelling should be able to circulate freely'. The Directive contains detailed Articles relating to energy value, nutrients and polyunsaturates. The overall objective is to benefit the consumer and at the same time avoid any possible technical barriers to trade.

Environmental influence on product

Where companies are planning to market a standard product across national frontiers, legal and social requirements in relation to environmental factors will be paramount.

There are differences in the degree to which consideration of the effect on the environment will affect purchasing behaviour across national boundaries. German and Dutch consumers are more aware of, and educated in, environmental issues than their British and French counter-parts. This means that a UK producer wishing to sell in Germany as well as the home market will need to take the more stringent environmental measures in Germany as the standard.

The number of Germans describing themselves as 'environmentally aware' increased from 35% in 1982 to 62% in 1989; 57% of the German population claim that preservation of the environment is more important to them than economic growth (Appleton, 1991).

This sea-change in attitudes has led to German companies taking environmental issues seriously, as they are aware of the potential impact on market share and profitability if they do not do so. It has led to the ecological positioning of new magazines, banks and management consul-tancies to a degree that is yet to be seen in the UK.

The EC is likely to introduce a scheme for 'green' labelling of ecolog-ically approved products (other than food, drink and drugs, which are to be treated separately). The European Environment Agency (EEA) will set the criteria and labels will be awarded by an independent panel of experts nominated by the Member States. The objective is to encourage the manu-facture of environment-friendly products. Consumer preference for goods so marked will be a strong incentive for manufacturers to cooperate.

There is increasing evidence of environmental claims in advertising, and the discerning consumer will look for these as well as maintained perfor-mance on other benefits. This will be costly for the manufacturer, but to neglect this requirement will be to jeopardize brand share in the longer term.

Protection of inventions, trademarks and intellectual property under EC law

EC competition rules are designed to promote free trade and fair compe-tition. However, there needs to be protection of industrial, commercial and intellectual property so that innovation and investment are encouraged. There are five areas in which EC legislation impinges on protection of commercial 'rights' to exploit an idea, invention or brand:

(1)   patents
(2)   trademarks
(3)   copyright
(4)   exclusive licence agreements
(5)   sharing of information

Patents and copyright are dealt with in Chapter 16 under the broader issues of new product development.

The Community trademark

A proposal for the creation of a Community trademark was presented by the Commission as early as 1980, and modified in 1984. Adoption of the proposal has been held up by differences over the site of the office and its working languages. It provides for a ten-year registration, renewable for further periods of ten years. Refusal of a registration would occur if it is already held by another Community trademark holder. It also sets out a procedure for settling legal disputes relating to counterfeit products or contested validity of a mark. Due to the fact that there are differences in national legislation, a Community Directive reducing these was finally adopted in 1988.

However, transition to such a Community trademark is likely to be slow, and so to protect a brand name and logo it is still necessary to file a trademark registration in each country where protection from passing off of another product under the same mark is required. In line with the recognition of the enlarged market, there are also procedures for holders of a trademark to get Member States' customs authorities to prevent the marketing of counterfeit merchandise originating outside the Community (European File, 1989b).

Exclusive licence agreements

The EC has powers to judge exclusive licence agreements in terms of whether they may restrict, prevent or distort competition. Companies may submit details of such agreements to the Commission and apply for an exemption from the provisions of Article 85(1) of the Treaty of Rome if their arrangements are not covered by one of the 'block exemptions'. These block exemptions are issued to ensure that certain sorts of agreements, the competitive advantages of which generally outweigh the disadvantages, are not caught by the competition rules. The judgements of the EC Commission and the European court represent an increasing body of case law from which companies may draw to determine what is acceptable practice.

A significant case arose in 1986, when a complaint was made by the Norwegian Elopak Group, which had been collaborating with the Liquipak Group over the possibility of developing a new packaging machine incorporating a process protected by Liquipak's exclusive licence. This licence had been granted to Liquipak by the National Research and Development Council in 1981. Tetrapak acquired Liquipak and the exclusive licence, and although the licence itself benefited from falling within the patent licence block exemption (which exempted it from the effects of Article 85(1) of the Treaty of Rome) the Commission declared that Tetrapak was in breach of Article 86 (abuse of a dominant position) from the date of the acquisition until the exclusive licence expired (Competition Law in the EC, 1990).

A converse decision was indicated in February 1990 in the case of the acquisition by Rhône Poulenc of all Monsanto's production units in the USA, UK and Thailand for the production of intermediates used chiefly by the pharmaceutical industry in the manufacture of analgesics and antipyrectics.

The EC Commission took the view that Rhône Poulenc did not hold a dominant position within the Community, as there were no real barriers either to entry from third countries or to trade between Member States. Patents for these products had expired many years ago (Competition Law in the EC, 1990). The same overall conclusion on this case was reached by the UK Monopolies and Mergers Commission (MMC) and the French authority responsible for competition.

Sharing of information

The Commission scrutinizes any arrangements between suppliers wherever market information is shared. Where such an arrangement is in place for the purpose of concerted action to maintain or increase market dominance, then the Commission, if there is an appreciable effect on the competitive structure of the market, takes the view that there is infringement of EC competition law.

The information-sharing arrangement of the European Wastepaper Information Service (EWIS) involved each member sending statistical data to EWIS concerning wastepaper usage, stock levels, consumption and historic market price levels. Information was then distributed by EWIS in the form of aggregate figures.

The Commission judged that this arrangement was not contrary to competition rules on account of the nature of the information shared, and because EWIS members remained free to act independently in the market (Competition Law in the EC, 1989).

Product liability

In the UK, the Consumer Protection Act 1987 marked the move from a need on the part of a plaintiff to prove negligence by the supplier of a faulty product to a position of strict liability on the part of the producer or supplier.

There was a general movement in Europe towards greater concern for consumer protection during the 1970s and early 1980s. After years of debate and lobbying, a draft proposal was adopted by the European Council in July 1985 (EC Official Journal No. L 210/29, 1985). The resulting Directive required harmonization of national laws and regulations by the end of July 1988, although not all Member States were ready to meet this deadline.

Key features of the Directive on Product Liability are as follows (a more detailed exploration of product liability in the EC is provided by Greer (1989)):

Article 1: Adopts the principle of strict liability. 'The producer (which includes not only the manufacturer but, for example, an 'own-brander' and a person who imports the product into the EC from outside the EC) shall be liable for damage caused by a defect in his product'.

Article 3: Defines potential defendants in terms of their role in the marketing channel. For 'own label' products, the retailer or wholesaler may be liable.

Article 4: The injured party must prove damage and product defect and the causal relationship between the two.

Article 7: Allows certain defences including, for example, that the defect did not exist at the time the product was distributed and that the state of scientific knowledge at the time the product was launched could not have predicted the outcome under dispute. This is broadly in line with the Development Risks Defence of the UK Consumer Protection Act.

Problems and assignments

(1) Discuss the relative importance of:
    (a) consumers' perception of added value
    (b) tangible or demonstrable benefits

associated with a brand. How important are advertising message and weight in determining the relationship between (a) and (b)?

(2) Identify areas of added value that could be the subject of promotion for the following services:
    (a) a general medical practitioner's (GP's) surgery
    (b) a retail bank
    (c) a lawyer's practice specializing in corporate work.

(3) Why has 'quality' become an essential component of any product offering? In what ways does the management culture within an organization help or hinder the process of achieving quality in all aspects of product delivery?

(4) Discuss the interaction of the design, research and development, engineering and marketing functions in achieving a successful new product launch.

(5) Why are brand attribute measures so important in tracking consumer brand performance? Identify how changes in consumer attitudes towards the environment could affect the relative importance of brand attributes for laundry detergent, personal stationery and petrol.

(6) What are the features of a consumer market which militate against the penetration of retailer's own brands or 'own labels'? Use the markets for petfoods, breakfast cereals, toothpaste and wrist watches to illustrate your answer.

(7) As a coursework project, for two Member States of the EC identify how the national profile on:

    (a)   design
    (b)   innovation (as measured by patents)
    (c)   technology (as measured by investment)

has contributed to the nation's relative strength or weakness in a specific global industrial market. Comment on the historic nature of government support within the market for both countries.

(8) What are the factors that need to be taken into account in pan-European positioning of a brand?

(9) Identify a company that operates in at least three EC Member States, and determine how far product positioning has been influenced by moves towards a unified market.

References

Aaker D. A. and Keller K. D. (1990). Consumer evaluation of brand extensions. *J. of Marketing*, **54**(1), 27–41

Accounting Standards Committee (1989). *Accounting for Goodwill*, SSAP No. 22 (revised)

Baker M. (1989). A new philosophy of management? *Quarterly Review of Marketing* (Winter)

Carroll Mohn C. (1989). Comparing the statistical quality of two methods for collecting brand image data: Coca Cola's experience. *Marketing and Research Today*, August

Caulkin S. (1987). The fall and rise of brands. *Management Today*, July, p. 45

Chambers N. (1987). Developing a consumer strategy in the NHS or getting things right. *Hospital and Health Service Review*, January

de Chernatony L. (1988). The fallacy of generics in the UK. *Marketing Intelligence and Planning*, **6**(2), 36

de Chernatony L. (1989). Marketers' and consumers' concurring perceptions of market structure. *European J. of Marketing* **23**(1), 7

Collard R. (1989). *Total Quality – Success Through People*. London: Institute of Personnel Management

Cowell D.W. (1984). *The Marketing of Services*. London: Heinemann

Economist (1989). The perils of greening business. 14 October

Euromonitor Publications (1990). *Brand Names: The Invisible Assets*, 2nd edn, pp. 7–8

Freeman C. (1982). *The Economics of Industrial Innovation*, 2nd edn. London: Frances Pinter

Goldstein S. and Howe R. (1988). Rockwell's approach to improving quality. *Personnel J.*, July

Hooley G.H. and Mann S.J. (1988). Adoption of marketing by financial institutions in the UK. *Service Industries J.*, **8**(4), 488

King A.M. and Cook J. (1990). Brand names: the invisible assets. *Management Accounting*, November

Lewis B. R. (1989). Quality in the service sector: a review. *International J. of Bank Marketing*, **7**(5), 4

Likerman A., Barwise P., Higson C. and Marsh P. (1989). *Accounting for Brands*. London Business School

Little Arthur D. (1991). *Technological Change* (quoted in *Financial Times*, 27 February)

Lorenz C. (1990). *The Design Dimension – The New Competitive Weapon for Product Strategy and Global Marketing*. London: Basil Blackwell

Morris D. (1979). The strategy of own brands. *European J. of Marketing*, **13**(2), 59–78

Olins W. (1989). *Corporate Identity*. London: Thames and Hudson.

Price Waterhouse (1990). *Value for Money Auditing*. Gee and Co.

Rothwell R., Gardiner P. and Scott K. (1983). *Design and the Economy – The Role of Design and Innovation in the Prosperity of Industrial Companies*. London: Science Policy Research Unit for the Design Council

Smith D. and Harbisher A. (1989). Building societies as retail banks: the importance of customer service and corporate image. *International J. of Bank Marketing*, **7**(1), 22

Teare R. (ed.) (1990). *Managing and Marketing Services into the 1990s*. London: Cassell

Watkins T. (1986). *The Economics of the Brand*. Maidenhead: McGraw-Hill

European perspective

Appleton E. (1991). The greenest of the green. *Marketing*, 28 March

Boodle Hatfield (1989). Construction Products Directive. *Facilities*, 7(9)

Cecchini Report (1988). *1992 – The Benefits of a Single Market*. The Commission of the European Communities

Competition Law in the EC (1989). *Information Agreements (Wastepaper): The EWIS Case*. November, **12**(11)

Competition Law in the EC (1990). *Abuse of Dominant Positions (Cartons): The Tetrapak Case*. October, **13**(10)

Competition Law in the EC (1990). *Acquisitions (Chemicals): The Rhône-Poulenc/Monsanto Case*. December, **3**(12)

European File (1989a). *The European Community and Recognition of Diplomas for Professional Purposes*. Commission of the European Communities, October 13/89

European File (1989b). *Patents, Trade Marks and Copyright in the European Community*. Commission of the European Communities, December 17/89

Gabb A. (1989). The professions' uncommon market. *Management Today*, January

Greer T. V. (1989). Product liability in the European Economic Community: The new situation. *J. of International Business Studies*, **20**(2), 337

Howcroft B. and Whitehead M. (1990). The Single European Market: the challenge to commercial banking. *International J. of Bank Marketing*, **8**(3)

Seal G. M. (1990). 1990s – Years of promise, years of peril for US manufacturers. *Industrial Engineering*, **22**(1), January

Ugeux G. (1989). 'Europe sans frontières': the integration of financial markets. *The Royal Bank of Scotland Review*, No. 162, June, p. 9

8   The pricing decision

Chapter objectives:

- to consider the importance of price across all departments of the company
- to account for the economic and strategic factors that should be considered in setting the list price
- to understand the short-term/tactical influences of the list price, e.g. discounts
- to consider the various ways of going about pricing a product and/or service

Introduction

All key functional departments of a company have a vested interest in the price that is charged for the product or service provided. The marketing department's concern is that the price is compatible with the product positioning and the benefits perceived by the target market. The salesforce will be concerned with the price relative to the market norm, and how easy or difficult the sale will be at the individual customer level. The finance department will be keen to see that all costs associated with the product are covered and that there is a healthy contribution made to overheads and profit. The production team will be concerned that a sustained level of sales leads to continued orders on the factory. The department responsible for personnel management would prefer to avoid laying off workers if sales decline as a result of a price increase.

All of these considerations point to the importance of the pricing decision to the company's survival and success. They also introduce the concept of an interdisciplinary framework necessary for examining the impact of pricing decisions on company performance. There is a need for the marketing professional to draw on the simpler rules from economics and accounting in order to understand fully the role that pricing plays in the production of a coherent marketing plan.

A major part of this chapter deals with the issues surrounding the setting of a **list price**, including the demand curve and price elasticity, business objectives and detailed methods for strategic decision-making on price. In practice, the list price is subject to a variety of short-term influences, not least of which is **discounting**. This invariably complicates analysis of the pricing environment and makes some of the theory which follows an over-simplification of the issues. However, an understanding of the underlying concepts is essential if the student or practitioner is to advance to the stage of multivariate analysis of the marketing mix as a prelude to market forecasting and setting of brand budgets. Practical approaches to discounting are included towards the end of the chapter.

Definition of price

A simple definition – money for which a thing is bought or sold – indicates the precise nature of the marketing dilemma on price. Will there be enough purchasers of the product at the price at which the company will cover costs and make a profit?

This is a cyclical question, since more purchasers will mean increasing economies of scale on a longer production run, and therefore lower costs per unit. However, management has to define the threshold level of operations for a new product at which there is commercial viability. This threshold level may rest on financial or production constraints if no minimum has been set on market share or unit sales.

For example, the decision regarding the minimum run for a promotional T-shirt will be beset by fewer longer-term considerations than that for the minimum run for viability of a new glass container. For the latter, mould costs, machine down-time for new settings, and possible changes in furnace temperature will need to be taken into account in deciding minimum run and price per unit.

Both examples illustrate that there is a **risk** attached to the pricing decision; the key to success in pricing is reduction of risk through three major considerations, which are explored in this chapter.

Reduction of risk in pricing

(1)   The pricing objectives should be derived from the total marketing strategy, and this in turn should be moulded by the corporate objectives.

(2) Market research to assess market response to price is essential (but frequently neglected).

(3) In today's complex marketing environment, a combination of pricing methods is more likely to produce results in keeping with management expectations. The exclusive use of one pricing method is unlikely to achieve the necessary level of sensitivity to market demand and internal constraints.

Before embarking on these areas, it is important that the student gains an understanding of the relationship between price and **demand**.

The demand schedule

The relationship between price and quantity bought is called the **demand schedule** or **demand curve** for a product.

For the purpose of illustration we can take the hypothetical example of sugar. Figure 8.1 is a graphical representation of the data in Table 8.1. The fact that the curve slopes downward to the right illustrates the important law that demand declines as price is increased; there is an inverse relationship between quantity demanded and the price charged. As with most laws there are exceptions, such as the increased demand for vintage cars as the prices escalated during the late 1980s, with speculators competing with collectors at auctions.

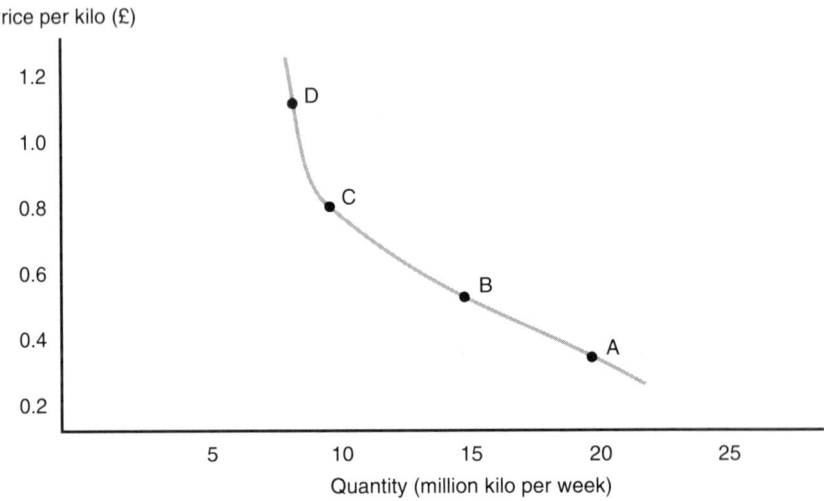

Figure 8.1 The demand curve for a particular good; inelastic demand (example: sugar).

Table 8.1 Data to support Figure 8.1.

	Price (£ per kilo)	Quantity (million kilo per week)
A	0.30	20
B	0.50	15
C	0.80	10
D	1.10	8

Elasticity of demand

Various commodities or products differ in the degree to which the quantity bought responds to changes in the price charged. For example, in Table 8.1 we can see that there is a 25% decline in demand when there is a price increase of 66% (from A to B). Put another way, for every 1% increase in price at this point, there is a 0.375% decline in demand.

The revenue generated by demand at a specific price can be expressed as shown below:

$$\text{Revenue } (R) = \text{quantity } (Q) \times \text{Price } (P)$$

From the data in Table 8.1:

R_A = £6.0 million
R_B = £7.5 million

A product is said to have **inelastic demand** when revenue increases with increasing price. In the case of sugar, this might be because there are few low cost substitutes, and dietary habits are sometimes difficult to change.

When revenue decreases with increasing price, this occurs because the fall in quantity demanded for a 1% increase in price is greater than 1%. This situation is called **elastic demand**.

When an increase in price results in an exactly compensating fall in quantity demanded, leaving revenue unchanged, then the **elasticity of demand** is **unitary**. Just as Figure 8.1 illustrates the situation of **inelastic demand**, so Figure 8.2 represents **elastic demand**, where the quantity demanded is more responsive to changes in price.

Table 8.2 provides the information corresponding to Figure 8.1, and represents the hypothetical situation for a volatile market in a precious metal with specific technical applications, where there are cheaper but less effective alternatives. From Table 8.2 it is clear that as price increases from 400 DM per gm to 700 DM per gm the quantity demanded declines in such a way that revenue is reduced. This is elastic demand.

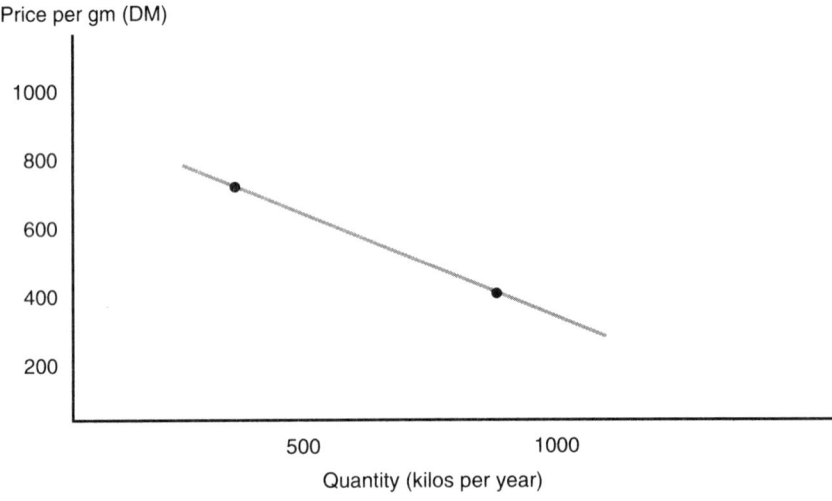

Figure 8.2 The demand curve; elastic demand (example: sugar).

Table 8.2 Data to support Figure 8.2.

	Price (DM per gm)	Quantity demanded (kilos per year)	Revenue (DM million)
A	400	900	360
B	700	350	245

It should be emphasized that this exploration of the behaviour of the demand curve falls into the area of marginal analysis as the assumption is made that price is the only variable changing. In practice, several features of the marketplace with an influence on demand could be changing at the same time.

Putting a value to price elasticity

Although the demand curve for a product will exhibit different values of price elasticity at different points along the curve, marketers need to be able to estimate the value in a limited region of the curve to understand the sensitivity of the market to price changes. One way of reaching a value is to take a 'straight line' approximation on a particular section of the demand curve. This can be represented as shown below:

$$\text{Average price elasticity (PE)} = \frac{\% \text{ change in quantity}}{\% \text{ change in price}}$$

$$\text{Average PE} = \frac{\text{change in demand}}{\text{average demand over range}} \div \frac{\text{change in price}}{\text{av. price over range}}$$

$$\text{Average PE} = \frac{Q_2 - Q_1}{\frac{1}{2}(Q_2 + Q_1)} \div \frac{P_2 - P_1}{\frac{1}{2}(P_2 + P_1)}$$

Where Q_1 and Q_2 are quantities demanded at prices P_1 and P_1.

The figure for PE will be negative, because Q and P are inversely related and the slope of the demand curve is downwards towards the right.

Using the equation for PE in the examples illustrated in Tables 8.1 and 8.2 the following calculations are derived. From Table 8.1 for sugar, using the values at points A and B:

$$\text{PE}_{\text{sugar}} = \frac{(15 - 20)}{\frac{1}{2}(15 + 20)} \div \frac{(0.5 - 0.3)}{\frac{1}{2}(0.5 + 0.3)}$$

$$= -0.57$$

This is an example of inelastic demand.

Taking the values for the precious metal illustrated in Table 8.2:

$$\text{PE}_{\substack{\text{precious} \\ \text{metal}}} = \frac{(15 - 20)}{\frac{1}{2}(15 + 20)} \div \frac{(0.5 - 0.3)}{\frac{1}{2}(0.5 + 0.3)}$$

$$= -1.61$$

The negative value of more than 1 shows elastic demand in the area of the curve under investigation.

Business objectives and the pricing decision

Pricing is a key aspect of marketing strategy. If the **pricing strategy** is set in isolation from the broader goals, then there is a high risk of a conflict of interest between functional departments when the results on performance begin to filter through the organization.

For example, the finance director has been set the task of achieving a 10% net margin after overhead recovery but before interest payment on loans. This is higher than the previous year. The marketing director has been commissioned to achieve a market share increase for the two leading products, which between them account for nearly 60% of company profits. It is common knowledge that the major competitors will not be increasing prices in line with costs in the foreseeable future because of over-capacity in the industry.

What pricing strategy is likely to be adopted from a marketing view-point, and will this conflict with the financial objectives for the company?

This simple example illustrates how corporate strategy must be interpreted into coherent and quantified objectives for each area of functional control. There should be internal consistency in the figures, which are usually generated through the forward budgeting process.

Assuming that this scenario would apply in a well-managed company, there are five alternative business objectives which might be used to formulate the marketing strategy and which will therefore influence pricing.

Market leadership

This approach is particularly relevant when a company is about to enter a new market which is either emerging or not yet dominated by a key player. The level of commitment in terms of product superiority, customer research and promotional support is generally high. The **market leader** is content to fund development of a consumer franchise longer-term, before a profit position is achieved. Timing is important with this approach, particularly in industries where products can become obsolete sooner than expected through the innovation of a competitor, for example, in personal computers.

Rewards from this market-leader approach are high in terms of market share, higher price compared with the market norm and improved levels of profitability. The price would rest on two advantages: firstly product superiority, and secondly being the first entrant to commit resources to awareness, which often assists in expanding the market and not just individual brand share.

In the field of fast-moving consumer goods, Procter & Gamble have used this strategy consistently to establish a leading market share in detergent and related markets worldwide. IBM used this strategy in the mainframe computer market, where the name became synonymous with the values of quality and reliability.

Market skimming

The strategy of **market skimming** is possible in market conditions very similar to those pertaining to market leadership. Market skimming can be defined as a company commanding a high price for a product leading to a high profit margin through two options:

(1) pioneering a new market sector through technical innovation, effectively being the first entrant to that sector, or
(2) appealing to a segment of an existing market in which the purchasers are prepared to pay a premium price for quality and service benefits.

An example of the first option is the relatively high prices charged for microwave ovens in the UK in the early 1980s, when the experimenters had sufficient disposable income to allow them to pay these prices for the benefits of novelty and convenience.

The service sector provides an example of the second route, with deluxe valet dry-cleaning services available in certain locations of major cities. Speed and quality are integral aspects of the service. The additional cost of providing the enhanced service will not absorb all of the price premium, so there is the increased margin available to the operator whether sole trader, company-owned multiple or franchised outlet.

Market penetration

The business objective with this scenario is to achieve acceptance and purchase of the product among sufficient mainstream users as to enable the company to obtain volume business and economies of scale. The market-share objective is likely to be set for the longer term, creating a significant force in the market. The pricing decision implicit within this business objective hinges on the way in which the marketing targets are set. If market share and volume sales targets are high by market standards then the price will be set in the middle to lower range, and will complement the image created by advertising.

Once again, **timing** of product entry or product modification is critical and the pricing element of the mix needs to be researched carefully to reduce the risk of under-performance on sales volume through too high a price.

Amstrad took the market penetration approach, reflected in their pricing strategy for personal computers. This pricing approach has the additional benefit of discouraging potential market entrants. In order to compete on price, a new entrant would need to have lower cost sourcing (which could be as a result of better technology) or would need to accept lower margins.

Survival

When a company is competing in a market with over-capacity then the relationship between supply and demand will exert a downward pressure on price in a free market. The nature of the competition in the market will determine just how responsive to this downward pressure a company must be in order to survive. (The nature of competition is explored in more detail later in the chapter.) With this scenario, the overriding company objective is to maintain sales at a level that will cover unit variable costs and overheads with sufficient margin to cover interest payments on loans if this is how the working capital is financed. This is a short-term measure as a company is unlikely to survive in the longer term without profit.

An alternative approach to meet conditions of a drop in demand is to raise prices rather than decrease them. If the demand is known to be price inelastic and long-term relationships have been forged with existing customers – particularly in industrial and business-to-business sectors – then revenue in the short term can be optimized in this way. Such an upward price movement could be accompanied by product enhancement to create additional value to the customer at little cost to the supplier.

The over-capacity for steel in Europe forced prices down and the fight for survival stimulated cost cutting exercises in British Steel. The rate of production is now on a par with Germany compared with 40% below in the 1970s, and financial losses became profits in the 1980s and early 1990s.

The fate of the small business when prices move downwards is often more precarious than that for the large corporation, as there is often little financial cushioning available against cash-flow constraints and overdraft limits.

Methods for setting price

A market-led organization will see price as a key element of the marketing mix, along with the product specification and features, the advertising message and media used, sales literature and distribution channels. Traditional techniques for setting price must be viewed in the context of the total marketing mix.

Perceived-value pricing

Price has to be viewed in the context of the added value that is created for the end-user, in real terms and in the perception that the user has of the value obtained. Some of this perceived value may be attributed to the advertising platform or branding that has been superimposed on tangible product features. Because these elements are working together, it is important that the positioning strategy is very clearly translated into price and advertising elements at an early stage in development, and that research does indeed confirm that there is no dichotomy between the two.

Since price is what customers are prepared to pay under prevailing market conditions, their perceptions of the value become critically important when it is not easy to compare products. Historically, perceived value pricing has been used for consumer products where the necessary research to link price with the 'halo' effect of branding is more easily accommodated.

For an industrial product such as bulk chemicals, the added value obtained from one supplier is directly comparable to another. The buyer is therefore less likely to make judgements about the price based on perceived value, and more likely to review spot market prices. However, as the chemicals purchased move into specialty-use areas, there are greater process cost penalties to the buyer if the product does *not* meet technical specifications. The expertise and track record of the supplier will form part of the added-value assessment prior to the purchase decision, and the higher-priced product could be chosen.

It is not always easy to value the elements provided within a product or service package, but competitive edge can be gained when some attempt is made to show the customers the hidden value of benefits they are receiving for the price. These may be training or service elements included within the price, giving the customer better value for money.

Going-rate pricing

Before setting a price for a new product or adjusting the price of an established one, the range of prices and product features of the competition must be assessed. This is part of the essential desk and field research that is a component of any product manager's tool kit, and is also part of the marketing audit process prior to setting forward plans and budgets. How strongly the pricing decision will be influenced by what the competition is charging depends on the nature of the market and the strength of competition. A summary of the different conditions that can exist is given in Table 8.3.

Table 8.3 How market structure determines the going-rate price.

	Definition	Examples
Perfect competition	When no firm operating in the market has control over price. The price will fluctuate without a seller appreciably influencing it.	Currency markets with no exchange controls or gold standards. Commodities – e.g. wheat, where there is no government intervention.
Monopoly	The extreme case of imperfect competition when a single seller has complete or monopolistic control over the supply, and therefore, the price of a product.	Government monopolies in public utilities.
Oligopoly	This means that there are few sellers in the market, and they all therefore exert some influence over price. (1) The first type of oligopoly is where the product sold is identical or almost identical across suppliers. (2) The second type of oligopoly is where there are few sellers who sell differentiated products.	(1) Road freight haulage. (2) Seats on scheduled airlines in Europe.

In practice, more prices are determined by a combination of monopolistic and competitive forces. Most markets are characterized by **imperfect competition**, where one or several companies exert a significant influence on price.

The series of privatizations of British utilities during the mid to late 1980s was an attempt to introduce greater competition into the markets for telecommunications, gas, electricity and water. In some instances this objective was frustrated by the maintained monopoly control over the market by one supplier, even though the status of that operator had changed from government-owned to a public company with a multitude of shareholders.

Oligopolistic markets include that for air transport in Europe. Where governments are keen to see the survival of national carriers, prices for the same journey are remarkably similar from one carrier to the next. Deregulation of air transport in the USA has brought with it greater price competition; however, it has been argued that this has also created greater pressure on cost reduction, with implications for safety standards.

What the competition is charging, particularly in a market for undifferentiated products, will set a **ceiling** on the price that the new entrant can demand.

Cost-plus pricing

Cost-plus pricing is adopted because it is simpler than alternatives, it suits a standard operating procedure and, given cost stability, it can result in lengthy periods of price stability. The method involves the simple addition of a predetermined mark-up to the figure for total costs to create the price.

The ability of management to set an optimal price where the product or service is complex will depend heavily on the accuracy and depth of information both on internal costs and on external market constraints. For the former, the costing procedures and accounting methods will be important, and for the latter, the degree of marketing expertise in assessing the added value compared with the competition will be paramount. What costs should a company consider in setting a price? These costs can be allocated to five broad categories as shown in Table 8.4. How a company allocates costs across products will depend very much on the conventions derived from operating practice. For example, a pharmaceutical company might wish to amortize development costs for several abortive ventures across the life of the latest new branded drug (easy to forecast because of known patent life). The company might also allocate marketing and selling costs across products according to set criteria.

Using the cost breakdown in Table 8.4, a company might choose to apportion by product all costs in groups (1), (2) and (5), and to assign all costs in groups (3) and (4) to a 'company overhead' category. Each product would then have to make a contribution, through the price set for

Table 8.4 Costs to be considered in the cost-plus method of pricing.

(1)	Development costs	Scientific research and development
		Engineering trials
		Design and tooling
		Patents, trademarks
		Product registration
(2)	Direct costs (to manufacture product or provide service)	Raw materials
		Components
		Direct labour
		Machine running costs
		Delivery
(3)	Indirect costs or overheads	Rents on leasehold buildings
		Rates
		Office running costs
		Office staff salaries
		Stationery
(4)	Capital costs	Freehold buildings and land
		Premium on leasehold buildings
		Machinery and equipment
		Vehicles
		Furniture
(5)	Marketing costs	Production of TV commercial, press advertisement, etc.
		Cost of media time or space
		Sales literature
		Special promotions
		Salesforce salaries and expenses
		Salesforce bonuses and commission
		Exhibitions, seminars, etc.

it, to this 'company overhead' category. The capital costs of group (4) would be amortized over a number of years depending on the accounting conventions of the organization.

The importance of having information on detailed cost breakdowns becomes apparent here, as it is only when all of these costs are estimated in a reliable way that the pricing level can be set to cover these costs and provide a mark-up – whether this is 10, 15 or 30% of total costs. The pricing level then has to be compared with the going-rate for similar products to assess competitive positioning. If the **cost-plus** price is too high to enable the product to compete, then the nature and level of costs must be re-examined. The company's costs will set the **floor price** for the product.

Another way of approaching the cost-plus method of pricing is the traditional way of dividing costs into **fixed costs** and **variable costs**. A break-even analysis will indicate the sales level at a given price at which both fixed costs and variable costs per unit will be covered. All sales beyond this level will then start to provide profit. Judgement is needed for assessing whether this level of sales can reasonably be expected, given market conditions. Knowledge is needed on how costs will vary at different levels of production, with higher production levels bringing economies of scale and lower unit costs. The benefits of the experience curve should not be overlooked, where efficient sourcing of raw materials, more cost-effective use of machinery and minimizing stocks against fluctuating demand all help to reduce unit costs over time.

Target-return pricing

Some companies have very clear objectives as to their target rate of **return on investment** (ROI). Investment may be defined in terms of costs in groups (1) and (4) in Table 8.4. The way in which major development and capital investment costs are amortized over several years and the way in which these are allocated to products will influence the target rate of return on investment on an annual basis. This will then define the price level necessary to meet this target.

So, for example, privatization of UK water authorities in 1989 meant that heavy investment commitments would have to be financed out of profits rather than government grants. This meant a thorough review of pricing to make sure that a reasonable level of investment could be maintained, and that earnings per share were adequate.

Development costs for new drugs constitute a very heavy risk investment for pharmaceutical companies. Taking the example of a new anti-viral drug administered by injection, variable cost per unit dose is set at £8. The costs of research and development and drug trials to obtain a product licence in key countries totalled £20 m. New machinery installed for production cost £6 m. If a target return on investment of 15% is set, then target price to achieve this can be calculated as shown. The sales level for the year is forecast at 0.5 million doses.

$$\text{Target return price} = \text{Unit cost} + \frac{(\text{Return} \times \text{Investment})}{(\text{Unit sales})}$$

$$= 8 + \frac{0.15 \times 26}{0.5}$$

$$= \text{£15.8 per dose}$$

This illustrates the importance of the ROI element in pricing for products requiring heavy investment in research and development or new technology. Management then has to decide whether the sales figure put into the equation is consistent with the price derived. There has to be an evaluation and revision process.

Mark-up pricing

A less complex way of setting price for a product or service where cost norms are well established is the method of putting a set **percentage mark-up** on costs. This method is traditional in retailing where, for example,

	£	%
Retail price (including VAT at 17.5%)	10.16	117.5
VAT	1.51	
Retail price (excluding VAT)	8.65	100
Retailer's margin	3.46	40
Wholesaler's price to retailer	5.19	60
Wholesaler's margin	0.87	10
Manufacturer's price to wholesaler	4.32	50

Figure 8.3 Example of relationship between manufacturer's selling price and final retail price for consumer products.

100% mark-up is the norm for fashion retailing. The mark-up would be lower than this for food retailing, however, where there is more rapid stock-turn on purchased items, permitting a different margin structure.

The flow diagram in Figure 8.3 illustrates the way in which mark-up is applied to costs at different levels in the supply chain, to provide the intermediary with a selling price. The level of the mark-up will depend on norms in the industry, the services provided by the intermediary and competitive forces. Note the difference between **mark-up** and **margin**. These terms apply to the same absolute amount of money, but the way in which each is defined as a percentage is different.

In the example, the retail price excluding VAT is taken as the index base of 100 and the various steps in the distribution chain to reach this price point are illustrated along with the mark-up at each stage. (In reality, VAT would apply at each stage in the chain but this has been excluded to show the real net gain to retailer, wholesaler and manufacturer.)

Psychological pricing

This approach to pricing draws on aspects that are not easily quantified, and is often used in conjunction with other methods. In markets where there is a cachet attached to the brand or where the pricing decision relates to a premium positioning of a brand in an array of products, considerable judgement is needed as to what the market will bear. Market research of a more qualitative nature, such as through focus groups, will help to establish the motivation behind purchase and will help identify the optimum price through consideration of lifestyle, disposable income and psychological needs. A higher price than the market norm will be indicative of quality and exclusivity. The seller is looking to meet the demands of possibly a smaller target market but at a higher price which generates sufficient volume sales at a generous profit margin. Where unit costs are low and price is high relative to the market, then a compensating investment is often needed in brand awareness through appropriate advertising. Fashion and accessory markets are examples, French houses in particular having capitalized on the ego-serving role of designer clothes, jewellery and luggage. Any significant reduction in price, once set, will have a damaging effect on the product's perceived exclusivity.

At the other end of the pricing spectrum, mass-merchandising stores and supermarkets are consistent users of price points which reduce the psychological impact of the actual money paid for an item – £19.99 appears a much lower price than £20.00, although the monetary difference is only one penny!

Sealed-bid pricing

In the area of large construction contracts or comparable project management and in certain areas of defence procurement, two or more leading suppliers in the field will be invited to bid or tender a price against a detailed specification of needs. The prices quoted by each supplier will be known only to the client company or government agency. A bid or tender will be accepted based on the product or service to be provided, the conditions of supply and the price. Where major contracts such as the building of the Channel Tunnel are concerned, reputation of the bidding company or consortium in the field is also a significant factor in the decision.

A company bidding for a contract therefore has to balance two risks:

(1) Bidding a high price to obtain a higher margin or provide cushioning against cost escalation, but with a lesser chance of winning the contract.

(2) Bidding a lower price for a greater chance of winning the contract, but with lower margins.

If a penalty clause is written into a major contract for overrun on completion date, then the risk of this occurring has to be built into the costing process prior to quoting a price.

Moral pricing

This method of pricing is based on the principle of a fair price, given the nature of the product or service and the customer's status and circumstances. For example, organizations providing meals or refreshments at places of pilgrimage or worship often charge below what the market would bear as they are driven by motives other than profit. Printers and other suppliers to reputable charities might wish to forgo normal margins in quoting special prices.

The question of what is a **moral price** for life-saving drugs can lead to heated discussion in the classroom, but must be considered in deliberate terms by pharmaceutical companies which must take into account the moral climate in which they are operating. Since a major purchaser of drugs in many countries is the government-controlled health service, the price that this service is willing and able to pay to prolong the lives of a finite number of patients has to be weighed against targets for profit and ROI.

Short-term price adjustments

The pricing methods reviewed in the preceding section are of specific relevance to strategic pricing, whether for an entirely new product or one already existing in the market, with the longer term in view. A great deal of day-to-day pressure on marketing management comes from the need to respond to competitive activity or a drop in sales over the *short term*. Within the strategic marketing framework there must be sufficient flexibility for management to manoeuvre on price, particularly where brand share is threatened or company survival is at stake. Very often, such response takes the form of price discounts or special deals.

Responding to competitor price reduction

The form of response to a price reduction by a competitor will depend on the following:

(1) The competitor's dominance of the market;
(2) The level of product differentiation in the market;
(3) The company's position: does it have a major or insignificant market share?
(4) Management judgement as to whether the price reduction is temporary or permanent;
(5) Estimated price elasticity of demand for the product.

If the move is seen as a temporary discount then a tactical price reduction or 'customer deal' may be planned in response, but timing is important. The loss of margin with the lower price should be temporary for both parties. If the move is seen as permanent, the nature of demand should be assessed. If there is a longer-term downturn in the market and all the major players reduce price, then there is the risk of a permanent reduction in operating margins. The company with the best operating margins is in the strongest position for survival.

Discounting

This is often the only option available when a slump in demand or over-capacity in the market brings the average market price down. However, this approach can also be used as a short-term positive tactic to gain sales at the expense of competition, provided the new price is communicated effectively through the distribution chain. Discounting can be effective in both enabling a company to survive and in gaining a tactical advantage. There are dangers inherent in this pricing decision, and the ways to avoid them are given in the following **ten rules of discounting**.

The ten rules of discounting

(1) Set a discounting policy that is known, understood and followed by all members of the organization who have to implement it. This way, gross margins can be protected from indiscriminate price-cutting, the level of authority to change price is established and the salesforce can refer to the policy to defend their sales position on price, and the reasons for it.

(2) Beware of devaluing the product image. The level of exclusivity, perception as market leader and the nature of the relationship with the customer could be affected by indiscriminate price cutting.

(3) Have a specific objective for discounting. This might be to reward loyal customers, encourage brand switching, clear stocks or boost sales in the low season. Quantified, but reasonable, targets help to define what is to be gained for a loss of margin caused by the discount.

(4) Make sure that the discount is understood and applied through the distribution chain on a planned basis. For example, if a discount is to be passed on to the ultimate end-user, then wholesalers must be encouraged to do this through sales literature, displays, special packaging and the prospect of additional sales and profit. If a volume discount is provided as a retailer incentive only, then it should be sold as such.

(5) Do not give away more margin than is necessary to meet the objective of the discount. A sensitivity analysis of sales and profit outcome for various price scenarios helps here.

(6) Put a time limit on the deal if it is a 'one-off'. At the consumer level, the time limit can bring forward a repeat purchase or encourage brand switching. At the wholesaler or retailer level, an extended period of price cutting can allow stocks to be built up at the lower price which are held over to sell at the normal price, if there is no promotional flagging of the discount on the packaging. This leads to excessive loss of margin to the supplier.

(7) Specify a minimum order quantity (MOQ) at which the discount applies. This MOQ should be set at a level which provides for a minimum margin on the deal. (This is an extension of the problem facing many businesses where servicing some small customers is just not profitable, unless there is the opportunity for developing future sales with them.)

(8) Charge for *special* deliveries necessary as a result of the discounting. Very often, customers will place a small order for discounted stock to assess offtake and then demand a further delivery.

(9) Discounting can be used as a vehicle for encouraging prompt payment. Such appetisers as '5% off list price for payment within six days of invoice' are common within the UK clothing industry, and this is a particularly useful cash-flow ploy for small companies servicing large retailing groups – both sides benefit.

(10) Care must be taken to see that any special terms and conditions attached to sales at a discount are displayed at point of sale for the general public, or on the order form or agreement for industrial or business-to-business transactions.

Such discounting techniques change the customer's perception of the price charged for the benefit received. This reinforces the need to evaluate the suitability of discounting on the basis of the product category and likely competitive response. It is in such evaluation that the contrast between the shorter-term considerations and the strategic pricing methods covered in this chapter comes into focus. Both are needed as professional marketing tools in an increasingly complex and competitive business environment.

The reduction of risk in those areas of the pricing decision that can be quantified and possibly researched is essential to companies for which environmental and competitive influences are unpredictable and outside their control. In these circumstances, a sensitivity analysis built around a few key assumptions can help identify the optimal marketing mix, including the pricing decision.

European perspective

While much is written and spoken of the advantages that will accrue from a unified European market in 1992, the implications of moves towards harmonization on the pricing decision are varied, interrelated and potentially complex. Considering the way in which an exporter from the UK to Germany might choose to set a price based on the cost-plus method, the flowchart in Figure 8.4 outlines the influencing factors at each transaction stage.

Other considerations which come into play here are exchange rate fluctuations, which can have dramatic short-term effects on price, and the protectionist measures adopted by countries either by national technical standards to be met by imported goods or in relation to procurement policies of government agencies such as in the areas of power and telecommunications.

When exports to a specific EC country expand sufficiently to justify the setting up of a subsidiary, then the company takes on the mantle of a multinational. The implications for the pricing decision then reach beyond a simple balancing of mark-up on costs with market forces in the export territory. The decision becomes one of how to set a transfer price from the country of origin to the local subsidiary in the context of the legal and corporate taxation environment in both countries, and how these will be affected by the move towards harmonization. Each of the key issues raised in this introduction is now examined in more detail.

UK ex-factory price (including manufacturer's mark-up)

    (1) transport to Germany
    (2) insurance
    (3) administrative delays at borders
    (4) manufacturer's mark-up

Delivered price to wholesaler in Germany

    (5) storage in Germany
    (6) delivery to retailer
    (7) wholesaler's mark-up

Delivered price to retailer in Germany

    (8) retailer's mark-up
    (9) VAT charged to buyer at end of chain

Final retail price in Germany

Figure 8.4 Factors influencing export price.

Harmonization of VAT rates

Exports from any EC member country are exempt from VAT, but VAT is levied from the final end-customer in his/her country. A company considering exporting to another EC country would need to view the final selling price to the end-user (after the mark-ups necessary through the chain) with the addition of the going rate of VAT applicable to that product category. This would mean that, assuming transportation and other transborder costs are the same for several destinations and that the same agent's commission applies, then the final price would be a function of differing VAT rates. Moves towards harmonization of VAT rates have been moderately successful. Different rates on luxury goods provide some justification for divergent prices for the same product across EC borders.

Administrative formalities and border controls

While representing physical and psychological barriers to trade, administrative formalities and border controls between EC Member Countries also constitute costs which have to be carried by the business as a loss in margin, or by the customer in the form of a higher price. Such costs have been quantified in a business survey among around 500 firms in six EC countries – Belgium, France, Germany, Italy, the Netherlands and the UK (Cecchini Report, 1988).

The findings from the survey indicate that these costs could amount to 2% of the transborder sales. There is also the hidden cost of turnover and profit that companies forgo because of these barriers. There is the cost to governments of the human resources needed to maintain these barriers, and the lost tax revenue where sales have been inhibited. Some of these border barriers will be alleviated by the harmonized system of commodity description and coding and a single administrative document to be used for the export, import and transit of goods over EC frontiers.

The research also indicates where the costs of border administration are low – as for the Benelux countries – and where they are high – as for Italy. The 'Benelux 50' document facilitates trade between Benelux countries and this reduces customs clearance costs. At the other end of the spectrum the costs of importing into Italy are estimated to be five times higher than for Belgium.

Protectionist procurement policies

Since the formation of the EC there has been a steady development in cross-frontier trade within the private sector. However, this has not been so evident in the public sector. The reasons for this are varied: national government support of emerging technology; regional development plans around historically localized industries with the implications for employment; political strategies in the area of defence procurement. These reasons and many more can be put forward to explain the limited opening of public sector tenders to cross-border bids. Perhaps one barrier underestimated is the language and convention of doing business in another country, heightened when the protocols, budget controls and administrative procedures of a government department represent a communication and negotiating nightmare to the foreign seller.

Until 1992, EC legislation on procurement excluded four sectors: energy, transport, telecommunications and water supply. However, where legislation has applied to other market categories, it has not had much direct effect because of the difficulties of enforcement, particularly where tenders are highly complex with the requirement for expert judgement on the relative merits of different bids.

The net effect of these barriers to cross-border procurement is national industries protected from competitive forces, which means artificially high prices. Although state-of-the-art technology could be a feature of national endeavour in one or two key industries, such benefits are unlikely to accrue across the board. This means that the best 'added-value' products or low-cost substitutes are not available to the buyer.

Viewing this situation across all EC countries, the total effect in artificially high prices paid would be a significant figure if viewed in the context of total EC gross national product. Breaking down these buying barriers would mean increased competition with accessibility of products and services better suited to national needs and, ultimately, lower prices.

Exchange rate fluctuations

International pricing of goods and services is sensitive to currency exchange rate fluctuations. Currently many small to medium-sized UK businesses quote export prices in pounds sterling. This means an effective fixed price to the seller, and the importer carries the risk of exchange rate fluctuation. If sterling weakens against the Deutschmark, for example, there is a price advantage to the German buyer. If sterling strengthens against the Deutschmark then the German buyer pays a price penalty. This company must decide whether to absorb this as a cost increase or to pass it on as a price increase to the end-buyer. This is when some knowledge and experience of the market are essential, to gauge how demand will respond to such exchange rate-induced price increases.

In the situation in which the exporter is quoting the ex-factory price in the import currency and sterling depreciates against this currency, then the exporter has gained an effective price increase in sterling.

As a general principle, for trade between EC members it is advisable to sell in a strong currency (that is, one which is likely to appreciate against others) and to buy in a weak currency. If the UK exporter is selling in Deutschmarks then it is advisable to sell Deutschmarks forward, and if a UK company is importing in Deutschmarks it is advisable for them to buy Deutschmarks forward against sterling to hedge against an appreciation of the Deutschmark against sterling. This gives the business the protection of a fixed exchange rate in a world of floating exchange rates.

The European Monetary System (EMS) has as its objective the significant narrowing of the band of exchange rate fluctuation of member currencies, thus reducing the currency risk of trade between Member States. The instability of the ERM in the period 1992–93 is explored in the European perspective section of Chapter 14.

Transfer pricing

When company exports from the EC country of origin to a second EC member reach the stage at which company employees handling importation, sales and distribution would be more cost-effective than the use of an importing agent, then it is appropriate to set up a subsidiary in the country of import. The new subsidiary will have to operate within the legal and tax framework of the host country, as well as reacting to market conditions there.

Where a subsidiary is set up to handle marketing, sales, delivery, servicing and administration with imported goods, then the pricing decision is influenced by a wide range of factors. The company must consider the profit objectives in the country of origin as well as the profit objectives of the subsidiary. What level of corporation tax is charged in both countries, and what special import tariffs or controls apply to the product category? Where is the major currency risk to the transaction and can this risk be minimized through pricing policy? Taking the example of transferring goods from a country with a corporation tax on profits applicable at 40% to an EC country where the subsidiary's turnover would attract corporation tax at 33%, it would make sense to reduce the transfer price to a minimum to maximize profit-taking in the low tax territory. A summary of different ways of setting transfer prices along with the advantages and disadvantages of each method is shown in Table 8.5.

Table 8.5 Methods of setting transfer price.

Method	Advantages	Disadvantages
Transfer at level of cost of export without any mark-up to headquarters.	(1) Enter market at competitive price. (2) Economies of scale possible with penetration.	(1) Subsidiary sets price without regard to wider EC market implications. (2) Not realistic for longer-term profit targets.
Cost-plus for planned level of profit to headquarters and subsidiary.	(1) Realistic on costs at each stage. (2) Straightforward to administer.	(1) Danger of disregarding market conditions.
Market-based (e.g. going-rate or penetration pricing).	(1) Realistic for longer-term market position. (2) Can establish new product or name and develop expertise locally.	(1) Danger of not covering all costs of subsidiary. (2) Care needed in deciding long-term profit objective allowing for change in market conditions.
Set price as if continuing to sell to import agent with separate legal identity.	(1) Mark-up will reflect market norm at each stage.	(1) May not cover overheads of sales and marketing subsidiary. (2) Difficulty in identifying market norms without prior knowledge of intermediary stages.

The effects of EC Competition Law on pricing

EC Competition Law has a very wide brief and anti-competitive practices in the area of pricing are covered by Article 85(1) of the Treaty of Rome. This prohibits:

> 'all agreements between undertakings, decisions by associations of undertakings and concerted practices which may affect trade between Member States and which have as their object or effect the prevention, restriction or distortion of competition within the common market...'

It goes on to give examples of practices which may fall within the scope of this prohibition, including horizontal price fixing

Horizontal price fixing is an agreement to fix price by undertakings at the same level of supply. Article 85(1) includes within its scope explicit agreement, concerted practice or the exchange of price information as well as discounts, rebates and credit terms. Pricing of services is included within the terms of reference, but some service industries such as banking and insurance exhibit features which may justify exclusion with a suitably argued case on a specific activity, such as the commission charges among banks for operating Eurocheque systems (Bellamy and Child, 1987).

Of concern to the exporter of goods to other EC Member States is price-setting at a different level in each country on the basis of local market conditions. Selling identical products of the same quality at the same port of entry to customers from different Member States at very different prices, to reflect local market conditions without consideration of intermediary costs, has been shown to be unacceptable to the European court in the case of United Brands UBC in 1978 (ECR 207, 1978).

Parallel imports

Parallel importing is the buying of goods in a low price area of the community and exporting them to a high price area at a price that is lower than that charged through the 'authorized' channel or intermediary. Growth of such parallel imports eventually renders the official higher price unworkable. In theory, any horizontal agreement which precludes the possibility of such parallel trading would be in breach of Article 85(1). However, there is the dilemma that if there was no protected territory available to a distributor, then the commercial viability of taking on a distributorship would have to be questioned. In practice, Community law seeks to strike a balance between these two.

Parallel importing situations tend to be features of export markets where currency controls mean that suppliers set transfer prices sufficiently high to guarantee profit-taking in the country of export rather than the country of import from where profits cannot be repatriated. With the freeing of currency restrictions of this type within the Community, this will eliminate a common reason for parallel imports.

Longer-term effects of EC harmonization on price

A border-free market of 340 million people will create the opportunity for companies to plan and invest for a sales potential far in excess of what they could possibly hope to achieve within the confines of an individual country. The gearing up to provide products or services on this wider scale will provide the incentive for the better use of corporate resources and the advantages of economies of scale. These factors will exert downward pressure on price whether there are several key players in any one market or a multitude of smaller, specialist suppliers. New patterns of competition will arise and the cost efficiencies obtained at one level in the supply or value-added chain will feed through as lower costs to the next level.

In the longer term, this will enable European companies that have responded to the new market dimension to compete with Japanese and US counterparts with their historic cost advantages which are a result of serving larger home markets. However, companies based in the EC must also be aware of the opportunity which the enlarged EC market will create for companies based outside the EC but which acquire companies operating in it. In the summer of 1988 the Swiss company Nestlé gained control of Rowntree, based in the UK, creating an organization poised to penetrate the EC market for chocolate confectionery.

Another longer-term consideration facing the truly 'European' company of the future is whether the streamlining of administration which would be facilitated by the Single Market would be matched by an appropriate tax arrangement. Currently Ford of Europe has a small army of lawyers and accountants to manage its subsidiaries around the EC. Even in 1993, Ford would still have to do separate tax accounting and separate pricing between subsidiaries.

This taxation problem relating to transfer price is one of several taxation issues that are being addressed by EC working parties. Meanwhile, the company with an eye to Europe has to draw on the best available marketing and financial expertise at its disposal to optimize pricing structure in the context of a changing corporate legal and tax framework.

Problems and assignments

(1) A company with experience in the industry wishes to launch a new roller-ball pen with extended cartridge life. Examine the product positioning and pricing structure of your home market. Outline the various pricing options facing the company and the methods that could be used for setting the price.

(2) What do you understand by the term **price elasticity**? Compare the demand response to price changes of products with **elastic** and **inelastic** demand. Use two markets of your choice to illustrate your answer.

(3) An industrial company lowered its price for a particular component on two occasions with the following results:

Price	Unit sales
$10	2500
$8.5	2850
$7.5	3100

Calculate the average price elasticity of demand for the component. What do you deduce from the figure that you obtain?

(4)　The management of a company manufacturing and marketing computers has noticed that the overall profit margin for the business has been declining. A price review is necessary. In a summary document to the management committee outline the key factors which need to be taken into account in deciding on the price in each of the following areas:

(a)　Mainframe computers with software to solve corporate data processing problems.
(b)　Desk-top personal computers suitable for small businesses.

(5)　The sweet biscuit market is dominated by three major suppliers in the mass-market sector, and there are five companies whose premium products have significant distribution. As one of the mass market suppliers, what are the alternative responses that you might make to a major price reduction campaign by one of the other two leading suppliers? Give the advantages and disadvantages of each course of action.

(6)　Arkwright Medical Instruments Ltd had pioneered the development of a high-resolution body scanner and had successfully tested it in two hospitals in the UK. A German private health company was very interested in acquiring one of the scanners, but due to the high capital cost was unsure about purchasing outright. It had enquired whether Arkwright had considered leasing the machines on one-year contracts, and had received a favourable response but without any details as to leasing costs.

Arkwright management had set the purchase price at £0.75 million and took a view that a private health-care organization could reasonably amortize the capital cost over eight years. Based on experience in the two hospitals in the UK, the machine could be used for 15 patients per week on average and these hospitals had costed its use at £500 per patient, whether paid for by public health funds or private health insurance.

Propose a one-year leasing price to the German customer taking into account the volatility of the sterling/mark exchange rate. Allow for a fluctuation of ±8% for the pound against the Deutschmark. The German company has asked for the leasing price to be quoted in Deutschmarks.

(7)　A new Anglo-French company marketing a colour copying service has requested advice from a marketing consultant on the pricing for their product. The colour copy produced is very superior to Canon photocopy quality, but slightly inferior to standard short-run printing. On specific sizes of runs for medium weight paper the break-even price (including overheads but not marketing costs) compares with actual prices for Canon photocopying and short-run printing as follows:

Length of run	Break-even price	Canon photocopy price	Short-run printing price
100	120	50	700
200	220	94	for any
300	300	135	run to
500	450	200	500
1000	700	350	850

The short-run market demand by size of order has been researched and shows the breakdown given below:

	(%)
up to 100	45
101–200	15
201–300	10
301–500	10
501–1000	20
	100

Some advertising will be necessary to attract the business community which will provide the majority of sales. The financial target for the new product is 15% profit on sales after covering all costs.

As the marketing consultant to this company what price structure would you recommend for the new service, giving your rationale?

(8) What are the marketing, financial and legal implications of pricing across EC Member States for a single product taking into consideration:

(a) Different prices based on what each Member State will bear?

(b) A consistent price across Member States based on product and transportation costs plus a standard mark-up?

References

European perspective

Bellamy C. and Child G. (1987). *Common Market Law of Competition*, 3rd edn. Sweet & Maxwell

Cecchini Report (1988). *The European Challenge 1992 : The Benefits of a Single Market*. Wildwood House

ECR 207 (1978). United Brands UBC

Financial Times (1989). Brussels dreams again of creating truly 'European' companies. 15 May

Financial Times (1989). Parallel import fears start alarm bells ringing for UK book industry. 24 July

Keegan W.J. (1984). *Multinational Marketing Management*, 3rd edn. Englewood Cliffs, New Jersey: Prentice-Hall

The Times (1988). Nestlé's chief views his prize. 20 July

Whish R. (1985). *Competition Law*. London: Butterworths

9 Distribution channels: choice for profit and growth

Chapter objectives:

- to understand the role of distribution within the marketing mix
- to look at how levels of service and competitive advantage are directly linked to distribution channels
- to examine how distribution can be managed by producer or the ever-increasing number of channel intermediaries
- to understand the increasing importance of logistics planning in tandem with customer service and just-in-time planning and management
- to consider the role of retailing and the increasing power of the major retail chains
- to consider how the Single Market will affect the distribution of goods

Introduction

How do British clearing banks view the prospect of reaching Spanish consumers with cheque account facilities and home loans? Why have American and Canadian companies chosen to invest in cable franchises in Britain where British investors have held back? Can a mail order company realistically expect to have a pan-European strategy after 1992?

The nature of these questions suggests that the traditional view of 'distribution' within the marketing mix – linked to the physical transportation of tangible goods and the associated paperwork – is inadequate for the logistical problems now facing companies where advances in telecommunications are having a major impact on the provision of goods and services.

For most organizations, the objective is to enable the target market to gain access to the product or service in a way that is convenient for the customer and cost-effective for the supplier. However, the difficulty which companies are now facing in achieving product differentiation means that the **way in which the product is presented**, including aspects of **quality** and **service**, is a means of achieving **competitive advantage**. The channel of distribution has become a key component of added value. Companies are no longer in the business of simply minimizing the costs of distribution, they are perpetually assessing the trade-off between level of customer service and the cost of delivering it. Where a company has made a commitment to holding sufficient stock on all lines to deliver 100% service, then this is a benefit to be used in advertising but it is an expensive promise, as consideration of the various channel functions will illustrate.

A **marketing** or **distribution channel** is composed of a network of interdependent companies or agencies involved in the movement or transmission of an item of value from the point of production to the point of consumption. The end-user will be concerned with *what* is delivered, *how* it is delivered, *where* and *when*. Assuming that the end-user receives the correct product to match the need, then each of the other three components has a value in its own right which contributes to the final purchase price.

These values can be created by the producer, in controlling the channel through which the product or service is delivered, or by **channel intermediaries** who themselves charge a price for the services rendered. The different types of intermediaries and the functions that they perform are examined in this chapter, in the context of the balance of commercial power within the channel.

The second part of the chapter deals with **logistics planning**. This focuses on how the level of customer service is to be defined and the integration of stock management (including warehousing and transportation) with the flow of information and payment to fulfil this service level. The implications of **just-in-time** planning and implementation for organizational culture and management methods are reviewed.

The importance of **retailing** in the national economy and the power wielded by major British retailers over other members of the channel are acknowledged by a section devoted to this area. The advanced operational skills which have evolved in this environment are examined, together with performance criteria and legal aspects of consumer protection and employment.

The impact of advances in telecommunications and the speed of information flow on modes of delivery and the balance of power within marketing channels are touched upon in this chapter. These issues are considered in greater depth in Chapter 17, where they are viewed in the context of their impact on traditional marketing methods over the next decade.

Why use intermediaries to reach the target market?

There are two overriding reasons for distributing through an intermediary: **access** to the end-user through the existing network of contacts or outlets of the intermediary, and the lower **cost** of using a third party rather than the principal carrying out all channel functions. In 1989, there were 99,751 food retailers in the UK. Farmers could not survive without these outlets providing access to their products for the general population. However, a clothes manufacturer has the choice of reaching the target market through the 59,286 clothing and footwear retail outlets (1989), or supplying direct to the customer through mail order.

Choosing a marketing channel is a key strategic decision with long-term implications. Once established, it is difficult to change without a major upheaval in both the relationships of the organization with its vendors, and in its operating methods. This frequently requires a fundamental change of culture and expertise within management.

Apart from the obvious need for a new company to decide the form of marketing channel to use, the trigger for a reassessment of marketing channel for an existing organization might be:

(1) The launch of a new product;
(2) Penetration of a new market with an existing product;
(3) Reappraisal of the cost/price structure;
(4) Acquisition of a company with complementary product and distribution strengths;
(5) Change in the external environment, such as legislation or taxation, or an economic downturn.

Channel choice is tightly interwoven with the other elements of the marketing mix, and it cannot be taken in isolation from considerations of product, price and promotion. Competitive edge is derived through availability of the right range of product with quality and service guaranteed. The channel chosen must deliver this, but at a cost which can be absorbed in the final price to the end-user, allowing each member of the channel to take profit for the functions performed, including promotion.

Types of vertical marketing systems

Marketing channels are traditionally viewed as facilitating the flow of goods and services on a sequential basis, from one intermediary to another. The linear representation of this through a **vertical marketing system** (VMS) is illustrated in Figure 9.1 where a personal computer might flow through two intermediaries before it reaches the end-user. The type

Manufacturer	**Government departments**
	sells direct

Distributor
- several hundred, but around 20 major players
- tries to sell outside dealer network to improve margins
- high cost of stockholding
- can back repeat-order business with tele-sales

Dealer
- approximately 3500 in 1986
- looks for best price from distributor
- tends to under-stock
- acts as order-taker rather than proactive seller

End-user
- may be small business or private individual
- 250,000 units sold in 1986
- demand here drives activity through the channel

Figure 9.1 UK personal computer market as an example of a traditional vertical marketing system.

of customer supplied direct from the manufacturer might also lead to conflict between the manufacturer and major distributors. Similarly, the dealers would want to protect the margins they make through supplying their customer base, and would not want distributors dealing directly with the end-user. These potential conflicts can be eliminated through unofficial 'gentlemen's agreements' between the two parties, or through specific clauses in a contract.

One option is for a manufacturer to own the distribution channel which secures control of the product from factory or source to end-user. This is a **corporate vertical marketing system**, and examples include petrol distribution through oil company-owned chains of petrol stations, and on-premise beer sales through the high percentage of public houses owned by the major breweries. Where several major companies have come to control over 50% of the market, then there is the danger of abuse of this power through restrictive market practices or excessive pricing, and both of the industry examples given have been the subject of Monopolies and Mergers Commission investigations for precisely these reasons.

This channel format can also come into being through **backward integration** where a major retailer acquires suppliers to guarantee continuity and quality of merchandise.

Alternatives to the corporate vertical marketing system are the **administered vertical system** and the **contractual vertical system**, and the relative advantages and disadvantages of the three systems are examined in Table 9.1.

The administered vertical marketing system excludes outright ownership of one intermediary by another, but is characterized by one member of the channel exerting power over the other channel members. For example, IBM has significant power over distributors in the

Table 9.1 Comparison of the different forms of vertical marketing system from the perspective of a primary supplier.

	Advantages	Disadvantages
Corporate VMS (e.g. petrol, beer)	(1) Total control of product, process, and price. (2) Match resources to volume and type of product flow. (3) Full information available on end-user demand.	(1) Need to develop or buy expertise outside the core business activity. (2) High cost: capital outlay for set-up or acquisition. (3) Responsibilities of central management increased. (4) Economies of scale for own operation may be less than for independent with other clients. (5) Risk of strike or other discontinuity.
Administered (e.g. Marks and Spencer plc, Burton Group)	(1) Set quality standards for other channel members. (2) Possess leverage on price. (3) Impose operating standards to suit own procedures, e.g. deliveries and payment.	(1) Difficult to switch to other channels if environment changes. (2) Information flow may be one-way only. (3) Imposed attitudes could lead to complacency about the market.
Contractual VMS (e.g. Body Shop (franchise), software via dealers)	(1) Immediate access to existing customer base. (2) Costs related to functions performed so less overhead. (3) Flexibility in case of strike or other discontinuity.	(1) Less control over quality, information and possibly, price. (2) May have to compete for priority with non-congruent lines. (3) Mismatch of payment and information systems generating internal costs.

mainframe and micro-computer markets through high market share. Marks and Spencer plc imposes quality specifications on suppliers. The incidence of this type of marketing system is influenced by the degree of concentration of market power in particular industries. Exploration of British retailing later in the chapter will reveal the effects that the administered system can have on operating methods and the physical distribution of goods.

The contractual vertical marketing system involves intermediaries whose responsibilities to each other for distribution functions are the subject of a legal contract. This contract might be loosely structured with only minimum requirements relating to the specification of goods and terms of payment in a written document as, for example, in repeat orders for goods within an ongoing relationship between intermediaries. Alternatively, the detailed responsibilities of an intermediary might be specified in a distributor's agreement or a franchise contract. The nature of these responsibilities is illustrated by the channel functions shown in Table 9.2.

Table 9.2 Different types of intermediary – responsibilities and functions.

Intermediary	Involvement[†]	Definition
Distributor	S L T F P N	Takes on full wholesaling functions; major commitment to principal on stock and market coverage.
Desk jobber	P N	Wholesale order-taker: used for bulky goods and discrete loads, e.g. commodities; telephone dealing common.
Rack jobber	S L T F P N	Monitors retail offtake and merchandises new stock; bills retailer for goods sold.
Cash and carry	S L F	Provides convenient service for small retailers needing frequent, small orders of wide variety of goods but no credit.
Voluntary group	S L T F N	Bulk buying on behalf of small retailer members; non-profit.
Retail cooperative	S L T F P N	Bulk buying and retail service on behalf of consumer members who also receive any profits.
Agent	P	Seeks and obtains orders on behalf of a principal over a defined territory; paid commission on sales. Specialization by merchandise or customer type common.
Broker	P N	Acts on behalf of principal, selling lots or loads, negotiating on price and other terms. Charges commission on sale.
Auctioneer	P	Sells on behalf of principal for best price obtainable at auction, possibly with reserve price; charges commission on sale price.
Factor	F N	Financing of principals by taking responsibility for accounts payable, charging percentage discount on invoice value.

[†] S: carry inventory; L: take legal title to goods; T: involved in transportation; F: financial involvement; P: responsible for promotion; N: involved in negotiation.

Number of levels in the vertical marketing system

Direct supply from principal to end-user is known as a **zero-level channel,** and mail order is an example of this form of supply, as is bulk chemical straight from producer to the factory where it is to be used.

A **one-level channel** involves one intermediary, as in the direct supply from manufacturer to large supermarket chain, which serves the general public. This has been the norm for major brands of packaged food for some years, where the economy of scale has warranted this relationship. More recently, this channel structure has emerged for supermarket own-label wine, where whole vintages from specific vineyards are purchased by the supermarket chain. Their buyers select the product and negotiate terms of trade.

A **two-level channel** is more appropriate for specialist, more expensive wine vintages, where a wine shipper will purchase a specific quantity in the knowledge that this will sell to a number of retail outlets with whom it has an existing relationship. This channel structure typically involves a **wholesaler** and retailer, both of whom take **legal title** to the goods and pay for the stock purchased. In a market such as ethical pharmaceuticals (which are available to the general public through a doctor's prescription), the wholesaler is the key to cost-effective distribution. He must balance stock levels against forecast demand to minimize stockholding cost. The wine shipper on the other hand, might choose to hold on to certain vintages of wine in the expectation of appreciation rather than depreciation.

A **three-level channel** might involve two levels of wholesale as well as the retail stage to give three intermediaries in all. For example, there is a highly efficient Dutch auction centre for flowers, where large wholesalers will commit to bulk purchases on a daily basis. They will then sell on to wholesalers in the UK who operate from their pitches at New Covent Garden. Here, they sell on to retailers, minimizing stockholding. These retailers will range from small local chains with three or four outlets, to the small stalls seen outside hospitals or by the roadside. The highly fragmented nature of this market could be viewed as adversely affecting quality, and therefore, demand.

Sales of houseplants and cut flowers doubled in value from 1986 to 1991 (Marketing, 1991), and one reason put forward is the availability of favourite varieties in fresh condition throughout the year through improved transportation and storage facilities. This illustrates the product enhancement and market growth that can be achieved through improved distribution channels.

Marketing channel functions

One way of describing the functions performed by channel intermediaries is in terms of **flows**, and six flow categories can be identified:

(1) Physical flow of goods;
(2) Flow of **legal title** or ownership of the goods;
(3) Flow of the order for the goods;
(4) Flow of payment for the goods;
(5) Promotion flow: personal selling, advertising and product literature;
(6) Information flow: about the status of an order, delivery times (planned and actual), customer needs, market intelligence.

All of the functions performed within the chain can be classified to one of these flows, but examination within these categories does not necessarily provide the ideal framework. The approach adopted here is to explain some of the more complex functions, and to illustrate how intermediaries become involved in different functions on a selective basis, with the aid of Table 9.3. The rapid growth in franchising as a distribution format is acknowledged through the responsibilities specified in the franchise contract, as illustrated in Table 9.4.

Table 9.3 Marketing channel functions.

	Wholesaler fresh fruit	Major food retailer	Cosmetics retail franchise	Fashion mail-order house	Ethical drug wholesaler
Carry inventory		X	X	X	X
Physical distribution		X	X		X
After-sales service		X	X	X	X
Negotiating terms	X	X		X	X
Developing products		X	X		
Merchandise Accumulation	X	X	X	X	X
Assorting		X	X	X	X
Allocation		X	X		
Consumer Promotion		X	X	X	
Credit		X		X	
Financing	X	X	X	X	X
Risk-taking	X	X	X	X	X

Table 9.4 Components of a franchise contract.

Defined by the contract	Parties to the agreement (these may be individuals or limited companies) Period of agreement, e.g. 5 years Geographical area of exclusivity Rights granted to franchisee Payments due from franchisee Responsibilities of both parties Conditions for termination
Rights granted	Can be of two types: *Business format* Franchisor assigns right to use trademarks and logos, know-how and operating methods (such as picture framing, printing services, fast food) *Distributorship* Includes all the features of a business format franchise, but these exist to promote the distribution of a product, which often bears the trademark assigned (Coca-Cola, imported cars, cosmetics)
Payments by franchisee to franchisor	Franchise fee Royalty on sales Start-up investment or interest on loan (if franchisor is selling the premises to the franchisee or providing start-up capital)
Responsibilities of franchisee	Operate to standards laid down Provide information/sales data Develop sales potential of territory
Responsibilities of franchisor	Provision of a 'blueprint' for conduct of business: often in the form of an **operations manual** Training for franchisees and their employees Field supervision and quality control Consistent supplies of merchandise (distributorship) and promotion material National advertising

One general principle underpins this analytical framework: where a function is necessary to the successful operation of a marketing channel, then that function cannot be eliminated when an intermediary is removed from the chain. The function moves up the chain (possibly carried out by the manufacturer) or down towards the end-user. In the personal computer market example of Figure 9.1, it might be possible to eliminate the distributor from the chain, but this would mean that either the manufacturer or the dealer would have to commit to a greater stockholding role to ensure that demand was met. The member of the channel taking on the function will depend on capability and cost-effectiveness. Can the computer manufacturer realistically expect to deliver frequent small orders to a large number of dealers located all over the country?

Where a marketing channel is committed to fulfilment of end-user needs in a matter of days rather than weeks, then one or more intermediaries has to **carry inventory**. This requires **financing** and a degree of **risk**, since there are very few markets where demand can be forecast accurately. This risk increases where stock is perishable or likely to become obsolete.

The nature of the market and the position of the intermediary in the chain will determine what inventory is needed to fulfil time and place added value for the end-user. The degree of merchandise variety provided by the intermediary is created through the **sorting** function, and there are three recognized modes (Stern and El-Ansary, 1988):

(1) *Accumulation* Bringing similar stocks together from a number of sources to produce a homogeneous supply, such as wholesalers provide for retailers.
(2) *Assorting* Bringing a wide variety of stocks together from a number of sources to provide a heterogeneous supply which provides for choice and associated items in one location, as illustrated by retail outlets.
(3) *Allocation* The most evident form of this is the allocation of a merchandise mix to each outlet by management of a large retail chain. Bulk wholesalers also break down job-lots into smaller loads for their customers.

The involvement in inventory or stockholding marks the traditional wholesaler from a manufacturer's agent. Different types of wholesaler are described in Table 9.2, and where these are involved in holding stock, then they also incur financial risk. The agent acts on behalf of a manufacturer or 'principal', reaching a specific target market in a defined territory through personal selling. The agent earns a percentage on sales achieved, and deliveries are made direct from manufacturer's warehouse to the customer's premises. This type of agent does not incur financial risk associated with holding stock.

The agent is unlikely to have significant authority over the terms and conditions of sale in consumer goods markets and will not therefore be expected to exercise negotiating skills. This contrasts with a major distributor in an industrial market, where the operating margin will depend heavily on the terms which are negotiated, firstly with the manufacturer, and secondly with customers. If market conditions are changing, such as a downturn or new competition, then this gives the distributor flexibility of response.

Choosing a distribution channel

This major strategic decision has an impact on profitability and growth prospects for a company entering a new market sector. For this reason, a number of factors will be taken into account:

(1) *The nature of the product* Is it highly technical, requiring specialist knowledge on the part of intermediaries or are handling capabilities for mass-market products more important?

(2) *The marketing strategy* Is high-penetration, intensive distribution required, or is the product satisfying the demands of a niche market with a select audience?

(3) *The structure of the market and the nature of competition* The historical development of channels within a market will often leave a new entrant with no option but to adopt the same channels as the competition. A decision to circumvent the traditional intermediaries and to supply the end-user direct could provide competitive edge but might also involve high risk.

(4) *The location of logistical capabilities and expertise* These key resources (physical distribution, computer processing and tracking facilities) might rest with a few specialists, as in the third-party contract distribution of goods to supermarket chains, which is discussed later in the chapter.

(5) *The financial resources of different members of the channel* A principal with capital to invest might choose to develop a corporate distribution system. A principal without this would need to rely on distributors, who would carry costs of a salesforce, outlets and inventory as appropriate.

(6) *Price and profitability* Intermediaries carry out specific functions in return for a mark-up on their buying-in price, or for a commission on sales. These are costs which have to be built into the final price to the end-user. This price has to reflect the quality of the product in the context of competitive pricing. If one method of distribution results in a non-viable price to the end-user, then costs through the chain need to be re-examined, or an alternative channel chosen.

(7) *Potential conflict of interest* An intermediary might be carrying competitive products in a market where exclusivity of product line is the norm. The principal might wish to maintain control of computerized order processing and data retrieval, where an intermediary might include these functions as part of a standard contract delivery service.

These issues can be translated into objective criteria against which to judge alternative channels. **Linear averaging** provides a method of quantifying value judgement on the suitability of different channels (this method is described in detail in Chapter 5). Four possible criteria that may be used are:

- effectiveness of reach
- profitability
- capital investment/risk
- level of expertise/market knowledge

These criteria would be assigned an importance weighting, and then each alternative channel would be scored against each criteria.

Alternatively, a channel can be judged against the general criteria of **efficiency, effectiveness** and **adaptability** (Magrath and Hardy, 1987). This requires a detailed analysis of measures such as cost and coverage across the alternative channels. Time and effort invested in evaluation of options give a clearer view of the trade-offs necessary to achieve channel objectives. This is consistent with viewing a marketing channel as a strategic issue, contributing to longer-term business viability and competitive edge.

The nature of the contract between intermediaries

A written order for goods is the simplest form of contract, since this incurs responsibility for acceptance of those goods and payment for them under the terms and conditions of the supplier. (A telex order also constitutes a contract, but a fax does not – this has to be followed up by postal confirmation.)

In contrast, a **distributor agreement** will be a lengthy document specifying the responsibilities of the distributor in return for the rights to sell the product. These might be exclusive rights in a territory or to a particular type of end-user, and the manufacturer must be sure that the distributor has the resources and expertise to exploit the market potential.

Clauses in the contract would relate to minimum purchase levels, prices and payment terms, inventory levels, level of service to be provided to customers, and promotion. Distributors are valuable for their salesforce coverage of a territory, and they would be expected to use objective criteria to assess performance here (see Chapter 13). The use of advertising and technical literature could also be specified in the distributor contract, together with the way in which such promotion is to be financed. One model is a levy on the distributor for materials and advertising provided by the manufacturer. An alternative approach is an obligation for the distributor to develop sales to a minimum level in a given period. Implicit within such an undertaking is a commitment to promotion.

The degree to which sales performance is specified in a **franchise contract** will depend on the country in which it has been drawn up. The outline in Table 9.4 relates to a typical franchise contract in the UK, where minimum sales performance might not be specified. However, a clause would be included to denote that if a territory was not being adequately exploited then this would be a reason for termination of the contract. In the USA, the **franchisor** (the party owning the rights to a trade-mark, operating format or distributable merchandise) has greater legal redress with regard to minimum performance, and this is a double-edged sword when the franchisor also has legal rights over the lease to the property from which the franchisee operates.

The legality of **exclusivity** clauses within distribution agreements will depend on the nature of the market. This has been common practice for beers sold through public houses "tied" to a brewery group, and for soft drinks sold in public houses, clubs and other leisure outlets in the UK. In 1989, the Monopolies and Mergers Commission required breweries to divest themselves of tied houses where they owned more than a maximum specified.

Contract distribution

A manufacturing company has the choice of using its own distribution system, encompassing vehicle fleet, depots and computer processing, or can contract out the physical distribution of its products to a specialist organization. The traditional view is for a manufacturing company to regard its own 'in-house' distribution system as a cost centre. A distribution company acting as a third party between manufacturer and customer will be operating as a profit centre. The transfer of the capital investment and risk associated with physical distribution to the third-party contractor, together with the specialist expertise available, is the rationale for using such services.

Counter-arguments for using an in-house system include the higher cost of contracting out, as the third party will be looking to make a profit on the contract, and a loss of control over the quality of delivery and associated services provided to customers. An assessment of capital investment requirements and distribution expertise available within the manufacturing organization will be necessary, along with a review of the value-added services offered by the contractor. These can range from strategic distribution planning to materials handling specifications and warehouse layout, and the most significant contemporary advantage is access to sophisticated electronic data processing customized for the distribution process (Wilson and Fathers, 1989).

Some companies have no option but to contract out distribution, but with due concern for the level of control over information that is relinquished in the process. Others are confident in handing over responsibility for distribution in the knowledge that their own computer information system maintains the balance of control in their favour. This is the case for major British retailers in the enviable position of dictating the mode of deliveries from suppliers via designated third party contractors (this phenomenon is explored later in the chapter).

The grocery retail sector is characterized by a higher level of contracting out than consumer manufacture, industrial manufacture and non-grocery retail. In these sectors, research indicates that organizations which contract out distribution outnumber those who do not by a ratio of two to one (Meredith and O'Sullivan, 1991). The research also indicates that only two thirds of organizations found that the move to contract distribution achieved the main objectives of reduced costs, improved service and increased flexibility. There was much lower perceived achievement on the objectives of reduced investment and better results in core activity. In general, there was no difference in level of satisfaction between those using a dedicated distribution facility and those serviced by joint-user companies.

Service failure is cited as the most significant cause of dissatisfaction, and poor contractor management is blamed for this and other shortcomings. However, there is also a recognition that the company itself must take some responsibility for unsatisfactory performance, notably in contract specification, controls and management information.

Logistic alliances

Some of the problems of contract distribution can be laid at the door of the limited nature of the relationship where specific services are provided at an agreed cost. The longer-term strategic objectives of the two parties are unlikely to be strictly compatible. An alternative approach is to view channel members as potential partners in the distribution process, where cooperative rather than adversarial relationships are the norm, and companies work together for many years on an informal understanding rather than a formal contract.

In Japan, such logistic alliances are cemented through a greater degree of mutual dependence than is found in Western Europe or the United States. The commitment seen in Japan to one supplier of a component and one distributor might be regarded as taking undue risk if it were not for the strategic benefits that accrue to each party from the arrangement. A move towards strategic alliances between channel members has become evident in the United States, where logistics costs in 1990 were estimated at about 10.5% of GNP. This compares with 15.4% of GNP in 1981. This cost advantage is a secondary benefit of forging closer relationships between channel members. The primary objective is competitive advantage and market impact, as would be achieved by the projected consortium of four companies in the women's ready-to-wear market: Du Pont who make the fibre, Milliken converting fibre into fabric, Leslie Fay producing garments and Dillard Department Stores selling them (Bowersox, 1990). This vertical alliance could respond to fluctuating demand with tighter inventory control than would be possible under traditional supplier agreements.

Shifts in organizational culture may be needed to progress towards this type of alliance, as the degree of information-sharing required to make efficiency gains cuts across the traditional boundaries of confidentiality. This becomes a prominent issue where one channel member has access to another's computer database, which is a feature of the kind of networks described in Chapter 17.

Logistics planning

Physical distribution management focuses on the flow of goods from the point of origin to the point of consumption. Effective management of the supply chain has become increasingly dependent on the speed and accuracy of information flowing between channel members. This enables management to plan for the longer term as well as react to short-term fluctuations in demand. High interest rates on bank loans to finance working capital have added urgency to companies' reassessment of inventory levels. Where reduction in these levels is necessary to maintain profitability, the 'knock-on' effects on production schedules, warehousing needs and delivery cycles are significant. However, the driving force for management of the logistics process for a company to maintain competitive position has to be provision of a predefined level of **customer service** at an acceptable cost.

The increasing emphasis on product **quality** means a greater allocation of resources to making sure that the product arrives when the customer wants it, and with installation, technical advice and training provided as part of a complete package. Where intermediaries such as distributors or dealers are involved in the process, then the split allocation of functions can mean considerable planning and training of personnel at every level.

Trade-off between customer service level and costs

The costs of the distribution (or logistics) process can range anywhere between 5 and 20% of turnover. In high value-added sectors, after-sales service and advice are critical to perceptions of the product and supplier, but the cost of this provision can be high and is often disguised under a general 'overhead' classification in the profit and loss account. Companies such as Wang in the computer market are very aware of the costs associated with customer service, and employ a system of time sheets for sales and system personnel so that the true cost of serving a client can be identified.

The setting of objective targets for the level of customer service provides a policy framework within which personnel from different functional areas can respond. In production, quality targets can be set. In distribution, delivery within seven days of receipt of order might be the norm. In after-sales service, a 24-hour response to all technical emergencies could be part of the standard contract. These types of targets would require investment in equipment and people, which would constitute visible costs. There are also invisible costs of not meeting high standards of service with the eventual loss of customers.

- *Visible costs*
  - transportation
  - warehousing
  - inventory
  - personnel
- *Invisible costs*
  - reprocessing of orders
  - substitution of damaged goods
  - special deliveries
  - cancelled orders
  - customer dissatisfaction

Implementation of a **first time right** policy will seek to minimize the hidden costs of customer service. Where quantitative standards have been set for different service elements then measurement procedures for monitoring actual performance will provide regular assessment of where performance is falling short of target. This **performance variance** may be evident in such areas as accuracy of order filling, frequency of deliveries, billing procedure and returns policy. Corrective action will restore performance to target levels.

Companies whose reputations are built on quality of product and service will take pains to monitor the level and nature of customer complaints. In the retail sector, Marks and Spencer personnel adhere to strict policy on how such complaints should be handled. In the industrial sector, selective telephone follow-up to identify levels of customer satisfaction can provide an early warning system before isolated problems turn into negative perceptions of product and service quality.

The integrated supply chain

The sequential approach to distribution planning requires step-wise decision-making in the following areas, once the customer service standards of performance have been determined.

(1) *Transportation* Factory to manufacturer's warehouse to whole-saler to end-user. How many stages and which intermediary is responsible at each stage?

(2) *Warehousing* Does each intermediary carry inventory? Where is the inventory held? Is there a need for special storage conditions in transit?

(3) *Inventory control* What is the length of the order cycle? What level of safety stock is needed? Which intermediaries carry the risk of excess stock or stock-out? How is stock replenishment triggered?

(4) *Order processing* Is the paper flow integrated with the flow of goods? Is the system computerized to provide stock reconciliation and management information? How are problem orders and customer queries handled within the system?

The degree of overlap between these key decision areas is enhanced by the increasingly sophisticated software systems dedicated to the handling of goods, orders, money and customer information for specific industries. For this reason, the supply chain can no longer be seen as a simple sequential process with different functional departments responsible for discrete activities. Instead, specialist activities have become interdependent as the time-scale for production, transportation and order fulfilment is shortened to accommodate financial targets and changing market conditions.

Management of the contemporary logistics process rests on inter-locking plans in key areas, with rapid and effective feedback so that adjustments can be made to reflect customer needs. These interrelation-ships are illustrated in Figure 9.2, where the marketing planning function is seen as the driving force behind production scheduling, inventory management and distribution planning.

There are three aspects of this logistics framework which are critical to success:

(1) The chain is only as strong as the weakest link. The weak area might be an internal department or a distributor, and constant monitoring of performance is necessary.

(2) Effective communication between commercial and technical/pro-duction departments is necessary to ensure that the integrated logis-tics process is responsive to the marketplace. This will require formal and informal lines of authority and responsibility, so that forecasts can be altered and decisions made regarding the use of resources.

(3) Information on sales performance, customer satisfaction and changing needs is required by the manufacturer at the aggregate level so that marketing plans and sales forecasts can be prepared. A corporate or administered VMS will accommodate these needs. A manufacturer serving a wide array of industries through different types of intermediaries will encounter more problems in construct-ing an effective sales reporting and management information system.

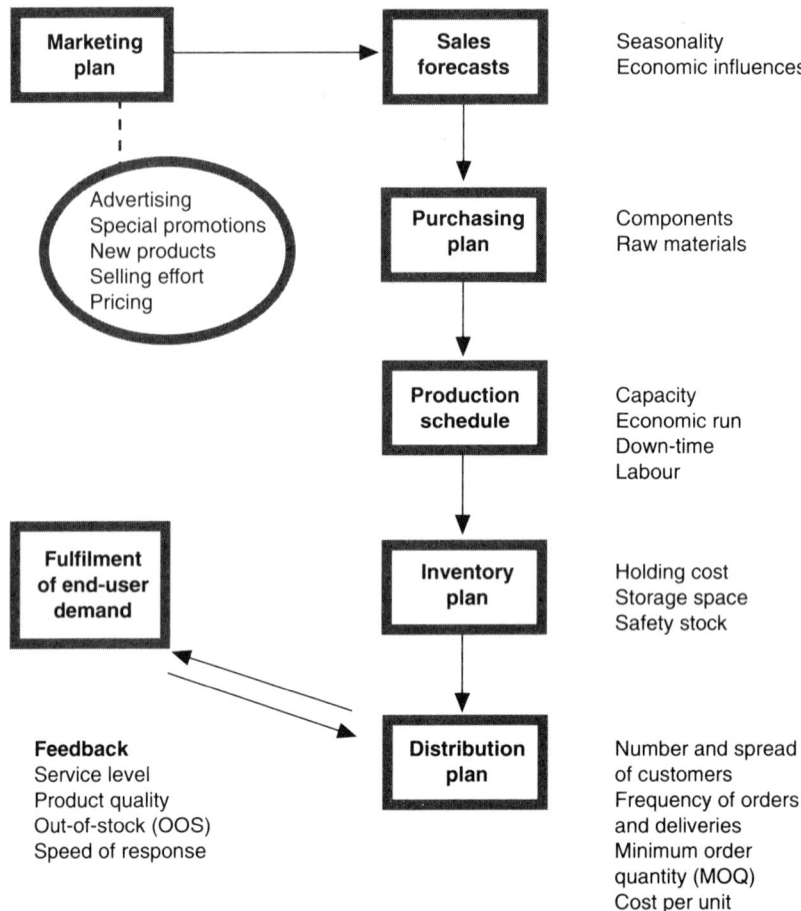

Figure 9.2 Decision flow-chart to show the relationship between the marketing plan and logistics for optimal fulfilment of end-user needs.

An alternative way of looking at the **integrated supply chain** is through the use of four key resources:

- facilities
- people
- finance
- systems

When strategic decisions have been taken, an organizational framework can be built which bridges traditional functional barriers (Stevens, 1989). This approach gives pre-eminence to logistics at the operational level, as a way of providing added value through enhanced customer service.

In 1980, deregulation of the transport industry in the United States brought greater competition in both costs and service. Combined with the high cost of capital and the increased price of oil as a legacy from the events of 1973, there was significant pressure on companies to improve logistics as a way of gaining competitive edge. Research has shown that companies that have integrated their logistics operations have gained increases of between 1.9 and 2.4 percentage points in operating margin. There is also research evidence to show that these companies tend to compete on customer service rather than price (Fox, 1987).

Inventory management

A high proportion of distribution costs for bulky industrial goods are attributed to holding inventory. As interest rates have moved inexorably upwards during the 1970s and 1980s, there has been a reluctance on the part of channel members to have significant amounts of working capital tied up in inventory. This has led to redistribution of the **risk** associated with inventory in some industries, as the most influential member of a channel has instituted new credit terms for intermediaries lower down the chain. It has also been the driving force to identify more efficient ways of operating the supply chain. This has led to implementation of **just-in-time** fulfilment which is explored in the following section.

Although the costs of **holding inventory** are the most significant, there are also costs associated with **processing inventory** and with the situation where an order cannot be fulfilled through an **out-of-stock** position (OOS). The major cost elements for each of these three areas are shown in Table 9.5, and range across both 'visible' and 'invisible' costs.

For many organizations, the investigation of how to reduce inventory costs reduces to a simple trade-off between the following two measures:

(1) Interest charged on working capital to finance inventory equivalent to one day's average sales, versus
(2) Profit on sales lost through a reduction in inventory level equivalent to one day's average sales.

Table 9.5 Inventory management: critical costs (visible and invisible).

Inventory holding cost	Inventory processing cost	Cost of out-of-stock
Interest charge on bank loan	Direct cost per order processed	Profit contribution on lost sale
Warehousing	Set-up cost per customer	Customer goodwill
Handling	Reconciliations	Product substitution
Insurance	Management information	Cost of creating back order
Obsolescence		

Where a company is not financing working capital through bank borrowings, then an alternative measure might be the **opportunity cost** of using the capital released from inventory in a different way.

The introduction of shorter lead times at some stages of the supply chain could mean that inventory levels can be reduced without affecting the level of service to customers. This efficiency gain for many organizations in the 1990s will be dependent on the harnessing of the most sophisticated information technology which, in itself, requires considerable capital investment.

Another trade-off which manufacturing companies employ is that between the **economic order quantity** for raw materials and components, their inventory holding cost, the **minimum production run** for the finished goods and their inventory holding cost. The involvement of four measures here illustrates the complexity of the analytical task facing many companies. Philips, the Dutch conglomerate, has invested in customized computer software to forecast and analyse **suppliers' costs**, which can then be fed into forecasts for Philips' own production and inventory holding costs.

Smaller companies are often tempted by the significantly lower prices of large production runs on components from their suppliers. The folly of ordering at this level becomes apparent when stocks from this delivery last far beyond medium-term requirements. This inventory has to be stored and financed, while the management hopes that product changes are not necessary, which will render the component obsolete.

There are standard formulae for the calculation of a range of inventory ratios, where historic sales patterns provide reliable guides to future needs and detailed costings are available. These include formulae for the following, and students are recommended to refer to a more specialized text for these and other quantitative methods associated with inventory management (West, 1989):

- safety stock levels where a number of locations are involved;
- optimum length of order interval for an inventory item;
- the economic order quantity (EOQ) for an item based on profitability, inventory holding cost and costs of initiating production.

Just-in-time (JIT)

The success of Japanese companies in reducing costs and prices by implementing JIT added to existing competitive pressures on Western companies to improve efficiency in the early 1980s.

Just-in-time is a logistics system in which inventory arrives at production and distribution points just as it is needed. Fulfilment of end-user demand as it arises is the driving force, so that there are two key benefits to the system: improved customer service levels and reduction of inventory holding costs. In effect, channel member cooperation replaces the need for buffer or 'safety' stock, and the working practices involved require a considerable change in culture, whereby traditional adversarial relationships between vendor and customer have to be moulded into partnerships.

Teamwork is also a prerequisite within the JIT organization, as changes in some of the functions within the logistics chain require more frequent communication and cooperation. Adoption of JIT affects the following functions:

- *Senior management*   Encourages commitment to JIT.
- *Marketing*   More frequent feedback of market and sales data.
- *Planning*   More critical coordination role.
- *Purchasing*   Different criteria for choice of suppliers and more frequent orders for lower quantities.
- *Production*   More frequent and shorter production runs.
- *Quality control*   More stringent standards at every stage in the procurement and production cycle.
- *Warehousing*   Implications of less inventory possibly at distribution points nearer to the customer.
- *Transportation*   Need for more frequent deliveries.
- *Data processing*   More frequent transactions with greater demands on management information system and computer support.

Changes in individual roles will not guarantee success of adoption of JIT; there has to be improved **communication** between departments and a willingness to work as a **team**. Suppliers themselves must be prepared to adopt JIT practices and to show a greater commitment to understanding the user's business. Perhaps the most difficult of all the requirements is a need for channel members to share what was traditionally confidential information on sales performance and logistical practices.

It is estimated that only about 40% of manufacturing companies use **manufacturing resource planning** software systems, and the majority of these are large companies (Horner, 1991).

Given the organizational changes necessary to implement JIT, management will need evidence that objectives are, indeed, being met. This requires monitoring of performance, and quantitative measurement criteria are necessary for success.

Although cost reduction is an important aim of JIT, the major objective for many suppliers is to gain competitive edge through improved customer service. Research indicates that this has been achieved in industrial markets: for example, back-orders declined by 20% to 30%, lead times were cut by over 40% and supplier delivery frequency increased by over 200% (Dion *et al.*, 1990). The same research indicated that half of the respondent companies found that purchase prices of goods bought JIT were slightly lower, while the other half did not perceive any price advantage.

The fact that this research did not find that companies had achieved increased profits through implementation of JIT is surprising if viewed from the perspective of reduced inventory levels. However, the increased customer service levels must come at a cost.

Adoption of JIT logistics management encourages organizations to take a closer look at **time-based performance measures** as well as traditional financial and output ratios. This approach can be used in evaluation of efficiency of processing and production, customer service, decision-making and new product development (Stalk and Hout, 1990). The closer that measures can get to the customer and the marketplace, the easier it is to judge levels of competitiveness.

Retailing

Retailing is the most visible part of the distribution chain. The 4.5% decline in the total number of UK retail outlets from 1986 to 1989 was evidence of the continuing trend towards concentration in retailing. However, the pattern is not consistent across all sectors; the most significant decline is evident in the number of food retailers (−17.5%), whereas the clothing and footwear and household goods sectors have seen a decline of less than 2%. The category classified by the Central Statistics Office as 'non-food' has increased by 12% and reflects the trend towards small, speciality 'niche' retailers filling the service gap in the high street left by the large retailing chains moving out of town or reducing the number of lines available.

The high level of concentration in the food industry, where five supermarket chains account for 50% of the market, has led to advantages of scale economy in buying and to investment in electronic data processing for more efficient logistics.

The concentrated nature of British food retailing, in contrast to that in other European countries and the United States, has given rise to considerable expertise in food-related logistics. This led to delegations of experts visiting Russia and other republics soon after the failed August coup in 1991. In spite of the political turmoil at the time, there was general acceptance of the need for expert advice on how to deliver the fruits of the harvest to the population centres, through improved food preservation processes and distribution.

Small, independent retailers do not achieve such a high national profile, and yet these are important to the economy in providing goods and services that the larger chains do not see as appropriate to their strategy or operations. They are also an important component of the small business sector, where lower entry costs than for manufacturing make retailing an attractive option for entrepreneurs and bank lending. The business dynamics for small, independent retailers are necessarily

Table 9.6 Comparison of strategic and operational features for large and small retailers.

	Large retail chain	Small independent retailer
Strategy options	Large target audience: (1) Price (2) Assortment (3) Quality	(1) Niche market (2) Specialist merchandise (3) Service
Property	Property portfolio may be core activity. Need prime site in high street or out-of-town development.	Can operate from non-prime site. High rental levels and 3–5 year rent review.
Physical distribution	Frequently contracted out to third party to consolidate deliveries. Tends to be administerered by retailing group with high market share.	Combination of supplier's own, contracted out and retailer collects. Small delivery quantities involve high cost passed on in price.
Inventory management	EPOS provides effective MIS to minimize costs. Stock-turn critical measure of performance.	Less sophisticated MIS. Wide assortment to provide choice and service is costly.
Personnel	Trained and experienced managers. Tightly rostered sales staff.	Owner/manager common. Family involved to reduce wages bill.
Finance	Strong balance sheet supports lower profit position in recession. High market share leads to higher margin.	Heavy debt burden leads to difficulties in recession. Mark-up dictated by market norm. Prolonged discounting erodes margins.

similar to those for the major chains, but the financial and operational constraints on the former mean that there are also significant areas of difference. These are highlighted in Table 9.6.

Economic aspects of retailing

The level of retail sales is a key monthly indicator of the state of the economy. Real consumer spending power is camouflaged in those economies where credit is freely available and where consumer confidence and interest levels dictate to what degree this is taken up. The use of credit was a major feature of the UK retail boom in 1986–89, when the savings ratio fell to an all-time low. Many new stores were opened and 12 million square feet of new out-of-town stores were planned for 1990. The subsequent tightening of the money supply through high interest rates led to a severe slump in sales which hit the clothing and household retailing sectors particularly hard.

Apart from the external influence of the state of the economy, there are six key factors which should be taken into account when examining the future economic viability of a retail outlet:

(1) *Location* There are three components to take into account; the catchment area in terms of the number and type of households, accessibility of the store by car or on foot; and the visibility of the store. Higher revenues and costs are associated with prime sites, and major retailing groups conduct store location studies to reduce financial risk. These are examined later in the chapter under a special heading.

(2) *Property costs* These include the purchase of a freehold site, or the annual rent on a leasehold site, and amortization of shopfitting costs. In some countries there will also be a commercial property tax or 'rate'.

(3) *Wage levels* These tend to be lower than in other industries. There is a lower incidence of unionized labour and a higher incidence of women and part-time employees compared with other industries.

(4) *Relationship between retail price and cost-of-goods* The absolute difference between these (before tax) is the gross margin, often expressed as a percentage of the retail price. Another way of describing this is as a mark-up on the cost-of-goods. For fashion and luxury goods this might be 100–130%, and for food it might be 20–60%.

(5) *Merchandise density* This affects sales per square foot (or square metre) and therefore profit per square foot (or square metre). High merchandise density is associated with budget items for the mass market. Low merchandise density is a feature of specialist merchandise aimed at a smaller target group.

(6) *Stock-turn* A financial ratio which measures the number of times the total stock is sold and replenished in a given period. It can be calculated by dividing the retail sales value in the period by the average stock value at retail price for the same period. Stock-turn for low-value, low-margin goods will be higher than stock-turn for high-value, high-margin items.

Store location

The importance of attempting to adopt a scientific approach to the forecasting of new retail developments is apparent to both retailer and local authority. The retailer is concerned by capital cost (£20 million for a superstore) and the return on this investment. The local authority needs to be reassured on the impact on existing retail provision and fit with environmental needs before granting planning permission. Instinct has to a large extent been replaced by the use of checklists (Nelson), customer spotting surveys, inter-store comparisons (Applebaum's analogue method) and gravity models (Reilly, Converse, Huff).

A detailed description of the above methods is not intended here. That can be found in many other texts, such as Dickson's chapter in the

Handbook of Retailing (West, 1988) and Davies and Rogers (1984). However, the most comprehensive review of Reilly's Law and the converse adaptations can be found in Schwartz (1963).

Huff's probability model, often credited to Lakshmanan and Hansen, was a considerable improvement on Reilly in that it was much easier to use in urban areas and introduced the concept of calibration (fitting the model to local conditions). This was demonstrated in the UK by planners in Lewisham, south east London.

Missing from the above-mentioned chapter in West (1988) is the section on the relevance of the Lewisham concept and methodology to forecasting turnover of new developments in the late 1980s. In theory, it is possible to calibrate the Huff formula to local conditions by:

(1)   'Forecasting' turnovers for previous years.
(2)   Forecasting turnovers without the new development.
(3)   Forecasting turnovers including the new development.

The difference between (2) and (3) shows the new development's likely turnover and impact on existing shopping provision. It would also indicate whether the size of the development is viable.

The major drawback to the use of such models is the availability of the data needed. No longer is there a Census of Distribution, and floorspace figures are less readily available than they used to be. Is this, perhaps, why local authorities with calibration models appear to rely on retailers' own impact studies? Local authorities could have made it easier for themselves by talking to each other and comparing notes and experiences.

Retailers are able to use sophisticated models because of the data bank that they have built up over the years – data not available to local authorities.

Site location models are useful tools, but their effectiveness depends on the availability of the necessary data.

There are two contemporary aspects of retailing which have contributed to sophisticated management control, and flowing from this, the financial success of major chains. The first of these is the advent of **electronic point of sale (EPOS)**, and the second is the technique for analysis of costs and profit associated with each item stocked known as **direct product profitability (DPP)**.

Electronic point of sale (EPOS)

This system for electronic scanning of the **universal product code** or bar code on each item at the check-out provides speed and accuracy in billing customers. However, the computerized information feedback to management also provides the following advantages:

- automatic computer re-ordering of purchased items;
- management information on fast- and slow-moving lines;
- elimination of the stock-room, with daily deliveries.

The existence of EPOS has also contributed to the balance of power swinging from the manufacturers of branded goods to retailers. Where manufacturers have to await the consolidated results of audit research, retailers can consult the previous day's sales when negotiating price, quantities and mix. The analyses available through EPOS enable the retailer to plan displays on the basis of actual sales of competing brands in the same product group, thus manipulating sales and profit per square foot.

The sharing of EPOS information with a supplier indicates the emergence of a channel alliance, but there is the risk that the retailer will relinquish negotiating power in doing this. The strength of this power is reflected in the increasing proportion of marketing budgets for consumer brands now allocated to retailer discounts, as opposed to advertising and sales promotion directed at the consumer.

Direct product profitability

The existence of discrete information available on each line stocked has facilitated an alternative way of analysing costs and profitability. The traditional approach has been to examine the absolute gross margin of a product group or individual line stocked. However, this approach does not take into account the retailer costs of handling, storing and displaying the product which are *not* included in the manufacturer's selling price to the retailer.

An alternative approach, called direct product profitability (DPP), takes into account the retailer costs of packaging, transportation, loading, storage and merchandising at the point of sale. By analysing and assigning these costs to individual lines and relating to the retail price, an individual product profit can be assigned.

So, for example, a toothpaste pack would carry an absolute value for gross margin lower than that for a kitchen roll multipack. However, the cost of transportation, storage and display for the latter would be higher, and could bring the actual line profitability below that for the toothpaste. This knowledge would enable the retailer to make decisions regarding shelf-space allocation and target stock-turn.

Research conducted by management consultants Touche Ross in conjunction with the Institute of Grocery Distribution (IGD) indicates that only a third of major UK retailers use DPP as a policy across a wide range of operations – from shelf space management and delivery method decisions to advertising (Fairley, 1990). The research indicated that, up to 1987, as many as nine out of ten major retailers still used gross margin techniques to calculate the profit made on each line stocked.

The complex analysis of all procedures and costs for every product necessary to implement DPP puts it within the scope of major retailers with sophisticated management information systems. However, manufacturers are also adopting DPP, and adjusting product size, weight and packaging to reduce sizeable cost elements that hitherto went unrecognized.

Legal aspects of retailing

The process of buying and selling requires all intermediaries, including retailers, to be aware of the consequences of entering into legal contracts. The simplest of these is the written order for goods or services, which is an undertaking to pay the agreed price on fulfilment of the order, or earlier, according to the terms agreed. Many contracts, for example in the area of wholesaling, are exercised after only verbal agreements. A long-standing arrangement of exchange of goods for payment may be viewed as a contract by virtue of the past actions of the two parties. Many of the uncertainties which might occur in such situations can be avoided in specially drafted **distributor agreements** containing explicit terms and conditions. This type of agreement, together with the more specific **franchise contract**, is discussed earlier in the chapter.

Apart from general consideration of the law of contract applied to the buy/sell activity of retailers, there are three important areas of law which impinge on retailing operations and management decision-making:

(1) Consumer protection
(2) Employee/employer relations
(3) Retail property – transfer of leases and restrictive clauses

Retailing groups offering credit facilities to their customers must comply with the Consumer Credit Act 1974. This specialist area will not be explored in detail.

Consumer protection

In the UK, the Consumer Protection Act 1987 contains elements of civil law, criminal law and codes of practice. There is automatic supplier liability for defective or dangerous products. One defence available is the 'development risks' defence. Under this, a manufacturer can claim that all risks associated with a product cannot reasonably be expected to be eliminated under conditions of commercial development. The onus is on the manufacturer to show that all reasonable steps were taken to test for safety and proficiency.

Retailers selling their own brands take on the liability of supplier under the terms of the Consumer Protection Act. Where the retailer is selling products supplied by, and under the label of, another supplier, then the retailer takes on liability for the goods under the terms of the Sale of Goods Act 1979.

In today's atmosphere of heavy price competition, where discounting is the norm, the consumer is protected from **misleading pricing** by Section 20 of the Consumer Protection Act:

> 'A person shall be guilty of an offence if, in the course of business, he gives (by any means whatsoever) to any consumers an indication which is misleading as to the price at which any goods, services, accommodation or facilities are available ...'

A criminal offence is committed if the reasonable consumer has found the price indication misleading. Trading standards officers are responsible for overseeing compliance with the law, and they will bring legal action as a result of their own investigations or in response to complaints from a consumer.

The most common area for concern is the advertising of a new 'offer' price compared with the 'original' or 'normal' price. Retailers are obliged to offer goods at the 'original' price for at least 28 days, but not necessarily at all outlets.

Codes of practice for different trade associations were encouraged under the Fair Trading Act of 1973. These have grown in number with the growth of service industries, but there is difficulty with enforcement as such codes do not carry the weight of law. There is the additional problem of traders who do not join a trade association, and whose practices damage the reputation of the whole industry.

The Association of British Travel Agents (ABTA) is an example of a strong industry association with emergency funding to support clients should the supplier find themselves in financial difficulty. Many clients look for ABTA membership before booking with an agent.

Employee/employer relations

Retailing and the distributive trades have been characterized by low wages. The viability of many small, independent retail businesses is secured on the basis of low wages balancing high costs of rental, business rates and bank borrowings. The low incidence of union representation has meant that the retailing labour force (predominantly women, many of whom work part-time) has not had strong negotiating power.

During the 1980s, a succession of Employment Acts reduced the power of the trade unions and weakened legislation relating to minimum wages. The position in 1989 was that the UK Wages Council minimum wage was £2.12 per hour, the EC minimum wage was £3.50 per hour and the average British hourly wage was £5.70.

The 1970 Equal Pay Act had serious implications for retailing only when the Act was amended in 1983. This allowed for 'equal pay for work of equal value'. This focused litigation on the informal practice of stereotyping the lower paid functions as women's work and the higher paid (and sometimes more physically demanding functions) as men's work.

In 1988 there was a Law Lords ruling that a woman's work as a cook in a shipyard was of equal value to men's work as painters, joiners and thermal insulation engineers. This set a precedent. In March 1990, three major retailing groups announced major pay awards to sales staff to bring their earnings into line with predominantly male warehouse staff.

Retailing property

Ownership of a freehold to a retailing site gives the retailer greater control over the future financial position, as there is no annual rent payable, and the value of the freehold can be shown as a capital asset in the balance sheet. However, a retailer considering purchasing a freehold must have access to the necessary capital.

Most small independent retailers become leaseholders in order to operate from a high street site owned by another party, which might be a major corporation, a university, or a private individual. The balance of power is held by the owner or freeholder, who determines the period of the lease, annual rental, and conditions of occupancy. A typical British lease might run for a three- or five-year term, with a rent review at the end of the term.

The freeholder will set the annual rent at the market rate for the type of retail site, without concern for the relationship between rental level and potential turnover of the retailer. However, this is a critical relationship for the retailer, particularly when rental levels are increased by anything up to 100%. The retailer must conform to the conditions of the lease, which might specify refurbishment and upkeep.

There is automatic occupier liability for the safety and care of persons entering the retail premises, and the possibility of legal action for negligence is a sufficient prompt for retailers to take out adequate insurance. Retailers must comply with the Health and Safety Act in the same way as all business proprietors.

Retail operations

The strategy of a retailing group will be reflected in a specific marketing mix involving the key elements of product, price, place and promotion, to meet the needs of a particular target group. However, these elements are translated into specific features of a retailing operation. For example, the location is critical to success, and promotion is effected through this location as much as through traditional forms of advertising. The product becomes a merchandise mix and the customer service to support it. A more detailed summary of the specific features of the retailing marketing mix are shown in Table 9.7.

The traditional power base in a retailing company would have been with the buying and merchandising functions. However, there is now evidence to show that the marketing concept has achieved almost universal acceptance in large retailing groups, with the existence of marketing departments in the majority of retail companies (Piercy and Alexander, 1988).

The effectiveness of the retailing marketing mix will be judged by a range of operational measures. The two key cost elements are **merchandise** and **personnel**, and these costs must be balanced against the desired standard of performance in providing customer service. Management information systems have evolved to provide senior management with instant access to consolidated figures for a retailing group. At the same time, power is devolving down the organization so that individual merchandise departments are responsible for performance, which is measured increasingly on the basis of gross margin as well as sales.

Table 9.7   Specific elements of the retailing marketing mix.

Key element	Example of implementation
Market segmentation	*Example* Department store chain: (1) Single price positioning for own lines such as for fashion or household merchandise (2) Multiple price positioning for agency lines (an agency is a supplier with branded merchandise who pays rental for space or commission on sales)
Image	Design of the store fascia and internal shopfittings Style and quality of merchandise Window display
Advertising	Visibility of store location Television and press Direct marketing to account customers In-store promotions
Location	Determines accessibility for target market within a defined radius
Customer service	Quality guarantee Free delivery Financing service Competitive price guarantee

The merchandising budget

The decision on the budget available for merchandise in each category is generally made at head office level in a group, and the **merchandise allocation** to each store takes place against historic sales performance. This procedure for fashion merchandise has to be tightly controlled because of the volatile nature of the market. Although cut, design and fabric might vary from one season to the next, there is a predictable trend in the pattern of sales between the major categories: coats, jackets, suits, shirts and so on. This trend is the core determinant of merchandising budgets, with the expertise and flair of fashion buyers combined with this to create a successful season's sales. The economic and demographic environment will be taken into account at the strategic level.

The merchandiser, with a team of allocators, will be responsible for getting the right merchandise to the right stores at the right time, and in the quantities necessary to satisfy demand. Procedures and control mechanisms revolve around individual **stock-keeping units** (SKUs). Using the example of men's fashion jackets, SKUs can escalate very easily as illustrated below:

$$5 \text{ sizes} \times 2 \text{ styles} \times 3 \text{ fabrics} \times 4 \text{ colours} = 120 \text{ SKUs}$$

In order to provide adequate control mechanisms in this type of merchandise situation, customized software for inventory control and processing is a feature of the management information systems of the larger retailing groups.

Stock-turn as a measure of performance

The pressures on retailing management to make optimal use of retailing space and to reduce the cost of holding inventory will mean that they are constantly seeking ways of improving stock-turn.

$$\text{Stock-turn} = \frac{\text{Sales during a specified period}}{\text{Average value of stock for the period}}$$

Example

Men's fashion jackets sold as an agency line in a high street chain. (An agency or concession arrangement is one in which the supplier takes a specific sales area for the merchandise, and in some cases, provides its own sales staff, with a commission on sales payable to the retail company.)

Year 1

Sales January to December 1989	£30,000
Average month-end stock (Jan to Dec 1989)	£8,000
Stock-turn 1989	3.75

Year 2

Sales January to December 1990	£28,000
Average month-end stock (Jan to Dec 1990)	£7,000
Stock-turn 1990	4.0

In the example, there is an improvement in stock-turn. However, there is a decline in the value of sales for the year. This might be due entirely to an economic downturn in the local catchment area or might also have been influenced by a reduction in stock held, which meant less choice for the customer. The ideal position would be an improvement in the annual sales *and* stock-turn figures.

Other measures of performance are 'sales per square foot' and 'profit per square foot'. These will give an indication of economic use of selling space. 'Sales per employee' and 'profit per employee' will indicate trends in productivity, but measures of **customer service level** are also important if this is not to suffer in the drive for efficiency.

Just-in-time retailing

Minimizing inventory at central warehouses or store stock-rooms is just as much an objective of retailers as it is of manufacturers and wholesalers. The advent of new technologies – EPOS and electronic transmission of purchase orders, invoices and data on stock availability (this is **electronic data interchange** or EDI) – means that retailers can also respond rapidly to customer demand.

In the USA, such systems have been designated 'quick response'. A study by Anderson Consulting has shown that, for the individual company, the savings by adopting such a system can amount to 5.3% of sales for mass merchants, 4.9% of sales for department stores and 5.0% of sales for speciality stores (Dolen *et al.*, 1989). However, these savings only accrue after sizeable investment.

New technology provides the tools of quick response, but managers thinking about every stage in the logistics cycle provide the catalyst for change in a fulfilment system. In the UK, B & Q were seen as the 'brash market leaders' in the do-it-yourself market. The appointment of a new logistics manager provided the opportunity to restructure the total supply chain for the business. However, there was a need to achieve short-term results as well as work towards longer-term goals (Bremner, 1990).

The success of the changes implemented at B & Q were attributed to the calibre of the project team – described as 'intellectual ownership' – and to managing the business culture. This involved co-opting suppliers, a software house and a distribution contractor onto the project team. B & Q chose to build the system around available software, rather than build the software to suit their own system. This way, they avoided many of the 'teething' problems typical of new system implementation.

Multi-channel marketing and channel conflict

Early in the chapter, different types of intermediaries were explored along with the typical vertical marketing system. The issue of several types of intermediaries being used in parallel to reach the same or different markets was not addressed. In many industries this is unavoidable in order to reach sufficient customers to achieve a minimum level of turnover with the available resources. Some examples are:

- sale of mainframe computers to major customers on a direct basis using the company's own salesforce;
- sale through distributors to a large number of smaller customers;
- sale of fashion clothing on a 'shop-within-shop' agency basis, where the manufacturer pays rental and/or commission on sales to a retail chain;
- sales through agents representing different geographical areas, who take orders from small independent fashion retailers;
- household furnishings sold through the manufacturer's own retail outlets;
- the same merchandise sold through mail order.

Where intermediaries are subsidiaries of the manufacturer or 'principal', the major issue with multi-channel marketing is whether this situation will lead to strategic problems as the business and market mature. For example, will the target market have different perceptions of a product depending on the channel through which it was purchased? Can a business support the costs of a retail and a mail-order operation in the longer term?

The launch of a new channel must be supported by strategic objectives which include the capture of a new customer base. Otherwise, there is significant overlap between the channels, and the major outcome is service provision to existing customers in the form of an alternative method of purchase.

Where intermediaries are distinct legal entities providing a service for the principal in order to make a profit, this type of overlap can have serious repercussions. For example, a manufacturer selling consumer products through retail outlets which are franchised by the manufacturer has certain responsibilities towards the franchisees. These might include exclusive sales rights in a specific territory. Should the manufacturer then decide to launch a mail order business with the same merchandise, with direct marketing to households in one or more of these exclusive territories, the franchisees' business would suffer. The legal redress available to a franchisee in this position would depend on the nature and content of the franchise contract. There have been European Commission judgements in relation to 'ownership' of customer lists.

The use of agents or distributors makes commercial sense when a principal does not have the resources to develop a customer base for themselves. When sales and resources grow to a point where the principal is able to reach the target market more cost-effectively themselves, the expedient business decision might be to eliminate the intermediary. This eventuality has to be considered at the stage of the initial distribution agreement, and accounted for by way of a limited-term contract, or by granting financial compensation linked to the business developed by the intermediary who is to relinquish rights in the future.

European perspective

Examination of the impact of EC harmonization provides an opportunity to explore issues of **physical distribution** of goods which have not been dealt with in the main body of this chapter. The effects of **Eurotunnel** on the flow of goods will also be considered. A second section will look at the implications for companies of **logistical operations** across borders, and some recent EC judgements on distribution agreements will be examined. Thirdly, developments in transborder retailing will be explored in the context of different legal, property and social scenarios in the various Member States.

Physical distribution of goods

The traditional choice facing companies on modes of transport for goods – road, rail, air or sea – based on cost/benefit analysis is virtually theoretical to all but a minority of businesses. This is for three key reasons:

(1) Air transport is costly and makes sense only for goods with a high value-to-volume ratio, or where speed of delivery is critical to the contract. This transport mode reduces storage costs in the destination market.

(2) Rail transport is an economic option only where goods are delivered in bulk and shipment journeys exceed 400 miles. This is because road transport links are needed at both ends of the journey for most goods.

(3)   Intercontinental shipments require sea transportation. The link with road transportation at either end has been the stimulus for growth of Roll-on-Roll-off (RoRo) services handling for containerized goods, where the container has a dual sea/road function. Consequently, the major issues of EC harmonization relate to road transport.

The reduction in trading barriers in relation to the physical movement of goods throughout the EC can be examined in two areas: deregulation of transportation of goods, and the reduction in the time and cost barriers created by national border controls for Customs and Excise.

Deregulation of road haulage

In 1986, 94% of the goods traded within the EC were moved by road vehicles. Whereas the 'free movement of goods' aspired to in the European Act applies to all forms of transportation, it is in the area of road haulage, the dominant mode, that there are the greatest hurdles to achieving this. Restrictions to be eliminated fall into three categories:

- permits and quotas
- price controls
- cabotage

Permits and quotas

Historically, international road haulage has been regulated by a permit and quota system. The **bilateral system** is an agreement between two countries in the form of one permit per journey. These permits are limited by quota in an attempt to protect domestic hauliers' operations. Around 75% of road haulage has been affected by this system, and it restricts traffic to hauliers from the despatching or receiving nation. Also, permits for UK/Germany traffic, for example, do not allow hauliers to take domestic business in the other country, such as backloading part of the way.

The **multilateral system** involves groups of countries with permits issued by the EC which are purchased by the user and are valid for one year. They enable the user to make multiple journeys through the specified group of countries.

From 1 January 1993, hauliers carrying goods for hire and reward have been issued with Community authorizations which enables them to make as many international journeys as they want between Member States.

Price controls

The free market in road haulage throughout the EC would be distorted by individual members setting their own pricing structures. An EC Council Regulation of 1989 clarified the position on the fixing of rates for the carriage of goods by road between Member States (EC Reg. No. 4058/89):

> 'With effect from 1 January 1990, the rates for the carriage operations by road between Member States for hire and reward even if part of the journey is performed in transit through a third country, or by a road vehicle which is carried by another means of transport, without intermediate reloading of the goods ... shall be set by free agreement between the parties to the haulage contract.'

Analysis of haulage rates for different payloads over varying distances among EC Member States has shown that Greek domestic rates are the lowest, with the rates in the UK the second lowest. The rates in West Germany were the highest at the time of the analysis, with France and Italy also featuring at the higher end of the rate spectrum (Gubbins and Hancox, 1990).

Cabotage

'Cabotage' means the freedom to transport goods between destinations within one country by an international haulier from another country. Article 75 of the Treaty of Rome (1967) laid the foundations for cabotage. However, only in 1989 did an EC regulation specify that conditions should be created so that haulage work may be performed wholly within one country by an international haulier from another country who has just completed an international journey (EC Reg. No. 4059/89).

This **consecutive cabotage** would allow a carrier to achieve extra revenue on homebound journeys through more efficient use of vehicles. This, in turn, could result in lower operating costs and reduced haulage rates.

An EC proposal of 1985 goes even further in proposing that all restrictions on non-national providers of haulage services should be removed. This would allow any haulier to compete for two-way domestic traffic in another country. All laws, regulations and tariffs applying in the Member State would apply to the non-resident carrier. This proposal also set out the condition for such a carrier to identify a fictitious place of business. This is equivalent to the non-national carrier setting up a company in the second Member State, but without the need to employ personnel and incur overheads.

The operation of cabotage should mean that hauliers from each Member State are free to carry goods in other Member States, provided that they have fulfilled statutory requirements. In practice, German hauliers would not find operating in Greece or the UK as profitable as transporting goods in their own territory. However, Greek and British hauliers might find German, French and Italian markets more lucrative than their own. In time, competition would exert downward pressure on prices in such markets as Germany, and there could be rationalization of the haulage market as a result. During 1991 and 1992 there was some move towards experimentation with cabotage by countries previously forbidding it (notably Germany). It is likely to be extended in subsequent years but complete freedom of international road haulage within the EC appears some way off, especially if EC membership is extended to other countries.

The gradual deregulation of the road transport market should increase both intranational and international competition with the effect of downward pressure on rates. Elimination of state-based restrictive practices in road transport in the USA in 1980 had this effect as well as improving the level of service through the disappearance of some carriers and the emergence of others prepared to invest in marketing and innovation.

Environmental considerations will also play a part in the move towards total cabotage, as road vehicles are heavy pollutants of the atmosphere. In February 1992, the EC Commissioner for Transport commented 'one third of the lorries travelling on German roads at any one time are empty' (BBC Radio 4 interview).

Such environmental pressure on German hauliers might cause them to consider obtaining a full or part load for return journeys, even at rates below the German norm. This might create competitive pressure for UK hauliers, particularly while the balance of trade with Continental Europe is in deficit.

Reduction in border controls

Research among 500 firms in six EC countries has shown that, EC-wide, firms pay around ECU 8 billion in administrative costs and delays through intra-EC customs procedures – or approaching 2% of these transborder sales (Cecchini Report, 1988). These trade barriers at the borders are created through differences in VAT and excise duties, health and veterinary controls, transport controls (such as compliance with national safety rules), enforcement of trade quotas and gathering of statistics.

A major industry of freight forwarders and import/export agents has evolved to deal swiftly and efficiently with the administration of paperwork created by these border controls. The cost of using these services bears particularly heavily on small businesses. However, all businesses have to tolerate the delays of up to five days at some border controls for clearing goods through Customs, regardless of the mode of transport.

The EC Commission is tackling the issue of border controls through a harmonized system of commodity description and coding, and a new Community Tariff (TARIC) – applied to goods classified under the harmonized system. However, the greatest problem to overcome is in harmonization of VAT rates, with differences in excise duties also giving rise to additional administration and delays at borders.

The impact of the Channel Tunnel

The Channel Tunnel, due to open in 1994, will provide British hauliers with a speedy and continuous land-based journey to Continental Europe. There are two benefits that will accrue from the Channel Tunnel: a lower cost of crossing, and speedier processing of Customs and other border documentation.

For traditional containerized road freight, researchers have estimated that a container-load going through the Tunnel will average 11.7 tonnes. At a cost of a ferry crossing to Dover for this load of £150, it is estimated that this represents around 0.4% of the value of the container-load (Centre for Business Strategy, 1989).

The researchers made the assumption that each load has a 20% gross profit margin, and that the cost of crossing fell by 40% with the opening of the Tunnel. This would represent an improvement of less than one percentage point on gross margin. On these assumptions, *the cost advantage of the Channel Tunnel for road freight is not significant*. This means that the streamlining of Customs and other formalities is essential for the Tunnel to have a significant impact on the import/export dimension through speeding up the process.

The cross-channel ferry operators will respond to competition from Eurotunnel through pricing and quality of service, although the significant percentage of traffic that will use the Tunnel could jeopardize the existence of smaller ferry companies.

Time for the Tunnel journey will be 30 minutes, or 75 minutes including the time at terminals in a frequency of three to six times per hour. This is significantly faster than the combination of terminal waiting time and Channel crossing time for freight moving by ferry.

The existence of the Tunnel will be more significant where a choice is to be made between road and rail transport for shipments between the UK and Continental Europe. Direct rail linkage between the two means that more freight journeys will pass the 400-mile qualifying distance for economic shipment by rail, for such journeys as Manchester/Milan or Lyons/Liverpool.

There are opposing views on the impact of the Channel Tunnel on freight traffic. The research of the Business Policy Unit of the London Business School suggests that this impact will be less than expected by other forecasters who predict 'The opening of the Eurotunnel will be the centrepiece of a revolution in traffic patterns in Northern Europe' (Warburg Securities, July 1987). Much will depend on the infrastructure links at both ends of the Tunnel, and the evidence points to significant investment in such road and rail links on the French side, but not on the British.

Logistics across frontiers

The moves towards a harmonized Europe are taking place in a business environment already in a state of flux due to the increasing role of information technology. This is particularly true of the logistics and distribution function, where the speed of information transfer means that response to customer needs is faster.

Where major companies are examining the trade-off between customer service level and costs and making different demands on distribution companies, these needs have to be matched against the feasibility of a pan-European network providing consistently high standards and flexibility.

The traditional way of breaking down transborder distribution into discrete functional areas is illustrated in Table 9.8. Major users of road freight services are examining whether this is the best way of managing an interactive chain across borders. At these borders there are, at the minimum, administrative barriers and, in the extreme case, language and cultural barriers together with a less developed infrastructure compared with the home market.

Table 9.8 Traditional transborder distribution management.

Function	Options
(1) Home market transport to port or border	Company's own transport Contractor in home market
(2) Customs clearance and documentation	Company's own department Freight forwarder
(3) Transport in export market	Contractor from home market making licensed journey Export market contractor

(4) Warehousing in export market	Managed by:
	  subsidiary
	  distributor
	  contractor

(5) Delivery to customer in export market	Subsidiary's own delivery Contractor

Such problems point to the need for even greater strategic planning of distribution, but with the advantage of pan-European expertise which is likely to exist in only the largest multinationals, and some specialist distribution contractors. An example of the former is the Philips electronics company based in the Netherlands, with 350 factories worldwide, and with 75 distribution centres or stores/warehouses in the EC (Jansen, 1990).

One major change in distribution, according to Philips, is likely to be direct delivery from factory to customer. This will eliminate the need for some intermediate warehouses, whether in the home or export market. *Reduction in cross-border transit times will be crucial to effective customer service with this scenario.*

Alternatively, where pipeline stockholding is inevitable, the traditional pattern of national warehouses will be replaced by a few regional warehouses located at 'hubs' throughout Europe. The location of these distribution 'hubs' will be determined by customer density and access to good roads, rather than by national boundaries. It has been estimated that 65% of the EC population will live within an eight-hour drive of a single warehouse, and that virtually all the population could be reached within two days (Hill, 1990).

Considering logistics higher up the supply chain, the location of production will be optimized on a similar model, taking into account location of key component suppliers as a determinant of speed and cost of delivery of parts for JIT production and delivery. Japanese car manufacturers are locating production facilities in Europe to cater for the enlarged market.

Types of physical distribution agreements

During the 1970s the increasing market share of food retailing in the UK held by the major supermarket chains, together with their cost cutting moves to improve margins at a time of price competition, led to a revolution in distribution. The major supermarket chains – Sainsbury, Asda and Tesco – identified two major cost elements in the supply chain: poor vehicle utilization and excessive waiting time for store deliveries to be made. This led to the move towards central warehouses owned by the retailer or a contractor, and **consolidated deliveries** from these warehouses to stores.

An example quoted in favour of this approach is that in which 130 vehicles making small deliveries to two outlets requiring 25 hours for unloading could be replaced by two vehicles delivering full loads in 45 minutes (Stanton, 1981).

In order to concentrate on retailing, the food multiples adopted the principle of **contracting out distribution to third parties**. Suppliers were required to deliver to a nominated contractor's warehouse at specific times. In some instances this reduced the economic viability of the suppliers' own delivery fleet, and the net effect was a restructuring of food distribution in the UK. Contract distributors had gained 70% of the UK grocery market by 1990, and they controlled one third of total UK distribution.

Forward-looking distribution companies responded to these changes by developing transport and warehousing networks to cater for specialist needs – such as temperature-controlled fleets for fresh or frozen foods. As a result, the large contract distributors in the UK were investing heavily during the 1980s, putting them in a strong position to expand into Europe. They have also increased their links with other companies within the Community.

Distribution companies will take strategic decisions to invest when the nature of contracts with major customers ensures significant business in the medium term. However, in much of Continental Europe the practice of contracting distribution is less developed than in the UK. Although 70% of domestic tonne-kilometres (and nearly 90% at international level) is undertaken by hired hauliers in the EC, the incidence of 'contracting' to a distribution company is low. This is because many shippers prefer to deal on the **'spot' market** for haulage where price rather than quality of service is the determining factor.

The informal 'gentlemen's agreement' is common in Europe to allocate traffic between hauliers, with no contractual undertaking for shippers to use a specific haulier or for the latter to have vehicles available even on a short-term basis. This can even apply to specialist transport services catering to such needs as those for hazardous chemicals or plate glass (Backler, 1990).

An influencing factor in the degree to which these informal arrangements will disappear is the existence of obligatory tariffs in some Member States. These have kept the proportion of own-haulage high, which is a disincentive to developments in the contractor sector. EC Directives on tariffs will stimulate change in favour of lower haulage pricing, and contracting will become more attractive.

A degree of concentration among hauliers is necessary before such investment commitments as **electronic data interchange** could be contemplated. Such concentration is significant in the Benelux countries, but is less developed in France and Germany. A multitude of small owner-operators is the norm in Italy, Spain, Portugal and Greece.

The European distribution market is forecast to be worth £81 billion in 1992. Those shippers favouring the spot market for haulage will rely on competition to bring rates down, and the speed of accurate information (with the increasing use of electronic data interchange) available to make the right decisions. Conversely, UK distribution companies that have invested in efficient networked services will take a more strategic view of the opportunities of the unified market.

Legality of distribution agreements

EC Commission and European Court judgements to date reflect the application of competition rules to the distribution process, whether related to cross-border supply of products with the same or different specifications, or to exclusivity of supply within a single Member State. Two examples are cited here to illustrate the way in which the Commission's judgements will affect supply of goods in the unified market.

Example 1

In its Nineteenth Report on Competition Policy, the EC Commission published its policy regarding the purchase of cars on the Continent by British consumers who would pay a higher price for the same cars in the UK. A number of complaints had been received over difficulties in obtaining right-hand drive cars. This was viewed by the Commission as an artificial obstacle to the free movement of goods.

As a result of this intervention, Volkswagen AG adapted its operating procedures so that right-hand drive customers could obtain delivery of cars with UK specifications within the normal delivery period on the Continent. The legal effect of this was to give the UK customer the right to buy a right-hand drive car ex-stock in Germany, where retail prices would be lower than if the car was purchased through a UK distributor (Competition Law in the EC, 1990a).

Example 2

An EC judgement relating to abuse of a dominant position in the market for soft drinks meant that Coca-Cola Export Corporation amended an offending clause in a distribution agreement with Italian firms (Competition Law in the EC, 1990b). Proceedings were first initiated against Coca-Cola in September 1987 under Article 86 of the Treaty of Rome. This was as a result of complaints that Coca-Cola was giving rebates to distributors who did not sell other cola-flavoured drinks, and in some instances, this **exclusivity** extended to other soft drinks.

The amended Coca-Cola contracts came into force in Italy in January 1988, although the company denied that it held a dominant position in the market or had abused this. The Commission's view was that it had strengthened competition in the soft drinks market, thereby extending consumer choice.

Both of these cases arose as a results of complaints to the Commission. In view of its limited administrative resources it is difficult to assess how far the EC will monitor distribution practices outside those officially notified by companies in search of Block Exemptions. Companies will need to judge how far their own distribution agreements might be in conflict with competition law, as aggrieved parties have recourse to the EC

Commissioner for Competition to assess and change a company's contractual arrangements; and, indeed, parties to a distribution agreement which infringes Article 85(1) can be subject to fines of up to 10% of their total annual turnover.

Pan-European retailing

According to the EC Commission Background Report on Retail, Wholesale, and the Single Market, the commercial supply of goods to consumers through wholesale and retail trades accounts for around 17% of output and employment in the Community. This means that there are significant economic advantages to be gained by the Community as a whole by the more efficient provision of these services through harmonization of laws and practices. However, the Community's subsidiarity policy is that there should be as few legal constraints in this area as possible, and that self-regulation should be the driving force for a code of good practice which is accepted across the Member States.

For retailing, the speed with which such a code will come into force will depend on the underlying differences in structure, operations and profitability of the industry in each country. These issues are explored under the following headings:

(1) Degree of concentration
(2) Social Chapter
(3) Retail property
(4) Retail margins

The section will then conclude by assessing how retailing groups are taking advantage of the opportunities provided by the enlarged market, and how EC Competition Law impinges upon these activities.

Degree of concentration

The share of retailing held by the top five retailing groups varies significantly across Member States. However there are some broad groupings:

- Concentrated with high incidence of supermarkets and highest population per outlet: UK, France, Germany, Denmark.
- Mainly small companies, but supermarkets beginning to appear: Benelux and Northern Italy.
- Large number of small shops: Spain, Portugal, Greece, Ireland and Northern Italy.

With the five major supermarket chains in the UK holding over 50% market share in food retailing, there have been major economies of scale achieved in buying, and in consolidation of deliveries by contractor distribution companies (see previous section). Apart from Aldi in Germany, retailers in Continental Europe have not used their buying power to dictate terms of business with suppliers to the same degree. In France and Germany, buying groups are large and integrated. In Denmark and Italy, cooperatives have a higher profile. Some companies have adopted the strategy of vertical integration, where the manufacturing function is controlled as well as retailing.

A high degree of concentration can lead to uniformity of merchandise available, as illustrated by the major clothes retailers in the UK, dominating each high street in cities and major towns. Easier access to shopping centres in other Member States and harmonization of value-added tax will encourage cross-border shopping as consumers seek greater variety.

The Social Chapter

With over 12 million retail and wholesale employees across the EC, any EC legislation relating to pay, working conditions and training will have an impact on the costs and operations of this sector. The EC Social Chapter is an Action Programme of 47 points which is likely to put continued pressure on the UK in spite of the 'opting out' at Maastricht. The areas of concern to the government and employers relate to minimum pay, protection for part-time workers (comprising half the retail workforce in the UK compared with 36% for all EC countries), maternity leave and obligatory training. Only the UK and Ireland do not have laws relating to minimum wages, and commitment to training is already significant in France, Germany and the Netherlands.

The Social Action Programme (Directive 89/568) is to be translated into a series of Directives and recommendations. Although voluntary in principle, legislation could follow if certain Member States were seen to be flagrantly disregarding the recommendations. Since retailers conforming with recommendations will incur additional operating costs, countries not conforming will lead to an 'uneven playing field'. However, where member countries build the recommendations into their own legislation, any retailer wishing to expand abroad will be constrained by these higher social provisions.

Retail property

A major determinant of financial success for a retailer is whether the retail property is owned outright (freehold) or rented (leasehold). The pattern of earnings for a company paying rent will generally be lower than where there is a freehold. UK retail groups with significant freehold portfolios are in a position to bolster their balance sheets in good times, and to divest themselves of less lucrative sites during recession. It is more common in Continental Europe for even small retailers to own rather than rent, which avoids the pattern of retailers 'closing up shop' when a short-lease rent review takes the rent to uneconomic levels.

The period of lease will also contribute to the ability to plan in the longer term. British leases are frequently 25 years, with rent reviews possibly every five years. Belgian leases are also for 25 years, French for nine years, Italian for six years, and the Dutch for five years with an option to renew for a further five years.

Rental levels are the highest in Munich and London, with Paris, Rome and Madrid not far behind. The difference in rent per square metre between the major city and other important cities is greatest in France, Spain and the UK, whereas there is not such a great drop in Germany suggesting that population catchment and spending power are equally strong across the five main cities there.

For retail companies wishing to expand across frontiers, the general pattern of choice is between modern purpose-built shopping centres (some out-of-town with good road access) or traditional city-centre locations. The national rules relating to planning and development will reflect economic and environmental concerns. In the UK the emphasis was on out-of-town sites as against town centre during 1989 and 1990. However, the recession hit retailing particularly hard, leading some analysts to predict that there was a danger of over-servicing some catchment areas. This was borne out by the mergers within the DIY sector during 1991/92.

Retail margins

Comparisons of financial results across European countries are made difficult by the differences in reporting requirements, and by complex ownership trails. Comparison of UK company reports with those of French retailers indicate that the former achieved significantly higher profit margins in the period 1987 to 1990 (Corporate Intelligence Report, 1991). However, UK retailers reported profits down by as much as half for 1991, reflecting the severity of the recession, although grocery chains appeared better insulated than others.

Higher margins for British retailers could be a consequence of not passing on economies of scale in buying to the consumer in lower prices, and the lower provision of employee benefits and training compared with Continental retailers.

The higher margins available in the UK attracted the German cut-price chain Aldi to enter the market. Allegations that suppliers had been under pressure from supermarket chains not to supply Aldi prompted an investigation by the Office of Fair Trading, which found 'no firm evidence' to back the allegations early in 1991.

Strategies for cross-border retailing

The USA was traditionally the target of European retail investment during the 1980s. For the period 1980 to 1986, the total level of foreign direct investment in the retail trades in the USA increased by over 260% from $3650 million to $9754 million. This was evidence of retailing companies aware of the limits to growth in their home markets looking for profitable expansion abroad. The EC moves towards an open market in Europe have switched retailers' attention to the opportunities available there, with three possible strategies for growth:

• Opening retail outlets in other Member States, with the same brand image and merchandise that have proven successful in the home market.
• Acquisition of suitable retail companies in other Member States, to extend or complement existing market strengths.
• Joint ventures with retail groups in other Member States.

The first strategic approach has been used very successfully by Ikea, the Swedish catalogue furniture retailer, and by Benetton, the Italian retailer of fashion knitwear and separates (Treadgold, 1989). Ikea is now trading in over 20 countries. Benetton was founded in 1965 and by the end of the 1980s had more than 4000 outlets in over 50 countries. Ikea's outlets are company-owned, whereas the majority of the Benetton outlets were opened as franchises.

The success of this 'international' approach to expansion depends on the uniqueness of the concept, and the universality of the merchandise in meeting the needs of populations with a diverse range of cultures and purchasing power. Both Ikea and Benetton identified significant demand for their products at the mass market level, and their respective distribution operations enabled them to overcome foreign property constraints.

The second strategic approach is facilitated by the increasing sophistication of the financial markets in cross-border deals. However, ownership of Continental companies tends to be in private hands compared with the large public retail companies in the UK. This makes successful takeover bids of the former by the latter less likely. However, British companies are not protected from takeover by such ownership structure or by legislation relating to monopolies, which tends to be tougher in Continental Europe (Whitefield, 1989).

The possibilities created by the third strategic approach were appreciated by the large UK retailing groups at the end of the 1980s. Before then, they had lagged behind their Continental counterparts in developing **strategic alliances** and **joint ventures**. In 1989, the European Retail Alliance was formed by Argyll (parent of Safeway supermarkets and Lo Cost discount stores) putting £70 million into a joint venture with Koninklijke Ahold of the Netherlands and Groupe Casino of France. This cross-shareholding deal was estimated to give the trio around 8% of the entire European market (Bidlake, 1989).

Joint ventures and strategic alliances as a way of developing pan-European retail activities have distinct advantages in an environment where complete legal and tax harmonization is some way off. A local operator will have mechanisms in place for dealing with property negotiations and planning authorities, employee relations and the distribution network peculiar to a particular Member State.

Dilution of the existing operational styles and lower profit margins might be the price that has to be paid by British retailing groups if they wish to take advantage of this strategic option.

The joint venture will provide strategic opportunities for retailing across frontiers. However, this type of alliance between retailing groups will be scrutinized by the European Commission for evidence of anti-competitive practices. The criteria used will be degree of concentration as measured by joint market share, and contractual restrictions on the parties to the agreement competing independently.

The case of ASKO Deutsche Kaufhaus AG (a German holding company with significant retailing interests) and Klaus Jacobs (a Swiss investor with principal activities in confectionery, chocolate and coffee) acquiring joint control of ADIA (a newly formed Swiss company) arose in 1991. The acquiring parties agreed not to compete with AIDA in its core business of personnel services. The proposed arrangement did not involve any of the parties in horizontal or vertical relationships, and market shares in the three sectors did not exceed 15%. The Commission cleared the joint venture arrangement (Competition Law in the EC, 1991).

Problems and assignments

(1) Outline the respective strengths and weaknesses of a corporate vertical marketing system using examples to support your answer.

(2) What are the strengths and weaknesses of franchising as a means of distribution (in a retail situation)? To what factors would you attribute its huge growth over the last decade? To what extent would you expect this trend to continue?

(3) Apply the seven steps of choosing a distribution channel to:
  (a) Launching a new countline (chocolate bar) product.
  (b) Launching a new, budget-priced, easy-to-use word processing system.

(4) Demonstrate with examples how information technology (IT) in the logistics process has an increasingly direct bearing on a firm's competitive advantage.

(5) To what extent could cultural conflict inhibit the imposition of just-in-time/material resource planning in a European company compared with its Japanese counterpart?

(6) What factors have contributed to the high levels of concentration in the UK grocery multiple sector compared with Europe and the USA?

(5) Given the fact that the EC has opened up the road haulage market and that British hauliers have been deregulated for a number of years and appear to be price competitive, what advice would you give to a large British haulier thinking about moving into Europe?

(6) Both Safeway and Asda have allowed themselves to be drawn into alliances with other European retailers. Sainsbury and Tesco have retained their independence. Suggest reasons for this strategy of non-involvement and make recommendations for a Euro-strategy for the next ten years.

References

Bowersox D.J. (1990). The strategic benefits of logistic alliances. *Harvard Business Review,* **68**(4), July/August, 36

Bremner D. (1990). B & Q: a supply chain revolution. *Focus on Physical Distribution and Logistics Management* (UK), **9**(8), October, 10

Davies and Rogers (1984). *Store Location Research.* Chichester: John Wiley & Sons

Dion P.A., Banting P.M. and Masy L.M. (1990). The impact of JIT on industrial marketeers. *Industrial Marketing Management,* **19**(1), February, 41

Dolen P.Z., Grottke R.L. and Lukes J.P. (1989). Quick response: a cost/ benefit analysis. *International Trends in Retailing* (USA), **6**(1), 25

Fairley A. (1990). UK stores wake up to direct product profitability. *Financial Director,* February

Fox M.L. (1987). Integrating logistics systems across functional lines gives companies a competitive edge. *Industrial Engineering* (USA), **19**(6), June, 34

Horner S. (1991). Factories plug in just-in-time. *Computer Weekly,* 28 February

Kenworthy J.G. (1989). Some practical hints on sales forecasting. *BPICS Control,* **15**(2), April/May

Lawless M.J. (1990). Effective sales forecasting – a management tool. *Journal of Business Forecasting,* **9**(1), Spring

Magrath A.J. (1990). The hidden clout of marketing middlemen. *J. of Business Strategy,* **11**(2), March/April, 38

Magrath A.J. and Hardy K.G. (1987). Selecting sales and distribution channels. *Industrial Marketing Management,* **16**(4), November, 273

Marketing (1991). The blooming sales of houseplants, 28 March. (Reporting on Mintel (1991) Cut flowers and houseplants. *Market Intelligence,* February)

Mehra S. and Inman R.A. (1990). JIT implementation within a service industry: a case study. *Int. J. of Service Industries Management* (UK), **1**(3), 53

Meredith C. and O'Sullivan D. (1991). Contract distribution in the UK: what the customer really thinks. *Logistics Today,* **10**(2), March/April, 15

Piercy N. and Alexander N. (1988). The status quo of the marketing organisation in UK retailing: a neglected phenomenon. *The Services Industry J.,* **8**(2), April, 155

Schwartz G. (1963). *Developments of Marketing Theory.* South Western Publishing

Stalk Jr G. and Hout T.M. (1990). *How Time-based Management Measures Performance.*

Stern L.W. and El-Ansary A.I. (1988). *Marketing Channels*, 3rd edn. Australia: Prentice-Hall

Stevens G.C. (1989). Integrating the supply chain. *Physical Distribution and Materials Management*, **19**(8), 3

The Independent (1991). MMC calls for a supply squeeze on soft drink duopoly. 16 August, p 22

West A. (ed.) (1988). *Handbook of Retailing*. Aldershot: Gower

West A. (1989). *Managing Distribution and Change – The Total Distribution Concept*. London: John Wiley & Sons

Wheelwright S.C. and Makridakis S. (1985). *Forecasting Methods for Management*, 4th edn. London: John Wiley & Sons

Wilson P.R.S. and Fathers S.J. (1989). Distribution – the contract approach. *Physical Distribution and Materials Management*, **19**(6), 26

European perspective

Backler G. (1990). Co-makership relationships in distribution: a European perspective. *Focus on Physical Distribution and Logistics Management*, **9**(1), January/February, 2

Bidlake S. (1989). Reaching across the seas. *Marketing*, 5 October

Braithwaite A. (1990). Managing European logistics assets. *Logistics Today*, Part 1, **9**(4), July/August, 22; Part 2, **9**(5), September/October, 17

Cecchini Report (1988). *1992 – The Benefits of a Single Market. Official Facts and Figures*. Wildwood House

Centre for Business Strategy (1989). *1992 – Myths and Realities*. London Business School

Competition Law in the EC (1990a). Distribution arrangements (motor vehicles): the VW case. December, **13**(12)

Competition Law in the EC (1990b). Abuse of dominant position (soft drinks): the Coca-Cola case. December, **13**(12)

Competition Law in the EC (1991). Concentrations (retailing): the ASKO case. September, **14**(9)

Corporate Intelligence Report (1991). *European Retailing in the 1990s – a Manual for the Single Market*. Corporate Intelligence Research Publications

Gubbins E.J. and Hancox P. (1990). Cabotage and the Single European Market. *European Business Review*, **2**, 14

Hill G. (1990). Guidelines for a distributor. *Director* (UK), **44**(3), October, 125

ISEC/B22/91 (1991). Commission of the European Communities: background report on retail, wholesale and the Single Market, 5 August

Stanton A.G. (1981). The case for third party distribution. *Retail and Distribution Management*, March/April

The Times (1991). Supermarkets cleared over Aldi, 1 March

Treadgold A. (1989). 1992: The retail responses to a changing Europe. *Marketing and Research Today,* **17**(3), August

Underwood L. (1989). Strengthening the supply chain. *Director,* **43**(1), August

Whitefield E. (1989). The prospectus for international retailing. *Admap,* June

10 Advertising: creative strategy, execution and media choice

Chapter objectives:

- to examine marketing communications known as the promotion mix
- to explore the advertising process in detail and models that explain how it works – the link between awareness and action as well as the intervening steps
- to understand the advertising briefing and development process
- to look at the nature of client–agency relationships

The promotion mix

Once the target market for a product or service has been identified using segmentation techniques, then the benefits have to be communicated to that audience, balancing impact and durability of the message against cost. A variety of promotion methods is available to organizations, and a combination of techniques used well can create the synergy necessary for a successful campaign.

The range of marketing communication methods is known as the **promotion mix** and includes advertising, sales promotion, personal selling and publicity. Most organizations marketing products or services to the general public would use a combination of at least two of these methods in order to achieve marketing objectives and sales targets. A conglomerate such as Unilever would use all four methods in a planned and coherent fashion at the individual brand level (for example, Birds Eye frozen foods or Timotei shampoo), but would use publicity to gain the attention of the city and key investors on corporate performance and strategy.

Conversely, a major computer company such as Unisys would focus advertising in the specialist business press and would devote a major part of the marketing budget to personal selling and sales support in the form of printed literature and sales seminars.

Each organization will have its own convention for marketing terminology so that managers, functional departments and external agencies can communicate effectively. The definitions and demarcations described in the chapters dealing specifically with the promotion mix (Chapters 8 to 13) have been chosen on the basis of the academic viewpoint combined with current marketing practice.

Chapter 10 explores the **advertising** process in detail, leading logically from attitude formation and the link between attitudes and buying behaviour discussed in Chapter 4. The theory and practice of **sales promotion** techniques are covered in Chapter 11. Discussion of **point-of-sale** material is included within the definition of **sales promotion** (some textbooks refer to this as **point-of-purchase** material).

Point-of-sale communication tools include displays, posters, stock-holding units (or merchandisers) and flyers which exist in-store to influence the choice, where there is a premeditated purchase, or to encourage an impulse purchase.

A complete chapter is devoted to the theory, advantages and tools of **direct marketing** (Chapter 12). The needs of companies in the industrial and business-to-business sectors plus the increasing use of databases by consumer goods companies means that the contemporary marketing manager needs more than a superficial knowledge of direct marketing methods.

Chapter 13 explores in depth the theory and implementation of **personal selling** and **sales management**. The spectrum of skills and knowledge is investigated – from the use of psychology in evaluating a buyer's needs, to the advances in the use of information technology to evaluate salesforce performance.

Advertising

Advertising is the use of paid-for media to communicate a message about the benefits of a product, service, organization or mode of behaviour to a predefined target audience, in order to stimulate action from the audience to the benefit of the advertiser.

This action may occur within a short time-frame relative to exposure to the message, or may occur in the longer term after multiple exposures to the message within the same or different media have brought about an attitude change consistent with the new behaviour. The process of

persuasion is highly complex and has generated considerable research to derive possible explanations and models from both academic researchers and advertising agencies. Considerable use is made of the techniques of clinical psychology, to attempt to construct frameworks within which to evaluate the effectiveness of different advertising messages and the media used to convey them.

The escalating demands placed by advertisers on existing (and often limited) media, most particularly television air-time, has led to a rapid growth in newer media – such as direct mail, freesheets (free, locally distributed newspapers), satellite and cable television channels and direct telecommunication links for home shopping (for example, Minitel in France).

The importance attached to advertising by companies marketing goods and services, and the intensity of legal restrictions imposed on what can be said in advertising and on the media available, are the major influences on the size and sophistication of the advertising industry in each country. Where, in 1987, the advertising industry in the USA was valued at $90 billion for a population of 220 million, that in the UK was $9.5 billion for a population of 56 million, and in France was $5.9 billion for a population of 58 million, these opposing factors begin to become apparent in the relative advertising spend *per capita*. (These figures are $409, $170 and $102 respectively.)

The need to differentiate the message from the plethora of stimuli facing any one audience has focused attention on creativity as the key role of the advertising agency in servicing the client's needs. However, this leads to an ever-present tension between the marketing company's need to create sales and the advertising agency's need to sell creativity. This tension is used to advantage through the briefing process, but a marketing company with sophisticated research and statistical back-up is in a strong position to monitor whether the message and media used are giving value for money in terms of effects on sales and profits. A company without these in-house resources is dependent on the advertising agency to provide these tools to measure advertising effectiveness in a self-monitoring capacity.

The persuasion process

The rationale for the link between attitudes and behaviour has already been explored in Chapter 4. This relationship is the basis of **segmentation by attitudes** in order to choose a target group with a positive disposition towards the message to be communicated. The purpose of advertising is to create a shift in attitudes through harnessing these elements.

A variety of models has been proposed to throw light on the consumer purchase decision-making process. Kotler (1988) proposes a concept of the **Buyer's Black Box**, where outside stimuli comprising the external forces (economic, technological and cultural) and the marketing mix from a range of products impinge on the buyer, who then makes a decision on how much to spend, what to buy, where and who from. This acknowledges the existence of buyer characteristics (some of which are attitudinal) and a **buying decision process**.

A model which addresses the objectives and desired response for advertising more directly is the **AIDA Model** (Strong, 1925) which sees the buyer passing through the stages of

Attention → Interest → Desire → Action

This is very similar in concept, albeit in simplified terms, to other models which have been put forward in the past three decades to explain the decision-making process. However, very few have been supported by empirical evidence which provides advertisers with greater confidence that a specific creative strategy or executional style will result in the desired attitudinal change and intention to purchase. Some of the more important models of consumer behaviour are explored in Chapter 4.

How do these models help advertisers?

These models of the persuasion process and consumer behaviour identify the ways in which the advertiser may achieve an attitude which equates to **intention to purchase** or other **behavioural intention**. The advertiser must decide which attributes of the product or service will be the key features of the communication, and the way in which the message will be conveyed in order to achieve the required level of attitude change. Whether these decisions are made by the marketing company or the advertising agency they have employed will depend on the nature of the relationship and contract between them. (This is explored later in this chapter in the section on the client–agency relationship.)

The advertising development process

The role of an advertising campaign within the total promotion mix will depend on the marketing objectives. If there is a long-term plan to increase brand share, then this will translate into **advertising objectives** such as higher **brand awareness** in order to bring new users into the fold, or reinforcement of brand values or benefits to improve **brand loyalty** and maintain **repeat-purchase** at the individual level. If the marketing objective is to bring forward purchases in order to smooth seasonality or reduce stock levels, then the advertising objective is to incite an immediate response, and the message will be designed to achieve this.

Advertising objectives

In a successful campaign the purpose of the advertising is provided in the form of **objectives** which should, as far as possible, be expressed in terms of targets which can be measured. Examples of such objectives might be an increase in **spontaneous awareness** (where the subject volunteers the name of the brand unprompted) of ten percentage points, or an increase of five percentage points in 'intention to purchase'. The use of specific targets makes it possible to conduct research before and after the message exposures to identify whether the advertising has had the desired effects.

Table 10.1 Advertising strategy statement.

Advertising objectives	Targets to be achieved by the campaign, which may be expressed in terms of increases in the following measures for the target audience: – spontaneous awareness of brand – prompted awareness of brand – awareness of new attribute Positive perception of performance on existing attribute Intention to purchase Purchase (time-scale defined by product type and campaign timing)
Target audience	The **segment** identified as most receptive to the message and most likely to undergo a positive attitude change which will lead to action (for a cellular telephone this might be AB males with an income of £20,000 or more).
Product position or key product benefit	The platform which raises the product above the competition: this can be demonstrable such as a quieter car engine, or the product is made desirable through the cues of casting (to create a role model) and setting. The use of a second benefit may provide an additional message argument, but may also confuse the audience (research will identify the trade-off here).
Supporting evidence	This will provide the scientific or other underlying reason why the end-result or benefit is achieved. For example, a headache capsule may be faster-acting because of the granule size of the active ingredient.
Executional guidelines	These are the cues viewed as essential elements of the total communication: they might be in the form of 'tone of voice' to convey authority or fun; an in-use situation might be specified; a type of atmosphere or ambience may be the desirable cue, such as romantic or workplace. Role models for casting may be specified.

These targets are essentially **communication goals** which are at the core of the advertising development process. The objectives or goals will be stated clearly in the **advertising strategy** which is the blueprint for discussions between client and advertising agency. This document will also provide an outline description of the **target group** for the advertising message, the key product or service benefit (or benefits), the supporting rationale for the benefit and the **'tone of voice'**, in-use situation or ambience suggested to provide the correct **cues** about the product. Each element of the advertising strategy is identified in the outline given in Table 10.1. The impact of advertising at the aggregate level, as measured through sales response, can in part be explained by the repeat-buying theory explored in Chapter 4.

Emotional response to advertising

As well as appealing to consumer cognitive processes, many advertisements also evoke an affective or **emotional response** which is arguably more difficult to research with the traditional techniques of social research. Aaker and Myers (1987) suggest the use of four elements in a model of the feeling response to advertising:

(1)   Feelings engendered: warmth, fear, desire
(2)   Attitude of liking or disliking the advertisement
(3)   Transformation of the use experience (**intangible attributes** added to the brand)
(4)   Each of the first three being associated with the brand (the classical **conditioning process**)

It is this association with the brand that advertisers are aiming for in their use of intangible attributes in television commercials, often created through messages that appeal to the senses (visual delight or evocative music), the ego, or the desire for social conformity. For luxury goods or leisure products, which often involve experiences rather than tangible benefits, **creative** use of visual and audio stimuli is critical in the audience's identification of the product with the pleasing experience. The creative process involves making the message memorable as well as persuasive and there are a number of techniques that are recognized as leading to a higher level of remembrance and persuasion. Four key techniques out of 12 that can be identified from the psychology literature (MacLachlan, 1984) are getting the audience aroused, giving them a reason for listening, using questions to generate involvement and casting the message in terms that are familiar to the audience.

Advertising execution techniques

In order to distinguish an advertisement from that of the competition and to make it memorable, a number of devices can be used. Some of these are listed below with examples of their use in memorable UK television commercials from the late 1980s. Some of the techniques reinforce the rational message arguments, others build on the emotional route to persuasion. Most television advertisements employ a mixture of the two. Press advertisements may employ some of the same techniques but the facility for detailed explanation of the product benefits means that the creative hook used is frequently less important than the substance of the message, particularly for complex technical products.

- *Slice-of-life* Family setting for the 'Oxo' commercials. This series is of particular interest as the role of Mother is changed gradually over the years to be less tolerant of the domestic impositions of other members of the family. A touch of wry humour softens this role shift for the more traditional audience.
- *Lifestyle* This approach appeals to aspiration, and featured in commercials for 'After Eight' mints (elegant dinner party in a period house) and Martini (roller skating waitress in a busy New York street).
- *Fantasy* 'Anything can happen after a Badedas bath': this usually meant the arrival of a 'prince charming' with romantic style of transport just after his paramour had emerged from the bath. Another example is the fantasy feats of the suitor delivering a box of Milk Tray chocolates.
- *Mood or ambience* The atmosphere and setting that is associated with the product: for example, the tough, Western American setting for Wrangler jeans.
- *Music* The commercial is built around a theme song such as advertising for Coca-Cola, or the commercial 'borrows' some well-known music so that the emotional responses to the music are associated with the product.
- *Celebrity* The use of the product is endorsed by a celebrity, for example Richard Branson and the American Express Card.
- *Technical expertise* The makers of the product imply superiority of expertise in a particular area, for example, Audi cars with 'Vorsprung durch technik'.
- *Expert endorsement* Usually combined with scientific support for superiority in product performance or **unique selling proposition**. If comparison with the performance of another product is made, the brand is not identified by name in UK advertising. Procter & Gamble have used scientific expert testimonials for Crest toothpaste and Vortex disinfectants.
- *Humour* The role model is supplanted by a character whose pathos or inadequacy to the situation invites humour, such as in the famous Hamlet cigar commercials.

- *Fear* This makes use of the impact of what would be the outcome *without* the benefit of the product: for example, gum disease and loss of teeth without the use of a toothpaste providing periodontal protection.
- *Product as hero* The storyline focuses on the product performance without endorsement from personalities or role models. Credibility can be stretched and animation is often used: Sure antiperspirant is an example of the former, and Tetley tea of the latter.

Effectiveness of alternative executional techniques

With the link between creativity and success for advertising agencies, time and energy have been devoted to creating memorable and award-winning television commercials. However, with many campaigns, a memorable commercial did not necessarily result in high recall for the brand. Some agencies reassessed the needs of clients and understood the wisdom of introducing a mechanism for linking the creative process with the desire to move merchandise. (In the USA, advertising had not moved far away from this imperative.) In the UK, **account planning** was introduced to align the objectives of creativity and sales. 'It is no coincidence that planning originated in the agency where creativity and research go hand in hand. BMP's mould-breaking work for Smash and for John Smith was vigorously researched yet remained "creative" and won awards' (Bernstein, 1989).

The relative success of celebrity versus non-celebrity endorsement was touched upon in exploration of the ELM theory of persuasion (Petty and Cacioppo, 1983) in Chapter 4. Credibility of the endorser is directly linked to measures of advertising effectiveness and purchase intention, and research has been carried out to explore ways of heightening this credibility (Kamins, 1989). This research showed that two-sided appeals (where performance is disclaimed on a less important product characteristic at the same time as the key performance claim is made) were more effective than one-sided messages (where only positive performance is communicated).

Press advertisements for a selected brand of home computer were developed for the experiment, and there was confirmation of two other hypotheses: firstly, the celebrity appeals were more highly rated than their non-celebrity counterparts, and secondly, there was interaction between sidedness of the message and type of spokesperson. This resulted in the two-sided celebrity appeal working best, and the one-sided non-celebrity appeal having the poorest result on the measure of expectancy-value brand attitude.

Comparative advertising, with the use of explicit reference to a named competitor, is a feature of advertising in the USA, but not yet in the

UK. Arguments have been put forward for this type of advertising being less effective than non-comparative advertising because it is less credible and induces more counter-arguing. Research across three product categories (cigarettes, golf balls and toothpastes) on a variety of variables such as perception, attitude and cognitive response showed that comparative advertising by a challenger, a brand that was not the leader, increased brand similarity between the challenger and the leader (Gorn and Weinberg, 1984). Comparative advertising claims must be substantiated with sufficient technical evidence to satisfy any challenges to an adjudicating authority. Expensive clinical trials are now the norm rather than the exception in markets where a few multinational companies vie for position in serving health and personal care needs through proprietary products.

Social influences and the advertising message

There is considerable debate as to whether advertising is part of the social environment which helps to shape people's attitudes, or whether advertising must reflect prevailing attitudes in order to be effective. National advertising bodies take a cautious view on this argument when reconsidering, for example, the advertising on television of products which could be the source of offence or embarrassment to a small percentage of viewers. The advertiser's concern is the possibility of alienation of a major part of the audience, which militates against positive attitudes towards the advertisement.

The role of women

The traditional woman's role of homemaker was the focus of much of the advertising up to the early 1960s, and there was no softening of the demarcation between the male and female responsibilities. Advertising to women as wives and mothers used the persuasion technique of product performance as a route to gaining the esteem of their family and satisfying social pressures. This meant that message arguments and emotional factors were necessarily entwined.

During the 1970s and 1980s there was a shift in fulfilment expectations on the part of younger women, who entertained the idea of a career as well as family life. As this shift was identified through research, advertisers were forced to change the **role model** and the circumstances of daily life to reflect the attitude shift in the target market. However, the key product benefits for household cleaners and food products remained more or less the same, that is, achieving a good result to satisfy the traditional emotional responses.

The **slice-of-life** approach provided the greatest opportunities for the shift in cues which avoided the alienation of the younger woman. Where such shifts would be the subject of interest to the social scientist and population at large, the primary aim of the advertiser was to satisfy the needs of the target market. The **segmentation** process gave the clue as to how these attitude shifts should be represented through analysis of demographic changes and research into lifestyle. How many working mothers are there? Is the largest target group really the family of mother, father and two children? What will be the impact of the increase in longevity, and the financial power of the over-60s?

Many of these questions have already been answered, as is evident by the increasing incidence of television advertising and direct marketing for financial services to single women and the mature couple. Similarly, no board room scene is complete without at least one woman seated at the table. However, when products for indulgence by the woman alone are advertised, there is still the appearance of **fantasy** experienced by women but as perceived by men.

The use of sexual overtones in advertising is a sensitive issue, and regulating authorities are diligent in overseeing standards on television, but rely heavily on complaints for breaches of taste and decency in poster and press advertising. The sheer impracticality of vetting every advertisement means that this reliance on public response also provides a barometer of changing attitudes.

The role of men

Changes in attitudes towards acceptable behaviour for men have been later and slower: the traditional norm of the Englishman enjoying a pint of beer in the company of his male friends is still the social setting for the heavy advertising spend by the brewing industry. Some unacceptable behavioural traits such as the emergence of the phenomenon of 'lager louts' led to informal pressure on advertisers to review the social impact of campaigns with heavy exposure over an extended period.

The sharing of household tasks is another area in which the slice-of-life approach has to reflect the reality of the young married couple where both partners play an economic role and young men have been brought up with different expectations from their fathers. Similarly, the acceptability of men showing a softer side to their characters is revealed in the increasing number of advertisements portraying the caring father or new man.

However, the advent of the 'enterprise culture' during the 1980s brought with it the acceptability of a more overtly competitive business environment which was manifest at the individual career level. The distillation of this philosophy was apparent in portrayal of city types or 'yuppies' with a killer instinct. Very often, a touch of humour would be used to soften the moral implications, and mixed reaction in advertising circles resulted where it was not. This illustrates the importance of advertising testing through a storyboard approach before shooting a commercial and putting it on air. Any alienation created by casting, setting or storyline will be revealed and amendments made to bring these executional features into line with what is acceptable to the target market.

The balance between message arguments and peripheral cues

The advertiser has to bring together considerations of **product positioning**, type of support necessary for the key benefits, target market attitudes and the media to be used to arrive at a possible **executional style**. This is where the creative desires of the advertising agency must be balanced against the client's need to achieve a measurable result in the form of awareness, attitude or sales. A further complication is the subjective views of senior executives on both sides of the 'battleline', although adherence to the advertising strategy and the pragmatic use of research should prevent disagreement from becoming disaffection.

The range of options on executional style fall along a spectrum. At one end is the scientific endorsement of a product, with little or no emotional appeal. At the other end of the spectrum is the use of ambience and life-style appeals without any cogent message arguments. Most advertisements fall somewhere in between. The position chosen will depend very much on product type, degree of financial commitment relative to economic circumstances, and the attitude shift required for a change in behaviour.

Media choice

The choice of advertising medium for a product message will be made early in the creative process, as this has a dramatic effect on the way in which the message is executed. The advertiser's decision is how to reach the target market most cost-effectively with the greatest impact. For consumer products, television is the focus of advertising attention because it has the widest reach. It is also a source of entertainment as well as information. It is a very powerful tool of persuasion as it has the attention of the consumer in the intimate setting of the home. However, the high costs of television air-time mean that this medium is only available to a small proportion of advertisers with a high budget and a product with mass appeal. It is therefore appropriate to look at the pattern of UK spending on different media including newspapers, magazines, posters, cinema and radio, before exploring the major influences on media choice.

Pattern of advertising expenditure

Total advertising expenditure in the UK was £416 million in 1964, and this increased to £6779 million in 1988. Taking out the effects of inflation, at 1985 prices, this means an increase from £2779 million to £6000 million over the same period, which means that advertising spend has more than doubled. The oil crisis caused a decline in spending in 1974 and 1975, but the strongest growth came from 1983 onwards, with an annual increase of almost 9% in real terms (Henry, 1989).

The continued consumer boom during the second half of the 1980s and subsequent high level of business confidence meant that there was strong demand for TV air-time in particular, where growth in spending was twice as great as for other media. Looking at the percentage breakdown of advertising spend shown in Table 10.2, television accounts for 31% compared with 63% for press, which includes national and regional newspapers and consumer and business magazines.

The constant 23% of expenditure accounted for by regional press in 1964 and 1988 disguises significant trends within this category. For example, there has been a tripling in the number of free, local, home-delivered weekly newspapers from 1980 to 1987. This medium relies heavily on advertising, with a minimum of editorial. The advantages of blanket distribution outweigh any losses of reader interest, and the distribution services which have grown on the back of this trend has provided the facility for the growth in household leafleting. In Britain, as in other countries in Europe and North America, this growth in 'free sheets' has coincided with a decline in the traditional local press.

Table 10.2 UK advertising expenditure by media type 1964 and 1991.

	Percentage all advertising	
	1964	1991
National newspapers	21	15
Regional newspapers	24	22
Consumer magazines	11	6
Business and professional magazines	9	9
Directories	<1	7
Press production costs	4	5
Total press	69	64
Television	25	30
Poster and transport	4	4
Radio	<1	2
Cinema	2	<1
Total	100	100

The growth in classified advertising (where a direct response is called for) has been far greater than for display advertising (where increased awareness and image enhancement are the primary objectives). Advertising effectiveness is more easily measured in classified advertising, and the faster growth here may reflect the increasing desire by advertisers for results that can be measured in terms of enquiries or leads created, and a conversion ratio of sales to enquiries.

The small share of total advertising expenditure accounted for by business and professional magazines is indicative of the difficulty of reaching a specialist target group through these media in industrial and business-to-business markets, and the limited amount of product detail which can be provided in a typical press advertisement. Hence the emphasis on direct marketing for more effective targeting of advertising, and on personal selling, to match the benefits against customer needs for complex products or services.

Influences on media choice

The major influences on the choice of advertising medium can be summarized under four key headings:

(1) *Target market* Can this be reached through traditional mass media, or does the specialist target group require 'narrowcasting'? Most households are in the market for a washing-up liquid so television is appropriate; however, only companies in specific industries would be interested in digital control panels for manufacturing equipment, so specialist trade magazines would be more appropriate here.

(2) *Message objectives* Is the purpose of the campaign to change attitudes over a prolonged period or to stimulate purchase in defined catchment areas over a short period? Theme advertising in the national press would fit the first objective, but local press with a purchase incentive would suit the second.

(3) *Costs versus budget* Some advertisers are precluded from media such as television or national newspapers and magazines because of costs. A minimum threshold of expenditure is needed in these media to have a measurable impact (see the later discussion of frequency of exposure).

(4) *Legal constraints* There are controls on the advertising media permissible for certain types of products: for example, cigarettes may not be advertised on television in the UK, and there are tight restrictions on the message and executional style in other media. Lesser controls exist for alcohol products.

Media planning

Having given due regard to the media options available against the advertising objectives and the available budget, an advertising agency will submit to the client an outline media plan for a specific campaign. This will show, on a week-by-week basis, TV or radio commercial slots, press insertions and poster bookings. In order to evaluate the benefits of alternative campaigns, media specialists make use of two measures:

(1) *Reach* The percentage of the target audience exposed to at least one exposure over a specified time-frame.
(2) *Frequency* The average number of times that the target audience is exposed to the message over the same period.

These two measures are combined to arrive at a single measure of advertising impact, defined as the **gross rating points** ascribed to a particular campaign or part of a campaign:

Gross rating points = reach × frequency

A single figure for gross rating points can be achieved in a variety of ways, and it is the job of the media specialist to analyse the relative merits of the different options and to advise the client accordingly. For example, 360 gross rating points could be achieved by:

Reach	Frequency
90	4
60	6
45	8

The objectives of the advertising campaign would help in this decision. For example, if a relatively new product needed an increase in penetration level (through increased awareness) then a route of maximum reach might be recommended, with a minimum number of exposures to ensure a baseline level of impact and hence recall. Conversely, if brand switching within a relatively small group of heavy users of a product group was the objective, then a low reach and high-frequency **media strategy** might be adopted. Decisions regarding number of exposures and spacing of these exposures for optimal impact and recall are more difficult, and historic practice is used as a guide in the absence of research evidence. However, there may be evidence on the decay rate of advertising influence on purchase decisions for a specific product category (discussed later in the chapter in the section on evaluation of advertising effectiveness).

Another measure used in the assessment of media is the cost of reaching one thousand of the target group. The **cost per thousand** for television in the UK increased by 48% in real terms from 1980 to 1988. By comparison, the same measure for press increased by only 18%. This heavy increase in the cost of television air-time reflected the situation of limited supply against increasing demand. However, even advertisers committed to television support are cost-conscious, and in 1988 there was a slight decrease in the number of brands using television, against a significant increase in the number using press.

Setting the advertising budget

The decision on how much money to commit in support of an advertising campaign is one that leads to considerable management debate within an organization. In multinationals committed to advertising support for major brands, this debate takes place months before the start of the financial year when **brand managers** bid for advertising money through the submission of **brand plans** which are agreed at successive levels within the management hierarchy. The management commitment to advertising support as essential for long-term success means that the bidding process tends to be one brand against another from a broad sum earmarked for advertising (and controlled by the marketing director for the business unit or product group).

In organizations where the advertising component of the promotion mix is relatively small, such as in high-tech or specialist service industries, the debate may focus unnecessarily on the isolated benefits of this advertising, rather than on its complementary effect in such areas as personal selling, which may command a larger percentage of the promotional budget. Whatever the type of organization, some criteria for determining the size of the advertising budget are necessary, and one or more of the approaches below are commonly used:

- Relate the budget to the **advertising objectives**. If a significant increase in awareness, penetration or market share is required, then the budget must reflect the reach (high circulation media) and frequency needed to achieve this. Media planners are in a position to cost an ideal media plan to achieve the objectives, and management can take a view on whether there is a match between the targets and the money set aside to achieve them.
- What is the **competitive advertising spend**? Long-term relationships between market share and advertising share are the accepted wisdom in consumer goods markets. Assuming an effective execution of the advertising message then the advertising spend or **'share of voice'** – the share of the product sector's advertising spend accounted for by the brand – must bear a relationship to the desired market share. This type of analysis is most relevant to **steady-state** market conditions, where the positions of market leaders and followers are more or less established. This type of analysis is less applicable to industrial marketing, where expenditure on personal

selling and the cost of trade deals with specific customers could heavily outweigh the advertising spend. Since this type of information would remain confidential, it proves difficult to put together the competitive picture in quantitative form.

- The **timing of market entry**. This can influence the level of advertising support necessary to achieve a target market share. If the market is already developed with some keyplayers already established, then market entry will require launch advertising spend as a multiple of the 'steady-state' support. This is particularly true of mass market products where initial awareness levels are critical to long-term success.

- Is there an **advertising threshold** below which there would be no measurable impact on awareness or purchase behaviour? This determines the minimum level of advertising support, particularly when national media are used. Where money is limited, there are advantages to testing, for example, the relative benefits of a smaller advertisement in a high-circulation magazine, compared with a larger space in a low-circulation magazine.

- What is the historic **advertising to sales ratio**? This can be measured against sales at manufacturer's price or at retail price, so long as there is consistency in the definition used. This approach provides a rule-of-thumb for an established product, where maintenance of market position and steady growth are required. This approach is not valid for an organization which is re-evaluating its advertising position because of poor performance. Inadequate spend on advertising might be at the root of the problem, and the matching of budget to the task at hand would be a safer route to success.

A survey among leading US consumer advertisers (Lancaster and Stern, 1983) investigated their practices in determining advertising appropriations. The results were consistent with the results of previous research with one exception, a reduction from 51% to 20% for those who used quantitative methods; 80% used the 'objective and task' method, 53% used the percentage of anticipated sales, and 25% matched competitors. The research indicated that the typical advertising budgeting process was quite complex, with executives seeming to choose advertising expenditure levels that maximize profits and/or sales. Communication effects and consideration of the competition were also taken into account.

In view of the significant annual expenditure on advertising by many consumer goods companies, there has been a considerable amount of research over the last 20 years to gain more knowledge about the relationship between the use of advertising media and resultant audience attitudes and behaviour. This is explored later in the chapter, in the section on media research.

Industrial practices for setting the advertising budget

The small size of advertising budgets in the industrial sector compared with those for consumer products means that there is less empirical evidence for relationships between advertising spend and sales response. A review of literature offers some clues in three areas (Lilien *et al.*, 1976). Firstly, evidence exists that supports the notion of **economies of scale**, that is, in some areas of industrial advertising, additional spend yields increasing returns. Secondly, there is evidence for a **threshold effect**, but where this threshold is to be found is not established. Thirdly, there is support for the hypothesis that industrial advertising and personal selling are complementary, but no framework for the split between spend on advertising and spend on personal selling has been put forward as an aid to managers in budget allocation.

One approach for an industrial company in setting its marketing communication budget is to identify its position on the scale running from non-awareness through awareness, knowledge, preference, purchase and repeat purchase, to set the advertising objectives against this position on the scale and to use the medium that will best achieve the objectives. Costs can then be estimated for the different media used, for example, press advertising at the 'awareness' end, and direct mail for initiating new relationships or 'reminding' existing customers. Hill points to evidence which suggests that more successful companies were spending a lower proportion of turnover on marketing than the less successful, and this may be because of use of objectives and the monitoring of results in order to achieve a more effective allocation of resources.

Managing the advertising process

Following on from the exploration of the persuasion process in advertising and consideration of the advertising strategy, media choice and message execution, it is appropriate to identify alternative ways of managing the advertising process. The nature of the relationship between an **advertising agency** and the advertiser or **client** will determine both the quality of the advertising (and of the sales response) and the costs. There are six areas of possible contribution by an advertising agency towards a company's successful marketing activity, and these are shown in an order approximating to the decision flow and chronology of activity for a particular campaign in Figure 10.1.

Some manufacturers choose to rely on their advertising agency for considerable input at the strategic level, helping with market analysis, *ad hoc* research and identification of the positioning of the product versus competition for the purpose of communicating benefits. The agency then

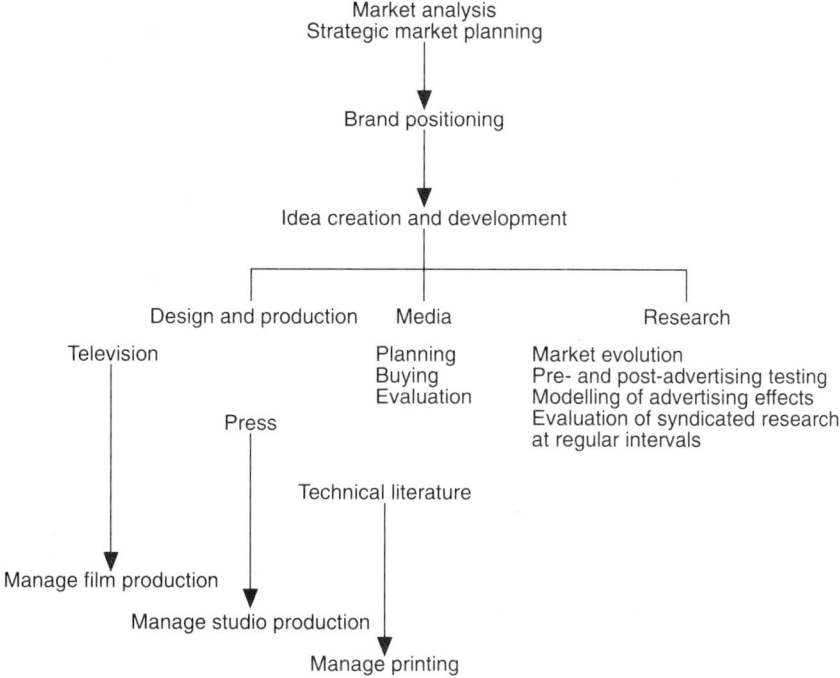

Figure 10.1 Stages in advertising development and areas of potential involvement of an advertising agency.

implements the chosen strategy through the creative, production and media functional departments. The client might choose this collaborative type of relationship where the in-house marketing expertise is limited, or where the agency has access to market data for the launch of a product in a new business sector.

Conversely, companies with an accumulated expertise in defining product strategies, and with departments whose role is to research and monitor advertising effectiveness (such as Procter & Gamble and Unilever) will use an advertising agency to devise the creative message and the media mix to exploit the product strategy to the full. These two approaches reflect differences in the balance of control of the creative function – the first assigns a greater level of influence to the advertising agency, with the concomitant danger of the creativity of message execution gaining dominance over achieving measurable results in recall and sales. The second approach ensures that the advertising strategy is closely adhered to in the final execution, and that there are processes for monitoring the success of a campaign which are independent of the agency.

Three ways of handling advertising

For small and medium-sized companies whose advertising needs are primarily creative and production support against a limited budget, there are three alternative ways of handling advertising. The relative advantages and disadvantages of these three approaches are outlined below.

(1) Full service advertising agency

This means that the agency performs all of the advertising functions: research, creative and media-buying. The agency is paid a percentage commission based on the cost of media purchased on the client's behalf. The agency will also add a 'handling' fee to the cost of production of commercials, artwork or printed materials which are managed on the client's behalf. Special research projects would be costed and charged as 'add-ons'. Within the 'full service' concept, the agency would be involved in overall strategy and continuity of the advertising message, possibly through an **account planner**. To ensure the efficient management of communications between client and agency and of the client's work in the agency departments, some agencies appoint **account managers**.

- *Advantages*
  - Client benefits from the all-round skills and experience of the agency.
  - Continuity of an account group with experience of the product.
  - Agency sees a campaign through from brief to final production, releasing client time and energy.
  - Agency acts as a sounding-board for strategy and ideas.
- *Disadvantages*
  - High costs.
  - Agency used would be generalist rather than market specialist.
  - Agency dictates working practices; sometimes inflexible, for example on speed of delivery.

(2) *Ad hoc* purchase of specialist services

This arises when a company identifies specific advertising needs, and is prepared to coordinate campaign management in-house. Services that are bought in are typically the creative function from specialist agencies, media-buying from specialist brokers, and research. The client will dictate strategy (unless a 'new product' consultancy is hired for the purpose), and will have clear views on media options.

- *Advantages*
  - Lower costs: agencies are paid against services provided.
  - Specialists can be chosen for specific tasks.
  - Specialist agencies are more flexible and can give a faster turnaround.

- *Disadvantages*
  - More control and coordination are needed from the client.
  - Difficulty of getting additional advice or services without negotiating extra payment.

(3) Do-it-yourself

Some companies do not wish to relinquish the advertising function to an outside agency for reasons of control or confidentiality, and prefer to employ and train in-house specialists. The assessment of the real cost of this approach is then made more difficult because of the assignment of staff costs to 'overheads' rather than 'marketing budget'. The smaller company might find that there is sufficient continuity of advertising approach with such a low budget and so this is the only practical approach, with a marketing executive taking on this role among others.

- *Advantages*
  - Total control of the advertising process.
  - Lower costs.
  - Highly flexible.
- *Disadvantages*
  - Lack of experience or specific skills.
  - Poor buying power on media.
  - Lack of second opinion on advertising.

With the increasing pressure on companies to control marketing costs, the decision whether to conduct advertising in-house (the 'make' decision) or whether to contract an external agency to perform this activity (the 'buy' decision) needs to be made within an analytical rather than intuitive framework. Company-specific capabilities, economies of scale, potential size of transaction and ability to monitor performance are four variables proposed within a framework for analysing what becomes a **'vertical integration'** issue – whether the advertising function should operate within the organization or not.

Assessing advertising effectiveness

For many organizations the advertising budget may be the largest area of discretionary spending, but this may be accompanied by a poor understanding of the results achieved. As Lord Leverhulme once remarked: 'I know that half the money that I spend on advertising is wasted. The trouble is that I don't know which half'. The past decade has seen significant developments in the techniques available for monitoring and testing the effects of advertising, although some advertising practitioners resist computerized research and forecasting methods being applied to what they consider an 'art' rather than a 'science'.

This section is devoted to an outline of some of the more advanced and contemporary approaches to identifying the optimal route for achieving specific objectives through advertising. It is divided into three areas:

(1) Consideration of *ad hoc* **research** methods which identify whether the advertising message delivered to a **test audience** or actual target group is achieving the objectives set for it;
(2) The use of continuous data to audit how well media are performing against tried-and-tested measures;
(3) The use of statistically derived relationships for the **model-building** approach to forecasting advertising response.

Ad hoc research methods

The purpose of advertising research is to reduce the risk in taking decisions about message and media. It should provide 'danger' signals if an advertisement is likely to be ineffective in delivering a persuasive message. Research should conform to industry standards of validity and reliability; it should provide results in time to be of help in decisions involving the allocation of funds and should be inexpensive relative to these advertising funds. **Qualitative** market research methods which support advertising development are explored in greater depth in Chapter 6.

Advertising copy development research involves the testing of a concept, proposition or claim among a group representative of the target audience, to see whether there is sufficient positive response to proceed along this creative route. Several alternative executions of one proposition could be tested at the next stage in the development process, to identify the most persuasive approach. This commonly involves the use of a storyboard approach in place of finished commercials.

Copy testing involves research on the finished advertisement to assess performance on specific criteria. These criteria might be measures of **spontaneous recall**, **prompted recall**, or perceived image using multi-dimensional scaling.

The **usage and attitude study** is a precise tool of measurement of brand-specific beliefs and is commonly used with a **test market** before and after a new TV commercial or press advertisement has run in a controlled region. Depending on the timing of the research, it will also be an indicator of **intention to purchase** in lieu of an actual purchase measure. This technique falls into the category of **quantitative research**, because of the larger samples of the target audience chosen so that the results obtained may be generalized with statistical validity.

The use of these advertising research techniques assumes a link between **awareness** or **recall** and **market share**. This has been established by the Profit Impact of Marketing Strategy (PIMS) programme of the Strategic Planning Institute, and this study is explored in depth in Chapter 15.

Use of continuous monitoring

The media department of any advertising agency depends on key **media research** sources to identify potential media for a campaign, to justify the inclusion of particular television spot times and press insertions to a client and to monitor the trends in the relative performance of different media. One measure of campaign effectiveness is the number of **'opportunities to see'** or OTS of the target audience. For a television commercial, this will depend on the proportion of the target audience viewing at the transmission time and the number of times the commercial goes on the air. For a magazine advertisement, OTS will depend on the readership of the magazine (which is often higher than the circulation figure) and the number of issues in which the advertisement is featured.

The media planner is concerned with the level of **exposure** that an advertisement will receive, and so is interested in **advertisement audience size** rather than vehicle or medium audience size. In practice, these are assumed to be the same. Sophisticated panel monitoring of television can now identify who within the household is watching at a given time. With the advent of satellite and cable television there is increasing competition for the attention of a static audience, and the viewing figures of the traditional commercial channels are under threat. This makes the monitoring process even more critical.

BehaviourScan

The most reliable form of advertising testing is empirical evidence that controlled exposure leads to a measurable change in behaviour, specifically, product purchase. In 1980, Information Inc., a Chicago-based research company achieved this ideal with the combination of three research capabilities:

- Supermarket check-out scanning equipment
- Household panels
- Split transmission cable television

By combining these three elements 'IRI created a real world testing environment for evaluating nearly all of the marketing variables that influence purchasing behaviour including advertising, pricing, shelf placement, trade activity and consumer promotions' (Poindexter, 1984). The BehaviourScan approach is to pinpoint a metropolitan area as a sampling point for the United States. Within each of these, UPC (Universal Product Code) **scanning systems** are installed in supermarkets and non-UPC items are recorded via key entry. IRI have direct telecommunication access to these data. A 2500 **household panel** is recruited in each market to track purchases at the individual household level through an identification number punched in at the supermarket check-out, and linked to purchases on computer file.

For the purpose of advertising testing, the unique feature of the BehaviourScan system is the split-cable television facility, which allows for the exposure of a sample of households to a 'test' strategy, and a matched set of households to the standard advertising approach, or an alternative test version. Also possible are tests of TV exposure versus no TV, **advertising weight** tests (how many exposures over what time-frame?) and copy tests. It is also possible to run test versus standard press advertising through the cooperation of local newspapers and leading women's magazines.

The net effect of this approach is that manufacturers of new brands are able to have evidence of consumer response to advertising in the form of sales rather than psychological measures of attitude and intention, whose relationship with the outcome of a major launch is at best approximate, and at worst, tenuous.

An alternative use of this scanner-panel approach to marketing research is identification of households with a specific buying pattern (for example, buyers of a particular brand of soup) and to transmit a new commercial at group A and the old one at group B and to monitor their purchasing patterns (Poindexter, 1983). Fears expressed over the possibility of intrusion of privacy and mass manipulation by such market research methods are dampened by consideration of costs, which will be a strong force for operating at a minimum sampling level consistent with validity of generalizing the results.

The model-building approach to forecasting advertising response

Where household panel and retail audit data are valuable in the type of *ad hoc* advertising testing already discussed, they are invaluable in providing a consistent framework of sales results for developing advertising/sales response models for particular markets. These models can then be used as tools for predicting volume response to alternative patterns of future media spend. There are two components to researching how to construct a campaign: **how many** exposures are needed and **how long** should the campaign last?

How many exposures?

The decision here is to expose the audience to a sufficient number of repetitions of the same execution of a product message to elicit the desired reaction in the form of a positive attitude change and new purchase behaviour. The number of exposures needed will depend on whether the brand is new or established (awareness versus reminder advertising), the market share and the purchase and use cycle. The shorter this cycle, the greater the number of repetitions needed, because of the opportunity for brand switching on each new purchase occasion. The degree of involvement of the audience in the product area will also be critical (cognitive processing of information versus emotional response) and the amount of competitive advertising (Ostrow, 1984).

How long should the campaign last?

There is considerable debate about the durability of attitude change after exposure to advertising, and indeed, about the level of **recall** after one advertising exposure. Very high levels of decay for **'unaided recall'** are the accepted wisdom in the weeks after advertising exposure, but the use of this measure assumes that purchase is heavily linked with it. **'Prompted recall'** is likely to decay less rapidly, and in-store brand choice bears a similarity to this measure.

This view is supported by such practitioners as David Ogilvy (1983) by his rejection of the 'day-after recall test'. The advertising agency Foote, Cone and Belding (Marketing News, 1981) claims that this measuring technique understates the memorability of commercials that employ emotions.

Translating this concept of a decline in recall into a workable quantitative tool means putting a figure to the **advertising decay rate** for a particular press insertion or television spot. What this means in practice is that one month after the exposure, there is a residual recall that has an impact on volume sales which is less than the impact at the time of the exposure. This impact then declines in successive months, until there is no residual effect.

The next question which must be answered is 'how long do these residual advertising effects last?' Examination of the findings of 70 published studies in the USA led to the conclusion that 90 per cent of the cumulative effects of advertising on sales occurs within three to nine months of the advertisement (Clarke, 1975).

The cumulative advertising effect of a campaign with multiple exposures over two or three months will therefore still be evident well after the last exposure. This leads into consideration of the short and longer-term effects of advertising. Those who argue for short-term effects are vindicated by the traditional response of the sales curve to an intensive campaign for a repeat-purchase or durable consumer product. However, companies that have sacrificed advertising spend for short-term financial benefits are subsequently dismayed by the progressive downhill movement of brand share in the longer term. This may only be manifest after 12 months or longer for an established brand, and adjusting the advertising budget to regain lost ground can prove very expensive, as the 'cumulative effects' of exposures on recall and attitudes have to be restored.

Advertising elasticity

Econometric modelling of the influences of advertising on volume sales can be carried out in the same way as the modelling of price effects. Traditionally, values for advertising elasticity (the percentage change in volume sales for a one per cent change in advertising spend) are smaller than for price elasticities. This has been put forward as an argument for the shift in marketing expenditure from advertising to various forms of promotional discounts. However, this simple view of the relative response of volume sales to changes in advertising versus change in price ignores both the composition of the brand's budget and the marketer's need to defend or improve contribution as well as volume (Broadbent, 1988).

Simon Broadbent compares the effects of a 10% price reduction with a 10% increase in the advertising allocation for a hypothetical brand with a **price elasticity** of -1.76 and an advertising elasticity of 0.22. The price cut leads to a lower contribution, so it is a way of 'buying' volume. In contrast, the extra spend on advertising leads to a higher contribution, and the brand image has been enhanced rather than diluted.

Econometric forecasting models which combine the effects of price movements and changes in advertising expenditure on a month-by-month basis provide the most sophisticated tools for the marketing manager to identify the optimal media and promotion plan for a brand to meet specific marketing and financial objectives. Such tools are only available to multinational consumer goods companies and the larger advertising agencies where the costs of the necessary market research data and in-house specialists are justified by large advertising budgets.

Some marketing practitioners would argue that this takes marketing decisions out of the hands of managers and places them firmly in the hands of computers. This is taking the role of such models to an extreme. However, these **expert systems**, once in place, provide the marketing manager with a means of testing the sensitivity of brand performance to various ways of spending the marketing budget. This is a very cost-effective way of reducing financial risk. This approach is explored further in consideration of the budgeting process for a repeat-purchase consumer product in Chapter 14.

By way of conclusion on the evaluation of advertising effects on sales, most companies would use a selection of techniques dependent on the size of the advertising budget, accumulated knowledge about brand performance and the degree of change in advertising strategy which involves increased risk. Pedigree Petfoods is one company that takes the view that while such tools are effective when taken together, no one method is sufficient on its own (Haselhurst, 1988).

European perspective

As early as 1988, Lord Cockfield, the then European Commissioner for the Internal Market and Britain's senior commissioner in Brussels, regarded television as an 'economic service' within the meaning of the Treaty of Rome. This led to the proposal that television required an EC framework,

Table 10.3   EC White Paper 'TV without Frontiers': key proposals.

(1)   Protection of the principle of free access for individuals to broadcasting channels from another Member State.
(2)   Harmonization of technical standards.
(3)   Provision for 60% of programmes originating from within EC states within three years of the proposal becoming law.
(4)   Restrictions on advertising for certain categories of products (such as tobacco).
(5)   A clause providing that 5% of programming (rising to 10% within three years) should come from independent producers.
(6)   Safeguards for younger viewers, with EC-wide standards on sex and violence.

outlined in the White Paper 'Television without Frontiers'. The key pronouncements of the White Paper are shown in Table 10.3; the implications were so far-reaching as to cause a strong lobby in opposition to individual proposals from a variety of interested parties.

Television is the most powerful of advertising media and accounts for over a third of advertising expenditure in the UK, with lesser ratios in other Member States except for Italy. Arguments in opposition to the proposals were based on unfairness of, or lack of need for, an additional legal framework for the **protection** of:

•   the EC advertising industry
•   the advertising industries of individual Member States
•   the viewer

The reaction from television production companies in the USA was sufficient to put proposed controls on programmes imported from the USA high on the international political agenda. The French took the lead in supporting the 60% quota, as the keenest Member State to retain 'national identity'. However, with British and German pressure against, the quota was removed as a potential Directive. European producers look to national quotas (such as the British quota of 16%) to protect their interests. It was argued by the British that television raises cultural rather than economic issues and it should therefore be covered by a 'convention' rather than an EC legal framework. This was just one of the many objections put forward by national governments and broadcasting authorities.

The issue of regulating broadcasting and advertising into the 1990s is further complicated by the opening up of the skies through **satellite television**. For the European, there may be as many as 120 channels available by 1995, financed predominantly by advertising. The laying of fibre-optic cable will bring **cable television** to millions more homes, with its potential for sponsored programmes and **home shopping**. Saatchi and Saatchi predicted that television advertising in Europe will grow from a $10 billion industry at the end of the 1980s to a $20 billion industry by the year 2000 (Feaser, 1989).

In the context of such growth in broadcasting power and fragmentation of audiences, the advertiser is looking at the economic issues raised by a pan-European campaign. The questions asked are the same as at national level:

- What message?
- What media?
- What costs?
- What results?

The answers to these questions are more complex at the pan-European level, and are affected by cultural responses of national audiences, the legal framework governing what is permissible, the availability of media in Member States and the comparative costs. These four areas are explored to provide an overview of the potential for global branding in the context of EC harmonization. First, it is useful to examine how far global branding has been achieved during the 1980s, and the link with organizational structure.

The extent of global branding

For the purpose of defining the **global brand**, a slight variation in name across national boundaries is accepted as a marginal difference due to language. All other key features of the global brand – target group, product presentation, form, benefits, image, pricing and accessibility – should be comparable.

Coca-Cola and Oil of Ulay have achieved this status across continents rather than countries. This means that the brand values and tangible benefits have transcended national culture and local conditions. The appeal of Coca-Cola is that of the 'young, carefree lifestyle' enhanced by a strong musical theme. That is not to say that the drink itself is not preferred in blind taste tests: possibly it is, but the image created through heavy advertising expenditure is an important facet of global success. For Oil of Ulay moisturiser, the emotive platform of 'anti-ageing' appeals to the thirty-something woman, whatever her skin colour or type and regardless of the climate. The credibility and trust built through advertising becomes more important than the texture of the lotion in the bottle.

This degree of global success is shared by major names in air transport or hotels, where the business traveller is confident of receiving the same level of service in each country. However, the nature of the product or service can inhibit such acceptance for cultural or economic reasons. The level of acceptance of specialist, convenience foods would vary significantly across national boundaries, heavily influenced by the availability and cost of fresh produce.

Table 10.4   Different organizational models for international brand advertising.

Central control	Advertising strategy dictated from centre; executional changes for local culture and conditions closely monitored. This requires a 'lead' agency at international level. *Examples:* Unilever (Lever Europe); United Distillers (Johnnie Walker)
Head office acts as resource centre	Local management free to develop advertising within broad strategic guidelines; central directives on agencies and media buying groups. *Examples:* SmithKline Beecham (Phensic, Macleans, Lucozade); Nestlé (Nescafé)
Complete autonomy of local management	Only minimal justification needed for product and advertising changes. *Example:* Heinz

One of the most successful global brands – Timotei shampoo – started life in Scandinavia appealing to the mood for nature and simplicity. This concept was easily transported to other countries as 'similar demographic groups within countries have more in common with their peers abroad than with their countrymen' (Hoggan, 1990).

The degree to which brands are global will reflect management strategy on the best way to exploit potential international sales. Some organizations exert tight control from the centre, and even small packaging or product changes have to be justified on consumer or technological grounds. At the other extreme, some organizations grant the local management total autonomy in the strategy as well as day-to-day running of brands. These two approaches are included in the summary of advertising management models in Table 10.4. The argument put forward for a centralized approach is that of economy of scale in the creative production process, and, to some extent, a saving in the number of experts involved. However, this often disguises the true objective of central management control of the advertising function, among others (White, 1990). The international benefits that can accrue from the same creative idea which has been proven to work in one or more major markets are self-evident in market share achievements of major brands in many countries.

Boots' plans for a pan-European advertising campaign for the over-the-counter (OTC) analgesic Nurofen led to the search in 1992 for agencies that had the network and experience to support this approach. A company with less developed international brand positionings might choose to work through the 'command' structure of an international agency network. This would facilitate the adoption of a common advertising strategy where the business management for the products was in the hands of distributors or autonomous subsidiaries.

Influences on the development of pan-European advertising

Different national cultures

Brands that have been successful on an international basis invariably harness the power of intangible benefits to differentiate themselves from the competition, and use heavy media expenditure to communicate these benefits. The values incorporated may rest on exclusivity, luxury, prestige, indulgence or concern for the environment. Cultural factors play a role in determining consumer response to these appeals, and both the brand platform and execution of the creative idea must respond to such national traits. The advertising industry would recognize the following broad differences in executional styles:

- Germany – rational, descriptive, informative
- UK – subtle, understated, ironic, humorous
- France – innovative, modern, attention-getting
- USA – emotional, lifestyle, glamorous

The predominance of press over television advertising in Germany reinforces the importance of technical fact over lifestyle considerations. Historically, the standard of living in what was West Germany has been high, so the 'exclusivity' appeal which works for many fashion and cosmetic labels would not be justified where a large percentage of the population could afford them.

These are just two influencing factors for the German consumer. There are many influences at work in the complex process of brand positioning – often heavily supported with **attitude** research. The link between attitude and behaviour can be tenuous, particularly where 'social value' research is used mechanistically to predict **buying behaviour**. The forecaster can make use of some key structural determinants to behaviour – the role of the home (owner-occupied versus rented), different family structures, the changing balance between work and leisure (particularly, the increase in the number of working women) and the ageing population (Lannon, 1988).

Different patterns for these characteristics of Member State populations will lead to intrinsic differences in purchasing patterns. A pan-European campaign can only go some way to shifting purchasing patterns towards convergence, under these conditions. There is now evidence that even in the homogenous market of the USA, segmentation is beginning to appear along geographical or ethnic lines. Where Europe's consumers are forecast to be spending $4.4 trillion by 1993 (97% of forecast US consumption), the motto 'Plan global – act local' appears increasingly appropriate (Economist, 1989).

French and British advertising agencies have traditionally been associated with taking the creative lead in Europe. However, this could become less relevant as serving the consumer needs of an enlarged Germany provides the economic base for a more powerful German advertising industry. Those working in what has been a more regulated environment will understand such constraints, unlike advertising agencies working in the more liberal environments of France and the UK. Developments in Eastern Europe will also provide a springboard for growth (Appleton, 1990). These three factors should combine to take the focus of advertising activity away from creativity (sometimes at the expense of sales response!) towards the rational Germanic approach. This trend will be reinforced if EC legislation also moves in this direction.

The EC legal framework

If the policy of the Commission is to maintain the concept of subsidiarity – leaving legislation to the Member States where it is appropriate to do so – then the controls at EC level should be less restrictive than suggested by the 'Television without Frontiers' White Paper. The total sum of the Commission's proposals and Directives can be viewed as an attempt to strike a balance between two potentially conflicting aims:

- consumer/viewer protection and public health;
- maintenance of the open market through the free movement of goods and services.

Advertising can be viewed as intrinsically good, in providing consumers with the information to choose between products which are freely available across borders; or it can be seen as potentially harmful, requiring a legislative framework for viewer and consumer protection (Denton, 1990).

An important EC instrument for consumer protection was the 1984 Directive on Misleading Advertising. This laid down definitions of misleading advertising and factors to be taken into account. It required Member States to have a process for advertisers to provide evidence for the truthfulness of their claims.

In contrast with this, the reality of Commission action during the period 1988 to 1992 was *ad hoc* Directives affecting specific broadcasting issues or product areas, without the appearance of a cohesive policy.

In respect of **broadcasting** issues, a Directive establishes the condition under which cross-border broadcasting can take place (Directive 89/552/EEC). It is based on the principle of home country control, and all transmissions from within a Member State must comply with the standards set by it. Articles of the Directive deal with restrictions on **television advertising** in terms of when it may be transmitted, in what quantity, the content and attitudes portrayed.

Product issues – tobacco products

The most controversial aspect of the EC regulatory framework for advertising has been in the area of **tobacco products**. A proposal was put to the European Parliament in March 1990 which regulated the information provided to smokers in press or on posters and the way in which advertisements were to portray tobacco products. The majority decision of the Parliament in March 1990 was to propose a more restrictive environment, with a ban on direct advertising and sponsored activities for tobacco. The Commission decided *not* to propose a total ban at that stage, but it cannot be ruled out as a consequence of the pressures created by the open market after the end of 1992.

The medical and consumer lobby groups will welcome this *status quo*, but muted reactions may be expected from some national governments whose tax coffers benefit from tobacco consumption. In November 1991 the EC Council of Health Ministers could not agree on the proposed tobacco advertising ban. The blocking minority of Member States comprised UK, Germany, Denmark, Netherlands and Greece (Advertising Association, 1992). The European Parliament is expected, ultimately, to approve the proposed ban.

Some experts take the view that the principle on which the original parliamentary view was based could open the door to broader advertising restrictions. The principle is that advertising rules for product sectors differ between Member States. This means that the sale of imported printed press from another Member State could be prohibited because the advertising it carries does not meet the required standards. As this contravenes the principle of an open market, then the EC is justified in setting the rules (Tempest, 1990). This could create a precedent for application to other product areas, or to more general broadcasting issues.

Pharmaceuticals

In 1990 the Commission published a working document relating to the marketing and advertising of **pharmaceuticals**, as this product area also falls under the aegis of concern for public health. The document harmonizes current practice in prohibiting advertising for prescription medicines, and sets out advertising conditions for non-prescription medicines. In response to this the industry proposed its own code of practice with self-regulation.

The Council of Ministers agreed a Common Pointer which is a compromise on the original proposal. There is concern over implementation as the wording of the Common Pointer is subject to different interpretation in each Member State (Advertising Association, 1992).

Alcohol

There is no EC legislation proposed to ban alcohol advertising. France plans to introduce restrictive legislation and this could spread to other Member States (Advertising Association, 1992).

Financial services

In the EC Second Banking Directive, banks were authorized to advertise by any means available in the Member State in which the bank had a branch or provided a service. This included foreign banks. There are further conditions for compliance in advertising life insurance, where the consumer undertakes a large financial commitment. Consumers must acknowledge that they are protected or controlled by the Member State in which a foreign provider is located, if that provider does not have an establishment in the consumer's country.

Broader issues of the legislative framework

If the European Parliament's policy on tobacco advertising were applied on a broader front then this would lead to a more restrictive legal framework, with the possibility for a gradual decline in advertising revenue across the EC. The only move towards a more lenient approach is in the area of **comparative advertising**. The proposal for a Directive on comparative advertising would amend the provisions of the 1984 Misleading Advertising Directive in this specific area. It takes a position towards the more liberal position in the UK and Netherlands.

There is also a moral dimension to harmonizing broadcasting controls. The ban in Ireland on the advertising for sale of contraceptives resulted in pressure on British press imported to Ireland which carried advertisements for contraceptives, pregnancy testing and pregnancy centres. Some British magazines removed the offending advertising in the export edition, in the face of possible prosecution.

This is an example of the complex legal scenarios of which an advertiser, broadcaster or publisher must be aware when contemplating expanding business across European borders.

Media availability

An advertiser wishing to communicate a consistent product message across European borders is constrained by the media mix within each Member State. The balance between television, national and regional press advertising is a result of national historical and cultural factors. Some governments have seen their role as protecting the public service broadcast ethic and commercial television has therefore less of a foothold (for example, in Germany and France). Other governments wish to avoid monopoly power in the national press, such as in Italy, where no more than 20% of daily circulation may be in the hands of one owner.

Television

There is a variation in the availability of air-time across Member States. The *per capita* expenditure on television advertising in the UK (£34) and Italy (£42) contrasts with France, where it is only half the UK figure, and Germany, where it is less than one quarter of it. The number of peak television spots available to an advertiser might be so low as to render unviable the type of intense campaign that has worked for a brand in other markets. This means a different media strategy is necessary.

Philips Whirlpool, a leading white goods brand, is committed to coordinating its high advertising budget across Europe through the advertising agency Publicis. However, media availability and lead times for booking television time have led to a more pragmatic approach to campaign planning. The German campaign is focused in press rather than television, there is a mixed media approach in the Netherlands, and television is used single-mindedly in France, Spain and the UK (Kavanagh, 1990).

The French television market is dominated by commercial station TF1 which is estimated to command over 50% of advertising revenue. Two independent rivals, La5 and M6, take a further 25% of revenue between them. Pressure for these two companies to merge has been resisted through powerful media groups behind each. Commercial air-time became available in Italy in the early 1980s, but the market was fragmented by hundreds of local television stations. These are networked for national advertisers.

The advent of satellite television in the UK was forecast to upset the traditional balance of viewing between BBC and ITV. Sky's four-channel system was launched in May 1989, and British Satellite Broadcasting (BSB) was launched the following year. After seven months of operation, BSB merged with Sky, and sales of satellite dishes were well below initial forecasts. The focus on music, films and sport provided satellite advertisers with well-defined audiences, but these were not large enough to provide serious competition to ITV. Research among homes receiving satellite or cable has shown that 60% of viewing is still devoted to the four traditional channels (Barnett, 1991).

Press

There have been attempts to create pan-European titles, such as the weekly newspaper *The European*, but circulation evidence suggests that the most successful strategy for press is the development of strong editorial coverage of European issues within established titles. Among English language publications, the *Financial Times* and *The Economist* have seen spectacular international growth in circulation during the 1980s, whereas *Business Week*, *International Management* and the *International Herald Tribune* have seen steady, but unremarkable, growth (Hook, 1989). The desire and ability to focus on European editorial content will determine the winners in this press race, and British-based titles appear to be gaining headway over their US competition.

The mass circulation figures which are a feature of British press advertising in the form of national tabloid daily newspapers are not representative of the *status quo* in other European countries. In France, there are 11 Paris-based newspapers with even *Le Figaro* having a circulation of under 0.5 million. The provinces are not heavy supporters of Parisian editorial. In Germany, the local and regional dailies dominate, and only three newspapers command readership outside the city of publication: *Die Welt* from Hamburg, *Frankfurter Algemeine Zeitung*, and *Suddentsche Zeitung* in the south, each with a circulation of under 0.5 million.

The fragmented nature of readership mirrors the regional cultures of France and Germany. Media planning becomes more complex, and the advertiser is faced with the question of whether national targeting is, firstly, appropriate and, secondly, feasible. The *Reader's Digest* is a rare example of a truly pan-European medium, offering advertisers a circulation of six million and being published in 15 languages. It is strong in the UK, Germany, France and Scandinavia (Fry, 1991). The readership profile of over-35s will not, however, suit all advertisers.

Free distribution newspapers have been successful in Germany and the UK. There are over 900 titles in each country, with circulation higher in Germany (50 million) than in the UK (38 million).

Media buying and costs

The demand for television air-time in the UK during the 1980s meant that national advertising revenue for this medium increased by between 15 and 20% per annum from 1981 to 1989. This reflects increased costs as demand outstripped supply, although Channel 4 came on air adding to available air-time. By 1987, there was evidence that average viewing time per day was beginning to fall; for January and February it stood at 4.2 hours in 1986, 4.1 hours in 1987, and 4.0 hours in 1988 and 1989

(Dunn, 1989). The impact of growth in VCR viewing will add to this downward trend. This means that advertisers were paying more for less in terms of 'OTS' ratings.

The rules of supply and demand appear similarly distorted when looking at the effects of growth in one medium on demand for another. In Italy, media expenditure grew dramatically in the early 1980s as commercial air-time became available, reflecting simultaneous growth in print advertising. There appeared to be a general stimulus to demand, as well as the inevitable cross-media promotion adding to press revenue.

With the differing balance between television and press advertising across EC Member States, there will not be a simple relationship between supply, demand and prices within each sector. As more companies seek a pan-European approach to media buying, only large media groups with a broad European base will be in a position to negotiate at this level. For example, the German publishers Gruner and Jahr, and Bauer (famous for women's magazines *Prima*, *Best* and *Bella*) are prepared to offer discounts to big spenders on a cross-border basis. The concentration of press power in the hands of just a few giant concerns is a feature of a market near to saturation. Targeting the new audience of eight million created as a result of German unification could give the German advertising industry a new lease of life (Fry, 1991).

The French media markets are dominated by brokers whose power arose in the 1970s and early 1980s, when magazines were offering heavy discounting for guaranteed revenue in the face of new competition from television. Four broking groups control 70 to 80% of magazine advertising. Price competition is just as fierce in newspaper advertising, and discount levels can be as much as 30 to 50% at a national level and 10 to 20% for local advertising (Masson, 1989).

The dominance of a few large media groups operating on a cross-border basis will attract the attention of the EC Commission if there is any sign of abuse of this position. A warning signal was given in the case of HUMO (Flemish programme guide) and NOS (Dutch broadcasters' association). Periodicals issued by Dutch associations holding broadcasting licences enjoy a form of monopoly over radio and television guides. Certain of these associations refused to provide HUMO with programming information when it went on sale in the Netherlands. The EC Commission intervened with the NOS. This resulted in programme information being available to magazines published in other Member States, and with possible import restrictions on these magazines removed (Competition Law in the EC, 1991).

There were formerly restrictions in the UK on the conditions for takeover of one independent franchised television company by another and the industry feared that the smaller companies would be vulnerable to takeover from larger European groups. France, Spain and Ireland all have a 25% ownership limit applying to companies from other Member States. Germany encourages 50% German-owned channels, and other countries have a 15% ceiling. This means that UK companies do not have the same opportunity to expand abroad as their European counterparts. There is a strong lobby from television companies for the UK authorities to create a 'level playing field'.

Problems and assignments

(1)   The role of the planner to align creativity and sales is largely superfluous and not relevant to the needs of most clients. Give reasons and examples to support or disagree with this point of view.

(2)   You have just received a brief from a prospective client asking your agency to prepare strategic and creative proposals for a financial services product, targeted at couples who are 50 years or over. While the target market is well defined and product benefits clearly explained, you must decide what further information you require. In the absence of such information, try to rationalize which creative execution or style you would adopt and why (e.g. slice of life, endorsement, humour, etc.).

(3)   Given the same target market and product as in (2), and also ample funds, what medium or combinations of media might you recommend for this client?

(4)   Your client, who manufactures printing presses, has decided to invest nearly all of their annual advertising budget in a series of quarter-page colour advertisements to run in one of the Sunday supplements. Their target market is very limited and, the client claims, almost bound to take this publication. What advice would you offer this client in order to ensure they spend the money to best effect?

(5)   As a brand manager, the product for which you are responsible is under-performing. You have asked to see both marketing and finance directors in order to make the case for more advertising funds. Without mentioning sums of money, try to build and present your case for more financial support.

(6)   As the newly appointed marketing director at a large consumer goods company, you are worried that your brand managers have historically been allowed to set advertising budgets as a percentage of anticipated sales. Make out your case for changing the method,as well as your preferred method and why.

(7)   'Culture, tastes and languages all prevent the effectiveness of a pan-European advertising strategy and execution. A more pragmatic market-by-market approach is far better advised.' Discuss this unfashionable point of view.

(8)   You are responsible for promoting a pop video with a very limited shelf-life. Your target audience is 15–24 year-olds, and you wish to advertise across Europe. Consider the options available and recommend your preference.

References

Aaker D.A. and Myers J.G. (1987). *Advertising Management*, 3rd edn. Englewood Cliffs, New Jersey: Prentice-Hall, pp 271–272

Anderson E. and Weitz B.A. (1986). Make-or-buy decisions: vertical integration and marketing productivity. *Sloan Management Review*, Spring

Bernstein D. (1989). Advertising and creativity: Some impressions of a generation. *Admap*, November

Broadbent S. (1988). What is a 'small' advertising elasticity? *Admap*, December, 34–36

Clarke D.G. (1975). *Econometric Measurement of the Direction of the Advertising Effect on Sales*. Marketing Science Institute

Gorn J.G. and Weinberg C.B. (1984). The impact of comparative advertising on perceptions and attitude: some positive findings. *J. of Consumer Research*, **11**, September

Haselhurst L. (1988). How Pedigree petfoods evaluate their advertising spend. *Admap*, June, 29–31

Henry H. (1988). Advertising and media trends over 25 years. *Admap*, November

Honomichl J. (1981). FCB: day-after-recall cheats emotion. *Advertising Age*, May, p 2

Kamins A.M. (1989). Celebrity and non-celebrity advertising in a two-sided context. *Journal of Advertising Research*, June/July

Kotler P. (1988). *Marketing Management*. 6th edn. Englewood Cliffs, New Jersey: Prentice-Hall

Lancaster K.M. and Stern J.A. (1983). Computer-based advertising practices of leading US consumer advertisers. *J. of Advertising*, **12**(4)

Lilien G.L., Silk A.J., Choffray J. and Rao M. (1976). Industrial advertising effects and budgeting practices. *J. of Marketing*, **40**, January, 16–24

MacLachlan J. (1984). Making a message memorable and persuasive. *J. of Advertising Research*, **23**(6), December/January

Marketing (1989). 'False' claims exposed in green ads purge, 13 July

Marketing News (1978). Repeating TV ads makes 2 factors snowball, 1 factor wear out, 7 April, p 1

Ogilvy D. (1983). *Ogilvy on Advertising*. New York: Crown Publishers

Ostrow J.W. (1984). Setting frequency levels: an art or a science? *Journal of Advertising Research*, August/September, I9–I11

Perloff R.M. and Brock T.C. (1980). And thinking makes it so: cognitive responses to persuasion. In *Persuasion: New Directions in Theory and Research*, Rioloff M.E. and Miller G.R. (eds). Beverly Hills, California: Sage Publications, pp 67–99

Petty R.E. and Cacioppo J.T. (1981). *Attitudes and Persuasion: Class and Contemporary Approaches.* Dubuque, Iowa: William C. Brown

Poindexter J. (1983). Shaping the consumer. *Psychology Today*, May

Poindexter J. (1984). Shifting sales into high gear. *Marketing Communications,* January, pp 15–21

Strong E.K. (1925). *The Psychology of Selling.* New York: McGraw-Hill p 9

European perspective

Advertising Association (1992). Special issues update (supplement to the *AA Newsletter*), January

Appleton E. (1990). Strategic planning 'United Germany' – the impact on European brands and advertising? *Admap*, **26**(11), 23–25

Barnett S. (1991). Why satellite television is pie in the sky. *The Independent,* 17 July

Competition Law in the EC (1991). Import restrictions (periodicals): the HUMO case, **14**(3), March

Denton R.L. (1990). Haphazard EC attitudes to advertising and the European legal minefield. *Admap*, **26**(5), 27–31

Dunn R. (1989). Greater freedom of the airwaves and advertising cost-effectiveness. *Admap*, **25**(6)

EC Directive on misleading advertising (Directive 84/540/EEC). Reported in *OJ* (1984) L250/17

EC Directives on conditions for cross-border broadcasting (Directive 89/552/EC). Reported in *OJ* (1989) L298/23

Economist (1989). The myth of the Euro-consumer, 4 November, pp 107–108

Feaser N. (1989). Stars and stripes everywhere. *The Observer,* 8 October

Fry A. (1991). The year of European media revolutions. *Marketing,* 28 March, pp 25–26

Hoggan K. (1990). Have ads will travel. *Marketing*, 26 April, p 38

Hook M. (1989). Press quest. *Campaign,* 27 January, pp 51–52

Kavanagh M. (1990). Marketing services – gateway to Europe. *Marketing,* 26 April, pp 31–33

Lannon J. (1988). The European consumer in the year 2000. *Admap*, **24**(11), 20–24

Masson P. (1989). Lessons from the changes in the European newspaper scene. *Admap*, July/August

OJ (1990). C/72/5 COM(90)46 final

Tempest A. (1990). New rules from Europe. *Admap*, **26**(5), 22–26

White R. (1990). 'L'Europe des Patries' and pan-European advertising. *Admap*, **26**(9), 15–17

11 Sales promotion: methods, tactics and results

Chapter objectives:

- to understand what constitutes sales promotion – its methods, tactics and results
- to understand why sales promotion is currently growing at a faster rate than advertising
- to examine how sales promotion can be both complementary and competitive

Introduction

Traditionally, sales promotion has been taken to encompass all those communication techniques which do not fall conveniently into any of the other categories – namely, advertising, personal selling and publicity. A further tradition in Europe has been the acceptance of sales promotion as the 'poor relation' of mainstream advertising. This has occurred through the greater emphasis by the leading advertising agencies on above-the-line campaigns where the opportunity for creativity is perceived to be greater, and where the profile of the agency can be enhanced.

This emphasis is now changing, partly as a result of manufacturer pressure and partly as a result of agencies wishing to be involved in the fast-growing sales promotion sector.

Reasons for the trend towards sales promotion

There are several reasons for the current trend towards sales promotion:

(1) Penetration in many consumer markets has reached a plateau, and manufacturers are striving to maintain market share through a balance between longer-term 'share-of-voice' and shorter-term incentives for the consumer.

(2) The minimum threshold for expenditure for a national TV campaign excludes many advertisers. The alternatives of press advertising or direct mail appear more cost-effective when combined with a specific type of sales promotion, more particularly where results are directly measurable.

(3) Escalating costs of TV air-time are leading advertisers to take a closer look at alternatives for reaching the target group more cost-effectively, and there is increasing acceptance of the idea of creative sales promotions supporting the brand concept.

(4) Developments in information technology, the falling costs of data storage and retrieval and the more sophisticated approaches to targeting on a geographical, demographic or need basis have provided the tools for implementing and controlling promotions more effectively than in the past.

(5) Very sharp peaks and troughs in the economic cycle which have borne particularly heavily on the sale of consumer goods have led to a greater emphasis on short-term marketing planning. This has meant a greater emphasis on promotions with immediate sales results.

Definition of sales promotion

In order to explore the different methods of sales promotion and their management and control, **sales promotion** in this chapter will be taken to mean:

> 'Those activities which provide an incentive, additional to the basic benefits provided by a product or service, and which temporarily change the perceived price/value relationship of that product or service'
> (Shimp and DeLozier, 1986).

Thus sales promotion can work at different levels within the distribution chain – with the salesforce, the retailer and the consumer (for the traditional consumer goods chain), and with wholesalers, distributors and agents in non-consumer markets. Direct mail and door-to-door leaflet distribution are often classified as sales promotion methods in their own right. Using the definition above, they should be viewed as the medium of delivery of a marketing message which includes the short-term incentive to purchase. Use of these media will be explored in depth in Chapter 12.

Example

Company   Batchelors
Product   Microchef Meals: a range of five different pre-cooked meals which do not need cold storage and which can be cooked in a microwave
Sales promotion   'Have a meal on us FREE'
Objective   Awareness of a new product and trial
Medium   Leaflet distributed to households
Response mechanism   Front of a Microchef pack sent with coupon from the leaflet, to claim the free meal
Additional benefit   Development of mailing list

Integration of sales promotion with other elements of the mix

Where there is a clearly stated product strategy and management is disciplined in following this through at every level of marketing implementation, then sales promotion activity will fit coherently into the total plan (the Example above illustrates the effective use of sales promotion to create awareness and trial of a new product).

However, the day-to-day pressures to achieve a sales target will often mean that a sales promotion is devised and implemented within a short time-frame without reference to the brand positioning and key benefits.

Table 11.1   Areas of interaction of sales promotion with advertising and personal selling.

Advertising	Personal selling
Target group	Target customer groups
Brand image	Product information
Key product benefits	Motivation
Media used	Training
Timing and frequency	Workload
Response mechanism	Timing and frequency
	Discretionary power over discounts

Interaction with advertising

Dealing in turn with each of the areas of interaction listed in Table 11.1, some areas lead to a greater synergy and others are fraught with danger. The final outcome depends on the experience and skills of the marketing team.

(1) *Target group*   This should be the same as, or a subsegment of, the target group defined within the product strategy. If an entirely different audience is chosen for the sales promotion, then not only will the promotion have to work harder at creating awareness but also there could be conflict between the needs of the new target group and the underlying brand benefits.

(2) *Brand image*   Is the promotion technique in keeping with the product image? For example, highly priced fragrances and cosmetics are frequently promoted by the offer of a free gift with a minimum purchase. A promotion built around a reduced price could damage the image of the line.

(3) *Key product benefits*   None of these should be abandoned for the sake of the promotion. Some companies have a policy of supplying a cost-reduced version of a product for a promotion. This is short-sighted in that repeat purchases are jeopardized for the sake of short-term sales. A more positive approach is to use one of the key benefits as a creative hook for the promotion. For example, low calorie versions of staple food brands invariably feature health or slimming themes in promotional activity.

(4) *Media used*   A special promotion can be announced using the same media as traditionally used for the standard image-building advertising, or by using complementary media. Retailers such as Boots tend to adopt the first approach in order to ensure wide reach through women's magazines. Convenience food manufacturers may choose to use a door-to-door distribution of coupon offers as inclusion of the offer would be inappropriate on a 30-second TV commercial.

The logistical support structure for the promotion must be in place for the launch through national media. This might include increased stock levels, printed literature, gifts, and the administrative support – whether in-house or contracted out to a promotion handler.

(5) *Timing and frequency*   Seasonality of the product will be an important determinant here. The gift buying seasons dictate the promotion cycle of many personal care and luxury items. Where TV and press commitments are seasonal, then sales promotions can maintain brand momentum outside these peak sales periods. An objective for the total media and sales promotion plan should be to optimize sales response over the whole year set against a specific budget for advertising and sales promotion combined.

(6) *Response mechanism* The need for customers to redeem coupons, enter a competition, claim cash against labels or place an order for the product means that the medium used has to provide the information and incentive to respond. Freephone telephone numbers on TV commercials and freepost coupons in magazines or newspapers are ways of minimizing the cost and effort of customer response. Planning such mechanisms at an early stage in the promotion is critical to a business which builds customer lists.

Example

Company   Courvoisier s.a.
Product   Courvoisier Brandy
Sales promotion   Free luxury chocolates with purchase of the large size
Objective   Repeat purchase in the larger size and brand-switching, without damaging the luxury image
Medium   Window posters, on-pack details
Response mechanism   Customer sends proof of purchase to get gift

---

Interaction with personal selling

For **consumer goods** markets, the major communication of the promotional message will be through traditional media, and the role of the salesforce is to reinforce the message through the distribution chain and to monitor how well it is operating.

Announcement of a consumer promotion will be to large retail chains in the first instance, and this will be the responsibility of key account management. Cooperation of the retail group will be necessary where the promotion involves abnormal merchandising, display material or additional personnel. This approach will also be needed at individual trader level if the promotion is not exclusive to a major chain.

These responsibilities mean that the sales force must be trained in the benefits and mechanics of the promotion and be sufficiently motivated to support it. Feedback from sales meetings on an outline promotion will enable marketing management to fine-tune the format and to solicit sales support before it is finalized. Additional incentives for the salesforce would take the form of competitions and bonuses. Considerations of promotion frequency and salesforce workload are dealt with later in the chapter.

For **industrial goods** and **business-to-business** marketing, personal selling is the major form of communication of the promotion, whether this takes the form of a price discount or additional value to the product for a temporary period. Support may well take the form of promotional literature combined with standard product information.

The target customer group may be specified by management, but there could be a degree of discretion in the new or existing customers who are approached with the promotion. This discretion could extend to the level of discount and extended payment terms in order to secure new or repeat business. This degree of responsibility demands professional skills and a motivation mix which focuses on profitability as well as turnover in the medium term.

Marketing budget allocated to sales promotion

Sales promotion activity costs money – whether through the additional cost of printing, free gifts, extra product, samples or competition prizes; or through the loss of contribution caused by discounting price. A budget must therefore be set aside to allow for these costs, but with recognition that certain objectives will be met.

How does the marketing department judge how much to spend on sales promotion, compared with the budget allocated to advertising, personal selling and publicity? There are some ground rules that can be used but the unique circumstances of the product should be the determining factor.

(1) *Is the market relatively new or mature?* A market sector which is gaining new buyers because of the inherent attraction of the product through innovation or fashion means that companies operating within it can achieve sales without recourse to sales promotion techniques. Awareness through advertising will generate demand. However, where the penetration of a product sector has reached saturation, then additional incentives will be needed to stimulate replacement purchase.

(2) *What market share does a product have?* If a product has achieved a dominant market share through superior benefits and heavy advertising then there will not be the need for additional inducement through sales promotion. It might be used occasionally for interest value. In contrast, a minor brand will need to reinforce awareness and provide an incentive for brand switching, but cost-effectively. Sales promotion would meet these objectives.

(3) *What is the purchase frequency of the product category?* Sales promotions for photographic films are more common than sales promotions for cameras. This reflects the greater number of 'opportunities to buy' for the film, and therefore the need for a brand to thrust itself towards the buyer with a pre-planned seasonality and frequency. This leads into considerations of the use of sales promotion to encourage brand switching where the market has reached an 'equilibrium' with no major new entries into the market and a fairly constant relationship between major and minor brands.

(4) *What is the degree of product differentiation in a market?* Some companies have built significant levels of turnover through establishing ranges without distinguishing features from the competition, but by selling persistently on a sales promotion platform. Such 'modus operandi' can be observed with mail order companies or fashion houses targeting to a mass audience through the classified section of mass circulation newspapers.

These are examples of a marketing mix with an extreme skew towards sales promotion, and can be justified by the absence of damage to brand image with strict merchandise planning and financial control to protect margins.

(5) *What is the historic sales promotion to sales ratio?* This should be considered in the same way as the advertising to sales ratio. However, the state of the market, competitive activity and future plans for the brand should be considered before simply repeating the pattern of the past.

(6) *What is the state of the economy?* National economic measures, such as high interest rates or increased taxation, can have a selective effect in causing downturns in certain markets. Companies might need to adopt sales promotion tactics to maintain volume sales at a reasonable level.

Along with the economic cycle, the business cycle for a specific industry will need to be observed, as well as seasonality patterns. Sales promotion can then be used to smooth demand fluctuation. Should a recession or market down-turn be prolonged, then the longer-term implications of the balance between theme advertising and sales promotion will need to be addressed.

Sales promotion techniques for repeat-purchase consumer products

Repeat-purchase consumer products offer the greatest scope for originality in sales promotion techniques as the large volumes of business involved allow sufficient financial returns to cover development costs. The creativity can reveal itself through the advertising medium, customer involvement, game, competition, prize or free gift.

An original promotional idea will gain attention, but the benefit accruing to the consumer must be clear and the mechanics of customer involvement or response must be straightforward.

Where a promotion is aimed at the target customer purchasing through traditional retail outlets, then the promotion has to be presented to – and accepted by – firstly the salesforce and secondly the retailer.

Failure to gain acceptance at either of these stages will mean that the promotion will be working at less than full potential by the time the message reaches the consumer. See Table 11.2.

Creativity in sales promotion can be extended to a continuation of the theme in order to provide incentive to both the salesforce and the retailer; thus there is a greater commitment to the success of the promotion, as everyone will be seen to benefit. The additional workload which a promotion demands of an independent retailer can be offset by increased sales and profit, but this benefit may need to be spelt out in terms of hard cash.

Table 11.2 Sales promotion techniques for consumer markets.

For the salesforce	For the retailer	For the consumer
Sales conferences	Training seminars	Demonstrations
Sales meetings	Factory visits	Factory visits
Competitions	Competitions	Competitions
Free samples	Free samples	Free samples
Incentive programmes	Promotion bulletin	Educational leaflets
Points system with gift catalogue	Discount on bulk buying	Sweepstake
Club for high achievers	Club for special customers	Club for repeat customers
Bonus scheme	Discount on parcel buying	Money-back guarantee
	Cooperative promotion	Reusable pack
	Discount for early payment	Reduced price pack
	Extended credit	Extra value pack
		Coupon for free or reduced price product
		Voucher with cash value
		Banded pack
		Premiums: Free with pack Free on pack Free mail-in Self-liquidating
		Joint promotion: Complementary product with charity
		Collector series

Example

Company   Virgin Atlantic
Product   Air route to Los Angeles
Sales promotion   Two free tickets to film preview
Objective   Travel agent awareness of new route to LA
Medium   Direct mail package with Hollywood theme sent to travel agents
Response mechanism   Phone-in to get complete information: respondents had names entered in free draw for trip to LA
Additional benefit   Building of mailing list of travel agents responsive to promotions
Next stage   Travel agents booking flight to LA receive two free tickets to cinema of their choice

---

Theory of consumer behaviour

The wide range of sales promotion techniques aimed at the consumer suggests that there is ample evidence that these promotions achieve their individual objectives in a cost-effective way. At the corporate level this would be true, and major consumer product companies would apply rigorous testing and monitoring of results to ensure this. However, the published literature tying in these types of promotion with the accepted theory of consumer behaviour is sparse.

The typical new food or personal care product is launched with a heavyweight advertising campaign possibly linked with a sampling or trial price promotion. The cumulative break-even position on the brand will be reached when there are sufficient regular repeat-purchasers at the standard price to more than offset the losses of the launch period and the current cost of maintenance advertising. The company will be 'buying' awareness and trial in the early period with the expectation of 'pay-off' later.

Table 11.3   The relative functions of advertising and sales promotion in the launch of a repeat-purchase consumer product.

	Awareness	Trial	Repeat-purchase
Advertising	Builds image Shows benefits	Encourages test of benefit against needs	Reminds consumer of benefits Reinforces positive attitude to brand following trial
Sales promotion	Supports image Serves as reminder	Creates easy access to product Provides inducement to test benefit	Incentive to: – bring forward next purchase – brand switch

The mechanisms by which advertising and sales promotion work in harmony to reach this 'pay-off' stage are illustrated in Table 11.3. It also helps to explain how the spending emphasis moves from advertising to sales promotion as the market reaches maturity, and heavy reliance is placed on brand switching for incremental sales.

Example

Company   McDonald's
Product   Hamburgers and related fast food
Sales promotion   General knowledge quiz with winners receiving free soft drink
Objective   Repeat visit to one of the fast-food outlets
Medium   'Scratch-off' card distributed from counter to each customer
Response mechanism   If correct answer 'scratched-off', customer can redeem prize
   at next visit

Developing the sales promotion

The initial brief

As most sales promotions cost money, it is important that the objectives, target customer, budget, operating constraints, measurement of results and timing are specified in a brief. This brief will then be the focus of a brainstorming session within the marketing department, or in the specialist agency hired for its expertise and track record in developing sales promotions.

Objectives should focus on a reasonable outcome and one which can be measured. As an increase in volume sales is the objective of most promotions, the brief should be specific about the level of increase and whether it will be achieved through new trialists, existing purchasers bringing forward a purchase, or by trading up on quantity purchased.

Subsidiary objectives might include increased awareness, and increased loyalty whether with the intermediary or ultimate end-user. Enhanced display at point-of-sale could result in a longer-term improvement in product profile.

The **budget** should be specified along with the costs that it is expected to cover. Estimates are generally available against a brief for costs of printing, gifts, media, leaflet distribution and coupon redemption. Two costs are frequently overlooked – design and development, and the agency's handling fee.

Operating constraints will determine what kind of promotion can be run through limitations on promotion handling within the marketing company or embargos that are placed by retailing chains on certain types of promotions. For example, some supermarket chains will not stock non-standard sizes; others will not permit demonstrations in-store; most provide clear guidelines as to acceptable dimensions of merchandising materials. Where a retail chain accounts for a significant percentage of sales of a product, it is advisable to obtain acceptance from the key account at an early stage in the planning of the promotion, before major costs are incurred.

Measurements of results should be built into the promotion handling protocol. This will be automatic for professional intermediaries handling coupon or gift redemption. The administrative implications need to be considered where the marketing company will be responsible for this.

An important aspect of the **presentation of results** is the link between the quantified objectives for the promotion and the cost budget. It should be clear at the outset whether incremental profit is expected from the promotion, or whether management are prepared to sacrifice profit for other benefits.

Timing of a promotion can be critical for seasonal products and a delay in implementation can result in lost sales which cannot be recouped, and heavy stockholding of premiums or gifts which will not be redeemed. Where a company has a portfolio of branded products each with sales promotion activity, then an outline year plan covering all the products is necessary to assess the combined impact on salesforce activity, the retail trade and cash flow. Smoothing of activity is easier for repeat-purchase items where the salesforce may have up to 12 journey cycles a year, and for mail order companies.

The detailed sales promotion plan

The brainstorming session will produce a short-list of promotional ideas which should be screened for suitability, feasibility and cost. Once the creative idea and the mechanics of the promotion have been decided, then the detailed plan can be constructed to identify all areas of activity and logistical implications for various departments. There are several key elements to the plan.

The idea or creative hook

This should 'add value' to the product by creating interest and activity through the distribution chain as well as providing money value through the offer. The careful choice of a gift, premium or competition prize can give it a very high perceived value, even though the cost to the company will be low through bulk ordering or a cooperative venture.

A creative form of customer involvement can divert attention from the more commercial aspect of the promotion. There appear to be fashions in promotional techniques. For example, some perfume houses use micro-encapsulated perfume cards with special introductory offers on new fragrances. There was at one time a wave of 'scratch-off' question and answer cards used by the brewing industry to promote particular beers. Development costs for these types of promotional tools are high, and the suppliers will want to maximize return on investment by seeking major clients who will require long print runs.

The headline that is used to announce the promotion and gain the attention of the reader should sum up the key benefit of the promotion in a creative way. However, care should be taken to see that it is not misleading.

Size of incentive

The size of incentive is crucial in determining the response rate. When an outside promotion agency is used, it will be able to provide guidance from past experience. When testing the promotion before launch is not possible, then some form of sensitivity analysis may be necessary based on reasonable assumptions.

For example, a coupon for 20 pence off a product would be expected to have a higher redemption rate than a coupon for 10 pence off. However, it would be unlikely that the rate would be doubled. In the absence of prior experience in running this promotion, management should calculate the outcome for a variety of scenarios to identify the route of optimal return with minimal risk. A balance invariably has to be struck between sufficient inducement to bring trialists and lapsed users into the fold, and so large an inducement that regular buyers stock up during the promotion such that profitability suffers in the medium term.

The redemption rate is often the most important item of information in the plan, as from this spring the estimates for product, gift or premium stock, and the labour required for processing and handling.

Conditions for participation

The nature of the promotion will dictate whether a purchase is necessary for the consumer to participate. If this is the case then any advertising or on-pack offer should state the condition clearly. Similarly, the requirement for additional proofs of purchase should be stated clearly, as should the closing date of the offer.

Competitions advertised on-pack invariably exclude from participation relatives or friends of employees of the company running the promotion.

Advertising medium

However creative or well-planned a promotion, its success will be limited if the target group does not know of its existence. The choice of medium in announcing the promotion is important in determining the response.

Direct contact with the target audience in the form of mailings or door-to-door distribution of leaflets or coupons is increasingly chosen by companies marketing repeat-purchase goods or services to announce special promotions.

Nearly 4600 million coupons were distributed in the UK in 1986. An advertiser has the choice of distributing these in newspapers or magazines, door-to-door, on-pack or through minor methods such as in-store. Couponing through newspapers and magazines attracts new users through the high circulation, but there are low redemption rates. There has been a dramatic growth in coupons distributed door-to-door during the 1980s, and this has been at the expense of newspaper coupons. The advantage of the former method is that targeting is now much more accurate with the computer databases now available, leading to higher redemption rates. On-pack couponing has as its prime objective the development of loyalty through repeat-purchase.

In-store promotions create high awareness with the store traffic, and the conversion rate from trial to purchase can be high with products such as novelty foods and drinks. However the cost of promotion personnel is high and training is necessary to provide product knowledge and selling skills.

Response mechanism

The easier it is made for the consumer to respond to an offer the higher the response rate will be. Each activity such as a second or third purchase or addressing and posting an envelope will act as another barrier to redemption.

In-store promotions benefit from the possibility of an immediate redemption of an introductory offer. There is no 'delayed action' as there would be with the redemption of a coupon received through the door. However, the former are less frequent due to logistics and costs of personnel.

Coupons redeemed through retail outlets are generally cleared through a handling house (such as the Nielsen Clearing House) which is paid a fee by the retailer for this service.

The mechanics of a sales promotion budget

When the objectives of a short-term sales promotion have been set, forecasts of costs and redemption rates can be inserted into a budget. This provides a framework for assessing the relative costs and results of different scenarios where there are the inevitable 'unknowns', as well as serving as the traditional vehicle for financial planning of marketing activity.

The costs of most promotions involving retailer participation are difficult to ascribe to particular customer categories. For example, it might not be possible to measure how many new customers have been recruited through a promotion without the specific use of direct marketing techniques (Chapter 12 gives more details on this approach). However, retailers are increasingly able to identify their customers' buying patterns through EPOS (electronic point of sale) and sophisticated databases. Where a promotion is run by a retailer with these tools, then it is possible to classify the customers for the promotion according to frequency and value of purchases and to compare the costs with the measured effects on buying patterns.

Considering the case of a typical manufacturer promotion, the **budget** outline in Table 11.4 illustrates the costing calculation that would accompany a coupon offer on a convenience food line. If the line retailed at 99p and the coupon had a face value of 10p, near-national household coverage would be expected for an established line. The figures assume door-to-door distribution of the coupon by a contract distributor (very often with free local newspapers).

The critical figure in the budget is the forecast redemption rate. Products with low awareness might be expected to achieve a low-percentage redemption rate (may be as low as 0.5%) unless there is a high novelty, utility or monetary value. Two different figures have been used for the redemption rate in Table 11.4, to illustrate the sensitivity of **cost per redeemed coupon** to this figure.

Table 11.4 Promotion budget for a coupon offer for a convenience food line showing two different redemption rates.

Normal retail price for convenience food line	99p	99p
Redemption value for coupon	10p	10p
Total coupons distributed	7 million	7 million
Forecast redemption rate	5%	2%
Number of coupons redeemed	350,000	140,000
Costs: (£000)		
Redemption cost at face value	35,000	14,000
Printing cost	70,000	70,000
Distribution cost (£20 per 1000)	140,000	140,000
Coupon handling cost	7,000	3,000
Total costs	252,000	227,000
Cost per redeemed coupon	72p	£1.62

Cost versus benefit

Some consumer promotions are designed to create a net profit, whereby the cost of the promotion is outweighed by the additional gross margin created by the incremental sales. It is often difficult to measure where sales are incremental. In most situations money is set aside for a promotion as part of an annual marketing plan to achieve an aggregate sales figure for the year. The impact of the promotion will show up in the monthly phasing of the sales budget.

In the example in Table 11.4, the gross margin on the convenience food line is unlikely to be above 25–30p. The cost per redeemed coupon far exceeds this, so the manufacturer would be prepared to suffer a 'net loss' on the promotion with the ulterior motive of recruiting new customers or increasing the frequency of purchase of existing customers.

Promotion budgets for industrial and business-to-business sectors

Control of promotional spending and measurement of effectiveness are just as critical in companies selling industrial products or services to other businesses. Because of the lower percentage of sales revenue generally apportioned to the marketing budget in such markets, it is even more imperative that these monies are used effectively. However, the traditions of such disciplines may be newer where special relationships develop with particular clients, or where the provision of a flexible range of services is seen as part of the total deal for a fixed price.

The starting point for promotion analysis is the protection of the **percentage net margin** at the aggregate 'business unit' level, whether defined as a single product or a product group. This hypothesis for analysis rests on the assumption that sales promotion should increase sales volume at a cost. This cost is measurable in one of three ways:

(1) As part of the total **product cost** (hence reducing the gross margin); this could involve additional services, deliveries or training provided within the standard price.
(2) As a reduction in **sales revenue per unit** due to **price discount** (again, reducing percentage gross margin).
(3) As an additional cost set within the **marketing budget**; this could be cost of printing, competition prizes, sample materials.

An example of case (1) would be the training of nursing staff in the use of a networked computer system for hospital patient management. If included within the standard system price (in the face of stiff competition), this training should be costed and the effect on gross margin assessed.

The highly competitive office services sector (printing, photocopying, fax service) is characterized by reduced-price incentives for instant purchase or volume deals. This reflects approach (2) where an attempt should be made to quantify the additional business gained through the price reduction. An assessment of the effect on the gross margin (in money terms) will reveal whether the promotion is cost-effective, or whether the list price has become notional for existing clients over the period of the promotion.

Scenario (3) is the more familiar, where additional expenditure is proposed, accepted and built into cash-flow forecasts. It has a more visible effect on final profits. It is also more vulnerable to cancellation if sales targets are not met.

This type of analysis of promotional expenditure has the added benefit of providing marketing management with a clearer understanding of the cost structure of the business, and identification of marketing activities that are key to success and those that are marginal.

Measuring performance of sales promotions

The shift in the allocation of marketing budget away from theme advertising and towards discrete promotions reflects the increasing pressure for companies to achieve value for money and, wherever possible, a measurable increase in sales. Larger corporations can afford specialist analysts to collect data, analyse trends and create statistical models to assist in the decision-making process. Research and consultancy services are available to companies that cannot afford such in-house services.

However, reliable data collected within a consistent framework are a prerequisite for determining the effects of a promotion on sales performance. Where such data do not exist, heavy reliance is placed on historical precedent for future promotion planning.

Measurement of consumer promotions

The traditional route to the isolation of the effect of a promotion on sales requires an identification of the causes of fluctuations in sales over an extended period before the promotion, usually through **regression analysis**. A forecast can then be made for base-line sale performance *without* the promotion. The additional sales created through the promotion can then be measured after the event. This is labour-intensive, and companies generally adopt this analytical approach for measuring advertising effects as well (see Chapter 10).

Another possible approach is **classical time series analysis** of consecutive sales volume measurements. An example of the use of this technique is the identification of the impact of giving away free miniature

Coca-Cola bottles with a specified volume purchase of Coca-Cola in a particular market area, as described by N. Carroll Mohn (1989).

In his rationale, Mohn proposes an eight-step approach to identifying the effect of a sales promotion, built around the core hypothesis that the actual sales observations (O) may be represented as:

$$O = T \times S \times C \times I$$

where

T = trend effect; S = seasonal effects; C = cyclical effects; I = irregular effects.

These four component types are generally assumed to be multiplicative in effect. Special promotions, along with strikes, material shortages and a heatwave, would qualify as irregular components of the equation.

The predicted Coca-Cola sales for the period mid-April to end-June 1987 (the period of the promotion) were calculated using weekly sales figures and number of working days for 1981 through to 1988. The actual sales for the period were then compared with the 'predicted' values to reveal the additional sales created by the promotion.

According to Mohn, a prerequisite of this method is that weekly sales observations should be available for the most recent three years of history, and that the length of data following the promotion period should be one and a half times the length of the promotion period. Judgement needs to be exercised as to what should be included as 'unusual' environmental factors during the pre-promotion and post-promotion periods, including significant competitive activity.

Single source data and more accurate measurement

'Single source' means the gathering of data on purchase from a panel of households and matching these with information on television commercials viewed, in-store displays seen, coupons received and price promotion exposure for the *same* households. The latter group of information would represent the independent variables of an analysis, or causal data.

The greater use of electronic monitoring and the bar coding of products (universal product code) have made it possible to collect accurate data on **sales** at the check-out through personal 'smart cards', or on **purchases** by a scanner in the home. Whichever route is chosen, a planned promotion can be tested in a predefined territory and the sales impact identified. On the basis of this experience – rather than forecast – the promotion can be extended on a national basis, adapted or abandoned.

The SCANTRACK National Household Panel was launched in the USA in 1989 by a joint venture between the NPD Group and Nielsen. This 15,000 household panel is geographically and demographically balanced to represent the US population (Tarshis, 1989). All purchases made in these households and coupons used are recorded electronically, television viewing is captured through meters attached to the television sets and households are in areas where there is a capability for electronic commercial recognition.

The final piece in the jigsaw is the SCANTRACK store level database which monitors trade promotion activity in 3000 supermarkets throughout the USA. The panel is designed around these stores as focal points. This is supplemented by the provision of promotion information direct from supermarket chains and other retailers. Some print advertising is missed, although the system measures magazines purchased and subscriptions.

Multiple regression analysis of the combined data for a specific product can determine weekly sales changes due to promotion factors in store and due to price promotions as well as coupon effects. The increase in the use of such single source data will not only encourage accountability in promotion management, but also allow for an assessment of the interaction of variables to devise the optimal marketing plan. (See Chapter 14 for an exploration of this approach.)

Trade promotions

Manufacturers of consumer goods employ a variety of incentives to encourage retailers to stock and sell their products (see Table 11.2). The degree of concentration of buying power, which is high in British food retailing, has a significant effect on the leverage and flexibility of the manufacturer in the use of such promotional tools. Even where there is pressure on the manufacturer to offer discounts or provide specific deals in return for product support, there is a need for measurement of the effects on sales and profitability, particularly as twice as much money is spent in this way as compared with promotions for the consumer.

The ability to measure the degree of support which the retailer gives in response to manufacturer trade promotions depends on access to audit data on retailer activity through either a commercial market research organization (typically Nielsen) or retailer cooperation in providing data on such factors as inventory level and display space. An outline of the ease of measurement of such retailer response against specific objectives for a promotion is provided in Table 11.5.

A major concern to manufacturers is whether trade promotions accepted by retailers result in promotional activity or support of the product at the retail level. The pressure exerted by retailing groups for discounts is motivated by the drive to lower costs and increase margins. The individual manufacturer has to set independent objectives for a promotion, making specific demands of the retailer. This calls for highly developed negotiating skills at the level of national account manager.

The reasons for a retailer to support one manufacturer's trade deal and not another can be specific to the retailing group (policy driven) or can be caused by the features of the product or promotion. Walters (1989), in an empirical study of 202 trade deals accepted by each of two US supermarket chains, revealed a surprising pattern of causality.

Table 11.5 Ease of measuring the results of trade promotions.

Objective of trade promotion	Ease of measurement[†]	Methodology
Incentive for retailer to carry new product	3	Test matched samples of retailers: one group with promotion, second group without (this method reveals tactics before national launch).
Incentive for retailer to increase inventory level	1 4	If commercial audit data purchased. If sample of retailers must be audited before, during and after the promotion.
Incentive for retailer to increase display space	2	Report of display achieved before, during and after the promotion, by salesforce or merchandisers.
Encourage off-season buying	1	Analysis of purchasing history of customer before, during and after promotion, and compared with seasonal pattern for previous year.
Offset competitive activity	3 5	If commercial audit data purchased. If customized protocol for research needed.

[†] 1 = very easy; 5 = very difficult.

In the study, positive relationships were identified between **level of merchandising support** from the retailer and the following variables:

- *Size of the trade incentive*   Retail support was greatest for those deals containing requests for small price reductions.
- *Size of the support advertisement*   Deals requiring small-sized advertising in support were more frequently supported than those requiring large-sized advertising, although support generally was high.
- *Size of the display*   Compliance was generally low.
- *Time since the product in the deal was last promoted*   Surprisingly, sales volume of product category, product rank within the category, price elasticity of the product and whether the deal was accompanied by a manufacturer to consumer sales promotion *did not show a positive relationship*. The limitation of Walters' research was that he used only two food and household product retailers.

A major problem to be overcome in the measurement of the effect of a trade promotion on sales is the inability to control other influencing factors (such as major competitive activity) and the difficulty in obtaining information on these factors to analyse and allow for their effects.

Salesforce promotions

Special promotions to the salesforce are an integral part of encouraging the team to focus attention and activity on specific products or sales objectives. Management has the advantage of a greater control over

Table 11.6 Phasing of salesforce promotional activities.

	Period 1	Period 2	Period 3	Period 4
Product A (launch)	Sell-in	(1) Stock delivered (2) POS in place (3) TV advertising	(1) Check offtake (2) Take re-order	
Product B (on-pack promotion)		(1) Check old stock level and facings (2) Sell-in	On-pack promotion stock delivered	(1) Check offtake (2) Take re-order
Product C (trade discount)		Check stocks	Sell-in	

implementation and measurement of promotions designed for the salesforce, assuming that the advances in information technology have been harnessed in this area of company operations.

The sales promotion might be designed to encourage effort against a new product, to stimulate prospecting for new clients or simply to provide a more creative form of reward for traditional tasks. The range of techniques available is more limited than for promotions to retailer or consumer (see Table 11.2), but there is a growing industry in which agencies specialize in the design and operation of salesforce incentives. A highly motivated salesforce is an important element of success in industrial marketing.

Chapter 13 goes into greater detail on salesforce motivation and rewards. An illustration of the type of detailed planning needed on a product-by-product basis is provided by the sales promotion activity plan in Table 11.6. This shows the activity loading on the salesforce for just three repeat-purchase household products over four journey cycles. The phasing of pre-selling activities such as stock checks, and post-selling activities such as display monitoring and delivery checks, is critical to the success of promotions that have to be implemented at store level.

Dangers and pitfalls of sales promotion

Although the benefits of sales promotion are clearly measurable, potential dangers are not always so apparent, particularly at the planning stage. Table 11.7 highlights the key problems or potential negative impact of sales promotion in the three target areas of the consumer, the trade and the salesforce, and proposes how the dangers might be avoided.

Table 11.7 Problems arising from sales promotion, and proposed solutions.

Target area	Danger	Solution
Consumer	Devalue the brand image	Choose a promotion theme or gift complementary to the image and control the frequency of promotions
	If the offer is open to all, existing customers stock-up at an advantageous price	Target carefully through promotion design and advertising medium, putting an appropriate time limit on the offer
Trade	Customers buy several months' stock at an advantageous price	Put a time and volume limit on the deal: use historic sales data to identify volume figures for major accounts
	Customers buy only when there is a special offer	Restrict the frequency of promotions and monitor the ratio of volume sales at discounted price to sales at standard price
Salesforce	Overload the salesforce with special promotional activity at seasonal peaks	Assess and agree forward 12-month promotion plan with sales management to achieve a balanced workload
	Similar promotional activity on two products coincides	Product managers should confer or a composite plan should be prepared and agreed before financial commitment to individual promotions
	Effort is put behind promotions that are known to work well and which yield the highest commission or bonus	Devise more attractive incentives for new or difficult promotions

The complete promotion plan

The theory behind, and implementation of promotions have been covered in sufficient detail to permit the fusion of key ideas into the format for an outline promotion plan.

Taking the example of an established brand of health snack promoted on a 'slim and fit' platform, the annual marketing budget of £4 million might be split in the fashion shown in Table 11.8.

The integration of marketing activities illustrated in Table 11.9 is a practical illustration of Hardy's view that '...successful promotions require sequential achievement of successes with the salesforce, trade and consumer' (Hardy, 1986).

The peak purchasing period for healthy snacks is traditionally after the indulgence period of winter and before summer clothes will reveal an unhealthy figure. Television and press advertising are scheduled to coincide with this tendency, although general awareness of healthy eating would have the effect of smoothing the hitherto sharp peaks and troughs. Some of the press advertising is used to announce the competition and free health booklet.

Table 11.8 Allocation of budget.

	£ (000)
Television advertising	1750
Press advertising	
TV Times	500
Woman's Own	300
Cosmopolitan	200
Sales promotion	
Couponed packs	350
Consumer competition	150
Free health booklet	300
Trade incentive	200
Salesforce incentives	
Holiday competition	50
'Salespoints' scheme with catalogue gifts	200
Total marketing budget	**4000**

To maintain awareness and usage levels, a further press campaign is inserted in September and October, and a trade incentive is planned for August and September to bolster awareness at retailer level and ensure that stock levels are high enough to cater for demand. Salesforce incentives are phased to maximize the results of the consumer and trade promotions.

Table 11.9 Outline promotion schedule for health snack with marketing budget of £4 million.

	Month											
	J	F	M	A	M	J	J	A	S	O	N	D
Television advertising			X	X	X							
Press advertising												
TV Times			X	X								
Woman's Own					X	X			X	X		
Cosmopolitan					X	X			X	X		
Sales promotion												
Coupon packs						X	X	X				
Competition			X	X								
Health booklet			X	X								
Trade incentive								X	X			
Salesforce incentive												
Holiday competition	X	X										
'Salespoints' scheme with catalogue gifts			X	X	X			X	X			

This scheduling example indicates the importance of planning a promotion programme well in advance (which could mean up to 12 months ahead) in order to gain the maximum commitment from all parties involved in implementation – from coupon handling house to key accounts, and from design agency to the salesforce. It is that commitment that will ensure that the money allocated will reap the planned rewards in terms of new or repeat customers.

European perspective

The opening up of borders within the EC to the free movement of goods will motivate companies marketing consumer products to devise pan-European promotions which provide the same short-term incentives to purchase across Member States. This ideal position would provide economies of scale on premium purchasing, logistics and administration. However, there are three constraints to working on a pan-European basis:

(1) The legal position in each Member State in relation to which promotional techniques are permitted.
(2) Cultural factors determining the degree of acceptability of the incentives within specific promotions.
(3) The degree of sophistication of the sales promotion industry such that specialist agencies and businesses exist to facilitate an individual promotion. Examples are coupon-handling houses and premium mailing companies.

Experts in the field take the view that the British sales promotion industry is significantly more developed than that of its European partners (Lyons, 1989). There are two reasons for this: firstly, sales promotion activities are relatively free from legal constraints in the UK with an industry code of practice as the basis for self-policing. The situation is very different in other Member States, notably Germany, where legal controls are much stricter. Secondly, the concentration of supermarket retailing in the hands of a few key players in the UK means that decisions relating to acceptance of promotions for manufacturers' brands are centralized, and the handling of coupons, leaflets and other non-standard materials is cost-effective as the handling house can make use of the retailing groups' administrative processes.

Cultural influences on consumer acceptance of a promotion are most evident from the comparative success rates for the same 'money-off' offer or gift with purchase across more than one country, assuming that implementation is broadly similar. Where significant financial commitment is involved, companies take the precaution of pre-testing ideas which are new for a particular market, and invariably use the services of specialist promotion companies for their local knowledge and experience. Links between promotion houses are increasingly common: Cato Johnson has links with Jean-Paul Lafaye in Paris; Diego Masi with Promotions Italia; Jacques Kieffer with Cerca. The major advertising agencies, aware of the trend in manufacturers' spending towards sales promotion, have built pan-European networks for their sales promotion divisions to parallel those for mainstream advertising. Ogilvy and Mather is a case in point.

Moves towards EC harmonization

Product harmonization is developing on the back of the general principle that a product which meets sensible standards in any EC Member State is deemed to meet the requirements of all Member States and can be sold there. (This principle was established in the famous Cassis de Dijon case of 1979, where the Federal Republic of Germany's prohibition of the import of the French drink was ruled illegal.) This means that, generally, **home country** rules rather than host country rules are to be adopted for harmonization. This applies to products but not to services such as **sales promotion**. If this principle were to be applied to sales promotion, then the freedoms associated with practice in the UK, Ireland and Spain would be permissible throughout the EC. However, there is the danger that the Commission will favour the more restrictive approach of Germany. A brief analysis of the historic development of EC policy will provide background to the position of uncertainty for practitioners.

Sales promotion has traditionally been viewed by the Commission as falling under the auspices of unfair competition. The most comprehensive study of this broader area was carried out by Ulmer and Beier (1967) at the Max-Planck Institut at the request of the EC Commission and was published in 1967. The **premium offer** field formed part of this study and the risk of unfair competition was identified under four categories (Braun, 1979):

(1) **Competitors** may be forced to be involved in premium offers.
(2) **Providers of premiums** may be adversely affected by market saturation.
(3) **Consumers** will have difficulty in identifying the true price/value relationship for the primary product.
(4) **The economy** may be adversely affected by the increased price of some consumer goods, necessary to cover the cost of premiums.

The impact on consumers has been the particular concern of the Commission, in their desire to protect them from unfair or misleading promotions. The Council's Directive on Misleading Advertising (1984) set the general framework for harmonization, and this appeared to favour the more stringent environment of West Germany. The **lobbying process** (on which the Commission depends for significant factual input as well as pressure for or against a specific legal framework from interested parties) has effectively blocked this move. This means that national sales promotion legislation remains the determinant of what is permissible in individual Member States.

There have been two EC test cases in relation to the application of the 'home market' principle to sales promotion. The first was Openbaar Ministerie v. Oosthoek. A Belgian publisher distributed certain reference books in the Dutch speaking areas of Belgium and in the Netherlands, offering free gifts which *did not* have a natural connection with the main product. Under Dutch law this was illegal, and the Amsterdam Court referred the matter to the European Court of Justice for it to decide whether the Dutch position was compatible with Article 30 (Lawson, 1991). In its judgement, the EC Court restated the principle of the Cassis decision. However, it took the view that the Dutch law contributed to **consumer protection and fair trading** since offering free gifts could mislead consumers as to real prices and could distort competition. There was judged to be no infringement of Article 30.

The second test case was GB-INNO-BM v. Confederation du Commerce Luxembourgeoise (9 March 1990). This involved a Belgian supermarket chain distributing leaflets in Luxembourg with the same advertising for offers of price reductions as used in Belgium. The advertising made reference to the previous price charged, and the local court ruled this as illegal in Luxembourg. The case was referred to the EC Court which judged the local ruling to be in breach of Article 30 because it denied consumers access to information fundamental to their protection (Lawson, 1991).

These EC Court rulings support the principle that if a promotion is lawful in the state of origin then national law cannot be used to prevent it being used in another Member State unless the local law protects the consumer from misleading information or upholds the conditions for commercial fair play. Each case of potential conflict between Article 30 and national law will need to be judged on its own merits by the EC Court.

Legality of specific sales promotion techniques across EC Member States

An outline summary of the legality of 20 different sales promotion techniques across 12 EC Member States is provided in Table 11.10. This provides a 'rule-of-thumb' guide for the early planning stages of a

Table 11.10 Which countries allow which promotion?

	UK	Irish Republic	Spain	West Germany	France	Denmark	Belgium	Netherlands	Portugal	Italy	Greece	Luxembourg
On-pack price reductions	●	●	●	●	●	●	●	●	●	●	●	●
Banded offers	●	●	●	?	●	●	?	●	●	●	●	?
In-pack premiums	●	●	●	?	?	?	?	?	●	●	●	?
Multi-purchase offers	●	●	●	?	●	●	?	●	●	●	●	?
Extra product	●	●	●	●	●	●	●	●	●	●	●	●
Free product	●	●	●	●	●	●	●	●	●	●	●	●
Reusable/alternative use pack	●	●	●	●	●	●	●	●	●	●	●	●
Free mail-ins	●	●	●	?	●	●	●	●	●	●	●	●
With-purchase premiums	●	●	●	○	●	○	?	?	●	●	●	?
Cross-product offers	●	●	●	○	●	?	○	●	●	●	●	○
Collector devices	●	●	●	○	●	?	?	?	●	●	●	?
Competitions	●	●	●	?	●	?	●	●	●	●	●	●
Self-liquidating premiums	●	●	●	●	●	●	●	●	●	●	●	?
Free draws	●	●	●	○	●	○	○	?	●	●	●	○
Share-outs	●	●	●	○	?	○	○	○	●	?	●	○
Sweepstake/lottery	?	?	●	○	?	○	○	?	●	?	●	○
Money-off vouchers	●	●	●	○	●	?	●	●	●	?	●	●
Money-off next purchase	●	●	●	○	●	○	●	●	●	?	●	●
Cash backs	●	●	●	?	●	●	●	●	●	○	●	●
In-store demos	●	●	●	●	●	●	●	●	●	●	●	●

Source: IMP, London.
● Permitted; ○ Not permitted; ?May be permitted.

pan-European campaign. Detailed restrictions on individual promotional types within countries are provided in *1992 – European Promotional Legislation Guide* produced by the Institute of Sales Promotion in the UK. Key facts relating to five commonly used promotions are indicated below.

'With-purchase' or 'in-pack' premiums

These are technically illegal in Belgium but are allowed where the premium is an accessory to the main product, or where it is of low value, indelibly branded and not generally available. In France the premium value must not exceed 7% of the promoted product's price where this is below FF500. Where it exceeds FF500, the premium value must not be more than FF30 + 1% of the main product's value. Premiums above FF350 are not permitted. All free premiums are unlawful in Germany, but they may be permitted where a realistic price is charged, where the value is negligible or where they represent a normal product accessory. In Italy the Ministry of Finance fixes the maximum value of premiums and specifies products which cannot be promoted in this way (usually food and drink). In the Netherlands, premiums must have a natural connection with the product and must not exceed 4% of the value of the main product. There are no restrictions on the use of premiums in the UK.

The non-EC markets of Austria and Switzerland have policies which reflect the restrictions of Germany. This means that there are laws against promotions that offer an inducement to buy which represents unfair competition, and disguises the true **price/value** relationship of the promoted product.

'Reduced price' offers

In the case of banded offers or multiple-purchase offers, the price reduction should not exceed one third of the combined price in Belgium, and the promoted product should be available separately at the usual price. The use of vouchers to redeem an identical product is also subject to the 'one third value' constraint. On-pack price reductions are permitted in France, Germany, the Netherlands and the UK. Such promotions in Italy require the permission of the Ministry of Finance, and advertising relating to the promotion must contain the official authorization number.

Competitions

In Belgium, a reasonably high degree of skill and judgement is required irrespective of proof of purchase. French and UK laws relating to competitions are similar. If no proof of purchase is required, then winners may be determined by chance, whereas if a purchase qualification is necessary then the winner must be determined by skill. In Germany competitions are legal if used as 'attention getters', but if they are judged as 'inducements to buy' then they are illegal. Competitions are legal in Italy but are subject to tax. In the Netherlands, games won by chance are illegal but promotional competitions won by exercising skill are permitted if prizes are in cash or a service with a value not exceeding 2500 guilders.

Collector devices

These are prohibited in Belgium although vouchers may entitle the purchaser to acquire cards or tickets for tombola or a competition. Collector devices are banned in Luxembourg and Germany.

Sampling

The use of sampling devices is banned in Germany if the product has been on the market for some time.

European Code of Sales Promotion Practice

In view of the diversity of the law in various EC Member States, there is a need for a coherent framework which embodies the spirit of EC law as set out in the Directive on Misleading Advertising. A set of guidelines has been prepared by the European Federation of Sales Promotion (EFSP) in Brussels. This provides a voluntary code and does not supersede the existing code in each Member State, where responsibility resides for ensuring that sales promotion activity complies with the law.

A summary of the general provisions of the European Code of Practice is shown in Table 11.11 under nine headings which focus on underlying principles. Application of two further principles in devising sales promotions requires expertise and judgement within the context of business ethics. These are, firstly, that any promotional activity should not

Table 11.11   Some key principles underpinning the European Code of Sales Promotion Practice.

Principle	Application
(1) Legality	Laws of Member States take precedence and the Code is meant to supplement the law.
(2) Spirit	The Code shall apply in spirit and to the letter, 'to eliminate practices prejudicial to the reputation of sales promotion': for example, the advertising of an 'offer price' as compared to a standard price relating to goods on sale in only one store out of many where the goods are available.
(3) Respect for the beneficiary	The advertiser must not exploit the trust or lack of knowledge of the beneficiary; the privacy of the beneficiary should be protected: for example, using winners for publicity, and ethical use of databases. Minors should be protected.
(4) Safety	There should be no risk to beneficiaries in distributing promotional products or services, and any potential risk should be highlighted in information provided.
(5) Presentation	Advertising for the promotion should not be misleading or deceptive, and it should be accurate in relation to quality, value usage and availability. The message at point-of-sale should be consistent across all media.
(6) Terminology used	This should be clear and include information on how to take advantage of the benefit, proof of purchase required or how to pay, and the name and address of the party offering the promotion.
(7) Participation conditions	Restrictions should be indicated clearly: who is excluded, what is required as proof of purchase, the date the offer ends, geographical limits, and the limit to the number of claims by an individual.
(8) Availability of promotional stock	The instigator should ensure that sufficient promotional stock is available to meet demand: the statement 'available while stocks last' does not absolve the instigator of this duty. Where demand outstrips supply, beneficiaries should receive items of equal or higher value.
(9) Administration	There should be adequate control facilities and procedures. Applications for the benefit should be honoured within six weeks of receipt.

Source: Institute of Sales Promotion (1991).

conflict with public interest in such areas as public order or material or moral damage, and secondly, that promotional products should be suitable for the target audience.

Impact of legislation in Member States on traditional multinational marketing methods

Taking the brand-building process illustrated in Table 11.3 , the legal constraints on sales promotion methods in certain countries will enfeeble traditional ways of achieving trial and repeat purchase. So, for example,

where toothpaste and shampoo have been sampled to millions of households in the UK, this would be illegal in Germany. Reliance would therefore have to be placed on price reduction to encourage brand-switching
there. Similarly, retailers in the UK may offer competition entry as a
reward for beneficiaries visiting an outlet (with the temptation to
purchase!). This technique could not be used across all EC Member States.

This has a significant impact on repeat-purchase products for which
there are frequent promotions attached to seasonal demand. A multinational company might choose to plan and implement promotions
through a pan-European team or committee. Legal and logistical barriers
to one single approach for each promotion would need to be identified
at the planning stage, as they would influence a range of decisions and
activities as outlined in Figure 11.1.

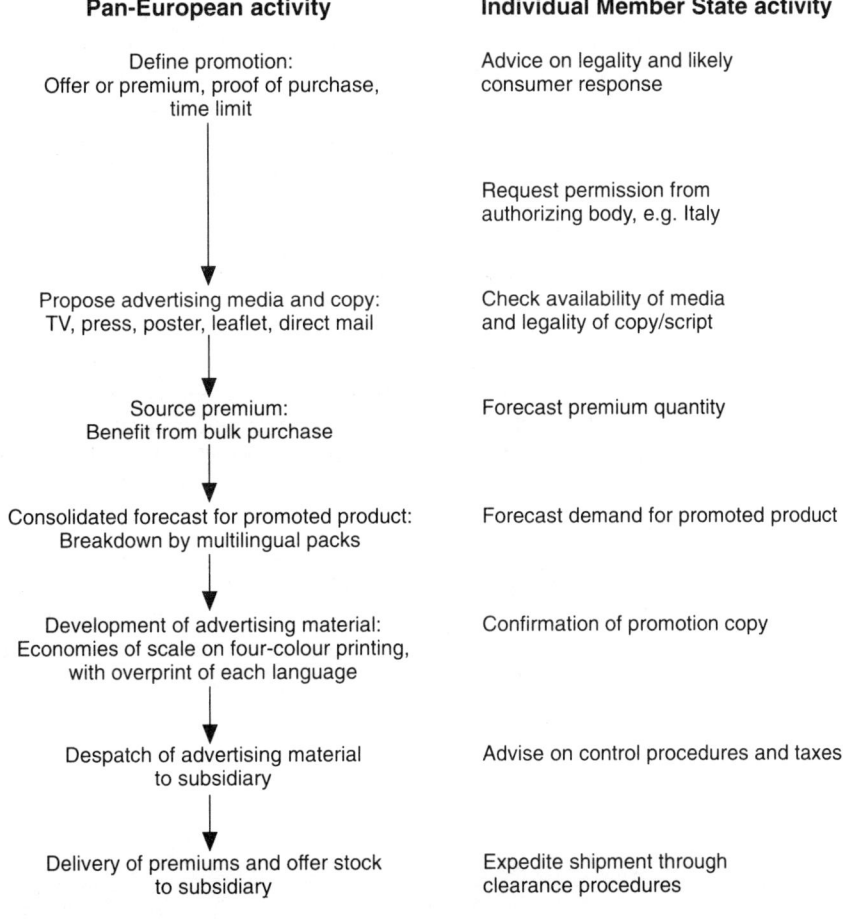

Pan-European activity   **Individual Member State activity**

Define promotion: Advice on legality and likely
Offer or premium, proof of purchase,   consumer response
time limit

                                             Request permission from
                                             authorizing body, e.g. Italy

Propose advertising media and copy: Check availability of media
TV, press, poster, leaflet, direct mail   and legality of copy/script

Source premium: Forecast premium quantity
Benefit from bulk purchase

Consolidated forecast for promoted product: Forecast demand for promoted product
Breakdown by multilingual packs

Development of advertising material: Confirmation of promotion copy
Economies of scale on four-colour printing,
with overprint of each language

Despatch of advertising material   Advise on control procedures and taxes
to subsidiary

Delivery of premiums and offer stock   Expedite shipment through
to subsidiary   clearance procedures

Figure 11.1 Decision and logistics flow in implementing a pan-European sales
promotion.

There are specific product areas which attract differing degrees of control over advertising and promotion in different Member States. Tobacco suffers from very stringent controls, and it is likely that there will be moves in a similar direction on alcohol promotions (Sambrook, 1990). Some companies are taking advantage of the new 'ethical' mood of the consumer, and are linking purchase of products to donations to worthy causes and charities. The 'green' movement is an obvious focus for consumer concern, and promotions using this as an 'attention getter' are likely to be scrutinized by some national authorities for legality and validity.

Impact on intermediaries

Companies providing expertise and services in pan-European sales promotion will benefit from a rapid expansion in demand as smaller client companies identify opportunities in new markets (multinationals have already established networks). However, the successful promotion agency will need resources or 'partners' in several Member States to give good advice on legal and logistical constraints, and to act as a handling house or broker across frontiers.

Sales promotion is an important feature of sales support at the regional level in the USA. The commonality of language, culture and, to some extent, the law, means that a promotion can be standardized and economies of scale achieved. These conditions do not apply across the 12 EC Member States and a very different approach is needed (Bantick and Hall, 1989). This will mean that agencies will need to develop client relationships over time in order to help build their European business. It will also mean that the 'roll-out' approach from one region to another so familiar in the USA will not be a viable option for Europe, without careful customization for the individual market.

While marketing companies and agencies alike gain experience in what remains a fragmented European market for sales promotion, the European Commission will decide where the 'battleline' should be drawn – near to the lenient terrritory of the UK, or closer to the more regulated markets of Germany and the Benelux countries.

Problems and assignments

(1)   Why might a brand manager with a brief to improve sales in the short term, turn to sales promotion before advertising?

(2)	In what ways might sales promotion be considered to be more flexible than advertising as a medium of communication and promotion?

(3)	Consider which sales promotion technique you would recommend for various audiences (e.g. trade, retailer, consumer) for the following products, and give reasons for your choices:

- (a)	new family hatchback
- (b)	recycled toilet paper
- (c)	a petrol brand.

(4)	Write a brief for your sales promotion agency requesting proposals for your liqueur brand. This is to be a summer promotion for a drink that is seasonally consumed at Christmas. Clearly state realistic objectives and supply all the information you believe to be relevant to assist the agency in its task.

(5)	In briefing the agency in question 4, you will need to lay down parameters of cost in order to supply a budget. What parameters would you use in arriving at the final figure?

(6)	What are the marketing, legal and cultural drawbacks of designing pan-European sales promotions for big brands?

(7)	Companies using the 0898 numbers for phone-in sales promotion competitions, which are usually self-liquidating or even profit-making, are becoming more and more prevalent. Examine the marketing and ethical issues behind this type of mechanic. Is it defensible and do you believe it will prevail?

(8)	In the light of the Hoover 'free flights to the US' sales promotion débâcle, what steps, if any, should be taken to safeguard the consumer? What do you believe are the short and long-term consequences of the promotion for Hoover?

References

Carroll Mohn N. (1989). Measuring the effect of a sales promotion. *J. of Business Forecasting*, Summer, 2–6

Cummins J. (1989). *How to Create and Implement Campaigns that Really Work*. London: Kogan Page

Farrar A. (1988). Sales promotion: the interface between discounting, money off and point-of-sale. *Admap*, May

Hardy K. (1986). Key success factors for manufacturer sales promotions in packaged goods. *J. of Marketing*, **50**(July), 13–23

McDonald C. (1988). Repeat buying' refreshed. *Admap*, September

Shimp T.A. and DeLozier M.W. (1986). *Promotion Management and Marketing Communications*. Dryden Press, p 446

Tarshis A.M. (1989). The single source household: delivering the dream. *The Age of Information Marketing* (AIM), Nielsen, No. 1

Walters, R.G. (1989). An empirical investigation into retailer response to manufacturer trade promotions. *J. of Retailing*, **65**(2), 253–272

European perspective

Bantick K. and Hall C. (1989). Do we mow the lawn or do we take sips of kir? *Promotions and Incentives*, January

Beier and Ulner (1967). *La répression de la concurrence déloyale dans les états membres de la CEE – France* (for the EEC Commission). Max-Planck Institute

Braun J. (1979). The present states of the sales promotions law in EC countries. April

Institute of Sales Promotion (1991). *European Code of Sales Promotion Practice* (prepared by the EFSP). European Federation of Sales Promotion, March

Institute of Sales Promotion (1992). *European Promotional Legislation Guide*, 3rd edn

Lawson R. (1991). Key problems in Europe: can you implement a pan-European promotion? ISBA Conference, July

Lyons J. (1989). German suppliers are jealous of us in the UK. *Promotions and Incentives*, January

Sambrook C. (1990). Who dares wins. *Marketing*, 26 April

12 Direct marketing: theory and application

Chapter objectives:

- to understand the different facets of direct marketing and appreciate its growing significance as a means of promotion
- to examine the two main features of direct marketing – building the database of prospects/customers and measuring response rates to different communications
- to explain the SACUDEF model and its implications/application to the business-to-business non-profit sectors
- to look at the role of creativity in a direct marketing campaign as well as control of the overall campaign and commensurate budgets

Introduction

In the USA it is estimated that 65% of advertising spend goes on direct marketing; in the UK, the figure is just 20%. The traditional UK image of direct marketing is one associated with low-profile, or even lower-quality, goods which are marketed to less affluent households whose prime reason for response and purchase is the ability to spread or delay payment. This image relates specifically to mail order and direct selling which are only two types of communication and distribution systems that employ **direct marketing**. The industry has moved a long way from this limited concept and now embraces direct mail, off-the-page selling, teleselling, electronic shopping and trade shows and exhibitions. Direct mail alone generated sales of more than £7 billion in the UK by 1988. The strength and flexibility of direct marketing in achieving highly specific and measurable results have meant that it is now the first choice of organizations, large and small, for reaching their target audience in a cost-effective way, rather than a method of last resort.

Definition

Direct marketing is defined as 'any activity which creates and profitably exploits a direct relationship between you and your prospect' (Drayton Bird, 1982). Once this relationship has been initiated, it can be developed and maintained with a variety of promotional techniques, from direct mail to personal selling. The key to establishing the relationship is capture of the name and address of the prospect. Once this information is entered on a computer database, the organization can target tailor-made messages at a group of prospects with certain features in common. The group may be identified by traditional segmentation techniques or by more sophisticated methods which are possible only with the facility of a computer database.

The second major characteristic of direct marketing is the facility for **testing** different communications and measuring the results in the form of a **response rate** for each different message, whether the difference comes in the form of the medium, the copy or the offer itself. This ability to test an advertising approach (for example, a direct mailshot introducing a new savings account to existing bank customers) against specific objectives (which may be the percentage response rate and the percentage that opens a new savings account) means that direct marketing methods provide the marketing practitioner with greater accountability for results against money spent.

These two features of direct marketing will be the common threads linking the main sections of this chapter. They are explored further in the reasons for growth in direct marketing, followed by a summary of the main types of direct marketing with examples. In order to provide a common framework within which to investigate and evaluate business units whose driving force for sales and profit is direct marketing, the **SACUDEF** model is explained and illustrated. This is then related in practical terms to the use of direct marketing in the business-to-business sector, in non-profit organizations (notably charities), and in the marketing of consumer products.

The later part of the chapter deals with issues and techniques of implementation: namely, creativity and direct marketing, with guidelines for mailshots and press advertising. A section on planning and control of direct marketing campaigns is complemented by a format for budgeting, to ensure that sales and profit targets that are identified through testing are, in fact, met. The advances in technology that will make direct marketing even more powerful in the future are discussed in the context of database management and telemarketing.

Reasons for growth in direct marketing

During the 1980s there were significant changes in the economic and technological environment which forced organizations to re-evaluate the effectiveness of their advertising in the context of the achievement of corporate and marketing objectives. Direct marketing has provided a more appropriate tool for a variety of companies, whether used in isolation, or as part of the total promotion mix, for the following reasons.

Precise targeting

Advances in computer technology have meant that prospects or customers may be identified on database by a wide variety of descriptors, from economic or demographic characteristics to details on the value and frequency of past purchases. This means that a narrow target group can be addressed with a message that exactly suits its needs, and money is not wasted on advertising to people who are not interested in the product or service. This is particularly valuable where there is a limited market for industrial products, and a database of prospects can be built over time using feedback from the salesforce. Similarly, a new supermarket serving a specific catchment area can be advertised through leafleting to households which fall within its boundaries.

Measurement of results

The degree of control that an organization has over a direct communication with a prospect means that it can collect and count responses, and analyse the aggregate result in a variety of ways. For example, the number of people responding to an offer for a collector series of porcelain figures advertised in a colour supplement to a Sunday newspaper could be compared with the number of respondents to a mailing advertising the same offer, and sent to prospects on a mailing list purchased from a **list broker**. The percentage response rate in the first instance would be based on the number of respondents and the circulation of the Sunday supplement; in the second example, it would be based on the number of respondents and the number of people mailed. It is this type of measurement that provides the facility for sophisticated testing of different offers, copy and media so that the format with the highest **response rate** can be extended to a wider audience, in the knowledge that the expense of generalizing the campaign will be justified in the results obtained.

Development of a database

The fact that a prospect's name and address are 'captured' for future use means that a continuing relationship can be developed. A variety of different communications can be used to maintain interest and affect purchasing behaviour. These can range from specific promotional mailings associated with book clubs, to 'house' magazines sent by higher educational institutions to schools and career officers in order to maintain a flow of information about student successes and new courses. Each organization is using an established data-bank of contacts to fulfil marketing objectives, whether these be new book subscriptions or improved awareness of local educational opportunities.

The ability to personalize a message

The more that a message is tailored to the needs of an individual, the greater the likelihood of getting a response and, ultimately, some form of financial commitment. At the simplest level, a mailshot is addressed to a named person, which has a higher chance of gaining attention than a general message on a poster or a circular. Modern technology in the form of laser printing permits the linking of various items of information about the named prospect or customer so that the printed material reflects not only the name and address in appropriate places, but also an indication of purchasing habits, so that a reward element can be introduced for maintaining or improving on this behaviour.

Range of creative options

Direct marketing has traditionally been shunned by some of the larger, prestigious advertising agencies because of its association with low-cost, hard-sell messages where product image over the long term is sacrificed to immediate sales response. These perceptions of direct marketing are changing rapidly, as the reality of the highly professional campaigns that are now evident in the media, and in mailings to businesses and households, become more widespread. Because of the wide variety of techniques that can be used, the scope for creativity is greater than would be possible if the product message were confined to traditional media only.

The challenge now facing advertising agencies or specialist direct marketing agencies is how to combine some of the lessons learnt from traditional brand marketing, with emphasis on building awareness through image, with the more immediate customer response required from a direct marketing campaign. The facility for measuring results with direct marketing has also led clients to begin to demand the same accountability from the agency for traditional advertising response.

Marketing flexibility

Where markets are volatile and unpredictable, some forms of direct marketing can be planned and implemented in a shorter time than can traditional advertising – for example, mailshots to existing customers or leaflet distribution to households in a defined catchment area. In contrast, the purchase of television spots or press space is subject to more forward planning, and this time-scale has to be extended for the production of new creative material.

The changing economic environment can mean considerable swings in the purchasing power of different types of households (for example, high interest rates hit households with mortgages particularly hard). A company with a sophisticated database can select target audiences for specific products or services designed to meet their changing financial circumstances.

Total control of the product message

With certain types of direct marketing, a company keeps total control of the way in which the product is projected to the potential customer. With mail order, direct selling, off-the-page ordering and direct response television spots (the use of 0800 telephone numbers in the UK) there is no intermediary between the advertiser and customer, so that the message and the fulfilment of the product or service can be quality-controlled. In many instances, a handling house may be instructed for fulfilment, but the service provided will be tailor-made to the needs of the customer. In contrast, the normal intermediary of wholesaler or retailer will be carrying a range of products and cannot guarantee to provide a 'bespoke' service. There is the additional advantage of **confidentiality** in areas such as computer technology, creative techniques and results of tests and campaigns when an organization decides to handle 'in-house' all aspects of direct marketing – from the creative function, through print buying and letter-shop management, to product fulfilment. Weighed against these advantages is the need for greater expertise and administrative back-up within the organization in order to ensure efficiency in each area. There could also be the need for considerable capital investment.

Types of direct marketing

The wide variety of media and response mechanisms used in direct marketing reflects the range of **marketing objectives** that can be met. These include awareness, identification of prospects, stimulus to first purchase, incentive for repeat purchase, reward for brand loyalty, product updates for existing customers and so on. The following summary defines the major forms used, together with main uses, common types of users, the advantages and disadvantages, together with a contemporary example.

Direct mail

This includes all forms of addressed material distributed by post bearing a message to prospective customers or subscribers. British businesses spent £483 million on direct mail in 1987, taking it into third place behind television and the media. By far the greatest use of direct mail is to obtain a direct response in the form of an order, a subscription or a request for further information in a **two-stage campaign**. Historically, this has been an important marketing tool for the industrial and business-to-business sectors where the target population is smaller than for consumer products and is easily identifiable through trade directories and leads generated by the salesforce.

There has been a significant increase in the use of direct mail by the financial services sector which became very competitive after the 1988 Financial Services Act. Charities and pressure groups are habitual users of direct mail. The major strengths of direct mail are:

(1) The capability for very precise selection of a target audience.
(2) The possibility of conveying a message with high impact in the personal home setting, and for conveying more detailed product information and a wider range of purchase incentives than is possible with some other media.
(3) Cost-effectiveness: although the **cost per thousand** reached may be higher than for other media, the precise targeting means that the total campaign cost will be lower and the response rate is invariably higher.

The disadvantages of direct mail become particularly apparent as a result of poor targeting, when wastage and a negative image for the company and for direct mail can result. The quality of **list management** will have a bearing on this issue, and can be costly for a small, specialist list of names.

Direct advertising

This invites a **direct response** or call to action by providing a mechanism through which the recipient can respond. A wide variety of media can be used: posters, television, radio, newspapers and magazines. Vital to this method is the name and address or telephone number to which the response can be made. 'Collector' albums of popular music are frequently advertised on television with a freephone number for response. Press advertising generally carries a coupon or voucher for response, and is sometimes referred to as **'off-the-page'** selling. A major advantage of this approach is that a wide target audience may be reached by these media where initial awareness and the development of a list of interested prospects or customers are required. The response is faster than with traditional brand advertising, and a facility for screening the prospects may be built into the process. The disadvantages of this approach are linked with the weaknesses of the media chosen: high costs for television and long copy dates or poor reproduction for press.

This form of direct marketing is particularly associated with consumer products and services because of the suitability of the media available. Its use for industrial marketing is limited to those sectors where suitable specialist and trade magazines exist to reach the appropriate target audience. The growth in the use of this approach for the 'business-to-business' sector is reflected in whole pages of national newspapers designated accordingly, with advertising objectives ranging from the recruitment of sales agents or franchisees to consultancies attempting to match new business ideas with potential investors.

Example

Organization   Midland Bank plc

Offer   New form of consumer banking service called 'First Direct', by which customers can bank by telephone 24 hours a day, 365 days a year

Objective   To create curiosity so that the audience would ring the freephone number to obtain more information

Medium   Intensive television campaign with a variety of settings and role models, supported by other media

Result   In the first four weeks of the campaign there were 40,000 enquiry calls

---

Catalogues

Historically, direct marketing in UK grew through the use of catalogues to describe a range of personal or household products which could be chosen and ordered in the home setting. The mail order market is dominated by three large organizations, GUS, Littlewoods and Freemans, whose combined share is around 75%. These organizations generally develop their customer base through two-stage marketing: the first step is to advertise the availability of a range of clothing or household products through a mailing or in magazines, and interested prospects then send off for the catalogue from which they place orders, or become agents to obtain orders from other parties. Agents can be rewarded for their efforts through payment of a commission or through a sliding scale discount on their own purchases.

Some organizations charge for the catalogue and refund the charge against the first purchase, while others provide this free, viewing it as a necessary marketing cost to encourage higher response rates. The greater incidence of regular mailings to households has meant that there are growing opportunities for an organization to offer the facility for **'piggy-back'** mailings of the sales literature or mini-catalogues of other companies. For example, the monthly mailings sent out by credit card operators to personal customers often include brochures from other organizations.

The advantage of a strategy of building business through this form of direct marketing is that a company does not need to use the traditional intermediaries of retailers to reach its market, thus maintaining high margins and total control. The attractiveness of the offers can also be enhanced by the availability of the merchandise through this route only, thus imparting a certain exclusivity. Customers who would otherwise be embarrassed by visiting a retail outlet are reassured of privacy. The company also has access to and control over the customer database, which would not apply if retailer intermediaries were used. Reliance on payment by cheque or credit instalment brings with this method the disadvantages of higher administration costs through the checking of credit references and a higher incidence of bad debts. There is also recognized to be a hard core of non-users of mail order who prefer the benefits of seeing and feeling the merchandise.

Household leaflets

There has been very rapid growth in this form of direct marketing with the escalation in the number of free local newspapers, which has given rise to companies specializing in household distribution. When these services are combined with market research tools that provide for accurate targeting (such as the ACORN classification of households discussed in Chapter 5), they become highly cost-effective as a way of delivering simple product messages, from the availability of local amenities to national promotions for consumer products, including samples and coupons. With an effective product message and appropriate incentive to respond, a response rate of 2% of circulation can be expected, even with a 'cold' audience.

Electronic media

The scope of this definition will be confined to the inclusion of those media where an offer is transmitted electronically through television, facsimile, teletext or a computer terminal, and the response may be made through the same medium. Where **cable television** has so far been available to only a minority of homes in Europe, its penetration should grow rapidly during the 1990s, providing mass access to **home shopping**. The major advantages of these forms of direct marketing are in savings on time and on the administrative 'paperchase' of traditional ordering systems. The response to an offer can be almost immediate, and the electronic command can flow through the sales channel, inventory control and payment procedure simultaneously. The company's departments work in harmony, using computer-matched information to provide the customer with a faster and more reliable service.

The advantages of such **electronic trading** are particularly apparent in industrial and business-to-business markets, where access to a supplier's database can allow a customer to know instantaneously if a component is in stock or if a service call can be made on a particular day. The order or booking can follow on immediately. However, this accessibility of the prospect can be abused as, for example, in the proliferation of advertising material arriving by facsimile machine. This gives rise to a cost to the recipient which can only add to an annoyance factor if the message is unsolicited and inappropriate. Electronic trading is explored in greater depth with industry examples in Chapter 17.

Telemarketing

This encompasses all direct marketing techniques that involve the use of the telephone in a 'proactive' way for outbound sales calls, or in a 'reactive' way for inbound calls involving an order, enquiry or complaint. The growth of inbound telephone marketing can be directly linked to the introduction by British Telecom in 1985 of the 0800 Linkline number which connects the prospect with the advertiser. Once converted to customers, they use the 0345 number whereby they are charged at the local rate. There were over 6000 companies using these lines in 1989, with around 10,000 calls an hour passing through them – a 50% growth on the previous year (Burnside, 1990).

Example

Organization   Technical Support Software Inc.
Offer   EXACT software at a cost of $495
Objective   To follow up by telephone all prospects who are mailed a demonstration disk of the program contained in a pack
Medium   A single telemarketer uses an IBM PC linked into the company's Novell network and, using a software package called SALEMAKER, the prospect data already imported generate a call list daily. The computer's modem dials the number and the telemarketer can add to the prospect file during the call. The program makes a note of any callbacks required. The program produces a record of the telemarketer's activity.
Result   An overall prospect to sale conversion rate of 14%. Direct mailings without telemarketing follow-up have an average conversion rate of 5%.

Trade shows and exhibitions

This type of direct marketing provides the opportunity for face-to-face promotion and selling to a relatively homogeneous audience who are self-selecting by virtue of their interest in the product or service category being exhibited. This type of marketing is of value to industrial companies who might not have other means for identifying prospects. However, exhibitions are being used increasingly for consumer interests such as skiing, sailing, and interior design.

The major advantage of this medium is the opportunity provided for obtaining **qualified leads** through discussion with new prospects and past and present clients. Small businesses in niche markets use trade shows for obtaining orders particularly where there is a seasonal sales cycle. There is also the advantage of reviewing the competition exhibiting, although this works in reverse and the company itself will be under the competitive microscope. Rapidly increasing costs of exhibiting at trade shows are driving many companies to examine the 'cost per lead' and to track the conversion of leads to orders. Companies organizing trade shows are sometimes disinclined to reveal evidence for the forecast number of visitors, which is the basis for charging exhibitors for stands, the rates varying according to position and size.

Direct marketing and traditional models of consumer behaviour

A great deal of advertising research is directed towards an understanding of the process that persuades an individual to act after being exposed to a message. In other words, it tries to answer the question: 'what goes on in the consumer's black box between exposure to advertising and the purchase decision?' Some of these theories are explored in Chapter 10.

There is a noticeable lack of interest in this type of research on the part of those actively involved in direct marketing. The reason is very simple: they are in a position to know the 'input' side of the consumer equation – how many people were exposed to the message at what cost? They can also measure very precisely the 'output' side of the equation – how many people responded to the message, how many became customers and what did they spend? It is the repetition of this framework of measurement which is behind the dependence of large direct marketing organizations such as Reader's Digest on the **testing** of campaigns, so that they are 'generalized' across the total list only when there is prior knowledge of the outcome in terms of response.

Such testing of campaigns or aspects of them on a sample of a mailing list is the direct marketing manager's research for reducing risk.

The traditional advertiser will use pre- and post-advertising testing, and image studies before and after the campaign to identify its impact. However, these measure have a tenuous relationship with actual sales, and the vastly more expensive test market is the nearest that the traditional advertiser can get to the hard results of a test mailing, for example.

The SACUDEF approach to direct marketing

The term **SACUDEF** is an acronym for the key components of the sales figure achieved through an organization's direct marketing activity over a specified period. In simple terms, the sales figure may be represented as follows:

Sales revenue = number of customers
× average debit (or value of sale)
× frequency of purchase (or payment)

This equation identifies three variables which are components of the final sales revenue figure, and which can vary under the influence of direct marketing activity to achieve the desired result. Depending on the market in which the organization is operating, one of these variables might be more susceptible to change than another. For example, a company whose core business is the sale of albums of popular music in cassette or compact disc form will be heavily reliant on methods of **customer recruitment** for achieving the annual sales target. Conversely, an organization marketing a range of luxury products through a mini-catalogue sent to a select, high-income group will focus on looking at the merchandise mix to improve the **average debit** of those that respond.

An outline of the ways in which each of these three components of the **sales equation** can be influenced by direct marketing activity is summarized in Figure 12.1. This also shows the non-campaign influences such as the nature of the market and state of the economy, as direct marketing campaigns cannot be carried out in isolation from strategic marketing. The items shown provide a checklist for planning at the early stages of developing a business area through direct marketing, and show where monitoring devices are necessary to identify the impact of various types of campaigns on sales. Before pursuing a detailed examination of the influence of direct marketing activity on each of these three components of sales revenue, it is useful to see how the total annual sales figure for a hypothetical company selling financial services can be analysed using the equation.

Sales are generated by

Number of customers	Average debit	Frequency of purchase
Non-campaign influences		
Market growth rate for sector product life cycle (PLC); classification of product as necessity or luxury	State of economy; level of discretionary spending	Usage rate for the product category; stage in family life cycle
Campaign influences		
(1) Method of reaching prospect: – build list – buy list (2) **Incentive** to respond (3) **Incentive** to purchase	(1) Pricing (2) Merchandise mix (3) Incentive for higher spend	Development of customer **loyalty**: (1) Maintain contact (2) Excellent service (3) Incentive or **reward** for loyalty
Longer-term factors		
(1) List maintenance (2) Rate of 'drop-out' in the list: how to replenish a customer base as well as developing it	Balance between product image and individual offers	Overlap between traditional theory of repeat-purchase and the pragmatic approach of direct marketing

Figure 12.1 SACUDEF model for planning and analysing direct marketing strategy and tactics.

Example

Lifeplan plc (a hypothetical company) sells a range of life insurance policies which incorporate a 'with profits' element so that the insured can look forward to a lump sum at the agreed redemption date There are three types of plan: the budget plan, whereby £200 a year is committed and paid in two half-yearly amounts, the standard, whereby the annual sum is £300 paid in quarterly amounts, and the premier, whereby £720 is paid over 12 months.

There is a total of 24,400 clients signed to an agreement at the start of the financial year, and the financial accountant can be sure of revenue of £6.7 million. However, this is of little help to the marketing department in determining where business has come from in the past and using this pattern to plan recruitment for the future. The following analysis is more helpful for identifying ways of improving the business mix through direct marketing. Frequency of payment is equated with frequency of purchase for other markets.

Revenue (000)	=	customers	×	average debit	×	frequency
Budget: 2640	=	13,200	×	100	×	2
Standard: 2850	=	9,500	×	75	×	4
Premier: 1224	=	1,700	×	60	×	12

Using the database for each of the categories of client, a profile of three different target groups can be built using commercially available research services, and three different communications targeted at specific audiences. The level of activity for each product area would depend on the market share, revenue and product objectives.

Detailed analysis of direct marketing using the SACUDEF model

There is a wide range of theory and rules attached to the practice of direct marketing, and the SACUDEF model provides a logical and analytical framework within which to explore these. It does this under three headings, which reflect the components of the revenue equation: number of customers, average debit and frequency of purchase. The influences of strategic economic, social and competitive forces are not included in this analysis as these are analysed in relation to all forms of marketing activity in Chapter 3.

Number of customers

Developing a customer base is the most effective but costliest aspect of building turnover for the short and longer term. Consideration of profitability will be left until later in the chapter, when the budgeting process for direct marketing is examined. There are three questions which have to be addressed when building this customer base or **customer list**:

(1)   *Who* is the **prospect**? How broad or narrow is the target group, how much information is available about its needs, and how well are these needs being met?
(2)   *What* is the product or service on offer? What are the benefits and features, and why should the prospect buy it?
(3)   *How* and *where* will you find these prospects?

These three questions follow the logic of traditional advertising development in that they require a definition of the **target group**, the **product positioning** and the **media** specification, which will be a form of direct marketing. The target group is reached through a prospect list obtained in one of two ways:

- by purchasing a list of suitable prospects;
- by building a list specific to the needs and products of the organization.

A **list** is usually sold for mailing purposes and will include the name and full postal address of the prospect. Lists may be purchased from other organizations direct, or through **list brokers** who offer a wide range of list varying in size, nature and cost 'per thousand names'. The more homogeneous the individuals on the list in terms of their needs, income and buying profile, the more effective the list is likely to be in eliciting a response and therefore the more expensive it is to buy. For example, a list of those over 60 years of age with a high economic and social profile will be particularly suitable for direct marketing of retirement homes, medical aids and special off-peak holidays.

The key to successful purchase of a mailing list is to match the profile of the list as closely as possible with the benefits of the product or service on offer. A second consideration is the **recency** of the list, which means 'how long ago have the names on the list responded actively to a direct marketing campaign?' If prospect's names have been obtained through a purchase two or three years previously, the response rate to a subsequent mailing for a different product category will be very much lower than in the first instance. In general, a mailing list that has been purchased has the advantages of providing a customer base faster and more cheaply than if it is built from scratch. However, such lists give rise to lower response rates to mailings than those that are custom-built, and this reduces cost-effectiveness in the longer term.

The names on a mailing list can be classified into three types: active customers, passive customer and prospects.

(1) *Prospects* These are names identified as within the target group for the product or service on offer. They can be identified by the marketing company or by the list broker, but the latter is likely to use less stringent conditions for membership of the target group and is less likely to have detailed knowledge about how the names were acquired. For example, if they were only prospects for another product category the response from the names will be much lower than if they were customers.

(2) *Active customers* These are names that have responded to an offer within recent history (to be defined by the marketing organization based on the frequency of purchase of the product category – or average frequency of payment for charities). A book club might define an active customer as one making a purchase in the past year, and this could be manipulated through an annual subscription requiring a minimum purchase level.

(3) *Passive customers* These are names that have not responded within the time-frame of an active customer but have, nevertheless, purchased in the past. The response rate to a common mailing would be expected to be lower for passive customer than for active customers, but higher than for prospects. This reflects an important feature of direct marketing: it is less costly to reactivate an old customer than to convert a totally new prospect.

List building is a slow and expensive exercise, but invariably provides a more effective marketing tool for a company that wishes to maintain long and profitable relationships with customers. The methods of **customer recruitment** that are used, such as national press and magazines, local press, direct mail and 0800 numbers in television commercials, provide the opportunity for obtaining 'warm prospects' in the first part of a two-stage process (by asking interested parties to respond in order to find out more), or for obtaining customers immediately by asking for an order. The high cost of media and mailings means that more organizations are tending towards the latter approach so long as there is the opportunity to describe the product in sufficient detail and to provide an **incentive to purchase**.

Other aspects of building and managing mailing lists are covered in the sections on **testing** and **database management**.

Average debit

This part of the revenue equation deals with the questions 'how much, on average, does each customer spend on each purchase occasion?' The total revenue figure for a specified period, such as a year, may include four purchase opportunities for each name on a mailing list. A proportion of the list will respond on each occasion, according to the percentage response rate for each mailing. Taking an aggregate of all these responses, there will be an 'average' amount paid for purchases.

Alternatively, a company might choose to take the average debit for each individual mailing or promotion as the criterion for evaluating its success, particularly when comparing the performance with past mailings of a similar nature. There are five major influences on the **average debit** for consumer products and services.

(1) *Price* Excluding the effects of inflation, upgrading the quality perception of the product on offer will permit a higher price. This could mean upgrading the complete merchandise mix by deleting lines at the lower end of the price spectrum, and adding more at the higher end.

(2) *Purchasing power* This reflects the economic circumstances of the target group or mailing list. Matching the merchandise and prices to the audience in order to maximize average debit requires a combination of knowledge on past response (often through **testing**) and judgement on needs and aspirations, where data on past performance are not available.

(3) *Linked purchases* Matching or complementary items, when attractively displayed in printed material, can have a significant effect on the average debit. A **special offer** or incentive linking the items will galvanize the effect. Whether these are features of seasonal 'one-off' mailings or 'collector series', the advantage for the marketing company is double-edged in that there are buying economies in linked items, and there is the revenue effect of the higher average debit.

(4) *Incentive for higher value purchase* Examination of the detailed budget for a promotion will identify gross margin levels against specific response rates and average debits. To increase the profitability of a promotion, a specific average debit may be identified as the ideal against which the company is prepared to offset the cost of an incentive, which may be a free gift or a discount, or free postage and packing. A more imaginative incentive might be the cross-marketing of an unrelated product or service appropriate to the

target audience (so that everyone benefits). One of the most success-ful incentives for increasing the average debit for repeat purchase consumer products is the 'line game', where every third or fourth line on an order form bears a common advantage such as '20% off', or two products for the price of one.

(5) *Frequency of customer contact* In the situation where there is an established relationship with the customer, response to an individ-ual campaign or mailing will depend on expectations of purchase opportunities in the future. In both consumer and business-to-busi-ness marketing, the customer will attempt to reduce stockholding unless there is sufficient incentive to reverse this behaviour. A common incentive is 'buy now before prices increase'. As with organizations selling through the traditional channels of wholesale or retail, a balance has to be struck between sales at standard and offer prices unless there is a deliberate policy to sell primarily on special promotion, with the list price as a reference point.

Frequency of purchase

This is now considered in the context of the third component of the direct marketing revenue equation, and is linked with the **customer's loyalty** towards the brand, company or cause. Identification of the repeat-purchase cycle for the market sector will assist in determining the ideal frequency of communication with customers, since there is the opportu-nity to describe benefits and incentives just as a product need arises.

A system of mailings that would yield optimal results on this theory is one in which each customer is contacted when a specific time has elapsed since the last purchase. This requires a sophisticated database which holds information on the date and nature of the last purchase, and is used so that a mailing is triggered just before the next repeat-purchase. There would be a high cost penalty for running such a system for frequently purchased items such as mass-market personal care products, where there is the additional disadvantage of low unit price.

This approach is, however, used successfully in the car market, where the average price and frequency of purchase can support the costs of database management. Volvo, for example, run a sophisticated mailing system to communicate with their customers, with the objective of encouraging servicing and repeat-purchase business for the large network of dealers. Rover has launched their 'Catalyst' magazine as the outcome of a culture based on thorough data collection and its imagina-tive exploitation. Each customer or prospect receives one of a series of magazines catering for specific and identified needs.

There is no reason why the principles underlying this approach cannot be adopted by smaller businesses providing services on a local basis; the execution of them, however, will be less ambitious on the grounds of costs and logistics. So, for example, dentists entering into new contracts with the National Health Service (as of 1 October 1990) are required to maintain specific records on their patient lists, conveniently managed on personal computers. This provides an opportunity to maintain contact with each patient when the time for a periodic check-up comes around.

As direct marketing provides the advantage of a continuing relationship with the customer, it has also generated a number of techniques for developing customer loyalty:

- Excellent, personalized service, based on knowledge of customer profile and purchase history.
- Personalized greetings sent on specific occasions (on the anniversary of purchase, birthday or Christmas).
- Operation of a **fidelity** system, by which the customer receives a benefit in return for continued custom or patronage; this can be shown in tangible form through a membership or customer card.
- Mailings about special events, targeted to specific groups of customers.

With prestigious products or retail outlets, individuals are prepared to pay for the privilege of being on such customer lists, since there is a cachet attached. A particularly successful form of 'special treatment' is the invitation to a preview of the season's merchandise. Very often, the exclusivity of the event is more perceived than real, but the additional revenue generated invariably outweighs the cost of advertising and staffing, and has created goodwill as a bonus.

The importance of testing

Much of the revenue generated by direct marketing activity is difficult to monitor and measure because of the inaccessibility of the information on performance, which remains confidential to the individual organization. This is particularly true of campaign testing, because if a company finds a way to reach a target audience more cost-effectively and with a higher response rate than previously, it is unlikely to reveal how this competitive advantage has been achieved. Therefore, each organization has to institute its own testing structure and its own criteria of measurement to achieve the optimal mix of offer, message and media.

New customer recruitment is generally the most expensive form of direct marketing activity for a business, and therefore is the source of many different testing techniques. In order to compare different recruitment methods it is vital that the following measures are taken for each campaign:

- how much the campaign costs in total, per respondent and per customer created;
- the percentage response rate;

- the number of new customers created;
- the total sales for the campaign;
- the **average debit** per new customer;
- how many of these new customers make repeat-purchases.

The **test protocol** will determine how this information is obtained through a **computer flagging** process, which means that each prospect or customer recruited and entered on computer file has specific information attached to that record. Every advertisement or mailing will have a specific campaign code and all responses to it will carry this code on the database.

What to test

A new direct marketing campaign will have a number of features that have not been used before. Some will be similar to those used in the past, and an organization might take the view that they are sufficiently comparable for deductions to be made on likely response rate. An organization might test:

(1) *The product, service or merchandise mix* The appeal of benefits, features and image will be under scrutiny.

(2) *The price* The normal rules of price elasticity will operate in a direct marketing campaign, although experience of a target market's spending power will help to eradicate a total mismatch of price to media or mailing list.

(3) *The offer or incentive* This might be in the form of a discount on standard price, linked purchase, exclusive collector series, free gift, sweepstake or a combination of any of these.

(4) *The message* This will take the form of a headline and body copy for press advertising, with supporting photographs or drawings. For direct mail, the main feature for testing is the personal letter.

(5) *The inserts for direct mail* The response rate for a mailing generally increases with the number of inserts, provided that these are relevant to the campaign objectives. These might include glossy brochures, vouchers, entry forms for competitions or sweepstakes or information leaflets.

(6) *The timing of a campaign* The audience is naturally more receptive to the idea of a purchase around pay day.

(7) *The list* This is particularly important for a list that has been purchased and where there is incomplete knowledge on the recency and purchase history of the names.

(8) *The medium for direct response advertising* Readership and circulation data are necessary to make an initial judgement on suitability, but testing for response will give clear guidance on whether the most cost-effective medium is being used.

(9) *Logistics* Where a campaign will set in train a complex series of administrative procedures and product fulfilment, then it is necessary to test whether the organization has the capabilities to cope with the level of demand, and to forecast stock requirement with greater precision.

Companies for which the greatest risk is the manufacture or buying of stock to meet anticipated demand will incorporate a permanent testing procedure within their promotional cycle. This way, there will be firm evidence of the percentage response to each of the offers, and stock can be produced accordingly.

With highly seasonal products or services the test may need to be carried out a full year before the full promotion, and this time-scale would also apply where there is a long production lead time. However, there are two disadvantages to testing under these circumstances. Firstly, a company will reveal its plans to the competition, and secondly, in markets where new technical features appear frequently, the product might be nearing obsolescence by the time of the full campaign.

As with other forms of market research, the cost of testing in direct marketing must be related to the financial risks involved in going ahead with a new campaign without a test. However, a test will also generate revenue, and the organization must decide whether any losses incurred on the test are outweighed by the information gained.

Guidelines for direct response advertising

The difference between traditional press advertising and direct response advertising is that the latter invites the reader to respond directly to the advertiser, and where an order is to be placed then sufficient product information is carried in the copy and instructions for payment are included. In terms of the persuasion process, many of the key features are common to direct response and traditional 'image and awareness' advertising.

Very often the products are neither glamorous nor easily illustrated and the media used far from ideal, as with black and white newsprint. This means that tight control needs to be exercised in areas of design and copy, to stimulate the reader into action. When the objectives of the advertisement have been set and the creative agency briefed, the following checklist can be used to evaluate the outcome:

(1) Does the advertisement attract attention? The **headline** should catch the readers' attention because they will want to know more and will read on. A question is a commonly used technique, and the answer to the problem should follow in the body copy.

(2) Is there one clear and overriding message? This will mirror the brand strategy in terms of major benefit and supporting features, or announce a specific offer to readers already familiar with these. There is a temptation to concentrate several benefits into the same advertisement. This is counter-productive as it leads to reader confusion and overload.

(3) Is it easy to read? This relates to the clarity of the print – black out of white is easier to read than white out of black or a colour – and the logical flow of the copy. Is the product described in clear and concise terms? Are simple examples provided which make the proposition more relevant to the reader?

(4) Are the visuals – whether photographs, drawings or technical diagrams – supportive of the copy and do they add to the text?

(5) Is it clear how the reader should respond to the advertisement – does the copy include a telephone number, response coupon or named individual within the organization? The use of a toll-free number or **freepost** address increases the response rate.

(6) Is there balance and harmony between the different elements of the advertisement? If the eye is pulled in several different directions at the same time, the logical flow of ideas may be lost and attention could wander. Too much space devoted to a visual could affect the amount of copy available to describe important features of the product.

Some direct marketing experts would go further than this brief set of questions and have derived checklists in which weights are assigned to up to 25 different criteria for judging a print advertisement (Egley, 1987).

The effective direct mailshot

Since the essence of direct marketing is the development of a relationship, the **personal letter** is the key to communication. It should convey a message that is relevant and demands action in a tone of voice which is appropriate to the target audience and which lends credibility to the product and organization. The copywriter who can understand what is going on in the reader's mind and can address that particular problem in simple terms will get a rewarding response.

The letter is the key medium of **persuasion**, which can follow the traditional AIDA model discussed in Chapter 10. Gaining attention is the most important step, as it is only by reading the letter that a prospect will identify the benefits of the product and any incentive to act. An imperative is often given in the form of a *'nota bene'* or 'NB' after the main body of the letter. Layout and typeface invariably reflect the common features of personal letters from a senior executive in the organization to an individual customer. The technology of laser printing permits the name and other details of the prospect or customer to be placed strategically within the copy.

When attention has been gained through the letter, interest will only follow if the **offer** is attractive to the reader and meets identified needs through benefits described in the letter and additional inserts. Transition from the reader's interest to direct action can be stimulated through incentives such as discounted price, free gifts, competitions and sweepstakes. A greater percentage of readers will be encouraged to respond if the act is made easy through the inclusion of an order form or reply coupon and addressed envelope. Reply paid postage is an additional and effective incentive.

The call for action may need to be communicated on the envelope so that it is opened by a higher percentage of the recipients than is usual for the type of mailshot. Reading the first lines of the letter and scanning other inserts is the next stage. These inserts should support or amplify the core message of the letter, and a considerable amount of testing goes into establishing the response effects of different incentives portrayed on different types of inserts.

As a general rule, response rates increase with the number of inserts in a direct mailshot. Each insert provides an additional opportunity for gaining attention and inducing action. Leaflets or brochures that promote the products should be of a quality and style which reflect the aspirations of the target audience and which reinforce the quality of the products, the range of merchandise and the value of the offer.

The most common form of direct mail incentive is the **sweepstake**. Its objective is to increase response. In many mailshots the sweepstake is the initial, major communication and the sales story for the product is secondary. These follow the rule that only one entity at a time can be sold effectively, and the highest possible response rate is the promotion objective. Many clients of experienced direct marketing agencies find this difficult to accept, and often demand a compromise between the impact of the sweepstake and of the product offer with a resultant dilution of the response.

The need to avoid illegal copy is just one of the three major constraints on advertising sweepstakes. The other two are sweepstake over-exposure which can cause devaluation of the technique and alienation of the audience, and demands by suppliers of prizes for exposure out of proportion to their contribution (Lewis, 1989).

Planning and execution in direct marketing

The involvement of a large number of different elements in many direct mail campaigns and the reliance on database management, sales administration procedures and fulfilment departments, as well as creative and

Key marketing strategy
Target market
Product image
Benefits
Differences from competition

↓

Campaign objectives
(1) New customers for existing products
(2) Reactivate existing but 'lapsed' customers
(3) Awareness and purchase of new products
(4) Increase average debit
(5) Reinforce loyalty
(6) Optimize sales of seasonal or obsolete products

↓

Select mailing list or media

↓

Establish budget

↓

Establish campaign performance criteria
Two stage: – % response rate and % conversion rate
– Average cost per lead
One stage: % response rate
Average debit
Average cost per customer
Average cost per new customer
Average contribution per customer

↓

Design the mailing package and copywriting
Personalized letter
Product leaflet/brochure
Sweepstake
Other incentives
Response mechanism

↓

Print and production
Time-plan
Quality control
Logistics
Costs

↓

Insertion and mailing
Capabilities and track-record of
mailing house (if contracted out)
Timing
Costs

↓

Response handling
Facilities of contractor or in-house department
Database management
Speed of order flow
Processing of payments or credit checks

↓

Fulfilment
Stock levels against order quantities
Efficiency and quality of packing
Speed of delivery
Customer service

↓

Analysis
Check mailing results against performance criteria
Check financial results against budget

Figure 12.2 Planning and executing direct mail campaigns.

printing functions, mean that the **planning** and **execution** of a campaign need to be carefully controlled to achieve a successful outcome. The stages of planning a campaign are shown in Figure 12.2, with some examples of detailed activity and performance criteria involved.

The logistical and quality control implications of a major national campaign, such as advertising the share flotation of British Telecom, British Gas or Abbey National, have led to the need for managers skilled in a wide range of direct marketing disciplines to act as coordinators on behalf of financial institutions. Contracts with **lettershops** for inserting and mailing on a large scale may be signed on the basis of the lowest quotation, but the track-record and facilities of the lettershop should be investigated fully to identify whether they can meet the deadlines without jeopardizing quality (Cobb, 1990).

Budgeting procedures

Large mail order houses operate strict budgeting procedures to ensure that the costs of individual campaigns are controlled within specified limits and that they meet broader marketing objectives in terms of number of customers, sales revenue and profits. There are necessarily some areas of uncertainty surrounding the customer which are outside the company's control, such as interest rates, inflation and the general level of confidence. However, the use of tests will identify key performance criteria that a major campaign should emulate in order to contribute to growth and profits. An outline format for a campaign budget is provided in Table 12.1. It illustrates the performance criteria that might be used for a small mail order company selling skin care and fragrance products.

With economic uncertainty, one of the major risk areas for a company selling manufactured items is a lower than expected level of orders against a high stockholding. When interest rates are high, this stock becomes expensive to finance or could become obsolete if demand drops off dramatically in that product category. Testing a particular merchandise mix or set of offers is crucial to avoiding over-exposure to financial risk where large mailing lists are involved.

The example in Table 12.1 shows three alternative financial outcomes for a mailing to 50,000 customers promoting a special offer on a fragrance and a skin care range. The customer is free to choose his/her own product mix so that the **average debit** is not automatically fixed. The mailing costs are the same for each outcome, but forecast (1) has a response rate of 12% where forecast (2) shows a response rate of 8%, with a resultant decline in profitability from 18.3% of revenue to 5.6%. Forecast (3) shows a decline in average debit from 11.90 to 9.90. Although this also results in a decline in profitability of the campaign, it is not as severe as for the lower response rate.

Table 12.1 Budget format for a direct mail campaign for mass market fragrance and skin care products (fictitious data).

	Forecast (1)	Forecast (2)	Forecast (3)
Number of mailings	50,000	50,000	50,000
Percentage response	12	8	12
Number of customers	6,000	4,000	6,000
Average debit	£11.90	£11.90	£9.90
Revenue (including postage and packing but excluding VAT)	£71,400	£47,600	£59,400
Mailing costs £			
Mailing components (letter, leaflets):			
Design	1,000		
Artwork	1,500		
Print	3,000		
Impregnated leaflet	3,000		
Postage	7,500		
Insertion and mailing	1,645		
Computer selection and labels	600		
Total mailing costs £	18,245	18,245	18,245
Mailing cost per 000	365	365	365
Fulfilment costs £			
Product	21,420	14,280	17,820
Freepost (response)	1,020	680	1,020
Order processing and packing	4,800	3,200	4,800
Parcel post	8,460	5,643	8,460
Leaflet insert	1,000	667	1,000
Order form insert	500	334	500
Free gift	2,820	1,880	2,820
Total fulfilment costs £	40,020	26,684	36,420
Mailing and fulfilment costs	58,265	44,929	54,665
Forecast profit	13,135	2,671	4,735
Profit as % revenue	18.3	5.6	8.0

It would be too costly to pre-test a mailing as small as 50,000, and this type of sensitivity analysis indicates the range of financial risk involved; the most probable outcome can be predicted from past campaigns. A great deal depends on the percentage response, and the figures given in the example in Table 12.1 are typical for customers – not prospects!

Database management

Many organizations converted to the techniques of direct marketing use databases as a way of accumulating information on prospects, so that promotions that have been seen to work in the past in the context of that specific market are repeated on a wider target audience. However, the British Direct Marketing Association sees 'database marketing' as not just the use of sophisticated software to build and control lists, but the innovative use of a database to identify new and potentially profitable niches in the market and thereby improve response rates.

In order to achieve such goals, data should not only be collected but enhanced by the overlay of demographic or geographic information from other sources. It can then be used for highly effective targeting to prospects whose needs and behaviour have been analysed and segmented. This facilitates more effective communication with the target audience and the building of relationships for the purpose of 'cross-selling' products, particularly in the financial services sector, and for offering products appropriate to different stages in the family life cycle (Coad, 1990).

This does not mean that the simple rules of **list management** can be ignored when the more sophisticated tools of information technology are available. When the database serves as the driving force behind a coherent marketing plan which includes the use of direct mail, telemarketing and personal selling, then it is even more imperative that the list of customers or prospects reflects recent and accurate history. This will ensure that response rates are optimized, revenue grows and profits are secured.

For list management, the following questions need to be addressed on a regular basis:

- When was the list of prospects purchased or built?
- Is it worth keeping on file prospects who have not responded to any communication?
- Has the list been 'cleaned' of names that have moved, of duplicate entries and of names who have requested that they should be removed from the list?

Telemarketing is an area that is characterized by a rapid evolution of software, and companies offering off-the-shelf software packages or tailor-made systems are essentially in the business of resolving some of the major problems facing marketing management. These include the sheer volume of information on customers, sales and market potential, the integration and analysis of data to aid in effective decision-making, and the coordination of the complex relationships between internal forecasting and planning and external researchers and agencies such as mailing houses and telemarketers (Simpson, 1989).

List renewal

The pressure to replace customers as they drop out of the database is particularly acute in the business-to-business sector during a recession. Management will have an insight into the percentage of customers or of the revenue base that this involves on an annual or cyclical basis. Resources in terms of advertising and personal selling are necessary in order to fill this potential revenue and profit gap.

As major multinationals marketing repeat-purchase consumer goods are tempted into direct marketing they will be looking for ways to predict and compensate for customer drop-out within their protocol for database management. It is in this sector that there is the greatest potential for overlap between the traditional theory of consumer behaviour and the more pragmatic approach of direct marketing.

The harmful effects of 'junk mail'

Every time an individual responds to an advertisement and divulges name and address, there is the possibility that the list so accumulated will be sold to other organizations. During the 1980s, the rapid growth in direct marketing and list broking meant that some households became inundated with unsolicited mail.

The personal reaction to a constant flow of inappropriate mailings can range from passive acceptance to such a level of hostility that the individual requests deletion from the mailing list through the Mailing Preference Service. Indiscriminate mailings which do not take account of segmentation, targeting and the needs of the audience create alienation towards all forms of direct marketing and, particularly, direct mail. As this hardening of attitudes of some members of the public affects the ethical and selective marketers as much as the more cavalier operators, there has been renewed effort to tighten the British Direct Marketing Association (BDMA) Code of Practice and to observe how it is followed.

Moving from the household to the business sector, a survey found that business people's disillusion with direct mail came from duplication and poor targeting rather than the sheer volume of letters (Marketing, 1989). So long as the Data Protection Act continues to provide the individual with the right to know and correct information held on them, and the BDMA Code of Practice discourages the proliferation of inappropriate mailshots, then direct marketing will continue to gain in importance as a cost-effective way of building a customer base and keeping customers loyal.

European perspective

There are considerable variations in the level of sophistication of the direct marketing industries of Europe. A major influence on its growth in individual Member States has been access to other cost-effective media.

Where these are restricted, the **direct mail** industry has blossomed. Across most north European countries, people receive between 38% and 90% more mailshots than in the UK (Gofton, 1990). A higher percentage of total advertising spend goes on direct mail in the Netherlands, Belgium and Denmark. Direct mail represents the largest sector of direct marketing, and is the form most adaptable to pan-European campaigns. Direct response advertising (through television and press) and telemarketing have seen a dramatic increase in use in the UK, but the cost, logistical and legal implications of operating across borders are complex.

Even where direct mail is a significant national marketing tool, it has been used predominantly for reaching the home market. It is estimated that only one per cent of companies use direct marketing for export sales. Those that do tend to operate in publishing (such as the *Financial Times*) or financial services (such as American Express), where problems of cross-border delivery and payment have been overcome. Companies successful with pan-European direct mail have started from a strong English language home customer base, and have applied the lessons l earnt to expand sales slowly across borders. The written word read in a second language can be more acceptable than face-to-face selling where this does not take place in the native tongue, when culture becomes more significant.

1 January 1993 was not celebrated by a sudden influx of mailings from one Member State to another. The major benefits of direct marketing over other forms of communication explored earlier in the chapter need qualification when viewed on a pan-European perspective. The differing pace of industry development across Member States has led to gaps in expertise and services. These can be particularly acute in relation to computer technology and campaign handling, from creative idea through to postcoding and mailing. These gaps in services add to more intractable problems of language, culture and individual Member State laws on customer databases. Some of these issues are identified in Table 12.2.

Precise targeting

Where customer needs transcend borders, the message can be matched to the prospect. Identifying the prospect for direct mail requires sufficient data to be held on individuals for effective segmentation of the database. A profile of representative members of a group identified through geography (postcode) or demographics may be sufficient for accurate targeting of a mailing against all households flagged with identical descriptors of purchasing behaviour or lifestyle. However, the proposal for a Council

Directive approximating certain laws, regulations, and administrative provisions of the Member States concerning the protection of individuals in relation to the processing of personal data would restrict the holding of such profiles (COM (90) 314 SYN 287 and SYN 288). If an EC Directive with such strict provisions became law, this would limit targeting and increase the incidence of **junk mail** (Pounder, 1990).

While the legal situation regarding consumer files remains unresolved, the major obstacle to systematic targeting across borders is the varying availability of **geodemographic classification** systems for customer files. The **ACORN** (CACI) and **PIN** systems are well established in the UK, and there is a growing service in lifestyle classifications provided by reputable market research companies. In Italy, three databases are available: SARIN, compiled from information on telephone subscribers, OLINET and CEMET (MacGinty, 1990). There are strict controls on the type of information that can be held on customer files in Germany.

There are three geodemographic systems available in the Netherlands: MOSAIC (CCN), Omnidata (developed through cooperation between the PTT and Reader's Digest) and Geomarktprofiel. No geodemographic system is yet available in Spain, and the French development of the Minitel computer-telephone link has provided companies with a telemarketing link where databases for direct mail are less sophisticated.

Ability to test response

A campaign that has produced good response in one Member State may be successful in another, but testing the approach on a sample of the mailing list will confirm this while reducing the financial risk. Points of difference in campaigns across borders should be reduced to a minimum when testing so as to seek out the common denominators, as customers from different cultures can behave in remarkably similar ways. Some differences will be imposed through local restrictions on sales promotion techniques. Each test will add to the reservoir of knowledge about customer response in a particular Member State. After several years, the pattern of what will work on a pan-European basis should become apparent, and economies of scale can be achieved.

The experience of some consumer goods companies using direct mail has been to carve Europe into two or three homogeneous areas: for example, German, Austrian and Swiss responses can be similar, and the legal structures are also comparable. The Scandinavian countries, the UK and the Netherlands may show similar patterns of response to product mailings, although differing standards of living can give rise to different

Table 12.2 Summary of key features of direct mail industry across some EC Member States.

Feature	France	Germany	Italy	Neth.	Spain	UK
Access to DM agencies	Adequate	Good	Adequate	Good	Poor	Good
Facility to personalize: laser printing	Adequate	Good	Poor	Good	Poor	Good
List availability	Good	Poor	Adequate	Adequate	Adequate	Good
Support and efficiency of post office	Good	Good	Poor	Good	Adequate	Good
Pre-sort rebates	High volume	Up to 30%			15–25%	15–32%

pricing expectations. Although southern European in culture, linking Spain and Italy with France would incur logistical problems as the first two countries do not have such developed direct marketing facilities.

Table 12.2 provides a summary of the relative position of six Member States with regard to:

• the range of creative options available for direct mail, through access to a number of experienced direct marketing agencies;
• the ability to personalize mailings through access to laser printing;
• list availability – either through companies habitually making their own lists available for rent, or through list brokers (for example, the UK has a highly developed industry, whereas the introduction of strict laws in Germany saw the number of lists available decline from 2500 to 250 in the space of five years);
• support and efficiency of the national postal service, including the availability of rebates where mailings are postcoded and bulk pre-sorted by district.

Precise targeting, the ability to test response, and the aspects listed above are critical to the success of a direct mail campaign where the list is selected and the mailing is created and posted in the individual Member State. Intrinsic to costs and smooth operations is the degree of integration available between the various stages of campaign implementation; for example, is one company able to offer list broking, postcoding, computer selection of names, laser printing, lettershop and warehousing, and fulfilment? Some large international companies prefer to coordinate these stages through their own managers, even if they are based in another country. The advantages to this are uniformity of approach, benefits of economy of scale in creation and printing, and **confidentiality** in relation to operating methods and response rates.

List availability

List availability is as important in business-to-business direct marketing as in consumer mailings. However, identifying potential users of the product and the name of the key decision-maker within the organization often requires a multi-stage approach. Lists available through brokers may suffer from being prospects rather than users of a product category, may not be sufficiently targeted towards a specialist sector, and may be out-of-date.

Gillette approached the marketing of a new plastic pencil which lasted three times as long as a wooden pencil (but sold at the same price) to office users through direct mail on a country by country basis. The first mailing involved sampling the pencil to the secretary and executive, with a broad spectrum of replies and information obtained, as well as sales. The second mailing was conducted on an international basis with a centrally controlled message, and this resulted in response rates across countries of between 10 and 20%. The third mailing produced a further 19% response rate; the sales budget had been met through this three-stage approach, and the company had developed a tailor-made list of stationery buyers with a detailed data-bank (Reed, 1990).

Apart from the strict application of direct marketing rules, there are two other lessons to be learnt from this success story; firstly, the needs of the European market must be researched to identify whether the product is acceptable to the new audience. Secondly, linguistic and cultural nuances must be properly understood, which means working with a specialist familiar with the local market (di Talamo, 1990). Where a list has been rented rather than built, the relationship with the list broker is critical to optimizing results.

Logistical implications of a pan-European mailing

Excluding legal considerations (which are dealt with later in the chapter), the greatest hurdles to implementing a pan-European mailing fall into four areas:

- computer software for list management
- format and content of the printed material
- product delivery
- payment procedure

The development of a 'European' list will involve compilation from various lists available at national level. For example, the *Financial Times* built a mailing list of 1.5 million names across Continental Europe from scores of lists. The software specifications will be different, there are differences in protocol for addressing an individual (particularly as a manager in a company), and the postcoding systems across EC Member States are different. How is the computer to identify the name of the individual, the company, the language of the recipient and country of destination (so that different offers, currencies and sort procedures can be triggered)?

Once these fundamental issues are resolved, the efficiencies to be gained through an international merge/purge facility and the separation of names into active customers and prospects need to be investigated. The profitability of campaigns for publishers of *The Economist*, for example, would be diminished if existing subscribers were to take advantage of introductory offers to new subscribers. International list management facilities are now offered by Printronic in the UK.

Response rates can be affected by the recipient's perception of the quality and authority of the message received. Cultural and language needs must be met in the method of address, the tone and the format of the mailing. Presentation of the incentive value may be significant, as illustrated by differences in response rates achieved by the *Wall Street Journal* when it presented the value of an offer in different currencies in two different ways. In one approach, a subscription offer was shown in the form of a table of European currencies whereas, in the second approach, a personalized, laser printed offer was used. The latter outpulled the original format, and was also cheaper (di Talamo, 1989).

International publishing companies have to balance the customer service/cost equation when making commitment to delivery times for daily newspapers or weekly magazines. The quality of editorial will not stand alone if information is no longer current. Strict adherence to delivery commitments is a possible contributory factor in the dramatic growth in European circulation for both *The Economist* and *Financial Times*.

American companies marketing financial services in Europe discovered that Europeans differ from Americans in the way that they pay for such services. Where use of the credit card is common in the USA, Europeans are used to paying by monthly direct debit. This is facilitated by a more accommodating banking system in Europe. The advantage for selling through direct mail is that the initial payment 'barrier' to the sale is much lower, as is the administrative cost of chasing payment (Lowen, 1990).

Mail order across frontiers

A major obstacle to mail order companies operating across borders is a lack of harmonization of Customs duties and taxes. Where discrepancies between Member States are significant there will be resistance to EC moves towards convergence on the part of the high tax country. For example, UK excise duties on wine makes this more expensive to the consumer than in France, Spain and Italy, and suppresses imports from those countries. A further lobby exists within the airlines, airport authorities and ferry operators whose revenues are heavily subsidized by duty-free shoppers.

The UK Post Office offers a service to overcome the problem of tax differentials for exporting, but it is cumbersome and costly for the advertiser to take advantage of this (King, 1989). It involves a deposit by the advertiser against the value of the goods before they are despatched, which affects cash flow.

A further obstacle to cross-border home shopping is the difficulty with which personal cheques are cleared by banks in another Member State. In most instances, this is just not an option and internationally accepted credit cards are the only workable alternative. Greater access to the 'Eurocheque' facility would ease barriers to mail order business, but processing or service charges need to be low enough for the advertised product to remain competitively priced.

The impracticality of cross-border shopping by mail order was acknowledged by the European Commission in a judgement in 1991. (This judgement was notified in a letter of 25 April 1991 from the EC Commission, and is reported in depth in *Competition Law in the EC*, 1991.) This related to the public takeover bid announced on 20 March 1991 by La Redoute Catalogue SA to acquire the entire issued share capital of the UK company Empire Stores Group plc, or at least 50% of it. The main business of Redoute is catalogue mail order sales of non-food products. It operates in a number of Member States, and is a wholly owned subsidiary of the French company SA La Redoute, which is controlled by the French retailing group Au Printemps. This group, in turn, is controlled by Swiss group MNG, and the indirect interest in Redoute is MNG's only activity in retailing or mail order.

The main business activity of Empire Stores is catalogue mail order of non-food products. Because the combined worldwide turnover of MNG and Empire Stores exceeded 5000 million ECU, and each had a Community-wide turnover of more than 250 million ECU, the proposed merger had to be investigated for concentration implications under Article 1(2) of the Mergers Regulation.

The Commission took the view that:

(1)   Mail order sales of women's fashion, household goods and home textiles in the UK were significant, and therefore retailing through catalogue mail order could be viewed as a market in its own right, and separate from other retailing.

(2)   Mail order businesses are essentially national in character, with facilities, catalogues and product ranges organized along national lines.

(3)   There are two features of UK mail order which differentiate it from other Member States: the use of agents who act as intermediaries in obtaining orders and receiving commission, and the inclusion of credit facilities in the catalogue purchase price of goods.

Taking into account these and other observations about the distinct nature of the UK mail order business in relation to Empire Stores, the Commission took the view that the merger could be permitted as it would not lead to an unacceptable level of market concentration in the EC.

EC moves towards harmonization of law on data protection

The draft proposal for an EC Council Directive on data protection goes significantly further than the UK Data Protection Act (1984) in protecting the rights of individuals to have access to personal data, to have them corrected, erased, and used only for certain purposes. The obligations of organizations holding personal data (on manual as well as computer files) under the proposal would give rise to heavy administrative procedures in relation to obtaining consent of the subject to the information being held. Some of the proposals would have implications for the type and use of personal information held by national security and other public sector departments.

The sizeable credit rating businesses developed in the UK on the basis of data files on court judgements regarding debt would be in jeopardy if one of the provisions became law. (Details of the main provisions of the draft proposal are given in Pounder (1990).)

Because of the disparity between this draft proposal and UK law, the EC Commission has been lobbied by representatives from the UK Advertising Association (AA), and alternative proposals have been put forward by the Direct Marketing Committee of the European Advertising Tripartite (EAT). The serious implications for the UK direct marketing industry if the draft proposal should become law has had the effect of raising the profile of direct marketing within advertising. This has led to efforts by the AA to encourage the industry to take a more cohesive approach towards representing its own interests (Wade, 1991).

Meanwhile, data protection law in other Member States reflects varying levels of control. That in Germany is the most stringent, while Italy has no data protection legislation on ownership or use of lists. France has had laws in force since 1980 which give individuals access to information held on file. In Spain, direct marketing legislation focuses on the types of offers and games of chance that are permissible. Data protection legislation came into force for the first time in the Netherlands in 1989, which some observers view as late for one of the most developed industrial countries in the EC (MacGinty, 1990).

Should the EC Commission respond to counter-proposals from the direct marketing industries of individual Member States and soften its approach to legislation, countries like Germany could oppose cross-border mailings for non-compliance with their own data protection laws. Such opposition could disguise attempts at protectionist measures.

In spite of these legal uncertainties, US direct marketing agencies have seen the opportunities to be gained from the open market, and have decided to invest in the future with the Netherlands as a base. The success of direct mail depends on the written word. The fact that 80% of all information stored in computers is in English and three quarters of the world's letters, faxes and cables are in English suggests that UK companies also have a significant advantage when the barriers come down (Linen, 1991).

Problems and assignments

(1)   List as many advantages as possible that direct marketing might have over mainstream advertising in the communication and promotion of financial services products.

(2)   As marketing manager for a firm selling reproduction porcelain figures, you have decided to experiment with direct marketing. In the first instance, what source(s) would you use to go about building your mailing list/database?

(3)   What spin-off benefits may accrue to a company that has successfully invested in direct marketing?

(4)   Direct response advertising can use the same media available to mainstream advertising. Given the request for the prospect to respond, which medium in particular may be best suited to direct response advertisements?

(5)   What steps might you recommend being taken to support a mailshot and improve the chances of response from prospects? What caveats would you add to your arguments?

(6) In which instances would you recommend a client to include a prize draw in a mailshot, and when would you recommend a client not to use this tactic?

(7) Think of an application where telemarketing would be more appropriate than other forms of direct advertising. Explain your reasons.

(8) You are investigating the feasibility of a pan-European direct mailing campaign. Which marketing and logistical barriers would you have to surmount to be able to implement the campaign?

References

Akaah I.P. and Korgaonkar P.K. (1988). A conjoint investigation of the relative importance of risk-relievers in direct marketing. *J. of Advertising Research*, August/September, 38

Bidlake S. (1990). Coming of age. *Direct Marketing*, 25 January, p 33

Bird D. (1982). *Commonsense direct marketing.* The Printed Shop

Burnside A. (1990). Calling the shots. *Marketing*, 25 January

Coad A. (1990). Data speak. *Marketing*, 25 January

Cobb R. (1990). Marketing services: direct marketing – keeping posted. *Marketing*, 25 January, p 27

Croft M. (1989). Mailshots right on target. Direct marketing special report. *The Times*, 25 September

Egley J. (1987). Everything you always wanted to know about advertising – but were afraid to ask. *Business Marketing*, June, p 138

Lewis H.G. (1989). Hey Ed McMahon …when are you gonna deliver my house? *Direct Marketing*, June, p 24

Marketing (1989). Exploding the mailshot myth, 13 July (refers to *The Real Truth about Business Direct Mail* (1989). London: Smith Bundy and Partners)

Miles L. (1990). Initiative tests. *Direct Marketing*, 25 January, p 39

Reed D. (1989). Life after data bases. *Campaign*, 14 July, p 51

Simpson A. (1989). All keyed up. *Marketing*, 5 October

European perspective

Competition Law in the EC (1991). Concentration (mail order): the La Redoute/Empire case, **14**(8), 179–183

di Talamo N. (1989). Mailing into Fortress Europe. *Direct Mailing*, August, pp 51–54

di Talamo N. (1990). Selling in Europe without a sales force. *Direct Marketing* (USA), **53**(1), 22–25

Gofton K. (1990). The direct route. *Marketing*, 26 April, p 36

King B. (1989). Why 1992 will be good for UK direct marketing. *Promotions and Incentives*, January, p 26

Linen C.T. (1991). Marketing and the global economy. *Direct Marketing*, **53**(9), 54–56

Lowen I. (1990). Eyes on Europe. *Direct Marketing*, **53**(6), 44–47, 111

MacGinty F. (1990). When the walls come down. *Direct Marketing*, **52**(10), 22–24

MacGinty F. (1989). If the walls come down. *Direct Marketing*, **52**(8), 53–55

Pounder C. (1990). EC sharpens the claws of data protection law. *Computing* (UK), 18 October, pp 24–25

Reed D. (1990). Opening up to export. *Direct Response* (UK), August, pp 44–45

Wade R. (1991). The AA to the rescue. *Direct Response* (UK), February, pp 30–31

13 Selling and sales management

Chapter objectives:

- to examine the factors involved in the personal selling process, including culture, personality and the buyer network
- to understand the various stages of the selling cycle from preparation to closing, with the addition of after-sale service
- to stress the importance of interpersonal skills in selling, together with training, as prerequisites for success
- to consider the role of motivation in selling – both in terms of self-motivation and incentives to sell

Personal selling: its role in the promotion mix

Personal selling is the element of the promotion mix which involves face-to-face contact between buyer and seller with the objective of gaining the buyer's commitment to an idea, proposal, product or service. For profit-making businesses, the end-result of this commitment will be a beneficial contract, with the seller supplying a product or service and the buyer paying a specified price, the transaction taking place within the time-scale agreed under the terms of the contract.

In some situations, the seller of an idea or proposal is looking for funding commitment for a project where the 'benefit' to the buyer may not be realizable in the short term or even measurable at the time the proposal is sold. For example, some charities sell the sponsorship of a child in a third-world country to secure health and education. The benefit from this form of donation is knowledge of the child's well-being and the possible development of a relationship in the longer term. A second example is the selling of a literary work as a film project by eminent directors or actors.

They require funding to set the film in motion, but the box office success of such a project cannot be guaranteed.

Personal selling differs from the other elements of the promotion mix in that it is **flexible** – the method, content and style of the sales pitch can be modified to suit the product or service, the buyer's needs and the seller's interpersonal skills. It is a **two-way communication** – feedback from the buyer must be used to change the story or style to best suit the needs of the buyer, which are identified through the listening and probing process. The degree of flexibility will depend on the level of autonomy given to the salesforce and the policies laid down regarding changes in key contract areas such as price, service level and warranties. The other elements of the promotion mix are less capable of adaptation to suit the individual customer, as the success of advertising and press relations in particular depends on commitment to a particular message reaching as many of the target group as possible within a set budget. When advertising through mass media, changes to the message not only dilute its impact but also give rise to additional costs.

The selling process

Figure 13.1 illustrates the structured approach to understanding the selling process, possible even though the flexibility and two-way communication are aspects that highlight the very individual nature of every sales approach, which evolves under some specific influence. The first such influence is **culture**; this moulds the social reference framework within which the seller and buyer respond to each other in the initial stage of a relationship. Education effects can be considered an extension of this framework. The second major influence on the way in which a sales presentation is given and received is that of **personality**. It would be an ill-advised sales manager who tried to manipulate the personality of a subordinate (Cooper and Makin, 1984).

Behaviour gives the tangible signs of personality traits and it is within the manager's remit to influence behaviour to achieve specific results or maintain harmony within a team. This, after all, is one of the primary reasons for training. Evidence of success and experience gained in the past will give clues as to future behaviour, as will recruitment questionnaires which are designed to reveal attitudes and past behaviour so that these may be used predictively, prior to investment in training or appointment of staff. The systematic behavioural analysis of prospective customers is not seen as a necessary preliminary to the sales approach, and yet this analysis is part of an experienced salesman's repertoire of skills, even though it is possibly occurring at an informal and subconscious level.

A third influence on whether there will be a successful sale is the recognition of a **buyer network**. This is the set of individuals within the buying organization having an interest in the purchase decision for

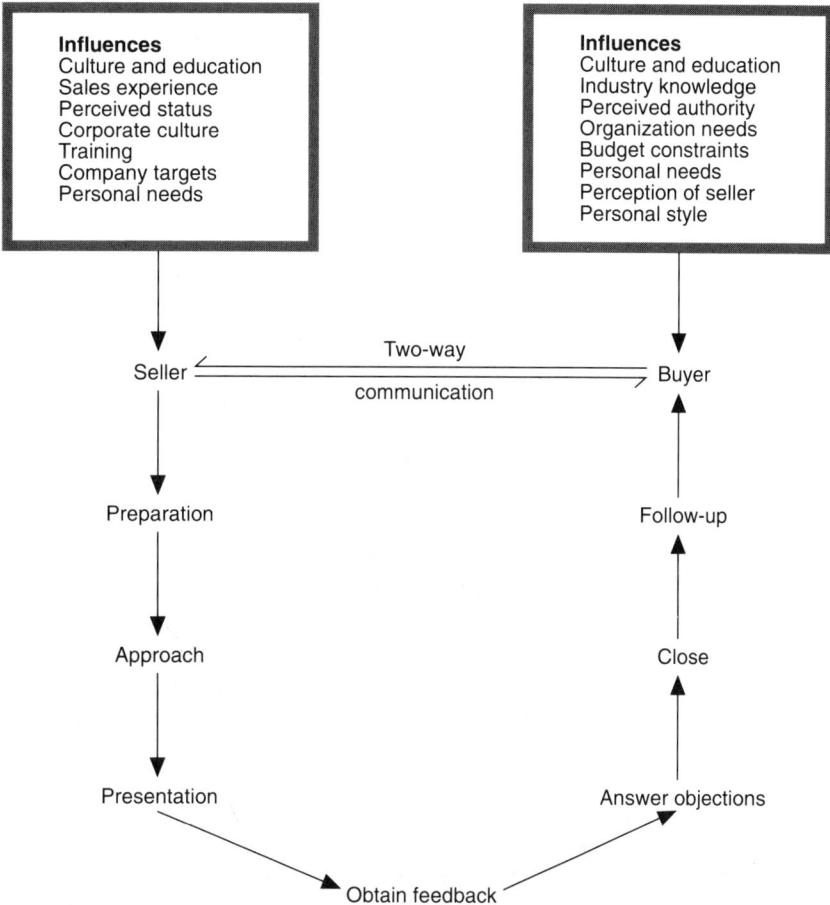

Figure 13.1 Influences on seller and buyer and the selling cycle.

high-value industrial products or services. Identification of individual needs within the buyer network, and how these overlap with organizational needs, is necessary to determine the form of communication and nature of selling tasks. The industrial buyer network is explored in detail in Chapter 4, along with the understanding of personal style in developing selling skills and the process of negotiation.

The selling cycle

There are key stages in the **selling cycle** which can be explored for the contribution that each makes to a successful sale. A high level of **preparation** will enhance credibility of the seller at the first sales interview and will permit optimal use of that initial contact time. How well the **approach** and first meeting is handled will influence the other stages in a developing relationship. The quality of **presentation**, including content and style, will be an indication to the prospect of product knowledge and professionalism.

At this stage, the sales process requires commitment to listening as well as presenting, for it is the analysis of **feedback** which will identify the key needs of the prospect and how they are best satisfied.

The successful completion of a sale will often depend on how well **objections** to the product, the person or the company have been handled, and part of the skill here is in determining which are the important objections. The timing of the **'close'** or the point at which the prospect is asked to commit to the proposal or product, is also critical to its success, and the choice of **closing** tactic will be influenced not just by the words of prospective buyers but also by their behavioural signals.

When the buyer and seller have differing ideas on the preferred outcome this could lead to a period of **negotiation**, in which each party is prepared to make one or more concessions in response to concessions from the other party, thus reaching a mutually agreeable conclusion. (The negotiation process is featured in Chapter 4.)

For some members of the sales team, the signing of a contract is the signal to ensure that the appropriate resources are available to meet the needs of the customer in a period of **follow-up**. This is important for keeping a satisfied customer and for obtaining new business through recommendation.

The key areas of the selling process which have been highlighted are explored through the integration of contemporary theory and current commercial practice. As there are limits to what can be assimilated through reading about what are essentially interpersonal skills, students are encouraged to focus on the development of these skills through group work and role-playing.

Consumer v. industrial markets: the nature of selling tasks

The consumer

Repeat-purchase consumer products and many consumer durables require mass-media advertising support if they are to achieve adequate market penetration and volume sales. The salesforce role then becomes one of facilitator, in making sure that the product has adequate distribution to satisfy the demand created through advertising. In fulfilling this

Table 13.1 Range of tasks involved in consumer and industrial selling.

Consumer	Industrial
Order-taking in the field	Order-taking in the field
Creative selling of new products	Research new prospects
Delivery of product	Visit new prospects
Stock-checking	Sales presentations:
Install promotion material	(1) Individual buyer
Merchandise product	(2) Seminar to buyer group
Support national account management	(3) Sales meeting with many prospects
at store level	(e.g. selling franchise)
Product advice	Provide technical back-up
Creation of goodwill	Service support
Educate on new policy	Develop testing protocol
Chase payment	Negotiation
Advise on discounts	Customer training
Provide market intelligence	Attend exhibitions
Cold-calling on prospects	Follow leads created by advertising
Give demonstrations	
At headquarters	**At headquarters**
Order-taking by telephone	Identify prospects and key personnel by research
Telephone selling: new clients	Liaise with service departments to satisfy client
Maintain customer files (manual or computer)	Telephone selling
National account management	Feedback to specialist departments on customer specifications

role, the salesforce also carry the key advertising message through to the intermediaries who need to share conviction in and understanding of the product.

This supportive nature of the selling role can be accentuated by the level of concentration of retailing power as, for example, a food retailing industry which is dominated by three or four major chains will significantly reduce the number of buying points where substantial decisions are made. The system of key account management will deprive the field salesforce of order-seeking responsibilities and will require instead a focus on skills of servicing and creation of goodwill at the individual store level.

The way in which selling time is allocated to preparation, sales calls, administration and other duties is more tightly controlled for repeat-purchase consumer products, as a journey cycle will be imposed by management to make sure that all accounts are serviced to the appropriate level.

The range of tasks required of a person selling consumer products is outlined in Table 13.1, and these can be compared directly with the range of functions involved in the sale of industrial products or business-to-business services.

The industrial market

In industrial marketing there has historically been a much lower percentage of sales revenue spent on traditional forms of advertising and sales promotion. This is because of the difficulty in reaching specific target audiences within the business community at a national or local level with mass communication techniques.

There are fewer customers with more specialist and highly individual needs, so personal selling constitutes the most influential, and often the most costly, form of communication of the product benefits. There are two reasons for the high costs of personal selling in industrial marketing. Firstly, where highly technical or scientific products are concerned, the seller must have the appropriate knowledge and qualifications to sell in a professional and credible way, which means a company must pay the going rate in salary and benefits. The second reason for high selling costs is that, if coverage of the market is to be achieved, there must be sufficient salespeople to reach the potential customers on a geographic or industry basis. Where there is not the facility for advertising through trade journals or other media, the sales call will be the only reliable way of providing information and establishing any form of relationship with the right person in the buying organization.

Industrial selling can involve a wide variety of responsibilities which will depend on the nature of the product and the characteristics of the potential customer. The key features, however, are the relatively high value of the contract or sale, the longer time-scale involved and the existence of more than one person in the client organization with an interest in the buying decision. A company buying new, high-speed engineering equipment will need satisfying on a range of technical information, customer endorsements and possibly engineering trials before committing to a new product. A hospital buying a high-cost body scanner will adopt a formal protocol in the way in which suppliers are vetted for technical superiority and reliability, and several expert users and managers will be involved in the final decision.

The selling cycle

A good sales representative will spend as much time as is necessary on non-interview activities, as the planning and organization that goes into the face-to-face contact will be a major factor in determining success. There are distinct and recognizable stages in the development of a relationship with a prospect for the ultimate goal of obtaining a sale or service contract.

Table 13.2 Preparation for selling: key information and sources.

Name of company, address, telephone number
Affiliation in group or legal status
Type of business, range of products/services
Number of employees
Names and titles of key executives
Credit rating (bank references at later stage)
Manufacturing methods
Testing procedures
Quality requirements
Purchasing procedures
Stockholding policies
Level of technical expertise
Investment plans
Product development or diversification plans
Competitive situation within their market

Sources of information
Enquiries to the company; sales literature
Company employees: receptionist, secretary, buyer, sales office
Regional and trade press
Company report and comment in financial press
Trade catalogues and trade associations
Industrial and trade directories
Exhibitions and trade fairs
Government reference services
National and local reference libraries
Town planning registries and departments
Distributors and agents
Suppliers

Preparation

As well as researching prospects and identifying a suitable approach strategy, attention has to be paid to the formalities and mechanics of identifying the right person for the sales interview and the ideal time to conduct it. Selling starts with convincing the person that he or she wants to meet you – what is in it for them? The seller's credibility will be enhanced at the interview by the level of knowledge about the buying company (Table 13.2 gives a checklist).

In many larger companies the market intelligence network created by the system of formal and informal information gathering is the key to formulating strategy for the future. Montgomery and Weinberg (1979) define three types of strategic intelligence systems: defensive (to avoid surprises), passive (for objective evaluation) and offensive (to identify opportunities). It is in the area of offensive information that sales management is in the position of suggesting strategic opportunities that may arise, and encouraging the sales team to react to new customer needs as they become evident.

The presentation

There are three possible approaches to the presentation. The first is totally structured with a 'script' format. The second alternative is totally open, unscripted and left to the personal skills of the salesperson in interpreting the needs of the moment. The third approach takes the middle route between these two. This is the approach of planned selling.

Totally structured presentation

Some companies adhere to a policy of consistent, structured presentations on the part of the salesforce. This might be necessary where the personal skills of those selling would not facilitate a more flexible approach, or where the company has evidence that the structured approach increases the likelihood of an order being placed. There is the requirement for more intensive training of new recruits and periodic retraining and refresher courses when this route is adopted. It has the advantage that the seller is confident of covering all the key aspects of the product without omissions, the seller maintains control throughout and there will be no repetitions unless these are planned as part of a closing summary.

Totally open presentation

In this approach the seller is free to run the interview in a way that best suits the situation and the personal style of the individual buyer. Training for this scenario would focus on the full range of product features and benefits, but would also equip the seller with a range of interpersonal skills enabling the identification of techniques that should be brought into play at the appropriate time. The advantage of this approach is that the seller is free to respond to the needs of the buyer as the interview progresses, and probing tactics will provide the feedback necessary for the seller to adjust the presentation to achieve a satisfactory conclusion.

A customer with a strong personality could manipulate this situation to take control of the meeting and divert the conversation away from the sale. There is also the risk of key benefits or supporting material being missed out of the presentation in a less structured approach.

Planned selling

The preferred route taken by many companies is that of **planned selling**. Here, a structure or outline exists to provide a reference framework of logical steps for making progress towards a sale. It is flexible enough to allow the story to be told in a way that suits the style of the buyer and the circumstances of the meeting or series of meetings. This approach is particularly appropriate where several stages will be necessary in the sales process and where the information imparted and responses to buyer needs will become more customized and detailed as the relationship develops.

There are two conditions necessary for planned selling: the salesforce must be recruited from the available pool of people with the right aptitudes and experience to tailor the presentation to buyer needs. There must also be adequate training in product knowledge, company resources and sales policies, and interpersonal skills. The ability to communicate with buyers with a range of knowledge and backgrounds will require innate skills of perception and response. However, these skills need to be bolstered with training on a regular basis, and included in this training should be seminars at which salespeople exchange experiences and ideas in order to improve the performance of the group.

A planned presentation will make the best use of time, include all the appropriate product benefits and will ensure that all objections or queries are answered. The astute seller will predict and prepare answers for objections prior to the interview. One approach to planning the information which should be used in the presentation is called the **features–advantages–benefits matrix** (FAB) (Balsley and Birsner, 1987). This involves the use of a matrix for each product, for the company represented and for the back-up services provided. It enables the new recruit to develop initial knowledge, and a repeat of the exercise by the more experienced members of the sales team will remind, reassure and provide confident answers to a range of possible objections.

Answering objections

A buyer will ask a range of questions about a product and the company supplying it during the course of a sales interview. Factual and confident answers will enhance the image of the seller and of the product. When these questions have been answered, whether in the same, or in a subsequent meeting, then the seller should be in a position to test whether the buyer is ready to make some form of commitment. It is in this stage of the selling cycle that the seller should probe the nature of any objections to the product, as very often the buyer will not volunteer these spontaneously. However, if there is hesitation or avoidance of a decision, then the seller has to determine the true reason for this. Most objections fall into the categories summarized below:

- Price objections
  - genuine
  - ploy to obtain discount
  - disguise for other category of objection
- Product objections
  - features inadequate for customer needs
  - product too complex for customer needs
  - evidence needed on reliability
  - reassurance needed on service provision

- training provision
- adequacy of warranty
- Company objections
  - new supplier with unknown track-record
  - existing supplier with poor reputation
  - dominant supplier in the market
- Timing objections
  - budget and current resources
  - stage in the planning cycle
  - change in individual responsibility
  - market conditions
- Salesperson objections
  - appearance
  - experience
  - knowledge of customer and market
  - personal style
  - inadequate response to client needs

A **negotiation** stage may be involved between answering objections and **closing** the sale.

Closing a sale

If the selling cycle includes a period of negotiation or if the buyer is in the right frame of mind once all questions and objections have been answered satisfactorily, then there must be a positive move to close the sale. Timing for this is of critical importance, and some experienced sales executives would argue that there is just one 'right time' to close a sale with a particular prospect. With a presentation depending on response to the buyer's needs and behaviour, the seller will fall back on experience and instincts to identify the right moment and the best way in which to close. Where the presentation fits a predetermined format, the seller will be trained to look for buying signals at one or more stages in the presentation and to capitalize on these opportunities.

Closing techniques

There are five classical ways in which a sale may be closed. Some contemporary literature expands these into nine discrete alternatives (West, 1987). The five most important techniques are:

(1) Direct – ask for the order!
(2) Multiple choice
(3) Last chance on special deal
(4) Scare – what loss!
(5) Move to progress the order

Follow-up

When industrial companies institute market research to identify the causes of a drop in sales and the lack of repeat business from past clients, one of the common findings is that customers were dissatisfied with the follow-up after placing the order or taking delivery. A common problem is lack of communication within the supplying company as to which department should take responsibility for client contact after delivery in such areas as simple enquiries, training, faults and malfunction, add-on orders and administration of non-standard contracts and payments.

All of these areas can be classified under the simple heading of **client account management**. In advertising agencies there is an executive assigned to the coordination of all dealings within the agency on behalf of the client company. This executive will have dealings with the creative team, production studio, media research, media buying, market research briefing, billings department and so on. This ensures the smooth running of all dealings with the client who is, after all, paying 17.5% commission on all that the agency does, and expects first-class service. This principle may be extended in some ways to providing customer service in industrial and business-to-business areas.

The larger computer companies operate on the basis of the front-line salesperson providing the pivotal link between them and the customer, drawing on the resources of technical and other specialist staff as well as service departments to fulfil customer needs, including comprehensive follow-up.

Where the product or service is not complex and the relationship is subsequently more at arm's length, then a follow-up telephone call or personal letter from a senior manager within the supplying company can act as recognition of the importance of that customer. This enhances the buyer's perception of company and product. It is a simple act, but the benefits can be great in the form of repeat business.

Role of sales management

Sales management is charged with the task of translating the corporate and marketing objectives of the organization into sales objectives and operational guidelines within which the sales team can achieve the desired result. This logical progression through the marketing strategy level of planning assumes that the organization is marketing-led in meeting the customer needs through product positioning, and that the sales strategy fits coherently with the other parts of the promotion mix.

This approach can be illustrated by reference to one key corporate objective which might be the increased profitability of existing products.

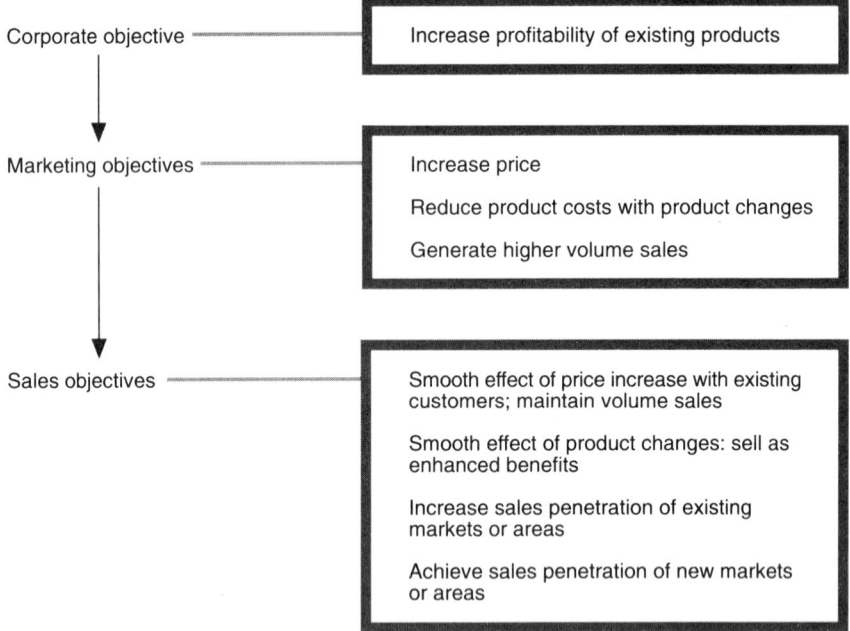

Figure 13.2 Translation of corporate and marketing objectives into sales objectives.

This would be translated into several marketing objectives, as shown in Figure 13.2. There are several ways of using marketing techniques to improve profitability through higher prices, cost-reduced products and higher volumes leading to economies of scale. These activities will have implications for the sales activities as the focus will need to be upon smoothing the effects of price rises and product changes and in developing new business in existing markets or geographical areas, or in new markets or areas.

Sales management has broad responsibility for obtaining sales volume, providing profit contribution and developing new business. The way in which performance is measured is focusing increasingly on profitable sales rather than 'volume sales at any cost', which usually means heavy discounting. In order for sales management to achieve success in these areas, top management has to provide adequate resources and the level of authority to allocate these resources to best effect.

Role of sales manager

The degree of **autonomy** which the sales manager has in controlling the way in which money is allocated to the appointment of sales personnel, their salaries and expenses, and ancillary running costs of the sales

Table 13.3 Areas of responsibility of the sales manager.

Responsibility	Areas involved	Working with
(1) Recruitment	Job description Advertising Screening Interviewing Short-listing Final selection	Personnel
(2) Sales force organization	Reporting structure Territory size Deployment of sales Personnel	Superior (marketing and sales director)
(3) Planning	Forecasting Budgeting Setting targets Planning journey cycles and promotional activity	Marketing and Finance
(4) Training	Field visits Nominate personnel for courses Run training programmes Improve standards	Personnel

(5) Rewards	Advise or decide on:
	    salaries
	    commission
	    bonuses
	    profit-sharing
	    promotion
		Personnel
		and
		Finance

(6) Discipline	Appraisal Develop positive attitude and commitment Monitor standards	Personnel
(7) Motivation	Show leadership Develop two-way communication Resolve conflict Solve problems in field Represent interests of salesforce with management and other departments	
(8) Administration	Monitor sales figures against targets Expenses, commission and bonuses Cars Agendas and schedules for meetings	Finance and Data Processing

operation will be balanced by the level of **accountability** to top management for the achievement of agreed targets. The size and nature of ancillary functions within a company will determine which aspects of sales personnel management are carried out by the sales manager. The traditional areas of responsibility of a sales manager are outlined in Table 13.3, which also indicates areas of overlap with other functional areas.

Relationships of a sales manager

The interpersonal skills of the sales manager are critical to the achievement of two-way communication and teamwork, which will be prerequisites for meeting sales targets. These skills will be used at a variety of levels inside and outside the organization.

The relationship with **superiors** such as the marketing and sales director or other members of the board of directors will influence whether targets are imposed from above or agreed on the basis of proposals from the sales manager adjusted to meet the corporate forward budgets. This relationship will reflect the corporate style of management: 'top-down' or 'bottom-up'. The sales manager's ability to communicate with **equals** such as functional managers in the areas of finance, marketing and logistics will facilitate smooth operations on a day-to-day basis and will mean that planning takes place across the traditional functional divides.

A greater part of the sales manager's time will be spent on communicating with **subordinates**. As well as maintaining a channel of communication for the downward flow of information relating to policies, targets, product changes, marketing activity and so on, this channel must be used for the upward transmission of problems in the field, grievances, feedback on customer response and market intelligence. The regular area sales meeting will be the contact point for management to listen, discuss and decide on the course of action where a problem exists. For example, if sales literature has not arrived on the due date prior to a promotion, the sales manager must act with other departments to rectify the situation. Failure to act will destroy credibility and will demotivate the sales team.

The sales manager's relationship with **competitors** will depend on the nature of the industry and the policy of the organization. At an informal level, it is likely that a regional structure will mean that some contact is inevitable. At the more formal level, the existence of a **trade association** for the industry to protect and further its interests will lead to the exchange of information and ideas. The danger of this leading to possible infringement of the law in such areas as price fixing depends on whether market power is held by the few rather than the many.

The degree of contact of the sales manager with **customers** will be an indication of the level of support that is provided in obtaining and servicing key accounts. It provides reassurance to the customer and valuable feedback to management. A final area of contact for the sales manager is with the **community**. At a regional level, visibility can improve perceptions of the product and the organization. At a national level, ethical and environmental issues will require the company to take a consistent position which is reflected in the actions of functional management.

Relationship between marketing and sales management

There are two alternative ways of managing the important inter-relationship between the marketing and sales functions. Each has its strengths and weaknesses, and an organization will choose the one that best suits the management style of the company and the nature of the market in which it is operating. These alternative models are shown in Figure 13.3.

Model (1) shows the situation in which the marketing director and sales director are of equal status in the organization and both report to the managing director. Whether they have equal levels of authority and responsibility will depend on the nature of their individual areas of control and the number and status of the personnel within them. The career history of the managing director will also play a part in determining the functional emphasis of the decision-making. The advantage of this scenario is that there is a director at the helm of each area who can concentrate time and energy on the functional performance of his or her subordinates. The narrower management responsibility means greater focus and a greater day-to-day knowledge of operations and potential problems.

However, the attendant disadvantage is that the quality of the integration of marketing and sales activities will depend on the level of communication and cooperation between the two functional directors. If

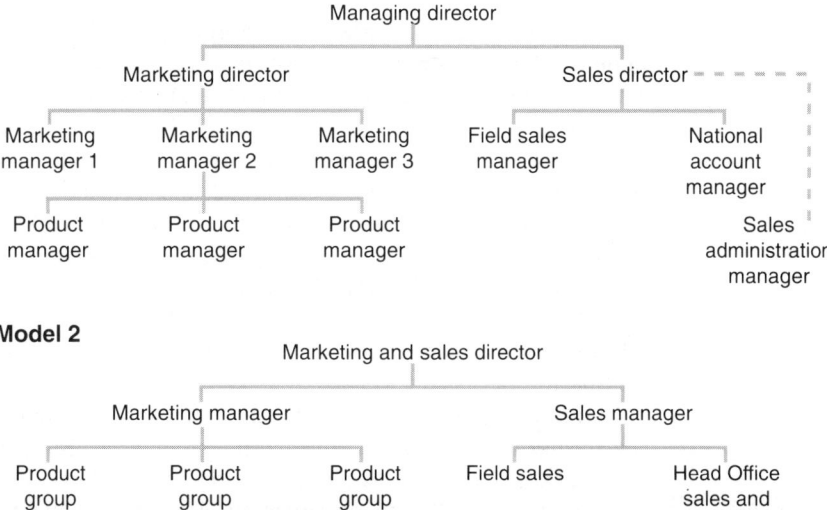

Model 1

Model 2

Figure 13.3 Alternative management models for the interrelationship between sales and marketing.

their personal goals are in line with the corporate objectives then this will be a successful structure. If this is not so, then rivalry and conflict will hinder integration of activities.

The alternative to this approach is Model (2), in which the marketing and sales director has authority over both functional areas, with responsibility for both sales and marketing personnel. This will allow for the optimal integration of marketing and sales plans without the danger of conflicting goals or interests. However, the success of this approach will depend on the competence of the director to motivate and control a greater number of subordinates. The skills and experience of both areas will be needed in this executive, or the management skills must be sufficiently developed to call on the experience and advice of the appropriate manager in order to solve specific problems as they arise.

Given the wide range of responsibilities of the sales manager it is reasonable to split these into two sections for clarity of exposition. Responsibility for recruitment, training and salesforce motivation will depend on the sales manager's ability to focus on the 'people' side of the business, and these functions will be covered in this chapter. In achieving the shorter-term targets, it will also be necessary for the manager to be 'task'-orientated. This will be important in salesforce organization, analysis of individual sales performance, journey planning and sales information systems, which are the subjects of Chapter 14.

Recruitment

A company that has a planned approach to salesforce recruitment will benefit from matching the right people to the vacancies, taking into account consistency in attitudes and performance, for a low turnover of personnel and lower recruitment costs in the medium to longer term. Robertson and Cooper (1983) identify two main elements in the recruitment process which govern the procedures adopted. Firstly, there are individual differences between people and it therefore makes sense to attempt to match people to jobs, and secondly, it is possible to predict future job success from current or past behaviour.

Most larger companies have an established procedure for preparing job description, hiring specifications and recruitment advertising. There will be the necessary period of discussion and agreement between sales management and the functional department responsible for processing recruitment. In some organizations, the term **Human Resource Management** has displaced the traditional title of **Personnel**. Smaller organizations will use recruitment agencies with the resources and experience to screen applicants and supply a short-list of candidates for interviewing by the client.

Table 13.4   The Seven-Point Plan and its application to selling.

		Desirable attribute for selling
(1)	Physical characteristics	Good health, ability to drive, high energy level, clear speech
(2)	Attainments: educational and career experience	Evidence of achievement of specific educational level, success in selling or other parallel career, training
(3)	General ability: cognitive skills and intelligence	Knowledge and understanding of product or market, ability to assimilate new information
(4)	Special aptitudes	Interpersonal and communication skills
(5)	Interests	Intellectual, practical or social implications for job
(6)	Personality	Level of self-motivation, self-perception, reliability, social relationships
(7)	Personal circumstances	Ability to relocate and travel

Interviewing

Probably the best-known of all assessment and interview formats is the Seven-Point Plan originally devised by Alec Rodgers (1974). This provides a framework for matching talent to occupation by obtaining specific information about people and the same information about the job. The plan was adopted for interviewing as it provides a simple and systematic framework for the inexperienced interviewer. The points of the original plan are summarized in Table 13.4 with an indication of the attributes appropriate to jobs involving selling.

Interviews may take the form of one-to-one meetings, panels, group activities or role-playing, psychological testing or product knowledge testing. Whatever the format or number of interviewers involved, it is important that the interview technique will allow different assessors to come to broadly the same conclusion about a particular candidate. This will apply in the initial screening stage for sales jobs, but the heavy dependence on interpersonal skills and personality factors will require the sales manager to assess how well the applicant would fit into the team, work without constant supervision in the field and match the manager's personal style.

If several interviewers are involved then an initial objective rating scheme may be applied to key attributes such as experience, commitment, development potential and self-motivation. These may be scored on a scale of 1 to 5 so that there is the facility for comparison between candidates. Bolt (1987) provides an example of such a rating scheme using the key attributes of ability to communicate, attitudes to change and competitiveness and general appearance.

Assessment by a combination of an objective rating scheme and subjective views on interpersonal skills and quality of self-presentation will enable the team of interviewers to arrive at a short-list of a few candidates, from whom the final selection will be made. At this stage, a more senior executive or sales manager will meet candidates as their assessment of how the individual will respond to a particular style of management will be important in the final selection.

Training

Companies that run their own sales training and executive development programmes, such as IBM, Unilever and Procter & Gamble, enjoy better results, consistently higher standards and lower staff turnover than competitors with a less positive attitude to training. Large organizations have the resources to develop and provide these courses, but at the end of the day they have to be paid for out of sales revenue. The level of this financial commitment will also see dividends in the standard of recruit that the company attracts, for a sound training is very attractive to the new graduate. Where a company invests in training it will also develop career paths to ensure that this investment is not wasted by early departure of the trained executives.

Smaller companies will not have the resources to conduct sophisticated courses themselves but can make use of the variety of training organizations to impart skills in selling, negotiating, time management or problem-solving. The company will need to train in product knowledge and procedures as these areas are highly specific to the organization.

Reasons for training

The rationale behind a company devoting financial resources and management time to training is embodied in one or more of the following tenets:

- inadequate supply of high-calibre sales executives;
- requirement for new recruits to acquire product knowledge and understand administrative procedures;
- improvement of sales performance and customer service levels;
- building of morale and the reduction of levels of salesforce turnover;
- development of more sophisticated selling and negotiating skills;
- keeping pace with technological change;
- response to competition – for example, from Japan;
- devolving of decision-making power down the organization – for example, the ability to grant customer discounts;

- expansion of sales potential through agents and distributors, possibly in other countries;
- improvement of foreign language capabilities.

Whichever of these dimensions is the focus of a particular training course, the net effect will be to improve performance in specific capabilities. For members of the salesforce who are relative newcomers to the company or the profession (or both), the learning curve for the individual will gain a steeper gradient and reach the plateau of optimal performance earlier through the training programme.

For more established members of the sales team, retraining will encourage the adoption of new attitudes and contemporary techniques. In some instances there will be resistance to change, and the perceptive sales manager will enlist the help of more senior members of the team to contribute to training. By this approach the authority and status achieved by taking on the training role will make it easier for senior sales executives to take new ideas on board while conveying them to others.

Motivation

Motivation is the driving force behind an individual's behaviour, and this might reflect several needs to be satisfied at any one time. A sales manager has to harness the energy and driving force of each individual in the team to satisfy management needs and as far as possible to reach acceptable levels of personal satisfaction. It would be impossible to provide a personalized motivation package for each member of the team. Instead, a set of rewards and working conditions has to be designed which provides the optimum level of incentive for the salesforce as a diverse group.

Some of the enabling conditions for a highly motivated salesforce are:

- good lines of two-way communication with sales management;
- clearly stated objectives on what is to be achieved;
- clear understanding of the sales role and responsibilities;
- credibility of sales management often linked to track-record;
- reasonable performance targets;
- fair system of rewards for achievements.

If these broader conditions do not exist, the resulting low level of morale is likely to result in poor sales performance and a high turnover of employees (measured by the percentage of the salesforce leaving in a 12-month period). The ripple effect of low morale through a team can be very harmful for future performance as well as current attitudes, as evident from increased importance attached to current outside interests, high expenses and small grievances taking on undue importance.

Motivation hinges on success in aligning sales goals with personal goals, which requires an understanding of how the individual satisfies personal needs.

Herzberg's hygiene – motivator theory

Herzberg (1959) focused on two distinct areas of personal need in the workplace which align more closely to the balance needing to be struck between security and challenge when a remuneration and reward system is being devised. **Hygiene needs** are satisfied by the conditions of salary, job security, fringe benefits and general working conditions. Relationships within the working environment will also play a part in satisfying these needs. If they are not met, there will be a level of **dissatisfaction** which will result in poor motivation and performance, and eventually the employee will seek a position where these needs are met.

The second area of need is described as **motivator needs** such as the nature of the work, recognition and achievement, and the status in the organization and level of responsibility. The provision of these conditions creates **job satisfaction**. Individuals will differ as to the level of motivator need and the ideal balance of constituent elements. So, for example, some members of a sales team will be content to remain in the same sales position servicing the needs of the same territory for a number of years because the financial rewards suit their personal needs for a secure income, and there is a low driving force for enhanced recognition through superior performance. Conversely, other members of the team will require more stimulus from the work itself and will respond to new challenges if rewarded with recognition.

Expectancy theory

Vroom (1964) put forward the hypothesis that for any group of goals set for an individual there are alternative paths to achieving them. The path chosen will depend on the individual's assessment of the likelihood of that particular pattern of behaviour resulting in the desired results, and on their perception of how well the rewards are balanced against personal effort and results achieved.

To make use of this approach, sales management must have a coherent view of the broad goals of individuals within a salesforce, and must adopt appraisal and counselling techniques to allow the individual to clarify his or her own goals. The next stage is to identify a reward structure which is in line with expectations. If the effort needed for the core compensation elements is within the capabilities for all the team, then there is scope for additional rewards for high-level achievement and for sanctions where effort falls short of what is required.

Table 13.5   Individual elements in the motivation mix.

Non-performance related	Performance related
Straight salary	Commission on sales
Pension contributions	Bonus plan
Health insurance	Share options
Company car	Sales contests
Training available to all	Training available to few
Sales meetings and conventions	Recognition and awards
Sales planning: forecasts on product or territory	Sales quotas
Appraisal system	Commendations as a result of appraisal
Standard form of supervision for all	Level of supervision dependent on performance
Pay increase and promotion dependent on length of service	Pay increase and promotion dependent on performance

The motivation mix

Having reviewed the theories that have influenced the ways in which reward structures have developed, a logical development from these theories is the separation of the different elements of the motivation mix into those that are critical for a minimum performance and those that are designed to take the 'average' performance well above this baseline. The latter group works through the varied response of individuals to incentives. These incentives may be based on material rewards, ego satisfaction or status, or self-fulfilment through job enhancement. A separation of rewards into these two groups is shown in Table 13.5.

This table does not give any clues as to how a company should strike a balance between straightforward compensation for fulfilling the basic requirements of a job, and incentive rewards. Very often, this balance is struck through trial and error, historical practice or the constraints of a company's financial position. This does not always provide an ideal solution, and may result in the extreme positions of either a well-rewarded but low-performance salesforce or a high-performance team with low loyalty and high turnover, motivated entirely by commission.

Requirements of a compensation plan

In deciding on the structure of a compensation plan, a company has to define the performance targets in the medium term and balance against these the financial resources available for rewarding the salesforce. With the benefit of experience in selling to particular markets, an organization will learn about going rates and incentive schemes which attract high achievers. On the company's part there will be the search for the highest achievement against the lowest sales costs. For the individual, there will be the requirements for a just reward for effort and results, and non-financial signs of recognition for the achievement.

As hard results of sales activities will not always be evident in the shorter term, for example when considerable sales support is necessary to maintain customer relations and goodwill or when prospecting for new business, there is a need for a sufficient and attractive fixed element of remuneration. However, where the major part of the individual sales effort will result in orders, revenue or contribution that can be attributed and measured, then the case for an incentive element to total remuneration is a strong one.

Ideally, a compensation plan should provide steady income for a threshold level of financial security and incentive income to encourage work patterns that will generate the desired sales result. This is not always feasible and a company has to make a choice of plan based on market conditions, pay norms and financial resources. Whatever mix is chosen, the elements within the plan should be fair, easily understood and as flexible as possible.

A company has a choice of three options when devising a salesforce remuneration plan:

(1) Straight salary
(2) Straight commission
(3) A combination of the two

If a company chooses the third option there is also the decision to make on the balance between the two elements; should it be 70% salary and 30% commission or is a high incentive element needed to guarantee performance?

One way of assessing the financial risk to the company of this type of remuneration plan is to use a **break-even analysis**. With a particular reward scenario, the volume sales at which all costs will be covered by sales revenue can be compared with the figure for a different scenario.

Analytical sales management

Where the discussion above focused on the responsibilities of sales management that call for good interpersonal skills, this section deals with the more analytical tasks of sales management. Sales planning and forecasting, sales force organization, supervision and control, evaluation of sales performance – all of these responsibilities make heavy analytical demands on a sales manager.

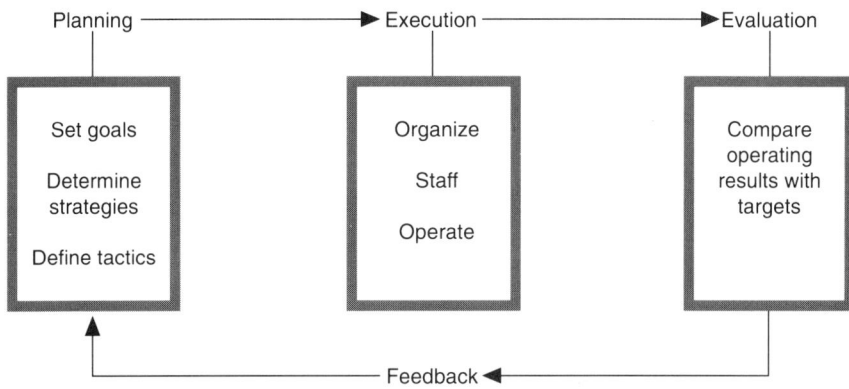

Figure 13.4   Salesforce management model.

These demands are magnified by key trends in contemporary business operations. Firstly, the need to integrate selling activities with production planning and delivery schedules in moves towards just-in-time performance standards imposes logistical constraints on an otherwise independent salesforce. Secondly, the rapid pace of technological change means that product or service improvements are constantly introduced into the sales portfolio. Thirdly, competition is more intense as product differentiation becomes more difficult. Fourthly, the information technology resources of some organizations means that the sales manager may be inundated with sales reports and analyses on a daily basis, at a level that hinders rather than helps in the profitable management of the salesforce.

Sophisticated sales management will turn this last feature to advantage by providing a clear specification of the data required to provide targets at an individual level and to evaluate performance against these targets. Information technology should be used to optimize the allocation of resources in achievement of sales objectives. However, a balance must be struck in management time spent with figures against the time spent with the people who are to achieve these figures.

The sales management process indicated in Figure 13.4 will be aligned with the forward budgeting procedures adopted in a company, whether these are organized on a product, divisional or total company basis. One of the limitations of sales targets or quotas is the reliance placed on sales volume or revenue as a measure of performance in many businesses. There is an increasing awareness of the need to make salespeople more profit-orientated. With the more sophisticated marketing analyses made available by computer and a more educated and trained salesforce, there would be considerable profit advantages to running each sales territory as an independent business unit (Schiff, 1983).

Sales forecasting

It is critical that there is sufficient attention paid to sales forecasts for the following reasons:

- to ensure consistency between marketing targets such as market share and market penetration and the sales forecasts;
- to identify whether resources are adequate for what is to be achieved;
- to confirm that the forecast breaks down into targets which are attainable at the individual level;
- to provide an identifiable link between sales forecasts and the remuneration system, where this is desired as a motivation tool.

The source of the sales forecasts will vary according to the policy, organization and size of the business. A survey of sales management practices by Dubinsky and Barry (1982) has shown that 'significantly more large firms than small firms tend to use extensively forecasts that are set by salespeople. Both groups, however, appear to establish forecasts primarily by using the opinions of top executives'.

It could be argued that where members of the sales team contribute to the setting of their own targets then there is likely to be a greater commitment to their attainment. However, management has to be aware of self-interest based on financial rewards, and balance this against the adjustments necessary at the individual territory level based on local market conditions. Only the individual salesperson will be able to provide the detailed market feedback to make such an adjustment to sales target or quota.

Salesforce organization

Few companies have the resources or expertise to identify the average 'return on investment' per sales call. Most companies, however, will be aware of the high proportion of total company costs which is allocated to the salesforce. This is particularly true of industrial markets, where personal selling is the most important (and often only) communication with the customer. This means that effective management of this resource is critical to corporate profitability and the way in which the salesforce is organized must reflect the needs of the market and the corporate objectives.

Steps in defining structure

Analysis of workload is a key preliminary stage in salesforce deployment analysis. Where there is a ceiling on total selling costs, as for a small but expanding business, then management will assess the salesforce size that is affordable and judge the results that can be achieved based on prior experience. This may give rise to limited geographic coverage, unless alternative solutions can be found such as the use of agents working in tandem with the company's own salesforce.

In the case of a larger and established sales operation, management will need to make deployment decisions based on the business targets that have been agreed. These decisions will include salesforce size, the number and size of sales territories and the allocation of effort to accounts, prospects and products.

The steps involved are identified by the questions that management must address:

(1) What is the distribution policy?
(2) What is the nature of the selling task?
(3) What are the customer needs?
(4) What is the range of products?
(5) What is the number and location of customers and prospects?

By answering these questions and having a clear idea of a realistic individual workload, then management can assign individuals to territories, products or customers, and determine the sales call frequency. From knowledge of, or forecasts for, the conversion ratio of orders to calls and an expectation of average order, the deployment decisions will be directly linked with global sales objectives.

Laforge and Cravens (1982) focus on the **sales potential** of a planning and control unit (PCU) as the major consideration for resource allocation. This PCU might be a territory, product, or set of customers. They acknowledge the range of approaches for making deployment decisions – the **intuitive** approach, based on experience, judgement and rules of thumb; the **systematic** approach, based on potential, workload and return on time invested; and the **decision model** approaches of empirical models or judgement-based models, or a combination of the two.

Factors influencing organization structure

A sales organization should reflect market conditions, but the choice of whether to deviate in approach from the competition or to emulate it depends on the distribution strengths or weaknesses of the company. In view of the rapidly changing market structure in some industries, there needs to be an inbuilt flexibility to the salesforce structure, although this poses some problems where territory limits are firmly defined and remuneration is linked to these. Also, it is not easy to contract or build a salesforce in response to fluctuating market conditions.

The number of vertical reporting layers will depend on the size of the salesforce, the amount of authority delegated down to the individual salesperson and the level of executive control deemed as reasonable within the industry. A span of control of eight to ten people is common, and reflects the traditional role of an area sales manager with specified territory managers under his or her control.

An operational focus on the tasks to be performed in order to achieve results should be balanced by considerations such as the skills, experience, training and personal needs of those who have to execute these tasks.

Geographical structure

This approach is common in consumer goods markets and where a uniform geographical penetration is necessary for industrial marketing.

For consumer products, and particularly those of a repeat-purchase nature, the selling role is supportive of the main customer communication through advertising, and the salesforce acts as a bridge between this advertising and the customer's access to the product on the supermarket shelf. Geographical coverage is therefore vital, as is the recognition of the importance of central buying points for major national chains. This then imposes a service or public relations role on the sales executive operating at the local level. The simple nature of the product means that highly specialist product knowledge is rarely necessary, or when it is, technical specialists from the company can be called upon, as in the case of a local health food chain querying the nature of additives in pre-packaged food before deciding to list the range.

This organization structure minimizes costs and travel time, and is also easier to monitor and control as sales are directly attributable to the territory manager, except where there is an overlap with national account management. Other advantages include the ability of the organization to respond to local needs, and the likelihood of building longer-term links with customers and trade organizations at the local level.

However, this feature of geographical organization can also turn against the company's best interests where a territory manager of long standing begins to put the customers' interests before those of the company employing him. The lack of flexibility of this structure is also a disadvantage. Individuals are loathe to move to new areas of the country where extra resources are required if it will mean considerable upheaval to personal or family life.

Product-based structure

The complex nature of many industrial products or business-to-business services means that the person selling needs sufficient product knowledge and technical expertise to identify customer needs and match the product to those needs. In some instances, this could require the preparation of a detailed technical specification for development or engineering departments. Such expertise will command high salaries, and a company is unlikely to deploy it on a regional basis but rather on a global basis for cost reasons. Such a product-based organization also allows for sales effort to be concentrated on new and potentially lucrative areas of business for prolonged periods.

This approach has disadvantages in that there will be loss of selling or negotiating time in increased travelling and this will increase costs. It is also possible that more than one person will be calling on the same customer with the potential communication problems that this can create in both selling and buying organizations. This makes greater demands on senior managers to know the broader picture and greater demand on the administrative system.

Customer-based structure

Industrial markets are characterized by the complexity of the buying process and by buyer–seller interdependence. The purchase of a new computerized production control system will require technical presentations and consultations with several key people in the buying organization, and the time-scale will be months rather than days. This situation favours a sales organization built around customer or industry type, as the needs and nuances of the industry will become second nature to individuals who specialize in this way. For example, ICL takes an industry approach to selling, and the different sales divisions focus on the different needs of the health service, education, banking and also office services.

In this way, a company can provide a highly specialized service to the customer, in which front-line sales executives will be spearheading a support team for solving the customer's problems rather than simply providing a product. It means that resources can be focused more effectively and it eliminates potential conflict that could arise with a product-based structure.

However, this customer-led approach is costly because of the highly trained and experienced salesforce. It is a feature of high value-added markets where the eventual purchase price is high and merits such focused allocation of resources. Defence and communication contractors such as Marconi would need to operate in this way with the defence procurement departments of individual countries.

National account management

This organizational approach to selling is also called **key account management** or **house account management**. It is a strong feature of sales in the consumer areas of food, clothing, furniture and household appliances in which major retail chains with national coverage will exercise considerable buying power. As a significant percentage of a manufacturer's total revenue and profit could depend on one of these chains, resources must be allocated to make sure that their needs are met and that special contracts are negotiated to the satisfaction of both parties.

Manufacturers accord high-level management responsibility to this function, which will often work in tandem with the field sales manager to make sure that policies and agreements made at head office are reflected in the support operations of the field saleforce. The key account manager will be responsible for drawing on the operational resources of other functional departments such as manufacturing, research and development and distribution to make sure that customer needs are met.

Calculating the size of the salesforce

The pressures of a business to maintain high growth rates in the short to medium term will lead to a periodic reassessment of the number of people selling and whether this is appropriate for the business targets.

In order to calculate the size of a salesforce a sales manager needs to know:

(1)   The total number of active accounts;
(2)   Classification of accounts by order size over 12 months (the number of groupings will depend on the nature of the industry and the sales mix);
(3)   The number of prospects to be called upon over 12 months;
(4)   The forecast conversion ratio of prospects to active accounts;
(5)   Call frequency for different account classifications;
(6)   Number of working days in 12 months;
(7)   Average number of calls per day.

In certain instances, a sales manager might wish to calculate the size of the salesforce needed to maintain and develop existing accounts, and then to consider prospecting as a separate issue requiring additional resources. With a salesforce organized along geographical lines, however, it would be logical to consider the two together. The worked example below considers the simple situation of existing accounts only.

Example

A wholesaler of tools, building accessories and general ironmongery sells to a range of customers including builders, independent ironmongers and do-it-yourself chains. The company has built a good reputation for product quality and service, and a key account manager has recently been promoted from the field salesforce to centralize dealings with the larger multiple accounts. The reorganization that ensued has permitted a reassessment of the number of people needed for coverage of the independent accounts and smaller chains.

A telephone ordering service has been instituted to support smaller accounts where the call frequency might not match their requirement for smaller repeat orders.

Total number of accounts to be
covered by field salesforce: 1730

These accounts are classified by size of order:

Number of 'A' accounts	150
Number of 'B' accounts	380
Number of 'C' accounts	1200

On the basis of past experience and industry norms, the call frequency for different accounts is as follows:

Calls per year:

'A' accounts	12
'B' accounts	6
'C' accounts	4
Number of selling days in the year:	220
Average number of calls per day:	5
Number of calls per year per person:	1100

Total number of calls	
'A' accounts	1800
'B' accounts	2280
'C' accounts	4800
Total calls	8880

$$\text{Number of people in field salesforce} = \frac{\text{total calls}}{\text{calls per year per person}}$$

$$= \frac{8880}{1100}$$

$$= 8.07$$

Based on the premise of call rates and number of accounts remaining as given throughout the year, then eight people would be needed to maintain and develop these accounts.

Supervising the salesforce

The level of supervision and control that is possible with a salesforce depends on the nature of the remuneration structure. Where the major part of the financial reward is in the form of a fixed salary, management is entitled to exert some control over the way in which sales executive time is spent; the degree of professionalism required for the selling role will also dictate the management techniques that are used.

Where all or the greater part of remuneration is in the form of commission on sales, then less control can be exerted on the way in which time is spent. The financial reward for results acts as an automatic supervisory mechanism. However, the company might wish to provide some minimum obligations attached to the rights to sell in a territory, and could build these into a short-term contract renewable at regular intervals.

Reasons for supervision

As well as an aid to improving performance, the formal and informal supervisory techniques that are common for a salesforce enable training and managerial assistance to become an integral part of the field operation. The regular pattern of sales meetings, briefings and individual appraisals sets the formal structure within which the informal communications network should develop. The balance between these two will depend on corporate policy and, in the case of smaller businesses, on the owner's personal style.

The system of management supervision should provide a two-way communication flow which is essential for high morale and to allow company policy to permeate through the sales team. This open channel of communication is particularly important where market intelligence can only reasonably be obtained through the salesforce, as in many industrial markets.

The sales manager's personal style will influence whether the overriding attitude to supervision is one of positive motivation with recognition and reward for good performance, or whether criticism, sanctions and warnings predominate. The manager with a broad range of interpersonal skills will focus on the positive, but use managerial authority where performance standards have fallen to unacceptable levels.

The three key methods of salesforce supervision are:

(1) Personal contact
(2) Telephone contact
(3) Printed communication

Each of these three can be built into a formal communication system, or used informally to deal with specific market, customer or personnel issues as these arise. The pressure on organizations to keep costs to a minimum has encouraged optimal use of time for sales-generating activities, with a resultant reduction in the number of regular meetings.

Performance evaluation can take the form of measurement of salesforce **inputs** or **outputs**, both of which feature in the 'quantitative' column of Table 13.6. Items in the 'qualitative' column are not so easy to classify this way.

Table 13.6 Criteria for evaluating and controlling sales effort.

Quantitative	Qualitative
Sales volume (e.g. units, tonnes)	Product knowledge
Sales revenue	Application of company policy
Number of orders	Ability to close sales
Average order size	Quality of customer relations
Conversion ratio of orders to calls	Time management
Coverage of potential accounts	Initiative in prospecting
Number of new accounts	Positive attitude
Number of lost accounts	Personal presentation
Profit contribution	Territory management
Total expenses	Acceptance of responsibility
Ratio of expenses to sales	Market awareness
Special promotions arranged with customers	
Sales quota plan	

Managing salesforce costs

The major components of selling costs are salary, commission and other performance-related rewards, car purchase (or leasing) and maintenance costs, hotel and subsistence, and other travel costs. Sales management is in a position to control both the absolute level of expenses and the ratio of expenses to sales generated, whether by the individual, or on a territorial, product or account basis.

The primary unit of cost control will depend on the depth and frequency of data available. Comparison of the ratio of selling costs to sales revenue by territory will indicate whether an adjustment is needed to territory boundaries to bring travel costs for larger territories into line with those for smaller geographical territories. Where this is not feasible, then an adjustment to call frequency or selling method for the larger areas might be more appropriate to equalize costs.

Where cost analysis by product line is available, a drive for increased profitability will prompt the sales manager to encourage sales of products with a higher gross margin. This can be done through structuring the quota plan to include a target for one or more higher margin products.

Analysis of costs by accounts

An ideal computerized information system would provide a cost break-down for every account as well as a sales history, and this would show up those accounts that were not cost-effective based on pre-set criteria. If the total sales for a specific account for 12 months are insufficient to cover costs of sales visits, deliveries and after-sale service, management would need to take a view as to whether a **minimum order quantity** (MOQ) should be instituted over a 12 month period, or at the individual order level for the account to qualify for sales visits or free deliveries. An alternative is a telephone ordering system for smaller accounts.

This type of analysis of sales and costs by account tends to reveal a pre-eminence of the 80/20 rule, which shows a pattern of 80% of sales being generated by 20% of accounts. However, the cost pattern of servicing these accounts is rarely in the same proportion, and can be at serious variance from it.

Sales information system

The ability of sales management to respond to fluctuating market conditions and to redeploy resources to optimize results will depend partly on the frequency, accuracy and relevance of sales information. The resources devoted to management information will reflect a company's position to capitalize on opportunities and to respond to market threats at the level of the individual sales territory.

Ideally, there should exist a computer information system which integrates data on orders placed and processed, invoiced sales, returns, payments made and outstanding, and discounts and credits given for each account. There are standard software packages to provide this facility or a company might choose to have a customized software system written to its own specification.

The company wishing to maintain a competitive edge in sales results versus costs will also have available specific analyses that monitor sales calls, average order by account classification and selling expenses versus orders gained for each salesperson. This does not make heavy demands on selling time in the case of a company that has invested in direct-input telecommunication lines from the field to central computer facilities.

Where such computer resources are available within a company, the degree to which they are an asset to sales management decision-making depends on the level of knowledge and confidence of management in making use of such computer technology. Research suggests that in the areas of sales forecasting, sales lead qualification and sales call planning, less than a quarter of industrial marketing managers would have extensive knowledge and more than two thirds would have little or no knowledge (Morris *et al.*, 1989).

Telemarketing: more cost-effective selling?

The escalating costs of face-to-face selling are forcing some organizations to question whether all of the account service activities which have traditionally been carried out by the field salesperson need to be handled on a personal basis. The sales office back-up provided to customers in the areas of account queries, order processing, billing, credits and complaints will depend on a variety of factors including data processing facilities for account management.

However, many companies now take the view that certain 'proactive' marketing roles usually assigned to the sales executive can be accommodated through a central department with clear guidelines as to what is to be achieved and the methods to be used.

Telemarketing has been defined as 'a system staffed by trained specialists who utilize telecommunications and information technologies for the purpose of implementing marketing and sales programs in a cost effective way' (Coppett and Voorhess, 1983).

One of the growth areas of telemarketing is in cold-calling to provide **qualified leads** to the field salesforce. This reduces the cost of providing a sales lead and releases personal selling time for calls that have a greater probability of resulting in an order. The telephone screening process increases the quality of the lead and should enable the salesforce to close on a higher proportion of calls (Lichtenthal *et al.*, 1989).

A particularly popular approach is to distribute a sales catalogue to existing accounts and prospects, and to enable the customer to use this with the back-up of a telemarketing support service. Digital Equipment Corporation started telemarketing in the late 1970s when it was determined that it was not cost-effective for DEC's sales personnel to be order-takers rather than sales engineers. By the mid 1980s the Accessories and Supplies Group had sold approximately 30,000 items in this way (Coppett and Voorhees, 1985).

Major computer suppliers have taken this a stage further by adopting an interactive computer system for their more important customers in the UK. When the customer has a query related to an existing product or service, they can log into the sales support software system. If the query is not answered satisfactorily by working through the menu presented, then the customer may request telephone follow-up.

European perspective

A central policy of the European Community is the free movement of labour, and this is enshrined under Article 48 of the Treaty of Rome. Ten Member States have been following this principle, and Spain and Portugal were due to fall under the same mantle from January 1993. The freedom with which workers can move from one Member State to another will vary according to the demand for specific skills and knowledge, language barriers, and the acceptability of educational, professional and vocational qualifications gained in another Member State.

The EC has been gaining ground in the universal recognition of diplomas and vocational qualifications through specific Directives (such as the Directive on Mutual Recognition of Professional Qualifications (89/48), effective from January 1991). Thirty eight professional institutes in the UK are affected by the Directive, excluding doctors, dentists and architects, who are subject to sectoral Directives. (A full list of affected professions is provided in Owen and Dynes (1989.)

However, clauses allowing for probationary periods of professional practice in the new Member State or additional learning programmes mean that it will be some time before there is exchange of professionals on a significant scale.

In the profession of selling and sales management, a major part of a flow of workers across borders will be through multinational companies initially, as these recognize the value to managers of experiencing new cultures and ways of doing business. At the same time, subsidiaries benefit from prior experience with more developed markets and an international team of managers is created.

Issues relating to this developmental approach to cross-border placements within larger organizations are explored below. The more general framework of the current European scenario relating to conditions of employment, recruitment, training and remuneration are covered in this section.

Terms and conditions of employment

EC legislation has so far had a major impact in only two areas of employment: equal pay and treatment, in particular as between the sexes, and employee rights during company transfer (or takeover). There have been a number of important judgements from the European Court, and the move taken by the UK in 1983 legislating for equal pay for work of equal value (outside the terms of an existing job evaluation scheme) was prompted by the EC legal view. However, there remain difficulties in application of this amendment.

Employee rights and conditions of service are dealt with comprehensively in the 1989 **Social Charter** and the associated Social Action Programme. This was a point of contention at the 1991 Maastricht summit, when the UK stood alone in opposing legislation that would give employees rights to a minimum wage, and improved maternity and other benefits. Many EC Member States already comply with the provisions, and the British fear is of increased costs to employers.

With such an uncertain future on EC policy, the prospective employer or employee must familiarize him or herself with the detailed law and conventions in relation to employment contracts for each Member State. The *European Management Guide on Terms and Conditions of Employment* (Burgess, 1991) provides a detailed summary across ten Member States.

One area in which the EC has left individual Member States to legislate without detailed guidance from the Commission is Sunday opening for retail outlets. In Germany and Denmark there are strict laws on shop opening hours, which tend to follow office hours. In France and Spain there is some flexibility, with climate influencing activity and differences in habits between town and country. In the UK, France and the Netherlands the law distinguishes between different classes of outlet; for example, the corner shop has more freedom than the major supermarket chain, although the latter suffers from being more conspicuous if it should break the law.

This was, indeed, the case in the UK in the period leading up to Christmas 1991, when major retailing chains took the risk of being fined a maximum of £52,000 in order to bolster poor sales during a recession. Some lawyers contended that restrictions on Sunday opening were in contravention of Article 30 of the Treaty of Rome, but this argument has now been rejected by the European Courts. Other pressure groups take the view that liberalising the local law would result in the contractual imposition of Sunday working for employees of major chains. Enforcement of the Sunday Trading law is the responsibility of Local Authorities who feel overworked and unsupported by Government in this complex task (Hawkins, 1989; Hedley, 1989).

Recruitment

In the absence of detailed EC guidelines in the form of proposals or Directives, the laws and codes of conduct of individual Member States reflect a wide spectrum of control on recruitment practices. This ranges from the strict regulatory framework in Germany, across the bureaucratic procedures of Italy and Spain, to the relative freedoms of France, the UK and the Netherlands. A broad outline of the degree of legal control and state of development of recruitment consultancies in six Member States is provided below. A comprehensive analysis of legal controls and the state of development of recruitment and interviewing practice for ten Member States is available in the *European Management Guide on Recruitment* (Burgess, 1990).

Belgium

The recruitment and selection of workers is covered by the National Collective Agreement (No. 38) of 1983. This is morally binding, but certain clauses are also legally binding as of 1984. The key areas included in relation to recruitment are equal treatment, respect for privacy and confidentiality.

France

Recruitment in some industries is affected by collective agreements. These include distribution and retailing, chemicals, metalworking, and hotels and catering. The right to privacy in the recruitment process is covered through Article L123-1 of the Labour Code. However, legal controls on recruitment are less of a problem than the general lack of language skills and a low level of employee mobility. Speculative letters from potential candidates constitute the largest single method through which graduates and young employees are recruited, although there is a growing profession of recruitment consultancy for more senior appointments. The central organization for these consultancies (APROCERD) has issued a code of conduct. French companies place heavy reliance on analysis of handwriting (graphology) in the recruitment process.

Germany

There is a statutory obligation for companies to consult works councils and seek their agreement in a number of areas related to personnel planning, internal advertising of vacancies, employee selection and application documents. The state placement system dominates recruitment and it has a special section dealing with managers. Private consultancy in executive recruitment is permitted, but there are strict guidelines – for example, in the areas of the use of application documents and the building of databases on applicants. Newspaper advertising is the commonest form of recruitment for managers and specialists, although German companies have a tradition of first looking for suitable candidates from within the organization. Trade fairs are also used by companies as a way of meeting potential new recruits.

Italy

Recruitment in Italy is slow and potentially expensive because of the requirements of the bureaucratic process. There is heavy reliance on personal contacts. The official system is specified as a route to recruitment, but direct recruitment by an employer through personal contact, unsolicited application or advertising is permitted for managers, workers in companies employing no more than three people and some other categories. The use of recruitment consultants is widespread and growing, and there is a Code of Professional Ethics published by the professional association (ACORD).

Netherlands

There is no specific legal framework regulating the recruitment and selection process. Draft legislation was prepared in 1982 but this did not become law. The Dutch Institute of Personnel Management (NVP) has a code of practice which gives the most detailed guidance for prospective employers and employees. Recruitment consultancies have become more important, and the professional body (OAWS) has a code of practice.

Spain

Article 64 of the Worker's Statute (law 8/1980) covers areas of employee participation, and under this the works committee has the right to receive reports on recruitment plans and to express views on major changes in the workforce. The practice of 'official notification' of vacancies has become a formality, although any advertisement for an appointment has to carry the state recruitment agency job number. Such direct advertising is the commonest method of recruitment for specialist and managerial staff. The executive search market is growing, and is unregulated if judged by the standards set by Germany.

Training

Differences in

- the level of qualifications attained on average across the population of Member States,
- the amount and quality of training provided to employees,

- the relative competence of managers as measured by national economic performance

reflect differences in attitudes and cultures in relation to the contribution by effective employees in industry to national economic wellbeing. In Chapter 7, the concept of **added value** was explored. The skills and knowledge of the workforce are an important component in deriving this added value, which is a necessary precursor of corporate profits. There are two complementary routes to building an effective workforce:

- recruitment of individuals whose formal education at secondary school and higher education levels creates a firm foundation in the form of technical knowledge and analytical skills;
- a planned route of vocational, technical or managerial training through the career to build on this foundation, developing the individual's potential and enhancing performance.

Differences in educational attainment of managers in different Member States are apparent. In France 49% of managers have a minimum of two years' higher education, and the greater part of this group has studied for four or five years following the Baccalauréat. A 1984 survey showed that 62% of German managers held a diploma denoting successful completion of a higher education course in a polytechnic or university. In the 100 largest companies, 54% of management board members have doctorates (Handy *et al.*, 1988). In contrast to this, a 1985 Labour Force Survey showed that only 12% of British managers had degrees, although a more selective sample of corporate managers in the 1987 CBI survey raised this figure to 40%.

These figures denote differing levels of educational attainment which will influence not just aptitude for managerial tasks, but also attitudes towards skill and knowledge improvement during the course of their own, and their subordinates', careers. Once again, this is reflected in training activities.

In France, there is a history of state commitment to training for administrators through the Grandes Écoles, and this is combined with an intellectual tradition, promoting a systematic and analytical approach to problem-solving. Companies of more than 50 employees draw up a training plan which is discussed with the Works Committee. Individuals have the right to training leave, and large corporations spend 3.36% of their wage bill on training, where the law requires only 1.2%.

In Germany, it is compulsory for companies to belong to a Chamber of Industry and Commerce. Through the membership fee, each company has access to courses and management development programmes offered by these organizations. The needs of medium and small companies are met through these, and through the Bildungswerke in individual federal states. The courses run for single companies can focus on presentation skills or selling techniques, and these are popular as the benefits are seen to be almost immediate.

Handy *et al.* (1988) identify three routes to management training in the UK: corporate, academic or professional. Many of the large multinationals based in the UK attract high-quality recruits because of the structured provision of training. Smaller companies benefit on a cascade basis when these highly trained employees are recruited by them at senior level. A structured approach to accumulating credits for prior training and experience is now evolving, so that those managers who missed out on formal qualifications when they were young can gain them later in their careers.

By far the most popular entry point to a career in business management in the UK is through the accountancy profession. There are 120,000 practising accountants, although many of these will not be involved in the traditional role of auditor. Instead they will be using the formal financial skills gained early in their careers in a general business or managerial role.

These differing routes to management training and development reflect culture and economic performance. The British emphasis on financial training and career progression has led to a short-term focus with corporate results geared to the needs of the City rather than the longer-term market development needs of the business (Hutton, 1991). Whereas in Germany there is acknowledgement of 'Technik' as an accomplishment in the art or science of making things, and persons qualified in such engineering areas are viewed as capable senior managers, this culture does not prevail in the UK where the accountant is 'king'. In Germany, over 30% of gross domestic product is furnished by manufacturing industry whereas this has given way to service industries in the UK, which are generally less exportable.

Skills and training in retailing

A significant proportion of a country's selling skills is to be found in the retailing workforce, which has traditionally been viewed in a different way from industrial sales management. There are 7.7 million people employed in retailing in the European Community and 4.4 million employed in wholesaling (Eurostat, 1991). These combined figures account for 11% of employment in the EC, and over one third of these employees are part-time (and predominantly women). France, Germany and the UK account for almost 68% of total Community retail employment.

According to the findings of the EC Labour Market Survey of 1990, across the eight countries surveyed, three quarters of the retail workforce was skilled. The largest proportion of unskilled workers were to be found in the Netherlands and the UK (where there are more part-timers) and in Spain. The highest share of skilled workers was in Germany and Italy.

The introduction of common European standards for retail competence and qualifications would have the effect of raising standards in countries not yet committed to investment in training in this important sector of the economy.

There is a central European initiative for the recognition of training and experience in the form of the European Centre for the Development of Vocational Training (CEDEFOP). This focuses on managers and the self-employed in the wholesale and retail trades and other service industries (Roney, 1990).

Remuneration

The national influences on levels and forms of pay in some selling and sales management functions are as follows:

(1)   National or regional collective agreements;
(2)   Statutory cost of living adjustments;
(3)   Cultural norms regarding merit rises;
(4)   Compulsory job grading with linked bands for remuneration;
(5)   The legality and acceptability of 'incentive' pay;
(6)   The incidence of share purchase schemes for employees;
(7)   The norms regarding fringe benefits such as pension contributions, health insurance and company cars.

In addition to these legal and cultural influences, companies operating across borders will endeavour to harmonize pay structures and job grading, where transfer of managers between head office and subsidiaries is commonplace. Any convergence of management grading and remuneration is likely to be a slow process. For example, Air Products took ten years and ICL planned a three-year process of convergence (IPM, 1988).

In Spain, it is compulsory to indicate a job grade for a new recruit, including duties, salary level and fringe benefits. Article 39 of the Workers' Statute defines a job grade as a band which represents groups of employees of similar ability, qualifications and responsibilities. This would be difficult to implement where management functions are highly specific and non-comparable. However, it excludes the possibility of 'incentive' pay, and this would be a disadvantage for companies in which performance-related pay is the norm for the home market salesforce.

Two further blocks to performance-related pay are compulsory disclosure of management remuneration to unions (as in Spain), and the need to divulge company results in order to implement it. Companies in Italy would be reluctant to do this.

Constraints such as these mean that companies must work in a pragmatic way towards harmonized pay structures, but take into account local employment law and common practice. Further influences on relative levels of remuneration for selling functions will be the cultural and economic significance attached to the role, and the qualifications and experience of those employed. For example, the German 'technical' sales engineer with a doctorate will be accorded appropriate status within the organization, and remuneration will reflect this higher perception of the role than might be the case in a company in the UK.

Problems and assignments

(1)   What distinctions would you make between the respective tasks of selling in the consumer and the industrial fields? Which tasks do you imagine may provide more scope for career development?

(2)   As a salesman selling industrial machinery, identify the information you would elicit from a prospect before you started to 'sell' your own product.

(3)   A prospect is concerned about buying from you. He has not previously dealt with you or your company, he is unsure that the service support matches his current supplier and your product is premium priced, leading to price objections. How would you deal with these objections?

(4)   To what extent would you accept the premise that the marketing and sales directors should be one and the same person in a medium sized company selling industrial goods?

(5)   'Good salesmen are born not trained.'
       'The best training is to get out on the road.'
How relevant are such attitudes for selling in the environment of the 1990s?

(6)   You have just won national distribution rights to sell a brand of lorry. Given the agreed national coverage, on what basis would you go about organizing your salesforce?

(7)   As managing director of a small domestic tool manufacturer, you previously organized your salesforce on a geographic basis. With the rationalization/concentration of fewer, larger retailers selling far more of your product, while small builder's merchants and DIY high street outlets have lost share, how would you reorganize your salesforce?

(8)   As your company expands you have anticipated market opportunities in Italy. Identify the constituent factors in your decision

on whether to employ an Italian who requires product/company training or an Englishman or woman who may require the same plus understanding of the local business culture as well as language training.

References

Adams A. (1987). *The Secrets of Successful Sales Management.* London: Heinemann, p 100–104

Balsley R.D. and Birsner E.P. (1987). *Selling: Marketing Personified.* Dryden Press, Chapter 9

Cooper G.L. and Makin P. (1984). *Psychology for Managers.* Basingstoke: Macmillan

Coppett J.I. and Voorhees R.D. (1983). Telemarketing: a new weapon in the arsenal. *J. of Business Strategy,* Spring, 80–83

Coppett J.I. and Voorhees R.D. (1985). Telemarketing: supplement to field sales. *Industrial Marketing Management,* **14**, 213–216

Dubinsky A.J. and Barry T.E. (1982). A survey of sales management practices. *Industrial Marketing Management,* **11**, 133–141

Herzberg F., Mausner B. and Snyderman B.B. (1959). *The Motivation to Work,* 2nd edn. New York: John Wiley & Sons

LaForge R. and Cravens D.W. (1982). Steps in selling effort deployment. *Industrial Marketing Management,* 11, 183–193

Lichtenthal J.D., Sikra S. and Folk K. (1989). Teleprospecting: an approach for qualifying accounts. *Industrial Marketing Management,* **18**(1), 11–17

Montgomery D.B. and Weinberg C.B. (1979). Towards strategic intelligence systems. *J. of Marketing,* **43**(Fall), 41–52

Morris M.H., Burns A.C. and Avila R.A. (1989). Computer awareness and usage by industrial marketers. *Industrial Marketing Management,* **18**(3), 223–231

Robertson and Cooper (1983). *Human Behaviour in Organisations.*

Rodgers A. (1974). *Seven Point Plan.* London: NFER

Schiff J.S. (1983). Evaluate the salesforce as a business. *Industrial Marketing Management,* **12**, 131–137

Vroom V.H. (1964). *Work and Motivation.* New York: John Wiley & Sons

West A. (1987). *Modern Sales Management.* London: Macmillan Education

European perspective

Burgess P. (ed.) (1990). *European Management Guides: Recruitment.* Incomes Data Services and Institute of Personnel Management

Burgess P. (ed.) (1991). *European Management Guides: Terms and Conditions of Employment.* Income Data Services and Institute of Personnel Management

Handy C., Gordon C., Goward I. and Randlesom C. (1988). *Making Managers.* London: Pitman

Hawkins E. (1989). Open defiance. *Local Government Chronicle* (No. 6346), 24 February, p 20

Hedley R. (1989). Trouble in store. *Local Government Chronicle* (No. 6346), 24 February, pp 18–19

Hutton W. (1991). Why Britain can't afford the City. *Management Today,* September

IPM (1988). *1992: Personnel Management and the Single European Market.* Incomes Data Services and the Institute of Personnel Management, October

Owen R. and Dynes M. (1989). *The Times Guide to 1992: Britain in a Europe without Frontiers – A Comprehensive Handbook.* London: Times Books, Chapter 7, pp 87–96

Roney A. (1990). *The European Community Fact Book.* Chamber of Commerce, London/Kogan Page, p 118

PART 3

Market planning and responding to change

14 The complete marketing plan and budget

Chapter objectives:

- to differentiate business and marketing plans
- to understand the full extent and composition of a marketing plan
- to look at the role of econometrics and market modelling in marketing planning
- to understand the interface between accounting and marketing planning
- to consider the implications of a single European currency

Introduction

The wide range of market opportunities facing a company in order to survive and grow in a competitive climate requires a forward-thinking management to take a realistic view about what can be achieved in the near future, what resources are needed and how the activity will be coordinated. However, the concept of **marketing planning** restricted to its association with the implementation of promotion decisions, and monitoring performance against sales targets, presents a narrow and dated view of its role in business management.

An organization that is driven by the needs of the marketplace will develop a plan that answers the questions:

- Where are we trying to get to?
- When will we arrive?
- What resources will we need to get there?
- How will we know that we have arrived?

These questions encompass the need for objectives to be achieved over a specific time-scale, with controlled use of financial and human resources, and with monitoring devices in place to measure performance against targets. The objectives may be expressed in terms of financial performance indicators, but their achievement will only be possible by fulfilling customer needs against a coherent operating plan which acknowledges the involvement of all functional departments. When the corporate objectives are translated into a marketing plan, this can act as a blueprint from which other functional departments can develop their own detailed plans for resource allocation and operating targets.

Planning is essentially the process of making strategy work through the coordination of departmental activity so that marketing, finance, production and human resource functions are moving in concert towards common goals. The nature of the product or service and **corporate culture** will determine the balance of decision-making power between these functional areas. However, the role of the marketing plan and supporting sales forecast is recognized by customer-led organizations as vital to the production of forecasts and action plans for other areas of the business, as illustrated for a manufacturing company in Figure 14.1. At every phase of its operations, an organization must strive to bring itself into a mutually satisfactory relationship with the customer *and* ensure an adequate return on investment.

The detailed marketing plan is the mechanism for ensuring that there is a balance between customer needs and organizational objectives and can highlight the areas of potential conflict well in advance. This chapter looks at the reasons for marketing planning, followed by the detailed contents of the plan, and exploration of current management attitudes and practices in relation to such planning. For some organizations, the marketing strategy and plan are the driving force for change and the effects on the organization are examined in this context.

The link between the marketing plan and the profit and loss forecast or budget is examined through the use of practical examples. The increasing importance of the effects of marketing decisions on logistics planning is highlighted, with an examination of the control mechanisms needed for effective contingency planning, particularly when there are marked changes in the economic or market environment. The need for testing the financial implications of alternative marketing plans leads into an investigation of the use of computer modelling as an aid to the marketing planner, and the wider role of information technology in effective management decision-making.

Because such sophisticated techniques are within the reach of only those companies with a large sales and capital base, there is also a section on marketing planning for the **small business**. Here, the principles and budgeting process are applied to show how profitability levels of different marketing scenarios can be assessed before critical troughs in cash flow occur. Spreadsheet analysis is a cost-effective tool for the small business where a team of econometricians and statisticians might be employed by the multinational concern.

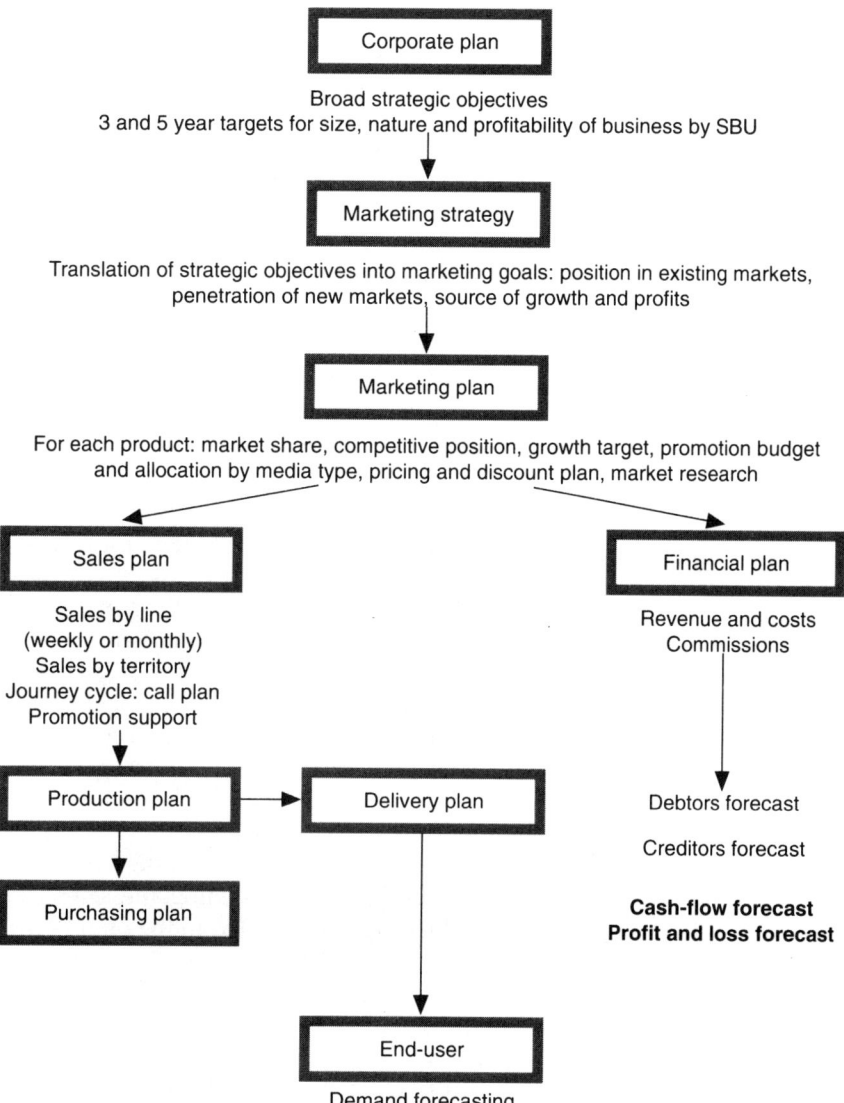

Figure 14.1 The role of the marketing plan in relation to operating plans for other functional departments.

Reasons for marketing planning

There are three discrete areas of business activity which are linked by the market planning process.

Strategic marketing provides the longer-term objectives and goals that give rise to a logical framework within which the different parts of the business can operate and by which their success can be judged. The time-frame for this might be three, five or even ten years, although the financial targets used to define these objectives will more frequently be restricted to one to three years into the future.

Operational marketing represents the day-to-day execution of the marketing plan in areas as diverse as media commitments, new product development, pricing and discounts and the setting of salesforce quotas. It is in this area that at least 80% of executive time is spent.

The **quantitative techniques** used as aids to marketing decisions involve a variety of measures to assess whether targets and budgets have been met. Depending on the degree of variance between actual results and targets, there will be feedback into the operational planning process or, at the extreme, into strategic decisions.

With this three-tier structure in mind, marketing planning is essential for the following reasons:

(1) To ensure that corporate objectives are met; these might be defined as return on investment, percentage net profit, price to earnings ratio, the divestment of certain peripheral activities or entry to new markets either through acquisition or organic growth.

(2) To translate corporate goals into marketing objectives which are reasonable and measurable. Examples of such measures would be market share targets, penetration levels of existing or new markets, awareness and attitude measures following product launch or revised advertising campaigns, percentage growth in sales and level of gross margin by product (to be defined and discussed in the section on the forward budget).

(3) To ensure the efficient deployment of the key marketing resources – the promotion budget and marketing and sales personnel – in order to meet the objectives highlighted in the plan.

(4) To facilitate coordination of the activities of the functional departments reporting to marketing management – market research, advertising, product development, field salesforce and sales administration.

(5) To encourage cooperation between departments with other functional responsibilities and marketing management, where the activities of these departments – such as buying, production, distribution, finance and personnel – are critical to the successful implementation of the marketing plan.

(6) To institute control and measurement devices on a regular basis to assess the degree to which marketing targets are being met.

(7) To allow for alterations to planned activities where there is under-performance against targets.

(8) To facilitate feedback to senior management where indicators suggest a change of strategy in response to competitor activity or a market downturn.

(9) To support forward budget proposals for individual products or strategic business units (SBUs) where there is a bidding process across all product groups for marketing support funds.

(10) To ensure that elements within the promotion mix are compatible and mutually supportive over a given time-frame (generally 12 months, with detailed activity planned on a monthly basis).

These ten reasons for marketing planning converge in the need for a disciplined approach to thinking through the allocation of marketing resources and amending action plans if targets are not being realized. This discipline and the associated planning conventions should be mirrored in the working patterns of other functional departments, if the needs of the marketplace are to be exploited successfully.

Marketing planning as a tool of strategic change

The introduction to this chapter assumed the establishment of corporate objectives which are translated into marketing objectives for the preparation of the marketing plan. This is the ideal, logical scenario which pertains to an organization whose culture facilitates and encourages this process.

The traditional power structure in a corporation might resist the formation of the organizational framework which is a precondition for such formal market planning. Industries which have been protected from the full effects of open competition are particularly prone to this phenomenon (such as state run industries with near monopoly powers). When this protection is removed, there has to be radical thinking about the way in which the organization can respond to market forces and meet the new objectives, which may include satisfying the shareholders.

Piercy (1990) puts forward three propositions in relation to marketing-led **strategic change**: firstly, that the corporate environment underpins not only the implementation of marketing, but also the perceptions of strategic choice; secondly, that the culture represents the 'institutionalized power' of the dominant interests in an organization; and thirdly that culture can be 'operationalized' through strategy and marketing implementation.

An example of how this can work in practice is the transformation of the culture of British Airways by a deliberate policy after privatization. A major programme of training seminars was instituted at every operational level within the organization so that every employee became aware of the importance of the quality of customer service. Thus the implementation of a key marketing objective became the pivotal force for culture change.

Contents of the marketing plan

Although each organization will have its own conventions regarding the format of management information and associated vocabulary, there are common elements across all marketing plans, and the core content is illustrated in Table 14.1. The key headings reflect information that is necessary for operational marketing. The additional bonus of this format for the marketing plan is that it guarantees a disciplined and rigorous approach to the preparation of the plan. What this means in practice is that considerable time is spent in collating information which reflects the *status quo* and supports decisions on the future allocation of funds.

Table 14.1 Contents of the marketing plan.

Management summary	Key points on state of the market, current position and prospects for the product, future marketing goals, human and financial resource implications of the operating plan.
The *status quo*	Position of the product in the market, market share, sales by line/variant, significant changes in patterns of demand, competitive analysis, the macro-environment, cost issues and profits.
Future for the market	Likely changes in the economic, social and technological climate affecting the market; probable competitive strategies, likely trends in product and marketing costs.
Market research	Identification of information needed to maintain and strengthen product position, and to enter new markets, with an outline of methods to be used.
Marketing objectives	Broad objectives: 3 or 5 years Detailed objectives: 1 year Sales growth, market share, introduction of new variants, relaunch of product with modifications, new promotion campaign, increased levels of awareness and attitude changes, heightened levels of sales enquiries, gross margin, net profit, control of expenses.
Product strategy	Statement of competitive position in the market with target market and key benefits; how this follows through into an outline promotion plan.
Promotion plan	Twelve-month plan showing timing and costs of TV spots, magazine and other press space, sales promotions, mailings, trade discounts and salesforce incentives. Operational details are given in sufficient detail to permit implementation.
Sales plan	Phasing of sales volume and revenue by line by month: how this translates into salesforce activity including the journey cycle, average daily call rate, average order size and mix, penetration of new territories or markets, changes in handling of major accounts. Implications for sales administration and customer service.
Detailed budget	Three-year 'P & L' – the revenue and profit statement which takes account of product costs, promotion expenses and overhead allocations. This may be accompanied by a month-by-month revenue and profit forecast for the immediate 12 months, to feed into the cash flow forecast.
Performance controls	Key criteria for monthly management meetings to assess how performance varies against the plan, so that each department affected can take compensating action.

In large corporations, there is a planning or budgeting 'season' at least six months from the start of the new financial and operational year. Where the traditional product management reporting structure exists, individual product or **brand plans** will flow up the organization for approval. These documents invariably support requests for research and development funds or money for advertising in competition with other brands in the portfolio. The senior management task is to allocate the resources in a way which will best meet the growth and profit targets of the organization. When the approval process is complete, plans are adopted for implementation (with or without amendments for optimistic market forecasts or ambitious promotion budgets). Where the brand manager is the champion of the brand and must use energy to gain commitment to it within the organization, senior management must take a realistic view of the current market and what is achievable given the internal competition for resources.

One of the most neglected areas of the marketing plan is the specification of **market research** required over the medium term to fill gaps in information and to identify opportunities for the future. Identification of the market research needed will be aided by a clear perspective on the future for the market combined with an analysis of the company's strengths and weaknesses in relation to the trends.

The way in which **marketing objectives** are defined will depend on the nature of the product and market and the level of accountability of marketing management for profit as well as revenue. The availability of syndicated market research and retail audit data for consumer products on a regular basis means that measures of brand performance such as market share, distribution, out-of-stock position, pricing and comparable measures for the competition can be tracked, and used as objectives in their own right, and also as **performance control** mechanisms.

In industrial markets where there may only be two or three key players due to the levels of investment needed in new technology, such performance tracking devices are neither available nor strictly suitable. Success of future marketing activity will depend heavily on refinements in product specifications to meet individual customer needs, and on negotiating skills in determining the terms of major contracts, rather than expert deployment of advertising resources. The contents of the marketing plan will reflect this bias and may also be confidential to senior management, with only limited information reaching functional departments.

Where divisional management is responsible for effective marketing as a route to achieving sales and profit objectives, the marketing plan will reflect the responsibility for achieving revenue against a specific marketing budget, and controlling product costs. An alternative scenario is that in which the marketing plan reflects more limited responsibility for production of advertising, media planning, implementing sales promotions and preparing sales support literature. This reflects the situation where line responsibility for performance is vested elsewhere in the organization and a department known as **marketing services** has a brief to propose and implement a plan to support targets within a budget. This situation of split responsibility means that agreement on the outline budget and constant communication between line managers and marketing executives are necessary for harmony and success.

Marketing planning: managerial attitudes and practices

The literature on planning in the business environment focuses on strategic planning, and only seven major research programmes have been identified as investigating the marketing planning that companies actually perform (Greenley, 1988). This literature search was the prelude to detailed research on attitudes and behaviour of managers with a particular focus on commitment to marketing planning. Responses in terms of improvements in the organization as a result of this commitment were split according to whether these were seen as **process** or **performance** improvements. Commonly cited process improvements were in the areas of information and communication, resource allocation, and control and coordination. Improvements in performance (profits and ROI, sales growth and market share) were cited less frequently.

The research indicated that the most commonly cited weaknesses of marketing planning were that programmes in the plan might not be followed, objectives might be ignored and that the plan was seldom used as a tool of control and cooperation. Greenley puts forward the hypothesis that there is a tendency for managers to be more committed to preparing a marketing plan than to its implementation. There is a case for arguing that senior management requires visible evidence of a planning process in the form of an official document and budget, but that the mechanisms for enforcing the plan through the hierarchy are less well defined.

A study of selected consumer, industrial and service companies operating in 20 countries throughout the world (Griffin, 1989) found that the format and vocabulary of the marketing plan was more likely to be similar to the accepted model in consumer and service companies than in industrial companies, and in larger companies (500 plus employees). The study found that consumer plans were more detailed and were more focused towards the promotion mix and subjective issues than their industrial counterparts.

The degree to which marketing planning plays a role in the strategic and operational success of an organization depends on three major issues:

(1) The commitment of management, and particularly senior management, to the process. This means a culture that provides moral support and practical accommodation to those who have to produce and implement the plans.

(2) An organizational infrastructure that facilitates communication and cooperation between functional departments whose brief it is to meet the objectives defined in the marketing plan.

(3) Regular and institutionalized use of checks and controls on performance (which may or may not be defined within the marketing plan), and a mechanism for feedback on performance measures into the decision-making process.

The greater convergence between the accepted norm of marketing planning and consumer goods manufacture and marketing suggests that the greater availability of regular and detailed information on product and market performance provides a ready-made structure for defining targets and measuring performance. Industrial and service companies have to fill in many gaps in the information jigsaw, and thereby propose a planning format which is founded on hypothesis and assumptions along with hard data. Gaining management and operational commitment to this plan is therefore likely to be a more difficult task.

Link between the marketing plan and the budget

The 12-month sales and profit budget can be related to the marketing plan in one of two ways:

(1) It is a product of the short-term financial plan derived from the business plan, and shows the performance targets and expenditure constraints within which marketing must operate and be judged. This requires collaboration between financial and marketing management to ensure that the marketing budget is adequate for achieving the sales objectives, before it is submitted to, and approved by, senior management.

(2) It is a short-term **financial projection** (using the **reporting conventions** of the organization) which supports the marketing plan in a bid to gain funds for the development of a product or business portfolio.

Three-year forecasts or budgets will have a greater degree of uncertainty attached to assumptions on the macro-environment, the market and product performance. However, some organizations see this as a necessary discipline to get the best available judgement on future performance potential in different areas of the business, so that outline plans may be formulated for resourcing and, if necessary, new sources of funds.

Bidding for marketing funds in the planning and budgeting 'round' is frequently competitive between brands or product groups. However, a market-led organization will not need to be convinced of the value of advertising support in building brands over time. Senior management will need to be convinced of the value that is achieved for every pound spent: this will be proven by way of product awareness and usage statistics as well as sales figures for consumer products, and by the number of new customers. The order to call ratio and average order size would be measures of performance for industries where the personal selling role is dominant.

However, some executives are in the position of having to submit marketing plans and forward budgets to company management who are not committed to marketing as an investment in the future, but see it rather as a short-term expense to be minimized, along with training and research and development. In this situation, the cost-effectiveness of different promotional activities included in the plan needs to be examined, and the lessons of past tests and promotions will be harnessed as supporting arguments.

An area of funding which gives rise to considerable debate is that of major advertising support for a brand. As the budgets for television support in particular can run into several million pounds, evidence on volume and value sales and market share compared with advertising expenditure over past years is the minimum requirement for a credible bid. The more sophisticated multinationals employ specialists to monitor audience quantity and quality against specific levels of expenditure in a range of media. This type of analysis is particularly relevant in times of high inflation of media costs.

Conversely, industrial goods require the commitment of a skilled and experienced salesforce to increase awareness and build on the existing customer base. Gaining additional resources in this area requires detailed information on past performance ratios and justification on the grounds of additional contribution to growth and profits. A call for increased resources just to maintain existing levels of business will rarely succeed without the promise of improved performance on other criteria. This is particularly difficult to achieve in recession or where there is market rationalization .

Lloyd (1989) suggests a range of techniques for achieving the maximum value for a limited budget. This includes the minimizing of overheads, using services not charged directly to the budget, charging other departments for services and negotiating with suppliers. Whatever the techniques employed to optimize the value of marketing resources, there must be measurement and control of expenditure in each area of promotional activity, with evidence of effectiveness in the form of cost per new customer, cost per thousand audience reached, cost per order and similar marketing ratios. These will provide a basis for performance reviews which act as a prelude to the annual budgeting round.

Forecasting

The planning process is dependent on management's best estimate of future demand for product or services. Best-guessing based on past performance and intuition is hardly adequate to make optimum use of resources, particularly where there are several hundred product lines and complex sourcing procedures. Military procurement is a case in point, and was undoubtedly the driving force for government agencies, along with academia, to be the predominant practitioners in forecasting during the 1950s. The advent of sophisticated computer technology and the competitive drive for efficiency led to the more widespread adoption of business forecasting methods by the 1980s.

Few businesses can operate in an environment devoid of **uncertainty**. Assumptions have to be made relating to future economic and market trends, so that a **forecast** can be made of the most likely scenario for demand for a company's products. Forecasting provides a way of reducing uncertainty, so that planned activity has a greater chance of coinciding with real need.

In the logistics planning cycle, **sales forecasts** are the starting point for the planning chain incorporating purchasing, production, warehousing and distribution. All operation departments can work to the same quantitative framework, although a degree of uncertainty requires flexibility in response to changing forecasts. The extreme form of this is **just-in-time** logistics planning.

The JIT focus on a short time-frame makes forecasting easier and more accurate, helping an organization to meet the objectives of reduced inventory and improved customer service. However, adoption of the shorter forecasting time-frame does not eliminate the need for monitoring accuracy and giving feedback to the forecaster. One practical way of achieving both is the use of a sales forecast request form, which includes comparison of actual performance with forecast.

Where economic cycles are characterized by extreme peaks and troughs, the forecasting and planning process is put under considerable strain. For example, few businesses would have foreseen the drop in demand of up to 20% in some industries triggered by a near doubling of UK interest rates in the period 1989/90. Where production capacity, sales organization and pricing are built around reasonable sales forecasts, companies have to make drastic structural changes when these forecasts are not met over a prolonged period.

In this position, a large corporation can fall back on financial reserves or sell peripheral assets. A smaller company with a weaker balance sheet might find itself in the straitjacket of paying higher levels of interest on loans taken out to buy machinery in order to expand capacity just as demand tumbles. An extended period of negative cash flow may lead to a company facing bankruptcy. This was the position of many small and medium-sized companies serving the construction industry in 1990/91. In contrast, the food industry is insulated from such cyclical demand.

There are three forecasting scenarios for demand:

(1) regular and predictable;
(2) irregular but mathematically consistent;
(3) irregular and unpredictable.

The demand for consumer banking services can be assigned to the first category, the demand for soft drinks and cold remedies to the second and the demand for securities (linked to stock market activity) to the third.

Forecasting methods

A wide range of quantitative methods of forecasting is available to management, from the simple calculation of moving annual totals on a personal computer spreadsheet, to econometric modelling using a complex array of internal and external data. Some of the more common methods are summarized in Table 14.2, where the data requirements and level of technical expertise necessary are indicated.

Table 14.2 Review of the more common forecasting methods.

Method	Comment
Simple time-series smoothing methods: – simple moving averages – exponential smoothing	(1) Assume an underlying pattern exists in the data series which can be isolated from random effects. (2) No attempt is made to identify individual components.
Decomposition method for time-series analysis	(1) Separates each time-series' actual value into four components: trend, cyclical, seasonal, random. (2) The relationship can be multiplicative or additive. (3) Forecast value (F) at time t is arrived at using the equation derived and a value for the random components: $F_t = T_t \times C_t \times S_t \times R$
Simple linear regression between two variables	(1) Assumes linear relationship between two variables. (2) Forecast is possible for the dependent variable based on reliable forecast for the independent variable (such as demand for bottled water based on temperature). (3) Requires little statistical knowledge and limited data.
Multiple regression	(1) Explores historic data to identify relationship between sales and at least two other variables. (2) Reliability of forecasts based on regression equation depends on the number of historic data points used. (3) Requires more sophisticated knowledge and computing support.
Econometric modelling (generally only used by major companies with specialists)	(1) Judgement needed in deciding which variables to include and the mathematical form. (2) Minimum number of data points needed for acceptable level of statistical significance.

When choosing forecasting methods, there are several criteria that can be used: the time-horizon, data availability, cost, accuracy, simplicity and ease of use. The most common trade-off is between cost and accuracy, where the major costs are attributable to expertise and reliable data. In practice, many companies are limited in the forecasting techniques that can be used by the availability of historic data on variables likely to be related to market demand or company sales. The forecaster is looking for appropriate dependent variables (unit sales, market value) and a set of independent variables to which one of these can be related (consumer spending, temperature, new housing starts). A second constraint is the type of management information system used and the computer back-up available, since the value of forecasting is seriously curtailed if it does not fit comfortably with internally generated data for planning purposes.

The choice of forecasting method (or combination of methods) can range from the highly subjective choice of consolidated figures, to sophisticated techniques that require understanding and acceptance by the user. The former approach involves high forecast error, and the latter, commitment of resources. There is therefore a case for looking at how credibility is achieved for the forecasting function by addressing user needs, and by being part of the logistics management process as opposed to taking an advisory or consultant role (Lawless, 1990).

Detailed explanation and illustration of the forecasting methods indicated in Table 14.2 are beyond the scope of this chapter, but are provided in texts devoted to the subject (such as Wheelwright and Makridakis, 1985). Econometric forecasting methods are also touched upon in Chapter 8, in exploration of how decisions are reached on economic levels of advertising expenditure against consumer brands.

Format of the marketing budget

This will vary according to the conventions of the organization, and the level of accountability of marketing management in the area of financial targets. The format shown in Table 14.2 is a 12-month sales and profit budget for a consumer durable. Marketing costs are itemized so that it is clear how the budget is apportioned between different areas of the promotion mix. There are three key financial measures shown in the format which enable marketing management to compare the performance of different products or business sectors.

(1) Gross margin

This is the residue left from the sales revenue when product cost has been accounted for. Some organizations choose to allocate a 'distribution' charge against the product at this stage in the accounting process; others include this in the overhead charge against the product. The former approach has been used in Table 14.3. The gross margin is generally expressed as a percentage of revenue.

The higher the gross margin on a product, the less vulnerable is the net profit position to increases in raw material costs, a sudden decline in the market or more aggressive competition. This is because the organization has financial manoeuvrability through the difference between the gross margin figure and the net profit. However, the higher the marketing expenditure necessary for the product to maintain a viable market share, the more dangerous it is to cut this expenditure as an expediency in lean times.

(2)   Marketing contribution

This is sometimes called the **marketing margin** and is the residue left from the sales revenue after product cost and marketing costs have been accounted for. It is the amount of money left to pay for the **overhead allocation** and provide a **profit**. The marketing contribution expressed as a percentage of revenue shows how far a product is contributing to the general expenses of the total business (which could be office rental, rates, administrative personnel and office machinery running costs) and to the final profit figure.

Products that are in the decline stage of the product life cycle are frequently candidates for de-listing if there is little profit being generated. However, the figure for the marketing contribution will show whether the product is contributing to general costs, and whether discontinuing the product would mean raising an additional contribution from elsewhere in the portfolio.

(3)   Net profit

This is the figure for the residue from revenue when product costs, marketing costs and overheads have been accounted for. It is a key measure of the long-term viability of a product, although in the launch stage this could be very low or even negative, while money is spent on promotion to create awareness and a customer base.

The figure for net profit shown in Table 14.3 reflects the position *before* interest charges are paid on loans and before corporation tax is paid.

The way in which general **overheads** are charged against a product's revenue will depend on an organization's accounting conventions. Some companies will charge a standard percentage of revenue for general expenses which is the same across all products or even across all SBUs (strategic business units). Others will segregate products into different categories, and a different rate will apply to each category. Other companies allow a 'honeymoon period' to new products, in which they are not charged any general expenses.

Link between marketing strategy and budget structure

The 12-month budget provides a 'snapshot' of the marketing rationale and support for the product. It shows, at a glance, the price positioning in the market and the resultant level of volume sales. It shows the level of product costs and the gross margin, the latter providing the funds to support the product with promotion; and it shows the contribution that the product makes towards expenses and profits, reflecting whether it is in the launch, growth or mature stage of its life, compared with other products in the portfolio.

The way in which a **marketing budget** can be analysed for marketing rationale is illustrated by reference to the three budgets in Tables 14.3 (Product A), 14.4 (Product B) and 14.5 (Product C).

Product A is an 'economy' line household durable with a manufacturer's selling price (MSP) of £25.80. It has double the volume sales of product B and over three times the volume sales of product C. To achieve this level of volume sales, product A is supported by a high advertising spend (17.5%), consumer and retailer promotions. Total marketing costs

Table 14.3 Twelve-month sales and profit budget for product A: 'economy' household durable (volume sales in units: 150,000; manufacturer's selling price: £25.80).

	£000	%
Revenue	3870	100
Cost of goods	1548	40
Distribution	155	4
Gross margin	2167	56
Marketing costs:		
Advertising:		
media	627	
production	50	
Total	677	17.5
Sales promotion:		
consumer	72	
retailer discount	160	
Total	232	6
Salesforce:		
direct costs	380	
commissions	66	
support materials	38	
Total	484	12.5
Total marketing costs	1393	36
Marketing contribution	774	20
Overheads	348	9
Net profit	426	11

Table 14.4 Twelve-month sales and profit forecast for product B: 'traditional' household durable (volume sales: 75,000; manufacturer's selling price £38.65).

	£000	%
Revenue	2900	100
Cost of goods	1479	51
Distribution	116	4
Gross margin	1305	45
Marketing costs:		
Advertising:		
media	–	
production	–	
Sales promotion:		
consumer	–	
retailer discount	203	7
Salesforce:		
direct costs	245	
commissions	58	
support materials	16	
Total	319	11
Total marketing costs	522	18
Marketing contribution	783	27
Overheads	261	9
Net profit	521	18

account for 36% of revenue, which reflects the product's mass market position. The gross margin of 56% permits this level of marketing support. It is likely that the product is in the growth stage when the current balance between marketing expenditure and net profit is taken into account.

Product B is a 'traditional' household durable selling at an MSP of £38.65. There is no advertising support or consumer promotions, but retailer discounts account for 7% of sales revenue. The low level of total planned marketing expenditure at 18% of sales would be typical of a mature line, where high levels of advertising support could not be justified in terms of additional sales generated. Also, the gross margin of 45% would not support marketing expenditure at the same level as product A. The net profit of 18% (compared with 11% for product A) suggests that the product is being 'milked' for profits before its deletion from the range when sales and contribution are no longer adequate to justify its continuation. The need to discount the price in order to retain distribution suggests the likelihood of a continuing erosion of margin.

Product C is the highest-priced product in the range at an MSP of £65.90, reflecting its 'designer' status. It is supported with advertising at a level of 20% of sales, but there are no consumer or retailer sales promotions planned as these could damage the prestige image of the line.

Table 14.5 Twelve-month sales and profit budget for product C: 'designer' household durable (volume sales: 45,000; manufacturer's selling price: £65.90).

	£000	%
Revenue	2965	100
Cost of goods	890	30
Gross margin	1956	66
Marketing costs		
Advertising:		
media	530	
production	63	
Total	593	20
Sales promotion:		
consumer	–	
retailer discount	–	
Salesforce:		
direct costs	227	
commission	50	
support materials	20	
Total	297	10
Total marketing costs	889	30
Marketing contribution	1067	36
Overheads	267	9
Net profit	800	27

Total marketing expenditure is 30% of sales, which can be supported through the high level of gross margin at 66%. This also supports a high level of net profit at 27%. This means that in terms of absolute profit, product C contributes much more than product A, although the latter takes up more management time in devising and implementing the marketing programme. There may also be the strategic necessity to be represented in the lower-priced sector of the market.

The ways in which management would decide on the allocation of marketing funds between products in a business portfolio are considered in detail in Chapter 15.

The marketing plan as a tool of coordination and cooperation with other functional departments

The detailed exploration of the relationship between the marketing plan and budget explores the areas of potential overlap between marketing and finance. The marketing practitioner of the 1990s cannot expect to survive on purely creative skills. An ability to analyse the results of decisions and actions expressed in terms of sophisticated ratios and trends is critical to an understanding of the contribution which marketing is making to the financial health of the business. Some of the most successful companies are characterized by constant dialogue between financial and marketing management.

The parallel driving forces of **competitive edge** and **cost control** have led companies to examine the logistical framework within which customer demand is satisfied. This means that the buying, production and distribution functions must be drawn into the planning network, and there must be an internal consistency in the allocation of resources in each area to meet common goals. An organization that identifies **logistics management** as the key to competitive superiority will set itself performance parameters on stock levels, speed of order processing, delivery times and level of customer complaints. These parameters may be included in, or derived from, the targets in the marketing plan, and will reflect the corporate philosophy on the level of customer service that is necessary for maintaining and developing the sales base, and which will give the level of profitability outlined in the budget.

Organizations that see the logistics function as a source of **added value** for the product or service are often applying the search for quality in all areas of operations. Bowersox (1988) sees this as linked to the **just-in-time** (JIT) environment where the order cycle will determine the framework of logistical control over the quality of customer service. It is claimed that order cycles are generally getting shorter, which reflects the desire to minimize stocks financed at high interest rates, and to maximize stock-turn. The way in which suppliers and their customers communicate is crucial to this process, and the availability of **electronic data interchange** (EDI) to a wide range of industries has improved efficiency and flexibility of meeting customer needs. Chapter 17 deals in depth with the technological advances that are benefiting logistical planning and execution.

An area of resource planning which is frequently divorced from the marketing plan is that of **human resources**. Traditionally, this has been seen as the remit of the 'Personnel' function in collaboration with senior management. Apart from the additional marketing executives needed to work on new product development, the link with the marketing plan is traditionally seen as the justification for growth (or contraction) of the in-house sales team to meet the targets. In industrial markets, the salesforce salaries and running costs will account for the major part of the marketing budget. It is therefore an important part of the budget review process to assess whether this key resource is being used to achieve optimal results. The traditional way of estimating the size for a salesforce is shown in Chapter 13.

There are also the wider issues of labour productivity in manufacturing industry, and the way in which developments in information technology have made a major impact on staffing levels in the traditional areas of administrative support, including sales, finance and production control. Cost control is a vital discipline which can be triggered by the requirements of the budgeting process, as any erosion of margins will lead to a weaker competitive position in the medium term.

Contingency planning

Associated with every marketing plan is a set of assumptions regarding market growth, competitive action and the company's product, pricing and promotional strategy and tactics. Behind these lie underpinning assumptions about the state of the economy and how this will affect demand. A good marketing plan will state clearly the assumptions on which forecasts are based, and will indicate that alternative scenarios have been examined to identify where the outcome proposed in the plan is vulnerable to macro-environmental and competitive influences.

It is not feasible or desirable to prepare contingency marketing plans for a wide range of alternative assumptions, but where areas of greatest uncertainty in the market are highlighted, then the promotional activity and budget should be proposed with sufficient flexibility to respond to a changing market environment. For a major consumer food brand, this might be the rapid adoption of a short-term sales incentive to retailers to counter the launch of a new, competitive brand. The onset of a recession in industrial capital goods markets will be accompanied by discretionary discounting of price. In such situations, competitive activity would need an active response from the individual supplier, whose margins would then come under pressure in the short term.

An organization that chooses a systematic approach to planning, implementation and control will adopt the following practices to ensure that feedback on performance against plan results in corrective action at tactical marketing or strategic level:

(1) A clear statement of assumptions to the marketing plan.
(2) Examination of the effects of alternative market scenarios, pricing strategies and promotion plans on market share, sales volume and revenue, gross margin and net profit. Ideally, such sensitivity analysis should occur before final budget and plans are submitted for approval.
(3) Indication of the assumptions with the greatest band of uncertainty and contingency marketing action that would be possible within the constraints of available budget and personnel. Adverse effects on financial performance as a result of such contingencies should be highlighted.
(4) Weekly and monthly monitoring of performance against targets, with management evaluation of variance.

(5)   Decisions necessary on amendments to advertising, salesforce activity, pricing policy, production scheduling and distribution as a result of variance from budget.

(6)   Feedback to strategic decision-making level where variance indicates radical changes needed in plans and operations to achieve an acceptable marketing and financial outcome.

Marketing assumptions

For the preparation of marketing plans and budgets for consumer products, figures for the following underlying assumptions should be provided so that management is clear on the probability of the proposed outcome, and so that the internal consistency of the calculations may be verified (a year-on-year basis is assumed). For industrial markets, hard data in these areas are not always available and plans and budgets may be based on historic precedent rather than quantitative assumptions. However, all marketing plans should strive towards this ideal.

For the market, figures need to be provided for:

- market growth (volume): gives size of market in units;
- average price increase across the market;
- market growth (value): gives size of market in money;
- percentage market split by sector: defined by product type or customer need;
- advertising expenditure for the market (current prices);
- increase in media costs;
- advertising expenditure for the market (constant prices).

and for the product:

- average retail price (with indication of price movement);
- average manufacturer selling price (with indication of price movement);
- market share in volume terms;
- market share in money terms;
- advertising expenditure: gives 'share of voice';
- indication of retailer discount levels and when available;
- estimate of percentage of volume sold at each discount level;
- level of incentive for consumer promotions, duration and effects on demand;
- product cost;
- convention used for allocation of distribution costs and overheads.

When the full range of assumptions given above is disclosed then the type of sales and profit budget illustrated in Table 14.3 can be justified. Without the provision of the full range of assumptions, the proponents of the marketing plan will find themselves having to justify individual figures in the budget without the support of a logical, numerical framework. Where calculations of sales and profit performance are based on only one or two assumptions, then there is also the danger that the proposed budget will lack 'internal consistency' with other assumptions, notably the relationship between total market performance and projected brand performance.

Examination of alternative market and brand scenarios

The relationship between price changes from one year to the next and sales projections will invariably rely on judgement. This will also be the case for the effects on sales of the various promotional activities. Investigation of and reference to historic relationships will provide even firmer ground for budget proposals.

Presuming that the 'best' forecast of the market and product scenario is contained in the marketing plan and supporting budget, what if several of these key assumptions are wrong? For example, the forecast on average market price might be too high, leading to a deterioration in competitive pricing for the product. Advertising costs might escalate much faster than expected, so that a smaller audience is reached with the proposed budget, leading to a lower level of new customers. A new competitive product might be launched just as an attractive retailer discount was expected to boost purchases by key accounts. The sheer number of alternative scenarios makes it impossible to cover every eventuality, but the shrewd market planner will identify the most vulnerable assumptions and calculate the effect on the sales and profit budget of reasonable alternatives.

The number of alternative projected scenarios that can be investigated is a function of management time available, and the level of understanding of the interrelationships between variables under examination will depend on the availability of forecasting specialists. Investment in the personnel with the required background and experience needs to be matched by investment in computing power to gain maximum benefit from their skills.

The marketing planning framework will vary for each organization because of differences in the tracking information available on the market and on product performance. This will be combined with judgemental input from marketing practitioners on future sales response to promotional activity, to provide a standard format within which the effects of different assumptions can be tested. Where there is unlikely to be a 'right answer' for a forward plan and budget, some assumptions will be more realistic than others and there is likely to be a range from 'optimistic' to 'pessimistic' on key assumptions.

A standard spreadsheet format for investigating alternative assumptions allows for greater depth of **sensitivity analysis** because of the relative speed and simplicity of the operation. It also provides the opportunity for all products or business units to examine alternative scenarios using common disciplines, which means there is likely to be greater consistency in the quality of the plans and budgets that are submitted for approval. Appropriate software developments can also provide the facility for aggregation of budgets and forecasts so that the 'global' business position is projected and examined against corporate objectives.

Multinational corporations active in the field of repeat-purchase consumer goods have invested in the development of **marketing models** that imitate as far as possible the market scenario in which an individual brand has to compete. Considerable time and expertise are necessary to build models that can usefully predict the financial outcome of a given marketing plan. Assumptions are necessary for **price elasticity**, **advertising elasticity** and **income elasticity** of demand for a particular product category. These are generally derived from complex statistical models built within the company using expensive and consistently available market audit data. This type of **econometric forecasting** is at the leading edge of marketing planning, and proprietary systems are rarely publicised because of the competitive planning.

Control, measurement and contingency management

A marketing plan is agreed in the knowledge that assumptions and forecasts have been made on the basis of limited information, and that there is the likelihood that results will differ from plan. A system of monitoring devices and management controls is necessary to identify where performance is at variance with plan, how much the variance is, whether it requires compensating action, and how this should be implemented. This **feedback** model of contingency planning is frequently operated through a formal system of monthly or weekly management meetings in which each functional department is represented to highlight serious variances between plan and 'actual', and where decisions are made on compensating action to be taken individually or as a group.

The **recency** of information on sales performance is crucial to an early warning system for marketing adjustments to plans. The way in which **information technology** has been used to provide a company with automatic feedback on orders placed, sales mix, revenue and gross margin by line will dictate how quickly management can respond to offset poor performance or to diffuse successful ideas through other product lines or operational areas.

An organization will develop its own conventions on when variances are sufficiently large to warrant a revision of the 12-month budget. This might be an automatic control mechanism halfway through the financial year, or will be instigated when it is clear that poor performance against plan is unlikely to redress itself during the remainder of the year.

Experience of control techniques used in multinational pharmaceutical companies has given rise to a comprehensive format for planning assumptions and contingency planning (Lidstone, 1987). Where assumptions have a major role to play in the sales and profit budget, the 'what if?' approach is taken to identify an alternative scenario, its probability of occurrence, the likely impact and action to be taken. Applying figures to these items produces variance estimates for revenue and profits so that management is forewarned of possible budget revisions in the future.

Marketing planning for the small business

Sophisticated marketing planning has the reputation of being a luxury associated with large companies, and proprietors of small businesses frequently take the view that they can ill afford the time that this process needs. It is true that matters such as credit control, staffing and day-to-day management take up a larger portion of the directors' time, but neglect of marketing planning can, in itself, lead to a range of short-term problems as well as a lack of direction for the business for the longer term.

Some of the most common problems facing small businesses are a direct result of a lack of planning for the future in the context of an understanding of the market that is being served, and how prospects are to be reached and converted into customers. A brief review of these problems will clarify this statement:

- As a business grows, the administrative support barely keeps up with the level of sales, deliveries, payments due from customers and purchase invoices outstanding. This day-to-day pressure clouds the issues of the longer term.
- Computerized support for a business is not generally planned at the start-up for the medium-term needs. Therefore the system becomes increasingly inadequate and can hamper efficiency and growth.
- A small business may be in the position of supplying to a narrow market and is vulnerable if this sector suffers a downturn or collapses in the face of cheap imports.
- There may be no built-in mechanisms for maintaining contact with existing or past customers, and the resultant gradual decline in sales is not recognized or compensated by marketing to a new customer base.
- The original customer base may have been acquired on purchase of the business or through the existing contacts of the proprietor on start-up. Marketing costs are frequently seen as an expense rather than an investment, and the marketing budget may be insufficient to achieve development of the customer base, through such promotional methods as direct mail or through the prospecting efforts of the salesforce.

- There may be incomplete knowledge of product costs, so that the level of gross margin on each product range is unknown. If pricing is decided through competitive positioning, the true level of profitability may be lower for the business as a whole than forecasts predict.
- The level of overheads may be too great for the business to support in the early stages, before the customer base has been developed. These overheads may be under-utilized.

In a small business the skills, energy and commitment of the owner/manager will be critical to its success, and in a family concern it is important that there is clear leadership. Very often the business has burgeoned through knowledge and skills in a narrowly based market. The determining factor in whether the business will survive and develop is an ability to understand the needs of a wider market and to reach and serve it. This is where marketing planning plays a major role. However, this cannot be divorced from the day-to-day operations which cut across the functional divides apparent in large corporations.

The names **business plan** and **marketing plan** will tend to be interchangeable in the small business environment. The major reason for producing a forward plan is as a support document in seeking a bank loan. For this reason, the financial content of the plan – profit and loss statement, balance sheet and cash flow forecast – tend to take priority over the rationale on *how* this financial performance will be achieved. If the bank is providing a loan secured against other assets, then the bank's interest in the **process** by which the client develops the business will be minimal. This situation was spotlighted in the early 1990s when the number of UK company liquidations was at a ten-year high, and some business commentators questioned whether banks should be more aware of how small companies can survive a downturn in the market.

The steps in marketing planning for a small business are outlined in Figure 14.2. This reflects a pragmatic approach to planning, where the marketing function cannot be isolated from financial planning and day-to-day operations of the business.

Sales forecasting for the small business

As for large corporations, the financial plan for a small business should be derived from a forecast of revenue and costs based on the level of customer demand. However, the way in which most small businesses evolve means that the customer base is industry specific or confined to a small geographic area. These factors limit the potential for traditional market research techniques which can lead to objective sales forecasts.

Much more reliance is therefore placed on judgemental forecasts based on knowledge of historic performance, local market conditions and future capacity. Such methods make little demand on limited resources,

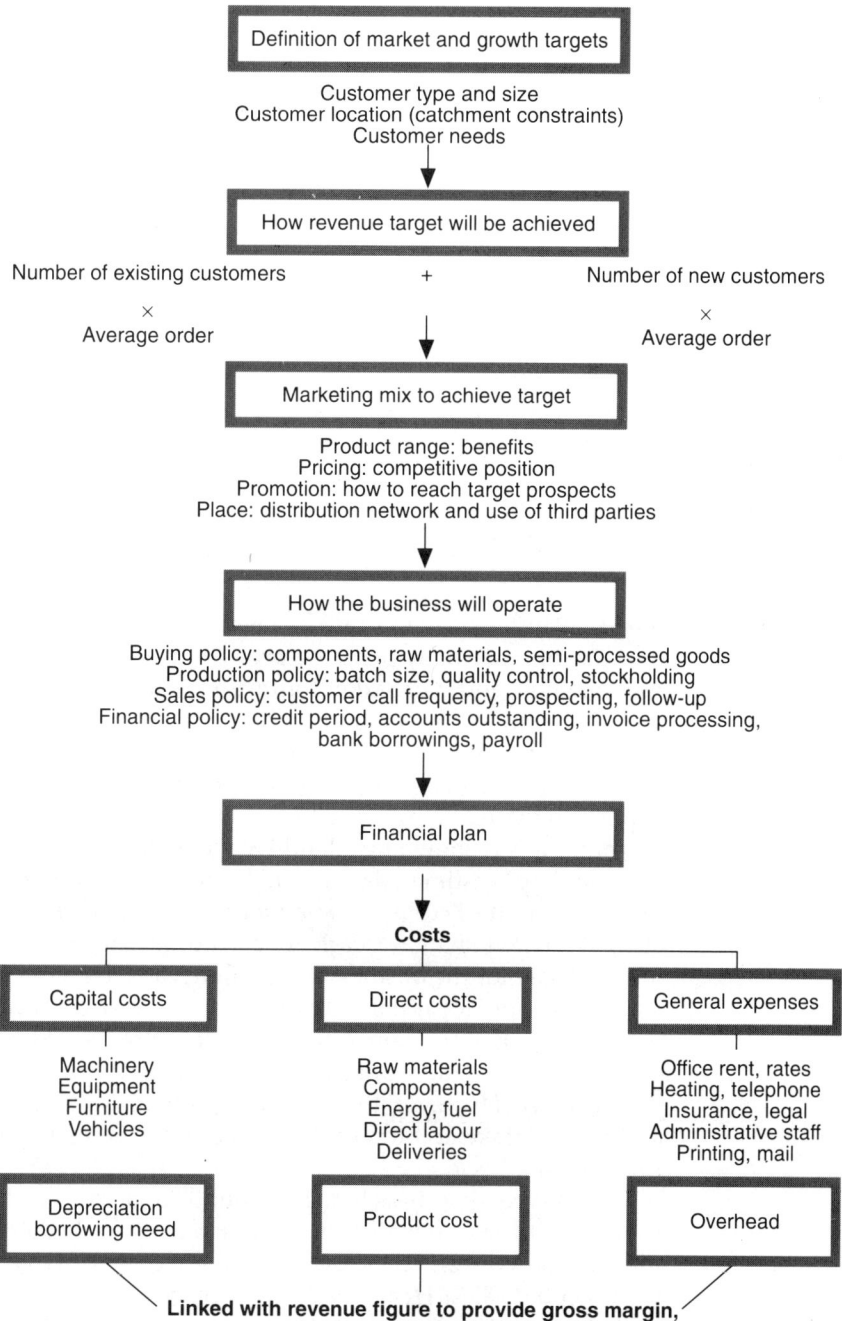

Figure 14.2 Planning process for the small business.

Table 14.6 Forecast of retail chemist sales potential with defined catchment area.

	Toiletries and cosmetics	Medicines and surgical goods[†]
National average weekly spend per household	£2.05	£0.90
Number of households	20,000	20,000
Total weekly spend	41,000	18,000
Total annual spend	£2.05 million	£0.90 million
Market share estimate:		
% multiple chemist	40	25
% multiple grocer	25	10
% independent chemists	35	65
Number of independents	6	6
% market share forecast for each independent	6	11
Annual sales potential for each independent[‡]	£123,000	£99,000

[†]excluding prescription dispensing; [‡]assuming equal potential based on site and merchandise mix.

but are likely to be inaccurate as a result. There are two general methods that can provide more accurate projections of sales. These are the **sales ratio** method, and the **market build-up** method.

The sales ratio method involves the use of general population data to derive a figure for aggregate demand; then, ratios for the way in which this demand is satisfied by product sector and suppliers within each are applied to reach a sales figure for the business in question. An example of this approach is shown in Table 14.6, where the retail sales potential for a chemist shop is estimated based on the number of households in the catchment area multiplied by the annual *per capita* expenditure on the product class. A market share for each competitor is estimated and the resultant market share for the business in question leads to a sales forecast.

This approach is particularly valuable in the absence of hard market research data before commitment is made to property leases or bank loans, since it can provide upper and lower limits to likely sales and profit performance. However, the new entrepreneur is likely to be an optimist and will not take account of the possibility of recession at some stage in the economic cycle.

The second approach, market build-up, involves identification and estimation of sales potential in discrete sectors – whether geographical or industry-based – and aggregation of these data to arrive at a total figure for potential sales. Heavy reliance is placed on market intelligence fed back through the salesforce, where there are no suitable industry statistics available.

More sophisticated forecasting techniques such as time-series analysis, regression models and input–output models are suggested as suitable for small businesses for which appropriate historic data exist (Frontistis, 1986).

European perspective

In the first section of this chapter, the marketing plan was identified as the mechanism for a company to reconcile the twin activities of fulfilling customer needs and meeting financial targets. It is the blueprint against which functional departments work in harmony towards agreed objectives. Where production is based in more than one European country to serve several Member State markets, the marketing plan and associated budget evolve from a more complex decision process than if they were limited to operations in just one Member State.

The language, culture, laws and accounting practices of each nation involved are influencing factors. This means that whereas they may have been five variables critical to the forecast at a national level (such as labour rates, advertising spend or bulk discounting), the involvement of several Member States will create an additional array of possible outcomes due to the effects of international factors. These are:

(1) *Production location* This raises issues of distance to markets, local corporation tax, regional development grants, labour productivity and restrictive practices, fluctuations in invoicing currency (for direct sales or intercompany transfers), and the availability of technical expertise.

(2) *Stage of market development* The timing of launch of state-of-the-art products in each Member State will depend on the level of sophistication of customers within it. For consumer markets this will relate to disposable income, lifestyle, education and media availability. For industrial markets, governing factors will be level of investment in new technology, the skills and expertise of the workforce and management attitudes to the quality/price relationship.

(3) *Financial resources* A company will be restricted in the number of markets that can be developed at any one time through the availability of cash generated by existing business, or by limited access to loans to finance working capital. There is also the decision to be made of where to raise such loans or whether an ECU bond should be issued.

(4) *Financial expertise* This relates to day-to-day cash management and the quality and costs of services available from banks, which are traditionally national in character and operating methods.

(5) *Information technology* To what degree can a database be accessed by subsidiaries for stock availability, costings or customer delivery dates? This raises questions of software capabilities, expertise and running costs, with the overriding need for compatibility of national data processing and storage systems as the basis for development of an interactive network.

Issues relating to location of production facilities and stage of market development are explored in the context of business and marketing strategy in Chapter 3. The focus of this section is the identification of moves towards harmonization in areas of financial management which play a vital role in underpinning the viability of a marketing plan. Linked to this is the importance of information technology in ensuring tight management control of the flow of goods and money across borders.

Moves towards fiscal harmonization

The European currency unit (ECU)

The ECU was created by the EC in December 1978 as the European currency unit based on a weighted 'basket' of the 12 member currencies. The contribution from each currency is determined by the economic importance of the Member State within the EC. So, for example, the Deutschmark has a 30.1% weighting and the Italian lire a 10.15% weighting. The conversion rates between the ECU and internationally traded currencies can fluctuate daily and are published in the *Official Journal of the EC*.

Currently, there is no ECU issue by a central European bank, but it is recognized by Member States and companies within them as a trading currency. This means that prices can be quoted in ECU, invoices can be issued in ECU, and the currency can be traded on the foreign exchange markets. Adoption of the ECU has been a slow process, but its use is expected to become more widespread during the 1990s. The ultimate objective of the EC is convergence towards a **single currency** by the end of the 1990s. If this is achieved, it means that the individual currencies of Member States will no longer be used after a certain date, and all business transactions across the EC will be in the single currency.

The benefits to companies of this scenario are:

- No currency risks in buying or selling goods in the currency of another Member State. Possible changes in exchange rates have meant that companies have had to trade in the foreign exchange market in order to reduce their exposure to the possibility of paying more for a product or service or receiving less for one sold, when prices are agreed in the currency of another Member State.
- Comparison of financial performance of individual subsidiaries will be simpler where there is the same currency unit.

- Consolidation of financial accounts will be facilitated. However, the legal requirements for whether this is performed and to which conventions will largely depend on EC moves towards harmonized reporting practice.
- There will be cost savings in the avoidance of currency transactions in the process of buying and selling, and in cross-financing of investment in subsidiaries. Savings will also accrue from less management time spent on these areas.

These advantages suggest that the corporate sector would make significant gains by the move towards a single currency. However, sophisticated financial management has resulted in profits being augmented by successful trading in the foreign exchange markets or simply by anticipating exchange rate fluctuations as part of trading in the core business.

Some Member States, most notably the UK, are resisting moves towards a single currency as this is viewed as a removal of national sovereignty in determining monetary policy. However, it is difficult to see how the major effects of removing barriers to trade can be exercised without true harmonization through creating a 'level playing field' in financial transactions.

An example of how the use of the ECU can reduce risk in cross-border transactions is its adoption by The Tioxide Group in May 1985 (Halford, 1991). The Group (which became a wholly owned subsidiary of ICI at the end of 1990) conducted a great deal of intercompany trade between the subsidiaries in France, UK and Italy. Tioxide found that the ECU could be treated like any other currency (it could be transferred, traded, borrowed and lent) and was a stable currency because of its aggregate nature.

The European monetary system

The European monetary system (EMS) was established in March 1979 for three reasons:

- to reduce exchange rate volatility and provide the conditions for convergence of interest rates,
- to coordinate exchange rate policies versus external currencies such as the US dollar and the yen,
- to control inflation.

The exchange rate mechanism (ERM) specified that the value of each Member State's currency may not fluctuate by more that $\pm 2.5\%$ of the agreed exchange value when the currency entered the ERM. Should there be signs that this condition would be breached then national banks would intervene in the foreign exchange markets to support the value of the currency.

On entry to the ERM in October 1990, the pound sterling was allowed a fluctuation band of ±6%, which also applied to the Spanish peseta. This allowed for a period of adjustment, as the discipline of the ERM had consequences for the economies of joining nations. Some economists took the view that the ERM represented too tight a straitjacket for sterling, and that it would prevent the kind of reduction in interest rates that in the past were a necessary condition for economic recovery. This could precipitate conditions for devaluation of the pound creating the kind of scenarios associated with the 1960s and 1970s (Gonnissen, 1991).

The pattern of interest rates across key Member States did indeed begin to show a trend towards convergence by April 1992, compared with those of April 1991. However, the financing of unification increased borrowing requirements in Germany, with a rise in interest rates. This had a profound effect on the rates of other Member States such as the UK, where high interest rates impeded economic recovery.

In September 1992, downward pressure on the pound sterling led to its removal from the ERM. In August 1993, other currencies came under similar pressure with high German interest rates supporting a higher parity for the Deutschmark. The effective suspension of the ERM has led to speculation as to whether:

(1)   the ERM will be reinstituted;
(2)   convergence across Member States on key economic indicators will be possible, to support monetary union;
(3)   a single currency is feasible or desirable.

Development of international accounting standards

The wide variety of accounting conventions across Member States means that even within one company operating across borders, there will be several different formats for accounts for subsidiaries. For most Member States, the format will be dictated by a tax focus, although this is not the case for the UK, Ireland, the Netherlands and Denmark, where Anglo-Saxon conventions apply. The degree to which universal rules are applied to presentation of financial results (and therefore, the budgets with which they are compared) will depend on the individual company's conventions for consolidation. Where there is no legal requirement for disclosure of **consolidated accounts**, then the purpose is purely one of internal management and control.

However, consolidation of accounts becomes compulsory for medium-sized groups (with over 250 employees) under the 7th EC

Directive of June 1983 relating to accounting standards. The objective of this is to move towards comparability of accounts, although progress here has been slower than in areas such as competition law or monetary policy. Consolidation of accounts was previously rare in Spain, Portugal and Greece, so implementation of laws to comply with the Directive will mean significant changes to past practices for these countries. Italy, Ireland and Portugal have been slow to implement laws, with other Member States complying with the Directive between 1985 and 1990.

The main provisions of the 7th Directive include articles relating to consolidation, exemptions, uniform formats and the treatment of goodwill. Compulsory items appear to have drawn inspiration predominantly from standards set in the UK, Ireland, France, the Netherlands, and to a lesser degree, Germany (Nobes, 1990).

The most contentious areas of harmonization are treatment of goodwill, deferred tax and foreign currency transactions. Further moves towards harmonization are likely to be based on the actions of such bodies as the International Accounting Standards Committee (IASC) where no further EC legislation is planned in the medium term. Following a 1990 conference, an Accounting Forum was established with members drawn from national accounting standards bodies (Irvine, 1991). This serves to advise the European Commission, and the opportunity for communication between members might serve to further the cause of harmonization even without EC endorsement.

European cash management

Where many marketing plans are accompanied by a sales, cost and profit analysis for the short to medium term, the cash flow projection inevitably remains the domain of the finance or treasury department. Yet this is possibly the most significant constraint on the timing of the operations through which the plan is achieved. Most noticeably in an economic downturn, cash flow determines when orders for raw materials may be placed, when commitment is confirmed for advertising space, and when additional contract staff can be hired to fulfil a service agreement.

Managers are increasingly adopting short credit term options with suppliers in return for discounts, but the cash flow implications need to be evaluated. The impact of a recession is to create a cash-conserving mentality as accounts receivable decline and yet stocks are still to be financed and salaries paid.

An economic downturn necessitates a review of cash management, and European financial deregulation was an additional catalyst for putting this high on the management agenda. An international survey indicated that the majority of companies interviewed planned to make changes to European cash management over the next three years (Kaess, 1991).

Two major trends have emerged from this: firstly, companies are identifying whether it is cheaper to pay fees for bank services rather than maintaining positive balances on which the bank, rather than the customer, earns interest. Secondly, electronic transfer of funds is taking place on an international basis – companies can pay foreign suppliers and expatriate workers, and make pension and other recurring payments at low cost. Progress in cross-border use of EDI will depend on resolving issues of common formats, cost effectiveness and security.

The importance of information technology

The speed with which a company may adopt a pan-European approach to planning and budgeting will depend, firstly on the ability of managers to comply through gaining the necessary expertise, and secondly, on the **information technology** support available within the group. For many organizations, an international system evolves from internal best practice in database management and reporting systems. The other option is to develop completely international bespoke software. This is an expensive and lengthy process, and this function invariably falls to US software houses whose development costs are amortized across an international customer base. Japanese companies are also building software for the international market, with the advantage of the DOS and Unix systems having become standards. European software companies have the experience base for greater understanding of pan-European needs, but frequently lack the resources for software development and exporting.

There are two major influences on the choice of an international system: **format compatibility** across regions, important for accounting and management information systems, and **language needs**, dictating requirements in translation functions and character handling.

Accounting conventions

Most accounting systems cater for currency conversion, and this is a core capability along with others which will be specified according to central management reporting needs. Peripheral functions may be added to cater for local accounting reporting laws and conventions. For example, in

Portugal, all credits have to be reported as negative debits. The move towards harmonization on consolidation of accounts will act as a focus for system development.

However, the different national approaches to accounting lead to some organizations choosing one of these for international management accounting to suit strategic needs. The Anglo-Saxon approach of the UK and USA splits management accounting and financial accounting into two separate functions. Entries are made into separate books of accounts for general ledger, accounts payable and accounts receivable. There is more flexibility than in other European states in the way accounts are prepared, with the general condition that they comply with the various Companies Acts and standard accounting practice. This approach means that data from different files (such as inventory, purchases, sales orders) flow into the general ledger, which facilitates consolidation.

In contrast, in France and other Continental countries, ledgers have been used in such a way that they appear to operate more like an integrated database. The French integrate four types of account: Auxiliare (third parties), Comptabilité Générale (general accounting), Budgetaire (budgeting) and Analytique (management accounting). Input data relating to individual areas of activity – sales orders, purchase orders, payroll, stocks and so on – flow into a more general database facilitating each of these accounts (Bannister, 1991).

Language capability

English dominates in software provision, and this can be a problem where foreign subsidiaries do not have users conversant with the language. Translation becomes necessary for help screens, menus and message facilities. One option is to have the two languages on-screen at the same time. Another is a facility developed by software vendor Kewill-Omicron which includes a 'term bank'. This provides for the translation of a particular term once, and this term is automatically adjusted on all screens (Classe, 1991).

Problems and assignments

(1) 'Marketing plans are simply the means by which the marketing strategy will be implemented and how resources will be allocated.' To what extent do you agree with this definition of marketing planning?

(2) Why do you think it is that marketing plans for consumer products are often described as being little more than promotional plans? Why are marketing plans for industrial products not so likely to be so afflicted?

(3)   Why are sales and revenue forecasts deemed to be so important by many companies?

(4)   Marketing plans are based on assumptions about the external environment and the marketplace. Since these assumptions will often be at variance with reality, what is the point of adhering to a fixed plan?

(5)   What level of financial data do you consider would be appropriate for inclusion in a marketing plan for a small start-up business? Specify what financial information you would include.

(6)   Critically assess the arguments for and against a single unit of currency for all EC Member States for commercial purposes.

(7)   What benefits for industry will be manifested as a consequence of the move to establish standardized/harmonized accounting practices and presentation formats?

(8)   What implications or bearings might a marketing plan potentially have on other non-marketing functions within a company?

References

Bowersox D. J. (1988). Logistics: the route to quality. *Focus on Physical Distribution and Logistics Management* (UK), **7**(7), 8–14

Chase Jr C.W. (1988/89). Short-range production based forecasting at the Mennen Company. *J. of Business Forecasting* (USA), **7**(4), 2–5

Frontistis T. and Apostolidis P. (1986). Forecasting applications in marketing and small business. *Marketing Intelligence and Planning*, **5**(2), 24

Greenley G.E. (1988). Managerial opinions of marketing planning. *OMEGA Int. J. of Management Science*, **16**(4), 227–287

Griffin T. (1989). Marketing planning: observations on current practices and recent studies. *European J. of Marketing*, **23**(12), 21–35

Lidstone J. (1987). How will we know when we've arrived? Implementing and controlling the marketing plan. *J. of Marketing Management*, **3**(1), 61–71

Lloyd T. (1989). Winning the budget battle. *Sales and Marketing Management*, April, 32–36

McDonald M.H.B. (1989). Marketing planning and expert systems: an epistemology of practice. *Marketing Intelligence and Planning* (UK), **7**(7/8), 16

Piercy N. (1990). Marketing concepts and actions: implementing marketing-led strategic change. *European J. of Marketing*, **24**(2), 24–42

Wheelwright S.C. and Makridakis S. (1985). *Forecasting Methods for Management.* (4th edn.) John Wiley and Sons

European perspective

Bannister G.A. (1991). Accounting systems and software in France – Part I. *Management Accounting*, **69**(8), September, 48

Bannister G.A. (1991). Accounting systems and software in France – Part II. *Management Accounting*, **69**(9), October, 46–48

Classe A. (1991). The right way to keep export options open. *Computing*, 7 November, pp 36–37

Gonnissen J.W.A. (1991). Treasury and the EMS. *The Treasurer*, **13**(8), 38–41

Gooding C. (1992). A global view of planning. *Software at Work, Financial Times Review*, Spring, 22–28

Halford D. (1991). Using the ECU in commerce. *The Treasurer*, **13**(8), 42–44

Irvine J. (1991). When the navel-gazing has to stop. *Accountancy*, (108/1175), July, 24–25

Kaess L.S. (1991). Cash management in the 1990s. *The Treasurer*, **13**(7), 26–29

Kavanagh J. (1992). Keeping tabs on 7500 product prices. *Software at Work, Financial Times Review*, Spring, 11

Nobes C. (1990). EC group accounting: two zillion ways to do it. *Accountancy*, (106/1168), December, 84–85

15 Portfolio analysis: longer-term strategy and allocation of resources

Chapter objectives:

- to examine how marketing decisions are made at the broader business level
- to consider how an organization should analyse its portfolio with regard to further investment or divestment of resources
- to understand what a company's long-term mission statement is and how its existing portfolio of businesses complements this objective
- to present a critique of the relative advantages and disadvantages of the various portfolio analysis techniques available

Introduction

The student has been taken through the journey of strategic analysis, planning and operational marketing as applicable to the single product or business sector. It is now appropriate to explore how marketing decisions are made at the broader business level. In a market-led organization, there will be periodic assessment of the way in which corporate resources are being used to take advantage of current and future opportunities for sales and profit. This requires a framework of analysis which makes use of historic data on performance and is capable of allowing for extrapolation into the future, keeping in mind the inability of the organization to control key external variables. This means that assumptions have to be made based on the latest information and the best judgement of management.

In the mid-1980s, BAT Industries group took a long, hard look at its business portfolio, which included tobacco, retailing and cosmetics, to identify where the best long-term potential lay, and how group resources should be redeployed. Where there is strong growth in all business sectors, then the decision is made more difficult as it is tempting for management to 'ride the wave' in all of them. However, where particular markets show slow growth or decline, convincing a managing board to divest itself of fringe activities in order to focus on the core business is more feasible.

The process through which such strategic decisions can be made is called **portfolio analysis**. It requires the organization to separate its activities into discrete **strategic business units** or SBUs so that performance can be evaluated on a comparative basis. An SBU can be defined in terms of a single product or a product group, the members of which share a common technology or the same end-market. Alternatively, an SBU may be a collection of different product groups which are linked through the same management and the use of common resources such as administrative support and distribution facilities.

At an early stage in the planning cycle, the performance of each SBU is reviewed according to the performance criteria that have been chosen as appropriate to the needs of the group and realistic in terms of the information available (both quantitative and judgemental). The questions which need to be asked are:

- What is the organization's mission statement and key business objectives in the longer term, and how well do the existing SBUs support this scenario?
- Which of the SBUs are the best source of growth and profits, and will this continue into the medium term?
- What resources will the organization have for the coming year (or possibly three or five years, depending on the planning horizon), generally formed through the net positive cash flow from existing SBUs?
- How should these resources be deployed through investing in those SBUs that show the best potential for performance, and drawing back investment from those product sectors where the pay-back is unlikely to continue?
- Which SBUs are subject to the greatest risk from factors outside the organization's control, such as recession, raw material supply constraints, new legislation or even war? How are such risk factors built into the analytical framework?

Whatever the mission of the organization, whether it is to provide the best earnings per share to the shareholder, to be the dominant force in an international market, or to provide the best service to the population at national or regional level on a limited current-cost budget (for a non-profit organization), certain **performance measures** will be necessary to look at the output of each SBU against the resources allocated to it.

One of the points of difference of the various portfolio analysis models that have been proposed over the past 40 years is the choice of performance measures. The more sophisticated models of the later decades have the advantage of powerful computing resources for their use and verification, with the attendant opportunity for identifying performance variables which are interdependent. This means that the focus of analysis can be even more narrowly defined in terms of key performance indicators. For example, the correlation between market share and profitability (which is explored in the PIMS research discussed later in this chapter) has become an accepted norm.

A search of the literature in the area of portfolio analysis reveals a division into the two branches of 'financial' and 'strategic' (the latter with heavy emphasis on marketing measures). Rather than adopt this rather artificial separation of two key disciplines, the important portfolio analysis techniques revealed in the literature are explained in chronological order of their publication, so that the impact of improvements in business management – particularly evident in large multinationals – can be given due weight. The chapter closes with a critique of the relative advantages and disadvantages of the various portfolio analysis techniques outlined.

Markowitz's portfolio theory

This was the first portfolio theory to be proposed and was essentially formulated for the management of **equity investments** (Markowitz, 1952). It acted as a foundation upon which other portfolio analysis techniques were developed. Markowitz hypothesized that the expected rate of return should not be the sole consideration in evaluating alternative equities, as this did not take into account the risk element of each.

An 'efficient' portfolio, according to Markowitz, was one in which the following computations were made for each security:

(1) The expected rate of return, measured as the mean value of all the likely rates of return.
(2) The risk measured by the standard deviation or variances of all the likely rates of return around the mean values.
(3) A further measure of risk in the form of the covariance or correlation coefficient of expected rate of return, with every other security under consideration.

With computing support, Markowitz showed that, from all the available universe of securities, a set of 'efficient' portfolios can be determined which would maximize the investor's expected rate of return for a given level of risk, or minimize the risk for a given level of expected return. An efficient portfolio can then be defined in terms of the securities to be held and the proportion of the available funds to be allocated to each.

Modern equity portfolio management has evolved from these principles, with the concept of diversification improving the reward/risk relationship or, in other words, 'spreading the risk'. Financial portfolio theory defines **risk** as variation in return rather than as a danger or likelihood of failure.

Applying financial portfolio theory to product portfolio decisions

Until 1983 there had been limited application of financial portfolio theory to individual product lines or SBUs within a corporate portfolio, as an aid in allocation of resources. Empirical research was then reported, based on the collection and analysis of data on 60 product lines and 33 SBUs from 21 US firms (out of 30 contacted), which explores the feasibility of this approach (Cardozo and Smith, 1983).

The objective of this research was to address three questions:

(1) Do product lines or SBUs vary from low return/low risk to high return/high risk, as securities do? This meant identifying whether there was a positive correlation between return and risk for all companies and for individual companies.
(2) What are the growth and cash consumption patterns of product lines with particular return and risk characteristics?
(3) Can operating managers follow the action implications of financial portfolio theory to improve the efficiency of use of the resources that they control?

To meet these objectives, frequency distributions and means and standard deviations were produced for the annual data for each product line or SBU, which then yielded average return, risk and relative cash flow for individual investments, companies and the sample as a whole.

The results of the analysis showed a consistent and highly significant relationship between risk and return for the sample as a whole and for several individual companies. Product lines and SBUs, like securities, range from low return/low risk to high return/high risk.

Regarding the second question addressed, the data revealed no consistent relationship between relative cash flow and any other variable. High return/high risk product lines consumed neither more nor less cash than low return/low risk product lines.

The research findings in relation to the third question indicated that action implications from financial portfolio theory appear to apply to individual companies (which intuitively would be expected to reflect the 'security'), but require modification for use in a product evaluation context. This is because the alternatives open to management in the allocation of resources include taking one or more products out of the portfolio (no resources allocated) at each end of the return/risk spectrum.

Such **divestment** decisions could not be made in isolation of considerations of longer-term growth prospects for product categories and of efficiencies created through shared production or administrative facilities. Therefore the decision tools of financial portfolio theory can be applied to product decisions, but take place over years rather than the minutes of equity portfolio decisions.

Ansoff's product/market expansion grid

Assuming that growth is a strategic end for all profit-making organizations, then the alternative paths to achieving this have to be evaluated regularly and systematically. A framework for identifying the options available for pursuing growth is provided in the product/market expansion grid (Ansoff, 1957). This approach is founded on **sales** as the parameter of growth, where other portfolio planning techniques use market share, market growth, cash flow, margin or return on investment as performance criteria (as will be illustrated later in the chapter).

Ansoff's approach is based on the potential for growth coming from a clear designation of the **product** areas in which the company is competent and of the **markets** which these products can serve. Firstly, a **market penetration** strategy involves the pursuit of growth through increasing the market share of *current* products in *current* markets. This is a low risk route for sales growth as there is minimal investment required on product development and the company has experience of the market.

Secondly, a **market development** strategy entails the launching of *current* products into *new* markets. This involves greater risk, as the company is dealing with different market characteristics and, possibly, different buyer needs. Even with comprehensive research, there is risk attached to the deployment of selling effort and the cost of advertising targeted to the new group.

A **product development** strategy is one in which *new* products are launched into *current* markets. Investment in research and development, new plant and promotion constitutes a much higher level of risk than for the first two strategies. Another attendant danger is the possibility of cannibalization of sales of existing products. However, where there is the likelihood of obsolescence, it is better that a company should replace its own product than allow a competitor the privilege.

The fourth, and most adventurous, option facing a company as a source of sales growth is the strategy of **diversification**. This involves *new* product activity in markets that are *new* to the organization. It should be viewed as a route to growth when the other three strategies have been explored and exploited. Only if these do not fulfil the growth targets that have been set for the future should diversification be a serious option. This is because of the higher risks, and these relate in particular to the company moving away from its core activities. An alternative approach is the acquisition of a company with a successful product in an established market. Expertise is purchased along with market share.

Acquisition can also be a route to achieving the other three strategy options:

(1) Market penetration: acquire a competing brand.
(2) Market development: acquire a distributor.
(3) Product development: acquire complementary technology.

In all three examples, the advantage of acquisition over an 'in-house' approach is speed of growth and the knowledge of proven success. However, the outlay in financial terms is invariably higher, and this will be evident in the balance sheet rather than simply as a current cost in the profit and loss account, as would be the case for **organic growth**.

Strategic vulnerability

One of the issues facing management is whether to view the business portfolio through the logic of the organizational structure or through the logic of the environment that impinges on business performance. Life cycle analysis attempts to identify key trends which will influence future performance. In later work, Ansoff proposed an approach which linked the life cycle position of an SBU with the firm's profitability relative to competitors (Ansoff and Leontiades, 1976). This approach could be considered a precursor of the Boston Consulting Group Matrix which is explored later in the chapter.

However, life cycle analysis cannot predict **strategic discontinuities** such as petroleum crises, a major technological breakthrough or marked changes in consumer behaviour. These events can offer threats or opportunities, and it is management's task to control and reduce the vulnerability of the total business mix to the external environment. Ansoff and Leontiades recognized this need to prepare the firm on the external and internal fronts to provide strategic flexibility. They suggested a three-stage approach:

(1) Identify if the firm has a **strategic vulnerability** problem. A simple approach to this is an assessment of the percentage of sales, profit, cash flow and invested capital accounted for by the top SBU, the top two SBUs and the top three SBUs, to give a measure of the concentration of the firm's success and resources.
(2) Compile a list of the **strategic issues** such as political, technological and social events which could have a major impact on the organization. Many of these would have an impact on all firms competing in

Strategic issues	Impact	Strategic business areas					Vulnerability of the firm to strategic issues
		1	2	3	4	5	
Competition							
Growth of societal markets							
Development of the Common Market							
Trade with socialist countries							
Economic & political pressures by developing countries							
Monetary trends							
Inflationary trends							
Emergence of the multinational firm							
Technological breakthroughs							
Bigness as a competitive tool							
Saturation of demand							
Emergence of new industries							
Government regulation & control							
Growth of the service sector							
Affluent consumer							
Total 0–5 years (N) 5–10 years (L) End 10 years (F)							
VULNERABILITY OF THE FIRM							

Figure 15.1 Impact of environmental trends. Reproduced from Ansoff and Leontiades (1976).

a market, but some events would be more critical to the performance of individual companies with a particular technological or customer profile.

(3) Assess the impact of the strategic issues identified for each SBU. An approach to this is illustrated in Figure 15.1. The grid allows the total vulnerability of the firm to a specific issue to be summed, and the total vulnerability of an SBU to all strategic issues is also assessed. This analysis offers the basis for decisions as to whether the firm's vulnerability through individual SBUs should (and can) be reduced, but this has to be counterbalanced by an assessment of the profit implications.

Profit impact of marketing strategy (PIMS)

Up to the early 1970s, there was no definitive research on which strategic factors could be linked with profitability. An attempt to remedy this was the unique research project called PIMS organized in early 1972 as a project of the Marketing Science Institute, a non-profit organization associated with the Harvard Business School. It was the second stage of the research, which involved 57 companies reporting data for 620 businesses for the years 1970–72, that led to significant findings in relation to the key determinants of profits (Schoeffler *et al.*, 1974).

The objectives of the research were to identify the factors influencing profitability in a business, and to evaluate how **return on investment** (ROI) varies in response to changes in strategy and market conditions.

The profit model used included 37 distinct factors which could be related to profitability. However, the research findings focused on three major determinants of ROI. These were **market share**, **investment intensity** and **company factors**.

The researchers suggested that the strong positive relationship between profitability and market share could be explained by companies with stronger market positions having the benefit of **economies of scale**. Another determinant of ROI identified by the researchers was **investment intensity**, which is defined as the ratio of total investment to sales. The *higher* the ratio of investment to sales, the *lower* the return on investment tends to be. The combination of this factor with market share accounted for a considerable portion of total variation in ROI.

The category of influence on profitability designated as **company factors** included such features as size and diversity. The findings of the lowest ROI for the 'average' size category was explained by the 'large' corporations benefiting from **economies of scale** and the smaller companies (under $750 million sales) having the advantage of greater flexibility.

The experience curve

The findings of the PIMS study led to further exploration of the relationship between market share and profitability, notably by the Boston Consulting Group, who focused on the 'experience curve effect' in their capacity as international advisors on corporate strategy.

As well as the traditionally accepted view that labour input per unit of manufacture tends to decline with increases in accumulated production, the Boston Consulting Group found that the type of relationship involved frequently applied to the *total cost* involved in manufacturing, distributing and selling (Hedley, 1976).

When real unit cost was plotted against cumulative production volume using a logarithmic scale, then a straight line normally results, as the Boston Consulting Group illustrates for industrial plastic products, an electronic component, a material processing business and the life insurance industry. The slope of the line is such that the unit cost drops to around 70 to 80% for every doubling of cumulative volume.

A discontinuity occurs in this straight line when there is a technological breakthrough to give much lower production costs per unit, or if there is very rapid market growth, as was the experience in the electronics market in the early and mid 1960s when the US market volume growth was regularly at more than 50% per annum. The cost declined and so did the price of the average germanium diode in the USA.

The strategic approach of Nissan in 1990 to counter the success of Toyota in the Japanese market was a management regime which revolved around a 'product-focused' project team to bring new car models to market. This gave scope for models which catered for the needs of emerging target groups. However, there was an underlying principle that there would be a narrow range of chassis on which the different models would be assembled. This maintained the major thread of 'economies of scale' which would guarantee longer-term profitability while being market-driven.

There are two areas in which the classic 'experience curve' theory is open to challenge. Firstly, increase in market share is adduced to come from reducing prices, as a result of advantageous costs due to economies of scale. This can lead to a 'price war' in which everyone is the loser (of margin!).

For some companies, market share leadership is achieved by product superiority, and a commitment to advertising is appropriate here. The price charged may be 5–10% above the market average. Investment in advertising is necessary to create the brand perceptions which justify the higher price. This means that the higher gross margin achieved must be allocated against marketing and profit to maintain the dominant share position and ensure the target rate of return on investment. This involves perpetual fine-tuning of the marketing plan, and detailed information on performance is critical to this balancing act.

The second area in which the traditional wisdom can be challenged is the scores of companies with a small share of a market, but who choose to provide specialist products and are operating at better than average margins. The example of Mercedes-Benz can be cited (Kiechel, 1981). The argument is put forward in defence of the theory that, in fact, the market should be correctly segmented to identify a separate market for *luxury cars*, in which the Mercedes-Benz share would, of course, be much higher.

This brings into focus the importance of an organization being clear about the markets in which it operates, and structuring performance parameters that are sensible, coherent and measurable, when using the kind of portfolio planning methods described below.

Boston Consulting Group's growth–share matrix

The findings of the PIMS study provided an empirical basis for the development of matrices which focused on market share as an intrinsic parameter for the evaluation of the relative performance of different products or SBUs within a portfolio. Significant among these was the **growth–share matrix** developed by the Boston Consulting Group (BCG) in the late 1970s (Hedley, 1977).

As well as using market share as a key indicator of competitive position, this matrix also identified **market growth** as an important strategic parameter. In a rapidly growing market it is easier to achieve growth for the product, in contrast to the static market situation when sales volume increases must be made at the expense of competition. Such growth also fuels the availability of cash that can be invested in the same product to improve the market share and, as economies of scale and the experience curve take effect, to improve profitability as well.

However, the additional cash generated can also be allocated to strengthening the competitive position of another product or SBU whose market share and market growth position indicate that this would be a more propitious use of funds. The structure of the growth–share matrix assists in just this type of decision, as shown in Figure 15.2. Relative competitive position is shown on the horizontal axis, measured as relative market share compared with the market leader and plotted on a logarithmic scale. Percentage market growth rate is shown on the vertical axis. SBUs shown on the figure fall into one of four quadrants formed by the matrix, each of which has a significance for the portfolio in terms of growth rate and cash generated for re-investment. The size of each SBU in terms of sales is indicated by the size of the circle.

SBUs falling within the upper left quadrant are known as **stars**, as they are market leaders and they exist in markets with high growth rates. These might be products at a relatively early stage in the product life cycle or those which have been established for some time and continue to dominate an expanding market. In either case, the product will be 'cash-hungry' to maintain investment and, particularly in the case of a relatively recent launch, could produce a net negative cash flow.

When a high-growth market becomes more established and the market growth rate falls below 10% then an SBU with a dominant market position falls into the lower left quadrant, in which case it would be called a **cash cow**. In this situation, the company provides advertising and production capacity support at a maintenance level such that there is a high positive cash flow from the product. The company is effectively 'milking' the dividends of the previously high levels of investment. These dividends can be used to finance new products which are positioned in markets with higher levels of growth.

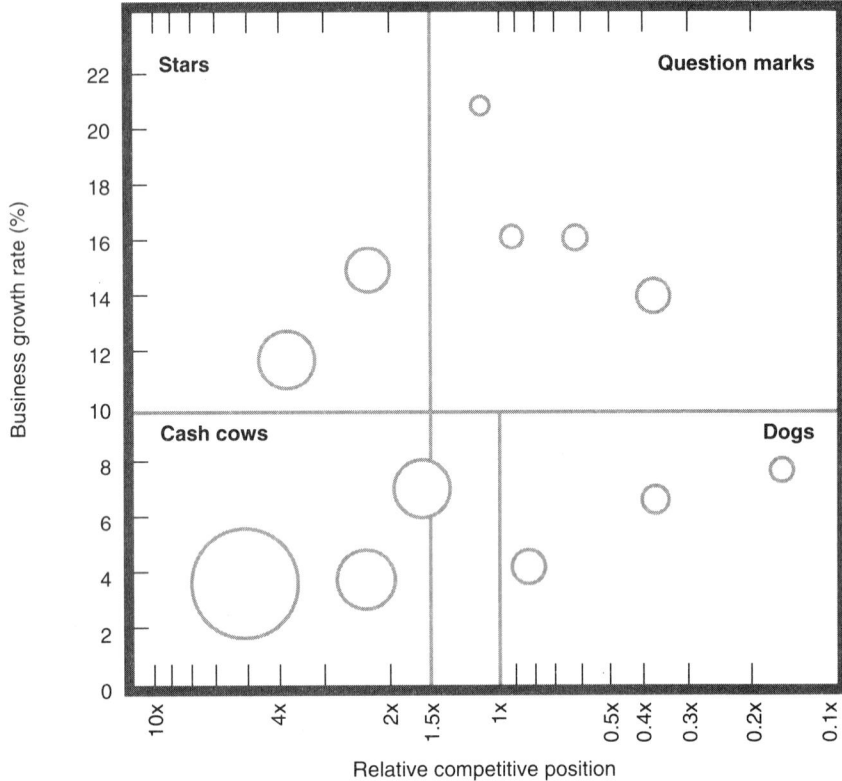

Figure 15.2 Boston Consulting Group's growth–share matrix. Reproduced from Hedley (1977).

Products or SBUs that fall in the lower right quadrant of the matrix are called **dogs,** as these are characterized by market growth rates of less than 10% and by a market share less than the major competitor. This scenario could reflect a product that was once a cash cow, but in a market that has become saturated and thus the brand has lost its dominant position through low advertising support. A dog could still be contributing positive cash flow but profitability would be low and prospects poor.

Products or SBUs in the upper right quadrant of the matrix are **question marks,** this classification reflecting the questions which an organization must ask itself about cash to be allocated. This is because the product has a low market share in a high growth market, and could be due to a recent launch with further market share attainable with continued support, or due to only modest success in a market dominated by other players. In either of these scenarios, the product is a net cash-absorber, as it will require investment to keep up with the demand created by a growing market, and a strategy of increased market share will require investment in advertising or sales effort.

In each of these four classifications, it is clear that the relative cash-generating or absorbing property of the SBU is the dominant theme for strategic decision-making, rather than sales growth as in Ansoff's matrix, and the risk/return balance of financial portfolio theory. The BCG matrix is therefore helpful in decisions related to allocation of resources for the future profitability of the total portfolio.

An initial question that an organization must face is 'how balanced is the portfolio?' Although the matrix can provide only a **static** picture of the portfolio for one year, it is a useful tool for strategic decisions, provided future market trends and competitive strengths and weaknesses can be predicted. These decisions might be:

- *Build* For question marks where higher market share can be achieved in a high growth market, and where there will be pay-off in the future.
- *Hold* For a cash cow that will continue in a strong positive cash flow position as long as its market position is protected through appropriate injection of funds and management effort.
- *Harvest* For a cash cow in a market that has poor future prospects or where short-term requirements for cash are paramount. There is the danger that, in the latter case, a cash cow becomes a dog before its time. Dogs can also be harvested if a decision has been made to allow the hastening of their eventual demise.
- *Divest* For dogs that are not providing sufficient profit to merit continuing with any management or sales support. One limitation of the matrix becomes apparent in situations where the gross margin on a dog might be high and it is contributing to overheads which would otherwise have to be allocated to other SBUs. A company should also divest itself of a question mark which will continue to be a drain on cash flow but with few prospects of becoming a major cash-contributor in the future.

Empirical evidence for differences in performance and strategic attributes between SBUs in different quadrants of the BCG matrix

Use of the BCG matrix for analysis of a business portfolio lays emphasis on relative market share and market growth rate. There is an implicit assumption that the positioning of its businesses against these two coordinates allows an organization to infer the prescriptions given above for 'remedial' action or rebalancing the portfolio in terms of cash flow performance.

Prior to empirical research on industrial companies from within the PIMS database (Hambrick *et al.*, 1982), there was no systematic evidence in existence as to whether the performance tendencies of businesses in the four cells actually warranted such prescriptions. The research which helped to fill this void covered data on 1028 businesses in the growth or maturity stages of the product life cycle. The two types of variable analysed across these businesses were **strategic attributes** and **performance**.

The strategic attributes included ratios of resource usage (such as capacity utilization and sales per employee), ratios of expense structure (such as manufacturing costs/revenue and advertising to sales ratio), working capital management and market domain. Four performance measures were used and these were: return on investment, cash flow on investment, return per risk (average ROI divided by the variability of ROI) and market share change.

Hambrick *et al.* found that the four types of business have significantly different tendencies to consume or generate cash. These tendencies were in line with the expectations of the BCG matrix for cash cows, question marks and stars, but the findings for dogs were contrary to expectations. The analysis of data for dogs included in the study indicated that they had an average net positive cash flow on investment while holding their market shares.

This finding has implications for management of business portfolios with a steadily maturing profile. Such management is naturally reluctant to divest itself of a high number of established products. Efforts would be repaid in examination of how established products can be rejuvenated on a periodic basis. This is certainly the approach taken by consumer goods' companies with brands that have existed for 30 or 40 years, where marginal changes in product and image are made to respond to contemporary needs.

General Electric's business screen

Taking the concepts of market attractiveness and business strength beyond the simple parameters of the BCG matrix requires input on a range of factors which will contribute to each of these more broadly based measures. This is the basis of General Electric's approach to portfolio analysis, and it provides a schematic representation of the relative strengths and weaknesses of a portfolio against the parameters identified by the organization as key to success (Day, 1986). These would be selected from the two alternatives shown below

Market attractiveness	**Business strength**
Market size	Relative market share
Market growth rate	Product quality
Profit margin	Brand image
Competitive intensity	Distribution strength
Economies of scale	R & D capability
Technological requirements	Unit costs

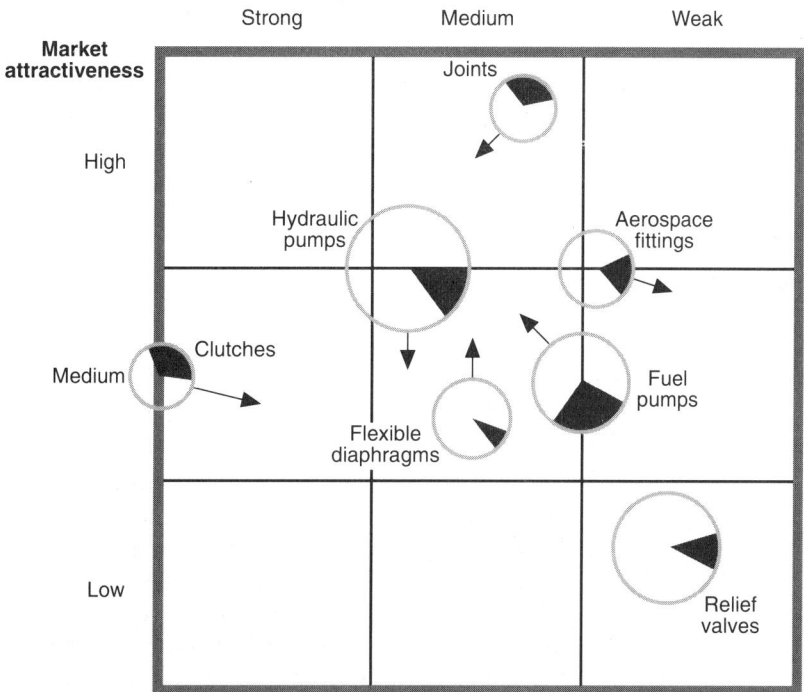

Figure 15.3 Market attractiveness – competitive position portfolio classification. *Source:* Day G.S. (1986). *Analysis for Strategic Market Decisions.* West Publishing Co.

From these, and other, factors pertinent to the two major parameters of success, a company chooses those that are most relevant to its current and future business profile, and assigns a weight to each factor, and a rating on the factor for each SBU. The value of (weight × rating) is summed across the factors for market attractiveness, and the same procedure is adopted for business strength. These two values are then plotted on a nine-cell business screen, as shown in Figure 15.3, to give a position for each SBU. The size of the circle represents industry size and the shaded slice of the pie indicates market share.

The business screen is divided into nine cells according to the strength or weakness of the SBU on industry attractiveness and business strength or competitive position. The advantage of this approach over the BCG matrix is that the position on the grid suggests certain strategies as more appropriate for the SBU than others. Thus it becomes a more immediate tool of decision-making. The strategy to be adopted tends to be clearer where the SBU score on either market attractiveness or business strength is very high or very low. The intermediate scores present situations where selective investment might be needed or divestment would be recommended, possibly at a later date.

In practice, a company might have the majority of its SBUs in these intermediate cells as in the case of a lack of attention to and investment in new products and emerging markets in previous years. This poses difficult questions in terms of where to allocate limited investment resources and which cash-generating businesses to 'kill off' through lack of future prospects. Such a dilemma points to the value of this business screen as a device for comparing current and future portfolio positions to determine the best strategies.

Strategies indicated by the GEC business screen

Each of the nine cells of the business screen is characterized by a high, medium or low score on market attractiveness (MA) or business strength (BS). Working from high to low BS, the nine strategies indicated are given below:

(1) *High MA/High BS*   It is necessary to *invest* to achieve further growth and to *protect* market position. Medium-term profits might be sacrificed to consolidate longer-term dominance of the market.

(2) *Medium MA/High BS*   *Selective* investment in the most promising sectors is indicated and a strategy to *build* on existing strengths.

(3) *Low MA/High BS*   Look for ways of *defending* market position without high-risk investment, so as to maintain good profitability. If profitability is threatened, look for rationalization.

(4) *High MA/Medium BS*   *Invest* to build on strengths, with possible challenge to the market leader if this does not involve unacceptable risk. Minimize business weaknesses.

(5) *Medium MA/Medium BS*   Concentrate investment in a *selective* way with focus on attractive market niches. Look for *low-risk* opportunities for *earnings*. Identify future vulnerabilities.

(6) *Low MA/Medium BS*   *Harvest* (optimize profits) and minimize investment. If a more attractive segment cannot be found then *restructure*, which may involve rationalization of product lines.

(7) *High MA/Low BS*   *Selective investment* in market niches is indicated and possible *acquisition* to strengthen business position. If these opportunities do not exist, then exit from the market may be desirable if earnings potential without investment is low.

(8) *Medium MA/Low BS*   Preserve *earnings* potential without significant investment. Look for the opportunity to sell while the market is attractive, or plan to rationalize.

(9) *Low MA/Low BS*   A *harvest* strategy is indicated with a view to *divestment*. Prune product line and reduce costs.

This business screen approach to strategic decisions would commonly be adopted by management at corporate level or by a specific unit whose task it is to advise senior management on forward planning for investment across the range of businesses within the portfolio, in order to meet corporate objectives.

The role of marketing management would be to identify the existing strengths in defined markets, and to project sales and profit performance by product group based on their best knowledge of future demand and competitive activity. The annual budgeting procedure may act as a trigger for the information, judgements and predictions to flow up the management hierarchy so that this input can be consolidated in a corporate planning review. Investment decisions will need to be made on a three- or five-year planning horizon, and planning tools such as the GEC business screen provide a coherent framework for pinpointing cash-generating and cash-hungry SBUs, present and future.

Armed with these comparative pictures, strategies may be adopted which are calculated to achieve corporate objectives over the planning period. Such portfolio planning tools provide **guidance** to management in determining these strategies: they should not be an end in themselves.

Margin-return model for strategic market planning

Although both the BCG growth–share matrix and the GEC business screen are tools for identifying sources of positive cash flow and the preferred areas for its future deployment, neither provides a direct yardstick of profitability. (Market share and business strength are used as surrogate measures of profitability, dependent on the PIMS findings on the relationship between market share and profits.)

The two most common goals of a 'for profit' organization are to maintain a target **net profit margin** and to provide an adequate ROI. This composite performance will be an aggregate of the varied performances of the SBUs within the portfolio. In the early 1980s an approach to business evaluation which focused on these two profit measures was proposed (Jagdish and Frazier, 1983). The basis for this model is whether or not a firm reaches targeted levels on both its net profit margin and ROI. The division of the model into four quadrants reflecting the success or failure of a business to meet these two targets is illustrated in Table 15.1.

The proponents of the model admit that there is a lack of specification of a time-scale for the targets to be met. Current one-year targets would be inadequate as these will fluctuate dependent on the position of major products within their life cycles, with the attendant cash flow and investment considerations. The setting of an average target over several years would appear to be more appropriate, as this would allow for variations in investment requirement (in both plant and marketing) and cost of capital per unit of sales generated.

Table 15.1   The margin-return model.

| | | Targeted return | |
		Satisfactory	Unsatisfactory

		Quadrant 1
		(1) *Marketing Entrenchment*
		    (a) Share protection strategy
		    (b) Repositioning strategy
			Quadrant 2
			(1) *Volume Improvement*
			    (a) Sales stimulation strategy
			    (b) System selling strategy

Satisfactory		(2) *Market Expansion*
		    (a) Multinational strategy
		    (b) Full-line strategy
			(2) *Capital Restructuring*
			    (a) Distribution productivity strategy
			    (b) Reseller alignment strategy

Targeted margin		**Quadrant 3**
		(1) *Margin Improvement*
		    (a) Repricing strategy
		    (b) Cost control strategy
			Quadrant 4
			(1) *Corporate Retrenchment*
			    (a) Overhead reduction strategy
			    (b) Reorganization strategy

Unsatisfactory		(2) *Product Improvement*
		    (a) Migration strategy
		    (b) Vertical integration strategy
			(2) *Corporate Restructuring*
			    (a) Divestment strategy
			    (b) Diversification strategy

Source: Jagdish and Frazier (1983).

The two functional management areas most affected by the strategies suggested in quadrants 1, 2 and 3 of the model are marketing and finance. It is the ability of managers in these disciplines to work together in seeking the best strategic options and to cooperate in their implementation that will determine whether there is a shift in margin and ROI performance. There will be some involvement of production and logistics management in co-determination of strategic options, for example when repositioning requires technological and production changes, or when a new intermediary specifies delivery and service criteria different from current practice.

Strategies proposed in quadrant 4 have wider implications for all functional management including human resource planning, as decisions relating to divestment or reorganization will be made at corporate level, with implementation delegated to business managers who will, in turn, rely on departmental support. The matrix management approach (functional management at corporate level and line management within the SBU) will make this a complex process, and different vested interests might render such changes nigh on impossible.

Looking in detail at the implications of strategies in quadrants 1, 2 and 3 for marketing activity and investment, the options shown in Table 15.2 emerge.

The margin-return model places strategic marketing decisions in the wider context of corporate financial performance. There is a balance set between short-term and long-term objectives through the options indicated in the four quadrants, and the link between marketing decisions and financial performance forces management to assess resources and functions in a multidisciplinary manner.

Table 15.2 Strategy options for marketing activity and investment under the margin-return model.

	Marketing activity	Investment
Quadrant 1	Reinforce brand position *or* Relaunch with product improvement *or* Expand into new geographical markets	Maintain advertising *or* Invest in new plant and advertising
Quadrant 2	Expand brand franchise *or* Delegate sales growth to distributor or licensee	Increase spend on advertising *or* Reassess if lower investment is preferable
Quadrant 3	Look for increased margin through cost reduction, or higher added value to give higher price	Invest only if stage in life cycle indicates adequate return

Corporate uses of portfolio planning

In the early 1980s academic and business interest in the application of portfolio theory was at its height. Amid the rhetoric and hyperbole, research was carried out to identify how far objective, analytical portfolio planning was used to strengthen the corporate decision-making process. Sponsored by the *Harvard Business Review*, Fortune '1000' industrials were surveyed (Haspeslagh, 1982).

The research found that 75% of organizations were practising portfolio planning at the corporate level, but only 14% of companies had reached the more advanced 'process' stage. Most companies considered that each SBU was a portfolio in itself and the more experienced companies were likely to treat the portfolio planning exercise as a multi-level operation. There was also evidence to indicate that companies practising portfolio planning separated the strategic planning review from the financial review, but that the process shifts emphasis from short-term profit and sales objectives to longer-term profit and sales targets and competitive analysis.

Comparison of portfolio planning models

A variety of alternative approaches to strategic planning models, where a number of products or SBUs are involved, have been explored. The complexity of some of these models means that the student of portfolio planning may find it difficult to:

(1) Compare the relative merits of the five models;
(2) Decide on the most appropriate to use for a specific stage in an organization's reappraisal or development.

For a straightforward assessment of the relative advantages and disadvantages of the five models, Table 15.3 provides this in summary form. It also highlights the parameters used for assessing the performance of SBUs within the portfolio.

Financial portfolio theory has been included in Table 15.3 to show how far the other models have moved from this initial concept of identifying the most 'efficient' portfolio of equities, based on the balance between the return that an investor deems acceptable and the risk that is acceptable to achieve this return.

The concept of risk is inherent within Ansoff's product/market matrix, but this has to be assessed by the user when pinpointing the quadrant in which there are opportunities for sales and profit growth. The market penetration strategy would represent the 'least risk' option for most organizations, unless a new, multimillion pound television campaign was necessary. Conversely, diversification would represent the 'greatest risk' option for most organizations unless, like the Hanson Trust, this was the nature of their business in order to achieve corporate financial goals.

Both the BCG matrix and the GEC business screen are constructed on the basis that relative business strength and market attractiveness are two performance parameters which can identify the position of a single SBU relative to others in the portfolio, with a prognosis on relative cash flow. The BCG matrix uses simple versions of these performance parameters – relative market share and percentage market growth rate. The GEC business screen goes further in the direction of devising composite performance parameters which are more suited to corporate needs. This latter approach requires more effort in identifying and computing the performance measures, but this is rewarded with a greater specificity of the strategic direction indicated for each SBU, and for the portfolio as a total entity.

The margin-return model moves further in the direction of financial performance parameters, with a grid formed by the two most common targets for a profit-making organization: net profit margin and return on investment. The position of the product or SBU in the grid indicates the strategy to be adopted for investment and marketing activity, and the latter is automatically set in the context of the broader view of corporate financial performance.

With regard to the choice of portfolio planning model, this will depend on:

(1) *The type of organization* The breadth and depth of products and the degree to which it is market- or finance-led.

Table 15.3 Comparison of portfolio planning models: performance parameters, advantages and disadvantages.

Portfolio planning model	Parameters for assessing SBUs	Advantages	Disadvantages
Financial Portfolio Theory (Markowitz, 1952)	Risk and return	Identifies the most efficient portfolio.	Needs modification for decisions relating to products or SBUs.
Ansoff's Product/Market Matrix (Ansoff, 1957)	Sales and profit growth from one of: (1) Market penetration (2) Market development (3) Product development (4) Diversification	Pinpoints the strategy and level of risk according to quadrant.	(1) Does not provide tool of quantification. (2) Does not indicate limits to resource allocation or rewards.
Boston Consulting Group Matrix (Hedley, 1977)	Grid formed by: Relative market share and % market growth rate. SHOWS RELATIVE CASH FLOW	Identifies alternative strategy for each quadrant: (1) Build (2) Hold (3) Harvest (4) Divest.	Is a snapshot at one point in time: need to compare with grid using forecasts for market and product performance.
General Electric Company Business Screen (Day, 1986)	Grid formed by: (1) Composite measure of market attractiveness (such as market size, growth, competitiveness, profit, technology) (2) Composite measure of business strength (such as market share, brand image, R & D and unit costs). SHOWS RELATIVE CASH FLOW	(1) Parameters more specific to corporate needs. (2) Identifies different strategies for nine cells.	(1) More complex of success parameters. (2) Danger of such an analysis becoming an end in itself.
Margin-Return Model (Jagdish and Frazier, 1983)	Grid formed by: Net profit margin and return on investment (ROI)	Marketing activity and investment type identified for each of four quadrants.	Lack of specification of time-scale for financial targets.

(2) *The stage of development of the organization* If it is a small company with relatively few products (or a great many products to provide an importing or retail assortment), highly sophisticated portfolio planning may *not* be appropriate. (The author has witnessed a student attempting to apply the BCG matrix to a company with a turnover of £3 million, importing and selling 300 different lines in a market where their total share was less than one per cent. Tutor guidance early on would have saved a lot of wasted effort.) In this situation, a disciplined approach to market and financial analysis will indicate the strategy to be adopted.

(3) *The availability of data for the performance parameters* This will be less problematic in the area of internal data, but for industrial and business-to-business markets, figures for size, growth and competitive

shares of markets are often a function of informed estimates based on salesforce intelligence rather than industry audits, and this will limit the value of such techniques as the BCG matrix and the GEC business screen.

As a general comment, it is important that a sense of proportion is maintained about the management time and specialist effort that such strategic tools require, balanced against the benefits that they can bring to the strategic decision-making process. The word **'process'** is critical in that there are keys steps to be taken:

(1) Identify the level of SBU for analysis (are discrete data available?).
(2) Choose the most appropriate performance parameters and, therefore, the most suitable matrix.
(3) Gather and analyse the data.
(4) Construct the matrix.
(5) Make decisions on strategic direction, as a result of evaluation of the matrix. (This may involve constructing a matrix to represent the future based on forecasts, and comparing with that for the present.)
(6) Convert strategic decisions into operational plans.

Companies that stop at step (4) can be accused of making portfolio analysis an end in itself rather than using it as an aid in strategic decision-making. Organizations that show management commitment to step (5), but which have not paid attention to organizational structure and lines of communication, are often unable to implement step (6) effectively, and are then in danger of under-achievement against the strategic plan.

European perspective

The general aim of portfolio planning – reducing risk and optimizing return in the medium to longer term – takes on specific dimensions when viewed in the context of Europe as a single market. A corporation will be seeking to enter new markets or consolidate existing market strengths, basing decisions on:

- growth potential
- risk from factors outside corporate influence
- profitability / return on capital

Taking the **Ansoff product/market expansion grid** explored in the main section of the chapter, the potential 'market' route for growth includes a geographical interpretation. The objective of the Single European Act (1987) is to provide for the free movement of people, goods and money across the borders of the 12 Member States. The question that arises for portfolio planning purposes is whether 'the market' should be defined in terms of a single Europe, or whether each Member State constitutes a separate market.

By the end of 1992, considerable progress had been made towards removal of barriers to the movement of people and goods between Member States. However, very little headway was apparent in fiscal harmonization. Allowing the European Commission greater powers over taxation and management of national budgets appeared to be a diminution of national sovereignty that some governments would not tolerate. This factor has a significant bearing on whether company resources are allocated to 'Europe' or to a Member State, in the portfolio planning process. This is because there is unlikely to be convergence in either **risk** or **return** across Member States.

To identify the reasons for this state of affairs, the issues are explored under three headings:

(1)   Corporate decisions on *where* to operate;
(2)   Corporate decisions on *how* to operate;
(3)   The likelihood of achieving economies of scale.

The section concludes with an analysis of how the prospect of a single European market acts as a magnet for outside investment, notably from the USA and Japan.

Corporate decisions on where to operate

In the first analysis, a company will be looking at the prospects for its products and services in a given geographical territory, based on buyer needs, level of competition and feasibility of distribution. A strong case for investment will then rest on the potential for an attractive return on investment compared with other strategic options. This will depend on five budgetary components of operating in a market over a given time period:

(1)   *Sales volume*   This will be influenced by disposable income, living standards and aspirations of the population. **Personal taxation** is one mechanism for the redistribution of wealth which will affect discretionary spending. There are no moves for direct personal taxes to be harmonized across the EC.

(2)   *Price*   There are moves towards convergence here. EC judgements on unlawful price discrimination together with Member States moving towards an agreed minimum rate of VAT of 15% have the effect of making differential pricing across borders more difficult to justify. However, the manpower resources of the Commission would not

permit scrutiny of pricing in every product or service sector, and there will be heavy reliance on pricing complaints made to the Commission.

(3)   *Costs*   This is the financial component where convergence is more complex and most elusive. It includes areas such as labour rates, productivity, social payments, factory and office rental, and local business taxes, which are all subject to conditions within each Member State. Raw material and component costs will respond to buying power across the enlarged market as more companies adjust to the new freedoms in movement of goods since 1 January 1993.

(4)   *Profit*   This is a function of varying costs across Member States, and is also dependent on levels of corporation tax.

(5)   *Investment*   Levels of investment vary with national business culture, interest rates and tax incentives for corporate investment in specific industries or geographical regions. Government **subsidies** can influence investment decisions by the private sector, but most transparent forms of government subsidy have been ruled out by the European Commission as undermining the principle of free competition in an open market.

The European 'supply and demand' equation

The brief summary of the influences on the five budgetary components of operating in a Member State reveals that the European Commission has made greater progress towards harmonization in the fiscal areas affecting consumption than it has in the fiscal areas affecting supply. If the European market is viewed in terms of a 'supply' and 'demand' equation involving companies and individuals, then there is an imbalance in the legislation which distorts the operation of a truly open market.

The Single European Act (1987) changed the provisions of Article 99 of the Treaty of Rome:

'The Council shall ... adopt provisions for the harmonisation of legislation concerning turnover taxes, excise duties, and other forms of indirect taxes to the extent that such harmonisation is necessary to ensure the establishment and functioning of the internal market...'

The focus on **indirect taxes** affects demand for goods and services through the price mechanism. However, the lack of legislation to harmonize direct taxation means that the concept of a level playing field is frustrated through differences between Member States in:

- corporation tax
- personal direct taxation
- social charges on corporations
- local business taxes

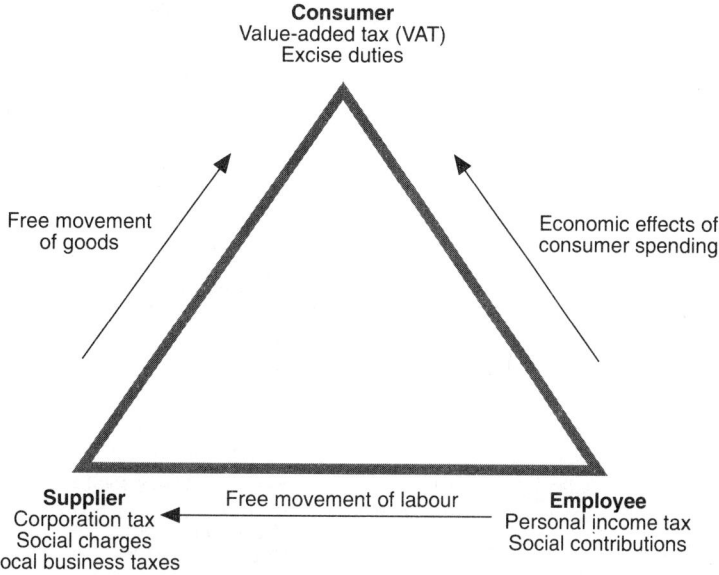

Figure 15.4 Supply and demand factors affecting the achievement of a 'level playing field' for markets in Europe.

The way in which these interact with the European 'supply' and 'demand' equation is illustrated in Figure 15.4.

Dealing first with the 'demand' side of the equation, there was formal ratification by the Council of Ministers of a minimum **value-added tax (VAT)** rate of 15% in July 1992. By this stage, Member States were broadly in line, with German and Spanish rates needing to rise to meet this requirement. Allowance was also made for the UK to keep the zero rate on food, transport and children's clothes.

The principle of reduced VAT rates applies to 20 items, and application of the reduced rate is discretionary, decided on economic, health, social or demographic grounds. Up to two reduced rates are legal, but these must not be less than 5%. There is no upper limit to VAT rates, and many Member States apply higher rates to luxury goods. Decisions here will be based on the need for tax revenue and consideration of market mechanisms (the potential for cross-border shopping in particular). A summary of VAT rates across Member States is provided in Table 15.4.

The prospect of significant cross-border sales also raises the issue of what level of VAT to charge the customer from another Member State. If a business in the UK charges 17.5% VAT to a home customer, should it not also charge 17.5% to a French or German customer? The loss of sovereignty in determining tax rates inherent in this question has led the Commission to defer a decision on this until 1997.

Table 15.4   Rates of value-added tax across EC Member States.

EC Member State	Rates of value-added tax (VAT)[†]
Belgium	Reduced rates: 6%, 12% Standard rate: 19.5% Luxury rate: 25% + 8
Denmark	Standard rate: 25%
France	Reduced rate: 5.5% Standard rate: 18.6% Luxury rate: 22% (restricted application)
Germany	Reduced rate: 7% Standard rate: 15%
Greece	Reduced rate: 8 per cent Standard rate: 18% Luxury rate: 36%
Ireland	Zero rate: books, food and drink, medicines, children's clothes Reduced rate: 16% Standard rate: 21%
Italy	Reduced rates: 4%, 9% Standard rate: 19% Luxury rate: 38%
Luxembourg	Reduced rates: 3%, 6% Standard rate: 15%
Netherlands	Reduced rate: 6% Standard rate: 18.5%
Portugal	Zero rate: food, pharmaceuticals, books Reduced rate: 8% Standard rate: 16% Luxury rate: 30%
Spain	Standard rate: 13%
UK	Zero rate: food, books, medicines, children's clothes Standard rate: 17.5%

[†] Rates apply as at 30 June 1993; Reduced rates generally apply to necessities assessed on social or economic grounds.
Sources: Ernst and Young (1991); Croner (1992).

Excise duties continue to differ across Member States. These are charged on tobacco, alcoholic drinks and mineral oils. The considerable contributions that these make to national tax coffers makes debate on convergence of rates a sensitive issue. Where the exports of wines are important to the French and Italian economies, imposition of high excise duties by other Member States is an effective barrier to a free market. Similarly, high excise duties on spirit imports is particularly damaging to free trade in Scotch whisky. Member States are free to increase excise duties or to add new ones, so long as they do not institute border controls to collect them.

The divergence in the rates of **personal taxation** across Member States has the effect of creating an unequal playing field in reducing **personal disposable income**, thus affecting market potential on the 'demand' side of the equation. The levels of personal taxation across the Community will also help to determine corporate location, based on the importance of attracting high-calibre employees. Euro-employees with language capabilities and the desire to work in several locations through their careers will also wish to preserve a consistent standard of living when relocating within Europe.

Social payments by companies towards employee welfare can be considered as another form of direct taxation. Figures available in 1990 showed that in France, these payments accounted for 12.1% of gross national product (GNP). Comparable figures were 7.2% in Germany, 3.6% in Great Britain and 7.7% in Italy (Delachaux, 1990). Divergence between these figures illustrates the difficulty in gaining agreement across all Member States to the Social Chapter laid before the Council of Ministers in 1992.

Special levies on businesses decided at local level within each Member State can contribute to regional infrastructure (such as the UK general business rate) or to industry training (as in Germany). Where these additional levies represent a significant percentage of turnover, a company may be deterred from legal and operational presence in a Member State.

Corporate decisions on how to operate

The strategic options open to a company for entry to markets in other Member States are explored in the European perspective to Chapter 3. Where a company chooses to export to another Member State directly through operations at the head office, or where an agent in the export market administers sales, liability under company law of the Member State representing the export market is minimized. However, laws on product liability could be enforced against a principal.

As soon as a company opens an office for the furtherance of business in a Member State, it will be liable to meet the requirements of company law there. It could take the form of a branch office, a subsidiary or the registered headquarters. Each EC member country has its own very specific legal requirements, so adding to the complexity of business operations at the European level.

The proposal for a European company statute (Societas Europa) met with considerable opposition and little progress has been made towards this. There have been 12 EC Directives relating to company law, and the subjects to which these Directives relate are summarized in Table 15.5.

Table 15.5   EC Directives on company law

Date of adoption	Subject of legislation
1968 1st Directive	Compulsory disclosure of information in readily accessible form, including name, address, directors, share capital and balance sheet, and profit and loss account.
1976 2nd Directive	Relates to formation of limited liability companies and to the maintenance, increase and reduction of capital in order to 'ensure minimum equivalent protection for both shareholders and creditors'.
1978 3rd Directive (implemented 1986)	Regulations for asset mergers at national level of public companies by **acquisition** and by the formation of a new company (precursor of 10th Directive).
1978 4th Directive (implemented 1987)	Presentation and content of annual accounts of individual companies, and valuation of assets and liabilities (research by the Scottish Accounting Standards Council indicates inoperability because of cultural influence on what is a 'true and fair view').
1972 5th Draft Directive (amended Directive 1983, 1988)	(1) Imposes a distinction between the members of the Board of Directors of public companies responsible for **management** and those responsible for **supervision** by introduction of two-tier boards. (2) Requirement for employee participation in the running of companies with more that 1000 employees.
1982 6th Directive (implemented 1986)	Relates to provisions for division or demerger of public companies, and to protection of rights and interests of employees and creditors.
1983 7th Directive (implemented 1987)	Coordination of requirements for preparation of consolidated accounts, including where one company has a 20% holding in another and exercises a dominant influence over it (definition of a **subsidiary**).
1984 8th Directive (implemented 1988)	Minimum standards for qualifications of auditors to declare that accounts are a 'true and fair view'. Adopted in UK, Belgium, Luxembourg, Germany, France, Greece, Portugal and Spain.
1985 Intended 9th Directive (formal proposal scheduled for end-1990 did not materialize)	Seeks to formalize the legal relationship between undertakings within a group that includes a public company, which are subject to unified controls by a single undertaking or managed collectively as a single entity.
1985 10th Draft Directive	Extends procedures for **mergers** and divisions (3rd and 6th Directives) to cross-border mergers by public companies.
1989 11th Directive (implemented 1 Jan 1993)	To place **branches** of foreign incorporated companies in the same position as regards disclosure and related requirements imposed on a locally incorporated subsidiary (by the 1st, 4th, 7th and 8th Directives).
1989 12th Directive (1 Jan 1992)	Relates to single-member private limited liability companies.
1989 13th Directive (amended 1991)	Proposal for a Directive on involvement of employees in management of the European company.

Sources: Croner (1992); UACES Conference on Corporate Strategy in the EC, December 1991.

There have been two cases taken to the European Court of Justice, and this court acknowledged only limited legal effect for one of these Directives.

One of the most contentious areas for harmonization of company law is the legal right for worker participation in decision-making. In a number of Member States – notably Germany – this is built into company law, with four types of worker participation. The Fifth Directive on company law related to employee participation in public companies employing more than 1000 employees, and this met with considerable opposition from the UK.

Any move towards a European company would meet with divergent views on the issue of worker participation. An alternative proposed is the European Economic Interest Grouping (EEIG), which is a hybrid between a partnership and a company. The EEIG would carry unlimited liability, but would take on a separate, legal identity from the partners or directors. It would *not* be formed with the profit motive, but for the purpose of cooperation across borders – such as to organize procurement. There were fears that the EEIG would be used to avoid employee representation, so a maximum number of employees was set at 500. The EEIG would *not* be exempt from EC competition rules.

A recent EC proposal for a European company statute included registration in one Member State, in which case the rest of company law would be derived from that Member State. This approach does not solve the problem of differences across borders, and the incentive remains for choosing a location where company law is least restrictive. This works against the spirit of the Single European Act.

The likelihood of achieving economies of scale

High market share is linked with high return on investment, and the prospect of penetrating several Member States with a standard product creates the opportunity for economies of scale, as barriers come down. Although this is put forward as one of the prime objectives of the open market (Cecchini Report, 1988), there is no guarantee that this will be the outcome for a range of industries.

For sectors specifically excluded from EC law on procurement until 1993 (telecommunications, transport, energy, and water supply), economies of scale have been achieved at national level through public or private monopoly. There is no immediate prospect of higher margins through economies of scale at the European level for these industries, or their suppliers.

In industries where barriers are starting to fall, increased competition means the elimination of some players, with economies of scale accruing to the survivors. In some chemical industries, closure of inefficient plant is the only route to survival, providing growth opportunities to companies which have invested in technology.

In the **financial services** sector, there are several reasons why economies of scale may not be achieved with an open market. This will affect investment decisions:

- In the wholesale sector, it is likely that any economies of scale have already been exploited, so that the events of 1992 are not significant (Dale, 1990).
- Differing consumer needs as a result of culture means that the retail banking sector cannot necessarily offer the same product with the same advertising and delivery format. This reduces the opportunity for scale economies.
- There is evidence that the regional banks in what was West Germany have fewer employees per dollar of deposit, and much higher profits per employee than their national counterparts. This suggests that economies of scale are achieved at a level below that of the top Community banks (Davis and Smales, 1989).
- A low-risk option for expansion across borders is for an insurance company, for example, to sell specific services in another Member State through a bank already established there. The return is then diluted through payment of commission and administration costs.

The type of alliance illustrated through this fourth point shows that typical routes for increased market share and higher return might be sacrificed for more innovative relationships between providers in different Member States.

The open European market as a magnet for investment

The flow of investment from the USA and Japan into Member States during the 1980s is evidence of the potential seen for return from the barrier-free market. However, US multinationals such as Ford and IBM were conquering European markets long before the benefits of 1992 became apparent. This took place through investment in production capacity within the Continent, to achieve market penetration.

A different picture emerges when US indirect investment in European markets (through foreign securities) is analysed. In 1990, American pension funds and life insurers each held only 4% of their portfolios in foreign assets. Among individual investors, international diversification is even lower (Turner, 1991). Despite an apparent free-market philosophy, US controls on capital outflow are highly effective. Retail banks are reluctant to allow individuals to hold foreign currency, and marketing restrictions imposed by the Securities and Exchange Commission make it illegal for American citizens to invest in most offshore equities, bonds and investment funds. The focus on direct market investment by corporations means a flow of profits back to the United States with consolidated returns in dollars.

Japanese corporations have also taken the direct investment route for European market penetration in such sectors as motor vehicles and consumer electronics. However, the picture for indirect investment is more positive. Life insurance portfolios have increased their foreign securities element from 9% in 1980 to 32% in 1990, although dollar assets tend to dominate.

The concept of a single capital market for Europe should be turned into reality by the abolition of all restrictions on movement of funds across borders. However, the reality of a single capital market is more elusive. In the period 1965–86, there was distinct correlation between investment rates and savings rates across Britain, Belgium, West Germany and France (within a study of eight countries in total). If there was a free capital market, there should be no connection between the two, as was the case for the period 1880–1913 when exchange rates were fixed to the gold standard (Economist, 1989).

An explanation is put forward for the lack of mobility of capital across borders on three grounds (Bayoumi, 1989):

- government intervention to redress the balance between savings and investment;
- the higher risk attached to foreign investment because of lack of information about foreign borrowers and lenders;
- uncertainty over currencies.

An alternative to raising finance in one European currency with the risks attached is the use of the ECU, the European unit of currency. The ECU is based on a basket of 12 currencies and, accordingly, there is less risk of large value fluctuations. One source of the ECU has been the Eurobond market. The European Investment Bank has used the ECU as its balance sheet currency since 1981. ECU bond issues increased nearly fourfold between 1987 and 1991, with General Motors, IBM, General Electric and Toyota as the largest corporate issuers in this period (Constandse, 1991). The major barriers to corporations making greater use of the ECU as a working currency are national accounting standards and tax laws requiring payment in the domestic currency.

Problems and assignments

(1) How useful do you consider the tools of financial portfolio theory to be in making investment/divestment decisions of a company's own strategic business units?

(2) Critically assess the utility of the Boston Consulting Group's growth–share matrix as applied in today's commercial environment.

(3) Summarize the strengths and weaknesses of the margin-return model. What advantages does it have over BCG and/or Ansoff?

(4) As a marketing manager within a strategic business unit and overseeing several brand managers, which models might you choose to operationalize to examine the long-term aspects of your marketing plan?

(5) You have been seconded by the CEO of an international pharmaceuticals company to conduct some form of portfolio analysis to provide commensurate strategic recommendations. Your first task is to decide at what level to discriminate, e.g. product, brand or SBU. Write a brief report to the CEO explaining your decision on this important issue.

(6) Continuing the task set in (5), write an interim report to the CEO rationalizing why you have elected to focus on using the GEC business screen model and how you intend operationalizing it.

(7) All models take account of the 'market'. In theory the EC is now a single market. Again using your work for the pharmaceuticals company, which definition of the market are you going to use and why?

(8) What are the implications for companies trading across European borders of divergent rates of VAT levied across different product categories? How important is it for national governments to realize greater convergence?

References

Ansoff I. (1957). Strategies for diversification. *Harvard Business Review*, September/October, 113–124

Ansoff H.I. and Leontiades J. (1976). Strategic portfolio management. *J. of Management*, **4**(1), 13–29

Cardozo R.N. and Smith Jr D.K. (1983). Applying financial portfolio decisions: an empirical study. *J. of Marketing*. **47**, Spring, 100–119

Day G.S. (1986). *Analysis for Strategic Marketing Decisions*. London: West Publishing

Hambrick D.C., MacMillan I.C. and Day D.L. (1982). Strategic attributes and performance in the BCG matrix: a PIMS-based analysis of industrial product performance. *Academy of Management*, **25**(3), 510–531

Haspeslagh P. (1982). Portfolio planning: uses and limits. *Harvard Business Review*, January/February, 58–73

Hedley B. (1976). A fundamental approach to strategy development. *Long Range Planning*, **9**(6)

Hedley B. (1977). Boston Consulting Group approach to business portfolio. *Long Range Planning*, **10**(1)

Jagdish N.S. and Frazier G.L. (1983). A margin-return model for strategic market planning. *J. of Marketing*, **47**, Spring, 100–108

Kiechel III W. (1981). The decline of the experience curve. *Fortune*, 5 October

Markowitz H. (1952). Portfolio selection. *J. of Finance*, **7**, March

Schoeffler S., Buzzell R.D. and Heaney D.F. (1974). Impact of strategic planning on profit performance. *Harvard Business Review*. March/April, 137–145

European perspective

Bayoumi T. (1989). *Saving-Investment Correlations*. IMF Working Paper, 89/66, August

Constandse A. (1991). Raising finance using the ECU. *The Treasurer*, **13**(8), 49–52

Croner (1992). *Croner's Europe* Update No. 44, May

Dale R. (1990). The future evolution of financial markets in Europe. *The Royal Bank of Scotland Review*, No. 165, March, 3–15

Davis and Smales (1989). *Integration of European Financial Services 1992 – Myths and Realities*. London Business School: Centre for Business Strategy, pp 104–115

Delachaux F. B. (1990). The effects of 1992 on European business. *Business Horizons*, **33**(1), 33–36

The Economist (1989). A Capital Mystery. 7 October

Ernst and Young (1991). *International VAT – A 21 Country Guide*. London: Kogan Page

Turner P. (1991). Capital flows in the 1980s. Bank for International Settlements. Reported in *The Times*, 13 May, p 23

16

New product development

Chapter objectives:

- to examine the demands for research and development (R & D) in the 1990s
- to understand the various reasons for new product development (NPD)
- to understand the inherent risk involved with NPD
- to look at the different sources of innovation

Introduction

A company must respond to change for survival, but it must make commitment to the products of the future to ensure longer-term success. This means investment in research and development, with inherent risk of inadequate pay-back if the product does not perform to expectation. There are, therefore, conflicting demands on management.

Companies will respond to pressure from shareholders, evident through the share price mechanism, by developing a strategy for growth in sales and profits. Alternative strategies have already been explored for the single product (Chapter 3) and for a portfolio of products or strategic business units (Chapter 15). One option open to management is the route of organic growth through the fullest exploitation of existing product ranges, with the addition of new products that are the best fit with existing business in terms of capitalizing on technological, distribution and image strengths. These new products are necessary to replace declining sales in mature markets as well as providing the seedbed of growth.

The speed of technological breakthrough in many market areas and the ease with which competitors can imitate innovations that cannot be patented means that the company planning such organic growth must devote considerable resources to the quest for, and development of, new product ideas a long time in advance of possible launch onto the market. This way, they are striving for continuous competitive edge, but there is the attendant risk of some of these ideas not materializing in the form of a marketable product, and the expenditure must be written off against the **research and development** budget.

Organizations such as 3M adopt a common approach across divisions to the evaluation of new ideas and subsequent development of those with market potential. More than 25% of sales each year are from products introduced within the last five years. This is achieved through financial commitment to research and development.

This commitment to new product development must be made in the context of national economic conditions and, for multinationals, the relative economic performances of the countries in which they operate will be taken into account. In what currency will the investment be made, and the profits taken? Should new technology be transferred to subsidiaries or held in the country of origin to maximize exports? Is a licence agreement with another company the best way of exploiting distribution strength? These are some of the strategic questions which have to be addressed at an early stage of a new commercial venture.

The average rate of return on capital in OECD countries was 16% for the period 1980 to 1986. This average figure disguises a wide range across individual countries – 17% for USA, 9% for UK, 12% for Germany and 14% for Japan. The reasons for these wide variations include differences in the contributions from the manufacturing and service sectors, the cost of capital (interest on loans), and the level of investment in new technology. The ways in which individual governments give subsidies and tax incentives to stimulate spending on research and development will influence commitment to investment by the private sector. In the USA over 30% of business enterprise research and development was financed by the government in 1987, compared with only 2% in Japan and 19% in the UK. The higher figures in the USA and the UK include a large element of defence research, which would then feed into export potential for armaments, missile guidance systems and communications.

Although the level of direct government financing of research and development appears low in Japan, the supportive infrastructure built around MITI encourages corporations to commit a higher percentage of profits to investment in new technology than is apparent in other OECD countries. This investment is primarily aimed at producing better and less costly versions of existing technology – in other words, applied research, whereas other nations will be striving to break new scientific or technological ground. Examples of this Japanese approach are evident in the success of the Sony Walkman and the global market leadership of Japanese companies in hi-fi and television.

Although the strategies for success might differ at national industry, corporate or product level, the reasons for pursuing new product development are invariably similar. For the purpose of this chapter, **new product development** will be defined as the creation of a new product form, entity or service which satisfies the needs of an existing or new market, and which involves the organization in a new manufacturing process, sourcing from different suppliers, or different marketing and distribution activities. This definition identifies a significant level of risk which is not so marked for **product improvement** or **product adaptation**. For these latter areas, the risk of failure is generally reduced through experience of the market and less investment in new plant than would be the case for a totally new product.

Reasons for new product development

The predominant reasons for companies to become actively involved in new product development are:

(1) To maintain market leadership or market share through maintaining technological, usership or cost edge over the competition. A position of dominant market share ensures the economies of scale which protect contribution to overheads and profit at a higher level than the competition is able to achieve. This is one insurance policy for future survival and success, as the higher profits can release further development funds.

(2) To safeguard margins through improved process technology and lower product cost when competitive pressure in a near-saturated market prevents price rises in line with otherwise rising costs.

(3) To provide for revenue and profit growth by increased penetration of current markets by serving the needs of new customers with more advanced products in existing areas of expertise, or by launching into totally new markets. This route of organic growth requires commitment to expenditure on research and development in the longer term, with controls necessary in the process to minimize financial risk.

(4) To optimize use of resources, such as production capacity, research expertise, distribution strength or information processing capability. The addition of new products or, increasingly, services (as in the finance sector) that an organization is able to provide will improve the revenue base over which the fixed costs can be absorbed.

(5) To improve return on investment. This objective is linked with longer-term planning for strategic growth. This outlook is difficult to

maintain when the economic climate is subject to sharp changes (such as the increase in bank rate from 8% to 15% over a period of 18 months in the UK). This type of environmental discontinuity leads to contraction in demand and higher cost of financing debt incurred for the purpose of development and launch of new products. The ultimate result is increased financial risk with a negative effect on return on investment.

The risk–reward relationship in new product development

During the 1980s it became increasingly difficult to launch a product which was demonstrably different from the competition and which could build and hold market share over an extended period. One reason for this is the high standard of living enjoyed by developed nations such that many of the markets which traditionally acted as 'hosts' to new products – repeat-purchase consumer goods and consumer durables – no longer enjoyed the high growth rates of the 1960s and 1970s. This meant that establishing the rationale for new product acceptance became more difficult and more prone to **financial risk**.

In 1987, 10,182 new supermarket products were introduced in the USA. Of these, 2039 were in the health and beauty sector and 7900 in the food category. It is estimated that between 80% and 90% of these new products will fail (Kane, 1989). One suggestion put forward for failure in consumer markets is the lack of unique information which facilitates segmentation based on contemporary influences on buying motivation, including self-esteem and 'traditional' versus 'modern' values. Kane suggests that too many companies rely on historic purchase and attitude data rather than using **focus groups** to explore underlying motivation.

A key role of marketing management charged with responsibility for new product development is to weigh the potential rewards of success against the **risk** of failure. Potential rewards can be measured in traditional terms of marketing success – market share, market penetration, sales and number of customers. There will also be the traditional financial measures of success – absolute profits, gross margin, net margin, return on investment, earnings per share.

Defining and evaluating the risk attached to a new product development programme is not so straightforward. The company wishing to develop and market new products has three possible routes: new markets, new functions and new technology. One way of viewing the interrelationship of these three routes is to consider each as an orthogonal direction; a specific new product strategy would be plotted on each of the three dimensions. Along each dimension, risk increases with newness and one way of measuring risk is to apply a four-level scale along each dimension (Abetti and Stuart, 1988).

Risk assessment for the new business start-up will depend on the nature of the market, the level of investment and the sources of finance. However, for the established company with a broad portfolio of products, there will be a framework of assessment of potential rewards and risks for new product proposals. Within this framework a balance is needed between allowing new product ideas to surface within the organization (and providing a formal mechanism through which they are explored), and minimizing time and money spent on ideas that are likely to fail.

Table 16.1 Successful new products from the 1970s and 1980s.

New product	Market sector	Comment
Golden Wonder's Pot Noodles	Instant hot snacks	Only one of several brands to survive
McCain Oven Chips	'Ovenable' frozen food	Revived a static frozen food sector
RHM's Cracottes	Savoury cracker	Tasty snack or bread substitute
St Ivel's Shape	Healthy food range	Satisfied trend to healthy eating but also tastes good
Dairy Crest Clover	Spreadable dairy product	Opened up new sector for butter substitutes
Quaker Oat's Harvest Crunch	Cereal bars	Satisfied consumer need for healthy snacks
Cadbury's Wispa	Confectionery countline	Launched with military precision
IDV's Piat d'Or	Mass appeal wine	Heavy TV support stimulated market
IDV's Malibu	Spirit-based drink	Aimed at the younger 'travelling' market
IDV's Bailey's Irish Cream	Pre- or after-dinner tipple	Many imitators but few survived
Grolsch	Bottled, specialist beer	Most successful of minority labels
Next retailer fashion label	Coordinated fashion wear for women aged 25–40	Rapidly followed by other fashion chains
Swatch	Low-cost fashion and leisure watches	Developed new sector
Christian Dior's Poison	Upmarket female fragrance	Massive marketing support
Giorgio	Male and female fragrances	Californian heritage no obstacle to success
L'Oreal's Freestyle	Hair-styling mousse	Capitalized on trend towards easy-care hair fashion
Shulton's Insignia	Grooming range for men	Timed to coincide with social acceptability
Filofax	Personal organizer	Created a product sector: cheap imitations followed
Crown Matchpots	Decorative paint	Satisfied consumer need for colour coordination

The success of the new product **screening process** will depend on:

(1) *When does it take place?* Should it be after concept testing or after pilot production? The former will be more critical for a new consumer product, and the latter will be a greater factor in the success of an engineering innovation for industrial customers.

(2) *Who evaluates risk?* Is it the new product development manager working in isolation or in consultation with the board of directors? Or is there a standing committee for regular appraisal of new product opportunities, combining the skills of marketing, technical and financial specialists?

(3) *How is risk evaluated?* Is it based purely on a set of objective parameters for screening projects at specific stages of development? Or is there the facility for combining these objective parameters with judgement based on a changing market environment and the evolving demands on resources within the organization?

Screening mechanisms to identify potential winners and losers among development projects are just one managerial component of the total new product development process, which is now examined in detail.

The new product development process

Sources of innovation

There is a variety of ways in which a company can obtain or create new product ideas, but there are two overriding factors if there is to be a reasonable expectation of financial return on some of these ideas. Firstly, an organization must be close to its market, and be prepared to listen to the needs of the customer. This can be achieved through primary market research or through analysing the changing demands of intermediaries or agents (particularly where export markets are concerned). Secondly, a company must be prepared to invest in the innovation process, through the time and energy of managers at every level and in the form of capital investment in manufacturing processes and in new ways of controlling the business to serve the customer in the best possible way.

Given these two commitments – to market needs and to investment – then the following can act as catalysts to development projects (see Figure 16.1).

Long-range studies

These are prevalent in markets where large sums of capital investment are needed to survive and succeed such as the civil aircraft market or pharmaceuticals. When investment in new products is measured in hundreds

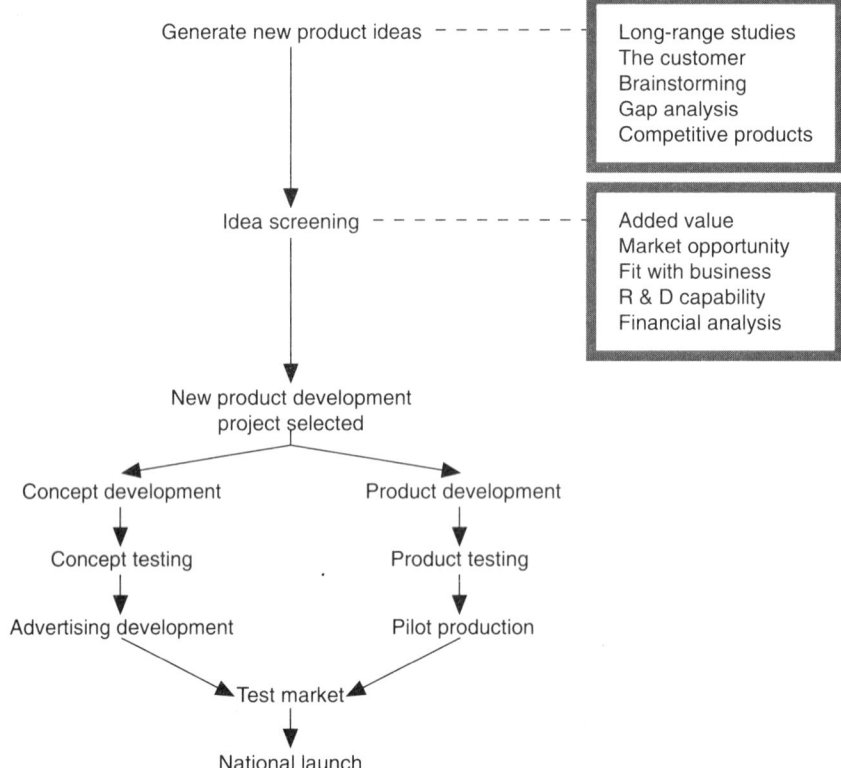

Figure 16.1 Key stages in the new product development process.

of millions of pounds rather than just millions, then the expense and labour involved in a large-scale study of potential customer needs 10 or even 20 years into the future is more than justified. With the increasing **globalization** of products at inception rather than halfway through their life, the need for research on a global scale means that major international research organizations can gain the commitment of just a few key players in a particular market in order to take on the costs of a multi-client study.

As well as cost sharing, this research approach provides data on total market trends through the aggregation of data on individual customers. This information is more willingly given to a third party on the understanding of confidentiality than to one supplier.

A second approach is the **Delphi technique** in which a panel of experts is quizzed in a structured way on their views for specific development in five, ten or twenty years' time. A panel of 25 persons is considered the absolute minimum (Parker, 1987) and panellists should be drawn from as diverse a range of industrial and cultural backgrounds as is appropriate to the task. Objectives should be clearly stated with all possible ambiguities eliminated, preferably through piloting the questionnaire. Questions should relate to customer needs and market trends as well as the environments in which these will exist, as it is invariably changes in the economic, social or technological environment which act as catalysts of changing needs.

The outcome of such a study for the individual company is a composite expert view of future market needs such that a decision can be made about the necessity or advisability of embarking on new product development to meet those needs.

The customer

In consumer markets this means a commitment to market research to understand the changing needs of the customers **as they perceive them**. Very often, such changes will be aspirational and fundamentally associated with attitudes shaped by economic, technological and social developments. Not all customers will change in the same way, and the research facility to understand newly emerging segments will provide the initiative for innovation to give competitive edge. Invariably, the key question within valuable research is not 'what will you buy?' but 'why will you buy?', however disguised this may be in a battery of attitudinal questions. The key to identifying the emerging segment is the facility for cluster analysis of responses to questions on a range of attitudinal dimensions.

For industrial markets, many innovations come from listening to the customers about unfulfilled needs or product refinements they require for their own special processes or systems. Particular attention paid to the customers who lead technology in their own markets can provide an early indicator of future needs of less adventurous (but possibly more numerous) prospective clients. A dilemma that can arise for the innovator is how much to invest in tomorrow's technology while at the same time protecting the market carved out through exploiting today's technology. Companies such as GEC and Black & Decker are committed to investing in change, but with a commercial eye to current market share.

Brainstorming

A flow of ideas around a predefined theme from a group of people with knowledge and skills associated with the markets or technology to be exploited can be one of the most productive routes for innovation. The brainstorming session should be held in a location away from the usual day-to-day pressures of business. The topic should be defined and the session led by a convenor prepared to focus the activity of the group but who will not allow the flow of ideas to be constrainted by traditional business criteria at this stage. The interactive nature of the session is a key requirememt for the cross-fertilization of ideas across disciplines and markets.

The same group might be involved in the second stage, when screening of ideas takes place according to a set of marketing, technological or financial constraints. However, the avoidance of an involuntary 'pre-screening' of ideas at the individual level is more likely if these criteria are explored by the group after the brainstorming session. An alternative approach is the screening of ideas by a multidisciplinary committee whose purpose is to identify the development projects for the future and to monitor how well they meet corporate investment criteria at successive stages before a product reaches the marketplace.

Gap analysis

This technique is associated predominantly with exploration of existing markets to see where needs are currently unfulfilled or likely not to be met in the future. Detailed information on demographic trends and future spending power, as well as investment in market research, are necessary to exploit this technique successfully. For example, the projected increase in the elderly population in many advanced industrial nations in the 1990s has led some construction companies to specialize in protected housing, and the decline in the 16–25 age group in the UK has forced fashion retailers to revise their strategies for specific chains. Companies like Boeing survey changing patterns of air travel and extrapolate findings 20 years into the future to identify the new civil aircraft needs of the major carriers.

Dissecting competitive products

The success of some companies rests on their persistent attention to product superiority, which is achieved through careful monitoring of the competition and market research into the end-user's perceptions of performance of different products. Japanese success in the hi-fi and television markets was built on use of the latest technology to provide products that were superior to American or European competition. Repeated success induced an association in the minds of consumers that 'Japanese' meant 'better', which led some British companies to give Japanese sounding brand names to home-produced television sets.

   This source of innovation spans the ill-defined divide between a totally new product and a product improvement. However, where new technology or a vastly superior way of using a product is introduced then the former description is justified, particularly where the product becomes accessible to a larger market through promotion and price, as in the case of the rapid penetration of the microwave oven in the UK and Minitel information and advertising services in France.

Learning from overseas

The differing stages of economic development across countries and continents means that ideas already showing commercial success in one area may be applied successfully in another, with or without changes to suit the local market.

Screening of new product ideas

The way in which an organization will select innovations to be pursued in order to develop the business and maintain or increase return on investment invariably reflects strategic approach. Some criteria that might be used, each attracting a specific weighting according to the perceived priorities of future performance are as follows:

- benefit of superiority compared with competition;
- meeting customer needs as identified through attribute profiling;
- identification of new market segments whose needs fall within existing technological and commercial expertise;
- degree of fit of new product concept with existing brand name strength and consumer expectation of product performance within the brand, to capitalize on existing franchise;
- value-added component of the product or process matches or exceeds that of products in the existing portfolio;
- diversification into totally new areas of activity where forecast financial return justifies the investment and risk;
- priority given to specific development areas where there is a limited financial budget for new product development, and where the time and energy of the development team needs to be focused: decisions can be made through cost/benefit analysis.

The degree of sophistication of the analytical approach used in the screening of ideas for development varies with the type of industry (Deschamps, 1989). There is traditionally greater dedication to detailed analysis of lifestyle, customer needs, perceived value and dissection of competitive products in fast-moving consumer goods and automotive product industries than in textile products and clothing and 'technical' or other consumer durables. Similarly, strategic approaches of these industry sectors follow a similar pattern, with creative segmentation, customer monitoring and systematic product improvement being more characteristic of fast-moving consumer goods and automotive products than of consumer durables. However, the link between the more analytical approach in both strategy and screening and new product success is not proven through quantitative findings, and the Japanese record of success in consumer durables would vindicate their success in analysis of market needs and provision of well-researched and targeted products.

The screening criteria above suggest a significant judgemental input from members of the development committee or team responsible for recommendations to the board of directors. There is the possibility that different criteria will be used at different levels in the management hierarchy. For example, the brief of the development committee (at middle management level and multi-disciplinary in composition) might be to focus exclusively on market needs and technological capabilities of the organization to meet those needs. Those development projects meeting the criteria at this level will then flow up to a more senior task force or a managing board for screening of proposals based on financial performance criteria, involving projected sales, profit, capital investment required, return on capital and projected cash flow.

To reduce the risk of new product proposals passing through the screening process which eventually prove to be 'failures' by the accepted corporate criteria, the more qualitative judgemental input can be translated into a scoring process similar in design to the **linear averaging** method illustrated for choice of market segment in Chapter 5. Financial risk can be translated into compatibility of the new product proposal along a range of functional dimensions – brand strength, distribution channels, research and development expertise, current production capability, investment required, skills and experience of the workforce. These dimensions are ascribed weightings (such that they total 1.0 for each product) and the product proposal is scored against each dimension. The total for 'weighting × score' against each dimension is summed to give a total rating for each new product proposal. This rating figure provides a simple benchmark of comparison of the relative merits of different new product proposals. It is a more consistent framework within which to suppress unfavourable projects and to give the green light to new product proposals with greater prospects of positive contribution to the business portfolio.

Projecting sales and profits for new products

An essential part of the screening process for new product ideas is an assessment of the contribution that the new product will make to future financial performance. The forecasting capabilities of a company will be an important determinant in the degree of analysis which can be applied to this process. For consumer products, a three or five-year projection is necessary to identify break-even point for investment versus new profits coming on-stream. In this situation, investment will be in advertising as well as plant and machinery, and the financial conventions of the organization will determine the criteria against which the projected performance will be judged.

For example, a company launching a new repeat-purchase consumer product such as a new hair-setting agent (this market grew significantly during the late 1980s) might project a sales and profit forecast for the first three years after launch. The financial conventions might dictate that advertising is considered as a current marketing cost in the year in which it occurs, although there is a heavy 'investment' in early years to achieve a significant market share by the third and fourth year. Other conventions might dictate that total investment in research and development and plant is written off over five years, and that return on capital for the product will be assessed on this basis.

One model for the **sales and profit forecast** for a new product is shown in Chapter 14 (Tables 14.3 to 14.5). It assumes that legal and administrative costs associated with the product launch are absorbed within a percentage overhead charge against sales of the product. This percentage figure might be the same as for well-established products or might be higher or lower, depending on the financial conventions of the company. Where Tables 14.3 to 14.5 show a one-year projection, this would be expanded to three or five years for a new product launch, with the profit figure moving progressively from negative or low positive to high positive across the years, as the advertising in early years pays dividends in terms of market share in the medium term.

For industrial companies, detailed information on the size and trends within a specific market is generally not available and market intelligence gleaned from customers as well as dissection of competitive products will tend to be the starting point for a new product proposal. Proven capabilities in research, technology and marketing will tend to sway decisions where definitive forecasts on the market and financial environments ten years into the future may not be realistic. The very large sums needed to compete in the technology race in some markets reduce real competition to two or three companies, certainly at the national and, increasingly, at the global level. Each company will have a clear view of its strengths and weaknesses, and the increasing trend for industry consortia to support research (as in the case of IBM and its rival AT&T supporting a research project into superconductivity at the Massachusetts Institute of Technology) reduces those risk elements associated with a company taking an independent path in areas of basic, long-term research (Reich, 1990).

Concept testing

Branded consumer products provide a 'reason to buy' over and above the mechanical performance elements common to generics. The reason why one brand will be preferred to another is that the advertised benefit matches the user's need. The changing needs of consumers may be monitored on a periodic basis to identify any quantum leaps in expectation from a product sector due to sharp changes in the social or economic environment. However, when a new product idea has been shown to have potential, it is critical that the way in which it is presented to the target audience will attract a purchase response. This 'trigger' mechanism is identified through the technique of **concept testing**. In the initial stages of a development project, most consumer goods companies would conduct exploratory concept testing through a series of **focus groups** among a broadly defined target market.

At later stages in the product and concept development process, this qualitative research approach would be replaced by a narrower range of concepts tested among a sufficiently large sample of the target group to qualify as **quantitative research**. The higher cost of this approach would be justified in the greater confidence which the findings would give management in the final choice of concept for product launch. The concepts might be tested in isolation of the product, as in the case of members of the target group being invited to give Likert scale responses to a range of concepts put forward in mock advertising form. Alternatively, the concepts might be presented with the product, and the respondent asked a range of questions about concept suitability for the product as it has been perceived to perform. The former approach gives a clear indication of the preferred benefit; the latter approach indicates how far the preferred concept and product are matched (or, in the worst case scenario, mismatched).

Each of the major consumer goods companies has a preferred protocol for taking a new product proposal through the concept testing stages. Some believe in the value of testing preferred attributes in isolation of a product, except to identify where the competition is *not* meeting the identified need. The task of the research and development team is then to produce a product that matches the preferred concept. This means avoiding the creation of **cognitive dissonance** through the gap between consumer expectation created by the advertising and the product performance.

Other companies take the view that a more realistic route is to test alternative concepts in the presence of the product so that concept and performance can interact in the same way as they would with the final branded product. The objectives for this type of research need to be clearly stated and the research methodology tightly controlled, as the number of variables is inevitably higher than for small-scale test concept testing. The approaches that might be used are **hall tests** or **in-home product placement tests**, both of which are explored in more detail in Chapter 4.

Example

With the increase in both the number of working women and the number of households with microwave ovens, there was a latent demand for pre-prepared oven-ready dishes which simply required a short cooking or reheating period. Major food companies, including supermarket chains, developed products to meet this new demand. To achieve optimal product positioning against the target group with the greatest propensity for repeat-purchase, concept testing would have included an exploration of the following key benefits:

(1) Use of quality ingredients
(2) Convenience and speed of preparation in the home
(3) Part of a healthy diet: no artificial additives
(4) Good tasting
(5) Inclusion of gourmet and exotic dishes

Testing of this range of concepts would need to be accompanied by exploratory research on the price range that the target group would be prepared to pay: were they looking for economy or middle-range pricing, or were they prepared to pay a premium for the right product? A clear direction on the preferred concept(s) and on pricing would enable the company to set costing parameters for the product in development, so as to guarantee a specific level of gross margin which would follow norms of the existing business or be sufficient to pay for a national advertising campaign. Researching the price after the product has been through a lengthy development and testing programme might result in incompatibility between product cost and acceptable price.

Reasons that a company might screen this new product development route as *not* suitable for continuing to the next development stage would be as follows:

(1) Insufficient demand: the target group is too small for the high-volume production criteria of the organization to maintain economies of scale.
(2) The range of meals necessary to interest the target group in repeat-purchase is too wide for the volume purchasing criteria on raw materials.
(3) There is a mismatch between the price that the target group is prepared to pay and the cost of ingredients and manufacture, leaving a gross margin that is unacceptable.
(4) The organization does not have access to a distribution network which can guarantee same-day delivery for chilled products at a cost that it can support.

The importance of pre-development activities

The example provided above illustrates the value of early market research to identify the purchase trigger and acceptable price. Detailed market analysis is critical in many market areas to identify market sectors, their size and trends, and to assess the degree of competitive edge afforded by development along a particular route. The speed of technological innovation is making the judgemental input of scientists and engineers crucial to assessment of how long an unpatented innovation can provide product superiority and marketing advantage.

There are many new product failures where greater investment of management time and energy in the pre-development stages of pre-liminary market and technical assessment, market research and project screening would have resulted in better product positioning against needs or abandonment of the project on the basis of technological or marketing capabilities or financial criteria. A study of 203 industrial product launches (123 successes and 80 failures) showed that the ways in which these pre-development activities were carried out were strongly correlated with product outcomes (Cooper and Kleinschmidt, 1986).

As it becomes increasingly difficult to achieve product differentiation in markets where the penetration level of the product sector is high, then there is greater risk attached to innovation. This increases the pressure on companies to operate a disciplined approach to concept development and testing, observing objective criteria for the 'stop–go' decision, particularly at the early stages of a project. A conflict of interest can arise when a senior manager or director is highly committed to a specific project, and this source of persuasion outweighs all the objective evidence or advice from specialists.

However, had the board of Beecham not given the go-ahead for a final period of research into synthetic penicillins in spite of the risk of no product breakthrough, then the company would not have achieved its outstanding success with this product group in the 1950s and 1960s. The inspiration of one individual can no longer be relied upon for such a venture when the research expenditure and cost of getting an approved drug onto the market is so much higher during the 1990s. Beecham acknowledged these market forces in the merger with Smith, Kline and French, whose access to the American market through a highly developed distribution structure gave greater financial justification to expenditure on Beecham's undoubted strength in drug research.

The link between innovation strategy, process and success

There are several alternative strategic approaches that an organization might pursue in its quest for successful innovation. There is no clear evidence to suggest that higher levels of investment are necessary to pursue an offensive rather than a defensive strategy, although this might be expected intuitively. Some of the most successful companies are able to sustain the double-edged strategy of defending their established positions within existing markets and at the same time attacking new markets with superior products.

The pharmaceutical industry in the UK provides an excellent illustration of how key players adopt different strategies towards investment in research and development. During the 1960s much tighter government controls grew on new drugs entering the market, with the formation of the Dunlop Committee in 1964 and the Medicines Act of 1968. This created a very much higher threshold of investment necessary in taking a new chemical entity through the necessary clinical trials to obtain a product licence. At the same time it was becoming more difficult to make a significant breakthrough in totally new fields of clinical performance. This meant that the risk factor was increasing with the levels of investment during the 1970s and 1980s.

One way of attempting to identify differences in innovative performance between companies which may be explained by contrasting strategies for innovation is the selective use of patent data combined with defined measures of R & D expenditure and the number of new chemical entities launched commercially at the company level (Steward and Peters, 1987).

The ability of an organization to respond to the need to defend existing markets and enter new ones depends heavily on an innovative culture promoted through formal management processes and supported by top management. One approach is high-calibre management of strategic business units with the autonomy to work on new ventures, but with a centralized corporate management team keeping an overview on financial performance and potential areas of overlap. This structure thrives during periods of economic growth, but stricter controls invariably operate during periods of recession. For example, the Japanese company Matsushita evolved a divisional organization during the 1930s but returned to centralized management during the post-war confusion and recession. During the 1950s, increasing competition required the greater flexibility of independent product groups with the addition of marketing, research and development and administrative functions. There was oscillation between the two models of management in subsequent years, with the oil crisis and stagnation of the mid-1970s provoking a trend back to more centralized control (Pascale and Athos, 1986).

Timing and obsolescence in the new product development process

Evidence from research and the judgements of informed observers indicates that product life cycles are getting shorter. There are two major forces at work creating this pressure on companies committed to innovation. Firstly, technology is changing at an exponential rate, and secondly, mass communications mean that conversion to a new product no longer relies on the traditional diffusion process as proposed by Rogers (1962). Speed of adoption invariably depends on advertising and distribution strength, provided that product benefits and price are matched to the needs and spending power of the target group. This reflects the increasing power of market leaders to dominate a sector through controlling the speed of innovation by sheer weight of advertising, the cost of which would be outside the resource capabilities of other companies operating in the same sector.

There are financial benefits to speeding up the development process. Firstly, the innovator in a market sector can command a premium price for the additional benefit and is likely to take and hold a significant market share when there is wholesale adoption. Secondly, the cost of financing research and development increases with the length of the development process if this is wholly or partly funded through borrowing (Rosenau, 1988). Where funding comes from an organization's own resources, then an appraisal of the **opportunity cost** at key stages in the project will identify whether funds are being allocated wisely. Opportunity cost is defined as the foregone opportunity of using resources on one project rather than another, and would be of particular relevance where different strategic business units are competing for central development funds.

Computer simulation of alternative project completion dates with projected costs for successive phases of development provides management with a tool for assessing the financial implications of shortening new product lead times or of meeting unavoidable delays for technological or commercial reasons. For some organizations, this use of computer software would extend into the practical management of projects, where the complexity and number of projects require sophisticated management information for tight control of the process.

It would be spurious to propose an outline timing schedule for new product development, as the time-scale differences between the development programmes for high-tech industrial products on the one hand and fast-moving consumer goods on the other would make this impracticable. However, the greater discipline that appears to be adopted by the major consumer goods multinationals in project management in order to optimize timing and efficiency of new product launches suggests that lessons can be learnt from a generalized approach to their logistical planning.

The phasing of the activities involved in the development and launch of a new consumer product are illustrated in Figure 16.2. The planning principles inherent in this process can be 'borrowed' for industrial goods, with the proviso that lead times will be longer (particularly where product licences or a government seal of approval are necessary) and certain aspects of branding and advertising development will not apply or will be fundamentally different (such as in the painstaking production of a technical sales manual rather than press advertising).

The separation of the planning process into 'product' and 'branding and advertising' has the shortcoming of missing the interaction between the two activities. However, if the planning schedules were integrated this would apply to only a narrow range of products, as the point at which, for example, product testing and advertising development coincide (if, in fact, they do at all) would differ from one product category to another. So this aspect has been sacrificed for simplicity of presentation and a greater potential for general application.

The pressure on companies to speed up the development process has implications for the degree of overlap between different activities and the inherent risk that this involves. For example, should the protocol for in-home placement market research for a new consumer product be written before the less costly panel testing within the organization is complete? Should final orders for components with relatively long production lead-times be placed before pilot production has taken place to the total satisfaction of engineers? These are the types of decisions that development teams face, for if 100% confidence is required at each stage then it is likely that the competition would have time to pre-empt the launch.

Companies are increasingly weighing the risk of an early decision on key stages in the development process against lost competitive advantage. This has led to the increasing adoption of development phases showing

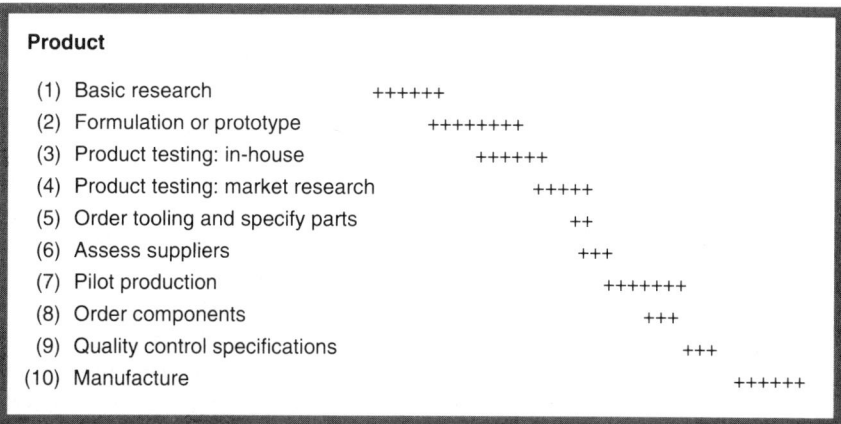

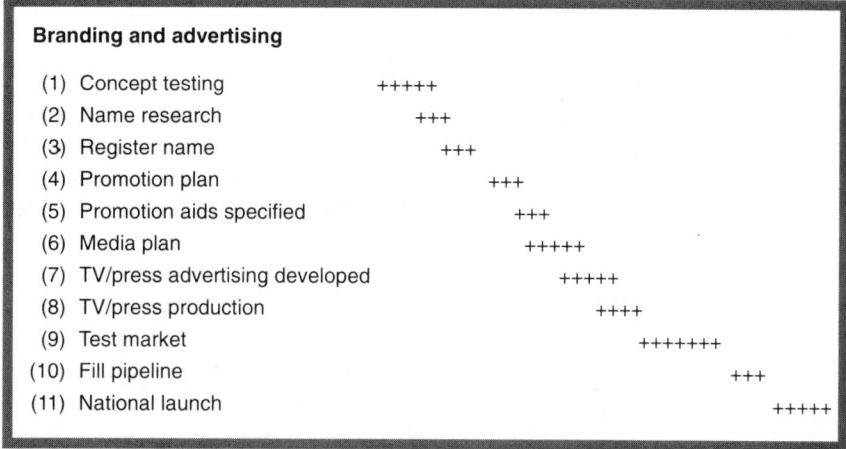

Figure 16.2 Phasing of new product development activities.

multiple overlap (that is, one phase overlapping at least two others), with the pressure that this places on multi-disciplinary teamwork to increase the probability that a new development project will result in a successful market launch (Takeuchi and Nonaka, 1986).

The test market

Where a company is committed to significant investment in engineering plant, computer processing and, increasingly, automated production through robotics, there is considerable financial risk in progressing to the engineering and production stages. Therefore, early soundings on customer response to concept, design and proficiency are necessary at an early stage in the project.

In contrast, where a significant share of the investment is in the marketing process, then there is wisdom in testing the message and the media for a new consumer product. Hopefully, earlier research will identify 'whether the customer will buy'. The **test market** should identify 'how much the customer will buy' against a given advertising spend and distribution weighting. In effect, the test market becomes a mechanism of fine-tuning when the launch has been given the go-ahead.

There are serious factors weighing against the use of test markets. Firstly, it can be difficult to delineate an area for retail distribution which exactly coincides with measurable media reception. Secondly, the market environment might not reflect that of the national market by way of consumer attitudes, competitive activity or salesforce effectiveness. (In fact, some areas used repeatedly for tests develop specific characteristics as a result.) Thirdly, a prolonged test market gives the competition an opportunity to counter-attack before national roll-out.

Where the conditions within the area of the test market can be controlled, and the test objectives are clear, then the advantages of running a complex test are illustrated in the UK launch of the Wispa chocolate bar (Table 16.2). Cadbury were able to identify sales offtake greater than predicted against a 'national equivalent' advertising campaign in the Tyne Tees area, and could therefore scale-up production for roll-out into other areas.

Table 16.2 Launch of Wispa chocolate bar illustrating the use of a test market and national roll-out.

Brand name:	Wispa
Company:	Cadbury Ltd
Market:	UK market for chocolate countline confectionery.
Product USP:	Novel technique for texturing chocolate to create a pure chocolate countline with a difference.
Market research:	(1) 1978/79 exploratory focus groups; favourable response to product but not to names. (2) Total pack test, firstly through hall tests, and then through an in-home placement test. Favourable response to product but not to names. (3) New name research; Wispa chosen.
Capital expenditure:	£12 million on new, technically advanced manufacturing facilities which took 20 months to build.
Test market:	April 1981 in the Tyne Tees television region. A full national equivalent television campaign resulted in demand exceeding supply.
National roll-out:	Started with the Tyne Tees region of 1983. As the product was launched in each area, managers moved in three days prior to the launch which was activated through the local sales team and a special 'task force'. Briefing on the launch took place only 72 hours beforehand to maintain secrecy and avoid competitive response through advertising or distribution.

Permission from Cadbury Ltd is acknowledged in inclusion of this table.

An approach to test marketing that has found favour during the latter half of the 1980s is the **test laboratory**, which is a form of artificial 'superette' in which the test product is merchandised along with competitive products and companion product sectors in as realistic a setting as possible. Consumers in the target market are then given spending money for the purpose of making a purchase decision after being exposed to advertising for the test product, among others.

There are obvious limitations to the way in which this reflects a launch situation, but the controlled conditions allow reliable comparisons to be made on the relative results of different advertising messages and on the effect of price of the test product relative to the competition. There is a significant advantage to the level of secrecy that can be maintained through this test procedure.

Organizational structure to manage innovation

Many organizations have difficulty in devoting sufficient attention to the management of innovation when there are considerable pressures on the successful stewardship of current business activities. This is equally true when a firm is going through a successful period and the need for new products is not so apparent, or when competitive pressures are the focus of attention and management is preoccupied with protecting the current business base. One way of resolving this dilemma is to create specific groups or teams whose sole task is the development of new products in isolation from the diversions of ongoing business activities.

Many large companies have been exploring the organizational route of **new venture units** (NVUs). These separate divisions or companies allow for the creation of an entrepreneurial culture for the adoption of new product initiatives outside the bureaucracy and reporting mechanisms of regular operations. This approach has the advantage of an enhanced profile for new product activities with, at the same time, freedom from the stringent control that might be the norm for ongoing business but would be inappropriate for new projects.

Research conducted among leading Canadian firms (Bart, 1988) indicated two key problems associated with the formation of NVUs. Firstly, if the new venture is related to existing business then possible rivalry between the two areas could have a damaging rather than net beneficial effect on performance. Secondly, motivation of managers in NVUs is problematic where the reward for new product success tends to accrue to the organization but the risk of new product failure falls on the shoulders of the individual manager in the form of damaged promotion prospects. The research indicated that chief executive officers were keenly aware of these problems and tried to address them within their own organizations.

An alternative way of scrutinizing organizational structures designed to accommodate new product development is on a spectrum, spanning a range from the assignment of the new project to relevant functional areas, with coordination by upper levels of functional management at one end of the spectrum. At the other end of the spectrum would be the **project team** approach, whereby a project manager is put in charge of a multifunctional team assigned on a full-time basis. The project manager has full autonomy over the project, with no formal involvement of functional management. At stages between these two 'models' there is a changing balance between the responsibility and authority accorded to functional management and to project management.

The benefit of the balance of authority residing with functional management is cost-effectiveness in the use of expertise and skill, and the assurance that those responsible for creating the business of the future are also in close contact with current market needs. However, a project manager and team devoting full attention to a new venture are more likely to cope with added complexity and possible new technology, and seek swifter decisions as 'champions' of the project.

The approach in which there is the combined input from functional and project management is commonly known as the **matrix** management structure. Problems have been identified in experiences with the matrix approach based on research among 62 successful companies, where the task force/project team approach was seen to be more successful in developing new products or solving complex tasks (Peters and Waterman, 1982).

Research findings which tend to provide equal justification for the project team approach and the matrix approach (with authority balanced between functional and project management or leaning to the latter) have examined four parameters of success (Larson and Gobeli, 1988). In this study of 540 development projects, in Canada and the USA, the matrix approach was adjudged to have similar performance capabilities to the project team approach in meeting schedule, cost performance, technical performance and overall performance.

The change of leadership at Nissan in the mid 1980s saw the introduction of the 'project manager', who was responsible for seeing a new car model through from the design stage to the sales showroom. The new management culture forbade interference in the development stage from the board or from the engineering unions as had been the case hitherto, and the focus of activity was the work of young designers and engineers who were perceived to be closer to the target market for the end-product. This new culture infiltrated through to Nissan dealers who were similarly encouraged to get closer to the customer and his or her needs. This approach improved Nissan's performance against Toyota in the home market, although the battle of the giants continues at home and abroad.

The success of Japanese companies in commercially applied innovation reflects a well-documented focus on the team approach to problem-solving. Other research among new product managers in high-technology companies has identified variables correlated to innovative performance, which fall into three broad categories (Thamhain, 1990). These are **task-related factors** (clear objectives, direction and leadership, experienced and qualified personnel and project visibility); **people-related factors** (including work satisfaction, good communications and job security); and **organization-related factors** (such as organizational stability, sufficient resources, rewards and recognition and supportive management).

These variables would tend to be identified by managers, regardless of culture, as the desirable features of an organizational framework for new product development. However, the political and resource constraints within many organizations mean that only some are attainable at any one time.

Reasons for new product success or failure

Following exploration of the new product development process and alternative organizational structures to facilitate innovation, it is valuable to identify the reasons why some new products are successful at launch and in establishing a strong market position and, conversely, why a large number of new products are commercial failures. There is no formula for a 'magic solution' to this inherently risk-laden area of business, but the following factors, if present in sufficient number and degree, will increase the probability of success:

- Company factors
  - The new product activity is in an area of established skills and expertise.
  - Top management is involved in promoting and supporting projects, within the organization.
  - A climate is created in which innovation can thrive in parallel with current business operations.
  - Managers of new projects have the benefit of experience of the market to be served, whether through existing employees, through hiring new expertise or through consultants or agencies contracted to work with the company.
  - An organization shows its commitment to a project through the allocation of sufficient resources.

- Process factors
  - Sufficient pre-development activity has been undertaken to establish a clear understanding of the needs of the target market.
  - The reporting structure for project and resource approval is not unduly bureaucratic, so that there can be a free flow of ideas in the early stages, and controlled development in the later stages.

- The interaction of managers and specialists in the development process makes the best use of expertise while ensuring that the speed of development is appropriate to the forecast pace of obsolescence in that market.

- Market factors
  - The size of the target market is sufficiently large to provide adequate return on investment.
  - The market growth rate is high enough to ensure a minimum level of adoption of the product in the launch phase.
  - The market is undergoing change.
  - There is no other dominant brand or company within the market.

- Product factors
  - The product has a distinct and unique benefit which has been identified as matching market needs.
  - This distinct benefit is capable of being communicated to the target audience.
  - Speed of adoption in the product sector is fast enough for adequate pay-back.

- Promotion factors
  - Sufficient money is committed for providing adequate reach of the target market through the chosen media, with a frequency of communication to establish the desired benefits in association with the brand or company name.
  - The right media are chosen to reach the target market.
  - The advertising message is clear, informative and relevant.
  - The sales plan and follow-through meet the requirements of the launch by way of training and performance of the salesforce, and intermediaries involved in the supply chain.

The importance of factors related to the company and the process in new product success is highlighted in research undertaken among 200 directors of British enterprises (Deloitte, *et al.*, 1988). This identified six chief factors that can hinder innovation: company culture (where failure is punished more than innovation is rewarded); poor staff involvement; the view that market forces preclude innovation; the way in which resources are allocated; poor or slow communications up the organization; and the role of the leader in fashioning a corporate culture which encourages innovation. A significant finding was that only two out of three directors interviewed rated innovation as 'very important'.

The importance ascribed to innovation within an organization will reflect corporate priorities in the quest for success, invariably measured in financial terms. Some researchers have argued that a preoccupation with such financial measures has an inhibiting effect on new product development. In an attempt to identify the truly independent measures of success, research into over 200 new product case histories in 125 industrial companies isolated three dimensions of success by applying factor analysis across ten performance gauges (Cooper and Kleinschmidt, 1987). These performance dimensions are financial, market impact and opportunity window. The financial dimension incorporates the traditional measures: **market impact** incorporates market share measures, and sales and profit versus objectives, while **opportunity window** portrays the degree to which the new product opens up new product category or new market opportunities to the firm.

The acceptance by a company of these broader, non-financial definitions of success requires a visionary chief executive who is able to gain commitment to longer-term projects against the shorter-term demands for financial success from shareholders and the financial community. The longer-term market share position which can arise from this strategy invariably brings with it the desired financial return. One proviso is worth emphasizing: where a country has consistently high levels of inflation over several years, then high levels of investment in innovation become even more difficult to justify in terms of the 'devalued' profits of subsequent years.

European perspective

The creation of the Single European Market has provided the innovative company within its borders with the opportunity to achieve economies of scale in the production of new products. However, the very high costs of scientific research and technological development prevent some European companies from even entering the race for market leadership.

The lower level of spending on research and development in Europe compared with the USA is one of the major reasons for loss of European eminence in key technology sectors of the future. In 1985, total European expenditure on R & D was 65 billion ECU, compared with 146.5 billion ECU for the USA. On a *per capita* basis, Japan's expenditure was also higher than that for Europe. Another important feature is the way in which money is spent. For the period 1950 to 1987, the USA achieved 115 Nobel prizes for physics, chemistry or medicine and physiology, Europe gained 86 and Japanese research attracted only four (EC, 1988). This was because Japanese research effort was focused on commercial applications of existing inventions rather than breaking new scientific ground.

The number of Nobel prizes gained by European countries is an indication of the quality and potential of European research, and it still takes the lead in controlled thermo-nuclear fusion and particle physics. Yet in fields of economic importance – electronics, information technology, material sciences and biotechnology – Europe has lost ground.

Apart from the lower financial commitment to innovation, other reasons have been put forward for this situation:

- the lack of financial incentives for companies to invest in R & D;
- inadequate venture capital markets;
- poor follow-through from scientific discovery to technological development and on to marketable product;
- lack of marketing support;
- corporate culture that does not encourage cooperation across disciplines and functional reporting lines to develop new ideas;
- too many research teams working in isolation, with inadequate resources, and with language barriers to the dissemination of information.

The policies of the EC Commission seek to address the fragmented nature of European research by encouraging technological cooperation without restricting free competition. There are two aspects to this:

(1) EC-funded research;
(2) EC judgements on technological agreements.

EC-funded research

In 1991, 2.3 billion ECU from EC funds were allocated to research. This is 4.2% of the total Community budget (and 4% of the total public expenditure on research in the 12 Member States). The EC research and development policy is aimed at cross-border cooperation, coordination and mobility between industry and science. The rationale for funding certain projects is founded on four general precepts:

(1) The scale of resources needed for certain projects would otherwise exclude European companies, particularly in areas of primary or 'speculative' research.
(2) It can provide a guarantee of excellence in those fields chosen for support, by ensuring that the complete range of equipment is available.
(3) Transfrontier problems need transnational solutions – especially in relation to the environment.
(4) A truly harmonized market will only work if product testing and standards are compatible; technical cooperation in the early stages of a project will encourage this.

The EC sets priorities and budgets on the basis of four-year framework programmes. The first started in 1984, and the Third Framework Programme runs from 1990 to 1994, overlapping the second by two years.

The Commission is trying to concentrate, as well as update, activities. Greater weighting is being given to environmental research and biotechnology with less spent on energy research, which dominated in the 1970s. However, information and communications technologies still take the largest share of funding (CEC, 1990).

Any industrial company, university or private or public research institute can apply for research funding, provided that there is at least one other partner from another Member State. Research proposals submitted for Third Framework funding had to fall within one of the eight key categories defined by the Commission. The nature of programmes supported within the Second Framework are shown in *EC Research Funding*, the official Commission guide.

EC judgements on technological agreements

There are two judgements which provide insight into the Commission's concern to encourage cross-border cooperation in R & D without reducing effective competition in a market. Firstly, in the industry for space electronic equipment for civil radio communications and broadcasting satellites, an agreement was signed in 1986 between Alcatel Espace and ANT Nachrichtentechnik. The agreement involved the allocation of devices for R & D and production, such that each partner specialized to their mutual cost advantage. However, allowance was made for royalty-free and non-exclusive cross-licensing of patent rights and for joint patents in some instances.

The Commission took the view in a judgement in 1990 that the general conditions for the Block Exemption Regulation on R & D were present. The cooperation deriving from the agreement would lead to technical progress and cost savings which could be passed on to customers. Although there would be collusion in marketing, the combined market share was not large enough to distort the nature of competition in the market (Competition Law in the EC, 1990).

The second case relates to the formation of a consortium, ECR 900, by AEG Aktiengesellschaft, Alcatel NV and Oy Nokia, for the joint development and manufacture and the joint distribution of a pan-European digital cellular mobile telephone system. The mobile telephones themselves were not included in the agreement. It was judged that this cooperation agreement did not restrict competition, as none of the parties would be in a position to market this equipment on an individual basis because of the high costs involved (Competition Law in the EC, 1990).

These judgements illustrate the necessity for parties to an agreement to ascertain whether they fall foul of the EC competition rules. The

Commissions's role is difficult in that it wishes to encourage scientific and technological collaboration which will enable companies to compete in world markets. At the same time, the competitive disadvantages of the collaboration must not outweigh the competitive advantages. The high costs of research in such areas as drugs, aerospace and telecommunications means that the likelihood of individual companies shouldering this burden alone is diminishing.

The risk/return relationship

World-class companies in Europe are now looking to research partnerships as a way of reducing the costs and risks that their shareholders are asked to carry. For example, GEC is working with MATRA in the area of satellite payloads, and with Siemens on telecommunications. A strategic decision has been taken to focus on these activities, with the result that individual patents from GEC will be fewer in number.

Where companies maintain a flow of patents through basic research, this has to be financed from existing, successful products. For example, Zantac, the anti-ulcer treatment, was launched by Glaxo in 1981. This proved a financial success, contributing more than half of Glaxo turnover in 1990, with a world market share of 41%. However, pressure has to be maintained on bringing new drugs to market, and the projected research spend of between £560 million and £600 million for 1992 came at a time when profits from Zantac were expected to plateau (Campbell, 1991). At such times, investors become nervous about profit forecasts in the short term.

Similar pressures were apparent for ICI in 1991, when there were expectations of a takeover bid from the Hanson Trust. ICI is one of the leading British investors in research and development. It spent £679 million on research and technology development for production processes in 1990. This high level of investment was seen as a central plank to defence against a takeover bid. However, some critics suggested that ICI was more successful in traditional, compared with new, areas of research. An analysis of ICI patents compared with Bayer, BASF and Hoechst indicated successful targeting of research funds (Leadbetter, 1991).

Collaboration between partners from different Member States within Europe does not eliminate risk, but careful evaluation of the projected R & D costs, market potential and economies of scale achievable by working in partnership can increase the chances of commercial success and reduce financial exposure.

Development of the Anglo-French Concorde supersonic aircraft is a case study demonstrating how national prestige attached to a highly visible innovation could cloud judgement in relation to commercial viability.

Table 16.3 Evaluation of the Anglo-French Concorde supersonic aircraft as a collaborative research project.

First prototype:	1967 at the Paris and Farnborough Air Shows.
Production:	Early 1970s in both UK and France.
Design specification:	Supersonic speed, to carry 100 passengers and cover unbroken distance of 4000 miles.
Marketing rationale:	Once BOAC (now British Airways) and Air France took delivery, other airlines would order to remain competitive (the 'me too' strategy).
Cost/price relationship:	Concorde tickets across the Atlantic were up to five times the price of an economy seat, in order to cover capital and running costs. This meant seating was rarely full.
Technical problem:	Noise levels for Concorde were high; airports such as Tokyo refused permission for take-off and landing.
Predicted sales:	200 aircraft
Actual sales:	16 aircraft
1990s status of European R & D into supersonic travel:	British Aerospace conducting low key 'maintenance' research.
1990s status of other R & D into supersonic travel:	Boeing (Seattle, USA) working on supersonic travel for the mass market to a new brief: (1) Number of passengers – 250 (2) Minimum unbroken distance – 6000 miles.
Focus of research:	(1) Improve fuel efficiency through aerodynamics. (2) Reduce aircraft bodyweight through use of new metal alloys.

Table 16.3 illustrates the difference between the reality of what the market needed and the product that was delivered. The fact that parallel production lines were built in UK and France eliminated major economies of scale that were to prove vital when orders for the new aircraft fell far short of plan.

The European patent

A patent is an official registration of a discovery which gives the author the exclusive right to use the invention for a specific period. The publication of the patent serves to provide information on the invention to interested parties.

The provisions of the Munich Convention (1973) came into force in 1977. A European Patent Office was set up in Munich. This issues the European patent which has the effect of a national patent in those countries belonging to the Convention, or those selected by the applicant. The European patent lasts for 20 years, and is published in any one of the Office's official languages (German, French or English). Despite its relatively high cost, the European patent involves fewer procedures than the obtaining of three or four national patents.

The Luxembourg Convention (1975) on the Community patent was signed only by the Community Member States, and it ensures that the European patent has the same effect in all the countries of the Community. There are two provisions of this Convention which are of commercial significance (CEC, 1989):

(1) Products protected by the Community patent and launched anywhere within the Community will be able to circulate freely within the Community. This is also true of a licensed product.

(2) If the exclusive rights conferred by a Community patent are judged by the Commission to have been abused, then these rights may be restricted, and compulsory licences issued by national authorities.

The legal integration which the Luxembourg Convention implies has been a slow process. Meanwhile, biotechnology inventions were covered by special provisions under a Commission proposal of October 1988.

Many inventions and processes critical to the financial success of companies remain the subject of individual national patents, where the length of protection varies. For pharmaceutical companies, increased safety and efficacy testing requirements have eroded the effective patent life. This was recognized by the European Commission in its proposal to restore effective patent protection for a pharmaceutical innovation to 16 years for a new product, with a maximum restoration period of 10 years. In line with this recommendation, France has approved a Supplementary Protection Certificate which confers 17 years' patent protection, and Italy has granted patent protection for 18 years. The British government was not as easily convinced of a need for a change in national patent law (The Independent, 1991).

Copyright

Where intellectual works cannot be protected by patents or trademarks, they can be the subject of copyright. This particularly applies to the printed word, music in the form of cassettes or discs, films, computer programs and the configuration or topography of a microchip. For areas such as computing, the speed of change is so great that only if companies can recoup on a pan-European scale will they contemplate investment in design and production.

The European Commission published a Green Paper in 1988 entitled 'Copyright and Technological Challenge'. The aim was to work towards a unified legal environment to encourage investment. Harmonization of copyright in the areas of television and books has been particularly difficult. The Commission has, however, focused attention on the British 'Net Book Agreement' which allows publishers to dictate retail selling prices.

Copyright in relation to computer software has been the subject of a Statement by the Commission of European Communities (Official Journal, 1989). This affirms the conviction that computer programs merit adequate legal protection, because of the intellectual effort and investment involved. Differences in the level of protection afforded by Member States led to the Commission initiating moves towards harmonization.

However, any unreasonable restriction of competition through the abuse of copyright would not be tolerated, such as, in certain circumstances, the withholding of information on a computer program to prevent other companies from providing link software.

Communication of innovation

New product adoption across the 12 Member States will be less predictable than adoption within each Member State because of the influence of culture and economic circumstances (explored in Chapter 5). A company marketing a new product can adopt two approaches: it can promote the new product to meet needs already diagnosed; or it can respond to requests for innovation when the client identifies the need. This latter *laissez faire* approach is likely to lead to greater risk and to enable the competition to gain market advantage.

Apart from the language barrier to the communication of innovation, the different cultures and economic circumstances of individuals across Europe mean that the source of the new idea or product is likely to be quite different from the receiver of the new product message. In other words, the source is **heterophilous** to the receiver. This would be the case for a British company marketing pre-prepared meals for the microwave oven to the poorer regions of Southern Italy where fresh food is abundant. A more **homophilous** interaction might exist between the company and consumers in the Netherlands. However, the nature of diffusion of innovation means that some degree of heterophily needs to be present between source and receiver (Rogers and Shoemaker, 1971).

Accurate and adequate information about the target market will define the level of heterophily, and thus the nature of the need (if any) and the best way to communicate the innovation. This theory provides support for financial commitment to market research, and the appointment of distributors or agents in markets where the level of heterophily is high, in order to reduce risk.

Significance of brand name

Concept testing remains one of the most valuable ways of gaining insight into consumer attitudes towards a product category. Many companies use the same focus groups to test possible names for a new product. This is an inexpensive and practical way of testing reaction to a product name. The stages for name selection for a new market (assuming a product already launched in the home market) are:

(1) Search in the name registry of the new regional market.
(2) If the same name can be used, what meaning does this convey in the new language? (consult nationals of that market).
(3) If this meaning is appropriate for the product, include among other possible names in concept testing.
(4) If reaction is positive in concept testing, include the name in large-scale product testing (hall test or in-home placement test).

The advantage of having a common brand name across Member States is the cost-saving that can be achieved in having common packaging and common advertising. Where different languages are involved, these will be catered for on packaging and through copy or voice-over in television advertising.

Some companies have made a strategic decision to have different names for broadly similar products on sale in different Member States with different packaging for each market. This is to avoid the possibility of 'parallel imports' where products have different competitive positions and prices in each market. In principle, this works against the EC competition policy. It remains to be seen whether the EC Commission will await complaints on such differential terms of supply, or whether it will take a proactive role in questioning such marketing practices.

Industrial new product development

The existence of the enlarged European market will accommodate greater economies of scale in production, but will also heighten competition. The full force of European competition is yet to be felt by those supplying the public sector in each Member State. There is substantial buying power in the hands of national utilities, telecommunications and defence. EC Directives relating to open tendering will encourage good practice in publicizing invitations to tender. However, cultural and language barriers as well as differing product standards will continue to inhibit cross-border tenders, unless there are significant indicators of potential success.

Where there has been major financial commitment to R & D from companies supplying these sectors, an adequate return on investment will only be available through serving several Member States. Three factors have been identified as enhancing the probability of commercial success (Frammerman, 1988):

- functional superiority – this might be manifest through lower cost or extended life;
- patent protection;
- cooperation of one or more major customers.

For the company wishing to market new technology in several Member States, the state of the art in each would need to be assessed. Choosing to focus on the needs of the organization at the leading edge could pose language and cultural problems for the supplier. The way in which such problems were tackled would depend on internal organizational culture.

Corporate culture and innovation for the enlarged European market

The influence of organizational structure, process and culture on the relative success or failure of new product development has been explored in the main body of the chapter. Where a company adopts a strategy of change in order to address the needs of the enlarged market, then the beliefs and values that have underpinned success in the past may not be appropriate for the future.

There are several ways in which new and more appropriate values can be injected into the organization so that it can take on the European challenge:

(1) *Organizational change* A restructuring of divisions to reflect the need for innovation to meet the needs of a wider market. For some multinationals, this has meant the creation of a 'European Division' whereas the line managers of the individual countries had previously had a different reporting structure. This creates the opportunity for an international new product development team in which the members retain general management responsibilities in each market.

(2) *Senior manager with European brief* A manager without a product portfolio is free to act as a catalyst at senior level, to give major company activities the necessary European dimension.

(3) *External director or consultant* This route to change can bring an outside set of values, but there will be less knowledge of the existing culture.

Approaches (2) and (3) are those recommended by Hassard and Sharifi (1989). In the longer term, recruitment of potential managers whose education and background have a broader European dimension will ensure that change feeds from the bottom of the organization, as well as from the top.

Problems and assignments

(1) To what factors would you attribute Japanese electronics companies' NPD success in the 1980s? Use examples in your answer and draw comparisons with Europe and/or the USA.

(2) In a high technology world, is it reasonable to expect marketing departments to provide the lead for R & D teams?

(3) Outline the advantages and disadvantages of concept testing in NPD.

(4) What are the advantages and disadvantages of approaching NPD through small project teams – new venture units – instead of more conventional departmental approaches?

(5) What distinctions, if any, would you draw between the NPD process for a manufactured product as compared with a service?

(6) How important is company culture in fostering a positive attitude towards NPD?

(7) What role should government take in supporting/funding R & D in a market economy? Put your answer into the context of the European Union, taking account of the situation in the USA and Japan.

(8) What are the implications for R & D expenditure, among large companies, of the advent of the Single Market and what is termed the European Union?

References

Abetti P.A. and Stuart R.W. (1988). Evaluating new product risk. *Research, Technology Management*, **31**(3), May/June, 40–43

Bart C.K. (1988). New venture units: use them wisely to manage innovation. *Sloan Management Review*, **35**, Summer

Cooper R.G. and Kleinschmidt E. (1986). An investigation into the new product process: steps, deficiencies and impact. *J. of Product Innovation Management*, **3**, 71–85

Cooper R.G. and Kleinschmidt E. (1987). Success factors in product innovation. *Industrial Marketing Management*, **16**(3), 215–223

Deloitte, Haskins and Sells (1988). *Innovation: The Management Challenge for the UK*. London

Deschamps J.P. (1989). Creating the products the market wants. *Marketing and Research Today*, February

Kane C.L. (1989). Overcome the me-too product syndrome. *J. of Business Strategy*, **10**, Part 2, March/April, 14–16

Larson E.W. and Gobeli D.H. (1988). Organising for product development projects. *J. of Product Innovation Management*, **5**, 180–190

Parker E.F. (1987). Delphi research. *J. of International Marketing and Marketing Research*, **12**(2), 65

Pascale R.T. and Athos A.G. (1986). *The Art of Japanese Management*. London: Penguin

Peters T.J. and Waterman R.H. (1982). *In Search of Excellence*. New York: Harper and Row

Reich R.B. (1990). Who is us? *Harvard Business Review*, **90**(1), 53–64

Rosenau Jr M.D. (1988). Speeding your new product to market. *J. of Consumer Marketing* (USA), **5**, Part 2, 23–36

Steward F. and Peters C. (1987). *Managing Product Innovation in the British Pharmaceutical Industry*. British Academy of Management

Takeuchi H. and Nonaka I. (1986). The new product development game. *Harvard Business Review*, January/February, 137–146

Thamhain H.J. (1990). Managing technologically innovative team efforts towards new product success. *J. of Product Innovation Management*, **7**, 5–18

European perspective

Campbell C. (1991). Glaxo faces life after Zantac. *The Times*, 1 March

Commission of the European Communities (1987). Research and technological development for Europe. *European File 19/87*, December

Commission of the European Communities (1989). Patents, trademarks and copyright in the European Community. *European File 17/89*, December

Commission of the European Communities (1990). A guide for applicants. *EC Research Funding*, 2nd edn, May

Competition Law in the EC (1990). R & D agreements (space electronic equipment): the Alcatel case. **13**(3), March

Competition Law in the EC (1990). Copyright (general): commission statement relating to legal protection of computer programs. **13**(2), February

Competition Law in the EC (1990). Cooperation agreements (telecommunications): the AEG case. **13**(10), October

EEC Publications (1988). *Research and Technological Development Policy*, 3rd edn. Periodical 2

Frammerman R. (1988). How to avoid the technical traps in product development. *Planning Review*, **16**(6), November/December

Hassard J. and Sharifi S. (1989). Corporate culture and strategic change. *J. of General Management*, **15**(2), 4–19

Independent (1991). Pharmaceutical patent protection. Letter from member of the William Harvey Research Institute. 8 November

Leadbeater C. (1991). ICI level of spending on research has far outstripped that of its UK competitors. *Financial Times*, 23 July

Lucas E. (1992). The trusting giant of the West. *The Independent*, 24 January

Rogers E.M. and Shoemaker F.F. (1971). *Communication of Innovations: A Cross-cultural Approach*. New York: The Free Press/London: Collier-Macmillan

17 Impact of developments in technology on traditional marketing methods

---

Chapter objectives:

- to examine the changing patterns of distribution as a result of new technologies
- to consider the effect of developments in communication and information technology (IT) on marketing channels
- to look in detail at the areas of retailing, business-to-business and the banking sector

Introduction

As early as 1980, there were predictions that 'non-store retailing' would make significant inroads into the traditional business domain of major retailing groups. The capabilities for rapid transfer of information, orders and payment through advances in telecommunications and computing were expected to create a generation of **home shoppers** (Rosenberg and Hirschman, 1980). This consumer group would abandon the habits of seeking out information and products to suit their needs, and providing their own delivery service to the home. Instead, they would select information from a range of transmission sources directed at the home, and respond immediately through computer link, with the product delivered to them at an agreed time.

All the pointers towards this shopping revolution that started to emerge in the 1980s are still evident in the 1990s:

(1) The increasing volume of telephone- and mail-generated orders for traditional retailers, and the increasing success of direct marketing spots on television.
(2) The expanding array of merchandise available by credit card operators.
(3) The increasing penetration of cable television, with the facility for interactive shopping.
(4) Changing consumer attitudes and behaviour in relation to shopping hours and shopping as a leisure activity.

The forecast revolution did not materialize during the 1980s, and instead there was a sizeable growth in retailing provision in out-of-town developments and town centre shopping malls. This corresponded with a growth in disposable income in the USA and Western Europe so that the expansion of retail provision was supported by demand.

However, the fact that **electronic home shopping** has not yet supplanted traditional methods has not been an obstacle to advances in telecommunications and computing affecting the operating methods and efficiency higher up the value-added chain. The advent of **electronic data interchange** (EDI) has revolutionized the way in which buyers and sellers 'talk' to each other through electronic mail boxes and provide information on stock status, place orders and pay for the goods, all through computer link. It is likely that when the technology does flow down to the consumer, the major retailing groups themselves will be in the best position to capitalize on the marketing opportunities through prior investment in information technology related to **quick response** distribution systems.

For the industrial and business services sectors, **value-added networks** (VANs) provide the facility for rapid information exchange. The type of system adopted will depend on whether there is a dominant member of the chain (as in the corporate, contractual or administered vertical marketing system). The efficiencies in operating methods created through such networks can apply at the corporate, industry or even national economic level.

The trading cycle would not be complete without the flow of money. The banking sector has prepared itself for **paperless trading**, although the rate of advance towards this varies with the type and size of institution. The working practices and efficiencies can be viewed solely on an inter-bank basis, or as a function of the role played in market-led logistics for the supply of other goods and services.

The range of technology developments means that there is the potential for a **totally automated customer service** – from computer-dialled communication of the 'offer', to robotic selection and despatch of goods from the warehouse. However, there is a range of intermediary positions that are likely to emerge in the 1990s. Most particularly, the acceptance of cable television by new subscribers will determine the feasibility of **interactive home shopping** on a large scale. The speed of adoption of new shopping behaviour on the part of these subscribers will then determine how far and how fast this shopping concept will displace traditional marketing channels.

As a first step to exploring these issues, the full impact of developments in communications and information technology on marketing channels is explained through consideration of the 'four flows'.

The four flows between provider and customer

The relationship between an organization providing a product or service and the customer can be described through four elements of the interaction, which are shown in Figure 17.1:

(1)   Information on the product or service flows from the organization to the prospective customer. This can take the form of unsolicited direct mail, television advertising, personal selling or technical seminars – all examples of a wide range of **communication** techniques.

(2)   When the prospective customer is satisfied that this product will satisfy his/her need or that of the organization they represent, then an **order** flows between the customer and provider.

(3)   The provider validates the order, and converts this into instructions for the selection and **despatch of goods** to the customer.

(4)   **Payment** for the goods is sent from the satisfied customer to the provider.

This is an over-simplification of the transactions, but identifies the stages of the business relationship at which advances in telecommunications and computing can have a significant impact on

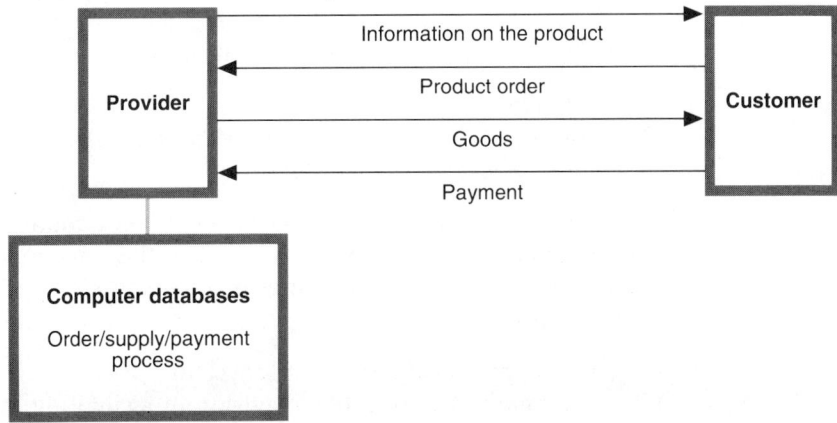

Figure 17.1   The four flows involved in the provider–customer relationship.

speed of response and efficiency. In any business system, integration of functions is crucial to effective customer service and financial control. As the cycle of the 'four flows' is compressed in time, so this need becomes more imperative.

Accurate and up-to-date **management information** facilitates integration of functions involved in the **process** – sales planning, forecasting, buying, production, order processing, and deliveries. The specification for this system and the database management which supports it will contribute to competitive edge for a profit-making company, or will permit cost control of provision for a non-profit organization. In the latter case, the process may be complicated by payment coming from a third party, such as a government department or insurance company in the case of health provision. Direct computer access between the provider and third party will reduce the need for administrative support for both.

Developments in information technology have created opportunities for providers to develop sophisticated **customer databases**, from which customers can be selected to receive promotional material based on past purchasing record or predicted future needs. **Market research** data provided on a syndicated basis or to a specific corporate brief can be manipulated or matched with internal data, provided that software is compatible.

The ways in which developments in telecommunications and information technology impinge upon the four flows and related databases are shown in Table 17.1. Each of these influences is unlikely to take place in isolation, so that it would be unrealistic to explore impact on marketing practices within this framework. Similarly, the speed of implementation will depend on state-of-the-art in each industry, the degree of competition (forcing companies to invest in customer service and efficiency), acceptance of new working practices and adoption of new technology by the individual consumer or household.

The impact of new technology will therefore be explored through examples of implementation and results under the following headings:

(1) Retailing
(2) Business-to-business (electronic data interchange)
(3) Banks and 'paperless trading'.

Success in these areas augurs well for adoption of interactive marketing on a broader front, as and when the consumer embraces new technology and adopts new patterns of behaviour. Some speculation is therefore justified in two areas:

(4) The future consumer 'offering system'
(5) The importance of cable television in facilitating interactive home shopping.

Table 17.1 Impact of advances in telecommunications and information technology on the provider–customer relationship.

Information flow to the customer on the product	More selective audience reach due to sophisticated database management. Customer can select product category for information through on-line facility, reducing time for sifting and printed material. Sharing of latest information by channel members through value-added networks (VANs). Penetration of interactive home shopping will reduce need for mailings and image advertising on traditional media (TV, press, radio) for some product categories. 'Narrowcasting' will be more prevalent through cable and satellite specialist channels.
Order transmission by the customer	Speed of response: will be seconds/minutes in place of hours or days. Quality of response: information structured to meet needs of provider. Immediate knowledge on stock status within VAN, and swifter management response to meet customer needs. Reduced paper flow. Possible involvement of salesforce with computer terminals, so technology supports face-to-face selling.
Provision of goods	Dominant member of channel dictates technology specification and mechanics of delivery (such as consolidated deliveries to central warehouse of grocery retailers). Higher level of customer service through swift response from the channel members to information – just-in-time (JIT) capability. Opportunity for alternatives to current distribution systems, such as **community warehouses** from which consolidated deliveries are made to cable television households. Computer ordering feeds through to automated warehousing and robotic selection of goods. Facility for product 'customization' by computer information on customer need flowing through to production.
Payment	Automated transactions reduce paper flow and need for administrative support. Reduced time-scale for payment 'clearing' improves cash management. Greater need for computer back-up and security systems to deal with fraud, human error and computer malfunction.
Customer database	More detailed segmentation and selection of target audience for promotions. Matching of syndicated demographic data with post-coded customer data. Advent of computer parallel processing will reduce file search time to facilitate customer-led logistics.
Market database	Immediate market research panel response through interactive facility. Automation of retail audit data transmission at collection, analysis and reporting stages.

Retailing

The success of the major UK grocery retailing chains in achieving net profit margins of three times their counterparts in Continental Europe is partly attributable to operational efficiencies gained through investment in information technology (IT). In other UK retailing sectors – clothing and do-it-yourself decorating – the same success is also apparent as companies gain sufficient market share to make the investment worthwhile. Two IT applications are gaining significant penetration: **EPOS** (electronic point of sale), and **EFTPOS** (electronic fund transfer at point of sale).

The advantages of EPOS are:

- speed at customer check-out through automatic bar code reading on products;
- capture of sales level by individual line, which provides information on reorder quantities;
- weekly or daily cash returns;
- automated credit/debit card processing;
- automatic cheque printing.

The larger retailing groups have invested in bespoke software which provides support for operating systems that are unique to a particular merchandise mix. The **management information** system is similarly customized and facilitates **direct product profitability** (DPP) analysis through tracking costs and margins for each product on its journey from delivery to a central warehouse or direct to the store to consumer purchase (see Chapter 9 for further details on DPP). The results from this type of analysis can then be channelled into production of financial plans and merchandising plans to achieve optimal levels of sales per square foot and profit per square foot of retail space.

EFTPOS is gaining slower acceptance both by retailing groups and the consumer, as the benefits of the debit card are not as transparent to the individual as those of the credit card. The costs to the retailer are also relatively high, both on an investment and individual transaction basis.

An example of the strategic importance of IT in retailing operations is provided below.

Example: The use of information technology for competitive edge at Texas Homestore

Texas Homestore has 229 stores in the UK, serving 2.5 million customers per week and stocking over 30,000 individual products.

Information technology objectives:	(1) To improve financial control.
	(2) To improve the timeliness and accuracy of information for business decision-making.
	(3) To improve merchandise management and control of the supply chain.
EPOS (IBM 4680):	First strategic system introduced in 1987 and fully implemented by 1989.
General business support:	The operating centre has two IBM mainframes from the latest SUMMIT range, which are upgraded with increasing demands of the business.
Private communications network:	Connects remote locations to the centre. Used for electronic mail (PSCICS), retrieval of data from the

	EPOS system, and on-line access to the merchandising and management information systems.
Executive information system:	Called COMMANDER, this allows access to merchandise and financial plans, showing results by product and location.
Financial systems:	Installed in 1988 based around the McCormack and Dodge ledger system. These were augmented with the M & D human resource system in late 1989. The latter controls the starter and leaver databases and drives the payroll.
Merchandise management:	The Texas Retail Integrated Merchandise (TRIM) system covers: • price file management • space and range management • stock control • ordering and receiving • margin tracking by line
Electronic data interchange	The JET system is based on industry standards, and is used to communicate with suppliers. JET links with the internal network PSCICS, allowing Texas users to communicate with suppliers.
Texas view of the future:	After a period of rapid growth, D-I-Y was a mature business by 1992, and future improved performance will need to come from efficiency improvements allied to new external opportunities.

Traditional mail order groups are even more dependent on the sophistication and flexibility of their information technology support systems to provide competitive edge. Costs of catalogues and promotion mailings have to be recouped by minimum levels of customer response, and sales lost against a particular campaign are difficult to replace. Clever manipulation of a customer database can realize sales to improve an otherwise static profit picture. This is illustrated by N. Brown, the mail order group which lifted pre-tax profits by 9% in the half-year to the end of August 1991. This was achieved through catalogues targeted at the disabled and at 40- to 50-year-old women. A special catalogue designed to reactivate dormant customer accounts was also a success (Hosking, 1991). (The traditional mail order process flow, including the role played by information technology, is examined later in the chapter.)

A 'half-way house' between the traditional retail and mail order operations is illustrated by the catalogue-based retailer Argos. The company prints 27 million catalogues a year and has over 260 stores. The computer support system linking stores to the centre is critical to adequate stock of each merchandise line being in-store for visiting customers.

Every night, the central Hitachi 9080 mainframe at Milton Keynes dials up stores on 42 simultaneous lines, to identify the stock shortages.

The information in the form of picking lists is relayed to six distribution centres for picking and despatch during the next day's shift (King, 1990).

New ways of looking at the customer database allows manufacturers to assess how to gain incremental sales using the same or additional forms of distribution. Levi Strauss & Co. has a leading position in the US market for jeans and related apparel. Increasing competition made it imperative that sales of core products through existing retail channels were sustained through mass media support. At the same time there was the need to develop a customer base for merchandise with less mass appeal (Ireland, 1987). Four opportunities emerging from use of the customer database were identified:

- testing of new product acceptance;
- spreading brand loyalty from core to non-core products;
- testing incentives for brand switching in retail;
- capture of the traditional mail order buyer.

Through direct marketing tests, the resultant customer was identified as a typical catalogue shopper rather than the traditional Levi customer; different product rankings appeared compared with retail and a different geographical pattern emerged. All of these pointed to incremental business through direct marketing techniques.

Business-to-business

Adoption of new technology in telecommunications and computing has led to integrated business networks in such industries as motor vehicles and shipping to gain efficiencies in time, operations and administration. These networks make use of **electronic trading**, which embraces a wide range of time and cost-saving facilities for transferring information between trading partners electronically rather than on paper.

Electronic trading encompasses three distinct areas: electronic mail, electronic data interchange and on-line interactive facilities.

Electronic mail

This facility provides for unstructured human messages to be transmitted at a time convenient to the sender and stored until read by the receiver. It operates through a series of electronic 'mailboxes' which act as the storage devices for the messages. Each organization that is a party to the system may have just one mailbox, or several individuals within an organization may have a personal mailbox each for different functional requirements.

An example of non-profit use of electronic mail is the UK network of ambulance services. When one regional service plans a trip into the area served by another, a message is transmitted two weeks in advance and left in the mailbox for the day of the trip. Scanning of the mailbox by the second authority will allow it to make use of the return trip for a patient, if appropriate. This facility has greatly improved journey efficiencies between the 25 participating regions.

Electronic data interchange

In EDI networks there is machine-to-machine transmission of structured messages with no human intervention. It involves automated routine transactions between trading partners such as transmission of orders, invoices, delivery information, acknowledgements and payments.

The use of EDI in the motor industry allows component suppliers automatic data access so that a just-in-time fulfilment policy can be implemented. This reduces the amount of money tied up in stock, and cash management is further improved by automated payment systems which remove the need for credit chasing.

The range of strategic and operational benefits of EDI is outlined in Table 17.2. 'Competitive edge' is cited as a strategic benefit, and this reflects the traditional view put forward in the literature. However, it has been argued that only in the case of a 'first mover' into EDI within a specific industry is there the likelihood of such competitive advantage (Benjamin *et al.*, 1990). In the cases used to support this view, EDI was a competitive necessity, with a level of cost-saving which did not equate to competitive advantage. Benefits to buyers were found to be greater than benefits to suppliers. A governing factor will be the member of the channel that has imposed system standards – if indeed these exist at all in the industry. A powerful buyer may impose the system standards on dependent suppliers. Other buyers may then have to follow suit to remain competitive through EDI.

Table 17.2 Strategic and operational advantages of EDI and barriers to implementation.

Strategic advantages	Operational advantages	Barriers to implementation
Competitive edge	Reduced paper flow	Customer resistance
Faster response to the market	Faster transactions	Lack of top management commitment
Better management information	Fewer errors in data entry	Lack of industry standards
Improved customer service	Elimination of duplicate activity	High investment cost
Total process planning and JIT	Instant access to information	Need changes in operations

The lack of an industry standard can be a significant barrier to adoption of EDI. In fact, this issue is of such importance that some experts believe it to be an alternative definition of EDI:

> 'Direct computer-to-computer exchange of standard business forms. EDI is not a system. It is a standard ... EDI consists of a communication standard defining how one computer is to talk to another computer over a network, and a message standard defining the sequence and format of data which is to be exchanged...'
> (Callahan, 1987).

A further significant barrier to implementation of EDI is lack of senior management commitment. One approach proposed is the appointment of a senior project manager with a high level of negotiating skills to ensure acceptance of the system internally and among key trading partners (Selby, 1989). The full implications of adoption must be recognized by senior management, including costs, operational changes, and the pilot period necessary where the traditional system and EDI operate in tandem so that problems can be identified and resolved.

Interactive data networks

Some of the most sophisticated telecommunication-linked computer applications involve on-line facilities whereby people interact with a software facility, the results of which can be transmitted for viewing or processing by another party. An example is the use of computer-aided design for architectural and engineering practices. The final agreed design can be 'exploded' into the various constituent materials and components for quantity assessment and costing using linked software. Purchase orders can then be generated from this process. Whether there is automatic transmission of these orders will depend on whether suppliers are linked electronically to the same system standard. For many industries, paper will need to be generated at this stage.

A simpler and more commonly implemented form is access to a database which provides the specific information necessary for a prospective customer to place an order or booking. There is the possibility of increasing the size of the market through such networks, which constitute more effective promotional and order mechanisms.

The insurance market is one in which the individual is dependent on getting advice specific to the problem. Computer links between high street brokers and the head office of the insurance company will ensure that this information is available almost immediately, once detailed parameters of the problem are communicated.

Suppliers in the travel industry – tour operators, airlines and hotels – require an efficient distribution system to reach their customers, whether in the holiday or business sector. In the retail travel sector, the first on-line reservation system became operational in 1982. The travel industry is an example of the success of **value-added and data network services** (VANs) encouraged by the UK government in the early 1980s.

In order to supply a **value-added and data network service** two components are necessary: a **network** and an **application** (Department of Trade and Industry, 1987). The network consists of telecommunication transmission links, switching capacity (exchanges) and processing capacity. In the UK, British Telecom and Mercury are the only companies licensed to own and operate a fixed-link network that can be sold to third parties. A company wishing to offer network-based services has therefore to lease transmission facilities to which processing equipment can be added.

The application is the special facility – often in the form of software for database access or manipulation – which allows the signals carried to be transformed in some way. This facility provides the added value to a service which can be proprietary to a particular insurance company, for example, or operated to an industry standard, so allowing travel agents to access data on flights or package holidays.

Importance of VANs in Japan

The harnessing of technological innovation to provide international competitive edge has been important for the Japanese distribution system which is frequently cited as a non-tariff barrier to import penetration. The system has had to respond to change as a result of three trends (Suyama, 1989):

(1) Lower growth rates, so there are not the same opportunities for oligopolistic manufacturers to benefit from increasing economies of scale.
(2) 'Individualization' of consumption, which could mean increased levels of stock of finished items, half-finished items and parts.
(3) Flexible manufacturing systems (FMS) and factory automation.

One of the ways in which the distribution system has responded to changing circumstances is by efficiencies gained through value-added networks. An example is 'Planet' – an industry network formed by eight manufacturers in the miscellaneous goods industry. The group includes Lion, Shisheido and Unicharm, forming a joint investment consortium with INTEC. The alternative to this arrangement would be an intermediary taking on the capital investment, with the possible absence of an industry standard for the network. Should one manufacturer dominate supply, then there would be the danger of 'administered technology' being used as a route to increased market power.

Example: Operation of a VAN in publishing

The focal point of newspaper and magazine distribution is the wholesaler – who manages a geographical area and distributes to retail outlets. In the late 1980s the traditional UK wholesaling arrangement changed when the Mirror Group chose to invite tenders for distribution of their major newspaper titles. This introduced the direct use of distribution companies to handle deliveries to wholesalers, and in some cases, direct to the retailer.

Publishers need accurate information on sales to react with future production runs. This is particularly critical when television promotion is used for special newspaper features. The traditional information route is through returns from the newsagent to the wholesaler, and ultimately back to the publisher. The involvement of all three in VANS will speed up this information flow, initiated by EPOS from the retailer, which then becomes available to both wholesaler and publisher through the data network. The reverse flow – information on prices, promotions and special editions from publishers – is immediately accessible to wholesalers and retailers for planned selling.

An illustration of this network is provided in Figure 17.2. INS, International Network Services Ltd, was established in 1987 by the STC Group and General Electric Company to specialize in the growing market for electronic data interchange both nationally and internationally.

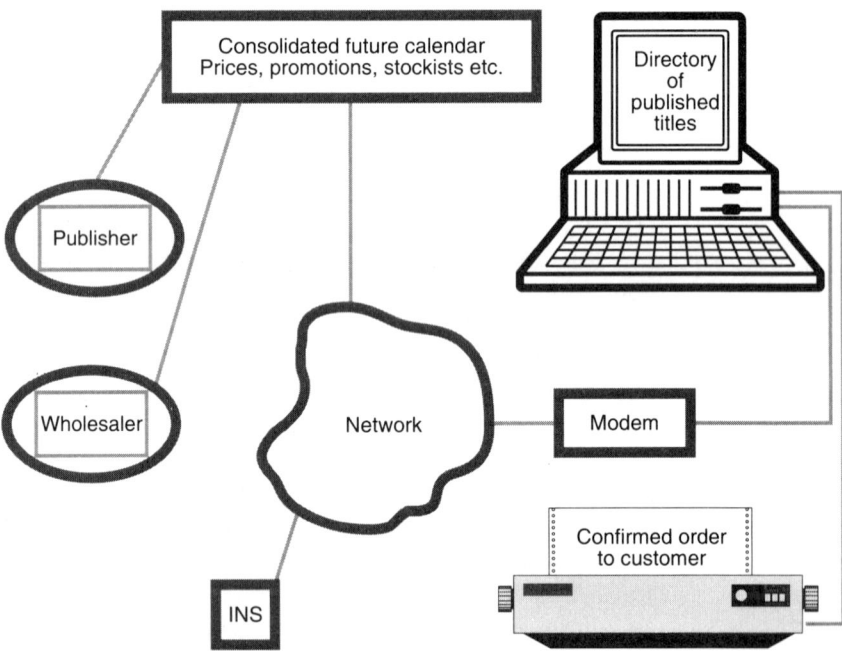

Figure 17.2 The use of value-added and data services in printing and publishing. *Source:* Department of Trade and Industry (1987).

Banks and paperless trading

Electronic trading within the banking sector can be viewed as a significant marketing tool in its own right, and as a route to facilitating a total consumer 'offering system' for a wide range of goods and services in the 21st century.

Competition in the UK banking sector is now so intense that the traditional clearing banks have had no option but to review their use of information technology, as the old building societies have entered the market as 'new banks' with up-to-date telecommunication and computing facilities. In the same way that grocery retailers have embraced new technology, so banking retailers such as TSB have looked at success factors in customer service and product delivery (Facilities, 1989). In 1989, one third of TSB's 1200 branches had been equipped for paperless trading with the total chain conversion taking three years and costing in the region of £100 million for hardware, software and training. The facilities include word processing, customer profile information, loan quotations, commercial accounts and balance sheet information.

Considerable 'back-room' space can be released as storage of all but legally required records can be eliminated, thus providing more space for customer contact and selling. The customer can access information on services and costs as well as retrieving more 'secure' data on personal accounts and transactions. Apart from the image and product enhancement gains, this investment provides the opportunity to measure performance in terms of sales or profit per square foot in exactly the same way as other retailers.

Banque Bruxelles Lambert (BBL), the second largest retail bank in Belgium, has gone further by providing not only the basic banking services through its automated 'banquettes', but also customer access to simulation models for financial planning and personal tax computation facilities (Knight, 1991). By removing the need for staff to spend time on simple transactions, this expensive overhead can be diverted to positive selling. However, there is a danger of depersonalizing banking with possible alienation of the customer. BBL's experience suggests that younger customers take to the 'self-bank' system more readily than older customers.

Database management is part of the information revolution within banking, and a critical element of the direct marketing approach used successfully by the leading exponents. Figure 17.3 illustrates the cycle of information, efficiency and profit gains from database investment.

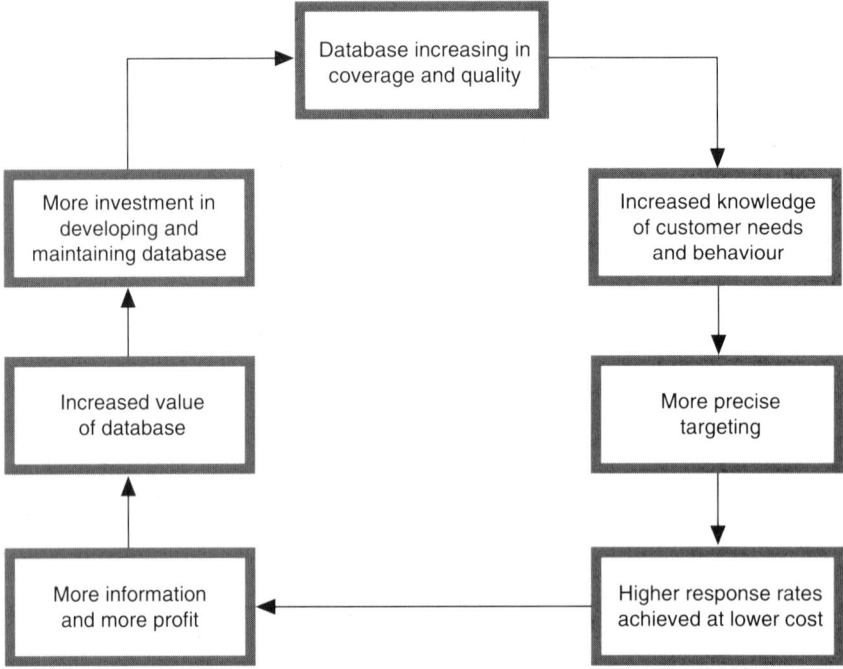

Figure 17.3 The benefits of database management in financial services markets.

The future consumer 'offering' system

The expanded services and efficiency gains from the availability of VANs and 'paperless trading' for banks are not the exclusive preserve of the business-to-business sector. However, adoption of advanced telecommunication and computing applications to serve individual households involves a very different economic equation. The facility for two-way communication between household and provider requires considerable capital investment in a cable network. The investor must be sure of a reasonable return on investment through the provision of profitable services to a customer base. The services might involve cable television, telephony and home shopping.

The initiative for such investment may come from the national government – through liberalization of laws and granting of licences in the area of telecommunications, or direct financial intervention in the market. Alternatively, the private sector may take the lead. For the UK, the latter approach is illustrated by companies from Canada and the USA taking on cable franchises for specific regions. These companies are prepared to take a longer-term view of financial return as a result of market experience in their home base.

At the same time as these developments, the consumer is becoming more discriminating, manifest through:

- Demands for more detailed information; a more educated population evaluates alternative 'offerings' before purchase decisions are made.
- The consumer expects this information to flow from provider at a time and in a form that is best suited to individual need.
- The propensity for individual needs to be specified and the expectation that these will be met marks the trend towards 'mass customization' discussed at the end of Chapter 5.
- Access to the product – delivery time for the tangible and flexibility for service provision – is seen as an integral part of the 'offering'.

In parallel with these needs, environmental pressures on car transport will increase and there will be a changed relationship between work and leisure for some of the population. It is highly likely that other forms of product access will evolve alongside traditional retailing.

Sequential marketing illustrated by mail order

To explore this evolution in terms of benefits to the customer and economics of operations for the provider, it is first necessary to examine the *status quo*. The step-by-step process of traditional **mail order** selling is illustrated in Figure 17.4. Eight stages can be identified in the process, each involving one of the four flows. Each step involves time, costs, the possibility of error and a degree of control over the activity on the part of the provider. The sequential nature of the process is its most distinctive feature:

(1) *Selection of customers for mailing* Accurate targeting depends on the level of sophistication of the database. The provider has complete control over this stage if the database is managed in-house; but only partial control if this is a contractor service.

(2) *'Personalized' promotion literature is produced* The quality of this bears a direct relationship with customer response, so provider control of computer-generated elements within printed material is essential.

(3) *Mailing of personalized message with, for example, catalogue* Provider loses control over delivery of message. Reliability of this stage depends on the quality of Post Office service.

(4) *Customer responds with order and payment* Speed of response dependent on whether by post or telephone/credit card. Sharp 'peaking' of response strains administration and packing lines.

(5) *Order is entered on computer* This generates documentation for fulfilment of the order, and simultaneously updates the customer database. The provider has complete control over this stage only if handled in-house.

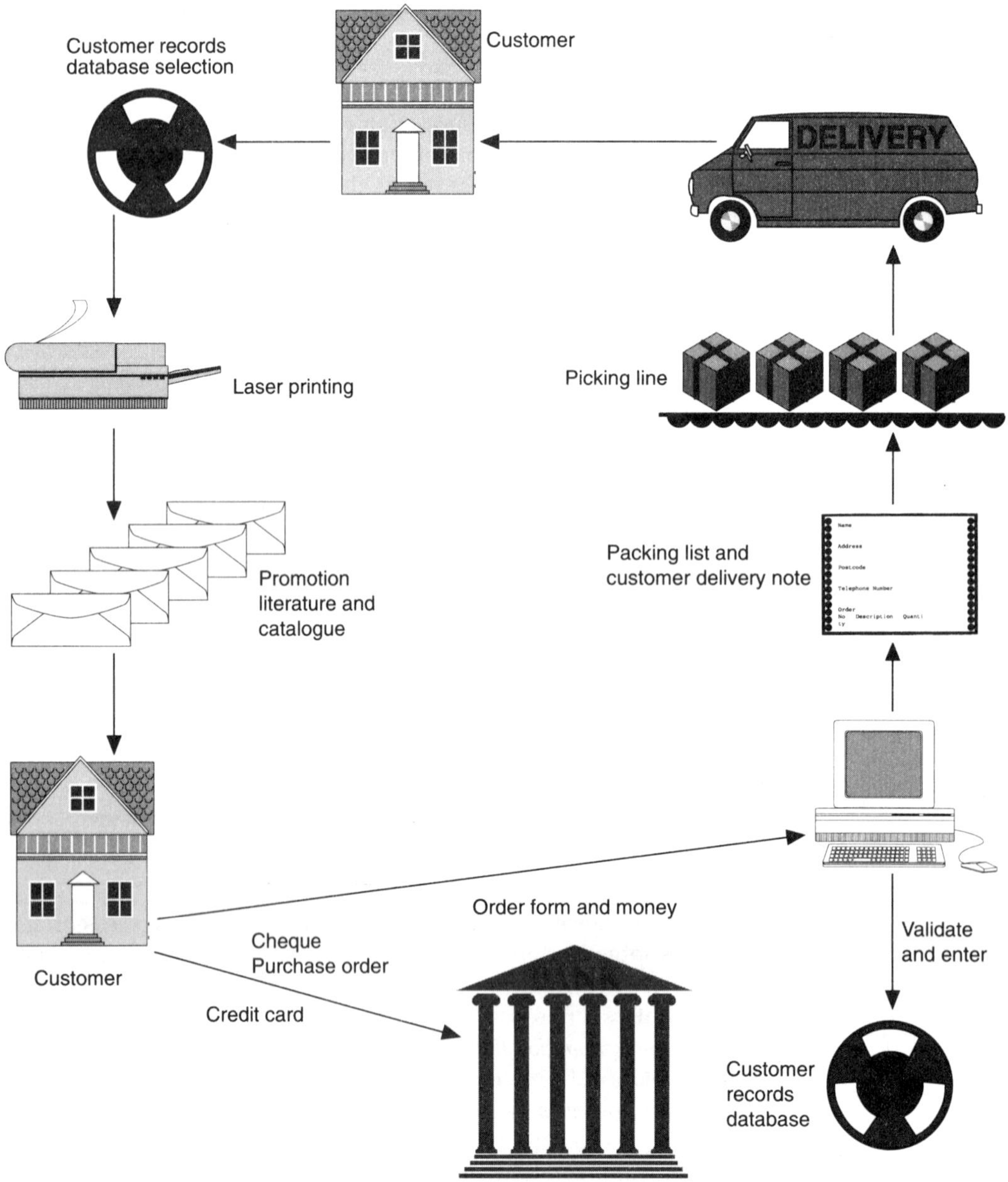

Figure 17.4 Mail order systems of the 1980s.

(6) *Monies paid into bank account* This takes place when the order has been validated and processed. There is the need for information to flow onto the financial management information system. A record of payments will also be required intermittently from the bank.

(7) *Selection of merchandise against order* There is excessive paper flow at this stage, and opportunities for errors in fulfilment.

(8) *Delivery of merchandise to customer* This generally involves use of the Post Office parcel service, or a contracted delivery service. The timing of delivery invariably suits the provider rather than the customer.

The 'offering' system of the 1990s and beyond

The provision of a cable facility for television and interactive computer services to the majority of homes is the first step towards the availability of a commercial 'offering' system. This will make use of the linkage between three technologies:

- Electronic media – dial-up capabilities for selected market information;
- On-air television catalogues and recorded videos;
- Interactive capability for ordering and payment.

These three technologies play specific roles in the 'offering' system illustrated in Figure 17.5, and which exhibits four unique features:

(1) The principal commercial members will act more simultaneously than sequentially.

(2) There is more competition between channel members for control.

(3) There will be greater involvement of financial systems in this form of 'retailing'.

(4) There is unprecedented consumer participation in the system.

The consumer will be the focus of service provision from each commercial member, as shown in Figure 17.6. However, the relationships between providers will be influenced by their interdependence: for example, the manufacturer may choose to operate through a merchandising company which consolidates a wide range of lines to provide consumer choice. There is the opportunity here for traditional retailers (particularly market specialists) to adopt this position, through their expertise in buying and logistics.

In another area of expertise, the telecommunications network provider will work closely with the company furnishing computer hardware to determine optimal configurations. Similarly, the merchandiser will need to operate to industry standards in the area of data transmission; if these do not exist, who will set the precedent? Manufacturers and banks will want to tap into a system that provides maximum business potential, as capital investment must be offset against future earnings.

Delivery systems must optimize routings and consolidate loads in order to be economic – whether as integral service units of marketing companies, or stand-alone businesses. Two conflicting forces will make this a difficult task in the future 'offering' system:

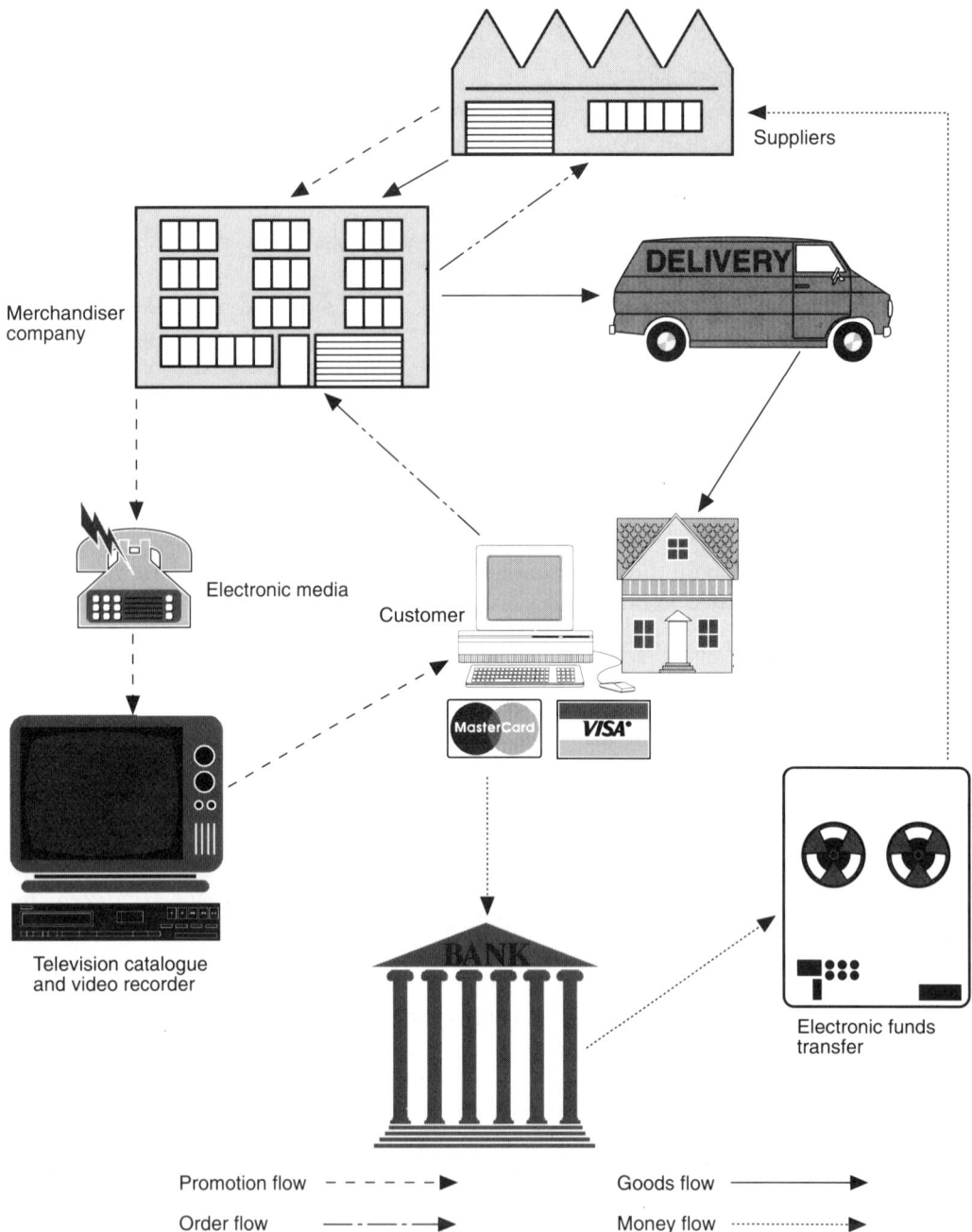

Suppliers

Merchandiser
company

Electronic media

Customer

Television catalogue
and video recorder

Electronic funds
transfer

| Promotion flow | – – – – – ▶ | Goods flow | ──────▶ |
| Order flow | ──·──·──▶ | Money flow | ··········▶ |

Figure 17.5 Offering systems of the 1990s.

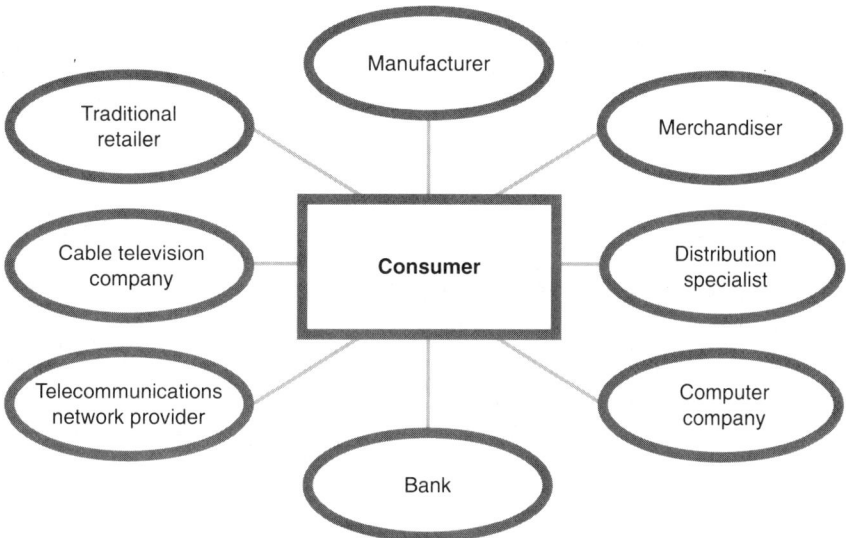

Figure 17.6   Members of the consumer 'offering' network.

(1)   Databases will tend to converge in format so that information can be matched or added, most commonly on a national scale.
(2)   Consumer needs will become more divergent, with the expectation of the needs being met on timing criteria as well as quality and price.

These conflicting trends point to the emergence of a different type of commercial member in the network, whereby competitive edge in computing, promotion and range consolidation and delivery result in significant power within the network.

Will consumers use the new 'offering' system?

Some limited market tests in the UK have not provided firm indicators of likely response to home shopping. In some instances, teleshopping has been directed at groups with special needs.

Qualitative research among women shoppers in the Glasgow region identified both positive and negative responses to the concept of shopping via computer link described as 'teleshopping' (McKay and Fletcher, 1988).

As in all markets, there will be innovators who adopt new shopping modes for a mixture of practical and status reasons. They are likely to be young, well-educated, familiar with computers and advanced telecommunication services, and who value the time released from shopping which can be devoted to work or leisure.

The unknown factor is how long these new habits will take to 'trickle down' to the majority of the population. Until this becomes evident, the capital investment in cabling (estimated at £4 billion for the UK) must be offset by the freedom to operate telephone services as well as cable television. This adds 21% to costs, but has the potential for doubling the cash generated from sales.

Importance of cable television in facilitating interactive home shopping

By the end of 1992, two million British homes were able to plug into cable television. In mid-1992, 300,000 subscribers paid around £20 per month to watch 35 channels. The cabling penetration level is much lower than in many other European countries (see the next section), but 1992 marked the beginning of a period of rapid development for the medium. Although the first cable television licences were issued as far back as 1982, doubts about viable return on the massive capital investment held back British investors. Two steps by the government have acted as a catalyst for investment by US and Canadian corporations:

- Rules limiting non-European Community ownership were dropped in December 1990.
- Regulations allow cable companies to provide telephone services as well as cable television. Rules introduced in 1991 by the government's telecommunications review gave cable a seven-year window during which time British Telecom is not allowed to send television signals down existing wires.

These changes have introduced the prospect of a reasonable cash flow in the short term, and viable return on capital in the long term. This has attracted overseas investors with cable experience. However, there are two features of the UK media environment which will have an influence on developments:

(1)   The resistance to a large influx of 'canned' television material from the USA, which is seen as a threat to the cultural *status quo* and future development. The threat of this is greater for the UK than other European countries because of the common language.

(2)   The opportunity that cable television will provide for advertising, and particularly 'narrowcasting' by way of highly geographically targeted messages, is a threat to the advertising revenues of established television companies.

Only when cable penetration is high enough to reach the majority of the population will these issues become serious. A computerlink in each cabled home will allow for two-way communication, and the option for an electronic order in response to promotion through cable television.

Even with the new electronic medium, perceptions of shopping from home could restrict uptake. UK perceptions of catalogue shopping were traditionally based on the availability of credit for purchases by lower socio-economic groups. The expansion of credit availability and new and successful entrants to catalogue shopping has helped to improve the image of shopping from home. There is a wider range of quality merchandise available, with niche retailers in particular benefiting from the requirements of more affluent groups for convenience shopping.

It is conceivable that a 'technological barrier' to interactive home shopping will need to be overcome through strong promotion of the benefits allied to reassurance that the system is user-friendly. The costs to the household of installation must not be prohibitive, and could be waived as an inducement to use the service (as in the case of the French Minitel service). The decision as to which member of the consumer 'offering' network should bear the capital cost could provide the catalyst for the formation of a consortium where financial exposure is reduced, and the prospective earnings shared.

The prognosis for interactive shopping in the UK

A positive view of commercial developments in electronic shopping is put forward by Michael Storey, former Chairman of the Cable Television Association.

Q. Do you see interactive home shopping becoming a reality in 10 years' time?
A. Yes, most definitely. Home shopping is already with us, through direct response to television advertising and the emergent home shopping channels – but the consumer currently has to make a telephone call to order products, which remains a barrier to immediate, impulse purchase. Research has shown that where an impulse reaction is possible, through the cable infrastructure, then there is an increased probability of making a sale.

Q. What service are you offering to the consumer?
A. Currently, the cable companies are selling films and entertainment to a target audience which classically has at least two television sets and a VCR in the home, and who tends to be the 'early adopters' of new ideas and technology. There is a significant opportunity to reach this audience with other products and services which constitute the potential market for home shopping.

There are two conditions necessary: firstly, the consumer must be able to make a decision to buy from home. This means that the product category must be right for this – beauty products, jewellery, home accessories, and such services as vacations, leisure activities and insurance.

Secondly, there must be a suitable delivery system to the home. For example, can the product be delivered by Royal Mail, or could there be a 'piggy back' arrangement with a current service such as Express Dairies?

Alternatively, **'community warehouses'** could develop, which act as delivery consolidation hubs.

Q.   Do you expect current mail order companies to become active in interactive home shopping?
A.   Currently, the catalogue is the most important feature of a mail order operation, and this overshadows the customer database. The advantage of interactive home shopping is the moving picture, which replaces the costly catalogue and is a more influential selling tool for the impulse purchase. If mail order companies see their business as home retailing rather than catalogue shopping, they will exploit aggressively the interactive home shopping opportunity.

The cable facility provides **reach** and **customer satisfaction**.

Q.   Do you see a merchandiser intermediary emerging, who provides the link between the cable company and the manufacturer?
A.   This is not necessary. The cable company acts as a distributor, providing an 'electronic highway' along which the cable company wants to see as much traffic as possible. The manufacturer or service provider can create the 'packaging' for presentation on cable television. Some retailers are already operating at the edge of technology in distribution, and it would be a small step for them to work with cable. If they don't, then intermediaries will emerge.

Q.   Why are you certain that interactive home shopping will be a majority rather than a minority activity?
A.   This has to be seen in the context of cable penetration levels. This year (1992), there are only 1.5 million homes in the UK passed by cable. Licences have been granted for cable facilities to almost 16 million homes (out of a total TV household population of 21.7 million).

By the year 2000 it is likely that at least 50% of these homes will be connected to a cable system – which means eight million homes.

How can I make this statement with confidence? Videotron, for example, had achieved 22% penetration level with its cable television service revenue averaging £20 per month.

Q.   What is the likely impact of interactive home shopping on current retail provision?
A.   As cable penetration increases, there will be a corresponding diminution in the need for traditional retail outlets. There are two possible strategic approaches:

(1)   The manufacturer or service provider (brands or generic products) bypasses the traditional retailer or distributor and advertises on cable with facility for delivery to the household.
(2)   The retailer uses cable provision to operate a dual-distribution strategy.

In either event, there will be less demand through traditional retail outlets.

The electronic age for the buying process and service format

The availability of technology and consumer demand for access to services from home is not sufficient in itself to give rise to the electronic age in shopping. There are barriers of system compatibility and investment to overcome. There will inevitably be power struggles between members of the provider network before decisions are made, unless a consortium approach is agreed.

The move to home shopping will not be taking place in isolation from the impact of advances in telecommunications and computing power on other facets of business and home life.

The development of **voice recognition systems** allows the link between telephone and computer to simulate a 'conversation'. This means that the customer can respond to an advertising campaign without the intervention of human operators. There are estimates that voice processing equipment sales in the USA could reach $2.4 billion by 1993, with 10% of the European telecoms market accounted for by such systems in 1993 (Whelan, 1989). This facility will permit total automation of the cycle – customer enquiry/order transmission/payment. Advances in robotics will ensure greater automation in warehouses, which leaves just product delivery reliant on human endeavour. Where the product is information or a service capable of electronic transmission, then this too will be automated.

Computing power available to most businesses, regardless of size, will provide for data manipulation and forecasting based on modelling methods best suited to the task in hand. This will replace reliance on traditional theories. In parallel with this, companies will be under pressure to use the most recent information on orders, deliveries and customer status. This requires adoption of new technology throughout the organization – from salesforce to van delivery network (Huff and McNaughton, 1991). There will be greater demands on new skills, acquired along with new attitudes through training.

Some services will be provided more effectively through interactive video: individual training, medical consultations, and a wide range of educational services will be available at regional centres initially, and then in the home. This will replicate the expertise and judgement of specialists through **expert systems**, where the computer takes the client through a series of steps to achieve an objective. This might be self-knowledge (counselling), subject knowledge (education) or a medical diagnosis and proposed treatment accepted by the patient (healthcare).

The British Telecom experiment with directory enquiry services, operating from the Scottish islands through **home workers** provided with the latest telecommunication and video links (Summer, 1992), marked the beginning of the **electronic revolution**. The adoption curve will be determined by organizational rather than individual needs, which means that the time-scale will be very much shorter than for the industrial revolution; in that historic event, the people moved to the work. In the new revolution, the work will move to the people. In the process, there will be significant environmental gains through reduced use of petrol and other energy resources, less pollution, and less need for new roads.

The degree of adoption of these new working patterns in the 21st century will not just depend on tangible cost and logistical variables. There will also be the social factor: just how much do individuals depend on the work environment for social contact? What alternative opportunities for human interaction may be necessary as part of the work package to retain motivation and social equilibrium? Companies will neglect these individual needs at their peril!

European perspective

Advances in telecommunications and information technology have provided the capability for transborder business transactions to be simple and instantaneous. This facilitates the move towards a single market in which other features of the business environment (such as technical standards, legal and physical constraints) will, in practice, create barriers for some years. Simultaneously, advertisers are gaining experience in reaching target audiences across Europe through satellite and cable television.

However, organizations may not be able to take full advantage of these developments because of constraints founded in lack of investment at the corporate and national level. Opportunities and constraints are examined in this section under the following themes:

(1) Corporate information systems
(2) Cable television
(3) Electronic transfer of funds
(4) International value-added systems (VANs)

Corporate information systems

By the end of 1992, some forward-looking businesses had established a European network to take advantage of emerging opportunities. Whether this has been done through acquisition, opening new offices or forging alliances with complementary organizations, effective sharing of information is critical to pan-European planning and operations. This, in turn, will be dependent on computer information systems that are adequate to the task.

The cycle of computer audit and upgrade within an organization will have the added momentum of meeting international requirements in the following areas:

- *Hardware compatibility* Standardized equipment requires significant capital investment. An alternative is network development based on core hardware with gradual upgrade on secondary sites.
- *Choice of software* Where different systems are in use across business units in individual Member States, the move towards a standard set of software will involve changes in data and file structure, with implications for working practices and training. This will impinge upon most operational areas including purchasing, stock control and distribution, marketing, finance and personnel.

  The costs of change must be assessed against the advantages of achieving economies of scale as a buyer, and of coordinating marketing and sales effort through access to a pan-European customer database.
- *Telecommunication links* The facility for data and document exchange will be essential at the internal level, with introduction of electronic mail and electronic data interchange of great advantage within an administered vendor network.

Planning of pan-European information systems will need to take account of EC Directives in a variety of areas that will affect the way information is stored and used. Four important areas are technical specifications and standards, coding systems for products and components, data protection legislation, and access to European databases (Kramer, 1988).

Cable television

The prospects for interactive marketing at the consumer level across Europe will be influenced by penetration levels for cable television in different Member States. The existence of a cable connection between the cable company and the individual household facilitates two-way electronic communication, enabling the household to make an immediate purchase decision after receiving a sales message. The penetration level in each European country is shown in Table 17.3, and this is influenced by a variety of factors:

Table 17.3   Level of penetration of cable television in Europe.

	Population (million)	TV homes (million)	VCR ownership (000)	Cable penetration (%)
Austria	7.58	2.75	827	22.3
Belgium	10.05	3.27	n/a	99.8
Denmark	5.14	2.10	504	53.5
Finland	4.96	1.87	840	36.4
France	56.00	20.0	5160	1.39
Germany[†]	77.63	32.53	8027	22.3
Greece	10.04	1.73	552	–
Ireland	3.55	0.98	373	36.0
Italy	57.47	20.0 (est)	4000	–
Luxembourg	0.37	0.13	44	69.6
Netherlands	14.79	5.80	2730	79.0
Norway	4.20	1.45	754	33.8
Portugal	10.23	3.19	905	–
Spain	39.90	10.54	4585	0.28
Sweden	8.44	3.31	2522	34.8
Switzerland	6.75	2.40	n/a	75.0
UK	57.19	21.70	13,889	1.4

[†] Post-unification.
Source: Cable and Satellite Yearbook (1991).

- variations in quality of aerial television reception;
- government investment in cable systems;
- private sector investment in the industry;
- degree of involvement and protection of utility companies;
- cable television programming availability;
- quality of competitive television channels;
- penetration levels of video recording equipment (VCRs).

The cable industries in Switzerland and the Benelux countries are the oldest and most developed. Germany has seen rapid growth since 1982 with nearly a quarter of households subscribing. In Austria and the Scandinavian countries, cable has a significant foothold. The cable industries in France and the UK are the least advanced, but heavy private sector investment in the early 1990s will mean faster growth to the end of the decade. Italy and Spain have yet to see cable television developed as a significant medium.

The relatively late development of cable television in the UK illustrates the influence of the factors listed above. Uncertainty about likely return on high levels of capital spending by the private sector inhibited development. There was also the fear that British Telecom (BT) would use its cable duct capacity to compete in media transmission. The seven-year moratorium on BT competing in this way and the issuing of regional cable franchises by the government have led to significant investment planned by companies with predominantly Canadian or US ownership. British television is also renowned for its quality, which means that cable services have tough competition. The high penetration level for VCRs also provides competition in the household's capacity to choose both the content and timing of viewing.

Signal transmission via cables is currently viewed as having national boundaries, reflected in the scope of the cable system itself. This avoids the anomalies that occur in controls of cross-border broadcasting, where the transmission must comply with the restrictions set by the country of origin.

In view of the dual nature of some cable systems (notably broad-band high capacity cables), in that they are capable of carrying telecommunication as well as television signals, national control is likely to continue for some years.

Potential for cable television in Europe

The European cable (or pay) television industry was estimated to be worth $4.5 billion in 1991, and forecast to grow to $16 billion by the year 2000. There are 130 million households across Europe, of which 32% were able to receive cable television by 1992. This includes SMATV (satellite master antennae television), such as flats in a block receiving transmission through a master satellite dish, with individual households connected through cable. By 2000, almost 54% of TV homes are expected to be passed by cable.

Success in individual European Member States will depend on alternative viewing quantity and quality. The choice available through cable will also be a significant determinant of penetration levels. Where Germany has only five programmes available through cable, Belgium has 10, France has 13 and the UK has 24 (based on 1992 availability).

Interactive home shopping

Assuming that the cable facility exists for households to react to television advertising by placing an 'electronic order', propensity to do so will vary across Member States according to culture, past experience and quality of the advertising message.

In the main part of this chapter, highly educated, computer-literate individuals who prefer not to spend valuable time on shopping were identified as the most likely target group for interactive shopping. The size of this group within the population of each Member State will influence the take-up rate of such a service.

The degree to which the national culture condones and supports more traditional methods of 'distance shopping' will also play a part. For example, the contribution of mail order to total retail sales and the percentage of the population who habitually places orders by telephone will be an indication of attitudes and behaviour tendencies which would support interactive shopping.

However, these arguments presuppose that the product message is sound and directed to the right target group. Cable television is subject to the same rules for effective advertising as other media. If there are legal or production constraints on the message, this can have a negative effect on sales response and future advertising revenue.

Electronic transfer of funds

The holiday traveller faces the reality of foreign currency dealings when confined to obtaining currency before travelling, using travellers' cheques or relying on the use of an international bank card when abroad. Each of these methods involves cost and inconvenience, with only the last option having the potential for an immediate transaction, technology permitting. Withdrawing money from a home bank account while in another Member State is usually a costly and slow procedure.

Moving from the retail situation to the corporate sector, cross-border payments in support of business transactions are even more complex and costly. Both sectors would benefit from the increased speed and reduced cost of financial transactions that would result from **electronic transfer of funds** operated at the pan-European level. This would be quite straightforward where one bank had branches in several Member States and transactions were essentially 'intra-bank'. With low levels of cross-border penetration of banks due to regulations and restrictions of Member States in protecting the home market, fund transfer is predominantly 'inter-bank'. Adoption of electronic fund transfer for retail and commercial banking will depend on the level of integration of European financial services.

The European Commission has prompted moves towards integration in three areas:

- free flow of capital
- free trade

- standardization of banking technology across Europe with a view to 'interoperability'

The principle of free trade in banking has taken longer to be adopted in practice than is evident for other business sectors. The Second Banking Directive (COM (87) 715) demands that '...each state recognise any financial institution licensed in another Community country to operate locally, as long as it does so under local rules'.

The licence is issued in the home country, which must ensure that basic operating standards are maintained. At the same time, the host country can enforce its own operating rules. For **mutuality** in electronic transactions, there would need to be convergence of regulations, security against fraud and service charges. One barrier to a bank being a member of such a transaction network is the level of capital investment needed. The return on investment needed is likely to come from offering services to customers in the home market, with the additional benefit of cross-border fund transfer. Would France, UK and Spain adopt new systems faster than Germany and Italy because of the higher penetration levels of credit cards in the former group? Alternatively, would a network be based on the existing clearing system for Eurocheques?

Standardization of technology would eliminate another potential impediment to formation of such networks. The Commission has promoted Europe-wide implementation of ATMs (automatic telling machines) and EFTPOS (electronic fund transfer at point of sale). As early as 1987, the Commission published the *European Code of Conduct relating to Electronic Payment*. Banks responded to the Commission with the *Accord for Payment Systems* published by the European Council for Payment Systems. This appeared to exclude areas of activity, such as building societies, which were to be included under the spirit of the Commission's proposals.

A Green Paper issued by the Commission in 1990 aimed to get national banking systems to simplify and speed up their systems for money transfers within the Community. Two committees were set up in 1991 to develop ideas on technical development for paperless systems and on the rights of payment system users (including retailers).

One result of the integration of the European market for financial services is competitive pressure on domestic cartels from outside. This will result in improved service and lower costs, particularly where domestic operators are forced to invest in technology in order to survive.

It is not surprising that banks are resisting moves towards integrated Europe-wide services, where current practice allows for higher profit per foreign exchange transaction. The Commission had initially been prepared for monetary union to resolve this issue. However, it is becoming clear to Commissioners that the banking sector is unlikely to take the initiative, and that the imposition of a common scale of charges will be a likely outcome for the intervening years, before the reality of a single European currency.

International value-added and data network services (VANS)

The same principles apply to VANS at the international level as are necessary for national networks. However, the operational constraints for each of several participating countries may well differ, resulting in a more complex scenario. There are three major issues to be resolved:

(1) Can the international network evolve through simple linkage of national networks? This will depend on the nature of relationships between 'transmission' providers.
(2) Who will set the standard for interfacing data and electronic decisions?
(3) Do industry needs differ from one country to another such that the specification for an international system needs to be flexible to accommodate these as well as language and currency differences?

National restrictions on telecommunication transmission mean that international networking is a specialist field, particularly where EDI is to be introduced. Where an international organization has the resources for an in-house network, interfacing constraints are apparent and technical standards can be set. Even under these conditions, the advice of a specialist network company can save time and money in implementation.

The networking needs of a major manufacturer requiring EDI links with suppliers and customers to provide for just-in-time operations are served predominantly by third parties. These network suppliers overcome problems of standards and software compatibility through evaluation of industry needs.

In the situation where a supplier is encouraged to adopt a particular software specification to meet the requirements of a network dominated by a major customer, there could be undue influence on the supplier's operating methods to the detriment of its business with other customers. This 'tying-in' of a supplier at a European level would be even more restrictive, and could fall foul of EC competition rules.

The European Commission is aware of the potential for electronic networks to be used to restrict competition. For example, in banking payment systems, insurance company dealings with agents and airline booking systems, barriers could be erected to prevent newcomers entering the system and, hence, the market. The Commission adopted Regulation No. 2672/88 which provides an exemption to airline computer reservation systems from Article 85(1) of the EC Treaty for certain types of agreements. Conditions attached to this exemption include the need for third parties to have access to the systems concerned (Competition Law in the EC, 1989).

Problems and assignments

(1)   Given that the communication and IT infrastructure was largely available in the 1980s, why has the home-shopping revolution failed to materialize?

(2)   To what extent do you believe that Argos' dual approach of catalogues and retail outlets is the way ahead? What are the marketing advantages and disadvantages of this system?

(3)   Describe the ways, for a business-to-business scenario, in which the application of IT can lead to marketing or competitive advantage.

(4)   First Direct has demonstrated the application of IT as well as the consumers' acceptance of new technology in return for greater convenience. How significant do you believe the advent of First Direct is for:
  (a)   its customers
  (b)   the Midland Group (which owns First Direct)
  (c)   the clearing banks as a whole?

(5)   Define the composition of a value-added network (VAN). How might a VAN be applied to achieve competitive advantage?

(6)   If manufacturers and service providers have so far failed to use new communication methods and IT to launch home shopping, what chances are there of applying the same principles across the Single Market?

(7)   Identify the primary reasons why cable television has been so slow in taking off in the UK. What is the significance of this tardiness for marketers?

(8)   What impact would you expect the advent of the Single Market (and accompanying legislation/Directives) to have on the provision of financial services across the EC, from the perspective of the consumer?

References

Benjamin R.I., de Long D.W. and Scott Morton M.S. (1990). Electronic data interchange: how much competitive advantage? *Long Range Planning* (UK), **23**(1), 29–40

Callahan D.K. (1987). *The Impacts of Electronic Integration on Buyers and Suppliers*. Master's Thesis, Sloan School of Management. Cambridge, Massachusetts: MIT

Department of Trade and Industry (1987). *The Economic Effects of Value-Added and Data Services*. A Vanguard Report

Facilities (1989). TSB: Designing for Paperless Trading. **7**(6), June

Hosking P. (1991). Customer database helps N. Brown to boost sales. *The Independent*, 16 October

Huff S.L. and McNaughton J. (1991). Diffusion of an information technology innovation. *Business Quarterly*, Summer, 25–30

Ireland J. (1987). Can direct marketing help Levi Strauss and Co.? *J. of Consumer Marketing*, **4**(3), 35–41

King J. (1990). Till changes help ring up the profits. *Computer Weekly*, 20 September, pp 32–33

Klein R.A. and Tyler Eastman S. (1982). *Strategies in Broadcast and Cable Promotion*. California: Wadsworth

Knight P. (1991). Banks cash in on automated future. *Financial Times*, 3 January

McKay J. and Fletcher K. (1988). Consumer's attitudes towards tele-shopping. *Quarterly Review of Marketing*, **13**(3), Spring, 1–6

Rosenberg L.J. and Hirschman E.C. (1980). Retailing without stores. *Harvard Business Review*, July/August

Selby M. (1989). Implementing EDI – a management problem. *Logistics Today* (UK), **8**(4), 41

Suyama K. (1989). Contemporary marketing behaviour and distribution system in Japan. *Review of Economics and Business*, **18**(1), 71–96

Whelan S. (1989). Telemarketing discovers its voice. *Marketing*, 13 July, p 17

European perspective

Ashman S. (1990). International networked manufacturing systems and the JIT concept. *BPICS Control*, June/July, 35–39

Cable and Satellite Yearbook (1991). *21st Century*

Competition Law in the European Community (1989). Market Entry (General): Commission Statement. **12**(12), December

Kramer A. (1988). Europe 1992: are your information systems going to be ready? *Management Accounting*, **66**(10), 32–33

Index